THE FATAL LURE OF POLITICS

'Deeply researched and eloquently written, this is a compelling study of a formidable socialist thinker and his intellectual milieux. *The Fatal Lure of Politics* is a work of prodigious scholarship: penetrating, engaging and authoritative.'

Phillip Deery
Emeritus Professor of History, Victoria University

'Finally, we have a definitive study of world-renowned prehistorian Gordon Childe, Australia's most famous left-wing intellectual. Terry Irving's extraordinary, investigative scholarship is enlightening and enthralling. This is an important book and biography at its very best.'

Verity Burgmann
Adjunct Professor of Political Science, Monash University

'Is science neutral? Why should Security Intelligence Services consider an archaeologist 'a very dangerous person'? Surveillance, espionage, and censorship were all part of the life of a young Australian, V. Gordon Childe, who became the most famous archaeologist of all time. This book offers a masterful account of the political context of his oeuvre and casts new light on his most famous book, *What Happened in History*. We have been waiting for a book like this for years.'

Margarita Díaz-Andreu
ICREA Research Professor, University of Barcelona

'Terry Irving's *The Fatal Lure of Politics* is a powerful work of immense scholarship that firmly situates V. Gordon Childe's life and work within his commitment to revolutionary politics. This is a well-written, remarkable piece of research that sheds important new light on one of anthropology's most daring minds and revolutionary figures. It is required reading for anyone interested in twentieth century intellectual history.'

David H. Price
Professor of Anthropoloyg, Saint Martin's University

The Fatal Lure of Politics

The Life and Thought of Vere Gordon Childe

Terry Irving

The Fatal Lure of Politics: The Life and Thought of Vere Gordon Childe
© Copyright 2020 Terry Irving
All rights reserved. Apart from any uses permitted by Australia's Copyright Act 1968, no part of this book may be reproduced by any process without prior written permission from the copyright owners. Inquiries should be directed to the publisher.

Monash University Publishing
Matheson Library Annexe
40 Exhibition Walk
Monash University
Clayton, Victoria 3800, Australia
www.publishing.monash.edu

Monash University Publishing brings to the world publications which advance the best traditions of humane and enlightened thought.

Monash University Publishing titles pass through a rigorous process of independent peer review.

ISBN: 9781925835748 (paperback)
ISBN: 9781925835762 (pdf)
ISBN: 9781925835755 (epub)

www.publishing.monash.edu/books/flp-9781925835748.html

Series: Biography

Design: Les Thomas

Cover image: Childe as he would have liked his friends in the 1920s to remember him. (Flinders University of South Australia, Evatt Collection Photographs: Evatt_1510_050)

A catalogue record for this book is available from the National Library of Australia.

CONTENTS

List of Illustrations vii

Introduction: A Death in the Cold War. ix

Part 1. Growing up into Revolution: Sydney and Oxford 1892–1917

Chapter 1	Living in a Divided City 3
Chapter 2	Students and Workers 18
Chapter 3	Socialists and Cooperators 34
Chapter 4	A Cold Northern Superculture 46
Chapter 5	More Outspoken than Any Other 65

Part 2. Labour Intellectual: Australia 1917–1921

Chapter 6	No Compromise. 83
Chapter 7	'A certain vacillation' 98
Chapter 8	'Yours for the revolution'. 115
Chapter 9	Labour's Mediating Intellectuals 130
Chapter 10	The World of Labour 146
Chapter 11	A State within the State 160
Chapter 12	The Intelligence Department 174
Chapter 13	The Premier's Minder. 184

Part 3. An Unknown Member of the Proletariat: London 1921–1926

Chapter 14	The Dismissal. 201
Chapter 15	A Pauper Colonial 217
Chapter 16	How Labour Governs and The Dawn 229
Chapter 17	'A movement that will have to go further' 253

Part 4. What Happens in History: 1927–1957

Chapter 18	Science as Communism	271
Chapter 19	A Grand and Hopeful Experiment	292
Chapter 20	An Absolutely Sincere Approach to the Party	311
Chapter 21	1956	334
Chapter 22	A Sentimental Excursion	346
Chapter 23	'Australia today is far from a socialist society'	357

Coda: Childe's Revolutions and the Fatal Lure 375
Acknowledgements 379
Bibliography 381
Index 405
About the Author 419

LIST OF ILLUSTRATIONS

Govett's Leap, Blackheath, where Childe's body was found xiv

The Rectory at St Thomas's, North Sydney, where Childe lived until 1900 4

St Thomas's Church, North Sydney, c. 1900 8

Herbert Vere Evatt as a young man 16

Harald Ingemann Jensen, c. 1910. 35

Childe's first gentlemen's club: Sydney University Union, c. 1910 43

Rajani Palme Dutt, as Childe would have known him at Oxford 51

Percy Stephensen at Maryborough Boys' Grammar School 123

Childe as the Premier's secretary, 1920. 187

Childe as a handsome young man 189

A smoko at the Labour Research Department summer school, 1922. 220

Douglas Cole in 1928 242

Mr Fat reading *How Labour Governs*, 1923 246

Professor V.G. Childe, Edinburgh, 1930s 273

O.G.S. Crawford setting out to democratise archaeology with his bicycle 282

R.P. Dutt, the communist cadre, in 1943. 285

The Marx Memorial Library and Workers' School, London, 1945 315

Jack Lindsay and Percy Stephensen at the Fanfrolico Press, London, 1920s . . . 321

Childe at the Isokon Flats, 1955. 346

Childe and Evatt outside the Great Hall, University of Sydney, 1957 359

In memory of
PETER GATHERCOLE
(1929–2010)

INTRODUCTION

A Death in the Cold War

The Australian-born archaeologist and prehistorian Vere Gordon Childe was one of the most distinguished scholars and public intellectuals of the first half of the twentieth century. His concepts of the Neolithic and Urban revolutions 'rank among the most important theoretical advances' in the study of human cultural evolution. He wrote 21 books, including the immensely popular *What Happened in History*, which sold 300,000 copies for Penguin Books in its first 15 years. He also wrote 281 articles or chapters and 236 book reviews in 99 periodicals. His reputation was not confined to the English-speaking world. His books were translated into 21 languages, and he travelled widely, finding appreciative audiences in Europe, Russia, Turkey and India, as well as North America and Australia.[1]

Publishers in the 30 years after his death issued more of his works than they had in the slightly more than 30 years of his career. The most recent of many conferences devoted to assessing his legacy was organised in 2007. Even outside the academy his name is known. In the 2008 movie *Indiana Jones and the Kingdom of the Crystal Skull*, the hero, after smashing his way into a college library on a motorbike, is recognised by a student who asks Jones for help to understand the diffusion of civilisation. The hero, an archaeologist who moonlights as a saviour of civilisation (although he has just done terrible damage to one of its achievements), resumes his teaching role momentarily to advise the student to 'consult the works of Gordon Childe'.[2]

---

1   Michael E. Smith, 'V. Gordon Childe and the Urban Revolution: A Historical Perspective on a Revolution in Urban Studies', *Town Planning Review*, vol. 80, no. 1, 2009, p. 5; Peter Gathercole, 'Allen Lane's Archaeological Best Seller', *The Penguin Collector*, no. 46, July 1996; Peter Gathercole and Terry Irving, with the assistance of Margarita Díaz-Andreu, 'A Childe Bibliography: A Hand-List of the Works of Vere Gordon Childe', *European Journal of Archaeology*, vol. 12, nos 1–3, 2009, p. 204; Sally Green, *Prehistorian: A Biography of V. Gordon Childe*, Moonraker Press, Bradford-on-Avon, 1981.

2   The papers from a conference organised by Margarita Díaz-Andreu at Durham University to celebrate Childe's legacy 50 years after his death are reprinted in the *European Journal of Archaeology*, vol. 12, nos 1–3, 2009; *Indiana Jones and the Kingdom of the Crystal Skull*, directed by Stephen Spielberg, 2008.

The film is set in 1957, at the height of the Cold War, coincidentally the year of Childe's death. There is a surprisingly subversive tinge to the film, as it reveals the existence of McCarthyite repression in universities. Prior to his library-vandalising moment, Indiana Jones had been captured by the Russians as they destroyed an American atomic research station. After an unlikely escape he resumes teaching (we hear him lecturing about Skara Brae, Childe's most famous excavation) only to be sacked by the college because the FBI thinks his presence with the Russians indicates that he is a communist sympathiser. His best friend in the college resigns in sympathy, suggesting that FBI interference was a wider problem, something Childe would have understood. As a pacifist, anti-imperialist and revolutionary socialist, Childe was spied upon by the state security bodies of Britain, Australia, the USA, and possibly the Soviet Union, for 40 years. On several occasions this surveillance derailed or hampered his career. When his body was found at the bottom of a cliff in the mountains west of Sydney, there was speculation that his death was neither deliberate nor accidental but the result of a sinister act.[3]

Childe's continuing reputation rests as much on the extraordinary range of his thought as on its particular usefulness to scholars of archaeology and prehistory. But his interest in social evolution, the theory of knowledge, and historical explanation were not just indications of breadth of mind; they placed him in a particular political setting and defined him as a left-wing intellectual. The connection between his politics and his career is the starting point for this study of his life and thought. It seeks to understand his life by placing him within the tradition of dissenting intellectuals of the left. It examines his thought to understand the political ideas that gripped that tradition in the first half of the twentieth century.

Childe's scholarly reputation, resting on work undertaken in Britain from the mid-1920s, was the product of what we might call his 'second life'. He was 33 when he published his first book on prehistory and 35 when he took up his first academic position. So there was ample time for him to have an interesting 'first life'; in fact, in his twenties and early thirties he contemplated devoting his life to politics. Since his days as an undergraduate at the University of Sydney before the First World War he had been active in left-wing politics, variously Labor, socialist, anti-war, and radically democratic.

At the same time, he had performed brilliantly in his university examinations in Sydney and Oxford, but when he applied for suitable academic posts

---

3   Ellen W. Schrecker, *No Ivory Tower: McCarthyism and the Universities*, Oxford University Press, 1986.

in Australia the university authorities, acting in concert with the business elite and the Commonwealth of Australia's military spies, made certain that he was not successful. So, he looked for employment using his political connections, and for most of 1918 to 1922 he was the beneficiary of Labor Party patronage. In his 'first life' he made his mark not in universities but in gritty Trades Halls and party offices, talking not to students of the human sciences but to agitators and Labor parliamentarians.

The knowledge of political philosophy and working-class politics that Childe gained in his 'first life', mainly in Australia, would influence his account of 'what happened in history'. For historians of archaeological thought, Childe's use of Marxism in his scholarship is a continuing area of disagreement (including the view of tiresome Marxist purists that he was not really one at all). The study of Childe's 'first life' reveals that if we want to understand his thinking, the question to ask is not 'What did Marxism mean?' for his archaeology, but 'What part did Marxism play in his life?' We have to consider, in other words, how Childe made the study of prehistory part of a political mission that began in his 'first life' and continued to his death.

As the First World War was ending, Childe wrote to an academic mentor in Britain that he intended to return there 'to escape the fatal lure of politics' in Australia. Ten years later he was well into an academic career in Britain that would bring him great esteem, but throughout that career politics continued to lure him. Indeed, politics were implicated in his death. There is a direct line between Childe's attraction to politics in his early life and his final – and fatal – political act. This is a book about the central place held by socialist politics in his life, and his contributions to the theory of history that it entailed. It is also about the conflict in socialist politics between radical revolutionary democracy and parliamentary social democracy, for Childe decided that 'politicalism' – his name for the latter – was fatal to socialism.[4]

* * *

Outside the Great Hall of the University of Sydney a small group of students listened through the side door as the Chancellor bestowed the honorary degree of Doctor of Letters on Gordon Childe. After the ceremony we waited on the asphalt outside the main entrance to see him walk in the academic procession,

---

4   Childe to Gilbert Murray, 17 November 1917, Gilbert Murray papers, Bodleian Library, Oxford, shelfmark 376, f. 86.

the collar of his green shirt just visible behind the academic gown and his heavy woollen suit. We were the campus radicals, gathered by the Labour Club to honour a fellow socialist on that warm April day in 1957.[5]

The previous year I had bought a copy of Childe's *Progress and Archaeology* (1944) because it promised to 'describe the progressive tendencies of mankind during the last 50,000 years'. It was number 102 in The Thinker's Library from the Rationalist Press Association (RPA), a series of cheap hardbacks that I recognised because there were several titles on our bookshelves at home, books by three of the great secularists and materialists, Thomas Huxley, Winwood Reade, Ernst Haeckel – and now Childe. He was part of something with which I could identify, a movement of 'forward thinkers' who, as the RPA asserted, believed that 'the relentless test of Reason' would eradicate superstition and ignorance while advancing human progress and welfare.

But as for Childe's politics, we campus radicals had only the vaguest idea: just that he was a Marxist scholar. Was there anyone among us who had heard of Childe's first book, *How Labour Governs – A Study of Workers' Representation in Australia* (1923)? It was out of print and rarely recommended in courses on Australian history, for in those dog days of the postwar boom we learnt about Australia only as a peripheral topic in British imperial history. In my Australian History class, we took bets on the date the lecturer would get to the moment when the first fleet sailed out of Portsmouth, usually a few weeks before the exam. Change was coming though, and a few years later I was part of the radical redirection of the humanities and social sciences liberated by the social movements of the 1960s. In 1960 the first issue of the journal *Labour History* appeared, and in 1964 there was a second edition of *How Labour Governs* – as a paperback. Meanwhile, Cold War emphases on consensus and conformity kept us in ignorance of our labour and radical past.[6]

In an interview in 1957, Childe referred to working in the 1920s as the private secretary to the Labor Premier, John Storey. Who? Storey didn't figure in our sketchy knowledge of labour history. Confusingly, *The Bulletin*, a right-wing magazine, reported that Childe had worked for Premier William

---

5   *Sydney Morning Herald*, 25 April 1957, p. 4 (and photo on p. 1); Kylie Tennant, *Evatt: Politics and Justice*, Sydney, Angus & Robertson, 1970, p. 21. The convention in labour history circles is that 'labour' refers to the organisations (parties, trade unions, bookshops etc.) in the 'labour movement', while 'Labor' refers to the parliamentary party, which adopted that spelling in the early 1900s. On the Sydney University campus in 1957, the Labour Club was not a Labor Party club.

6   V. Gordon Childe, *How Labour Governs – A Study of Workers' Representation in Australia*, London, Labour Publishing Company, 1923; 2nd edn, Melbourne, Melbourne University Press, 1964.

Holman, which didn't seem right because Holman was a Labor renegade, expelled by the party for supporting conscription in the First World War. We certainly had heard of Holman and Prime Minister Hughes and the other Labor Party rats; they were part of the labour movement's folk memory of defeats and setbacks. Subsequently I learnt that Childe did *not* work for Holman. Moreover, I discovered that this mistake has a curious provenance, for it turns up in the file compiled in 1957 by the Australian Security Intelligence Organisation (ASIO) on Childe. Perhaps the same informant, as ignorant as we were about labour history, misled both the magazine and the security service.[7]

Six months later the newspapers carried the story of the finding of Childe's body a thousand feet below a lookout in the Blue Mountains west of Sydney. Early on the previous day a taxi had driven him from the Carrington Hotel in Katoomba, where he often stayed, to Govett's Leap at the western edge of the Grose Valley. The taxi driver waited, but at midday went looking for Childe and discovered his hat, compass and glasses outside the fence at Barrow Lookout. Receiving no answer to his calls, he drove to Blackheath to alert the police. Constable Morey returned with the driver to Govett's Leap and descended into the valley but had to suspend his search at dusk. The following day Childe's body was found on a ledge near the Bridal Veil Falls. The news was on the front page of Sydney's *Daily Telegraph*: 'Seventeen men took five hours to get the body to the valley floor, then carry it up 6000 steps hewn from the rock to the top of Govett's Leap'.[8]

I followed the story not only because I had a political interest in Childe but because I was familiar with that part of the Grose Valley. In January, with five others, I had walked to the Blue Gum Forest from the end of Hat Hill Road. We scrambled down 275 metres at Perry's Lookdown, lunched and swam at the junction of the Grose River and Govett's Creek before following the creek to Junction Rock. Here we turned west and followed Govett's Leap Brook to the base of the Bridal Veil Falls. Just east of here Childe's body was found. Then we climbed the cliff track to Govett's Leap.

---

7   *Daily Telegraph*, 23 April 1957, 'The Sherlock Holmes of History's Dawn'. Australian Security Intelligence Organisation, 'Childe, Vere Gordon', National Archives of Australia, A6126/279 (released 1993), see f. 18; *The Bulletin*, 8 May 1957.

8   *Daily Telegraph*, 21 October 1957 (with photo of police party taking the body up the steps); *Sydney Morning Herald*, 21 October 1957. References at the time to Luchetti's Lookout were wrong, as Peter Rickwood has shown in his 'Forensic History: Professor Childe's Death Near Govett's Leap – Revisited', *Blue Mountains History Journal*, issue 3, September 2012, p. 47.

Govett's Leap, Blackheath, and the Grose Valley. Childe's body was found below
Barrow Lookout, the high point to the left of the waterfall.
(Museum of Applied Arts and Sciences, Sydney, Tyrell Collection, 85/1284-1589;
Kerry and Company, Sydney, c.1884–1917)

Since then I have discovered many more coincidences linking Childe to my experiences on that expedition. We were staying at 'Rostherne', owned by the family of George Arnold Wood, who was the first Professor of History at the university between 1891 and 1928. During the South African War (1899–1902), as the founder and President of the Australian Anti-War League, Wood was vilified in the press and censured by the Senate of the university. Sixteen years later, when Childe was victimised for opposing the First World War his supporters in the peace movement used Wood's trials to publicise the existence of a tradition of jingoistic intolerance in the university. Another coincidence: in the Blue Gum Forest we had swum naked just as Childe's friend, John Le Gay Brereton, and his friends had done in the mountain streams in the summer 50 years earlier. We took a taxi from Blackheath to 'Rostherne'. The driver was Stefan Siedleckie, whose daughter, Dr Stefania Siedleckie, carried out the postmortem and signed Childe's death certificate. Both Stefan and Stefania were socialists: the father in the Labor Party, the daughter in the Communist Party. Stefania was a prominent advocate of family planning and birth control in the early 1970s, helping to set up the Leichhardt Women's Health Centre in Sydney.[9]

* * *

The obituaries duly appeared, but their content was not always as the left would have wished. In *The Times* of London, Rajani Palme Dutt protested that its obituary had omitted any mention of Childe's Marxism. Dutt had good grounds for linking Marxism and Childe. In 1917 he had shared digs with Childe in Oxford: 'There in the somewhat cramped surroundings of a tiny common working and sitting room we pursued our arguments on Hegel and Marx far into the night'. Childe was 'in the forefront of archaeologists of our time', Dutt wrote, precisely because of his Marxism, 'since archaeology is by its very nature compelled to use consciously or unconsciously the methods of Marx, and build up the history of civilization from the records of tools and material objects'. Although Dutt, who was a founding member of the Communist Party of Great Britain, did not claim that Childe became a party member, he insisted that Childe 'remained ... heart and soul with the Marxist movement'. There was another weakness detected by Dutt in the obituary: its neglect of Childe's first book, *How Labour Governs* (1923), 'a very striking analysis of the limitations of a reformist Labour Government'.[10]

In Australia, where there were no obituaries in the daily press, it fell to the left to commemorate Childe and incidentally to expose the impact of Cold War ideology on Australian historians. Since the early years of the century the labour press and worker education movements had nurtured a distinctive tradition of historical writing – anti-imperialist, radical and class-focused. It had produced scholarly histories of importance by H.V. Evatt, Lloyd Ross and Brian Fitzpatrick, all path-breaking in their own way and worthy successors to the seminal work, Gordon Childe's *How Labour Governs*. In the 1940s and 1950s this radical and nationalist tradition was gaining acceptance among university historians, as revealed in publications by Robin Gollan, Bob Walshe and Russel Ward. In the

---

9   R.M. Crawford, *'A Bit of a Rebel': The Life and Work of George Arnold Wood*, Sydney, Sydney University Press, 1975; photograph of nude bathing in J. Le Gay Brereton papers, University of Sydney Archives; Australian Peace Alliance, 'Sydney University and the Progress of Knowledge' (press release), 12 September 1918, MF 1805 169/9-16; personal information on Stefania Siedlecky, confirmed by information from Roger Milliss.
10 R. Palme Dutt, 'Prof. V. Gordon Childe', *Times* [London], 24 October 1957, p. 14.

meantime the political environment changed with the election of the conservative Menzies government in 1949 and the retreat of the labour movement, weakened by internal fighting over communist influence in the unions. The moment was favourable for a counterattack, especially on historians, by conservative intellectuals. So puffed up were they by the turn of events, and by CIA money, that the main organiser of the attack claimed to be fighting 'a counter-revolution in Australian historiography', and of course the phrase suggested ever-so-subtly that left historians were promoting a communist agenda.[11]

Those under attack could see the political dimension of what was going on and two of them took the opportunity to strengthen their position in their obituaries for Childe. In *Overland*, a left-wing literary magazine, Brian Fitzpatrick, whose anti-imperialist economic histories were being criticised by conservative historians, got straight to the point:

> It may not be obtrusive to remark now, as I did when I made a little speech in praise of Childe last September, that Dr Evatt and I are proud to find ourselves placed in Childe's company when detractors of the labour movement and its historians offer their MA and PhD theses on labor [sic] to university examiners.

Fitzpatrick, the author of a short history of the labour movement and a regular contributor to *The Rationalist*, reminded his readers of Childe's 'rationalist, socialist convictions'. Fitzpatrick, a working journalist, praised Childe's commitment to popularising the story of man's evolution. Then he summarised Childe's academic career, but he ended by scorning the Melbourne dailies for failing to carry an obituary for Childe, who was 'among the greatest Australians, men who made substantial contributions to knowledge'.[12]

Russel Ward published his obituary in *Outlook*, Helen Palmer's independent socialist magazine, which already had an indirect link to Childe, for Helen's uncle, Esmonde Higgins, had been an associate of Childe's in London's Labour Research Department in the 1920s. Ward began in Fitzpatrick's manner, by striking a political note:

---

11   Terry Irving, 'Rediscovering Radical History', http://radicalsydney.blogspot.com.au/p/rediscovering-radical-history-essay-by.html; Peter Coleman, *Australian Civilization – A Symposium*, Melbourne, Cheshire, 1962, see p. 6 of his introduction. Coleman was a founding member in 1954 of the Australian Association for Cultural Freedom which was funded by the CIA, an arrangement that became public knowledge in 1967.

12   Brian Fitzpatrick, 'In Memoriam – V. Gordon Childe', *Overland*, no. 11, January 1958, p. 22, and *Meanjin*, vol. 16, December 1957, p. 424; Don Watson, *Brian Fitzpatrick: A Radical Life*, Sydney, Hale & Iremonger, 1979.

INTRODUCTION

About forty years ago V. Gordon Childe and H.V. Evatt were close friends at Sydney University. A couple of years ago Mrs Evatt told me that she was often warned by her elders to have nothing to do with either young man, as they were too much given to dangerous thoughts. Such visionary dreamers would come to nothing.

When, some weeks before his untimely death, I told Professor Childe the story, he hooted with laughter, and went on to recall how he had been 'persuaded' to leave the University as a result of his public support for the anti-conscription campaign during World War I. By bestowing an honorary degree on him this year, the University of Sydney did, perhaps, more honour to itself than to Childe, who had in no way recanted his unpopular principles in the interim.

His work will always have special interest for socialists ... because it is an all too rare example of how to apply Marxism to a specific problem. Childe was a life-long Marxist, but one for whom Marxism was always a method of attack and never a ritualistic incantation or a set of holy dogmas.

And that was virtually all his obituary did: claim Childe as a fellow socialist who 'like other really first-rate scholars' found it 'quite unnecessary to shield his work from the common gaze behind a smoke-screen of pretentious and polysyllabic jargon'. Ward made thereby an argument for the kind of approachable radical history that was under attack by academics and conservatives. It was the kind of history found in his *The Australian Legend*, published the following year and reprinted 15 times, through three editions, since then.[13]

There was an unstated personal motivation behind Ward's obituary, arising from an experience of discrimination not dissimilar to Childe's. Two years earlier Professor R.M. Hartwell had recommended Ward for a lectureship at the University of New South Wales, but Vice-Chancellor Philip Baxter and Chancellor Wallace Wurth vetoed his appointment because Ward 'had been active in seditious circles in Canberra'. Hartwell resigned in disgust and went to Oxford. It was not until Hartwell broke his silence about this act of covert political interference that we learnt that Wurth unofficially but routinely consulted ASIO about appointments. Meanwhile, Ward had accepted

---

13   Russel Ward, 'Death of Professor V.G. Childe', *Outlook*, vol. 1, no. 4, November–December 1957, p. 11; Russel Ward, *The Australian Legend*, Melbourne, Oxford University Press, 1958; Russel Ward, *A Radical Life: The Autobiography of Russel Ward*, South Melbourne, MacMillan, 1988.

a lectureship at the University of New England and begun a distinguished academic career.[14]

A third person went public with praise for Childe, his old friend Herbert Vere (Bert) Evatt. They were still close. Childe had spent a few days at the home of Evatt and his wife Mary Alice, when he first arrived back in Sydney in early April 1957, and Evatt, as a member of the Senate of the university, probably had a lot to do with the decision to award Childe an honorary degree. When Childe's death was announced, Evatt issued a press statement saying Childe was one of the University of Sydney's most distinguished graduates. Evatt was also feeling the anti-communist winds of the Cold War. A secretive conservative Catholic organisation known as 'the Movement', set up in the 1940s, was using opposition to communist influence in the trade unions to infiltrate the Labor Party. In 1954 Evatt publicly exposed their machinations, a move that resulted in the expulsion of Movement members. Beginning in Victoria, these former Labor Party members campaigned against Labor on an anti-communist platform. By 1957 'the split' in Labor had reached Queensland. In the issue of *The Sydney Morning Herald* reporting Childe's honorary doctorate the main story was that the Labor Party in Queensland had expelled its leader, the Premier Vince Gair, for his right-wing policies. Within a few months his followers had joined the small anti-Evatt groups in other states to form the Democratic Labor Party. For the next 15 years the DLP would direct its supporters to give their second preference votes to the conservative coalition, thus keeping Labor out of office federally until 1972.[15]

* * *

One of the main things that the Cold War meant for most people in the 1950s was Soviet espionage. A series of sensational exposures of British and American citizens who had passed information to Russian intelligence agents captured the front pages: Nunn May in 1946, Klaus Fuchs in 1950, Guy Burgess and Donald Maclean in 1951, Julius and Ethel Rosenberg, who were executed by the Americans for spying in 1953, and Kim Philby in 1955. In Australia the

---

14   Hannah Forsyth, 'Knowledge, Democracy and the Russel Ward Case', unpublished paper, 2011. Ward had resigned from the Communist Party in 1949.
15   *Sydney Morning Herald*, 21 October 1957, p. 1, 'Tribute by Dr Evatt'; *Sydney Morning Herald*, 25 April 1957, p. 1, 'Crisis in Queensland Labor Party'; Bradon Ellem (ed.), *The Great Labour Movement Split in New South Wales: Inside Stories*, Sydney, Australian Society for the Study of Labour History, 1998.

INTRODUCTION

Australian Security Intelligence Organisation was set up in 1949 after the United States counter-espionage operation, code-named Venona, revealed the existence of a Russian spy ring within the government and public service. Then in 1954 Vladimir Petrov, the acting head of intelligence in the Russian Embassy in Canberra, defected, and the Menzies government set up a Royal Commission to investigate Petrov's material on Soviet espionage. Evatt believed (incorrectly as we now know) that Menzies and ASIO had timed Petrov's defection to harm Labor's chances in the 1954 elections, and, when it became known that Petrov's material mentioned several of Evatt's staff, he was convinced that the whole affair was an anti-Labor conspiracy. He decided to appear for them before the Royal Commission, but the Commissioners withdrew his leave to appear. Later, Evatt would show in parliament that the Commission was a legal disgrace. No Australian was ever charged with spying for Russia as a result of the Royal Commission, mainly because the USA insisted that the evidence from the Venona decrypts should not be made public. In fact, the Petrov Commission damaged ASIO, for in subsequent years the left in the labour movement took every opportunity to discredit it. The role of ASIO in the Russel Ward case, for example, was made public when Jim Cairns, the Labor left-winger who would become a doughty leader of street protests against the Vietnam War, raised it in parliament in 1960.[16]

Suspicion as to the kind of Australians who might spy for Soviet Russia fell of course on the members of the Australian Communist Party and its associated organisations. The party was beholden to the Russians financially and ideologically, although after Khrushchev made his notorious speech at the 20th Congress of the Communist Party of the Soviet Union in 1956 many members regarded Stalinism with revulsion and the Russian version of state socialism with distaste. We also know now that Wally Clayton, a high ranking but elusive member of the party, ran a spy ring of public servants passing material on to Russian intelligence agents at the embassy. But for most party members in the 1950s, the Soviet Union was not central to their adherence to communist ideals. Yes, there had been a proletarian

---

16 David Horner, *The Spy Catchers: The Official History of ASIO, 1949–1963*, Sydney, Allen & Unwin, 2014; Desmond Ball and David Horner, *Breaking the Codes: Australia's KGB Network, 1944–1950*, Sydney, Allen & Unwin, 1998; Michael Thwaites, *Truth Will Out: ASIO and the Petrovs*, Sydney, Collins, 1980; Robert Manne, *The Petrov Affair: Politics and Espionage*, Sydney, Pergamon Press, 1987; Ken Buckley, Barbara Dale and Wayne Reynolds, *Doc Evatt: Patriot, Internationalist, Fighter and Scholar*, Melbourne, Longman Cheshire, 1994, see pp. 378–80; *House of Representatives Official Hansard*, No. 49, Tuesday 6 December 1960, p. 3619 (Jim Cairns, speech).

revolution in Russia in 1917; it was world-historic if you accepted the simplistic version of the materialist conception of history then current in the party; but it was not necessary to suppose that Australian revolutionaries had to slavishly follow the Russian path. Such was the comforting rationalisation of most Australian communists as they digested the revelations of Stalin's crimes in Khrushchev's secret speech. Complete rejection of the militaristic, manipulative model of communist politics that produced the Stalinist 'cult of the individual' and the police state – that would not occur until the collapse of the Soviet Union more than three decades later. In the meantime, there was a steady exodus of thoughtful members, including most of its intellectuals, some of whom were expelled for demanding an open discussion of Soviet communism.[17]

Revolutionaries expect surveillance; they are after all intent on overthrowing the capitalist state. They will accept assistance from allies at any time and from wherever, but in the last analysis they are only as authentic as the support they receive from the oppressed in their immediate surroundings. As for ASIO, according to its official history, it responded to directions from the government but it was also a deeply conservative organisation that equated the Communist Party with the interests of the Soviet Union. All communists, in its view, were psychologically capable of espionage, and that applied to those who sympathised, the 'fellow travellers', as well. Indeed they were even more dangerous because they could hide behind a facade of liberalism. Many artists and academics were targeted unjustly, and some such as Russel Ward suffered harm to their careers. Hence the oft repeated depiction of ASIO as an enemy of civil liberty, harassing individuals who are acting within their rights. But this misses the point. When anti-capitalist ideas are in the air, as they were in the 1950s and 1960s, ASIO's basic function, its real importance to the state, is gathering information about, and in the process disrupting, movements of revolutionary change. And that was the situation in 1957 when Childe returned to Australia. The main issue for the state ought to have been subversion, but although ASIO had separate departments for subversion and espionage, as long as conservative politicians exploited the fear of espionage for electoral purposes, ASIO found it difficult to stop looking for Soviet spies,

---

17   Tom O'Lincoln, *Into the Mainstream: The Decline of Australian Communism*, 2nd edn, Melbourne, Red Rag Publications, 2009; Mark Aarons, *The Family File*, Melbourne, Black Inc, 2010; David McKnight, *Australian Spies and Their Secrets*, Sydney, Allen & Unwin, 1994. The author of this book left the Communist Party in the early 1960s.

although said spies would have been working fairly fruitlessly in a country at the periphery of world capitalism.[18]

Gordon Childe was accustomed to surveillance. He had had a dossier with the British intelligence service, MI5, since 1917. He would have been aware of this because his application to travel home via the USA in that year was refused. Arriving in Australia (via the Cape) the censorship of his mail began immediately, Military Intelligence having been tipped off about his anti-war activities by MI5. He knew this too, because he joked about it in his correspondence and attacked the censors publicly. When he returned to Britain in 1921 the MI5 dossier was reopened, remaining active until he left for Australia in early 1957. In the 1940s he turned down invitations to lecture in the USA because he expected the State Department would deny him a visa. Just before he embarked on the ship to Australia, he revealed that he was annoyed that he would be spied on in the country of his birth. Sure enough, ASIO opened a file on him.[19]

In Childe's file there is a memorandum that reveals clearly the Cold War espionage frame in which ASIO placed revolutionaries. On the day after Childe's body was found, the Director-General of ASIO wrote to the Regional Director in New South Wales:

> Local press reports indicate that Professor Childe recently met his death near Katoomba in circumstances which suggest that he may have committed suicide. If there is any justification for this view, and in the light of earlier allegations against him, we should be glad if you could discover whether his action in taking his life could have been influenced by factors of counter-espionage significance.

The press reports, however, when they tried to explain Childe's death, assumed it was an accident – and the subsequent inquest confirmed their assumption. Why, then, did the head of Australia's counter-espionage organisation pursue the possibility that Childe had committed suicide? What circumstances suggested suicide rather than an accident? And if an unnatural death by someone

---

18 McKnight, *Australian Spies*, p. 85.
19 Military Intelligence Section 5 (MI5), 2005 KV2/2148 and 2005 KV/2149, 'Childe, Vere Gordon', files held at National Archives (UK), released in 2005; ASIO, 1993 [279], 'Childe, Vere Gordon', A6126/24, held at Australian Archives, Canberra, released 1993; W.J. Peace, 'Vere Gordon Childe and the Cold War', in Peter Gathercole, T.H. Irving and Gregory Melleuish (eds), *Childe and Australia: Archaeology, Politics and Ideas*, Brisbane, University of Queensland Press, 1995, pp. 128–43.

with a security record has to be treated as suspicious, why did the suspicion suggest a spy in trouble rather than a disillusioned subversive?[20]

The Russian Embassy in Canberra had been closed since the Petrov affair so Soviet spooks would have had to have had very good cover indeed to keep operating in Australia. Nor is there any evidence in Childe's ASIO file that he had made contact with foreign intelligence operatives. But that was the possibility raised by the Director-General's memo. The various consequences of such imagined contact for explaining Childe's death are so unlikely as to be delusional. Perhaps Childe jumped to escape exposure as a Soviet agent of influence? Did he jump to get away from a Soviet agent? Or did someone push him? The memo was an instinctive response by an official with Cold War paranoia. When, at the inquest, a witness was recalled to testify that he 'had no reason to believe that the deceased had to fear violence from anybody' it may have been the result of ASIO's interest, because only in ASIO was this being implied as an explanation for the possibility that Childe took his own life in a counter-espionage context of fear.[21]

The Director-General was not the only person to be paranoid about Childe's death. When Mary Alice Evatt, Bert's wife, heard the news she immediately concluded that he had been murdered, because he knew too much. About what and by whom? We don't know, but the context in which she came to that conclusion is easier to imagine, given Bert's suspicions that ASIO had become a dangerous and reactionary force in Australian politics. In which case, perhaps Mary Alice thought that ASIO had done the wicked deed.[22]

There was also a strange and uncomfortable echo of his death in a 1964 novel. In *The Dangerous Islands*, Russian agents are secretly installing devices in remote places along the Celtic Fringe – the Hebrides, Ireland and the Scillies – to allow their satellites to guide nuclear-armed rockets with greater accuracy. A Russian fishing trawler nearby carries technicians and spies to maintain the devices, but they are also reliant on the local knowledge of an archaeologist, old and white-haired Professor Burbage, who is excavating a Bronze Age burial site on one of the western islands. The Russians are blackmailing him

---

20   Director-General to Regional Director NSW, 22 October 1957, Childe's ASIO file, as in footnote 7 above.

21   Inquest into the death of Vere Gordon Childe, evidence of Alexander Gordon, 22 November 1957, Inquest no. 2389 of 1957, NSW State Records Office, 13/8459.

22   Bill Peace to Terry Irving, 19 March 1988 re Peace's correspondence with Kylie Tennant: 'Mary Alice Evatt was convinced that Childe was the victim of a political murder! Apparently Childe wrote to Evatt a note the day or two before he died stating that I'll see you next week or something to that effect. Mary Alice Evatt, according to Tennant, was convinced that Childe knew "too much about something".'

because in 1936, while digging in the USSR, he had an affair with the wife of a high-level Russian official. The climax of the novel occurs on a cliff on Bryer in the Scillies. Burbage has worked out that the heroes of the novel, an MI5 man and his girlfriend, want to question him, and he is determined to avoid this. A chase ensues along the cliffs, observed by a Russian spy who has come ashore from the trawler. Burbage slips and falls to his death, whereupon the Russian shoots him twice to make sure he is dead. Later the body of the would-be assassin washes up on a beach, murdered by his own comrades. The MI5 man ensures the Russian has a proper burial with a headstone reading 'A communist, known to God'.[23]

Was the unfortunate Burbage based on Childe? He had made a visit to Russia in 1935 and he had excavated archaeological sites in Ireland and Scotland, including the Neolithic village at Skara Brae, in the Orkneys. This was public knowledge at the time, but the author of the novel knew Childe personally. The name on the title page was Ann Bridge, but her real name was Lady Mary Dolling Sanders O'Malley. She was an amateur archaeologist, and archaeology turns up in several of her novels, one of which, *And Then You Came* (1948), includes an archaeologist, Professor Porlock. She dedicated this novel to Childe, who had provided her with archaeological information to help with her 'romantic reconstruction', as he called it, of the legend of Deirdre of the Sorrows. Childe told her he did not see much of himself in Porlock but he was grateful for the dedication:

> To Professor V. Gordon Childe, D.Litt., D.Sc., F.S.A., F.S.A. Scot., Professor of Prehistory at London University, who more than any other man has made their own prehistory live for the people of Britain. With very great respect.

This respect is perhaps the source of her sympathetic treatment of the character Professor Burbage in *The Dangerous Islands*. The heroine describes Burbage's pro-Russian activities as 'silly' but 'innocent', and discounts the value of his unwilling assistance to the Russians.[24]

Childe and Lady Mary had a mutual friend, Mansfield Forbes, a lecturer in English at Cambridge who had dug with Childe at Old Keig and Finavon in Scotland. Another connection was between her husband's cousin, Angus

---

23   Ann Bridge, *The Dangerous Islands*, London, Chatto & Windus, 1964.
24   Ann Bridge, *And Then You Came – A Novel*, London, Chatto & Windus, 1948; Childe to Lady Mary O'Malley, 12 July 1948 and 16 December 1948, Ann Bridge papers, 22/2, Harry Ransome Humanities Research Center, University of Texas at Austin; Bridge, *The Dangerous Islands*, pp. 118, 178.

Graham, a Scottish archaeologist who worked with Childe on the Royal Commission on Historical Monuments of Scotland. A still further connection was through Mary's flatmate in her single years, Ethel Graham, the sister of Angus Graham, who married the historian R.G. Collingwood, whose writings on Roman history Childe admired and whose theory of history challenged Childe to develop his own ideas. Nothing untoward here: it was a typical friendship and professional network of the British elite.

There was, however, another connection, one with Cold War overtones, through Lady Mary's husband Sir Owen St Clair O'Malley. With strong anti-Soviet views, he was a high-level diplomat and Foreign Office counselor who was knighted in 1943. Earlier that year, on the discovery of a mass grave of nearly 22,000 Polish officers near Katyn, he wrote the report for the FO that pointed overwhelmingly to Russian guilt – a verdict confirmed in 1990 by Mikhail Gorbachev. There is a distinct possibility that O'Malley would have known that his wife's friend had an MI5 dossier, and that in 1941 this friend was under suspicion because of an excavation near a defence site in Orkney. During the Cold War, O'Malley's important diplomatic role in Europe was followed in the press, so he was precisely the kind of person to whom the FO's Information Research Department would have fed its propaganda. He might have known, and told his wife, that in 1949 George Orwell had 'fingered' Childe, along with others, as a communist sympathiser who was therefore an untrustworthy British subject.[25]

Childe was never a spy, not even an agent of influence consciously collaborating with Soviet power. As we shall see, he was sceptical of the benefits of that power for science and liberty. But as his ASIO file pointed out, in Britain he was a member of several Communist Party front organisations and his 'recent utterances have generally been in accord with the prescribed Party line'. In 1957, in the context of the Cold War, this was sufficient for a chief of ASIO, the wife of a Labor political leader tormented by hostile political and security forces, and a conservative novelist married to a ruling-class diplomat to wonder about his involvement with disloyal forces. What each of them missed was a simple truth: that Childe was an intellectual who had committed himself to the idea of historical progress and the role of revolutions in history.[26]

---

25 Alan J. Foster, 'O'Malley, Sir Owen St Clair (1887–1974)', *Oxford Dictionary of National Biography* online edition, accessed 21 June 2011; 'Archaeologist Fingered by Orwell', *British Archaeology*, 73, November 2003, online edition accessed 1 May 2011.

26 File note in Childe's ASIO file, A6126/24, f. 18.

Part 1.
Growing up into Revolution: Sydney and Oxford 1892–1917

Chapter 1

LIVING IN A DIVIDED CITY

Gordon Childe was born in Sydney in 1892, the middle year of a pivotal period in Australian politics. Since 1890, 'great strikes and lockouts' had brought the turmoil of bitter class war to the Australian colonies. Armed troops supported the police in the maritime strike of 1890, those in Melbourne ordered by their commanding officer to 'fire low and lay them out'. Sabotage and incendiarism punctuated a long shearers' strike in 1891. During a strike of metalliferous miners in Broken Hill the following year, the militancy of a Women's Brigade was the union's most feared weapon in its campaign of violence against strikebreakers. Then in 1894 there was a second shearers' strike, even more violent than the first. Australia's national song, 'Waltzing Matilda', recalls an incident when a striker, pursued by three troopers for setting fire to a woolshed, killed himself near a billabong. As these strikes one by one went down to defeat, union leaders and socialist intellectuals piggy-backed a political movement on the mobilisation the strikes had created. They formed labour parties, and almost immediately the voters sent labour politicians into the colonial parliaments of New South Wales, Queensland, Victoria and South Australia. Now the labour movement had two wings, one characterised by industrial organisation and militancy, the other by parliamentarist caution. Could they work together? Which one should take the lead? As a young man, Gordon Childe devoted his energies to answering these questions, writing a study of labour organisation, *How Labour Governs – A Study of Workers' Representation in Australia*, that labour activists continue to consult.[1]

To his family none of the political and industrial turmoil of the 1890s mattered very much. They lived on Sydney's leafy North Shore, without even a bridge to link them to the gritty suburbs on the southern side of the harbour where the struggle between capital and labour was being fought

---

1   Childe, *How Labour Governs, 1st edn*, pp. 4–5 on the formation of Labor parties; Stuart Svensen, *Industrial War: The Great Strikes 1890–1894*, Wollongong, NSW, Ram Press, c. 1995.

out. Proper as well as conservative, the family announced his arrival in the 'Births' column of *The Sydney Morning Herald*, just one of seven listed that day: 'Childe – April 14 [1892] at St Thomas's Vicarage, North Sydney, the wife of Stephen H. Childe, of a son'.[2]

The pretty but damp Rectory at St Thomas's where Childe lived until 1900.
The family shown is that of the first Rector, W.B. Clarke.
(State Library of New South Wales: PXA 2137/11 (60), item 40)

The colony was sliding ever faster into economic depression: at its worst moment about 30 per cent of workers were unemployed, according to the Sydney Labour Council. In February 1892 the government opened a Labour Bureau that registered nearly 14,000 unemployed men and women in its first six months. Destitute men and women began sleeping in the Domain, but as the nights became colder and the socialists began to proselytise among them, the government arranged for the single men to go to the Brown Brothers Stables in Castlereagh Street, where they slept amid the stench of manure and fermenting straw. On the night Childe was born another 800 were sleeping in

---

2   *Sydney Morning Herald*, 20 April 1892, p. 1.

the Exhibition Building, where the charitable ladies and gentlemen comprising the Citizens Committee were surprised to discover that the unemployed men became more dissatisfied the more they were given! Six 'objectionable' agitators (who were telling the men to demand the resumption of public works) were expelled from the building that night and the Committee decided – following a logic still relied on by conservatives to punish the ungrateful recipients of charity – to reduce their free meals to one a day. Then it made a point of giving the men the same blankets issued to the Special Constables who helped to break the maritime strike of 1890.[3]

The vicarage where Childe was born was damp and had no drainage or gas but it would have seemed a palace to the Ladies Committee for Relief to the Indigent, one of whom wrote to the *Herald* on the same day as his birth was announced. She had been visiting the homes of married men in the working-class suburbs south and west of the city centre: 'No pen could describe the destitution and misery. Houses void of furniture, families without food and clothing. In many cases we had to provide immediate food to stay starvation. The men all ask for work, offering to take any wages, that their wives and children may have shelter.'[4]

The *Herald* was in favour of private philanthropy rather than public works. For over 50 years, its owners, the Fairfax family, had aligned it with the interests of the business and professional communities. In 1892 its columns reflected and reinforced the mix of fear and relief that the bourgeoisie felt during a lull in the class war of the early 1890s. Its writers congratulated the forces of order for mounting 'a spirited resistance' to labour's attempt 'to seize control of capital', and for surviving a 'period of domestic anarchy', by which they meant the clashes on the streets between supporters of the maritime strike and government-organised Special Constables and volunteer militias in September 1890. Now the labour movement was in retreat, although who could tell whether its newly elected parliamentary representatives in Macquarie Street would not introduce socialism by stealth?[5]

Abroad, the *Herald* saw signs of the fragility of the rule of capital everywhere, reporting in eye-popping detail the 'anarchist outrages' in Paris, Rome, Berlin, Brussels, Barcelona, and New York in the days surrounding Gordon's birth. It inferred that Sydney would not be free forever from 'the chaos of

---

3   *Sydney Morning Herald*, 1 April 1892, p. 6, and 15 April 1892, p. 7; Raymond Markey, *In Case of Oppression: The Life and Times of the Labour Council of New South Wales*, Sydney, Pluto Press and Lloyd Ross Forum, 1994, p. 13
4   *Sydney Morning Herald*, 20 April 1892, p. 6, from 'Stanmore'.
5   *Sydney Morning Herald*, 15 April 1892, p. 4 (editorial); 4 June 1892, p. 13 (letter).

strikes, riots and dynamite'. Moreover, the colony's labour politicians were part of the same threat to the social order as the overseas anarchists because they too aimed to create a socialist utopia 'from the debris'.[6]

The *Herald's* readers had reason to feel uneasy. Despite the defeat of organised labour, the unorganised multitude had not got the message. Indeed, in the mind of the most disaffected, it was almost as if the use of 'official' violence against labour's organised 'physical force' during the strikes now justified spontaneous and unofficial eruptions. A hall in Darlinghurst was wrecked during a tug of war event when the management tried to close it; 25 police were needed to break up the riot that ensued. Outside the Water Police Court at Circular Quay, two factions in the local Chinese community fought with iron bars and sticks with iron knobs over a gambling dispute. Later that day the nine arrested men tried to storm their way out of the watch-house. In working-class Redfern, the Waterloo 'push' and the Chippendale 'push' (rival larrikin gangs) fought with sticks and stones on Regent Street. When the police arrived, the two pushes joined forces and 150 youths beat the police back along the street. There were 12 arrests. Larrikins attacked a dairyman in Burke Street, Redfern, terrorising the residents for an hour. Even employed workers were unruly, despite the spectre of unemployment and the collapse of the trade unions, starting strikes without the backing of the Trades and Labour Council, as did the non-unionised miners excavating the Bondi sewer in June 1892.[7]

How to account for the existence of people who seemed to delight in rioting? A letter writer to the *Herald* answered the question by opining that it was all the fault of the socialists agitating among the working classes. The remedy was left to the readers' imagination. But for the larrikins, as another letter brutally declared on the day Gordon's birth was announced, only the lash could deter such 'fiends in human form'. Finding scapegoats to blame and punish diverted readers from considering the class forces underlying the experience of social disorder. Recent scholarship has argued that the larrikins were working-class youths unhappy about having to repress and sublimate their natural instincts as they were corralled into the 'respectable' and disciplined working class of industrial capitalism.[8]

---

6   For reports of the overseas 'outrages', see *Sydney Morning Herald*, 20 April 1892, pp. 1, 12, 14; 1 April 1892 for editorial on them.
7   *Sydney Morning Herald*, 20 February, 2 March, 18 May, 20 June 1892; the Bondi sewer strike reported on 17 June 1892, p. 6.
8   *Sydney Morning Herald*, 20 and 23 April 1892 (letters); Kylie M. Smith, 'Subjectivity, Hegemony, and the Subaltern in Sydney, 1870–1900', *Rethinking Marxism*, vol. 19, no. 2, April 2007, pp. 169–79.

***

Gordon spent his youth in a loving family residing in a prosperous suburb. His father received from the Church of England a house and a comfortable annual income of 475 pounds. To ordinary workers, living in the conflicted southern and western suburbs and, if they were lucky enough to be employed, earning less than half that amount, North Sydney must have seemed idyllic. On the waterfront there were clusters of working-class terraces and a few small shipyards. Further up the hillsides there were substantial houses and streets of middle-class villas. The elite school that Gordon would attend, the Sydney Church of England Grammar School ('Shore'), was established in 1889 in the mansion of the entrepreneur B.O. Holterman, who had discovered the largest nugget of reef gold in the world at Hill End in 1871. From the terminus of the steam ferry at Milson's Point, North Shore professionals returning from business in the city could catch either the Miller Street cable car that ran up the hill to St Leonard's Park, or the North Shore railway line (its construction vigorously pushed during the depression of the 1890s) that linked the scatter of settlements north to Hornsby. After 1893 commuters could ride the electric tram that ran east along the ridge from St Leonard's Park to Spit Junction. Growing up in North Sydney's go-ahead decades, Gordon would have found few signs of inequality or political contention to prick his social conscience.[9]

The Childe family would have alighted from the cable car at McLaren Street, where St Thomas's church stood just off Miller Street on a large site near the top of the hill. In 1881, soon after Stephen Childe became the rector, two of Queen Victoria's sons, Prince Albert and Prince George, laid the foundation stone for a new church building, which was completed in 1884. Designed by the well-known Anglican architect Edmund Blacket in the decorated Gothic style, it acknowledged the social and economic aspirations of North Shore residents. Cathedral-like, large and squat (the spire on the tower was never built), it had an attractive pattern of coloured slates in its roof. Seating up to a thousand worshippers, it is still the largest Anglican parish church in Australia.[10]

---

9 Isadore Brodsky, *North Sydney 1788–1962*, Municipal Council of North Sydney, 1963; Cable Clerical Index.

10 *A Sense of Time Past and Future: The Building of St Thomas's Anglican Church, North Sydney*, The Church, 1971; Jeannie Walker (convenor), *What God Has Done: 150 Years at St Thomas's Anglican Church, North Sydney*, The Church, 1996.

An imposing statement of North Shore wealth and faith – St Thomas's Church, North Sydney, c.1900. (State Library of Victoria; F. Henningham, printer; H20294)

Stephen Childe conducted services while the new church was built over and around the old (eventually it was removed stone by stone out the front door) but his family was not able to live in the new rectory until 1900. More salubrious their new home might have been, but it did not protect Gordon from illness. In his early teens he spent two years in bed with polio, according to Angus Graham who in the early 1940s worked closely with Childe. Perhaps his father hired a private tutor, but it is more likely his elder brothers and sisters as well as his parents would have seen to his education until he was able to walk around the corner to Berry Street where H.N. Crisford, BA, ran the North Sydney Preparatory School. Crisford advertised that he prepared boys for Shore, where Childe's brother Lawrence had been a pupil, and where Gordon attended from 1907.[11]

From the surviving documents it is not possible to catch a glimpse of the everyday lives of the family. When Sally Green wrote her biography of Childe she relied for information from Gordon's niece, Mary, the daughter of his

---

11   Angus Graham, 'In Piam Veterum Memoriam' in A.S. Bell (ed.), *The Scottish Antiquarian Tradition*, Edinburgh, 1981, p. 222; *Sydney Morning Herald*, 19 June 1907, p. 3 (advertisement).

half-brother Laurence, and his cousin Anne, the daughter of his mother's brother Alexander Gordon. Neither could have had useful personal memories of Gordon or of the Childe family in North Sydney, because Mary was born in 1913 and Anne in 1912. In relation to the affectionate bonds between Gordon Childe and his three much older sisters, however, Mary may well have provided reliable information, because in the 1950s she was looking after Ethel, the youngest of his three sisters, who was then in her eighties. When Green concludes that Alice (born 1871), Marion known as 'May' (born 1874), and Ethel (born 1876) doted on Gordon as an infant and young boy, it has the ring of truth, for Gordon kept in touch with his sisters throughout his life, and in 1922 he was helping Ethel with a generous allowance when she was an invalid. We also know, from a letter written by their father, that he always regarded Gordon as 'a good son'.[12]

Again, there is no documentary evidence about Gordon's feelings for his mother. Harriet Gordon married Rev. Stephen Childe in 1886 after his first wife had died, leaving Stephen with five children. When her son was born in 1892 she was 39 and her husband was 48. She was an ideal wife for a widowed clergyman, for her father had been one of the grandees of the Church of England in the colony since the 1850s. Alexander Gordon, QC, was the main legal authority for the Sydney diocese, serving on many of its committees until the 1880s, and publishing several pamphlets on church law and polity. He and his wife Anne, who grew up in India where her father was a missionary, were friends of Frederic Barker, Bishop of Sydney. In the 1880s Harriet's father, as a member of the appointed Legislative Council, opposed the introduction by the Premier, Henry Parkes, of 'free, compulsory and secular' schooling to the colony. In 1889 he published *The Future of the Empire; or a brief statement of the case against Imperial Federation*, arguing that the bonds of empire were sufficiently protected by the loyalty of its separately governed and self-governing colonies of British settlers. Meanwhile, Harriet's mother set up the Sydney branch of the Church of England Girls' Friendly Society. Together they were typical, as was Stephen Childe, of the imperial English men and women of the Victorian era who established the 'sense of colonial subordination' in the psychology of Anglicanism. No-one in this circle sympathised with 'the democracy' of the colony.[13]

---

12 Green, *Prehistorian*, pp. vii, 148; Stephen Childe to Sir George Fuller, 21 April 1922, NSWSA, Premier's Dept Correspondence, A22/1477 in 9/4885.
13 Hilary M. Carey, *Believing in Australia, 1851–1900*, Sydney, Allen & Unwin, 1996, p. 85; Ken Cable, 'Alexander Gordon (1815–1903), barrister', *Australian Dictionary of Biography*, Melbourne, Melbourne University Press, Vol. 4, 1972, p. 269.

Stephen Childe is an enigma. On the one hand he was extremely conventional in his beliefs and politics. He was related to a well-established county family – the Childes of Kinlet in Shropshire – and he had been educated at Corpus Christi College in Cambridge, where as well as a BA (1868) he was awarded the Chancellor's Medal in Law (1869). Perhaps it was this social background that led to his appointment and long incumbency as rector of St Thomas's, where he remained for 33 years, rising to a senior role in the diocese as Rural Dean of North Sydney. In his personal relationships, however, he was unpredictable, distant and outré. As a young clergyman in England he had been unable to settle in any of the six positions he had held, and within two years of arriving in Sydney he was causing consternation among the clergy and lay members of the synod. In 1882 he organised an 'Old English Fair' at the Garden Palace in Macquarie Street where young ladies from North Shore congregations, in period costume, collected donations. This use of 'female beauty' to aid church finances so outraged a Rev. Hodgson that he referred to them in the synod as 'daughters of Moab' (who had slept with their father to carry on his line). There was uproar as defenders of the virtue of the young women of the north threatened Hodgson with violence. Stephen, it seems, appreciated female beauty. Perhaps this was the origin of the dislike of Stephen in his second wife's family, the Gordons, who privately called him a 'womanizer'.[14]

Among his congregation there was also disquiet, although the evidence for this may well reflect the views of later commentators. The Sydney diocese was and is strongly evangelical, but the Rev. Stephen Childe is remembered by the congregation of St Thomas's as leaning towards the high church Tractarians in church politics. The evangelical party in the Church of England regarded the Holy Scriptures as the only source of revelation, and believed the central spiritual experience was conversion. In the 1840s a movement critical of the evangelicals emerged in Oxford and soon spread through the Church of England at home and abroad. To the Tractarians, as the members of the Oxford Movement were known, the non-rational 'enthusiasm' of the evangelicals was embarrassing, and their indifference to church traditions distressing. The Tractarians liked to show the continuities between the Church of England and the Church of Rome, especially those visible in the rituals of worship, such as the wearing of the chasuble, and they believed that the episcopacy was divinely ordained. To

---

14 Green, *Prehistorian*, p. 5; The Cable Clerical Index; *Sydney Morning Herald*, 12 May 1882, p. 3.

the evangelicals, these were dangerous ideas, undermining the lessons of the Reformation.[15]

The only documented evidence for Stephen Childe's opposition to the evangelicals is a well-publicised incident at a synod meeting in 1898. Speaking to a resolution aimed at curbing the influence of the High Church movement, a Rev. J. Vaughan referred to the 'extreme ritualism' to be found in some churches in London because 'the Archbishops and Bishops had forgotten their vows and betrayed their trust'. This caused general uproar, amidst which Rev. Stephen Childe asked the Archbishop whether such 'abominable views' should be allowed in synod. When the Archbishop from the chair refused to disallow the view, Childe walked out of the meeting. Otherwise the evidence suggests that while he might have sympathised with the High Church position, he did not actively oppose the Archbishop, for there were several churches where the chasuble was worn, but St Thomas's was not one of them.

Like many followers of the Oxford Movement, Stephen Childe was keen on music in church services (several of his children taking part in the ensemble at St Thomas's), and Alice and Ethel joined Anglican religious orders, a favoured project of Tractarians, and it may also not have been a coincidence that he was forcibly retired in 1913, when the new Archbishop, John Charles Wright, decided to rid the Sydney diocese of the last traces of Tractarianism. His estrangement from his congregation, however, was not necessarily doctrinal. It is just as likely that in a middle-class congregation at a time of awakening national consciousness there was a mixture of cultural and personal issues creating dislike of their Cambridge-educated parson. It might have been enough that he was aloof, that he had a speech impediment that amused the young people in the pews, and that he was frequently absent from the parish while visiting his second home at Wentworth Falls, 100 kilometres to the west of Sydney in the Blue Mountains.[16]

Whether Gordon Childe inherited his independence of mind from his father we can only conjecture. There would have been a literature of religious argument in the kind of home that Gordon grew up in, especially one in which the parents drew on different church traditions. More to the point, religious argument could cover awareness of social problems, and from there to criticism of the inequalities of the social order that gave rise to them. The

---

15   Stephen Judd and Kenneth Cable, *Sydney Anglicans: A History of the Diocese*, Sydney, Anglican Information Office, 2000; Stuart Piggin, *Evangelical Christianity in Australia: Spirit, Sword and World*, Melbourne, Oxford University Press, 1996.

16   *Sydney Morning Herald*, 23 September 1898, p. 6; Stephen E. Judd, 'Wright, John Charles (1861–1933)', *Australian Dictionary of Biography*, Vol. 12, 1990, pp. 585–6.

conversion of the lower classes, seen as 'missionary' activity, could easily mutate into support for reform. The Christian Social Union (CSU), which attracted many second-generation followers of the Tractarians as well as evangelicals, endorsed the emerging labour movement in the 1890s (although the CSU was never proletarian in composition). And then there was the general influence of 'the social gospel'. As far as we can tell, in the St Thomas rectory 'the social gospel' was not a guide to religious purpose, but Harriet was dedicated to the good works normally expected of a parson's wife. At the very least, she would have brought awareness of the social problems affecting individual parishioners into the family circle, and into the life of her son. Beyond that, however, it seems unlikely that Gordon would have formed radical attitudes while at home. The family's horrified reaction to his later anti-war activities suggests that politically it was a thoroughly conservative household.[17]

In any case, the family's influence would have diminished soon after his 18th birthday. In 1910 his mother died, a few months before he was due to sit for his Senior Matriculation to the University of Sydney; in 1911 his uncle, Judge Alexander Gordon, took him into his home in Elizabeth Bay, where he lived for the next three years while he attended university; and in 1913 his father, having resigned from St Thomas's, went to live in Wentworth Falls accompanied by a new wife with whom Gordon was never comfortable.

* * *

The death of Gordon's mother might have been the moment when he began his walk away from religion. In December of that year, in Shore's school magazine, he published a translation from ancient Greek of 'Elegy No. 2' by Xenophanes of Colophon, a philosopher and theologian who was born about 570 BC. There were elements of the life and thought of Xenophanes that might have appealed to Gordon in 1910.[18]

---

17   May to VGC, 20 July 1917, Childe's MI5 file, KV/2; Alice to VGC, 5 May 1918, National Archives of Australia, Directorate of Military Intelligence, MP95/1, Intelligence reports on enemy trading and other suspicious actions, 168/1-7; Alice to VGC, 22/6/1918, Intell. Reports 168/8-14; Laurence to Alice Childe, 10/11/1918, Intell. Reports 167/56.

18   *Sydney Morning Herald*, 29 July 1910, p. 6, death notice for Harriett Childe; *The Torch-Bearer*, vol. 19, no. 7, December 1910, p. 229 (I am grateful to Robin

If he contemplated leaving home (a step he took a few months later), perhaps he wondered about what it would be like to spend most of one's life in exile, as Xenophanes did in Sicily. Perhaps he appreciated Xenophanes's criticisms of Greek militarism and athleticism. The 'Shore' school, modelled on Dr Arnold's Rugby, sidelined the intellectual formation of its pupils to concentrate on developing an ethos of moral rectitude, gentlemanly conduct, and respect for authority, enforced through prefects and embodied in strenuous exercise. Gordon was never a prefect, and never wore the uniform of the school's cadet unit nor excelled on the sporting field. Or more pertinent to the moment, grieving for his mother, and finding the heavy religious atmosphere at home irksome, Gordon might have been drawn to Xenophanes because he was a religious sceptic, poking fun at the traditional Greek idea of a pantheon of gods whose images were reflections of the Greeks themselves.

While criticism of the Greek obsession with the Olympic Games is central to the elegy, Gordon's translation highlights the connection between the (city) state and religion. The brute strength that the city prizes is displayed in the precinct of Zeus, the father of the Gods:

> If with swift feet one be a victor there
> Where Zeus's precinct by Pisean stream
> Stands at Olympia – or in the wrestling bouts
> Or through possession of the grievous art
> Of boxing – he would be more dear
> For all his countrymen to look upon
> And at the games the foremost seat would take,
> And would be nourished from the public store
> Of that, his city, and receive such prize
> As should for him be treasure evermore;
> Yea with swift horses he might gain all these
> And yet might not be worthy as am I.
>
> For better is our wisdom than the strength
> Of men or horses. 'Twas right rashly formed
> That other judgment. No, it is not right,
> Right to prefer brute strength to wisdom good.
> Small any gain to the state might come

Derricourt for drawing this to my attention); Tim Whitmarsh, *Battling the Gods: Atheism in the Ancient World*, London, Faber & Faber, 2016, on Xenophanes see Ch. 4; Michael Patzia, 'Zenophanes (c.570–478 BCE)', *Internet Encyclopedia of Philosophy*, www.iep.utm.edu/xenoph/ accessed 1 April 2016.

> If any, striving by Pisean flood
> Should conquer; for that victory does not fill
> The treasure houses of his city – No.

Xenophanes, in Gordon's translation, not only takes the side of wisdom, but he denies that it is served by the pact between Zeus and the political power that the city (state) embodied and the brute athletic strength that it rewarded. 'It is not right that religion is harnessed to power; there is something unworthy about it.' If Gordon were attracted to Xenophanes's atheism, it did not prevent him becoming the Honorary Secretary of the Social Services Department of the Men's Christian Union at the University of Sydney a few years later. It does suggest, however, that he might have taken a critical step away from the orthodox view – his father's view, no doubt – that the role of religion was to support the status quo.[19]

* * *

The move Gordon made in 1911 across Sydney harbour may have been doubly significant. He had finished his schooling, his mother had died a few months earlier, and he was leaving the vicarage in North Sydney for his mother's brother's house in Elizabeth Bay. Ostensibly, this would make his travelling to Sydney University easier. By this time, however, Gordon was showing the independence of spirit that would lead him into unorthodoxy. In the light of the family's dismay a few years later when he opposed the First World War, it is not difficult to imagine that he was also running away from the conservative political leanings of High Churchmen such as his father.

Elizabeth Bay was a prestigious upper-class suburb, but it was cheek by jowl with one of the oldest and meanest parts of working-class Sydney. Because Gordon loved to walk – he played golf in the university vacations – it is not impossible to imagine him striding off after breakfast to the university, a distance of about four kilometers. The most direct route would have taken him south through Darlinghurst, east of the city centre, along the ridge where many substantial mansions had been built before the middle of the nineteenth century. Reaching Liverpool Street, he would begin to descend into the valley behind Woolloomooloo Bay, to walk past the narrow terrace houses of East Sydney, with their front doors opening onto the footpath,

---

19   *Hermes*, vol. XIX, no. 1, June 1913, p. 31 re Childe and the Men's Christian Union.

built for the labouring classes in the same period. Then he would climb up a short hill to reach the city proper, turning south and then west up the street now known as Broadway, passing the city's oldest brewery to reach the gates of the university at Camperdown.[20]

Vere Gordon Childe enrolled in 1911 and Herbert Vere Evatt in 1912; although they had very different upbringings, otherwise they had much in common. From the country, Evatt, raised by his widowed mother in the Bank Hotel in East Maitland, and fiercely determined to make his mark in the metropolis, had set his heart on a legal career. Meanwhile, Gordon, from the leafy side of the harbour, and a professional milieu that kept its distance from that of publicans, was already showing the academic prowess that would bring him distinction as a student, having been awarded the Cooper Scholarship for Proficiency in Classics at the end of his first year. Whether because they shared the unusual name of 'Vere', had similar political ideals, or because Evatt saw a useful legal connection in the making – Gordon was lodging with a judge – Bert and Gordon began a friendship for life in 1912.[21]

They would walk together discussing their personal philosophy, finding common ground in their dislike of selfishness and delight in overcoming difficulties. They disdained the infrequent motorcars that passed them as anti-social: 'you just get in your motor car and you drive along and don't talk to anybody'. Sometimes they hiked in the Blue Mountains, where the Childe family had a palatial holiday home overlooking Wentworth Falls. They also took many walks in the city, perhaps between the university and Uncle Alexander's comfortable mansion on Elizabeth Bay Road. Evatt, who lived in St Andrew's College in the university grounds, might have appreciated visits to the home of the Gordon family, where there was a young toddler, born in 1908, and an infant born in 1912 – and of course an eminent judge.[22]

---

20 *Sydney Morning Herald*, 21 June 1910, p. 6.
21 Kylie Tennant, *Evatt: Politics and Justice*, Sydney, Angus & Robertson, 1970, Ch. 1; Childe's academic record: University Archivist to Miss S. Green, England, 5 February 1976, University of Sydney Archives, Biog 353/2; K.J. Cable, 'Gordon, Alexander (1815–1903)', *Australian Dictionary of Biography*, Vol. 4, p. 269; Martha Rutledge, 'Gordon, Margaret Jane (1880–1962)', *Australian Dictionary of Biography*, Vol. 9, 1983, pp. 55–6 (also details on her husband (Sir) Alexander Gordon, 1858–1942).
22 'Interview with Mary Alice Evatt, 1973', National Library of Australia oral history tapes (I am grateful to Barbara Dale for her transcript of this tape); Mrs Gwen Silvey to Terry Irving, 13 June 1990 re the Childe houses in Wentworth Falls.

Another visionary dreamer: Herbert Vere Evatt as Childe would have known him in the early 1920s. (Flinders University of South Australia; Evatt Collection 1537 001)

As Arts students, they attended lectures in the two-storey, sandstone main building, a Gothic Revival version of a medieval Oxford or Cambridge College with internal courtyard, bell tower and crenelated parapet, set on a rise overlooking Victoria Park. Begun in 1855, the only parts completed when Childe arrived were the imposing east range facing the city, the Great Hall and the Fisher Library, diagonally opposite each other on the north-east and south-west corners. He could take tea in the undergraduates' 'ramshackle wooden common room', crossing the muddy quadrangle to reach it. At lectures, university custom required him to wear an academic gown, and elsewhere on campus to take the initiative in greeting any passing professor, to whom you were very possibly known, for it was a tiny academic community. In Gordon's first year, there were only 386 students in Arts, of whom about 270 attended lectures during the day, taught by six professors, five other full-time teaching staff and a few part-timers.[23]

Despite its elitism and stuffy traditions, the university could not but be unaffected by the democratic ferment at home and abroad, not to speak of the reformist political discourse encouraged by the recent accession to government of the Labor Party, federally and in New South Wales. The signs of campus radical activity and thinking were small, but for our story they are significant because Gordon was involved in all of them.

---

23   *University of Sydney, A Short Description prepared for the use of the Congress of the Universities of the Empire*, published by the University in 1912; Sydney University Christian Union, *The University of Sydney Students' Handbook*, Sydney, G.B. Philp and Son, 1913; Clifford Turney, Ursula Bygott and Peter Chippendale, *Australia's First: A History of the University of Sydney, Volume 1, 1850–1939*, University of Sydney, 1991, p. 647.

Chapter 2

STUDENTS AND WORKERS

University life could not be quarantined from the turbulence of the city, and students with radical sympathies could not ignore the contradictions of representation. In the years when Childe was an undergraduate at Sydney (between 1911 and 1913), workers defied their leaders to engage in spontaneous industrial warfare, and students defied their professors to challenge how the university was run. Although we have no direct evidence about the impact of these events on Childe at the time, they must have contributed to his radicalisation – and we have indications in his later writings that they did. The important point here, in the light of his development as a socialist, is that these were proto-revolutionary years, in Australia as in other parts of the world. Indeed, as we shall see, the outbreak of the First World War has been attributed to the desire by the ruling classes of Europe to head-off radical democracy and socialism. This chapter is intended to suggest how the seeds of Childe's radical politics were sown in those years: his sympathy for militancy, his contempt for 'politicalism', and his interest in alternative working-class parties and industrial organisations.

* * *

When Gordon Childe was writing *How Labour Governs*, he remembered a strike that occurred almost a decade earlier, while he was at Sydney University. In 1913, workers in the local gas works struck for a wage increase of six shillings a week – 'a bob a day'. As gas supplies dwindled, the street lights were turned off and thousands were thrown out of work. There were demonstrations, street-corner meetings and violent attacks on the strike-breakers. Although the strike was soon over, eight weeks of industrial war followed, a 'strike epidemic' according to the *Herald*. For Childe, there was an event during the gas strike that he could not forget. Twice in *How Labour Governs*, he referred to the Premier of the Labor government, 'Honest' Jim McGowen, a former boilermaker and a good unionist, calling on members of the public to assist the owners by volunteering to take the place of striking workers. Some did, and Childe, disowning the politesse of his middle-class background and privileged life, was quite comfortable calling them 'scabs', the dirtiest word in the labour vernacular. Among the scabs were some of his fellow students.[1]

The supply of gas had been a matter of great public sensitivity ever since the election of the Labor government. The three privately owned gas companies were not loved. They supplied watery gas at three times the price of publicly owned English gas companies and used their monopoly position to exploit consumers. Their managements provoked strikes by sacking union delegates. As the cost of food and housing rose, gas workers felt they had a right to higher wages. When the union in late 1912 decided to ballot its members about a strike, the Labor Minister of Labour took out an injunction to stop the ballot. When the union applied for a special wages board, the Arbitration Court rejected the application. So, on 3 February 1913, against a background of rising prices, unemployment, and strikes for wage increases in other industries, the union decided to approach the companies directly, asking for a pay rise of one shilling a day. The gas companies refused to negotiate.[2]

The union said it could do no more, but the workers could. On 28 February, ignoring the union, but with 'an unswerving and unquestioning loyalty that would do credit to a highly disciplined army, every man on the works "took a holiday"', as the *Herald* reported. Retaliating, the court turned its attention to the informal processes of mobilisation, issuing an injunction against the main rank and file spokesman. Undeterred, the 2,000 gas workers, without the support of arbitration or their union, continued their campaign relying instead on popular support in the working-class suburbs of the inner city. They organised street-corner meetings and pickets as well as regular mass meetings of the strikers, where they elected delegates for particular tasks and heard reports of developments. These meetings repeatedly resolved not to return to work without a guarantee of 'a bob a day' extra, despite appeals from union leaders, Labour Council officials, and the Minister of Labour to leave the campaign in the hands of the government. They gave a better hearing to the anti-political ideas of Peter Bowling, the radical miners' union leader who had gone to prison in 1909, charged with conspiracy to cause industrial conflict.

---

1   Childe, *How Labour Governs*, 1st edn, pp. 37 and 59.
2   *Sydney Morning Herald*, 19 January 1911, p. 9; 20 January 1911, p. 4; 2 June 1911, p. 6; 15 and 16 November 1912, p. 19; 20 November 1912, p. 19; 4 February 1913, p. 7.

Bowling explained at a mass meeting that, if the workers were to triumph over the bosses, they needed to ignore the politicians and form a new industrial federation of coal miners, wharf labourers, coal lumpers and gas workers:

> They would find that they could only look after themselves. No law passed by any government, no matter how administered, could determine what conditions men should work under. That could, and would, be determined only by the men themselves.

That seemed to be true already; or else as in this case, if the workers were prevented from determining their conditions, they would make the public suffer.[3]

The police, with reinforcements from country districts, were on stand-by orders. Using their batons, they restored order at the Lord Mayor's public meeting in the Town Hall called to promote the recruitment of 'free labour', after supporters of the strike presented the Mayor with a stoker's shovel. But short of declaring a curfew and martial law the government could not guarantee the safety of the volunteers, for the militants of the working class were on the offensive. The boot factory 'girls' in Chippendale, the Australian Woollen Mills 'girls' at Marrickville, the casual labourers and waterside workers at the Darling Island wheat depot, and the riveters at Cockatoo Island – all soon followed the example set by the gas workers, and the ferry workers were threatening to do the same.[4]

No scab leaving the Kent Street gas works to walk through the darkened streets was safe from attacks by local residents in this waterside precinct. On Friday 7 March a group of about 30 students, after playing at being gas workers, exited by the Sussex Street gate and were met by boys calling them 'scabs' and 'blacklegs'. At every street corner, more hooting youths turned up to join the mob, which began attacking the students with volleys of blue metal from the road. The students ran down Grosvenor Street but were overtaken at George Street where blows were exchanged. They broke away but were followed down Bridge Street, dispersing at the Pitt Street corner. Ten of them ran along Pitt Street, as one of them would later tell a reporter:

> Near the 'Herald' office matters became worse. One of our fellows (a cricketer) had his eye so swollen that he was completely disabled. But

---

3   *Sydney Morning Herald*, 1 March 1913, p. 19; 3 March 1913, p. 9 (Judge Heydon's injunction); 4 March 1913, p. 9 (for government proclamation and Bowling's speech); 5 March 1913, p. 13; 6 March 1913, p. 8; 7 March 1913, p. 13.
4   *Sydney Morning Herald*, 3 March 1913, p. 7.

we stuck to it. The mob attacked us with such vigour that we deemed it best to keep to the wall.

The reporter continued the story:

> A disgraceful scene followed. A line of students in Pitt Street with their backs against the display placards of the 'Herald' Office, faced an angry crowd of unscrupulous fighters. There was punching and kicking, wrestling and stone-throwing. And through it all the 'Varsity men, so long as they could keep to the wall, used their fists only. Three of them held up leather bags as shields, which stopped many a piece of blue metal. At length, the scuffle having assumed a very dangerous aspect, one of the students made a dash for the front office of the building. This was the signal for the other nine, who followed with difficulty. One, the cricketer, fell, and was kicked several times before rising. Later the police arrived.

The scabs were saved; at the university, gentlemanly games of cricket would continue; and the angry crowd of hoi polloi, dispersing to avoid arrest, would feed their class resentments in the city's dark purlieus until the next clash.[5]

To limit the strike's damage to the government, the Premier called a conciliation conference of all the parties. The gas workers bypassed the union to elect their delegates; the workers heard their delegates report back: they had won. The government agreed to support the wage increase at a new wages board, allow the gas companies to pass the increase on to consumers, and there would be no victimisation. But the *Herald* saw it differently: the government had caved in to lawlessness, and other workers would be quick to take advantage of this weakness. Over the next six weeks conservatives had many occasions to remind the government of its weakness. By 8 April, there had been nine strikes in the past 32 days, according to a deputation to the Premier from the Employers' Federation. Why, they asked, was the government not enforcing the law?[6]

* * *

---

5   *Sydney Morning Herald*, 5 March 1913, p. 13, and 6 March 1913, p. 8, for undergraduate meetings; 7 March 1913, p. 9, for attacks on scabs; 8 March 1913, p. 19, for attack on students.
6   *Sydney Morning Herald*, 8 March 1913, p. 19, and 10 March 1913, p. 9.

The University of Sydney, founded in 1850, was the pinnacle of the system of public education in New South Wales. It was 'public' in several good ways: admission to the university was by examination, not by religious test or social standing, as in Oxford and Cambridge, and, by Childe's time, women could enrol in all undergraduate courses, and government-funded scholarships and evening courses made it possible for talented young men and women from the working and lower middle classes to aspire to higher education. Yet there was no escaping the fact that the university existed in a society divided by class, gender and race. The university was tiny, and dominated by the faculties of law, medicine, and engineering, each of which had links with powerful conservative professional and business circles 'downtown'. While its intake might aim to be socially inclusive (at least for white people), its output was inevitably exclusive. This was expected. The university's purpose, as the lawyer and leader of the Liberal opposition in New South Wales, Charles G. Wade, told the students, was to educate the 'leading men' of the country.[7] It was not just their higher education but their induction into a top-down system of rule that students were meant to value. In this sense, the university was a key institution for reproducing a white, masculine, professional and commercial culture of leadership in the state. Being public, therefore, did not make it a nursery of democratic knowledge, although some of the students would have been up for that.

In the Senate of the university, old men of power and status, with lifetime tenure, ruled the students. In 1911, Sir Normand MacLaurin, 75 years of age, a Macquarie Street doctor and shrewd businessman, had been Chancellor since 1896. Not counting the oldest and the youngest, the average age of the remaining 18 Fellows of the Senate was 60. Their ranks included seven knights of the (British) realm, Australia's first Prime Minister and four other lawyer-politicians, as well as three judges, five professors, and four medical doctors. Almost all of them had business interests, and two were leading industrialists.[8]

Their lives had been formed in 'the long boom' that followed the gold rushes of the 1850s, but by 1911 they were governing students with a very different generational experience and mental life. Like Childe, these students were born in the early 1890s, reaching maturity in a newly federated Australia,

---

7   Wade, the former Liberal-Reform Premier of NSW, used these words in his address to the students on Commem Day 1911 (*Sydney Morning Herald*, 15 May 1911, p. 10); Julia Horne and Geoffrey Sherington, *Sydney: The Making of a Public University*, The Miegunyah Press, 2012.

8   University of Sydney website for Fellows of Senate.

and entering university in the midst of the 'reaction against politicalism'. This was Childe's phrase in *How Labour Governs* for the enthusiastic embrace of direct action by workers 'wearied by the slowness of parliamentary methods' and disgusted by 'the treachery of Labour Ministers'. In 1911, few students would have sympathised with militant workers but there can be no doubt that they recognised the spontaneous, unofficial and combative industrial unrest as a challenge to 'the accustomed restraints of authority'. Moreover, traditional beliefs were bending before a gale of modernist ideas: idealism in philosophy, voluntarism in social thought, statism in political ideology, and immanentism in religion. Ten years after Federation there was a shadow over the Commonwealth's bright morning.[9]

Shaken out of their conventional moulds by these developments, the most articulate of the undergraduates were eager for more radical ideas, and the changing composition of the student body was suggesting what they might be. Of the 1,342 enrolled in 1910, 12.5 per cent were women and 18 per cent studied as evening students. Employment relationships and gender were becoming part of the student experience, and coincidentally so were the advanced remedies of cooperative production, Christian socialism, guild socialism, and radical feminism (as long as it wasn't militant) that aimed to mitigate the constricting and servile-making impacts of 'wagery' (as Alfred R. Orage's *New Age* called it) and patriarchy. In 1911 Sydney's radical students founded a Socialist Society on campus, probably for the first time at any Australian university.[10]

This was the context in which the Undergraduates' Association, believing students had a point of view that might make the university more relevant to a changing, turbulent world, was demanding representation on the University Senate. As *Hermes*, the university magazine, put it in July 1911, foreshadowing the student power rhetoric of the 1960s, they wanted a 'share in the management of themselves'. In fact, *Hermes* was full of examples of this desire for self-government. It reported in December 1910 that evening students faced peculiar difficulties (for example, anomalies relating to course equivalences), which the Evening Students Association was 'strenuously' trying to remove through discussions with the government, having decided unanimously that

---

9   Childe, *How Labour Governs*, 1st edn, p. viii; Michael Roe, *Nine Australian Progressives: Vitalism in Bourgeois Social Thought, 1890–1960*, Brisbane, University of Queensland Press, 1984; Mark Bevir, *The Making of British Socialism*, Princeton and Oxford, Princeton University Press, 2011, Ch. 11 on immanentism.

10   Enrolment figures from University of Sydney, *A Short Description prepared for the Use of the Congress of the Universities of the Empire*, Sydney, 1911, Appendix; *Hermes*, vol. XVII, no. 3, July 1911, for Socialist Club.

it would be futile to approach the Senate. In 1911 the lead article in *Hermes* complained of a 'want of sympathy, if not actual hostility, which the governing body ... has consistently showed towards the undergraduates'. The students were especially aggrieved by 'the iniquitous anomalies of the curriculum' that Senate had been 'cajoled into passing and retaining'. The leaders of the Undergraduates Association as a result were 'most emphatically asserting their right to representation on the Senate'. Now, with university reform 'in the air', *Hermes* was hoping for change, 'the triumph of green hearts over sere'.[11]

* * *

Since the 1890s, on a date in May the undergraduates had celebrated the annual Commemoration of Benefactors by a procession of satirical and jokey floats from the university to the Sydney Town Hall, where the official ceremony was held. It was an expression of saturnalia, when the world turned upside down for a moment as students laughed at their professors and the public saw politicians exposed to ridicule. Unruliness, however, could be infectious. The newspapers were full of reports of 'outrages' against authority overseas, and Australia was in the midst of a strike wave. In 1910 student rowdiness had prevented the Chancellor finishing his speech at the official ceremony. Early the following year, the city establishment was shocked that striking workers had taken over Martin Place (the banking and commercial hub of the city) to make inflammatory speeches. Something had to be done. The Martin Place outrage was probably in the minds of the Fellows of Senate, because we know that Wade reminded the students of it. The Fellows would certainly have remembered the previous year's humiliation of the Chancellor. Something was done: in April 1911 the Senate banned the Commem procession and cancelled the Town Hall ceremony.[12]

The reaction of the students was historic: for the first time they directly challenged the structure of authority on campus. It began at the next University

---

11 On the demand for student representation, see *Sydney Morning Herald*, 18 May 1911, p. 8; for 'green hearts and sere', apparently from a student song, see 'The May Scene', *Hermes*, May 1911, p. 5. There was no Fellow of Senate elected by undergraduates until 1937: Julia Horne and Geoffrey Sherington, *Sydney: The Making of a Public University*, Melbourne, The Miegunyah Press, 2012, p. 24.

12 For the reaction to workers' speeches in Martin Place, see Wade's speech to the students, *Sydney Morning Herald*, 15 May 1911, p. 10; for the Senate decision, see *Sydney Morning Herald*, 15 May 1911, p. 10 (student president's speech).

Union debate where a motion was carried deploring the decision, the mover saying that the Senate 'was a body of hidebound conservatives, whose ideas were not in keeping with progress, civilisation, or common sense'. Another speaker likened the Senate's decision to a Russian ukase. But the Senate stood firm, as the Tsar did at the start of the 1905 revolution. The Students' Association then defied the Senate by staging a replica of the official ceremony, in the Town Hall as usual, and they carried it off so successfully that the leader writer in *The Sydney Morning Herald* applauded them.[13]

At about 10.00 a.m. on Saturday 13th of May 1911, an old man was seen making an undignified rush down Hunter Street to the police station, with the derisive cheers of his tormentors following him. It was Sir Normand MacLaurin whose house on the ridge at 155 Macquarie Street was under siege from students. They sang:

> What's the matter with our Commem today?
> O, why has the mighty Sir Normand stayed away?
> O, no one can speak for six hours or more,
> Except our eloquent Chancellor.

For over an hour, contingents of hooting students had arrived at number 155:

> Then loads of wood and coal. Then the postman bought an extraordinary big mail. Then the telephone worked overtime. Streams of taxis passed and repassed, firing salutes as they got broadside on. At last Sir Normand MacLaurin felt that the joke had gone far enough. He determined to run the gauntlet, and bring reinforcements.

The police mobilised, cordoned off Macquarie Street and the demonstration was over.[14]

But not the repercussions. Within a few days both the Professorial Board and the Senate met to consider how to punish the students responsible for the Chancellor's 'molestation', as Professor Tom Anderson Stuart called it. At the Board meeting he proposed that those responsible should be 'rusticated' for two years; that is, suspended from their degree candidature. The Professorial Board wisely rejected this, resolving instead to summon the committee of the Students' Association for an explanation on the following Friday. The Senate issued a similar summons. On Wednesday, 1,000 students (Childe would have

---

13   *Sydney Morning Herald*, 22 April 1911, p. 15, for Union debate. Tsarist decrees were called ukases.
14   *Sydney Morning Herald*, 15 May 1911, p. 9.

been among them) attended a meeting called by the Students' Association. The response was clear and militant: if any students were rusticated, the entire student body would strike for as long as the rustication continued. They resolved to meet again on Friday to hear the decisions arrived at by the Board and the Senate. The *Sydney Morning Herald* predicted an angry demonstration if the university authorities decided to punish the students.[15]

The city elite, through the *Herald*, counselled the Senate and the Professorial Board to 'take a mild and reasonable view', saying that the Students' Association ought not be held responsible for 'the temporary overflow of youthful spirits' outside the Chancellor's residence. Besides, any drastic reaction by the authorities would leave a legacy of bitterness which might be dangerous in unsettled times. The advice was taken. On Saturday the *Herald* was able to report that the Commem affair had been 'smoothed over'. The Chancellor asked the Professors not to take any action in so far as anything affecting him was concerned, and the Chair of the Students' Association apologised to the Board for the songs lampooning the Chancellor. The students had won, and for much the same reasons as workers did when they prevailed in industrial disputes. The more adventurous among them had taken direct action; the greater part of them had supported the direct action by showing their determination at a subsequent mass meeting, and then they had escalated the dispute by threatening a mass strike if their grievance was not resolved. Next year the Senate allowed the Commem procession.[16]

* * *

Meanwhile, outside the university, in all manner of workplaces, young workers were also challenging authority. There was a strike wave in Australia in the years leading up to the First World War, part of what *The Sydney Morning Herald* called in 1911 'The World's Unrest': '[It is] symptomatic of some gangrenous core hidden deep in the heart of things'. In nearly every issue, there were reports of the spreading turmoil caused by this disease: the sabotage, the general strikes, the riots and violence occurring in other parts of the world. In August 1911 the epicentres were Mexico, Cairo, Barcelona, Northern France, various towns and cities in the USA and most alarmingly the major cities

---

15   *Sydney Morning Herald*, 18 May 1911, p. 8 ('Students' Strike – Trouble Threatened – Will Support the Undergrads' Committee – May Down Books on Friday').
16   *Sydney Morning Herald*, 20 May 1911, p. 15.

of Britain. In May 1912 the reports dealt with cities in the USA, Budapest, and London. Much of the paper's labour coverage in July 1913 focused on the rebellion of miners in Johannesburg. And so it went, with the editorial writer hammering the point that these labour uprisings were caused by workers refusing to accept the advice of their leaders and rejecting state-approved conciliation. Such insubordination threatened not just trade unionism but, if disrespect for authority spread, the hierarchy of social relations that was essential for orderly civil life.[17]

Nor was Australia free from these spontaneous outbreaks and rebellions against authority. Workers often decided to 'take a holiday', striking before informing the union, as the gas workers did in 1913. Worse, there was an epidemic of strikes involving workers rejecting the advice of their leaders. In October 1911 a section of the Sydney waterside workers went on strike for higher pay. The federal President (and founder) of the union, W.M. Hughes, Attorney-General in the Commonwealth Labor government, and Mr Harrison, the union's local branch Secretary, told a packed meeting in the Town Hall that work should be resumed pending negotiations with the employers. But 'amid a perfect hurricane of excitement' the workers voted to continue the strike, 'the densely-packed masses of wharf labourers shouting out their approval and waving their arms to accentuate their assent ... Then, with faces beaming ... the strikers came forth into the open – all apparently full of fight and fun.' In 1911, the *Herald* discovered symptoms of the disease among the sulphide workers at Newcastle (who rejected the offer of the Minister of Labour to mediate), the agricultural implement makers in Melbourne (who rebuffed a similar offer from the Prime Minister), and the Bundaberg cane cutters (who brushed off Labor Minister Frank Tudor). In 1912, the disease had spread to the Lithgow iron workers, and in 1913 to the Sydney gas workers, ferry workers, lumpers, textile workers, coopers, farriers, and brick workers, and to the Melbourne coal movers. Labor politicians were furious. State Ministers in New South Wales, A.H. Griffiths and A.C. Carmichael, vented about the damage to state socialism caused by unruly workers, and even the Secretary of the Trades and Labour Council, Mr E.J. Kavanagh, MLC, admitted that most

---

17   *Sydney Morning Herald*, 15 August 1911, p. 8, 'Labour Unrest' (editorial), 9 September 1911, p. 14, 'The World's Unrest'. I have used this data in Terry Irving, 'Rebellious Workers: Insubordination and Democratic Mobilisation in Australia in the 1910s', in Peter Sheldon, Sarah Gregson, Russell Lansbury and Karin Sanders (eds), *The Regulation and Management of Workplace Health and Safety: Historical and Emerging Trends*, Routledge, 2020.

of the recent strikes were brought about by workers ignoring their unions or acting contrary to union rules.[18]

This atmosphere of insubordination among workers was infectious, and soon other parts of the community were becoming stroppy. Now any form of protest involving a challenge to social custom or economic power was called a strike. When the undergraduates threatened to boycott classes, that was a strike. When Methodist local preachers in rural Victoria were in dispute with their church supervisors, they were said to be on strike. In working-class Wollongong bus customers who protested a fare rise by walking were called strikers. Bookmakers in Bathurst, negotiating with the Racing Club, were said to be on strike. According to the press, when doctors at the Kurri Kurri hospital resigned over a colleague who was not a member of the BMA, and when the matron and nurses at Mudgee hospital walked out, their actions were strikes too. In Auckland, players in a touring rugby league team from Sydney threatened 'to strike' over the suspension of a team-mate, and in Wollongong the volunteer gunners in the local Artillery Corps who resigned rather than attend repeated training sessions were called strikers. If this was mimicry in the thinking of conservatives it was nonetheless an indication of the power of the conflict between workers and employers to frame the discourse of politics in the state.[19]

Even when the term 'strike' is applied narrowly to the withdrawal of labour-power it is clear that there were many atypical strikers, at least if we have in mind a masculine blue-collar proletarian directed by an organised labour movement. By March 1913, according to the *Herald*, New South Wales was in a state of 'lawlessness' and the Labor government had 'become the servant of the law-breakers'. The only solution was for 'the community to break the Government'. The *Herald*'s words invoked violence rhetorically,

---

18   *Sydney Morning Herald*, 18 June 1913, p. 13 (Botany), 1 March 1913, p. 19 (take a holiday), 26 October 1911, p. 19 (full of fight and fun), 2 February 1911, p. 9 (sulphide), 17 February 1911, p. 7 (agricultural implements), 7 July 1911, p. 5 (Bundaberg), 19 March 1912, p. 9 (Lithgow), 1 March 1913, p. 19 (Sydney gas), 25 March 1913, p. 9 (Sydney ferries), 4 April 1913, p. 9 (lumpers), 18 June 1913, p. 13 (textile), 23 September 1913, p. 10 (coopers), 18 October 1913, p. 21 (farriers), 7 November 1913, p. 10 (brick workers), 16 August, 1913, p. 17 (Melbourne coal movers), 10 April 1913, p. 8 (Griffith, Carmichael), 14 February 1914, p. 21 (Kavanagh).

19   *Sydney Morning Herald*, 18 May 1911, p. 8 for undergraduates; 5 February 1912, p. 11, and 14 February 1912, p. 22, for Methodists; 4 June 1912, p. 8, for bookmakers; 11 April 1912, p. 9, for bus passengers; 19 July 1912, p. 9, for Kurri Kurri doctors, and 19 August 1912, p. 9, for Mudgee hospital; 7 September 1912, p. 15, for rugby league players; 12 September 1912, p. 9, for gunners.

but there was a lot of actual violence. There were assaults on individual scabs, intimidation of scabs collectively, particularly as they were marched to work by the police, stoning of police, and the destruction of property belonging to employers and scabs. It was like a civil war, according to the *Herald*. There were several hotspots: the Sydney waterfront, the northern and south coast coalfields in New South Wales, the Broken Hill metalliferous mines, the Lithgow iron works, and, outside of the State, Renmark during the wheat harvest, the sugar towns in north Queensland, the port of Townsville, and the Brisbane tramways. Labour-instigated violence was in fact widespread in these years, and as likely in strikes involving shop assistants as in those of labourers. It could involve and energise the wives of strikers as well as young men and women. Some dramatic examples: the destruction of the blast furnace in Lithgow and the torching of boss Hoskins's beloved Renault car, an 'act of rebellion' according to the *Herald*. In north Queensland, bands of armed strikers stalked scabs through the cane fields, guerrilla-like, during the sugar strike of 1911. In the Brisbane 'badge strike' of 1912, strikers used explosives to sabotage the trams. In October 1913, miners at Beaufort, Victoria, after firing shots at four scabs, chased two into a mine shaft, where they hid until rescued, and ran the other two out of town. Two miners were subsequently arrested and charged with attempted murder.[20]

In these years, when the working class was on the offensive, violence was just another weapon of class mobilisation, but it had a revolutionary potential – not in the acts of violence themselves but in their relationship with the violence of their class opponents. The workers were getting an education in the role of force in class relations. No-one committed to constitutional government could countenance such violence, because representative government was meant to take force out of politics. By the same token, workers who got used to using violence collectively had taken a step away from liberal parliamentarism. This step was in fact the social foundation of the process Childe in *How Labour Governs* called anti-politicalism. The workers using force in their industrial struggles were the same workers rejecting state-appointed arbitrators, politicians, and union bosses.

---

20   *Sydney Morning Herald*, 30 August 1911, p. 14; 31 August 1911, p. 9 (Lithgow); *Sydney Morning Herald*, 2 August 1911, p. 15 (sugar strike); 26 January 1912, p. 7 (Brisbane explosives); 8 March 1913, p. 19 (student scabs); 18 October 1913, p. 21, and 20 October 1913, p. 9 (Beaufort). Mick Armstrong, 'Disturbing the Peace: Riots and the Working Class', *Marxist Left Review*, no. 4, winter, 2012; Kay Saunders, 'Masters and Servants: The Queensland Sugar Workers Strike, 1911' in Ann Curthoys and Andrew Markus (eds), *Who Are Our Enemies? Racism and the Working Class in Australia*, Canberra, Hale & Iremonger, 1976.

* * *

In February 1911, the Broken Hill Amalgamated Miners' Association wired the striking sulphide workers in Newcastle, commending them for having nothing to do 'with professional politicians and strike-breaking politicians'. In Perth, a few months later, a mass meeting of striking brick-makers condemned the interference of Labor politicians. In New South Wales, the Colliery Employees' Association, the union covering coal miners, disaffiliated from the Labor Party in 1911 because its policy was 'not in keeping with the march of democracy'. In 1913, a delegate of the iron workers' union told the Western District Labour Council in New South Wales that workers were 'disgusted' with the present Labor Party. The Council resolved that financial union members should in future select parliamentary candidates, not the Political Labour League. In October 1913, the *Herald* published a letter from Arthur Sim. He wrote that 'as a member of the Newtown Political Labor League, and an executive member of the Amalgamated Railway and Tramway Services Association I am disgusted with the present Labor Ministers'. In the same year, the Barrier Labour Federation (Broken Hill) resolved to select its own candidates to run against official Labor candidates in the next election.[21]

As these examples show, the reaction against politicalism among the rank and file was taking two forms. Disillusioned by Labor Ministers who issued appeals for scabs and who encouraged the Industrial Court to punish strikers with fines, the militants' first response was to break the connection between the unions and the Labor Party. The easiest way to do this was to ignore the existing unions and set up a new independent body, an industrial union federation. This was the strategy of the labourers' unions who decided in 1911 to set up an Australia-wide federation which other unions could join. Envisaged as an industrial union, which would equip the working class for the future Socialist Commonwealth, its rules prohibited parliamentarians from holding office. As we saw, during the strike wave of 1913, Peter Bowling made a similar proposal, concluding that only 'the men' can and should determine their working conditions.[22]

---

21 *Sydney Morning Herald*, 7 February 1911, p. 10 (sulphide workers), 2 October 1911, p. 6 (brickmakers), 19 October 1911, p. 9 (disaffiliated), 19 July 1913, p. 20 (Western District), 28 October 1913 (Arthur Sim), 14 October 1913, p. 9 (Broken Hill).

22 *Sydney Morning Herald*, 22 November 1911, p. 19 (labourers' union), 4 March 1913, p. 9 (Bowling).

This was the lesson Bowling drew from the disastrous defeat of the 1909 coal miners' strike which he had led and for which he had been gaoled by the conservative Wade government. That strike had been defeated by political action, especially by Wade's illiberal 'Coercion Act' which imposed gaol sentences for planning or participating in a strike in 'an essential industry'. Bowling redoubled his efforts to encourage 'spontaneous' action among workers as soon as he was released from gaol. A few weeks after his speech to the gas workers, he addressed a Trade Union Congress in Sydney, in another attempt to break the nexus of the unions with parliamentarism. He failed by a small margin. Now he was calling for a new party, an industrial labour party.[23]

The idea of a different kind of workers' party was the second form of the revolt against politicalism. The need for it was not only discovered when Labor governments let the workers down, for a limited form of anti-parliamentarism was actually part of Labor's history, an incipient strain in Labor's 'novel theory of democracy', which insisted on the control of politicians by the movement. Just before the 1910 State election, the New South Wales General Secretary of the party received a letter of resignation:

> After careful consideration and close scrutiny since the Federal elections I am compelled to sever my connections to the Political Labour League. To my mind it is no longer a working-class party ... You have amongst yourselves men who only a few months ago were the direct representatives of the capitalist class ... Your actions of late in brushing aside the [selected candidates] of local leagues – the people qualified to say who should represent them ... [and] accepting the cast-off Liberals ... is a disgrace and scandal in Labour's cause.

The disaffected member was Timothy William McCristal, a 30-year-old agitator who had recently been elected President of the Sydney Wharf Labourers' Union. To his disgust he discovered that a faction loyal to the Central Executive of the party was resisting his attempts to rid the union of its criminal element and expose the corruption of former officials. He was also angry that the party flirted with the business elite (he was outraged that the President of the Political Labor League and member for Belmore was Paddy Minahan, a manufacturer, known as Sydney's 'Boot King'),

---

23 Childe, *How Labour Governs*, 1st edn, p. 114 (reaction against politicalism), p. 121 (1909 coal strike); *Sydney Morning Herald*, 25 March 1913, p. 10 (Bowling).

ignored corruption in the unions, and showed contempt for rank and file control of the party.[24]

McCristal epitomised the working class's savage democrats. His desire for a real 'working class party' led him in 1910 to form the Social Democratic Party of New South Wales, 'to represent the democracy of the country'. It aimed 'to secure the full results of industry for the producers' by nationalising the land, the banks and factories, to abolish the State Parliaments, and to make Australia a republic. He startled a wages board hearing by declaring that he did not believe in employers. Rather, he said, 'the unions should elect those in charge from amongst them'. Sensing his power to shock, he went on to tell the board that he had tried to alter the union's objective to the attainment of 'an Australian republic and the ultimate emancipation of labour by the abolition of the wage slave system and the establishment of a co-operative Commonwealth'. The *Herald* called this 'a curious notion'. In 1910, standing for his party in the working-class electorate of Pyrmont, McCristal secured about 8 per cent of the vote. The Social Democratic Party lasted until in 1914 he enlisted in the Australian Imperial Force.[25]

* * *

Early in 1913, members of the parliamentary Labor Party rebelled against 'the do-nothing policy of the McGowen cabinet' and replaced their leader with the ambitious William Holman. The party had been in existence for almost 25 years, its annual conferences affirming and reaffirming a core of demands: that the undemocratic upper house, a barrier to Labor legislation, should be abolished; that rural land should be nationalised and freehold tenure converted to leasehold; that a state iron and steel works should be established; that public works should be carried on by public employees, not contracted out to private companies; that the state housing scheme should be extended and a Fair Rents Court set up. None of this was revolutionary but when Childe and Evatt were campaigning for Labor at the end of 1913, after three years of Labor government, not a single plank of this program had been implemented by legislation. Three years later, the parliamentary party

---

24 *Sydney Morning Herald*, 8 September 1910, p. 12 (resignation letter), 23 August 1910, p. 9 (WWF Sydney branch), 3 August 1910, p. 9 (Minahan).

25 *Sydney Morning Herald*, 3 August 1910, p. 9 (Social Democrats), 16 September 1913, p. 10 (wages board), 15 October 1910, p. 15 (election results).

would split, expelling Holman, Hughes and their supporters. Ostensibly the reason was the attempt to introduce conscription, but the roots of the split went deep into the soil of working-class disillusionment with parliamentary politics. Evatt and Childe would have to choose which side to join: the militant workers or the cautious parliamentarians.[26]

26   Childe, *How Labour Governs*, 1st edn, pp. 9, 36.

Chapter 3

SOCIALISTS AND COOPERATORS

In April 1910, 30 graduates and undergraduates met on the eve of the federal elections with the intention of establishing the university Socialist Society. Downtown, conservative citizens were shocked. On election day, while the voters shifted to the left, and Andrew Fisher was getting ready to lead his second Labor government, *The Sydney Morning Herald* called the formation of a socialist club at the university 'The Last Straw'. It was unusual for the *Herald* to adopt a calm tone for such an event, but then these socialists were middle class, not militant workers.[1]

The university socialists preferred a different metaphor. In 1911, one of their speakers, the Sydney graduate and geologist Harald Jensen, published a book called *The Rising Tide – An Exposition of Australian Socialism*. Jensen addressed the university socialists on 'Work and Wages', and it is probable that Childe was present. Certainly, when Jensen arrived in Brisbane in 1918, Childe spoke as if he already knew him. Born in 1879 in Denmark, Jensen accompanied his parents at the age of six to a mining town in north Queensland, where his father became an active member of the Australian Workers' Union. Harald won a scholarship to Brisbane Boys Grammar, went on to the University of Sydney and completed an honours degree in geology. He secured the Macleay Fellowship of the Linnean Society and in 1908 the university awarded him a DSc and the University Medal on the basis of his scientific publications. At the same time, he was emerging as a socialist intellectual, writing regularly for the labour press. From 1900 he wrote on science and politics for the Brisbane *Worker*, and in 1908–9 he published a series of articles that became *The Rising Tide* in the Sydney *Worker*. A rare recruit to labour from university-trained professional circles, Jensen dazzled the movement's leaders and activists, so much so that at the

---

1   *Sydney Morning Herald*, 13 April 1910, p. 11.

1911 and 1912 New South Wales Political Labour League conferences he was elected to the State Executive with strong support.²

The socialist intellectual and bushman, Harald Ingemann Jensen, about 1910.
(John Oxley Library, State Library of Queensland)

We have a photograph of Jensen in 1910, as Childe would have seen him. Lean and handsome, coatless but with tie and wing-collar, he sits at his study desk, turning toward the camera. Behind him is his Gladstone bag, above the cupboard is an axe or a geologist's hammer, and in his hand a metal mug, raised as if to invite a toast – objects suggesting that his real life lay outside the

---

2   H.I. Jensen, *The Rising Tide: An Exposition of Australian Socialism*, Sydney, The Worker Trustees, 1909; *Hermes*, vol. XVII, no. 3, July 1911; Childe to Le Gay Brereton, 23 December 1918, Mitchell Library MSS 281 vol. 4, pp. 125–6; B.J. McFarlane, 'Jensen, Harald Ingemann (1879–1966)', *Australian Dictionary of Biography*, Vol. 9, 1983, pp. 480-1; Michael Hogan (ed.), *Labor Pains Volume II (1906–11)* and *Volume III (1912–17)*, Sydney, The Federation Press, 2008, p. 436 (Vol. II) and pp. 11, 59 and 62 (Vol. III). Some of Jensen's letters to *The Worker* (Queensland): 17 March 1900, 21 January 1902, 3 September 1904, 7 January 1911, 8 April 1911.

study. During a scientific career analysing soil and prospecting for minerals and oil in outback Australia, he became a superb bushman, and when he died it was said that his great loves were 'geology, grog and women'. In *The Rising Tide* he romanticises the bush and idealises its men (he says nothing about its women): 'Usually much travelled and well-read, kind and sympathetic, noble-minded and liberal; of such it can be said "Here is a man"'. This literary apotheosis of the 'nomad tribe' of bush workers contributed seamlessly to the making of labour's masculinist 'Australian Legend'.[3]

While Childe was an undergraduate, the Commonwealth Government appointed Jensen Director of Mines in the Northern Territory. In *The Rising Tide* he had set out his belief that the development of northern Australia depended on public ownership of land, minerals and railways, and as he knew he was Prime Minister Fisher's personal choice for the job he naturally assumed that he was appointed 'to carry out the platform and objectives of the Labor movement as far as mining is concerned'. The Administrator of the Northern Territory, John Gilruth, conservative and autocratic, thought otherwise. Soon Jensen was forced to resign, having precipitated a Royal Commission into Gilruth's administration and embarrassed the Commonwealth by publicly opposing Australia's support for Britain in the war. However, he had the satisfaction of correctly predicting in the labour press that either Darwin would become an independent soviet or the Territory would receive representation in the Federal Parliament. In December 1918, led by Harold Nelson of the Australian Workers' Union, Darwin workers rebelled against Gilruth, who virtually became a prisoner in Government House before fleeing to Melbourne on a gunboat two months later. Nelson became the Territory's first elected representative, a post he held until 1934. At the time Jensen followed these events closely, and in 1966 published the first and only scholarly article on 'the Darwin rebellion'.[4]

Jensen was radicalised by his experiences in Darwin. He became a supporter of the Russian Revolution and the One Big Union (a revolutionary

---

3   Photograph of Jensen by Sidney Riley, State Library of Queensland; Jensen, *The Rising Tide*, p. 84; Russel Ward, *The Australian Legend*, Melbourne, Oxford University Press, 1966 (first published 1958), see Ch. VIII on the 'nomad tribe', and the contributions to Frank Bongiorno and David A. Roberts (eds), 'Russel Ward: Reflections on a Legend', *Journal of Colonial Australian History*, vol. 10, no. 2, 2008.

4   Letter by Jensen, *Daily Standard*, 24 December 1918; H.I. Jensen, 'The Darwin Rebellion', *Labour History*, no. 11, November 1966, pp. 3–13; David Day, *Andrew Fisher: Prime Minister of Australia*, Sydney, Fourth Estate, 2008, p. 256; David Carment, 'Nelson, Harold George (1881–1947)', *Australian Dictionary of Biography*, vol. 10, 1986, pp. 676–7.

industrial union), and an enemy of government bureaucrats, especially those who resisted radical initiatives proposed by learned people like him. A few years later, the Labor Party in Queensland expelled him for complaining that the party was neglecting its socialist objective. At the time he wrote his book, however, he supported the attainment of socialism through gradual reforms, arguing that Darwinian evolutionary theory justified this strategy. From the 1870s intellectuals had been harnessing Darwinian theory to the idea of historical progress, resulting in what we now know as Social Darwinism. Conservatives were to the fore in this development, expressing its central ideas as 'the struggle for existence' and 'the survival of the fittest' – phrases closer to the ideas of Herbert Spencer than those of Charles Darwin. In their hands Darwinism legitimated laissez-faire policies, individualism, and programs to preserve racial purity.

In response to the intensification of the class struggle in the 1880s, another reading of Darwin and history emerged – one often forgotten in these neo-liberal days. It was developed by radical thinkers: Edward Bellamy, Henry George and Louis Gronlund in the USA; and Belfort Bax, A.R. Wallace and Morrison Davidson in Britain. Jensen in *The Rising Tide* read Darwin as they had done. He argued that, in *The Descent of Man* (1882), Darwin 'distinctly maintained that in the human species the fittest consist of the bravest, the most intelligent, and most self-sacrificing, for these are of the greatest value to the race'. As social life became more complex, according to Jensen, 'Mutual aid gradually became a habit, morality grew inasmuch as the more persistent social instincts conquered the less permanent selfish instincts ... [and] man became a moral being'. Jensen refers to Bellamy and George, but his greatest debt is to the 1902 book *Mutual Aid: A Factor of Evolution* by Peter Kropotkin, in which the Russian zoologist and anarcho-communist drew on Darwin to show that 'the sociable instinct' of cooperation or mutual aid 'was the chief element for the preservation of the race'. As John Laurent has shown, interpretations of Darwin claiming that socialism was the evolutionary pinnacle of human society were well known in the Australian labour movement, but Jensen's scientific credentials gave them a rare authority.[5]

---

5   Some of Jensen's letters to *Daily Standard*: 7 March 1918 (in defence of Russian revolution), 24 December 1918 (the Darwin soviet), 20 February 1919 (One Big Union), 1 August 1919 (bureaucracy and socialism), 6 August 1919 (arbitration's weaknesses); John Laurent, 'Tom Mann, R.S. Ross and Evolutionary Socialism in Broken Hill, 1902–1912: Alternative Social Darwinism in the Australian Labour Movement', *Labour History*, no. 51, November 1986, pp. 54–69.

The university socialists also heard a speaker from a Marxist organisation, the International Socialists, who, according to *Hermes*, attacked the Labor Party as 'a mere collection of wolves in sheep's clothing, who sigh for the flesh-pots of capitalism, and exploit the workers for the purpose of keeping the ministerial benches warm'. Childe may well have written this unsigned report for the university magazine, for he would later refer ironically to his own preference for the *bios apolausticos* – fleshpots – of professional status over the privations of revolutionary politics. If so, we might detect the beginnings of Childe's disillusionment with Labor's parliamentary politics. The report also noted that the speaker's attack on parliamentarism elicited less adverse reaction from the audience than did his criticism of compulsory military training. Labor's politicians might be fallible, but its program – nationalist and progressive – had to be defended. So, as the world's first majority socialist government set to work – with Jensen as a Commonwealth employee, surveying for minerals in the Northern Territory and advising Fisher to take the mines into public ownership – these middle-class university socialists, patriotic and compassionate, thought they were rising with the tide.[6]

But what part would the Labor Party play in this future? The university socialists had adopted a set of principles, 'the creed' (as they called it), that remarkably omitted to mention the Labor Party. That must have been deliberate, given the party's recent electoral advances. The creed opened by affirming, in religious fashion, some fundamental truths: the organic nature of society and its historical continuity. Similarly, in its second article reformers were warned that they wasted their time if they meddled with the nature of man. With these two beliefs the members signalled that they were not going to contemplate ideas about structural contradictions in society, the necessity of revolutionary ruptures, or the historical relativism of morals and human nature. Then, in a gesture towards 'new liberalism', the third belief was enunciated: that the good society should balance the fullest expression of individual needs with the best interests of the organic social whole. The fourth showed the radical edge of new liberalism: that some class distinctions were good (those based on 'social and moral worth') while others needed to be eliminated (those based on birth, wealth and occupation). Then the creed enters completely new territory: the good society would be governed by the communist principle: from each according to his capacity and to each according to his needs. With Biblical roots, it was a principle deeply embedded in the masculine Christian

---

6   *Hermes*, December 1910, p. 126; R.P. Dutt, letter to *The Times Literary Supplement*, 3, 1965, p. 539.

tradition, finding notable expression in the writings of F.D. Maurice, Charles Kingsley and other mid-nineteenth century Christian socialists. Finally, the sixth article at last puts some politico-economic flesh on these principles: the members rejected private monopolies but welcomed public monopolies that contributed to the welfare of all.[7]

Such was the 'creed' of the university socialists when Childe encountered them. They were young radical intellectuals moving from conventional Christianity to ethical socialism with Christian roots, via new liberalism's political philosophy of government action for social amelioration. They embraced the current drift towards collectivist politics but only if it were initiated, as well as carried out, by the state; they were not in favour of *working-class* collectivism. Hence their ambivalence about the Labor Party. The creed was, however, too eclectic and vacuous to hold the allegiance of middle-class sympathisers — and it was already out of date. By 1905 Labor had announced its embrace of state socialism, a program of state activity around which new liberals (with misgivings about working-class pressure) and labourists (confident in their ability to withstand it) could coalesce. When Gordon Childe and Bert Evatt campaigned for Labor in the State election of 1913 it was plain that the university socialists had failed to counter the appeal of the popular mass party to radical intellectuals.[8]

* * *

Another radical development on campus occurred in 1912, when the Men's Christian Union set up a Social Service Department. It aimed to research working-class 'social problems' (discovered when members took walks in 'the slums' surrounding the campus) and to ameliorate them through voluntary Christian service: lectures, entertainment and assistance at boys' clubs and other 'institutions for social betterment'. Its leader was the Christian socialist and promoter of cooperative enterprises, Frank E. Pulsford, and its Secretary in 1913 was Gordon Childe.[9]

---

7   *Sydney Morning Herald*, 13 April 1910, p. 11.
8   Bruce O'Meagher (ed.), *The Socialist Objective: Labor and Socialism*, Sydney, Hale & Iremonger, 1983, see his 'Introduction: Labor Ideology and Socialism'; on the 'mass party' stage of representative government, see Bernard Manin, *The Principles of Representative Government*, Cambridge University Press, 1997, Ch. 6.
9   B.J. McFarlane, 'Jensen, Harald Ingemar (1879–1966)', *Australian Dictionary of Biography*, Vol. 9, pp. 480–1; for Jensen's membership of the Labor Executive, see

Born in 1873, Pulsford trained as an accountant. In 1910 he stood as the Liberal candidate in the federal seat of Newcastle against long-time miners' union leader and Labor moderate David Watkins, who retained the seat easily. By 1912 he had given up his parliamentary ambitions, finding them incompatible with his role of champion of cooperativism. In fact, his liberalism was never pure, at least not in comparison with the laissez-faire and free trade dogmas of his father, Senator Edward Pulsford. Like many liberal intellectuals in the early twentieth century, Frank Pulsford was a 'new liberal', a liberal with a collectivist tinge, dedicated to the social welfare of the people. But even in the company of new liberals he stood out, because he resisted the idea that state intervention was the only way to express the age's growing collectivism. Reason? Because it was undemocratic, imposed by top-down methods as a result of political action, and because the party most likely to set the agenda, at least in Australia, was the Labor Party, a party with socialist 'class' baggage.[10]

He took his message to the people by organising and addressing public meetings. The *Herald* reported one of his speeches under the heading 'A Substitute for Socialism':

> The old destructive methods of unionism could no longer serve the workers. The time had come when unionism must be constructive. A small weekly levy on the trade unionists of the State would rapidly accumulate to a vast capital available for co-operative enterprise. Co-operation was the way for industrial salvation, and offered unionism a new lease of magnificent usefulness. Socialism could end only in chaos and tyranny.

Workers had to be taught thrift and self-control. This aim had a venerable history among liberals, but Pulsford sought as well to empower workers through cooperative stores and producers' cooperatives.[11]

The popular-democratic tone of his liberalism, his radicalism in relation to his liberal peers, indeed his attraction to collectivism, had theological roots. In 1909 he published a pamphlet, *The Society of Tentmakers*, drawing on his experience as a lay preacher. He urged the Protestant churches to set

---

'Executive Report of Political Labor League for 1911' reprinted in Michael Hogan (ed), *Labor Pains Volume III*, p. 11; *Hermes*, vol. XVIII, no. 2, August 1912 for Social Service Department.

10   W.G. McMinn, 'Pulsford, Edward (1844–1919)', *Australian Dictionary of Biography*, vol. 11, 1988, pp. 307–8.

11   *Sydney Morning Herald*, 13 January 1910, p. 7.

up part-time courses in Divinity so that 'practical men' of business and the professions, with university degrees, could study for the Christian ministry while supporting themselves. They would then pursue their ministry without financial support from the church, just as the Apostle Paul did in Corinth while working as a tentmaker. Following his own advice, Pulsford enrolled in an Arts degree in the same year as Childe. After graduating, he completed a theology course and was ordained as a Congregationalist in 1915, attracted by that church's adoption of two key democratic forms: the priesthood of believers, and 'congregational', that is, non-episcopal, church governance.[12]

The Social Service Department that he and Childe set up in the Men's Christian Union at the university in 1912 was modelled on the Social Service committees of the Christian Social Union in Britain. The Anglo-Catholics and Christian socialists volunteering in these committees were mentally fixated on 'the slum', a term that when decoded meant a working-class culture beyond the reach of middle-class influence. In 1913 Pulsford published his major work, a book called *Co-operation and Co-partnership*, printed by The Worker Print in Sydney. There was a connection between the two projects: the tradition of personal middle-class interventions to service the social needs of the working class would be enhanced if the recipients were empowered to improve their lives through common effort. But that was already happening. The problem was that the labour movement was framing its collective action in class terms. Instead, Pulsford proposed in his book that 'social salvation' would only come about through interweaving 'self-interest with mutual interest', liberalism with socialism. This showed a sharp awareness that politics was moving in a collectivist direction, but it also implied that liberals urgently needed to redirect it.

He made several points that Childe might have agreed with. Collective solutions imposed from above were not only undemocratic, they did not work. State enterprises did not prevent 'the captains of industry' controlling the economy, and even in state enterprises labour is still treated as 'a mere commodity':

> Oh, ye wage-earners of Australia! Why have you not already achieved the Democratic control of industry? It is what you seek and it is within your grasp. Triumphant indeed has been your march these 25 years, and great your achievements; but who directly controls the great industries of the State? Not Labour. Many restrictions have you placed around

---

12 F.E. Pulsford, *The Society of Tentmakers*, Sydney, Bible House, 1909 (36 pages).

the profiteer, but in spite of what you have done, human labour is still bought and sold as a mere commodity, like soap and leather. ... Is it not true that still, in spite of all your victories in the realm of politics, the actual control of industry is in the hands of those captains of industry, to whom profit and service is the master motive?

Childe, in 1919, would also promote the idea of the 'democratic control of industry', but unlike Pulsford he did not accept that it must or could be realised through the accumulation of capital in a separate cooperative sector of the economy. As he would ask about the Labor strategy of building socialism through state enterprises, why would the powerful masters of private capital permit public, or in this case cooperative, capital to limit their activities and ultimately private capital's power to determine the direction of society? In the meantime, however, the meliorist, evolutionary, class-collaborationist and Christian socialism that he took with him to Oxford – assuming it was based on the ideas of Jensen, Pulsford and the university socialists – was not wildly different in practice from the collectivist thrust of new liberalism. Except for one thing: in 1913 Gordon was campaigning for the Labor Party, and whether he realised it or not he was involving himself with a party committed to a new model of political representation – as we shall see.[13]

* * *

Gordon was also active in the University (Men's) Union, but here he might have been radicalising as much as radicalised. The Union moved into its own building in 1913, and the increased facilities – including a common room, tea room and a hall capable of seating up to 300 – necessitated a more elaborate form of governance. In 1913 Gordon's name appears as a member of three of its committees, for the reading room, the archives and debating. Deciding on topics for the weekly Union debate was an activity Gordon clearly enjoyed because he remained on the committee in 1914, after his graduation. The topics often enabled the presentation of arguments then agitating thinkers and activists outside the university. The nationalisation of medicine was a perennial; other topics included socialism, industrial cooperation, compulsory

---

13 *Hermes*, vol. XVIII, no. 2, August 1912, and vol. XIX, no. 1, June 1913, re the Social Service Department; Frank E. Pulsford, *Co-operation and Co-partnership*, Sydney, The Worker Print, 1913; Pulsford, *A Leave-time Study of the Democratic Control of Industry*, Sydney, The Worker Print, 1918, p. 3 (16 pages).

military training, secret diplomacy, female suffrage, and pacifism. Whether Gordon tipped the balance towards such topics we cannot know. We do know that he took part in the debate held at the first meeting of the reconstituted Union because it was reported in *The Sydney Morning Herald* and *Hermes*. He spoke in support of the nationalisation of medical services. According to the university magazine, in the amusing style traditional for reporting Union Night debates, 'The Child [sic] then rose and prattled innocently in his own intimate way for some considerable time' in support of the proposition, but the motion was lost by a large majority.[14]

The first of Childe's men's clubs – Sydney University Union.
(University of Sydney Archives; G3_224_MF374_0195)

Although Gordon's studies centred on classics – in his last year at Shore he had shared the top spot for Latin in the Senior Matriculation examination – in his first year at university he took courses in Geology, Algebra, Geometry, Trigonometry, as well as Latin and Greek. The foundations of his later interest in science and mathematics as elements of prehistoric civilisation may well have

---

14 *Sydney Morning Herald*, 29 April 1913, p. 7; *Hermes*, vol. XIX, no. 1, June 1913, p. 28; University of Sydney Archives: University of Sydney Union, S.U. Debates Committee Minutes, 1913, 1914, 1917, 1918.

been laid in these courses. Beginning in his second year he added Philosophy to his Greek and Latin studies. He was successful in both Philosophy and Classics, receiving the Cooper Scholarship for Proficiency in Classics at the end of his first and second years, and the University Medal for Classics and the Professor Francis Anderson Prize for Philosophy in his third year.[15]

Francis Anderson is a significant figure in Gordon's political development, because it was Anderson who steered him towards the Workers' Educational Association (WEA), which he joined in 1913. Anderson was, for the time, a most unusual teacher. He encouraged questioning in class and approached the study of philosophy critically, emphasising its historical context. Moreover, in the final year course he threaded the study of philosophy through a series of political and social topics, almost as if he were teaching social theory. In fact, in 1911 he published an appeal for the teaching of sociology in Australia. A surviving notebook for a part of his third-year course is titled 'Philosophy of the State; The Real End of the State; Interpretation of Theories of the State'. Under this topic he included the study of Marxism and historical materialism. Anderson had a huge influence on Gordon's thinking. For several years after his graduation he would continue grappling with questions that he had first encountered in Anderson's classes, especially the meaning of truth, and the theory of the state; and with Marxism he had a lifelong engagement. Most importantly, he never forgot the experience of placing knowledge in a social context, and of thinking holistically. At the end of his career he referred to an interest in philosophy that had begun in 1913, an interest that led to his *Social Worlds of Knowledge* (1949) and *Society and Knowledge* (1956).[16]

Gordon took his final examinations at the end of 1913. A few weeks later he and Bert Evatt were campaigning for the Labor Party in the State elections, providing secretarial services to its leader, the Premier W.A. Holman. Labor was victorious; Bert and Gordon had begun their careers as labour intellectuals.[17]

---

15   Childe's academic results: University Archivist to Miss S. Green, England, 5 February 1976, University of Sydney Archives, Biog 353/2.

16   W.M. Anderson, 'Anderson, Sir Francis (1858–1941)', *Australian Dictionary of Biography*, Vol. 7, 1979, pp. 56–9; Sir Francis Anderson papers, University of Sydney Archives, P027, box 2; Childe, 'Retrospect', *Antiquity*, vol. 32, issue 126, June 1958, p. 73.

17   National Library of Australia, Oral History tapes, Interview with Mary Alice Evatt, 1973; Terry Irving and Sean Scalmer, 'Labour Intellectuals in Australia: Modes, Traditions, Generations, Transformations', *International Review of Social History*, vol. 50, part 1, April 2005, pp. 1–26.

Gordon's other career, as a scholar, was foreshadowed the following year in April, when he graduated in a ceremony in the Great Hall of the university, which awarded him First Class Honours in Latin, Greek and Philosophy, the University Medal for Classics, the Professor Francis Anderson Prize for an essay in philosophy, and the Cooper Graduate Travelling Scholarship worth 200 pounds. He intended to go to Oxford and postgraduate studies, guided there by the Professor of Greek at Sydney, W.J. Woodhouse, whose interests were as much in archaeology as in Classics. The English academic year started in September, and in the meantime Gordon had to find something to do. He hung around the Union debating circle until late April and then took a post in remote Glen Innes as a master at a private grammar school. Apparently, it was not a good experience, for after a few weeks he moved on to become a private tutor on a large property outside the town. In the meantime, the university allotted him one of the free passages to England offered by the Orient Line, travelling first class. Whenever he could he took the train to Sydney and stayed with Evatt at St Andrew's College, until on 1 August he embarked on SS *Orsova* for Plymouth, just three days before Britain declared war on Germany.[18]

---

18   Registrar to Childe, New England Grammar School, Glen Innes, 5 May 1914, Registrar's Letter Book, 1914, p. 179; Childe resigns from Debates Committee, 19 May 1914, Records of The Union, University of Sydney Archives; Timothy Champion, 'Childe and Oxford', *European Journal of Archaeology*, vol. 12, nos 1–3, April 2009, pp. 13–14; interview with Mary Alice Evatt, 1973; *The Glen Innes Examiner*, 26 March 1914, p. 4; Green, *Prehistorian*, p. 12; *Sydney Morning Herald*, 1 August 1914, p. 1 (Childe listed as 'through saloon' passenger, sailing today).

Chapter 4

A COLD NORTHERN SUPERCULTURE

Arriving in Oxford in September 1914, Childe found 'a hurly-burly of enthusiastic unauthorized activity', a microcosm of the 'vast reorganization' of British society caused by the government's decision to declare war on Germany. All over the town, Kitchener's notorious 'Your Country Needs You' poster admonished indecisive patriots. Recruiting sergeants patrolled the High Street, great military rallies and torchlight processions targeted the townsmen, and on the Balliol cricket ground older men, including prominent dons, drilled as the Oxford Volunteer Corps. In Alfred Street, undergraduates, hoping to enlist as officers, waited in a dingy room to present their case. Outside, children played soldiers and nurses, and 'ladies' formed emergency committees to relieve the expected economic distress in working-class families.[1]

It was a confronting scene, made worse by constant rain. In his rooms at Queen's College, Gordon felt Oxford's desperate excitement and fear. At night the town was dark, a rumoured Zeppelin raid having persuaded the local government to impose a blackout. Until military trainees filled them, the colleges were more than half empty even after term began. How long would the upheaval last? Would it interfere with his studies? He had no idea that it would turn his thinking upside down. Three years later, when he left Oxford to return to Australia, his religious and political ideas had changed forever, his activism had developed a sharp anti-authoritarian edge, and MI5 had categorised him as 'a very dangerous person'.[2]

Gordon's only surviving comment about his early months in Oxford was made four years later, when he wrote that in 1915 he came reluctantly to the

---

1   The observer was Rachael Poole, quoted in Malcolm Graham, *Oxford in the Great War*, Barnsley, UK, Pen and Sword Military, 2014, p. 25; *Oxford Magazine*, 16 October 1914.
2   'a very dangerous person': George Crystal (Home Office) to Lieutenant Kell (MI5), 19 June 1917, Childe's MI5 file, KV2/2148, UK National Archives.

conclusion that for him orthodoxy was impossible, and he informed the college accordingly. The implication is plain: until then he had accepted wholeheartedly the orthodox view that Britain's involvement in the war was justified. This is startling in the light of his later reputation as an opponent of the war.[3]

The Pro-Provost of Queen's, asked later in the war about Childe's pacifism, told the Home Office that in 1914 Childe had volunteered, and when he was rejected on medical grounds had decided to drill with a Civilians' Battalion. The records of Queen's say that he drilled with civilians, but did he *volunteer* and get rejected on medical grounds? In 1917, having embraced pacifism, he said that he feared he would be forced to contribute to 'the prolongation of this senseless slaughter' by being conscripted. By this time a revision of the 1916 Military Service Act gave the government the right to re-examine men previously declared medically unfit, so if Gordon feared being caught under this provision it would support the idea of his attempted enlistment in 1914. But he never referred to this provision. On the other hand, he did mention to his mentor, the Professor of Greek at Oxford, Gilbert Murray, that the original Act gave the government the right to direct men below the age of 41 into 'national employment'. He imagined himself, having refused such a direction from a military tribunal, emerging 'from an English gaol – a gaol to which a prolonged stay in this country would probably lead me as I am not yet 41'. The critical phrase here is 'a prolonged stay in this country', because the Act did not apply to men who were ordinarily resident in one of the Dominions, or resident in Britain only for the purpose of their education. Gordon therefore could rely on his being a visiting student to claim exemption from the Act – unless at the end of his studies he took up employment in Britain. Apparently, that was his intention.[4]

Did he try to enlist in 1914? It is at least possible that malicious college gossip invented the story later to harm his standing as a pacifist, or that conventionally minded persons, with little direct knowledge of Childe and limited knowledge of the exceptions under the Act, could not imagine a young man behaving in any other way. In fact, sometimes even radical socialists at first supported the war, as the future communist leader Clemens Dutt did. In 1916, applying for exemption from military service, he told a military

---

3   Childe to Portus, June 1918, Biography file M223 (Childe), University of Sydney Archives.

4   Armstrong to Home Office, 17 June 1917 in Childe's MI5 file, KV2/2148; Green, *Prehistorian*, p. 22; Childe to Murray, 16 March 1917, Gilbert Murray papers, shelfmark 376, ff. 136–7, Bodleian Library, Oxford; Childe to Murray, Wednesday, [July?] 1917, Murray papers, shelfmark 376, ff. 157–9.

tribunal in Cambridge that he had succumbed to 'war fever' and applied for a commission in the army in 1914, but now he had reverted to his true anti-war beliefs. Dutt and his brother Rajani were foundation members of the British Communist Party in 1920. Regarding Childe, who was a friend of Rajani, we may reasonably infer from his own admission that during his first term in Oxford he was a supporter of Britain's role in the war.

This stage of Gordon's radicalisation was characterised by mental struggle. We have to imagine an impressionable young colonial at the centre of the empire for the first time, socialising with imperial patriots and encountering jingoism wherever he turned. He wanted to fit in, and the pressure to do so was impossible to ignore. Yet just a few months earlier he had defied the conventions of his class by campaigning for the Labor Party. He had looked at the conservative religious morality of his class and said, 'no, it is not right'. Now he was in Britain, at the centre of the system that gave power to that class. It was going to take time to find a balance between his principles and his career. The scholarly achievements would come easily; it was more difficult to sort out the relationships between the principles that he was most deeply committed to: truth, conscience and revolution. And he had to reconcile being an Australian with living in the imperial heartland.[5]

* * *

In the meantime, he was meeting the university's radicals, and making friends, for, in Peter Gathercole's words, 'despite a minor myth to the contrary', Gordon was 'not a recluse'. Moreover, as we shall see, his most enduring friends were as politically minded as he was, even among his later professional colleagues. In Queen's, he met Robert Chorley and Philip Taliessen Davies, both members of the Oxford University Fabian Society. Chorley was called to the Bar in 1920, became a legal academic and an office bearer in the Association of University Teachers, before being raised to the Peerage as Baron Chorley in 1945 by the Attlee Labour government. Gordon's friendship with Davies, known in the family as Tal, was shorter but more intense. Davies, whose father was a Church of England clergyman in the northern working-class town of Oldham, described himself to the Oxford Military Service Tribunal in March 1916 as an atheist and international socialist. Although it is likely

---

5   On Clemens Dutt: Imperial War Museum, https://livesofthefirstworldwar.org accessed 19 July 2016.

Gordon was already heading in the same directions, his friendship with Tal Davies might well have helped, for they were close enough for the college Pro-Provost to assert that Childe had formed a 'romantic attachment' to him. Tal had a younger sister, Leila, a student at Somerville College, whom Gordon met, and he may have visited the family in Oldham, but he seems to have lost touch with them after the war.[6]

Childe also made friends with fellow socialists Raymond Postgate from St John's College and Rajani Palme Dutt from Balliol. They were very different young men. There is a portrait of Postgate painted a few years later by the Australian painter Stella Bowen that captures his dark handsome features, hair flopping over the forehead. He looks out thoughtfully at the world through small round glasses, pipe resting on a full lower lip, but he has taken care to seem indifferent to what the world thinks of him. He is dressed in a lounge suit and waistcoat, tie and matching handkerchief, but the suit is brown and rumpled, and the tie is red. The date is 1922; by this time, he had been a founding member of the British Communist Party and editor of its weekly, *The Communist*. In 1923, Postgate partly financed the publication of Childe's *How Labour Governs* and wrote a favourable review of it. In later life he was a social historian, author of mystery novels, and the founder of *The Good Food Guide*. He and Gordon often crossed paths, on one much photographed occasion while accompanying his father in law, the Cabinet Minister and future Labour Party leader George Lansbury, to Gordon's most famous excavation at Skara Brae.[7]

Unlike Postgate who left the Communist Party in 1923, Rajani Palme Dutt remained loyal to the party for the rest of his life. He was its leading theoretician, the founder and editor of its widely read *Labour Monthly*, as well as an officer of the Comintern, or Communist International, the Moscow-based body providing leadership to the world communist movement. Because of his prominence in the communist movement, there are many formal photographs of Dutt, or Palme Dutt as he was known in the communist movement. In keeping, however, with the convention in revolutionary politics that leaders only have a public identity, there is no 'candid camera' record of him as a private

---

6   Green, *Prehistorian*, pp. 40–1 for Chorley and Bloomsbury House Club; Armstrong to Home Office, 17 June 1917; for Davies: Imperial War Museum, https://livesofthefirstworldwar.org; Peter Gathercole, 'Childe the "Outsider"', *Royal Anthropological Institute News*, no. 17, 1976, pp. 5–6.

7   The portrait is reproduced in Lola Wilkins (curator and editor), *Stella Bowen: Art, Love and War*, Canberra, Australian War Memorial, 2002; John and Mary Postgate, *A Stomach for Dissent: Life of Raymond Postgate 1896–1971*, Staffordshire, Keele University Press, 1994.

person in those years. Always centred on his penetrating gaze, these 'official' photographs are assertions of intellectual dominance, slightly menacing and controlling. The features are regular and unblemished; the hair parted in the middle; and the lips closed firmly. Greatly admired among communists, Dutt's reputation was for 'dispassionate assessment of political situations', or to put it another way, for his inflexible adherence to the Comintern line. He was seen as distant and cool. But he did have close personal relationships, and one of those was with Gordon Childe with whom he shared lodgings in Oxford in 1917. There is an unofficial photograph of Dutt, and it dates from his time in Oxford or just after. He is in profile. The nose is large, the cheeks soft, the hair full and wavy. This is the brilliant young man whom Postgate and Gordon sought out for congenial walks and tea, as well as for interminable discussions of 'the Communist dialectic', as one of their friends remembered.[8]

* * *

In February 1915 Gordon was admitted to membership of the Oxford University Fabian Society (OUFS), a club for Fabians and their sympathisers. The London-based Fabian Society drew its membership mainly from the professional middle classes. Detached from their bourgeois moorings by the example of militancy among the oppressed – workers, women, the Irish – and radicalised by cultural modernity, the middle classes could be attracted to socialism if, as Fabians proclaimed, it meant three things: gradual change, progressive administrators permeating the civil service, and democracy with an elitist inflection. The Fabians were well reported in the journals of political comment, but they remained a small bunch, about 2500 nationally. They had a strong following in the universities. There were 500 members of the Fabian-initiated University Socialist Federation in 1915, 200 of them in the OUFS. Fabian policies were moderately reformist – on social and economic matters slightly more radical than those of the Liberal Party. In foreign affairs, however, Fabians were just as imperialistic. When the war broke out the Fabian Society supported Britain's involvement.

---

8   John Callaghan, *Rajani Palme Dutt: A Study in British Stalinism*, London, Lawrence & Wishart, 1993, Ch. 1; Graham Stevenson, *Encyclopedia of Communist Biographies*, https://grahamstevenson.me.uk/category/commiepedia/ entry on Dutt (for photos); H.D. Hall to Walter Kendall, July 1973 (draft), in H. Duncan Hall papers, National Library of Australia MSS 5547 box 60.

Rajani Palme Dutt, or Raji as Childe would have known him at Oxford.
(Labour History Archive and Study Centre, People's History Museum,
Manchester – Dutt Papers)

Outside the universities the model for socialist organising was either a doctrinaire band of Marxists, like the British Socialist Party, or a secular religious movement like the Independent Labour Party, which to its credit stood by its pacifist principles and opposed the war. But almost entirely independent of all of them – Marxists, Fabians and ILP – a rebellious working class was remaking British radicalism. From 1910 a huge strike-wave swept over Britain, swamping conservative union leaders and socialist intellectuals alike. As historian Walter Kendall described it, 'a wild, elemental, pent-up force seemed suddenly let loose, disregarding precedents and agreements, impatient of compromise, shaking the old complacent trade unionism by the ears'. It revived an almost forgotten radical model of organisation and way of thinking. Worker intellectuals, out of their experiences of workplace militancy and local control, and with the input of a small group of leaders influenced by French syndicalism, began to imagine social reorganisation at a distance from the state, and to theorise a decentralised industrial socialism based on democracy from below.[9]

Some of the younger Fabians in the universities were excited by these developments, both as harbingers of change and as justification for their growing interest in the ideas of guild socialism. Since 1907, *The New Age*, a modernist journal edited by A.R. Orage, had been promoting a return to the medieval guild system to counter the decline of craftsmanship and the loss of self-government by workers in industrial capitalism. At the same time, the threat to democracy posed by a powerful state and its bureaucracy was pushing the younger Fabians in more radical directions, especially because the leaders of the labour movement, whose idea of socialism was state-based, seemed unaware of the danger. These Fabian rebels thought that the collectivist socialist tradition of relying on the state to provide for the welfare of its citizens, together with the continuation of capitalist ownership of the largest enterprises, could only lead to an even greater loss of control for workers, to a 'servile state'. With a nod to the idea that guilds should be revived, they proposed to rethink socialism. They would abolish capitalist ownership and the wages system by basing a socialist society on devolved self-government, civil society pluralism, and the vesting of economic resources not in the state but in cooperatively run, industry-based, occupational groups – that is, in a modern version of the medieval guilds. Thus, guild socialism emerged, most

---

9 *Fabian News*, vol. xxxvi, no. 6, May 1915; Oxford University Fabian Society, Minute Book, 18 February 1915 (Childe elected to membership), Bodleian Library, Oxford; *Bulletin of the University Socialist Federation*, May 1915; *Labour History Review*, vol. 79, no. 1, April 2014, Special Issue, 'The Great Labour Unrest', particularly the 'Introduction: Revisiting the Great Labour Unrest' by the editor, Yann Béliard, pp. 1–17; Walter Kendall, *The Revolutionary Movement in Britain, 1900–21*, London, Weidenfeld & Nicolson, 1969, p. 26; Logie Barrow and Ian Bullock, *Democratic Ideas and the British Labour Movement*, Cambridge, Cambridge University Press, 1996, especially Chs 12 and 13.

clearly after 1912 in articles in *The New Age* and in S.G. Hobson's 1914 book, *National Guilds: An Inquiry into the Wage System and a Way Out*.[10]

When Childe joined the Oxford University Fabian Society, guild socialism was already a source of internal dispute, chiefly because of the activities of G.D.H. Cole. Three years older than Gordon and a Fellow of Magdalen College, Douglas Cole was the leading exponent of guild socialism in the central Fabian Society. In May, however, he resigned from the Fabian Society when at its 1915 Annual General Meeting the members rejected his resolutions to restrict the Society to research so that Fabians would be free to proselytise for trade unionism and guild socialism. Meanwhile the OUFS had independently decided to adopt a new constitution proclaiming that the aim of socialists was 'political and industrial democracy' through militant and class-conscious trade unionism. This was a clear rejection of permeating the state as the road to socialism. It was thus inevitable that the Oxford Fabians would secede. In June they set up the Oxford University Socialist Society (OUSS) as a federation of self-governing groups, one of which was to accommodate those members who remained loyal to the traditional state-centred Fabian collectivism. Tal Davies was the first Secretary of the OUSS, and Ray Postgate its first Chair. By this time, Gordon was a full member of the Fabian Society, but he did not join the society's Fabian group, which was anyway quite small because many of the students committed to traditional Fabianism had enlisted in the military.

Philosophically, the path to guild socialism was underpinned by a wave of pluralist thinking about the state and popular sovereignty, reaching a peak at about the time Childe reached Oxford. It was an important theme in a 1915 book surveying political thought in England written by an Oxford History don Ernest Barker:

> A certain tendency to discredit the State is now abroad ... [resting partly on] the new doctrine of the rights of groups ... In the sphere of economics this doctrine assumes the form of Guild Socialism ... [It] has tended to produce a federalistic theory of the State ... as a union of guilds.

---

10   Margaret Cole, 'Guild Socialism and the Labour Research Department', in Asa Briggs and John Saville (eds), *Essays in Labour History: 1886–1923*, London, Macmillan, 1971, pp. 260–83; 'Guild Socialism: The Storrington Document', also in Briggs and Saville, pp. 332–50; S.G. Hobson, *National Guilds: An Inquiry into the Wage System and the Way Out*, London, Bell and Sons, 1914; Frank Matthews, 'The Ladder of Becoming: A.R. Orage, A.J. Penty and the Origins of Guild Socialism in England', in David E. Martin and David Rubinstein (eds), *Ideology and the Labour Movement: Essays Presented to John Saville*, London, Croom Helm, 1979, pp. 147–66.

Childe was already primed for awareness of this tendency by his course on the state with Professor Anderson at Sydney. As a young Fabian rebel, he would have been aware of Cole's reliance on the 'doctrine of the rights of groups' when attacking the state-centred version of socialism, even more so after Cole delivered a paper to a symposium organised by the Aristotelian Society on 'The Nature of the State in View of Its External Relations' in 1915. Cole's target was the 'absolutist' idea 'in modern ethical theory' that the state is an end in itself, has 'the right to demand absolute obedience of its subjects', and possesses 'a general will'. On the last point, he was denying the claim made by the early nineteenth century German philosopher G.W.F. Hegel that history 'is the process whereby the spirit discovers itself' as it progresses towards 'the consciousness of freedom', beginning with the creation of the state, 'the first realisation of freedom', and ending with the bourgeois constitutional state which at last embodies the general will of society. It was a claim repugnant to both liberals, for whom only individuals might be said to have a consciousness of freedom, and pluralists, for whom the state was just one of the groups to which individuals belonged, and for whom the real basis for sovereignty was the group life of society. The democratic state, Cole insisted, only has the right to compel obedience 'in so far as it respects those obligations which the individual owes to other forms of association'. If it does not, then the individual's conscience should prevail over the State's right to demand obedience. As the British state extended its sphere of authority into markets and civil society in order to coordinate the war effort, a combination of individualism and pluralism became a powerful weapon in the hands of anti-war radicals. And it opened the door to other ways of thinking about democracy.[11]

* * *

The dominant group in the OUSS, comprising Cole and his supporters, was opposed to the war, but to avoid being banned by the university, as well as being rent by internal disputes, the OUSS had to take steps to fool the

---

11   Ernest Barker, *Political Thought in England from Herbert Spencer to the Present Day*, London, Williams and Norgate, 1915, p. 249, https://archive.org/details/politicalthought00barkuoft; A.W. Wright, *G.D.H. Cole and Socialist Democracy*, Oxford, Oxford University Press, 1979, pp. 32–34; G.W.F. Hegel, *Philosophy of Right* (1821), www.marxists.org/reference/archive/hegel/works/pr/prstate.htm#PR260, accessed June 2018; Paul Q. Hirst (ed.), *The Pluralist Theory of the State: Selected Writings of G.D.H. Cole, J.N. Figgis and H.J. Laski*, London, Routledge, 1989.

authorities. Postgate, an open pacifist, resigned as Chairman, and Cole and Theodore Chaundy sponsored a resolution declaring that the Society was not a pacifist organisation. This had the positive effect of pushing many of the most committed anti-war socialists, including Gordon's friends Chorley, Postgate, Dutt and Davies, into debating the war in other forums such as the Oxford Union. They also used the Society to host visiting speakers with controversial views. In March, at a meeting organised by Oxford's socialists, the speaker was Bertrand Russell, whom Ray Postgate referred to as 'an amiable stork' because of his habit of standing with shoulders and head bent forward. Russell told them that secret diplomacy and the deceitfulness of the British state were largely responsible for the present war.[12]

Resistance to the war came not only from socialists but also from a movement to protect civil liberties. The Defence of the Realm Act, passed four days after Britain declared war, began a period of authoritarian government that dismayed liberal intellectuals, especially because the Act provided for censorship and restrictions on free speech. Considerable publicity for the liberal position occurred when Bertrand Russell, Fenner Brockway, Clifford Allen and other leading anti-war intellectuals were gaoled under the provisions of the Act. But for the upholders of civil liberty worse was to come. When it was clear that voluntary recruitment could not be relied on to replace the soldiers slaughtered in the first year of the war, compulsion was introduced. Beginning in January 1916 a series of Military Service Acts conscripted an ever-wider circle of men. These acts made provision for exemptions but the treatment of conscientious objectors in the military service tribunals set up under the Act caused liberals great distress, even those supporting the war, such as the Australian-born Gilbert Murray, the Regius Professor of Greek at Oxford, whose help Childe would seek in 1916.[13]

Foremost in response on a national level were the No-Conscription Fellowship, which supported conscientious objectors and meticulously documented their cases, and the National Council for Civil Liberties, in whose London office Childe worked in the summer vacation of 1916. Also critical in

---

12 Margaret Cole, *The Life of G.D.H. Cole*, London, Macmillan, 1971, pp. 50–80; L.P. Carpenter, *G.D.H. Cole: An Intellectual Biography*, Cambridge University Press, 1973; A.W. Wright, *G.D.H. Cole and Socialist Democracy*, Oxford, Clarendon Press, 1979, Part 1; M.P. Ashley and C.T. Saunders, *Red Oxford: A History of the Growth of Socialism in the University of Oxford*, Oxford, 1930, pp. 18–25; *The Oxford Magazine*, 15 March 1918, referring to a decision of March 1916; John and Mary Postgate, *A Stomach for Dissent*, p. 58.

13 Martin Ceadel, *Pacifism in Britain, 1914–1945: The Defining of a Faith*, Oxford, Clarendon Press, 1980.

organising intellectual resistance to the war was the Quaker-funded Union of Democratic Control (UDC), a pressure group that advocated popular control of foreign policy and blamed secret diplomacy for the war. According to the *Oxford Magazine*, however, it gave support 'to the enemies of this country'. Childe was a member of its Oxford branch. At first, anti-war agitation was mainly confined to holding meetings, publishing leaflets and lobbying politicians, and the main thrust of anti-war propaganda was pacifist and moralistic: 'We cannot assist in warfare. War, which to us is wrong; war, which the people did not seek will only be made impossible when men who so believe remain steadfast to their convictions.' These defiant words appeared in a leaflet issued by the No-Conscription Fellowship, a leaflet that led to heavy fines for eight of its leaders for prejudicing recruiting.[14]

Russell publicly defended the right of conscientious objection to aiding the war after the passage of the first Military Service Act in February 1916. Although already a world-famous philosopher, this was the signal for the press to pillory him and the British Government to harass him. In April 1916 he was convicted under the Defence of the Realm Act and fined 100 pounds for being the author of a leaflet issued by the No-Conscription Fellowship (NCF) criticising the severity of punishment inflicted on conscientious objectors. Citing this conviction, his enemies ensured that he lost his fellowship at Trinity College, Cambridge. He was not deterred; in fact, his activism increased. When two of the leaders of the NCF were gaoled, he took over their roles. In pamphlets, speeches and articles he attacked the government and argued for negotiations to end the war. In the summer of 1916 he planned to make 35 speeches in South Wales where there was considerable industrial unrest. By this time, in response to growing working-class militancy, and the horrifying casualties of trench warfare, the anti-war movement presented a harder face. Internationalists and revolutionaries came to outnumber the pacifists, and workers' and shop-stewards' committees were organising strikes against industrial conscription. This prompted the government to reimagine its most feared scenario: a radicalised working-class seriously impeding the war effort, or worse, embarking on a revolutionary course, a prospect that seemed distinctly possible after the February 1917 revolution in Russia. The

---

14 *The Oxford Magazine*, 12 November 1915, p. 65; on the UDC, see Marvin Swartz, *The Union of Democratic Control in British Politics during the First World War*, Oxford, Clarendon Press, 1971; H. Hanak, 'The Union of Democratic Control during the First World War', *Historical Research*, vol. 36, issue 94, November 1963, pp. 168–80; *The Manchester Guardian*, 18 May 1916, p. 6; Childe, 'Personal Statement' included with Childe to Murray, 8 June 1918, Murray papers, shelfmark 376, ff. 44–6.

government therefore banned Russell from speaking in the industrial cities and along the coast and prevented him from travelling to the USA. When he warned the labour movement in 1918 that American troops in Britain could be used as strike-breakers, as they had been used in the USA, he was given a gaol sentence of six months.[15]

* * *

It was not unusual for graduates from British universities to take a further degree from Oxford or Cambridge, and this was also true of graduates from British Empire universities. Gordon enrolled in three degrees: a research degree called the BLitt, the BA in classics called Literae Humaniores ('Greats'), and the Diploma in Archaeology. It might appear as if he was setting himself a heavy program of study, but that turned out not to be the case. After a few weeks he dropped out of classes for the Diploma, perhaps because, as Timothy Champion suggests, he found sketching Greek vases pretty mindless. He took his research degree much more seriously. He went on a research trip to Greece in 1915 and by June of the following year his thesis on Indo-European influences on Greek prehistory had been accepted and the BLitt degree awarded. For the next 18 months all he had to study for was the BA in Greats, a course that he had already completed very successfully at Sydney. So, for at least his last 18 months in Oxford he was not academically stretched. Gordon had time for politics, and as Dutt noted in his diary, by November 1916 he became 'obsessed with his manifold activities'.[16]

As a resident of Australia visiting Britain for educational purposes, Childe was not affected by the Military Service Act, but his anti-war friends were. Under the Act single men between the ages of 18 and 41 were automatically enrolled

---

15   Olivier Estèves, 'Bertrand Russell, The Utilitarian Pacifist', *Revue Française de Civilisation Britannique* [Online], vol. XX, no. 1, 2015, http://rfcb.revues.org/308; DOI: 10.4000/rfcb.308, accessed 1 August 2016; Robert Duncan and Arthur McIvor (eds), *Militant Workers: Labour and Class Conflict on the Clyde 1900–1950*, Edinburgh, John Donald, 1992; J. Hinton, *The First Shop Stewards Movement*, London, Allen & Unwin, 1973, pp. 239–41; *What Happened at Leeds*, Council of Soldiers' and Workers' Delegates, Pelican Press, 1917; Martin Ceadel, *Pacifism in Britain*, pp. 318–19.

16   Timothy Champion, 'Childe and Oxford', *European Journal of Archaeology*, vol. 12, nos 1–3, 2009, pp. 13, 20; R.P. Dutt diary, entry for 3 November 1916, CP/IND/DUTT/22/02, Communist Party of Great Britain Archives, National Museum of Labour History, Manchester.

in the military unless they were ministers of religion or a local military tribunal had granted them a certificate of exemption on the grounds of being engaged in work for the national interest, ill health, hardship, or conscience. Although some opponents of the war were able to claim exemption because their work was regarded as significant for the national interest – as Cole did because he was an advisor to a trade union whose members might damage the war effort, and it was assumed Cole would advise them against going on strike – nearly all of them had to argue for exemption on the grounds of conscience. This was an ordeal because the tribunals, drawn from local elites, relied on a narrow definition of conscientious objection. A religious basis was just acceptable to them, but if the applicant declared himself an atheist, or worse a socialist atheist, the tribunals were decidedly unsympathetic. A successful case before a tribunal usually resulted only in an exemption from combatant service.

About 16,000 men sought exemption as conscientious objectors, most of whom accepted service as non-combatants, but there were about 6,000 'absolutists' who refused to make any contribution to the war effort or to recognise military authority. They were imprisoned. When about 40 were sent in May 1916 to France to join the British army, where the penalty for refusing to fight was death by firing squad, Gilbert Murray persuaded Prime Minister Asquith to issue an order that no conscientious objector was to be executed. Like Asquith, Murray was a Liberal, and he supported the war, but he also defended the liberal principle that men should not be compelled to act against their conscience. The army sent the absolutists back to Britain to rejoin their comrades in British gaols, there to suffer the brutality routinely dealt out to 'shirkers'. At the end of the war, 800 'absolutists' had spent more than two years in prison, including one of Gordon's closest friends.[17]

Conscientious objectors had until the second of March to apply for exemption. On 23 February 1916, Raymond Postgate applied to the Oxford tribunal for 'unconditional exemption' on moral and political grounds, supported by a letter from Professor Murray. On the same day, Dutt met with Phillip 'Tal' Davies, David Blelloch and Alan Kaye in his room to discuss what to say at the tribunal, and later that day Gordon gave his advice as he and Dutt walked up Headington Hill in the snow. Over the next few weeks the leading anti-war students faced the tribunal. As they expected, Postgate and Blelloch were deemed 'ECS', exemption from combatant service. Postgate, ignoring the order to present himself to the military, was arrested. His elder

---

17   John and Mary Postgate, *A Stomach for Dissent*, p. 65; Ceadel, *Pacifism in Britain*, pp. 38–41.

sister, Margaret, a Cambridge graduate, was often in Oxford to support Ray so she probably met Gordon then. They became friends when they worked together in the Fabian Research Department, and, when she came to write her memoirs, she believed that Gordon put on a party to celebrate her engagement to Douglas Cole. As we shall see, she was confusing parties – of which there were many in 'the movement' at that time. There was no party when Ray was sentenced to serve a month in prison. As Margaret walked away from the Oxford Courthouse, Gilbert Murray solicitously held an umbrella over her head, although it was not raining.[18]

In gaol, Postgate refused to obey orders or sign documents. Wanting to get rid of him, the prison authorities discovered in his medical history a childhood heart complaint and after a few weeks discharged him on fake medical grounds. Blelloch, who was Secretary of the Oxford branch of the No-Conscription Fellowship, chose non-combatant service by joining the Friends' Ambulance Unit. A few years later he was working as an economist for the International Labour Office, where he received letters from Gordon in 1921 about the possibility of employment there. Meanwhile, in Alan Kaye's case the tribunal found that the Military Service Act did not apply to him because his father, Julius Kaufmann, a Liverpool merchant, was German. Nonetheless the British state pursued him. Just weeks later he was arrested for distributing a leaflet that the court ruled was prejudicial to recruiting and sentenced to two months in prison. Childe got to know Kaye better when they both worked in the Research Department in 1917. When Kaye was 24, suffering from suicidal depression, he and his girlfriend gassed themselves in a flat in Kilburn.[19]

Rajani Palme Dutt was determined to defy the authorities, but he had to fight them to get the chance, for at his first hearing in March the members of the tribunal doubted that the terms of the Act covered Anglo-Indians. Their doubts were reinforced by a suggestion from the military representative at the hearing that the India Office did not want Dutt called up. This may have been because any defiance in the army by Dutt could have emboldened the Indian nationalist movement, many of whose leaders visited the Dutt family home in Cambridge. At a second hearing, Dutt had

---

18   John and Mary Postgate, *A Stomach for Dissent*, pp. 42–7; Dutt's diary, entry for 23 February 1916 CP/IND/DUTT/ 22/06; Margaret Cole, *Growing Up into Revolution*, London, Longmans, 1949, p. 59; Margaret Cole, *Life of G.D.H. Cole*, p. 42.

19   John and Mary Postgate, *A Stomach for Dissent*, pp. 42–7; Conscientious Objectors' Register, files on Kaye, https://livesofthefirstworldwar.org/lifestory/7649228#evidence, and Blelloch, https://search.livesofthefirstworldwar.org/record?id=GBM/CONSOBJ/3395.

to insist that as a British subject the Act did apply to him, and the tribunal reluctantly agreed. He was exempted from combatant service only, which meant that as an absolutist he would be well positioned to create mischief in the military system. Childe understood his friend's intention and gave it an added gloss. He told Professor Murray on 5 June that Dutt's refusal to accept 'the illegal escape' offered to him demonstrated his moral character. 'When the sympathizers with the C.O.s [conscientious objectors] are always prepared to cry out at the illegalities of the tribunals when it's against them it is very fine that a man should protest against illegality even when it is in his favor [sic]'.

Childe carried on a long correspondence with Murray about Dutt's plight, beginning on the day after Dutt presented himself at Cowley Barracks. Dutt was in good spirits. On the previous day, Thursday, according to his diary, he spent 'the most glorious afternoon in the world': five hours with Childe on the river and then tea at The Mill. On Friday morning he picked up Childe on his way to Cowley Barracks. There they joined a group of conscientious objectors. Dutt noted 'fearful heat; atmosphere of high walls, grand whitewash, and stiff soldiers; but the criminals beautifully and defiantly civilian'. As expected, he was arrested. He refused to eat or put on the uniform and was (in Gordon's words to Murray) 'vilely treated'. A week later he was transferred to Aldershot, from where several drafts of conscientious objectors had been sent to France. Gordon was alarmed, but Murray reassured him that this practice had ceased. Gordon wrote again, and Murray took Dutt's case to the Cabinet. Dutt compromised by ending his hunger strike and wearing khaki, but as he still refused to obey orders on 21 July he was court-martialed and sentenced to 56 days in a civil prison. Becoming ill, he was transferred to a military hospital and placed in a ward for prisoners with venereal diseases, but he saw this as another opportunity, describing the appalling conditions in letters that were used as propaganda by the no-conscription movement. Then unexpectedly on 12 August 1916 the War Office discharged him. His letter of discharge stated, 'This man will be liable to a fine of 100 pounds and two years' imprisonment if he is caught trying to enter the Army again'. Obviously, the government feared that any further incarceration of Dutt might weaken Indian support for the war or even encourage a nationalist insurrection. His biographer, John Callaghan, wrote, 'Dutt returned to his studies at Oxford hardened by his experience and more determined than ever'.[20]

---

20   John and Mary Postgate, *A Stomach for Dissent*, pp. 65–7; Callaghan, *Rajani Palme Dutt*, p. 16; Dutt's diary, entry for 18 May 1916, CP/IND/DUTT/22/06; Childe's letters to Murray, 27 May, 4 June, 5 June, 7 [?] June, 12 October 1916, Murray papers, Bodleian Library, shelfmarks 375 and 376, various folios.

That summer of 1916 Childe and Dutt met up in London to work in the Fabian Research Department, now heavily infiltrated by the guild socialists. Gordon also volunteered at the offices of the National Council for Civil Liberties. Back in Oxford, when the October term began, they toured the colleges recruiting for the Socialist Society, of which Gordon was the Secretary, replacing Philip Davies after he was arrested in April. For the next eight weeks Gordon and Rajani were together almost every day. They walked up Boar's Hill to visit Postgate who was 'in exile', studying in lodgings because, until 1917, his college would not take him back as punishment for bringing the college into disrepute. They celebrated with Kaye when he was released from prison. They discussed Gilbert Murray's letters to Gordon and wrote amusing pretend letters to members of the government. They saw *The Gondoliers* together. And nearly every night Dutt recorded their meetings in his dairy, of which the entry for Thursday 9 November is typical: 'out with Childe in afternoon and much pleasant philosophy'.[21]

Not long after the October term began Dutt persuaded Gordon and a few others to 'set up an unofficial group – a group for ourselves'. The group, which met nine times during term, discussed socialist theory. Since the Socialist Society's constitution allowed the formation of autonomous self-governing groups, why was it necessary to set up an unofficial group? Was it a revolutionists' cell in formation, perhaps? Dutt at least acted as if it were. He expected a degree of greater than usual commitment from its members, recording in his diary that the absence of one of them at a meeting raised the 'question of his turning away'. Robin Page Arnot, the Secretary of the University Socialist Federation, visited Oxford in 1916, later recalling that Childe impressed him as 'a young Marxist undergraduate'. Arnot, a future foundation and lifetime member of the Communist Party, would have filtered this recollection through an ideology that sharply divided reformists from revolutionaries. Childe, he was saying, was a revolutionary. The first paper to the group was delivered by Dutt, and its topic was 'The Class War', a war that in Marxist theory entails revolutionary crises as one mode of production gives way to another. It looks as if what the 'unofficial group' were studying was the possibility of socialist revolution.[22]

In that Autumn of 1916, while the would-be revolutionists met unofficially, Rajani took over from Gordon the position of Secretary of the Socialist Society.

---

21   Dutt's diary has 21 entries mentioning Childe for the eight weeks of term.
22   R. Page Arnot to P. Gathercole, 4 February 1960 (copy from Gathercole). Dutt's diary, CP/IND/DUTT/22/06.

He did not enjoy it, summing up his impression of left activity on campus as: 'Very empty – nothing much going on except a poor mechanical continuance of the Socialist Society. Balliol filled with freshers, mostly Americans, all silly. Childe the only person of interest.'

* * *

Gordon was determined to confront the government's system of oppression, particularly because it inflicted such suffering on his friends. In late 1916 he sent off a reply in high ironic mode to an article on conscientious objectors in *Hermes*, the magazine of the University of Sydney. Claiming it as 'a belated appreciation' of *Hermes* from Oxford's 'cold Northern superculture' of state worship, he welcomed its 'ray of barbaric sunlight':

> It dispersed the doubts and perplexities that the hypocritical whims of so-called Liberalism, and a yet more inconsistent Socialism, had evoked with cant about 'rival loyalties'. This spirit from the warm south breathed the true spirit of Hegelianism which has made our great foe able to rise above all silly sentimentality and present a terrible and united front to the world. Away with cant about the brotherhood of man! Let us frankly admit that no duty to truth, religion or humanity can possibly override the claims of the State. Even the Universities in England are not free of the scandalous crew. Young men who might have had honourable commissions in the Army and a 'war-degree', or even served their country in a 'funk-hole' at the War Office, have to be held up to ridicule at tribunals, brought up in police courts as deserters, and sent to prison for disobedience. But have no fear. A conscience-clause loses no useful men to the Army. Those who will face the full fury of public opinion, the vilification dealt out by tribunals, the shame of the police courts, the jeers and horseplay of the barracks, and, finally the soul-destroying monotony of the gaols, are too hardened in cowardice and hypocrisy to be soldiers. Nor does this end their punishment. Their actions have involved loss of positions or scholarships which would have been kept for them till 'after the war' had they joined up. Some twenty 'swats' from the sister University after cleaning up all the best places in the final 'Trips' are now cooling their ardour in Wormwood Scrubs with all their prospects gone for ever. Strangest freak of all, many of these outcasts claim to be Socialists, and this despite the fine lead the German

Socialists – save a few dreamers of the Liebknecht type – have given in patriotism by rallying to the cry (false and lying though we know it was) of the 'Fatherland in danger'. But in my indignation, I wax verbose.

One last word: never for a moment let yourself think that there may be two sides to any question like this, or that calm consciousness of national virtue that the Briton loves above life itself will be imperilled for ever.

Vere Gordon Childe, B.A. (Syd), B.Litt (Oxon), Queen's College, Oxford.[23]

As confutation, the mocking tone of the letter was offensive enough, but the real clincher was the intellectual ambush. While British patriots were attacking conscientious objectors, because the claims of the state overrode duty to 'truth, religion or humanity', their intellectual leaders were diligently broadcasting arguments about the pernicious nature of German state theory. One line of attack was quite sophisticated, drawing on a history of opposition to the impact of G.W.F. Hegel on British philosophy and the ensuing debates about philosophical idealism. Among the leading voices raised against Hegelian idealism was that of the radical liberal, L.T. Hobhouse, Britain's first professor of sociology, whose 1904 book *Democracy and Reaction* vigorously criticised its 'absolutism' and 'reactionary influence'. When the war broke out, he became even more strident, singling out for condemnation the statism of German philosophy. He coined the phrase 'the Hegelian theory of the God-state' to account for Germany's militarism, and its contempt for humanity, the sanctity of treaties and international law. Less sophisticated were the articles saturating the journals of opinion attempting to show that German intellectual life and culture were fixated on the country's supposed special 'spirit', its 'superbeing' or 'superculture'. The consensus among patriotic intellectuals was that a German philosophical deficit underlay the outbreak of the war.[24]

---

23 Childe, 'Conscientious Objectors', *Hermes*, vol. XXIII, May 1917, pp. 69–70.
24 Philosophical idealism is the branch of metaphysics that holds that reality can only be known through mental construction and that ideas have autonomy and primacy in relation to social forces. L.T. Hobhouse, *Democracy and Reaction*, London, Fisher Unwin, 1904; L.T Hobhouse, 'The Soul of Civilisation', *Contemporary Review*, 108, 1915, pp. 161–2; L.T Hobhouse, *The Metaphysical Theory of the State – A Criticism*, London, George Allen & Unwin, 1918; Stefan Collini, 'Hobhouse, Bosanquet and the State: Philosophical Idealism and Political Argument in England 1880–1918', *Past and Present*, no. 72, 1976, pp. 86–111; Gregory Moore, 'The Super-Hun and the Super-State: Allied Propaganda and German Philosophy during the First World War', *German Life and Letters*, vol. 554, no. 4, October 2001, pp. 310–30.

Childe's daring implication was that a similar deficit explained the British state's attack on conscientious objectors. He was also intent on reminding readers that there was another Germany, and another Britain, where liberal-minded people considered all sides of a question, and socialists remained true to their internationalist convictions. Karl Liebknecht, who founded the Spartacus League with Rosa Luxemburg in 1914 to rally fellow members of the German Social Democratic Party against the war, was still able to dream when Childe wrote to *Hermes*. In the Spartacist uprising in 1919 he was captured and executed by the Freikorps, precursors of Nazism. In Childe's life there was never a moment requiring that kind of physical courage, but this letter was intellectually brave. He sent it for publication indifferent to how it would be received in the common rooms of his alma mater and by its graduates in Sydney's professional circles. The letter was consciously provocative. He meant it to discomfort those Australians who relied on imperial sentiment rather than reason in their approach to the war. He meant them to know that he rejected their unthinking worship of the state.

Chapter 5

MORE OUTSPOKEN THAN ANY OTHER

In 1917 Childe had two more terms in Oxford. His friendship with Dutt continued to be close, and despite looming final exams he remained politically active. In February he delivered an address to the Oxford branch of the Union of Democratic Control, which Dutt attended. The next day he promised to be Dutt's second speaker at a debate with the Cambridge socialists on the topic that the class war was fundamental to socialist theory. Dutt wrote in his diary later that they 'got it passed by 16 to 9'. On 7 March they drank tea in Dutt's rooms and after some earnest discussion decided 'to abandon England as beyond redemption and English politics [as] a hopeless and blood-boiling occupation'. It doesn't appear that their political mood was improved by news a week later of the February revolution in Russia and the overthrow of the Czar, for it left no mark in the record of their lives. The press reports, however, enthused about the strengthening of the Duma – the role of the St Petersburg Soviet was largely ignored – and presumed that the Russian military would now pursue the fight against Germany with greater vigour. Why would this news excite a pair of anti-war activists – or of socialists whose preoccupation was socialist theory?[1]

In April he moved into Dutt's lodgings in Richmond Road: two bedrooms and a sitting room, all found for 25 shillings a week. About their term sharing lodgings in Oxford in 1917, Dutt was effusive, underlining in his diary that 'Living with Childe's pleasant and constant companionship' made it 'without question the best term I have ever had; glorious weather, tennis, punting, bathing, speaking, bridge or interesting work; everything rushed through in

---

1   Communist Party of Great Britain archive, papers of R.P. Dutt, Labour History Archive and Study Centre, People's History Museum, Manchester: Dutt's diary, October term 1916, CP/IND/DUTT/22/02, and March 1917, CP/IND/DUTT/22/06.

high spirits ... Lodging with Childe went off perfectly ... we did not tire of one another's company or even found our work really interfered with.'²

* * *

For some months Gordon had been coming to the realisation that staying in Britain to pursue a scholarly career in archaeology would result in his being called up for military service, and, besides, while the war continued it was impossible to carry out his research plans in Central Europe. But if he wanted to return to Australia, there was also a problem. In November 1915 the Australian Government, as part of its campaign to boost recruitment, ordered that no male of military age would be issued with a passport to leave the country 'unless satisfactory reasons were forthcoming'. Childe had read about this but wanted confirmation: would his passport be confiscated if he refused to join the army? In March 1917 he wrote to the Australian High Commissioner in London making it clear that he would not return to Australia if he had to give up his passport, declaring that he would not help 'however indirectly, in a war which I believe to be destructive to civilization and true liberty'.³

Making such a forthright statement of his anti-war views was a direct challenge to the authority of the state. Did Childe feel able to make it because he thought it unlikely he would have to surrender his passport? The strength of anti-conscription sentiment in Australia might have reassured him that he would be able to leave the country if he so wished. He knew of the defeat of the 1916 referendum to introduce conscription, and the insurgency in the Labor Party, which had led to the expulsion of its leader, the Prime Minister William Morris Hughes, the NSW Premier William Holman, and other supporters of conscription. The High Commissioner's response to his letter has not survived, but it may well have included the assurance that travelling abroad to further one's career was an appropriate reason for being able to leave the country on a passport.

---

2   Dutt's diary, various entries for 1917, in CP/IND/DUTT/22/06, and for his summing up of sharing digs with Childe, CP/IND/DUTT/22/02.

3   Childe to High Commissioner for the Commonwealth of Australia, 3 March 1917. That this copy is in Childe's file, M223, in the University of Sydney Archives indicates that Australia's intelligence service supplied it. On passports, see Ernest R. Scott, *Australia during the War – Vol. XI of the Official History of Australia in the War of 1914–18*, Sydney, Angus & Robertson, 1936, p. 311.

He was also playing with the idea of becoming a citizen of the USA, and, as Gilbert Murray had just returned from a visit there, he sought his advice. But the letter to Murray was again strident rather than conciliatory, and much more declarative than might be expected from a student supplicant writing to his mentor:

> My scholarship will be over as soon as I have taken Greats in June & I have no private means. I naturally can take no sort of 'national employment' in this country as that would be indirectly to assist in the prolongation of this senseless slaughter and to connive at the complete destruction of liberty and justice and the continued persecution of the finest men I have ever had the honor of meeting. I cannot well remain deliberately in a country to resist its laws & unless something turns up shall presumably have to return to Australia where there are still some vestiges of freedom. This means finally abandoning all hope of any academic career & the social exil [sic] of a political heretic.[4]

The 'vestiges of freedom' in Australia no doubt referred to the defeat of the referendum to introduce conscription in 1916. It seems he was fairly convinced by March 1917 that he could return to Australia without risk

At the end of term Gordon sat the examination papers in Greats. Dutt wrote in his diary: 'Childe, after taking the best first (Dodds was the other) for which I backed him with confidence, is now being given fifty pounds by the College to go to Australia now and return when the horizon is clearer'. Gilbert Murray wrote to congratulate him. Although this was a degree in classics, and Murray was a Professor of Greek, he annotated one of Childe's letters at this time thus: 'A very clever archaeologist. Australian. I have asked him to lunch on Sunday and walk.'[5]

The American option came to nothing, or perhaps Childe changed his mind after discussion with the authorities at Queen's, for in his next letter to Murray, written after his First in Greats, he was more confident about his academic future. After thanking Murray for his letter of congratulations, he wrote:

> I now purpose [sic] returning to Australia but I hope only temporarily. I certainly should not do so if I thought it would involve giving up archaeology permanently. The College however have made me

---

4   Childe to Murray, 16 March 1917, Murray papers, shelfmark 376, ff. 136–7.'
5   Childe to Murray, Wednesday [7 or 14] June, from Regent's Park, Murray papers, shelfmark 376, letter 157, replying to Murray's congratulations; Childe to Murray, 16 March 1917, Murray shelfmark 376, letter 136.

certain generous offers of financial assistance at present and in certain eventualities for the future. They consider I believe my chance of getting the Craven when that Fellowship is awarded in the post-war period would be less damaged by the absence of the applicant than if he had recently emerged from an English gaol – a gaol to which a prolonged stay in this country would probably lead me as I am not yet 41. One feels of course fears of being forgotten & it is frightful to be banished to wilds where no one had ever heard of Minyan ware, but it is perhaps the wisest course.

Childe was very proud of his first academic article, dealing with the dating and origins of Minyan ware, which had appeared in 1915.[6]

* * *

In May 1917 Childe had written to the Home Office for permission to visit Philip Davies in the prison at Dorchester to discuss his career after the war. He had closely followed Davies' defiance of the military machine, writing to Gilbert Murray for help and issuing a press statement about his sufferings (and those of another absolutist, W.B. Stott). After detailing his prison sentences and pointing out that the sincerity of his motives had been proved by his refusal three times of comparative liberty – that is, by taking up non-combatant work – Gordon concluded: 'I should think that the appeal to physical restraint to make a man untrue to his ideals (however wrong) is of the essence of persecution'. Davies had been court-martialled three times, and there would be a fourth before the war was over. By the time he was freed early in 1919 he had served nearly three years in gaol. He lost his exhibition and never returned to Oxford.[7]

On 1 June, Childe visited Davies in Dorchester Prison. The warden overheard their conversation and reported it to the authorities. Gordon apparently said that he was disappointed the German submarine blockade was failing

---

6 Childe to Murray, Wednesday, [July?] 1917, Murray papers, shelfmark 376, ff. 157–9. Childe applied for his passport on 3 July 1917. V.G. Childe, 'On the Date and Origins of Minyan Ware', *Journal of Hellenic Studies*, vol. 35, no. 2, 1915, pp. 196–207.

7 Childe to Murray, 5 June 1916, 7[?] June 1916, 12 October 1916, with press statement; Philip Taliessen [sic] Davies in Pearce CO Register Transcription, in http://search.livesofthefirstworldwar.org/record?id=gbm%2fconsobj%2f3493 accessed on 19 August 2015.

because he had hoped the suffering it was causing would force the British Government to sue for peace and the British workers to rise in revolt, as in Russia. The warden also reported that Davies was less than impressed with this argument, saying 'that it seems rotten to have to starve people to end the war'. Does this suggest that Davies was not as committed to radical action as Childe, and hence a reason why their friendship did not survive the war?[8]

Childe's confidence in the benevolence of the college authorities was misplaced. The prison warden's report prompted the Home Office to ask the college for its assessment of Childe. The Pro-Provost, Edward Armstrong, replied that Childe's case was causing the college a good deal of anxiety. After initially supporting the war, Childe, a brilliant student, had undergone an 'unfortunate change in his opinions'. Armstrong continued:

> This seems to have been wholly due to a romantic affection for P.T. Davies. Childe is repulsively ugly, probably the ugliest man in the world, and Davies in spite of his cantankerousness and wrong-headedness, has a certain personal attraction. Childe also got to know the Davies family, who all apparently have the same views.[9] The misfortunes of Davies became a monomania with Childe, entering into all his work and spoiling it, and perverting his moral and mental attitude. [He] is priggish and conceited, and would rather pride himself on belonging to a minority. To judge from his letters, his wish is to be ordered to serve in some capacity or other and to be put in prison for refusing.
>
> Our aim is to get him back to Australia ... I don't see any prospect for him in England, as able as he is. I doubt if he is a propagandist in a general way, though he talks freely and foolishly to his friends ... It is difficult to have any pity for these people, but in view of the ruin of a very promising career, it is a tragic case.[10]

The college thought Childe's career in Britain was over, and the Home Office tried to make sure that it was, drawing the attention of MI5 to Childe

---

8   C.E. Tolley (Warden, HM Prison, Dorchester) to Home Office, 1/6/1917, Childe's MI5 file, KV2/2148.

9   Leila Davies, a third-year student at Somerville College, Oxford, in 1916 was the elder sister of Philip Davies. Extracts from her letters to Joseph Dalby, a member of the No-Conscription Fellowship are here: http://blogs.some.ox.ac.uk/thegreatwar/2016/04/01/april-1916-the-court-martial-of-a-conscientious-objector/ accessed 15 August 2016.

10 E. Armstrong (Queen's College) to S.W. Harris (Home Office), 17/6/1917, in Childe's MI5 file, KV2/2148.

because of his apparently pro-German remarks to Davies. Childe, it declared, was 'thoroughly perverted and probably a very dangerous person'.[11] Although the Home Office noted Armstrong's doubt about his effectiveness as a propagandist, it was apparently convinced of the need to put him under surveillance, partly as a result of Armstrong's hint that Childe was homosexual. The logic of this is revealed in the use of the term 'perverted'. Being pro-German was deviant, but the fault was compounded if the subject's sexuality was also deviant. It became perversion. So, MI5 opened a file on Childe and advised their Australian counterparts to do the same.[12] Vindictiveness followed. When Childe applied for an extension of his passport he indicated that he wished to travel to Australia via the USA to view collections of antiquities. This request was refused, MI5 noting with relish that he would travel direct to Australia 'by the long sea route … [and] as he is in favour of the German Submarine campaign the voyage will make him realise what it means'.[13]

* * *

So, by June Childe had made up his mind that his only option was to return to Australia. While waiting for a suitable berth, he went to London and volunteered at the Fabian Research Department, studying industrial and welfare legislation, continuing work that he had begun in the summer vacation of 1916. Then he received a request from another Oxford student, Hessel Duncan Hall, that must have kept him busy for a few nights. Childe knew Hall from Sydney, where he had graduated BA from the university in 1913, and MA in 1915. Arriving at Balliol that year Hall mixed in socialist circles, taking tea with Dutt and Childe, but he was not a member of 'the unofficial group'. In later years he worked for the League of Nations and the British Embassy in Washington and wrote books lauding the British Commonwealth. Hall had received a letter from another Sydney student, Raymond G. Watt, whose

---

11 George Crystal (Home Office) to Lieutenant Kell (MI5), 19/6/1917, in Childe's MI5 file, KV2/2148.

12 The Home Office Warrant authorising the interception of Childe's mail was dated 25 June 1917. It was cancelled on 25 October. He applied for a renewal of his passport in early July. On 22 October, Kell wrote to Major Steward (Australian Military Intelligence) informing him of Childe's return and advising 'a discreet watch' on him. Steward replied on 21 January 1918 that they already had Childe under observation. Source: Childe's MI5 file, KV2/2148.

13 Kell (MI5) to Harris (Home Office), 23/7/1917, Childe's MI5 file KV2/2148.

studies at the university also overlapped with Childe's. In later years Watt was a prominent member of the League of Nations Union in Australia.[14]

Disturbed by the war's carnage but impressed by the dedication that it had elicited and wishing to harness it for international harmony, Watt had written to Hall for information about 'the true position with regards to the war'. Hall thought Childe was the right person to provide the information. Childe accepted the task, writing a long letter, in fact a quasi-article of over 2,200 words with endnotes and bibliographical information. From internal evidence we can date it to about 21 July 1917.[15]

Childe began by rejecting the idea that the only truth attainable in historical matters was 'that embodied in the generally accepted opinion of a particular country or nation', a view 'that might find support in certain passages in Hegel':

> This view, of course, ultimately leads to the doctrine expressed as 'my country right or wrong'. On this theory it is 'true' in Germany that this is a defensive war forced on Germany by the Russian mobilisation and the corrupt agreements of British and French imperialists: while across the border it is 'true' that this war was caused simply and solely by the unprovoked aggression of militarist Germany. A 'truth' of this sort seems in my eyes a contradiction in terms.

Instead, 'any genuine TRUTH must be equally acceptable to all men of all races who choose to seek it, laying aside all personal prejudices and bias'. Childe is here echoing an argument about truth that became part of the rejection of Hegelian idealism in British philosophical debates. According to this argument, reality is external to the human mind and truth has to correspond to reason's discoveries about that reality. To take this step one had to move beyond the 'generally accepted opinion of a particular country or nation'. This is the only way to discover the 'true position in regard to the war' – which he intends to describe in this letter for Watt's benefit.

First, however, he needed to convey the moral outrage felt by opponents of the war, for whatever the material losses – 'the rivers of blood', the 'steady

---

14   B.H. Fletcher, 'Hall, Hessel Duncan (1891–1976)', *Australian Dictionary of Biography*, Vol. 14, 1996, pp. 356–7; Nicholas Brown, 'Enacting the International: R.G. Watt and the League of Nations Union', in Desley Deacon, Penny Russell and Angela Woollacott (eds), *Transnational Lives: Australian Lives in the World*, Canberra, ANU E Press, 2008, pp. 77–8.

15   Childe to R.G. Watt, undated but internal evidence suggests late July or early August 1917, R.G. Watt papers, National Library of Australia, MS 1837, item 15.

increase in expenditure' defrayed by loans 'at ever rising interest rates' now costing 'six and a half million pounds a day' – they were slight compared to:

> [the] moral losses that have been sustained. Scarcely one of the bulwarks of British freedom are still surviving. Citizens may be interned without trial, even without any specific charge being preferred, by a mere order of the Home Secretary over-riding even Habeas Corpus.

In a footnote he gave the figure: 74 British subjects as of February. Speech and publication deemed as likely to prejudice recruitment or discipline in the armed forces were prohibited; not just Bertrand Russell, 'Crowds of insignificant people have been imprisoned under this regulation'. Again, 'you have the continued persecution of conscientious objectors', supported by another footnote: '1200 Conscientious Objectors are still in prison serving 2nd, 3rd, or 4th sentences for disobeying military orders'. Worse, they are tortured: 'Tortures admitted in the House include confinement in a pit half full of water, beating with scrubbing brushes, systematic kicking by parties told off [chosen] for the purpose etc.' He added a personal note: the fact that 'men are at this very moment in prison' for seeking 'the genuine truth about the war' was 'brought home to me very painfully in Oxford last year', and it 'made me suspect that the position of the allies in the present conflict might not be so unassailable as it seemed at first sight; for surely the truth could never be seriously imperilled by free discussion'.

Then he moved on to making a case against the war in four propositions. First, the Allies were not unprepared for the outbreak of war (although Britain 'wholly miscalculated the new conditions [of warfare] especially the importance of heavy artillery'). The British White Paper insisted that German aggression was the culmination of a long period of preparation. But, said Childe, 'Germany, we must remember, lay between two powerful countries', revanchist France and 'the aggressive autocracy of semi-barbaric Russia'. He presented the military and naval expenditure figures for the decade before the war and concluded, 'That Germany was preparing against war is clear enough, but so were France and Russia and they were doing it faster than Germany. It doesn't really look as if the Central Powers were out for aggression. Nor was [Germany] prepared as is always alleged at the outbreak of war. Russia, France and Britain were much better prepared.' Moreover, citing Lord Haldane, Childe wrote that Britain sent 160,000 men to France in 12 days. 'In the light of this the usual allegations that we were unprepared looks [sic] rather silly.'

Second, Britain was 'in the war' before Belgium was invaded – this in answer to the pathos invoked by British propaganda about German atrocities in Belgium. In fact, Childe wrote, Germany had offered to respect the neutrality of Belgium if British neutrality was guaranteed, but Britain could give no such guarantee because of the secret promise made to France for military and naval support. 'It really turns out that ever since the Entente with France, we had been committed to support her and incidentally, of course, her ally Russia against Germany.' And Childe then cited books detailing British connivance at aggression by France (in Morocco) and Russia (in Persia) in the years before the war. 'I do not see myself that the Prussian Militarists were any more of a danger to Europe than the Russian bureaucrats with whom we were allied through France.'

Third, Britain was in no real danger in 1917. 'There has been from a military point of view no change since November 1914 ... No one can imagine that either England or her colonies are threatened in any way or even have been since 1915. Though Germany occupies Belgium and portions of France and Russia, her advance is everywhere checked while all her colonies – a far greater area than the occupied territories [by Germany, in Belgium and France] – are in the hands of the Allies.'

Fourth, Britain was not interested in ending the war through a negotiated peace. It had rejected a proposal of this kind from US President Wilson, and ignored numerous openings for negotiation: a German offer to negotiate in December 1916, a vote in favour of negotiations in the Reichstag in July, and a speech expressing support for that vote by Germany's new Chancellor, Dr Michaelis.

Childe thought that the conclusion to draw from these propositions was inescapable: Britain was now engaged in a war of aggression – as were all the Allied powers. They had made secret deals for territorial expansion at the expense of Germany and her ally, Turkey. Britain would be able to keep Mesopotamia, France would get large tracts of Syria and of course Alsace Lorraine 'which is by now largely Germanised', and Italy would get large sections of Dalmatia 'which ethnically are certainly less Italian than Magyar'. He asked, 'I don't know if you can see any particular reason why British money, British lives and British liberties should be sacrificed to attain these objects' and answered:

> In the circumstances, then, it seems the duty of a free man is to stay at home and fight for the retention of the remnants of liberty there rather than allow himself to become an instrument of capitalists and diplomats ... Now the peril is from within; from home-grown junkers and bureaucrats, capitalists and profiteers. To fight them is a harder

and bitter task for it means opposing the mass of public opinion as it is manufactured by an unscrupulous press and wicked censorship.

As far as we can discover, Watt made no use of the information in this letter, perhaps because its anti-capitalist conclusion went beyond the Union of Democratic Control sentiments that framed the preceding propositions.

* * *

At the beginning of the war, Britain's Trade Union Congress, the official leadership of the working class, declared a unilateral industrial truce. Given the prewar wave of worker insubordination this was never going to work. In June 1915, the government's Munitions Act introduced industrial conscription – that is, workers could not change jobs without the employers' permission, a pass equivalent to the 'ticket-of-leave' used in colonial Australia to control convict labour. Additionally, industrial action that was deemed to restrict production became a criminal offence under the Act. Still, unofficial strikes continued to break out, fuelled by working-class anger over stagnating wages while food prices and rents kept rising. Gordon was outraged by the way employers could manipulate the wartime industrial regulations, making a note of one particularly blatant example. During a strike in August in 1916 on the Yorkshire and Lancashire railway the company, armed with exemption cards received from the local military tribunal, offered them to unemployed men willing to break the strike. These 'blacklegs' took the railway workers' jobs, and the strikers were conscripted into the trenches.[16]

He also bitterly resented the way employers were able to enrich themselves. After the war, the former Chancellor of the Exchequer in Asquith's Liberal government, Lord Buckmaster, boasted in the House of Lords that the war 'produced the most amazing profits this country has ever witnessed'. Childe knew this from his own reading during the war. In one of his notebooks he used reports of Select Committees and Government White Papers to record elements of the system that allowed munitions manufacturers to rip-off the government:

---

16   Childe provided the details of the railway strike to his friend William McKell who used the strike as an example of the dangers of conscription to Australian workers in a speech in Adelaide during the 1917 conscription referendum – see *The Daily Herald* (Adelaide), 6 December 1917, p. 6. I am grateful to Chris Cunneen for this reference.

> In the aggregate, 26 firms selected at random earned during one year nearly five times the amount of standard profit. Of this they retained as special depreciation on new capital expenditure more that [sic] half the standard profit and a slightly larger [amount] for added output. After deduction of munitions levy the firms retained nearly twice their standard profits …

Then he gave examples of the profits of particular engineering and chemical products firms. This section of his notebook is headed 'War and Capitalism'.[17]

As the war dragged on, the rank and file committees became more active, sometimes with spectacular results. In Glasgow and nearby Clydeside towns, a rent strike, led by the Glasgow Women's Housing Association, became a regional rebellion in the second half of 1915. By November, 20,000 tenants were refusing to pay rent, women were to the fore in the violent resistance to evictions, and the Clyde Workers' Committee, led by the anti-war socialist Willie Gallacher, was threatening in sympathy to close down the Clydeside factories. The local authorities retreated, dropping legal actions against rent strikers, and in December the government acted, freezing rents at prewar levels. Then in November of the following year a mass meeting of all the skilled trades in Sheffield, called by the shop stewards of the engineering union, decided to strike if a skilled fitter at Vickers was not released from the army. Skilled men were exempt from the call-up, but employers wanting to get rid of a worker could pull strings to have him served with a call-up notice and then hang on to his papers until it was too late to appeal. This is what happened to Leonard Hargreaves. While the unions' leaders in London dithered, delegates from the new city-wide shop stewards committee fanned out across the country spreading the strike call to all the major industrial centres. The strike started, the production of weapons ceased, and then the government gave orders that Hargreaves was to be returned to civil life. It was a short strike, but it had huge ramifications. In January the Sheffield Workers' Committee called another mass meeting to consolidate a rank and file movement, aiming to coordinate all the committees in the country and to cover all workers – skilled, semi-skilled and unskilled, men and women. In May 1917 a nationwide strike, the greatest in wartime, pushed the movement towards this goal. The issue was dilution – the practice of replacing skilled with unskilled workers. The government, faced with 200,000 striking workers in 48 towns, led by 100

---

17   Jim Horton, 'The First Shop Stewards' Movement', *The Socialist*, 16 November 2011, www.socialistparty.org.uk/issue/694/13154, accessed June 2018; Childe papers, Institute of Archaeology, University College London, item 55 (notebook).

shop steward delegates meeting in permanent session, again gave in, placing limits on dilution. A few months later a National Administrative Council of Shop Stewards and Workers' Committees was set up.[18]

In this heady moment for rank and file insurgency, the various groups on the left gathered at a 'Great Labour, Socialist and Democratic Convention' in Leeds on 3 June 1917. The main impetus for the convention, however, came not from this upstart movement for workers' control but from sections of the labour movement long committed to constitutional methods. The issue that united both insurgents and constitutionalists was the need for peace: it was the war that divided the Labour Party, and wartime laws that hamstrung workplace activists and sent working-class men into the trenches. Beyond differences over working-class strategies was the general feeling of war-weariness, and the sense that the war would never be ended by 'a knockout blow'. It was time for a negotiated peace. Anti-war sentiment had been strengthened by the February revolution in Russia. When a 'Russia Free' meeting was held in London's Albert Hall in March, 'nearly 20,000 tickets were asked for, whereas 12,000 was our limit. The meeting became the first great public expression of the demand for peace, and it moved hitherto silent people all over the country to call for peace', recalled one of its organisers, Francis Meynell. Radicals saw the overthrow of the Czar as a sign that democracy could overthrow even the most despotic of regimes. Surely, in the allied countries a democratic movement could force their war-obsessed governments to alter course. It was time for 'a people's peace'. If it were achieved it would be nothing less than revolutionary, yet its achievement would not subvert the role of the Constitution in British politics.[19]

The Leeds convention met under difficulties. Meeting halls were denied to the organisers until the Chief Constable, concerned about thousands of radicals holding impromptu meetings in the streets, intervened to ensure the Coliseum was made available. Hotel owners cancelled bookings. The town

---

18   Hinton, *The First Shop Stewards Movement*; https://en.wikipedia.org/wiki/Red_Clydeside accessed June 2018; Bill Moore, *Sheffield Shop Stewards 1916–1918*, Pamphlet 18, Communist Party History Group, London, 1960, http://banmarchive.org.uk/collections/shs/pdf/18%20moore.pdf, accessed June 2018.

19   Stephen White, 'Soviets in Britain: The Leeds Convention of 1917', *International Review of Social History*, vol. 19, no. 2, August 1974, pp. 165–93; Ken Coates, introduction to reprint of *What Happened at Leeds*, Nottingham, The Russell Press, 1974 (originally published 1917); Pete Jackson, 'The Russian Revolution and the British Working Class', *International Socialism*, issue 156, posted 13 October 1917, http://isj.org.uk/the-russian-revolution-and-the-british-working-class/ accessed 26 June 2018; Hinton, *The First Shop Stewards Movement*, pp. 239–41; Francis Meynell, *My Lives*, London, The Bodley Head, 1971, pp. 104–6.

council refused permission for an open-air meeting, and local larrikins, misled by the press about an influx of pro-Germans, harassed the delegates. Despite these setbacks, Robert Smillie, the President of the Miners' Federation declared the conference open before an audience of 3,500 of whom 1,150 were delegates. Among the latter was Gordon Childe, representing the Oxford Branch of the Union of Democratic Control. Perhaps he was met at the railway station by an organiser and offered a billet in a local home, as Dora Montefiore was.[20]

The importance of the conference was partly symbolic, a demonstration of the growing power of anti-war opinion, and partly opportunistic, a moment to bring together the pro- and anti-war sections of the labour movement and to harness the energy of the workplace militants to this project. Labour notables made speeches but there was little discussion. The resolutions had been prepared and circulated beforehand. Only the fourth resolution was controversial: to set up local councils of workers' and soldiers' delegates to coordinate working-class activity and to support the work of the trade unions and the organisations of women and soldiers.

The conference left an indelible impression on many of the participants, but mainly in retrospect. They wrote about the conference after the Bolshevik victory, after November rubbed out March in the left's political memory. Their accounts suggest that the conference ended with Britain about to turn red. Was Childe similarly unrealistic? He left no account of the conference except the fact that he attended it as a delegate, calling it simply 'the Leeds Conference'. In fact, at the time, knowledge about Russian revolutionary developments and the role of soviets in particular was almost non-existent. In Britain, the councils hardly got off the ground, and those that did were directed not to get in the way of existing organisations. They were a sop to the militants, who could do nothing with them because they had lost the initiative. Pacifism had trumped revolution. Childe would have been more excited by the resolution demanding peace and national self-determination, and by the resolution demanding a charter of civil liberties. But he followed the news of industrial conflict, for the idea of the class war was already firmly lodged in his mind.[21]

---

20   Moore, *Sheffield Shop Stewards*, p. 20; White, *'Soviets in Britain'*, pp. 172–3; Dora Montefiore, *From a Victorian to a Modern*, London, E. Archer, 1925, Ch. XVI, www.marxists.org/archive/montefiore/1925/autobiography/index.htm accessed June 2018.

21   White, *'Soviets in Britain'*, pp. 176–8: Childe, 'Personal Statement', included in his letter to Murray, 8 June 1918, Murray papers, shelfmark 376, document 43.

***

Rajani Dutt could draw on a family background of Indian nationalism to suggest the importance of connecting ideas to an actual movement. There was no such movement in Oxford, but at least he could proselytise for it. In October 1917, he addressed a student meeting on 'Socialism and War', arguing that the class war, if followed to its revolutionary conclusion, was the surest way to end the war between imperialist states. A riot broke out in the hall, windows were broken, Dutt was blamed and sent down from Oxford until his finals in 1918 (in which he did very well). In 1920, he joined the newly formed Communist Party, and remained loyal to it until his death in 1974. Communism was his way of escaping 'Bloody old Britain', to use a term later used by Childe's friend and Marxist colleague O.G.S. Crawford.[22]

Gordon had even less understanding of movement politics. Revolution was an event in history, or in a remote part of contemporary Eastern Europe. In fact, we might question how committed he was to revolutionary change at this time. In Dutt's college rooms he could endorse the idea of class war, but in his day-to-day life the pressure-group politics of the Union of Democratic Control (UDC) were just as important as the arguments of the Socialist Society or Dutt's 'unofficial group'. He was President of the Oxford branch of the UDC longer than he was Secretary of the Socialist Society, and when he returned to Australia he became Assistant Secretary of the Sydney branch. Perhaps another clue to his preferred kind of political strategy can be found in Dutt's comment that he had to induce Childe to take part in a debate with the Cambridge socialists. They would propose the topic 'That Class War was a fundamental part of Socialist theory'. But the kind of topic Childe favoured dealt with civil liberties. Although no copy survives of his paper to the Oxford UDC on 'Morality Versus Nationality' we know that he was preoccupied with the power of the nation state to deny the right of conscience in public behaviour and to corrupt the search for truth. These were the issues that motivated his campaign on behalf of conscientious objectors, and they formed the underlying reason for his letter to *Hermes* a few months earlier.

***

---

22   Callaghan, *Rajani Palme Dutt*, pp. 18–19; Kitty Hauser, *Bloody Old Britain: O.G.S. Crawford and the Archaeology of Modern Life*, London, Granta Books, 2008.

The Pro-Provost Armstrong thought that Childe became an opponent of the war because of his affection for Philip Davies, but perhaps he got the matter back to front: Childe became a war resister and then discovered a kindred spirit with 'a certain personal attraction' – his fellow socialist and Queen's man. Reading Armstrong's letter, it is hard to ignore the sense that he had seen something in Gordon's behaviour that led him to focus on the nature of the relationship with Davies. It may have been romantic, but then again it might have been the kind of friendship that blossoms in the warmth of a beleaguered fellowship of brave men and women who were prepared to sacrifice themselves to be true to their ideals. Gordon told Murray that Davies was 'a dear friend' of both Dutt and himself. And perhaps he knew how Leila, the elder sister of Philip, regarded that fellowship:

> It's rather absurd but I feel hot with joy when I am reminded that numbers are nothing, and that majorities are less than nothing, and that a handful of excellent people are stronger than the whole rest of the world. It's great to know what force there is in that few … The only place fit for decent people of my convictions is prison.[23]

It is certain Gordon felt that painful joy. In 1918 he said about his Oxford years: 'many of my friends were in prison for opposition to militarism and I was inclined to stay in England to join them'.[24]

Having posted his letter to Watt, Childe prepared to leave England's 'cold northern superculture'. He was 'thoroughly perverted' but only 'probably' dangerous. His 'manifold activities' remained in the collective memory of Oxford's student socialists for a few years at least. In 1919, when Esmonde Higgins arrived at Balliol College he wrote to his mother in Melbourne about joining the Oxford University Socialist Society, and the informal induction he received, including a history of its recent 'rows' with government and university authorities, and of its leaders, including a man recently returned to Australia called 'Childs [sic], of Queens, more outspoken than any other'.[25]

When Childe tried to emulate Dutt's escape from Oxford's restricted political arena, it was to the left's grand effort at regrouping in Leeds where the militants and revolutionaries were outgunned. Continuing his escape, he

---

23   Leila Davies to Joseph Dalby, no date but about May 1916, http://europeana1914-1918.eu/pt/contributions/19473 accessed 19 August 2015.

24   Childe, 'Personal Statement, 8 June 1918', in Murray papers, shelfmark 376, ff. 44–6; Childe to Murray, 5 June 1916, Murray papers, shelfmark 376, f. 152.

25   E.M. Higgins to 'Mother', 8 February 1919, Higgins papers, Mitchell Library (Sydney), 1174/1/2046.

arrived a few months later in Australia, where he discovered a Labor Party with working-class inflections and, in his words, 'a novel theory of democracy', a discovery that led him to write that the 'staunchest advocates' of revolution always leave it 'alluring [but] vague'. He learnt that in England.[26]

At Gordon's farewell party in Soho, there was too little food and far too much alcohol, and Douglas Cole got drunk for the first and only time. Anti-war to the end, Childe and his friends toasted the failure of the coming offensive against Germany. Much of this was known to MI5 as a result of a Home Office Warrant for the interception of his mail. On 12 August he sailed on SS *Rimutaka*, whose captain was instructed by MI5 not to allow Childe to leave the ship until it arrived in Australia. He was back in Sydney in October 1917.[27]

---

26   Dutt's diary, 21 February 1917, CP/IND/DUTT/22/06; Childe, 'The New Unionism and State Socialism', *Daily Standard*, 4 January 1919.

27   Page Arnot to Munster, 21 April 1978, Munster papers, Mitchell Library (re LRD); Green, *Prehistorian*, pp. 24–5 and Margaret Cole, *The Life of GDH Cole*, p. 42 (re Soho party; Margaret Cole mis-recalls this as her engagement party, but that occurred in May 1918 when Childe was in Australia); George Crystal (Home Office) to V.G.W. Kell (MI5), 19 June 1917; Kell to Crystal, 22 June 1917; Kell to Harris, 23 July 1917; Kell to Captain F.A. Hemming, SS *Rimutaka*, 31 July 1917, Childe's MI5 file, KV2/2148.

Part 2.
Labour Intellectual: Australia 1917–1921

Chapter 6

NO COMPROMISE

The *Sydney Morning Herald* reported Gordon Childe's arrival on 22 October 1917, alongside news of the sputters of a failing mass strike: workers arrested in Wollongong for attacking 'loyalists' (aka scabs); militant seamen in Melbourne delaying a vote to return to work even though many seamen were signing on; defeated waterside workers in Sydney begging the employers to take them back although a union of scabs had first call on jobs. The strike, often incorrectly called a general strike, began in early August, when railway and tramway workers in Sydney walked off the job over the introduction of a speed-up system using cards to record the duration and execution of tasks. As other workers refused to provide 'black' services or handle 'black' goods that might weaken the position of the railway men, it grew and grew until almost 100,000 were refusing to work, especially in the docks, railways, mines, ships, and gas works. Recent scholarship by Robert Bollard explains this surprising growth: the strike triggered 'an explosion of solidarity' that 'revealed the depths of underlying anger and bitterness' generated by the war. Moreover, this 'was not a passive bureaucratic strike, but a tumultuous carnival of protest', driven from below. For intellectuals on the left it was a liminal moment. Gordon's friend, the Sydney University Librarian, John Le Gay Brereton, thought that even if such a strike were defeated it would 'knit the workers more strongly together for the coming revolution'.[1]

But fail it did. The timing was off (there were huge stockpiles of coal) and the spontaneity demonstrated by the strikers was a weakness as well as a strength. Their leaders – the union officials, the tiny bands of organised socialists – and the labour intellectuals had no idea how to guide a mass strike. What were its aims? How could it be sustained? While the cadres of the working class

---

1   *Sydney Morning Herald*, 22 October 1917, p. 6; Robert Bollard, *In the Shadow of Gallipoli: The Hidden History of Australia in World War 1*, Sydney, New South Publishing, 2013, Ch. 6; Brereton to H.D. Hall, 25 August 1917, File M235 (Brereton), University of Sydney Archives.

dithered, the federal and NSW governments were acting. Laws were passed, police were deployed, but most importantly middle-class strike-breakers were mobilised. They were called 'loyalists' and my 50-year-old grandfather was one of them. Together with thousands of other volunteers he camped at the Sydney Cricket Ground waiting for deployment before he was sent to the southern coalfields. From Bellambi he wrote of the 'black work' he was doing and the refusal of local shopkeepers to serve his fellow strike-breakers. By early September the ad-hoc Defence Committee from the Trades Hall was looking for a way out. Undergraduates were driving the trams, unqualified firemen were driving the trains, new laws stole the job benefits of strikers, and gave scab unions preference for employment when the strike was over. On 9 September the Defence Committee at the Trades Hall called off the strike. The miners, wharf labourers and some of the seamen were furious; they held out until November – a few until December. My grandfather came back to Sydney and resumed his business as a commercial traveller. He framed the illuminated certificate the government sent him, praising his 'patriotic action' during 'the recent industrial crisis' as a 'National Service' in defence of 'Constitutional Government', and hung it in his lounge room where it remained for the rest of his life.[2]

The decision to call off the strike made Sydney's labour radicals angry. They complained about the inadequacies of labour leadership and the divisions in the movement. Among them were some who would become Gordon's comrades. Henry Boote, the editor of *The Worker* (Sydney), worn out from walking every day because he refused to catch trams or buses manned by scabs, felt 'wild'. What was the sense of the struggle when so many refused to join it? Luke Jones, the Secretary of the new Social Democratic League, was almost in tears describing to Boote how he was abused at a meeting of strikers for suggesting the strike was lost. Jennie Scott Griffiths, Texas-born feminist and socialist journalist who had campaigned in support of the strike in the coalfields with another of Gordon's friends Vance Marshall, a left union official, was knocked sideways by the capitulation. She detected a ruling-class conspiracy to provoke labour into a strike it could not win. Labour's leaders were stupid to fall for it, she said, but having endorsed the strike they were gutless to call it off. Even a year later the radical mood was pessimistic, and Childe shared in it. He noted the 'charges and counter-charges after the defeat' that distorted the truth about the strike and divided the left, confusing the task of understanding

---

2   Bollard, *In the Shadow*, Ch. 6; S.G. Spink to Marjorie (his daughter), 24 September 1917, held by the author; government certificate to S.G. Spink (born 1868) held by the author.

what it meant for working-class politics, one of the tasks he would set himself in *How Labour Governs*. In the meantime, there was an exodus of radicals to Queensland, where the last remaining Labor government had earlier in the year been re-elected with an increased majority.³

* * *

With details of his academic success at Oxford appearing in Sydney's daily press, Gordon began to look for employment. He discovered that his old school, Shore, had a vacancy, and went to an interview. Perhaps forgetting that he was not in Oxford, and that Sydney could be primly provincial, he dressed untidily. He was also more honest than necessary, mumbling that he was unfit for the job but would like to try it; he was not hired. Then the Principal of St Andrew's College in the University of Sydney rescued him, creating the post of Senior Resident Tutor and appointing him to it. This was more to his liking and it made use of his knowledge. He was popular with the students, according to the college magazine, for his 'scholarship was of the first order and his tea and cigarettes were second to none'. But elsewhere in the university it was a different story.⁴

John Le Gay Brereton reported that in the upper levels of the university he was called 'that swine' and regarded 'with shuddering dismay and horror'. It was rumoured that he had been sent down from Oxford. Campus gossips repeated the defiant phrase from his March 1917 letter to the High Commissioner in London, about not helping 'however indirectly, in a war which I believe to be destructive to civilization and true liberty'. The letter was provided by Australia's Military Intelligence, which had placed Childe under surveillance from the moment he stepped ashore, having been tipped off by MI5. There was a close relationship between Military Intelligence and the top echelons of the university, which had released some of its staff to work for Intelligence as censors, including a son of Professor Mungo MacCallum (the Dean of

---

3   For Boote and Jones, see Mary E. Lloyd, *Sidelights on Two Referendums, 1916 and 1917*, Sydney, William Brooks, 1952, p. 75; for Childe's pessimism, Le Gay Brereton to H.D. Hall, 4/11/1918, University of Sydney Archives, M235; Childe, *How Labour Governs*, 1st edn, Ch. XI, especially p. 176.

4   Le Gay Brereton to H.D. Hall, 19 February 1918, University of Sydney Archives, Le Gay Brereton papers, M235; R. Ian Jack, *The Andrew's Book: St Andrew's College within the University of Sydney*, St Andrew's College, 1989, p. 32 (Childe's appointment); *St Andrew's College Magazine*, no. 16, November 1918, p. 12.

Arts), and Professors Wilson, Holme, Todd and Nicholson. Childe would later name MacCallum and Professors Todd and Holme, together with the Warden Henry Barff, as those making 'violent statements' against him at the University Club and elsewhere. Any one of them could have been the conduit through which the letter reached the campus.[5]

Meanwhile Gordon was putting his mark on the left. Like many an antipodean traveller then and since, he found an audience interested in his experiences in the Northern Hemisphere. He joined the Labor Party and met a young Labor parliamentarian, William (Bill) McKell, whose speeches used information from Gordon about the effect of conscription in England on workers' rights, for Gordon had returned a few weeks before Prime Minister Hughes announced a second referendum to test public support for conscription. Childe would have been relieved when the referendum in December was defeated, and by a larger margin than in 1916. In January 1918 Childe gave a Sunday night lecture for the Labor Party on 'The Policy of the British Labour Party in Wartime', and he began writing anonymously for *The Worker*. In April he started teaching a course on political philosophy for the labour movement under the auspices of the Workers' Educational Association.[6]

He was also assisting the trade union left. For five nights in May and June 1918 he attended the weekly meetings of the Trades and Labour Council (TLC) to advise delegates opposed to the federal government's latest attempt to involve the unions in a national campaign to boost military recruitment. The Secretary of the TLC, W. Morby, proposed that the Council support the resolutions on recruiting adopted at a conference called by the Governor-General. Led by the socialists Ernest Judd and Henry Boote, the left was

---

5   Le Gay Brereton to H.D. Hall, 19 February 1918, University of Sydney Archives, Le Gay Brereton papers, M235; Childe to Dr Harper (Principal, St Andrew's College), 2 May 1918, included in Childe to Murray, 8 June 1918, Murray papers, shelfmark 376, 44/6; Secretary of St Andrew's College to Childe, 21 May 1918. National Archives of Australia, Commonwealth Military Forces, Intelligence Reports [henceforth NAA, CMF Intell. Reports] 168/1-7; K.J. Cable, 'MacCallum, Sir Mungo William (1854–1942)', *Australian Dictionary of Biography*, Vol. 10, 1986, pp. 211–13; Patricia Morison, 'J.T. Wilson and the Fraternity of Duckmaloi', *Clio Medica*, vol. 42, 1997, on the Censors; Childe, 'Personal Statement', included in Childe to Murray, 8 June 1918, Murray papers, shelfmark 376, ff. 44-46; Robin Derricourt, 'The Making of a Radical Archaeologist: The Early Years of Vere Gordon Childe', *Australian Archaeology*, vol. 79, December 2014, pp. 56–64 covers much of the material in this chapter.

6   Christopher Cunneen, *William John McKell: Boilermaker, Premier, Governor-General*, Sydney, UNSW Press, 2000, pp. 56, 64; ALP, State of NSW, *Report of the Executive for the Year 1918*, Sydney, The Worker Print, 1919; Le Gay Brereton to Hall, 19 February 1918, University of Sydney Archives, M235; *Australian Worker*, 11 April 1918 (philosophy course).

determined to make the debate revolve around the question of supporting or opposing the war. Then Labor's leader in New South Wales, John Storey, intervened, and the results were unexpected. Thinking to strengthen the case for the recruiting campaign he revealed that at the conference Labor had offered to support recruiting if the conservative governments stopped exploiting their victory in the 1917 mass strike by victimising workers and deregistering unions. Instead, it produced uproar and wild scenes, as pacifists joined with 'industrialists' (as the militant unionists were called) to accuse the politicians of another sell-out. The debate was adjourned week after week as each side jockeyed for control, with Gordon providing 'private advice' to 'the pacifist section'. Finally, Judd's motion to oppose both the war and recruiting was passed by 104 to 75. Two developments followed quickly, revealing the divisions entrenched by the debate. Judd was charged with 'encouraging disloyalty to the Empire' for moving his resolution, and in the election for Secretary of Council, Morby was defeated by Jock Garden, a future foundation member of the Communist Party.[7]

Gordon was proud of his behind-the-scenes role, writing to Murray that he was now convinced of the importance of socialist societies and liberal intellectuals in the class struggle: they mediated between classes and prevented revolutionary clashes. Was this written with tongue in cheek? After all, Murray was not a revolutionary but a prominent Liberal as well as his mentor. From this time his own intermediations increased, so he was clearly serious about this role, and he may well have remembered Cole admonishing middle-class intellectuals for ignoring the labour unrest in *The World of Labour*.[8]

He was becoming a well-known figure on the Labor Party's left. He conscientiously attended the meetings of his branch in Darlinghurst to support the left's campaign to get the June 1918 Inter-State Conference in Perth to adopt resolutions advocating a negotiated peace and an end to recruitment. When the Perth conference went some way to adopting the left's line, he was quick to portray it as a pacifist victory, sending an article, 'Australian Demand for Negotiation', to the *Labour Leader*, the newspaper of the Independent Labour Party in England. Although it was unsigned, Childe's authorship is indicated by the details it provided about the Judd versus Morby contest in the Sydney Labour Council. He probably sent it to Dutt, for we know from an intercepted letter from 'RPD' to Childe that Dutt was placing information

---

7 Childe to F.J. Williams, 3 May and 22 May 1918, in NAA CMF Intell. Reports MF 904, 169/1-8 and 169/9-16; *Australian Worker*, 2 May, 9 May, 16 May, 23 May, 30 May, 6 June, 27 June, and 4 July 1918 for reports of the TLC meetings.

8 Childe to Murray, 8 June 1918, Gilbert Murray papers, shelfmark 376, ff. 44-6.

taken from Childe's letters in various publications, the 'respectable portions' in the *Labour Leader* and the 'disreputable portions' in the *Socialist*.[9]

The article contains the Perth resolution in full, which allowed for recruiting on condition that the Allies issue a 'clear authoritative statement' of their 'readiness to enter into peace negotiations upon the basis of no annexations, no penal indemnities'. This was headline material, which the *Leader* abbreviated in its subheading as 'No recruiting unless Allies declare for no annexation', but it missed the passion for ending the war that energised the party branches in the weeks leading up to the Perth conference. Childe was impressed by the class-conscious character of this energy. He began by informing British readers of the 'rapidly increasing tension between the Labour Party and the Nationalists (Liberals and Labour seceders)' since the anti-conscription vote, and the recent strengthening of the 'anti-war tendency' in the party and labour councils. He described in detail the 'violent opposition' to Morby and Storey from a 'strong body of class conscious Unionists' which now 'commands a majority on the Sydney Trades Council'. He provided the text of Judd's successful resolution, which was much more forthright than the Perth resolution:

> We refuse to take part in any recruiting campaign and call upon workers of this and other belligerent nations to urge their respective Governments to secure immediately an armistice on all fronts and initiate negotiations for peace.

He reported the similarly 'drastic' resolutions on peace adopted on 1 June by the NSW party at a conference that Childe probably attended. The resolutions declared that the war was 'being prolonged for imperialist and capitalist ends', demanded 'an immediate armistice for discussion of peace terms', and affirmed 'that the white race were being exterminated'. He recorded that these resolutions 'were, after a long debate, carried with enthusiasm'.

In another sign of his standing, the State Labor Executive and the Social Democratic League asked him to lead a deputation to the Minister of Justice seeking indulgences (for example, more visitors and better food) for Vance Marshall and other 'political prisoners' in line with those in Britain for 'First Class Prisoners' – a topic on which Childe was knowledgeable because of his

---

9   *Labour Leader* (UK), 22 August 1918, p. 3; Major H.E. Jones (Australian Counter-Espionage Bureau, Melbourne) to Colonel (Frank) Hall (MI5), enclosing letter to Childe from RTD' (which meant RPD, according to later notation on the letter from Jones), 25 June 1919, KV2/2148 (Childe's MI5 file).

work in support of conscientious objectors in England. Marshall was serving his second term for making speeches detrimental to recruiting.[10]

He also met up with his university friend Bert Evatt, and introduced him to William McKell, the three of them frequently lunching together. McKell, who had entered the State Parliament for the seat of Redfern earlier that year, had left school when he was 13 to become a boilermaker, so when he decided to study for the Bar he needed help. Gordon tutored him in Latin and made précis of the books McKell had to read for the qualifying examinations. Childe, who was growing suspicious of the 'fatal lure of [parliamentary] politics', kept in contact with them both as they rose to eminence in state organisations. McKell became Premier of New South Wales and Governor-General of Australia; Evatt became a High Court Judge, Minister of External Affairs, President of the United Nations General Assembly, and leader of the Federal Parliamentary Labor Party in opposition.[11]

Gordon was also active in the peace movement proper. He joined the Sydney branch of the Australian Union of Democratic Control (AUDC), and when it amalgamated with the Australian Peace Alliance he became the Assistant Secretary, that is, he organised the meetings and sent out the circulars. He was particularly associated with the push to persuade peace activists towards involving workers' organisations. In July he gave a paper to the Australian Peace Alliance on 'The Manchester Guardian and The Nation: What Are They Saying?' Since the British Government had banned the sending of *The Nation* to 'the colonies', Childe was adopting a defiant stance in the paper. One imagines its content was similar to that in his letter to Watt. Not being a liberal internationalist like the better-known pacifists, his role has been neglected, but when he moved to Brisbane his fellow socialist and anti-war activist Isabel Swann lamented that Sydney was losing all of its 'best people … and now last but not least, Gordon Childe'.[12]

---

10 Childe to Byrne, 13 September 1918, Meanjin Archive, University of Melbourne Archives; Vance Marshall, letter to *Truth*, 15 September 1918.
11 Cunneen, *William John McKell*, pp. 64–5.
12 *Social Democrat*, 15 March 1918; *Federal Independent*, 15 April 1918; Australian Peace Alliance papers, Mitchell Library, Uncat. MSS 166, item 2; Rose Scott, Printed Leaflets and Newspaper Cuttings, 1904–24, Mitchell Library MSS 38/55, item 1 (Ann-Mari Jordens kindly provided this source); S.F. Allen to Childe, 13 June 1918, NAA CMF Intell. Reports, 168/8-14; Rose Scott Correspondence, Mitchell Library MSS A2281, circular from AUDC re Childe's paper on 9 July 1918; Isabel Swann to Jennie Scott Griffiths, 27 September 1918, NAA CMF Intell. Reports 176/36-45; Ann-Mari Jordens, 'Anti-war Organisations in a Society at War, 1914–18', *Journal of Australian Studies*, vol. 14, no. 26, 2009, pp. 78–93.

Most nights Gordon would go into the city to Mockbell's Cafe on Elizabeth Street where a group of young rebels met, 'Frank Nelson, Jim Bell and Turner' among them. Lost now to history, they were at the time sufficiently active – rank and filers from the Industrial Workers of the World (IWW), perhaps – for Childe to record their names. He was writing to Russell Pearce, a medical student at Sydney University, encouraging him to join the group. Russell had already done Gordon a favour, sending him an application form for teaching in Queensland public schools. In their letters they exchange thoughts about the war and socialist tactics, but rationalism was another common interest. Russell's father, George Pearce, was Brisbane's leading rationalist and it was probably George who obtained the form. Childe's Rationalist contacts also included William J. Miles in Sydney, who had founded the Rationalist Association of New South Wales, 'a peppery, authoritative little man with a strong nose, heavy moustache and booming voice'. Russell Pearce's trajectory was to the left – in the 1940s he had an ASIO file as a Communist Party sympathiser – but Miles shot off to the right, publishing a pro-fascist monthly that he passed on to Percy Stephensen. As we shall see, Gordon's life intersected with Stephensen's on several occasions.[13]

Gordon was also a friend of Fred Williams, another medical student, but at Melbourne University. During the second referendum on conscription in 1917, when offices, printeries and homes were being raided by police searching for subversive material, Williams hid the leaflets of a left group calling themselves the Militant Propagandists of the Labor Movement, possibly at Melbourne Hospital. In 1918 he helped to set up a Public Questions Society at Melbourne University. According to the Censor in Melbourne this effort showed the 'insidious methods of the Socialist Pacifist Groups'. When Williams came to Sydney, Gordon put him up at St Andrew's. The censors paid particular attention to the overlapping circles that made up the radical community, and in Sydney that overlap was secured by radicals using the newspaper and meeting rooms of the Social Democratic League. Formed in opposition to the conscriptionists who were expelled from the Labor Party, its promotion of 'Internationalism, Anti-militarism, Industrial Unionism and the recognition of the class struggle' attracted activists from a range of campaigns, but

---

13   Chris Cunneen, 'Miles, William John (1871–1942)', *Australian Dictionary of Biography*, Vol. 10, 1986, pp. 501–2; Craig Munro, 'Stephensen, Percy Reginald (1901–1965)', *Australian Dictionary of Biography*, Vol. 12, 1990, pp. 70–1; Russell Pearce to Childe, 21 October 1918, NAA CMF Intell. Reports, 167/56; Childe to Russell Pearce, 28 October 1918, NAA CMF Intell. Reports 168/30; File on Thomas Russell Pearce, NAA ACT CRS A6126/xm, item 66 (ASIO).

without posing a direct challenge to the Labor Party. Childe was probably a member, because many of the names of League members turn up in his correspondence, or they refer to him in theirs, including Percy Brookfield (the Socialist MLA from Broken Hill), Rev. A. Rivett (President of the Australian Peace Alliance in Sydney), Isabel Swann, Jennie Scott Griffiths, Luke Jones, and Vance Marshall.[14]

* * *

We saw earlier that in 1914, before he left for Oxford, Childe had joined the Workers' Educational Association (WEA), an organisation that was meant to reach out to working-class adults and bring them an advanced education based on liberal pedagogical principles. At the same time the university was committed to an extension program for non-matriculated students, so following the English model the university partnered with the WEA to deliver its 'tutorial classes'. Controlling the program was a Joint Committee for Tutorial Classes made up of WEA and university representatives.

In March 1918, in response to the hostility to Childe among the university elite, David Stewart, the Secretary of the WEA and an opponent of the war who had been a Vice-President of the Union of Democratic Control, decided that an act of solidarity with a fellow WEA member was necessary. He suggested informally to the Joint Committee that Childe might be appointed to a Tutorship in Ancient History, and because there was no evidence of his teaching ability the WEA would form a class for him so that the Acting-Director, Jerry Portus, could inspect it. This was done and in due course Portus reported that Childe was a satisfactory tutor. One of the university's representatives, and the Chair of the Joint Committee, was

---

14 'Extract from Melbourne Censor's Secret Intelligence Report dated 13 April 1918', included in Childe's file M223, University of Sydney Archives (re Public Questions Societies and Childe putting up Williams at St Andrew's); Lloyd, *Sidelights on Two Referendums*, p. 69 (entry in H.E. Boote's diary re Social Democratic League); 'Social Democratic League', *Australian Worker*, 31 May 1917, p. 4 (the League published *The Social Democrat*, and had a hall in Wentworth Avenue); Fred J. Williams to Childe, 28 May 1918, NAA CMF Intell. Reports 168/7; M. Brodney, 'Militant Propagandists of the Labor Movement', *Labour History*, no. 5, November 1963, p. 16. Ernest Scott, *Australia during the War*, Sydney, Angus and Robertson, 1936, describes the system of district and local censors in Ch. 3 'The Censorship'. According to Scott, by the end of the war, about 15,000 persons 'were being systematically watched' (p. 83).

Professor Francis Anderson, who had taught Childe and persuaded him to join the WEA, so Childe looked to be a shoo-in as far as the tutorial classes people were concerned. But would the university allow the appointment of a socialist? Portus was doubtful. Meanwhile, Childe, according to his friend Brereton, wandered the campus like the 'lost spirit' of one of the gargoyles on the university's faux-Gothic main building.[15]

At this time, the anti-war forces were mobilising, and over Easter 1918 the Third Inter-State Peace Conference took place in the Friends Meeting Hall in Foveaux Street. There were 100 delegates, including Gordon who was one of three from the Australian Union of Democratic Control. He delivered a paper on 'Peace, Imperialism and Internationalism', and his influence may also be seen in the conference resolution against Australia retaining the captured German colonies in the Pacific, about which he had earlier published a letter in *The Australian Worker*. Vance Marshall remembered him from this time, perhaps at this conference:

> In those days, when the fiery spirits of war antagonism were gathering together, he would rise in ungainly fashion to his feet ... His speech was slow, measured, scholastic – no vigour, no fire, but insistent, relentless, hammer-like ... One theme alone marked the tenor of his logic – 'No compromise! No compromise! No compromise!'

Privately a 'lost spirit' perhaps, but in public Childe could not easily be ignored.[16]

At the end of April, Gordon's enemies struck. Somebody complained to the Principal of St Andrew's, Dr Andrew Harper, about his participation in the Peace Conference. Harper then spoke to Henry Barff, the university's Warden (equivalent to a Vice-Chancellor today), who showed him the copy provided by Military Intelligence of Childe's letter to the High Commissioner in London. The Warden told him that the university objected to Childe's

---

15   Frederick Todd to Sir William Cullen (Chancellor, University of Sydney), 15 July 1918, File M223 (V.G. Childe), University of Sydney Archives; E.M. Higgins, *David Stewart and the WEA*, Sydney, Workers' Educational Association of New South Wales, 1957, p. 37; J. Le Gay Brereton to H.D Hall, April 1918, File M235 (J. Le Gay Brereton), University of Sydney Archives.

16   *Social Democrat*, 15 March 1918; [Rev. A Rivett] 'Interstate Peace Conference', 15 April 1918, *The Federal Independent*; *Australian Worker*, 11 April 1918; V.G. Childe, 'The German Colonies in the Pacific', *Australian Worker*, 7 February 1918, p. 19; Australian Peace Alliance papers, Mitchell Library, Uncat. MSS 166; Ann-Mari Jordens, 'Anti-War Organisations in a Society at War', *Journal of Australian Studies*, vol. 15, no. 26, 2009, pp. 78–93; Vance Marshall, 'Gordon Childe – Scholar and Thinker', *Daily Standard*, 2 January 1924, p. 1.

presence in the university and would never employ him. Harper conveyed this to Childe, saying that Childe's continuing membership of the college would jeopardise financial support from the City and embarrass the college in its dealings with the university. He then offered Childe the chance to resign.[17]

Gordon's first reaction was an indignant refusal, pointing out that he had been given 'no reasonable, just or legal grounds' for dismissal. He contemplated embarrassing the university by asking his Oxford academic contacts to write letters of support. But in the meantime, he had to respond to the Principal. Further thought persuaded him that Harper's concerns about the college's prospects if he continued as a member of college were realistic, and that as he had no desire to harm the college he should resign. So, he started to negotiate. He asked for his salary to be paid to 1 October, and, when the college agreed, he offered his resignation. The college released him from 1 June. His letter of resignation was not bitter but, for the enlightenment of members of the College Council, it did set out the principle they were violating: that a public teacher was entitled to express political opinions. It was regrettable, he wrote, that by giving in to 'the machinations of a secret junta within the University' the Council had 'become partners in the guilt of suppressing freedom of thought in the University'.[18]

Childe decided that he would only let his letter of resignation become public if it were used against the university, not the college. Accordingly, the university was his target when he put his case to his federal Labor member, James H. Catts. Nothing came of this, but he found a more sympathetic advocate in his friend, the Labor member for Redfern, William McKell. On 27 June McKell placed three questions on the notice paper of the Legislative Assembly for the Minister of Public Instruction. The first sought to establish that under the Act governing the university and its colleges no political or religious tests should be imposed on the selection of public teachers in the university. The second question sought to show that such a test had been applied in Childe's case and that in consequence he had been forced to resign from his position at St Andrew's. The details in this question clearly came from Childe:

---

17   Childe to Portus, no date but between early June and 9 July 1918, File M223 (V.G. Childe), University of Sydney Archives; Frederick A. Todd to Sir William Cullen, Chancellor of the University, 15 July 1918, File M223.

18   'Blessed are the Persecutors', *The Federal Independent*, 15 October 1918; Childe, 'Personal Statement' and the covering letter to Murray, 8 June 1918, Murray papers, shelfmark 376, ff. 44-6, Bodleian Library; Childe to S.J. Carruthers, 1 June 1918, in Murray papers, shekfmark 376, f. 41.

> ... The Warden and Registrar of the University stated that the Senate would refuse to employ Mr Childe because he was believed to hold views on war and peace similar to those affirmed by the Australian Labor Party in conference assembled in June 1917, despite the fact that Mr Childe's academic record at Oxford surpassed in brilliance that of any former Sydney scholar, and that his work on Greek archaeology has gained him a European reputation?

In the third question McKell asked the government to 'proclaim an immediate election of the Senate' if it were found 'to have abused its trust in this manner'.[19]

The government could not have been unaware of the falling out between the college and Childe, for the Colonial Secretary, George Fuller, was a member of the College Council. But how should McKell's implicit point that Childe was forced to resign because his views were those of the Labor Party be answered? As it was clear this had happened, either it was morally wrong and should be condemned, or the government would be seen as supporting the right of anti-Labor conservatives to dominate the university. Unwittingly McKell had given the government a way out. He had focused his attack on the university, not the college, as Childe had wanted. The Minister of Public Instruction seized on this distinction, replying that he had no control over appointments to the college, and suggesting McKell refer to the College Council. He added that Childe's name 'had not been before the University for employment or for any other purpose since the extension of his scholarship for a third year in 1915'. And in answer to McKell's first question he simply affirmed the principle: 'no religious or political tests are ever applied'. Six weeks later Childe would discover how hollow that affirmation was. That these answers were prepared at the university, by either Barff or MacCallum, underlines the duplicity involved in this exercise. Childe was being victimised by conspirators whose self-belief in their right to rule was unassailable by evidence or a sense of justice.[20]

Uncertain about his chances for the tutorial classes position, Gordon investigated other possibilities of employment. He thought he might approach

---

19   Childe to Williams, 3 May 1918, NAA CMF Intell. Reports 169/1-8; Government of New South Wales, *Parliamentary Debates, Legislative Assembly*, 1918, second series, vol. 72, p. 1453.

20   Jack, *The Andrew's Book*, p. 96. In Childe's file M223, in the University of Sydney Archives, the draft of the answers to McKell's questions is written on the back of university stationery with the letterhead, 'Memorandum from the Warden and Registrar'. At the end of the draft someone has written at a later date, 'Sir Mungo MacCallum', as if the handwriting was recognisable as his.

the miners and other unions about setting up a Labour College, similar to the Victorian Labour College, just recently started, which was modelled on the Central Labour College in London. He wrote to the Very Reverend M.J. O'Reilly, Rector of St John's, the Catholic college in the university, seeking his endorsement for teaching in religious schools 'even though I am not a Catholic'. O'Reilly replied that he would try to help in the future, but he could not at present. Childe thought there might be a current of political sympathy flowing between them because O'Reilly had publicly opposed conscription and earlier that year had invited Cardinal Mannix, an Irish nationalist and opponent of the war, to lay the foundation stone of a new wing at the college. The Chancellor wrote a rude letter to the Rector about Mannix and the university elite boycotted the event, but in attendance, under the red flags displayed in solidarity by some of Sydney's pacifist left, was Childe's friend Brereton. More promising was the possibility of finding a job with or through Australia's only remaining Labor government, so he interviewed the Queensland Treasurer, Ted Theodore, but that possibility would take time to come to fruition.[21]

In the meantime, Gordon formally applied for the Tutorship in Ancient History. He had been consulting his supporters since Stewart first mooted the appointment in March, fully aware that his candidature was a challenge to the most powerful men in the university. His supporters would need ammunition. As the date approached for the meeting that would consider his application, he prepared for the Director of Tutorial Classes 'a true and unvarnished statement of the facts' to counter the 'false or exaggerated rumours' about his 'heretical views on certain questions of national and international importance'. It was not a defence of those views but a comparison of how they were received in Oxford and in Sydney. In Oxford, the College Provost and 'others of the Fellows' accepted his 'unorthodoxy' whereas in Sydney Dr Harper asked him to anticipate the Council's decision to sack him by resigning. At the meeting of the Joint Committee to consider his application, Portus reported that he had inspected the WEA class on political philosophy and found that Childe was a satisfactory tutor. He then revealed that he had received a statement from Childe, but the Chair of the meeting, Professor Anderson, advised him not to read it 'unless the

---

21   Childe to F. Sinclaire, 20 August 1918, NAA CMF Intell. Reports, 169/35-42; Childe to F.J. Williams, 22 May 1918, NAA CMF Intell. Reports, 169/9-16; Childe to O'Reilly, 31 May 1918, NAA CMF Intell. Reports 168/7, and 10 June 1918, NAA CMF Intell. Reports 168/8-14; Le Gay Brereton to Hall, 11 March 1918, University of Sydney Archives, file M235 (Le Gay Brereton).

question should be raised'. Anderson obviously knew the reason for Childe's written statement, as did another member of the Joint Committee, Professor Irvine, the pro-Labor economist, who said as he was leaving the room before the agenda reached the matter of Childe's application that he thought the meeting might recommend Childe, despite the 'young man's radicalism'. Portus was also ready to recommend Childe, believing that it was not the responsibility of the Committee to consider Childe's political opinions. As the WEA members supported Childe, it seemed as if the statement would not be read. But then one of the university's representatives, Professor Todd, disagreed. He said he objected strongly to placing 'in an office of trust in the University a man whose opinions are contrary to the national interest', so giving such a man the opportunity 'of infecting the students in his classes'. Nonetheless the Committee voted to recommend Childe.[22]

Known as 'the Metternich of the University', Frederick Augustus Todd (1880–1944), Assistant Professor of Latin and Assistant Censor, unmarried at the time, enlisted in the AIF just 26 days before the Armistice. His was the sole vote against Childe. So outraged was he that Childe might persuade students not to fight for the empire that he wrote a letter of protest to the Chancellor. At that time the Chief Censor for Sydney's military district was G.G. Nicholson, the university's Assistant Professor of French. The university Chancellor, Sir William Cullen, would have known whom to turn to for advice. Nicholson after contacting his Military Intelligence counterpart in Victoria, wrote to Professor MacCallum that 'Col. McColl says the Secretary of the Department of Defence will probably communicate with the Chancellor about C'. The form suggested was: 'It is not considered desirable that … should be appointed … during the war'. At its August meeting, the Senate, with MacCallum an ex-officio member, rejected the Committee's recommendation, its minutes recording no evidence of dissent or argument.[23]

---

22   Childe, to 'Dear Sir' (undated statement for Portus), in M223 (Childe), University of Sydney Archives; Frederick Todd to Sir William Cullen, 15 July 1918, M223 (Childe), University of Sydney Archives; Portus to Atkinson, 10 July 1918, in Department of Tutorial Classes papers, file marked 'Victoria 1920–63', University of Sydney Archives.

23   A.J. Dunston, 'Todd, Frederick August (1880–1944)', *Australian Dictionary of Biography*, Vol. 12, 1990, pp. 237–8; Ivan Barko, 'Nicholson, George Gibb (1875–1948)', *Australian Dictionary of Biography*, Vol. 11, 1988, pp. 26–7; J.M. Bennett, 'Cullen, Sir William Portus (1885–1935)', *Australian Dictionary of Biography*, Vol. 8, 1981, pp. 167–8; Le Gay Brereton to Hall, 22 August 1918, University of Sydney Archives, M235; Nicholson to 'Dear Professor' [MacCallum], no date, File M223 (Childe) University of Sydney Archives; Minutes of the Senate of the University of Sydney, August 1918, University of Sydney Archives.

After this knockback Gordon's contempt for the university's leaders hardened, and he stepped up his campaign to shame them. He had already written to academics in Oxford asking them to protest to the University of Sydney. The Provost of Queen's, John Magrath, gave him the brush-off: 'I'm sorry you don't get on better with the authorities. The fault in these cases is seldom wholly on one side.' The Camden Professor of Ancient History at Oxford, Francis J. Haverfield, havered: it is always difficult, he wrote, to discover 'the real reasons' for actions; it is bad to mix politics with learning; he has little contact with the Sydney University authorities; and one should not expect anything different if one articulates unpopular views. Now Childe went public. He provided details of his victimisation by the 'junta of jingoes' to the Australian Peace Alliance, which issued a press release. He persuaded his political friends to write to the press. Although the government, advised by the university, refused to act, Childe remained defiant. On 8 September he delivered a lecture for the Labor Party on 'Freedom of Speech'.[24]

---

24   J.R. Magrath to Childe, 27 May 1918, NAA CMF Intell. Reports 168/15-20; F. Haverfield to Childe, 3 November 1918, NAA CMF Intell. Reports 167/68-76; W.J. Miles to Editor, *Daily Standard*, 10 September 1918, NAA CMF Intell. Reports 167/36-45, eventually published 25 October 1918; W.J Miles to E.N. Free, MLA (Qld), NAA CMF Intell. Reports 167-45; Childe to O'Reilly, 18 August 1918, NAA CMF Intell. Reports, 168/21-29; Australian Peace Alliance, Sydney, 'Sydney University and the Progress of Knowledge' (press release) 12 September 1918, NAA CMF Intell. Reports 169/9-16; W.J. McKell to Childe, 21 September 1918, NAA CMF Intell. Reports 167/36-45; Labor Party of NSW, State Executive, Report for 1918.

Chapter 7

'A CERTAIN VACILLATION'

When Childe returned to Sydney he was philosophically a Marxist and therefore a revolutionary. Revolution, however, when applied to Marxist political practice in the early twentieth century, was a capacious term. The pre-eminent example of political Marxism was the mighty German Social Democratic Party. It combined parliamentary campaigning with a 'cradle to the grave' policy of creating a separate socialist community for the working class and its Marxist intellectuals. Until the German party destroyed its leadership of international socialism by voting in 1914 for war credits in the Reichstag, Marxists understood its strategy as the 'orthodox' path to revolution. It was under challenge, however, from the 'radical Marxists': the revolutionary syndicalists who leaned towards anarchism and refused to engage in parliamentary politics; the left social-democrats in Western Europe who warned that parliamentarism was breeding a revisionist Marxism that envisaged capitalism changing peacefully and gradually into socialism; and the Bolsheviks of the Russian Social Democratic Party for whom a mass uprising of the working class and its allies would be needed to abolish capitalism.

Childe dismissed the orthodox Marxist and anarcho-syndicalist understanding of revolution as 'alluringly vague as far as its initial stages are concerned'. But what was the alternative? While he was in Australia he was not impressed by the Bolshevik example. Rather, as he was drawn into the anti-war movement, he discovered the militancy of the industrial unionists, and Labor's experience of government. He was no longer in Britain where everything to him seemed so bloody because of the Labour Party's 'loyalty' to parliament and constitutionalism. In Australia, the militancy of the 'industrialists' had swept many thousands of workers into a mass strike. Was it possible that Australia's different balance of class forces and the role of the unions in forming the Labor party might provide a non-violent but still revolutionary transition to socialism? If so, what role could a trained intellectual play? And what aspects of political philosophy – what ideas about democracy, the state and socialism – could he use in this revolution? Childe was entering a period of intellectual and political questioning – of vacillation.[1]

* * *

'Our Neo-Hegelians in Oxford and elsewhere had not been remiss in adopting and applying to the purposes of our nation and empire the characteristic features of the German state theory.' These words appear in one of Childe's notebooks, surrounded by notes that he had taken about the British Government's annexationist aims and its rejection of German offers to negotiate an end to the war. Their author was John A. Hobson, and they came from his November 1917 book *Democracy after the War*. Childe would have noted them with approval, for he had embraced the radical argument that the British state was using the war against Germany to pursue its own path to absolutism. Then, immediately below those words, he quoted Hobson again: 'By Prussian-Australianism I mean a combination of the capitalist-bureaucratic organisation of industry and commerce practiced in modern Germany with the nationalist-labor policy of Australia'. Reading this second sentence in Sydney, Childe may have raised an eyebrow. Was there an affinity between the Australian state and Prussianism? How did Hobson arrive at this position and what did it mean for socialist politics in Australia?[2]

John A. Hobson (1858–1940) would have first attracted Childe's attention as a fellow member of the Union of Democratic Control, and then as a radical economist and a critic of imperialism. His economic theory of underconsumption, foreshadowing elements of Keynesianism, proposed that, as the purpose of production was consumption, any saving meant that an amount of goods produced could not be sold. Because of the inequitable distribution of income, it was the wealthy who saved while the poor could not afford to buy. The implication for government was confronting: tax the rich and redistribute the savings to increase demand. Social unrest and a 'Crisis of Liberalism' (the title of his 1909 book) that might be solved if the state adopted a more positive role made his theory timely. It became a rationale for the program of

---

1   Childe, 'The New Unionism and State Socialism', *Daily Standard*, 4 January 1919, p. 4.
2   Childe papers, Institute of Archaeology, University College London, item 55 (notebook); J.A. Hobson, *Democracy after the War*, London, George Allen & Unwin, 1917, pp. 117–9 and 169.

'new liberal' welfare and taxation reforms after 1906. Turning to the contemporaneous expansion of European nationalist states beyond their boundaries, Hobson defined it as a modern form of imperialism and extended his economic theory to account for it. The new territories conquered in the late nineteenth century – for example in Africa – were not significant as export markets nor as colonies to absorb surplus population. Rather, they fulfilled the need to redirect the excess savings of the wealthy into investment in the empire. He showed that the return on this investment was nine times the value of the trade generated within the empire. But this new imperialism was a malign force. At home it created a parasitical rentier class, while abroad tensions caused by the expansionist greed of local capitalist elites could lead to war – as it had in the Boer War, of which Hobson was an outspoken critic. Lenin relied heavily on Hobson's theory, especially its connection to the causes of war, when writing his *Imperialism: The Highest Stage of Capitalism*.[3]

Hobson was not a Marxist, not even a socialist (guild socialism, he said, was an idea 'bred of political despair'). And *Democracy after the War* was not an exercise in systematic social thought. But given Hobson's standing in radical intellectual circles, Childe felt compelled to read his book. But to what effect? What might Childe have learnt from this book?

He would have been immediately impressed by its focus on 'democracy' as a popular ... something. Not a movement but something else, an unmistakeable trend at least. Hobson argued that individuals were now able to challenge the 'sham democracy of self-government' because of the impact of the war and social discontent, 'the solvent' of modern thought:

> Active-minded men and women have been sitting more loosely by their institutions and attachments. The critical spirit has been abroad. The rapid ferment of thought and feeling on the status of women and sex problems during recent years has been at once an index and a source of revolutionary energy directed to the very foundations of society. Coincident with the new and startling ebullitions of revolt in the world of labour, this new sex consciousness has transformed the whole nature of social discontent, and helped to turn it into broader channels. The shattering experience of war will have broken the taboos and sanctities

---

3   J.A. Hobson and A.F. Mummery, *The Physiology of Industry*, London, Murray, 1889; J.A. Hobson, *Problems of Poverty*, London, Methuen 1891; J.A. Hobson, *Imperialism: A Study*, London, Nisbet, 1902; Michael Freeden, *J.A. Hobson: A Reader*, London, Unwin Hyman, 1988; Jan Toporowski, 'Imperialism, with Special Reference to J.A. Hobson's Influence on Lenin', *Bulletin of the Marx Memorial Library*, no. 133, Spring 2001, pp. 6–18; V.I. Lenin, *Imperialism: The Highest Stage of Capitalism*, 1916.

> which warded off close scrutiny into the basic institutions of State, Property and Industry, the Family, Religion and Morals. (p. 160)

When it came to describing the then-current regime, Hobson does have a sense of its material props, the institutions and supporting ideas that constitute a system of rule. But when it came to the 'revolutionary energy' that might overthrow the system, he cannot identify the material forces and their interests that produce it. He can only point to its expression as a 'spirit', a 'discontent', a 'close scrutiny' – an idea, a feeling, and a gaze.

Childe might have pondered, therefore, on the social composition of Hobson's ideal democratic phenomenon, its dynamic and field of action, because Hobson was clear that it was not co-extensive with the labour movement. According to Hobson, the labour movement was sectional in its appeal, and it relied on 'rules and usages' at work to restrict output and hence the national wealth. Hobson offered instead an indistinct entity called 'the people', an aggregation of everybody whose interests were denied by 'the different sorts of reactionary agents in the fields of politics, industry, education and social life'. 'The people' would come into its own through education. It would advance with the help of rootless intellectuals, 'a minority of liberal-minded leaders' who were 'deserters from the upper-class and bourgeois creeds … For they have liberated themselves and can therefore help to liberate others from that fear of thought …'. This reads like an account of Hobson's own path to radicalism, but it is hardly a plan for collective mobilisation. Nonetheless, he believed that individuals united only by democratic sentiments would be able to defeat the reactionaries. How would they do this? The democrats would eventually get control of industry, education, 'the credit system', the press, the civil service, the magistracy and courts, the local councils and so on. The implied strategy was a kind of upside-down and unfocused Fabianism, in which democrats permeated random parts of civil society and the economy rather than the upper reaches of the State.

But what about the state? Childe at this point would have been bemused by Hobson's understanding of Prussian-Australianism, which was his characterisation of the British state's reactionary objective after the war. The centrepiece of its program would be the continuation of economic protection, which 'makes an easy appeal to every other obscurantist, bellicose and reactionary element'. But because not all workers will succumb to its appeal, given the recent upsurge of labour militancy, reactionaries will 'try to divide democracy and to protect Protection by surrounding it with other more attractive appeals to labour'. So, the Australian example of 'fastening tariff regulations to a labour policy of guaranteed wages and pensions' is called into the argument. Hobson overlooked the fact that 'the fastening' lasted all of seven months, before the High Court struck down the 'new protection'. Henceforth, wage increases for the Australian working class were won through the arbitration court and wages boards fearing to be outflanked by industrial militancy; the protectionist manufacturers had no legislative inducements to pay higher wages and opposed all efforts by workers to get them. Childe would have known this.[4]

Hobson's book was part of the intellectual transition among radical liberals from the positive state of the early twentieth century 'new liberalism' to the powerful, directive state of mid-century social democracy. He was quite explicit about the need for an enhanced role for the state after the war. Calling it 'state socialism', he welcomed the way 'new economic and political movements' would put pressure on the state to expand its functions: first, to 'supply fuller public services to the people in their general capacity of producer-consumers'; second, to enlarge 'State ownership and administration in various special economic fields'; and third, to make possible 'a large increase in taxing power'. His blueprint for social democracy, however, was premature. It was not enacted after the First World War because post-1918 governments did exactly what Hobson said they should not do: they deregulated industry, throwing half the workforce previously directly or indirectly supplying goods and services to the state onto the labour market and into unemployment, and they re-established 'the old condition of private profiteering ... cut-throat competition and secret combination'. But after the Second World War, the Attlee Labour government was prepared to introduce this version of socialism. Hobson in the meantime had become a trusted advisor to the Labour Party.

Hobson insisted in his book that democrats could not afford to neglect the politics of working within the state. 'Whatever the vices of a capitalist State, there is only one remedy, viz. to convert it into a Democratic State.' Labour in particular had to avoid syndicalist and pluralist ideas and embrace the sovereignty of the state. He ridiculed guild socialism as a recipe for chaos, because it proposed to divide that sovereignty by separating economic control from political control. Childe might have found this challenging. After all, at Oxford his socialism was formed in the pluralist guild socialist mould. His exposure to Marxism via Dutt occurred before the Bolsheviks triumphed; at that stage 'smashing' the capitalist state was understood as what had happened in Paris during the Commune of 1871. It still held the promise of an

---

4   Phil Griffiths, 'Labor's Tortured Path to Protectionism', in Robert Hood and Ray Markey (eds), *Labour and Community*, Australian Society for the Study of Labour History, Illawarra Branch, Wollongong, 1999, pp. 91–5.

increase of popular self-government. On both fronts, he was reflecting the shift away from the state as the centre of political and moral thought. But here was Hobson, a respected radical intellectual, arguing at length that the process of breaking 'the vicious circle of reaction' by democratic permeation had to culminate in state action to legislate for social democracy.

Could this strategy perhaps be turned to the achievement of revolutionary change? Dora Montefiore thought so. Born in Britain, she married into an Australian family and moved to Sydney, where the first meeting of the Womanhood Suffrage League was held in her home in 1891. Returning to Britain she became a Marxist, a militant suffragette, and in 1920 a founder of the British Communist Party. In 1918 she wrote in the paper of the British Socialist Party (BSP) that Hobson's account of the fight against the vicious circle of reaction was incomplete (because he wrote before the Bolshevik Revolution proved that striking at capitalism was the best way to transform society) but his call for the concentration of progressive forces was positive. The revolutionary BSP, she wrote, would remain part of the Labour Party, its weapons aimed at capturing the state.[5]

Childe, after he returned to Australia, would refer to Hobson several times in his writings, and his paper to the Inter-State Peace Conference in Sydney was based on Hobson's *Imperialism*. Like Montefiore, he would be active in the Labor Party. In late 1919 he would begin working for a Labor Premier, and he would argue that creating a 'real' Labor government was a route to socialism. But he would also call himself a revolutionary. Such political shape-shifting was of a kind with Hobson's political trajectory, and with his conflicted analysis of democracy, anchored in individualism but veering towards collectivism.

* * *

In February 1918, the Sydney branch of the UDC, in which Childe was active, organised a public meeting at the Protestant Hall to consider resolutions calling for a negotiated peace and opposing imperialism. For some months, as a result of the Bolshevik government's publication of the secret treaties between the Allies for carving up conquered territories, the Allies had

---

5   Dora B. Montefiore, 'Democracy during the War', *The Call*, 11 July 1918, p. 4 (from Marxist Internet Archive); Judith Allen, 'Montefiore, Dorothy Frances (Dora) (1851–1933)', *Australian Dictionary of Biography*, Vol. 10, 1986, pp. 556–7.

been under pressure to clarify their war aims. Lenin had announced that the Russian Government adhered to self-determination for conquered peoples, a principle that could also be applied to colonies. Prime Minister Lloyd George and President Wilson hastened to announce the same principle in January 1918, as if that had been their aim all along. In Australia this caused consternation, because it implied that the colonies of a defeated Germany might be restored to her on condition that the interests of the colonial population were recognised. The Australian press was not having that. The Pacific, at least south of the Equator, was Australia's trading sphere; New Guinea should be under Australian control because it was vital for the country's security. 'When the Germans wantonly bombard peaceful watering places like Scarborough, within reasonable distance of the British fleet, what abiding safety can there be for Townsville, for Brisbane, for Sydney, and for Melbourne?' – if New Guinea was restored to Germany. As expelled Labor Premier, W.A. Holman, told a New York journalist, 'Australia will never allow Germany to retain a foothold in New Guinea'.[6]

On the same day as the notice for the peace meeting appeared, there was a letter in *The Australian Worker* from 'V.G.C.'. Childe had come across an article in *The Nineteenth Century*, a British monthly literary magazine, by the former Bishop of North Queensland, George Frodsham, which asserted that Australians dreaded 'the return to Germany of her late colonies in the Pacific'. Childe thought: who were these Australians? His letter identified a different set of Australians, the 'Democracy of Australia'. His democrats were 'intelligent and experienced'. They would not be not 'bamboozled' into supporting the retention of German New Guinea after the war. The workers of Australia, he wrote, were not 'thirsting to secure fresh dependencies for the Commonwealth'. But in Britain there were propagandists who asserted the opposite. 'It is really up to the Labor Party ... to take some solid steps to dispel this new cloud of capitalist mythology', because acquiring colonies was a trap for the working class:

> Stripped of all sentimental gilding, the annexation of an uncivilised region by a civilised government has always meant just this – that the money of the taxpayers as a whole is to be spent on the defence and

---

6 *Australian Worker*, 7 February 1918 p. 4 ('Peace Demonstration'); Ernest Scott, *Official History of Australia in the Great War of 1914–18*, Sydney, Angus & Robertson, 1936, pp. 767–8; *Sydney Morning Herald*, 9 October 1917, p. 7 ('German Colonies – No Chance of Restoration'), and 10 November 1917, p. 8, and 24 November 1917, p. 8; *Brisbane Courier*, 5 March 1918, p. 8; *The Age*, 23 March 1918, p. 13. *Sydney Morning Herald*, 9 October 1917, p. 7 (Holman).

government of a territory in which the investing classes or capitalists shall find a profitable field for speculation. ... [The] capitalists gain a new field for investment, offering tempting opportunities to the company promoter and the manipulator of securities. And let us not forget the politician; for he gets something too – bless his patriotic soul: what J.S. Mill called a system of outdoor relief.

Then he concluded:

But this manoeuvre means something worse. Over ten years ago J.A. Hobson warned us that the privileged classes of Great Britain would attempt to induce the democracies of the Dominions to go in for an imperialism of their own, to buttress up the system with which, as he then showed, the retention of these privileges is intimately bound up. Hence it is another phase of the plot to implicate Australia in that vicious circle – Capitalism, Imperialism, Militarism.[7]

Two references to Hobson in one paragraph: by name, a reference to *Imperialism – A Study*, and as an echo of his *Democracy after the War* in the last five words. And in the previous paragraph another echo, because it was Hobson, in *Imperialism*, who was the latest commentator to revive the 'system of outdoor relief' phrase. Unfortunately, Childe mis-remembered his source, for it was James Mill not his son J.S. Mill who described colonies as 'a vast system of outdoor relief for the upper classes' – as Hobson correctly stated. The extension of the idea to politicians was Childe's novel contribution. It reflected his current preoccupation with the manipulation of public opinion in the interests of patriotism, as in his letters to *Hermes* and Watt. Childe had been in Australia just four months, but already he was talking about its democracy in the most extravagant terms, identifying it with the country's interests and encouraging Labor to lead it.[8]

And the same set of connections is evident in the next letter he sent to *The Australian Worker*. It appeared a few weeks later under the heading 'The Need for Clear Thinking', a phrase that echoed Cole's call in *The World of Labour*:

One great need of the democratic movement in all countries, especially in Australia, is clearness of thought. It is easy for the people to be led

---

7   'V.G.C.' [Vere Gordon Childe], 'The German Colonies in the Pacific', *Australian Worker*, 7 February 1918, p. 19; John Charles Vockler, 'Frodsham, George Horsfall (1863–1937)', *Australian Dictionary of Biography*, Vol. 8, 1981, pp. 590–1.
8   Hobson, *Imperialism*, p. 51.

astray by specious phrases. How many, for example, have a clear notion of the meaning of that liberty in the name of which the Allies are fighting today? Conscriptionist and Trade Unionist alike appeal to it to justify dramatically opposite policies. Neither side is clear as to how far liberty and compulsion are irreconcilable, though both seem to recognise that some sort of pressure is justified in order to 'compel men to be free', as Rousseau puts it. The orthodox Socialist pins his faith to 'the State'. But has he ever considered the real nature of that institution, and how it can fulfil the boundless task he lays upon it? In the past the State seems to have betrayed its votaries, and this even seems a justification for the syndicalist and anarchist.

Political philosophy, whose task it is to give precision to thought upon such subjects, has been seized and utilized by the governing classes. The reactionaries have twisted philosophy to suit their purposes, as in former ages they wrested religion to subdue the spirit of man. They have a seemingly coherent interpretation of the catchwords of democracy, and thus have been able to impose a theory favourable to their interests upon the leaders of the democracy. Even the revolutionary Rousseau has been made 'respectable' and adapted to their ends. They have a system there ready – a dangerous weapon for use against unwary thinkers. To meet it Labor must have a philosophy of its own. But this it can only get by resolutely tackling the sources from which their opponents likewise claim to draw their wisdom. Only so will the Labor Movement secure itself from battling for vain shadows and empty phrases.

V.G.C.[9]

Childe had returned to Sydney just before the second referendum on conscription. Apart from advising McKell, he took no part in the 'No' campaign, but in this letter he showed that he understood the central mobilising idea for the protagonists on both sides: the idea of liberty. And each side recognised that it could not be realised without some kind of pressure, some limitation to prevent the Hobbesian war of all against all. From where? Childe does not say, but the reference to Rousseau is telling. For Rousseau the general will, expressed in the rule of law, was sovereign; the government merely interpreted the general will. People submitted to the general will because it guaranteed

---

9   V.G.C. [Vere Gordon Childe], 'The Need for Clear Thinking', *Australian Worker*, 28 March 1918, p. 19; G.D.H. Cole, *The World of Labour: A Discussion of the Present and Future of Trade Unionism*, London, G. Bell & Sons, 1913, pp. 52–3.

that the individual would not be subordinated to the will of other individuals. Each individual was free but also constrained by their own understanding of the common good. But liberals were sceptical. According to Rousseau, the general will needed to be affirmed by direct democracy, in an assembly where every citizen was equal; to liberals that meant that the liberty of a rich person might be compromised by the liberty of a poor person. Liberals preferred a representative form of government in which the rich could claim to represent everybody. Liberals wanted government and sovereignty to be one. They wanted to smother popular sovereignty. Childe would have been familiar with this radical interpretation of liberty and compulsion from Cole's introduction to a 1913 edition of Rousseau's *Social Contract*.[10]

The antithesis of Rousseau's general will is the state, an expression of a will that is external to society and imposed on it. Nonetheless, as Childe pointed out, orthodox socialists have pinned their faith to the state. Not all socialists, just 'the orthodox' ones. He was thinking of the Fabians and the German Social Democrats, especially the Marxist revisionists among them. But did they understand its real nature, its limitations as a state in capitalist society, structurally incapable of fully realising working-class interests? It had let them down in the past, and 'this even seems' to justify the anti-statism of the anarchists and syndicalists. Note the 'even seems'. He was being careful, when considering their contribution to socialist theory, not to endorse their hostility to the state. After all, he was now a member of the Labor Party – but was he still an *unorthodox* socialist, a revolutionary?

At least in political philosophy the answer is 'yes'. He could have written: 'democrats need to understand the philosophical principles underlying parliamentary government because there is disagreement about how they should be interpreted'. Instead, he called out reactionaries for 'twisting' political philosophy (even the 'revolutionary' Rousseau had been made 'respectable') to suit the interests of the ruling class, just as they had made religion into an instrument of oppression in the past. The system of ideas they created out of the catchwords of democracy was dangerous because it was 'seemingly coherent' and because the leaders of the democracy were susceptible to it.

---

10 Robin Archer, 'Labour and Liberty: The Origins of the Conscription Referendum', in Robin Archer, Joy Damousi, Murray Goot and Sean Scalmer (eds), *The Conscription Conflict and the Great War*, Clayton (Victoria), Monash University Publishing, 2016, pp. 37–66; Frank Bongiorno, 'Why Did Australians Get So Emotional over Conscription during World War I?', unpublished paper, National Archives of Australia, 4 November 2016; J.J. Rousseau, *The Social Contract & Discourses*, translated with an Introduction by G.D.H. Cole, London & Toronto, J.M. Dent & Sons, 1913.

'To meet it Labor must have a philosophy of its own', based on the interests of the class it represented.

The sources of 'clear thinking' lay in the writings of the classical political thinkers and Childe was ready to interpret them in a radical way. Two weeks after his letter, *The Australian Worker* carried a notice submitted by the Workers' Educational Association announcing a course of lectures on political philosophy 'to be given by Mr V.G. Childe, M.A., B.Litt.'. The lectures were to start four days later, in the Assembly Room of the Department of Education in Bridge Street, so presumably the WEA expected a crowd:

1. Outline of the Problems – what do we mean by (i) The State; (ii) Citizenship; (iii) Self-Government; (iv) Liberty?

2. Historical Review of the Solutions Offered –

Hobbes – the state of nature is 'anarchy' – the negation of freedom

3. ditto – The State rescues man from Anarchy

4. ditto – the condemnation of revolution

5. Locke – the natural freedom of man

6. ditto – Revolution and popular sovereignty

7. Rousseau – the general will

8. ditto – The theory of majority rule

9. ditto – Freedom and self-government

10. Austin – Sovereignty and Law

11. Hegel – The national spirit

12. ditto – The State as the realisation of freedom

13. ditto – Contrast of the freedom of citizenship with (i) legal freedom, (ii) freedom of conscience

14. ditto – The State reconciles the economic and moral needs of man

15. ditto – Classes in the State

16. Mill and Spencer – the liberal reaction against the State

17. Tolstoy and the anarchists

18. The State and Labor (Cole)

Conclusions:

19. The State and the Individual

20. The State and Voluntary Associations

21. The State and other States[11]

Each meeting, according to the announcement, would be in the form of a tutorial class. There was a reason for this. In March, as we have seen, the Joint Committee for Tutorial Classes at the university was informally considering Childe for a Tutorship and wanted evidence of his suitability. As the Tutorship was to be in Ancient History, the choice of political philosophy as the topic must have been Childe's. Apart from the title of each lecture, we have almost no knowledge of this course. No evidence, for example, about its impact on students; but Portus, the Acting Director, reported to the Joint Committee in July that he had inspected the class and found Childe to be a satisfactory tutor. We also don't know if Childe reflected on the paradox of delivering lectures on freedom and conscience while he was being persecuted by college and university authorities for his political beliefs and activities.

But maybe there was a connection between his experience of persecution and the topic, because as a syllabus it broadcasts erudition rather than partisan philosophy-building. We can imagine him saying to his enemies: 'Your attacks imply I am not a fit to teach at university or adult education level, but how many of you have the knowledge of political philosophy that I have? Look: five weeks on Hegel! And look, in case you haven't noticed, not a single week on Marx!' If he imagined the syllabus in this way, he was undermining its capacity to provide a foundation for a philosophy that the labour movement could own. What would auto-didactic workers, in a Workers' Educational Association, have made of a lecture (number 15) on social classes in relation to Hegel's idealised state, especially as Hegel's social classes – agriculturalists, businessmen, and civil servants – bore no relationship to their experience as

---

11   *Australian Worker*, 11 April 1918, p. 6.

members of the modern working class? Perhaps the last six lectures would have moved closer to answering Labor's need for a philosophy of its own. They appear to be pointing towards embracing the state but in the critical, pluralist fashion of Cole attacking Fabianism. Later we shall see Cole demolishing the Hegelian 'God-State' and making a radical defence of Rousseau from the same position.

In Britain, the ruling idea was that the socialist state was simply against human nature, which was irrefutably individualistic, while on the other hand the success of the British state proved the utility of self-interest.[12] Childe was primed by his talks with Dutt to try to refute this idea, but what was the Marxist theory of the state? In contrast to Hegel, Marx and Engels held that the state could not be understood abstractly and in isolation from civil society but only in the context of economic and social relations. The state had to be understood critically and with practical, political ends in mind, for it played a role in the struggle between classes. The philosophical underpinnings of the materialist conception of history were constructed by Marx and Engels in a series of articles and treatises written in the 1840s as they worked out their position in relation to the ideas of a new, radical generation of Hegelians. These works, however, were not available to their followers until the 1920s and later. Childe would have been hard pressed to make Marxist materialism seem 'respectable' in 1918. Perhaps he did not want to, given his difficult relationship with the university. It was a better tactic to leave all the questions hanging.[13]

* * *

Having been forced to resign from St Andrew's Childe was now worrying about his future. At Oxford, campaigning for conscientious objectors he had cultivated Professor Gilbert Murray for his political connections, but later he sought Murray's advice about how to pursue his career during the war. He had returned to Sydney only to discover that the university's leading men were determined never to appoint him. In the imperial university network, however, Sydney was a junior partner to Oxford, where Childe had succeeded

---

12   K. Willis, 'The Introduction and Critical Reception of Marxist Thought in Britain, 1850–1900', *The Historical Journal*, vol. 20, no. 2, June 1977, pp. 451–4.

13   Ralph Miliband, 'Marx and the State', in R. Miliband and J. Saville (eds), *The Socialist Register 1965*, London, The Merlin Press 1965, pp. 278–96; Stuart Macintyre, *A Proletarian Science: Marxism in Britain 1917–1933*, London, Lawrence & Wishart, 1980, pp. 177–80.

so brilliantly. This was cultural capital that he could use. He resumed his correspondence with Murray in two letters written in June 1918, the first on 8 June bringing him up to date with his misfortunes and the second on 24 June asking for a reference to use publicly against his calumniators, the 'junta of jingoes' whose 'terrorism' has silenced all the liberals on the staff.[14]

His first letter to Murray, defiantly written on St Andrew's letterhead, was actually part of a package of letters. The package included a 'Personal Statement' describing his academic attainments since 1914 and his political activities in Oxford and Sydney. It concluded with a short account of 'the underground campaign' against him by the university's 'secret junta'. In this 'Personal Statement', he refers to four enclosures: his letter to the Australian High Commissioner of 3 March 1917 declaring he would not help the war effort, a letter from Queen's College suggesting he return to Australia until the war was over, his letter of 2 May 1918 offering to resign from St Andrew's if his salary was paid until 1 October, and his letter of 1 June 1918 to the Secretary of St Andrew's officially resigning. The 'Personal Statement', with its enclosures, reads like a press release and there is evidence that it was used by Childe's friends in the peace and socialist movements when they responded to his request to publicise his case. The intended effect of these documents was to establish that he acted towards the college with the utmost propriety, and that Oxford academics could extend collegiality to a scholar with radical opinions while Sydney academics could not.[15]

Childe constructed the letter to Murray of 8 June as a commentary on the 'Personal Statement'. He began by hinting at the imperial hierarchy of university education. His Statement, he told Murray, was an 'account of the "freedom of thought" allowed in colonial universities', controlled as they are 'by a clique of bigoted and narrow-minded men'. He listed their hostility to radical thought, the Labor Party, the WEA and the tutorial classes movement, and their leading role in advocating conscription. 'The result is that the University has become ... a glorified technical college. ... In the public life of the State the university is justly ignored ... Most especially in the great Labor Party and among the wage earners is the university becoming daily more suspect as a class and party institution.' Childe presents himself, in contrast, as committed to scholarship in this defective environment. The

---

14   Julia Horne and Geoffrey Sherington, *Sydney: The Making of a Public University*, Melbourne, The Miegunyah Press, 2012, pp. 244–5; Childe to Murray, 24 June 1918, Murray papers, shelfmark 376, f. 49.

15   Childe to Murray, 8 June 1918, Murray papers, shelfmark 376, ff. 41–6. The 'Personal Statement' is at f. 43.

Statement contained a new and relevant piece of information. On his return to Sydney, he wrote, 'I was contemplating applying for the Lectureship in Ancient History at the University should this post be established, and my intention was known to the Principal of this College [St Andrew's] and to many of the University staff. As however the proposal to establish the post was rejected on financial grounds, no application was sent in.' In like manner, in his letter to Murray he describes his paper on imperialism to the Easter peace conference as 'purely academic'.

This paper, referred to in the Statement as well as the accompanying letter, stands as the only indication by him of political involvement. He thus gives the impression that he was a propagandist, not an activist, a scholar providing words not deeds to his favoured radical causes. This of course was false. The peace conference was a conference of delegates and he was there as an activist in the UDC. He was a member of the Labor Party and was trying to alter its policy on the German colonies. He was a tutor, a lobbyist and an on-the-spot advisor to anti-war socialists. As we have seen, he had led a delegation to the government on behalf of Vance Marshall and spent many nights at the Labor Council meetings in the Trades Hall advising the opponents of the official Labor line on recruitment. They were successful, a fact that has a bearing on how he concluded his letter, attacking the bigotry of the 'intellectuals' because it really 'plays right into the hands of the extremist section among the industrialists and makes it even more difficult for impartial or moderate advice to be given or taken'. Was this written from personal experience at the Trades Hall? He described the situation and its dangers:

> There are no middle-class socialist societies to interpret the proletarian movements to the governing classes on the one hand and on the other hand to give some councils to revolutionaries and IWWs. So, there is no UDC or League of Nations Society of any weight to come between the extreme pacifists and internationalists and the dominant jingoes and annexationists. The result is an ever-growing bitterness … that may well lead to a very grave state of affairs in the near future.

Then he reflected on his own practice:

> When in England I was I'm afraid inclined to be impatient with a certain vacillation of the intellectual liberals. Now I can appreciate the enormous service such a class renders when I see the deplorable results of its absence. In many ways I am delighted with the growing radicalism of the Labor Party and the Trade Union Movement here, but I would

infinitely prefer reconciliation and compromise to revolution. If the latter is forced upon the Labor Movement it will be entirely due to the unscrupulousness and bigotry of the professional and educated classes. Excuse this somewhat hasty epistle. The mail is just going out.[16]

He sees himself in England, perhaps in Dutt's company, taking a hard line against expressions of liberal doubt about the class struggle. For the purposes of the argument he forgets his own insistence on the need for impartial truths about the war. Then he arrives in Sydney and is impressed by 'the great Labor Party' and welcomes the growing radicalism of the working class, but is alarmed by the savagery of their opponents, not only towards the working class but towards radical intellectuals like himself. In this moment of personal uncertainty and political change, he imagines middle-class socialists and pacifists as missionaries to the ruling class, explaining the inevitable victory of the 'world of labour'. At the same time, they could produce a philosophy for labour that would make revolutionary extremism unnecessary by showing that modern social thought was revitalising the idea of popular sovereignty. But the bitterness between classes in Australia was dangerous. In reaction, drawing on his own experiences of the Australian situation, he recognises the strategic possibilities of persuasion and compromise in the class struggle, reached after mediation by formally-educated labour intellectuals. Suddenly 'a certain vacillation' is not a weakness but a strength that was needed for 'the democracy' to triumph over the militarists and capitalists.

* * *

Gordon was spending his last 100 pounds slowly. He had now decided to apply to the Queensland Public Instruction Service for a teaching post, and to make his case he persuaded Brookfield, who thought Childe was 'head and shoulders above any other tutor', and Miles, to write to Queensland Labor politicians. Certain now that his chances were better in Queensland, he departed for Brisbane on 18 September 1918. On the same day, he wrote to the Chancellor, whom privately he called 'a deep-dyed ruffian': 'As the University of Sydney has set its face against all freedom of the teacher, and ignoring academic merits, enquires into the private views on politics of its professors and teachers, you will be relieved to hear that the enclosed section

---

16 Childe to Murray, 8 June 1918, Murray papers, shelfmark 376, ff. 44–6.

of my will whereby the University stood to gain about 2500 pounds has been altered in favour of a more enlightened body.' The favoured body was the Labor Council of New South Wales.[17]

---

17   Le Gay Brereton to Hall, 4 July and 4 November 1918, file M235, University of Sydney Archives; Pearce to Childe, 8 May 1918, Intell. Reports 168/1-7; Brookfield to C. Butler MLA, Qld, 10 September 1918, NAA CMF Intell. Reports 167/36-45; Childe to Chancellor of Sydney University, 18 September 1918, University of Sydney Archives, M223 (re his will).

Chapter 8

'YOURS FOR THE REVOLUTION'

Arriving in Brisbane, Childe did not quite know what to make of its political atmosphere. There were many positives. He was exhilarated by its 'refreshing air of revolutionary optimism', coming as he was from Sydney, where the industrial mood was defensive since the defeat of the mass strike of 1917. He also felt he had more freedom because there were no secret policemen taking notes at the regular Sunday night gatherings of radicals in the Trades Hall. He asked himself what was different about Queensland. He noted the more 'harmonious' relations between the Labor Party and the unions, a consequence of the absence of a split in the party over conscription. He applauded the impact of the left-wing newspaper run by the radical unions, the *Daily Standard*, which was 'doing good work, even on the war'. And Premier Ryan was a big asset. His implied support for the Perth conference resolutions enabled the party in Queensland to take a more definite stand against the war. Most important was his adroit handling of industrial disputes, of which there were many at that moment, especially among government employees in the railways, the state hotels, and the state butchers' shops. Ryan appeared 'to give way every time but to hide his surrenders even from the Tories'.[1]

Yet he was uneasy. Militants were coming to Queensland – the pacifists Margaret Thorpe and Arnold Holmes, the anti-war feminist Jennie Scott Griffiths, the socialist Cleeve Ullman – because they thought that if there were to be an Australian revolution it would start in Queensland. Gordon anticipated the revolution too, signing off his letters, 'Yours for the revolution', but he was contemplating two questions: What kind of revolution? And would it succeed? His answer to the second question revealed his thinking

---

1   I have gained insights into Childe's responses to Queensland from the very detailed account of his year in Brisbane written by Raymond Evans, '"Social Passion": Vere Gordon Childe in Queensland, 1918–19', in Gathercole, Irving and Melleuish (eds), *Childe and Australia*, pp. 1–26; Childe to W.J. Miles, 15 October 1918, NAA CMF Intell. Reports 168/21-29; Childe to Le Gay Brereton, 23 December 1918, Le Gay Brereton papers, Mitchell Library MSS 281, vol. 4, pp. 125–6.

about the first. He foresaw a 'sinister outlook' for Australia: the revolution defeated by the capitalist class's ability to manipulate working-class 'boneheads and bourgeois university students' – the same forces of scabbery that had cruelled the 'great strike' in New South Wales. And there was another problem. As he wrote to Brereton in Sydney, 'I now realise that ideals are an expensive luxury that should be left to poets and visionaries of independent means but no sort of authority'. It was a comment on the costly effect of ideals in his own life, but it also applied to his comrades, blinded by their unrealistic enthusiasm for revolutionary ideals. He found it hard to square the Trades Hall radicals' revolutionary optimism – which he partly shared – with his observation that the working class, trained in servility, would prefer pragmatism to idealism.

The rapid advance of Brisbane's labour movement had created a mood of radical expectancy among its intellectuals, and utopian socialist novels from overseas, such as Edward Bellamy's *Looking Backward* (1888), William Morris's *News from Nowhere* (1890), and Ignatius Donnelly's *Caesar's Column* (1890), sold really well. In the 1880s and 1890s, journalist William Lane had promoted Bellamy's vision of socialism, which was highly technicist, industrial and organised on military lines. Would this be the form Australia's revolution would take, given the passivity of its working class? Radicals preferring a more arcadian, artisanal and democratic socialism read *News from Nowhere*, which Morris had written partly to counter Bellamy's robotic socialism. Childe, who knew of Bellamy's influence in the 1890s, leaned towards Morris. When he was writing *How Labour Governs* he said he was glad that Bellamy's socialist utopia 'was never translated into fact' in Australia. He might have been thinking of William Lane's journey in the 1890s with several hundred labour movement militants to the interior of Paraguay to set up a communist utopia, which failed in part because of Lane's authoritarianism.[2]

One Sunday night at the Trades Hall Gordon decided to counter the 'absurd optimism' of Norman Freeberg and the other would-be Leninists. Exposed now to the possibilities for socialism provided by Queensland Labor's more unified and intellectual movement, he was changing his mind about the path to revolution. As the Censor in Brisbane noted, with more insight about Labor politics than most censors possessed, Childe, since coming to Brisbane, had been converted 'from "direct" to "political" action, and his Sydney friends are astonished by the change'.

---

2   Childe to P.R. Stephensen, 29/12/1918, Mitchell Library MSS 1284, Y2150; Anne Whitehead, *Paradise Mislaid: In Search of the Australian Tribe of Paraguay*, Brisbane, Oxford University Press, University of Queensland Press, 1997.

It was still very perplexing to Gordon: 'I don't really know why I've been transformed from pessimism to optimism'. In Brereton's view, he was consumed by 'despondent irony'. Meanwhile he was suffering from the heat ('97 degrees with a hot wind on Monday') and, unable to find congenial drinking companions, he had not been 'tight' since he left Sydney.[3]

Gordon stayed for a few days with Russell Pearce's father George, who was the Secretary of the local branch of the Rationalist Press Association, before moving into the bungalow of Rev. T.C. Witherby, an Anglican with High Church leanings like Childe's father. An activist in the WEA and Acting Director of Tutorial Classes at the University of Queensland, the Oxford educated Theodore Witherby had a reputation for eccentric behaviour. On one occasion, during a boring meal with two ladies at a restaurant, he disappeared under the table to read. He was also a supporter of the Russian revolutionaries of 1917. Gordon and he would have recognised that they had much in common, although not on the question of Bolshevism.[4]

* * *

After a month without a job, Gordon accepted a position as classics master at Maryborough Grammar, arranged for him through the Department of Public Instruction, to commence in 1919. No doubt he was hoping for something more demanding – as a government advisor or researcher – because his earlier stint as a schoolmaster in Glen Innes in 1914 had been a disaster. But his funds were running out. Then, in late October, his patrons in the government told him that he could start teaching in Maryborough at once. Four days later the local Labor MP escorted Gordon into the school and announced to the surprised Headmaster that Childe was the school's new classics master. Earlier that year the Labor government had reconstructed the school's board of trustees. Grammar schools, run by local businessmen and professionals, supported

---

3   We will look at Freeberg's ideas in the next chapter. Isabel F. Swann to Jennie Scott Griffiths, 27 September 1918, NAA CMF Intell. Reports, 168/1-7; Childe to Russell Pearce, 28 October 1918, NAA CMF Intell. Reports 168/30; Le Gay Brereton to Hall, 4 November 1918, University of Sydney Archives, M235; for the censor's comment: Witherby to Childe, 21 February 1919, NAA CMF Intell. Reports, 167/85-91; for 'yours for the revolution': Childe to Reg Byrne, 14 March 1919, in Meanjin papers, University of Melbourne Archives.

4   Childe to Miles, 15 October 1918, NAA CMF Intell. Reports, 168/21-29; Evans, 'Social Passion', pp. 6–7; Jack Lindsay, *Life Rarely Tells: An Autobiography in Three Volumes*, Ringwood, Victoria, Penguin Books, 1982, pp. 124–5.

by state funds but charging fees affordable only by wealthy families, were an affront to Labor, which was trying to promote public secondary schools. The President of the party's Central Political Executive, Billy Demaine, lived in Maryborough, owned a local newspaper, and was prominent in town affairs, so its grammar school was an obvious target, especially because the school was not performing well. The new board of trustees, which included Demaine and other Labor sympathisers, gave the masters notice that their contracts would end on 31 December. Morale among the staff dropped and misconduct among the pupils increased. So, when two teachers resigned unexpectedly the Minister for Public Instruction contacted Demaine, who in turn contacted the Chair of the board of trustees, who contacted the Headmaster. Along the line the message passed: appointing Childe would be 'a good thing'. That was how Childe had reached the school: propelled into the job by the government's policy of reforming secondary education, and the party's desire to exercise its patronage.[5]

By this time Gordon's radical past was no secret. His political friends were using it privately in Labor circles to help him find employment, and publicly to expose the prejudices of their opponents. The *Daily Standard* reported his imminent arrival in Brisbane under the heading 'University Intolerance – Tutor Victimized'. His friends, however, were unprepared for their opponents using this information against him in a campaign of deliberate mischief. The fuse was lit by an article in Demaine's Maryborough newspaper, *The Alert*. A few days after he arrived, under the heading 'Class Bias', it provided its readers with the phrases that would be bruited around by Childe's conservative opponents. The article stated that Maryborough's new grammar school teacher had been turned down by the Senate of Sydney University, that he happened to be a labour man, an anti-conscriptionist, a member of the peace alliance, and a speaker at the peace conference last Easter. It was read by a local resident, Mr G.Y. Harding, who had two sons at the school and wanted their education to continue 'on British lines'. He wrote to the *Maryborough Chronicle* the day after Childe's appointment was announced to ask if this 'Mr Child' was the person referred to in *The Alert*. He then repeated the incriminating phrases from *The Alert* so the readers would know what he meant. Harding attacked again a few days later in another letter, this time focusing on Labor interference in the running of the school. In Brisbane, a conservative Member of Parliament used the same phrases when asking the Labor Minister of Public Instruction, Herbert F. Hardacre, what he knew about Childe. (The Minister, in an answer that came

---

5   Childe to Miles, 15 October 1918, as above; Childe to Murray, 25 October 1918, Murray papers, shelfmark 376, f. 84, Bodleian Library; J.T. Noble Wallace, letter in *Maryborough Chronicle*, 21 November 1918; Evans, 'Social Passions', p. 8.

close to misleading parliament, told him to ask the trustees of the school.) In the town, recruiting sergeants made allusions at rallies to a traitorous teacher in their midst. Meanwhile, in the classroom, Childe's pupils, whipped into patriotic fervour, were uncontrollable. They drowned out his words by singing 'Rule Britannia', and they peppered him with shots from their peashooters. It was a difficult, perhaps dangerous, time for Gordon, and finally he had had enough.[6]

Under the heading 'Who is Mr Childe?' he wrote to the *Maryborough Chronicle*, which published his letter on 29 November 1918:

> Sir, To anticipate further repetition of this question, may I be allowed through your columns to address a few words to the critics who, fastening upon my alleged personal convictions in politics, and ignoring the scholastic record on which I was appointed to a temporary post here, have seen fit to prejudge my academic fitness.

He went on in ironic vein, likening his enemies to the anarchist followers of Kropotkin and Bakunin who created chaos with the aim of subverting the established order, an order that he identified as the school and his role in it. Despite the disorder his enemies had created, he had persisted with the task of teaching the pupils, who had been deserted on the eve of their examinations. That task fulfilled, he resigned:

> I do not feel it the business of a scholar to struggle against the violence of reaction learnt at home.

> If in future the political opinions of masters instead of their academic qualifications are to be made the subject of inquisitional researches by persons who once boasted the name of 'liberal', the future of education here will indeed be dark. If, moreover, when the persons in question are found to fail in the standards of political orthodoxy set up by this unseen tribunal, the methods of secret incitement to unruly pupils be continued, Maryborough may yet boast so unique an institution as a school for anarchists. I am, etc.,

> V. Gordon Childe.
> B.A., B.Litt. (Oxon)
> November 28, 1918

---

6   *Daily Standard*, 16 September 1918; *The Alert*, 4 October 1918; G.Y. Harding, letters to *Maryborough Chronicle*, 1 November and 5 November 1918; *Brisbane Courier*, 8 November 1918; Evans, 'Social Passions', pp. 11–12; S.E.A. Walker, 'School Days with Percy', Fryer Library, University of Queensland, MSS 55/18.

Ex-Scholar and Medalist of Sydney University, formerly Research Student of Queen's College, Oxford.

This defiant letter vindicated his role. As for the role of the Labor Party and the government, privately he was very angry, telling Brereton: 'It exemplifies if nothing else how not to do things'.[7]

* * *

When Gordon returned to Brisbane from Maryborough he stayed at 'Gowrie', a guesthouse in Wickham Terrace, Spring Hill, on the northern edge of the city. It was a street of big houses and medical suites, high enough to catch the breezes and perfectly situated for Childe, who could walk down the hill and across the centre of town to his job clerking in the State Land Tax Department, and on Sunday nights to the socialist gatherings in the Trades Hall in nearby Turbot Street. He was still assuming that his stay in Queensland would be temporary, and he had his eye on several possible jobs in Sydney. He had applied for a teaching post at Newington College, a Methodist school in Sydney. Indeed, in January 1919 the Headmaster wrote to Childe that he could start either at Easter or in June. Two weeks later the offer was withdrawn. On the intercepted letter the Brisbane Censor noted that the Headmaster had presumably 'become acquainted with Childe's eccentricities'. He had no need to name the clandestine body that did the acquainting. So Childe kept on clerking in the Land Tax Department, where he had been since late December, after an interview with Treasurer Theodore. It was 'very, very dull mechanical and monotonous work', mainly sorting papers, for which he was paid 10 shillings a day. When a Labor man, John English, was elected Lord Mayor of Sydney in December 1918, Childe contemplated working for him, perhaps as a private secretary cum advisor. Bert Evatt was keen for this to happen, but nothing came of it, perhaps because English was ill; he died suddenly in March 1919. Childe also advertised that he would coach students for university and bar examinations, 'Logic and psychology a speciality'. As Gordon entered the private education market his medal in philosophy had become an unexpected – but not very lucrative – asset.[8]

---

7   Childe, letter in *Maryborough Chronicle*, 29 November 1918; Childe to Le Gay Brereton, 23 December 1918, Le Gay Brereton papers, Mitchell Library MSS281, vol. 4, pp. 125–6.
8   G. Prescott to Childe, 7 January 1919 and 21 January 1919, NAA CMF Intell. Reports, 167/69-76; Childe to Le Gay Brereton, 23 December 1918, Le Gay

He knew he would have to delay his return to England, because he calculated that the Allies would not sign a peace treaty any time soon, as they would have to 'pacify' Germany and defeat 'the bloody Bolsheviks', and until then the Defence of the Realm Act and conscription would remain in force. Bored by his day-job shuffling papers, he needed a project to occupy his mind. In early December, Bert Evatt suggested to him that they might write a book 'renouncing bourgeois radicalism', Evatt's *Liberalism in Australia* having just been published. Nothing came of this idea, perhaps because Gordon wondered whether Bert's leftward drift from liberalism would take him as far as the camp of proletarian radicalism which Gordon was ready to explore. In Bert's book, Labor's program of state intervention was painted in new liberalism's colours, whereas Gordon was looking for signs of Cole's 'Greater Unionism' in the Australian working class. But he was encouraged that his articles about the anti-war insurgency in the Australian labour movement were being given 'great prominence' in British labour journals and 'hailed with joy in the I.L.P. etc'.[9]

So, by the end of December 1918, he had decided to write a book for the Fabian Research Department in London. Its Honorary Secretary was G.D.H. Cole, whose influence on Childe's politics we have already noted. In 1913 Cole published a hugely influential book in socialist circles, *The World of Labour*, whose argument we will examine in more detail in Chapter 10. Here we need only note that when Childe described his own book as 'a Monograph on the Political and Industrial Labor Movement in Australia' he was signalling that it would not be about either parliamentary labourism or Cole's class-conscious 'Greater Unionism', but rather the relationship between them. This relationship was only indirectly touched on in Cole's work because the British Labour Party was so puny and the British working class '75% loyal' to capitalism and the empire. In Australia, the labourist tradition was stronger, but so too was the grip of militant industrialism on a much smaller but more geographically concentrated working class. The two 'wings' of the movement had to be considered in relation to each other if the dynamics of Australian labour were to be understood.

His monograph, he told Brereton, would be:

Brereton papers, Mitchell Library MSS 281/4/125-6; Evatt to Childe, 6 January 1919, NAA CMF Intell. Reports, 167/69-76; *Brisbane Courier*, 26 April 1919, p. 1.

9   Childe to Brereton, 23 December 1918, Mitchell Library MSS 281, vol. 4, pp. 125–6; Evatt to Childe, 3 December 1918, NAA CMF Intell. Reports 167/57-68; for Evatt's book: Ian Tregenza, 'Are We All Socialists Now? New Liberalism, State Socialism, and the Australian Settlement', *Labour History*, no. 102, May 2012, pp. 87–98.

a connected account of Labor History say from 1910 on, aiming rather at analyses of tendencies and ideals than actual successes and failures, and paying more attention to movements like the I.W.W., the Industrial Vigilance Committee and the O.B.U. than election results or legislative enactments. But a comparison of the McGowen-Holman Governments with those of Ryan should make instructive reading – the real attitude (not the excuses in the Labor press) of the two administrations to strikes among their employees is rather a critical point. Ryan seems really to give way every time but to hide his surrender even from the Tories. H [Holman] used the true capitalist methods if I remember rightly.[10]

He did remember rightly. As we shall see, he made sure the reader of *How Labour Governs* knew that Labor in New South Wales condoned the punishment of strikers and encouraged scabs to take their jobs. As for Ryan's government, Childe had arrived in Queensland in the middle of a long dispute over wages in the State butchers' shops, that were part of a program of state enterprises set up by the Labor government. As meat became scarce, the union outsmarted the government by approaching local councils with an offer in which the council would procure meat for the shops and employ the workers – at the higher wage. At this point the Brisbane office of this state enterprise – no doubt encouraged by the government – gave in.[11]

A few days later he wrote to Percy Stephensen, whom he had met as a pupil at Maryborough Grammar, about his project:

> I am surrounded by reports re conferences and conventions. It is an interesting if depressing task. Incidentally, Billy Demaine was almost unrecognizable in a beard. We have retrogressed terribly since William Lane and the A.L.F. [Australian Labour Federation]. Still, despite many political traitors it has been mainly due to democratic pressure – bonehead pressure one would say. Nor am I sure that I would like to have seen 'Looking Backward' translated into fact. It is far from the ideals of the Newer Unionism.[12]

---

10   Childe to Brereton, 23 December 1918, Mitchell Library MSS 281, vol. 4, pp. 125–6.
11   *Daily Standard*, 22 November 1918, 10 December 1918, 24 December 1918, and 28 December 1918, and *How Labour Governs*, 1st edn, p. xvi (on State butchers' shops).
12   Childe to P.R. Stephensen, 29 December 1918, Stephensen papers, Mitchell Library MSS 1284, Y2150.

Many of the themes of Childe's approach to labour history are present in this letter: the criticism that labour has lost its ideals; the suspicion of utopians; the contempt for political traitors; the endorsement of Cole's view that a new form of trade unionism may save the movement's idealism; and his disdain for a form of democracy that empowers uneducated voters. The term 'boneheads', just a decade old when Childe used it, reveals the attraction IWW imagery had to Childe – as it did to other middle-class radicals during these years of labour unrest.

The handsome Percy Stephensen holding the ball with the Maryborough Boys Grammar School rugby team, 1918.
(Fryer Library, University of Queensland;
P.R. Stephensen papers, UQFL55, box 5, photo 9(a))

While at Maryborough Grammar, Gordon's chief tormentor, the organiser of the pea-shooting and jingoistic rowdiness, was Percy Reginald Stephensen. Tall and fair-haired, the 17-year-old Percy caught Gordon's attention. Was Percy surprised to receive Christmas greetings from 'V. Gordon Childe' on the back of a postcard showing the head and shoulders of a youth, described as 'Bas-relief trouvé à Achlada Crete'? Perhaps not, because there had obviously been some earlier non-curricular conversations between them. In 1957, Percy told Gordon that his radicalisation began in 1918 when 'ideas you then [at Maryborough] planted helped me to attain a satisfactory *contra mundum* outlook'. Presumably these ideas could not have been imparted in the classroom. A friendship quickly developed, one that was close enough to support a regular correspondence between them, using their private addresses. A few days after Christmas, Gordon again wrote to Percy, referring to their previous correspondence. Gordon congratulates Percy on passing the Senior examination in Latin, and then proceeds to tell him about his 'projected history of the Labor Movement in Australia'. He was one of the first to know about this. Gordon signs off with, 'Hope to see you if and when you come to B'bane. Meanwhile long live Anarchism. Yours sincerely, V. Gordon Childe.'[13]

Percy's political education continued at the University of Queensland, but in a decidedly un-anarchist direction, for in 1921 he joined the Communist Party. At the university he was introduced to the bohemian left by Jack Lindsay, a year ahead of him in the Arts faculty. Jack, the eldest son of the artist Norman Lindsay, met Witherby through a family friend, and Witherby arranged for him to teach a course on English literature at the WEA in 1919. Through Witherby it was not long before Jack met Gordon, and because Jack was a student of classics, a friendship between them developed. Jack would visit Childe at 'Gowrie', and both of them were often weekend guests at Witherby's shack on Mount Tambourine, about 75 kilometres south of Brisbane. From the train station one had to walk 'across the flats to the slopes and then wind one's way up', an expedition that Gordon enjoyed. In his autobiography, Jack describes Gordon on these mountain walks 'bent a little, listening equally to the noises of the earth and my meandering hypotheses':

> I remember him in those days as a bubble-pricker, a mildly caustic iconoclast, whose glasses took on an unholy glimmer as he demolished somebody's illusions with sardonic kindliness. He was the most detached person I knew, and yet one felt all the while there was a warm core to his gently spoken and deadly sarcasm.

On another occasion, Jack recalls him standing on the edge of a cliff, 'staring with vague intentness into immensity, swaying a little with bent shoulders and sliding his glasses down to the end of his nose'. In the 1940s Jack and Gordon resumed their friendship in England, drawn together by their common interest in Marxism.[14]

---

13 S.E.A. Walker, 'School Days with Percy', Fryer Library, University of Queensland, MSS 55/18; Childe to Stephenson (postcard), Stephensen papers, Mitchell Library MSS 1284, Y 2150; Stephensen to Childe, 15 April 1957, Stephensen papers, Y2141; Childe to Stephensen, 29 December 1918, Stephensen papers, Y2150.
14 Craig Munro, *Inky Stephensen – Wild Man of Letters,* Carlton, Vic., 1984; Lindsay, *Life Rarely Tells*, pp. 124–30.

In 1919 Gordon read a controversial novel of English public (i.e. privately funded) school life, Alec Waugh's *The Loom of Youth*. Seemingly part of a popular genre of boarding school stories, in which boys learnt how to be gentlemen and defenders of the empire through sport and inflicting punishment on younger boys, Waugh's book had an uncomfortable message for the ruling class. Its hero, Gordon Carruthers, is shown as disillusioned by his experiences at Fernhurst school, where 'success lay in a blind worship at the shrine of the god of Athleticism. Honesty, virtue, moral determination – these mattered not at all' (p. 126). His friends are pagans, they despise the cadet corps, and they cheat at their studies. Their code of honour 'is very elastic. Masters are regarded as common enemies; and it is never necessary to tell them the truth. Expediency is the golden rule in all relations with the common room' (p. 69). This is what the public-school system is really like, Waugh was saying, and it is the source of Britain's philistinism and failure to understand the threat posed by the advance of Prussian militarism. To contemporaries, Fernhurst was easily identifiable as Sherborne, the school Waugh had attended.[15]

Publishing such a message in 1917 naturally provoked upper-class outrage and masculine defensiveness. The controversy raged in the press for weeks, but there was one theme of Waugh's story that the champions of the public-school system never mentioned: the homosexual relationships created by 'the monastic herding together for eight months of the year of thirteen year old children and eighteen year old adolescents' (p. 12). The novel refers to these 'romances' several times, accepting that they are natural, even though subversive of 'bourgeois morality' (p. 33). If one were involved in such a relationship it was OK as long as you were not caught. Near the end of the book, in a chapter called 'Romance', Carruthers, an older boy, begins 'a friendship entirely different from any he had known before. He did not know what his real sentiments were; he did not even attempt to analyse them. He only knew that when he was with Morecombe he was indescribably happy' (p. 242). These were feelings Waugh himself had experienced; indeed, he was expelled from Sherborne in 1915, when he was caught *in flagrante*. Gordon Childe

---

15 Alec Waugh, *The Loom of Youth*, London, Grant Richards, 1917. The version consulted here is the Project Gutenberg EBook, 2006. There were eight reprints of the first edition in the two years before Childe read it. 'Old Shirburnian Society, identity of characters in Waugh's *Loom of Youth*', http://oldshirburnian.org.uk/the-characters-in-the-loom-of-youth/, accessed 13 May 2017. Jeffrey Richards, *Happy Days: The Public Schools in English Fiction*, London, Manchester University Press, 1988; J.A. Mangan, 'Conformity Confronted and Orthodoxy Outraged: *The Loom of Youth*: Succès de Scandale in Search of a Wider Reality', *The International Journal of the History of Sport*, vol. 29, issue 12, 2012, pp. 1701–14.

would have found much to ponder in Waugh's novel. As he wrote to Le Gay Brereton, *The Loom of Youth* was 'rather a shocker for the bourgeois panegyrists of the playing fields of Eton'. Having survived 'Shore', an Australian version of Fernhurst, Childe was presumably not at all shocked, but he may have reflected on his time at Shore and concluded that his 1915 declaration that 'orthodoxy was impossible' applied to his sexuality as well as his politics.[16]

* * *

Gordon kept his distance from the Bolshevik supporters among Brisbane's socialists. He was not impressed by 'the absurd optimism' of Norman Freeberg, 'who spouted for an hour last Sunday' about the coming revolution. Perhaps he was glad to be in Maryborough when his comrades organised a meeting to celebrate the first anniversary of the Russian Revolution, and even gladder that he escaped the possibility of injury when it was attacked by returned soldiers. He certainly took no part in the 'red flag' riots. In March 1919 there were three days of street violence against the left, instigated by police and right-wing mobs, encouraged by the conservative daily newspapers, directed by a cabal of military officers and wealthy men, and connived at by Acting Premier Ted Theodore. On the first day, the soldiers attacked a small procession of socialists, industrial militants and pro-Bolshevik Russian exiles marching from Trades Hall to the Domain with red flags (which had been banned in September 1918). That evening a larger mob attacked an open-air meeting of industrial militants and then surged into South Brisbane to lay siege to the hall that served as the headquarters of the Russians, who drove them off with gunfire. On the second day a huge mob of perhaps 7,000 clashed with armed police in South Brisbane before destroying the Russian hall. On the third night the mob rioted in both South Brisbane and the city centre, where they attacked the offices of the *Daily Standard*. At this point their leaders decided that further vigilante violence was not necessary, especially because the police were arresting prominent industrial militants and Russian Bolsheviks and raiding the homes of others, including Jenny Scott Griffiths.[17]

---

16 Alexander Waugh, *Fathers and Sons: The Autobiography of a Family*, London and New York, Penguin Random House, 2008; Childe to Brereton, mid-May 1919, Mitchell Library MSS 281/4, pp. 127–8.
17 Childe to Pearce, 28 October 1918, NAA CMF Intell. Reports, 168/30; Raymond Evans, *The Red Flag Riots: A Study in Intolerance*, St Lucia, Queensland, University of Queensland Press, 1988.

On the day after the first riot, however, the *Daily Standard* published a letter from Childe, and a month later another. Both were occasioned by the riots, yet neither defended the right to fly the red flag. Instead their focus was on the response to the riots by the ruling class and the government. The first letter was published under the heading 'Is it the Black Hundred?' He explained that in Czarist Russia, when the regime was threatened with popular rebellion, the secret police worked through 'a notorious organization' called 'The Black Hundred' to inflame the 'ignorant populace' against the Jews. Similarly, Australia's 'real rulers' – the 'trusts and combines' – faced with 'a stiff opposition' from ex-servicemen, 'bitterly disappointed' at being deceived by promises of reinstatement, were using 'secret agents' and *'agents provocateurs'* to divert this legitimate anger onto Brisbane's Russians, 'refugees who have sought asylum on our free shores'. The second letter, headed 'Treatment of Political Prisoners', appealed to the government to ameliorate the conditions of the 'red flag' prisoners. After the riots, although there were many arrests, only the Russians and members of the IWW were gaoled, 15 of them, now treated 'on the same terms as thieves, drunken brawlers and wife-beaters'. In Britain and New South Wales, however, political prisoners were separated from common criminals and allowed indulgences in the form of visits, letters, clothes and food. Using his own experience of advocating for war resisters in Britain and of leading the deputation on behalf of Vance Marshall to the Minister for Justice in New South Wales, Childe suggested the arguments that the Home Secretary could use to reform the prisons to achieve the same result in Queensland.[18]

Gordon was moved to write these letters by two of his deepest impulses: to expose the exploitation of difference and to decry the oppression of idealists, in both cases by the combination of governments and business. In the first letter he is shocked by 'the unreasoned hate of the unknown and strange' on the part of the 'pimps' and 'the yellow press' who mislead 'the masses'. In the second, thinking about the war, he rails against the 'pretext that full political and religious toleration exists in Britain'. How could that be when nonconformists are forced into 'passive resistance' and suffragettes, 'inspired with altruistic ideals', have to embrace violence? Both impulses were on display during Gordon's time in Oxford when he was constructing his identity around difference and conscience as he opposed the war and defended those who resisted it. His letters thus are pointing to a continuing personal concern with these markers of his identity. But

---

18   V.G.C. [Vere Gordon Childe], 'Is It The Black Hundred?', *Daily Standard*, 27 March 1919; V. Gordon Childe, 'Treatment of Political Prisoners', *Daily Standard*, 28 April, 1919, p. 4.

in what way was he different? Why was he so insistent that conscience must not be compromised? The Censor in Brisbane, who read Gordon's correspondence forensically, thought that he was simply arrogant, motivated by pacifism and 'unbounded intellectual pride', but also by 'some burning sense of injustice'. With that last comment, the censor came close to the truth about Childe's politics. It was injustice, not inequality, that moved him – the unwillingness of the ruling class to tolerate difference and respect conscience.[19]

Meanwhile, Gordon's financial position was secured when he was given a temporary tutorial classes post at the university. This was the result of Ted Theodore extending his political patronage of Childe. At a conference of the WEA in March, Gordon made quite an impression on the university contingent, particularly Professor Mayo, who proposed to the Department of Tutorial Classes that he be hired to teach a class in economics. The patronage run-around began: money was provided by the Department of Public Instruction (Hardacre again) and earmarked for his course by Witherby, the Acting Director; and at the crucial University Senate meeting, Theodore, who had been lobbied by Gordon, attended, and the Senators 'accepted my name like lambs'. According to Gordon, wherever Theodore went his presence was awesome. At the previous meeting, when the Senators were 'plotting vengeance' against Witherby for a public lecture in which he compared the red flag to the crucifix, Theodore unexpectedly turned up and 'terrified them into sense and silence'.[20]

The Senate and the professoriate, however, were not finished with Childe. They kept secret that there was a vacancy for a lectureship in classics until the very last moment. The professors had already decided whom they wanted to appoint by the time Gordon heard about the position and hurriedly applied. The decision of the University Senate was predictable: to appoint a less qualified ex-soldier on the grounds that as Childe had no record of military service his 'fitness personally for dealing with university classes' was 'open to grave doubt'. This travesty of academic reasoning was written by Professor of Classics J.L. Michie, after whom the Arts building in the university is named.[21]

---

19   Censor's comment on Childe to Russell Pearce, 28 October 1918, 168/30.
20   Childe to Brereton, mid-May 1919, Brereton papers, Mitchell Library MSS 281/4/127-8; Joint Committee for Tutorial Classes, Minutes 1 May 1919, and Correspondence, Reports etc, Minutes of Senate 16 May 1919, University of Queensland Archives.
21   Correspondence and Reports, Senate Meeting, 12 September 1919, 'Temporary Lectureship in Classics', University of Queensland Archives; *Daily Standard*, 19 September 1919; Evans, 'Social Passion', pp. 24–5.

Within a week of learning of his failure to get the job, Gordon had left Queensland for Sydney, so he probably indicated his acceptance of his next position, as NSW Labor leader John Storey's private secretary, before learning of the Senate's decision. Obviously, he wanted the political job more than the academic job. Jack Lindsay recalled that Gordon 'never gave the least impression of a wish to return to the archaeological world' in 1919, a return that the lectureship would have facilitated, so we may assume that his application was only half-hearted. In fact, he took the opportunity to lambast his academic enemies. On 19 September the *Daily Standard* published an unsigned item headed 'University Bias – A Staff Appointment – Brilliant Scholar Turned Down – Crime of Being a Laborite – The Case of Mr. V.G. Childe'. The details of the application process, and of Childe's publication in the *Journal of Hellenic Studies*, could only have been provided by him, and the article finished with Gordon's customary acerbic dash. The University of Queensland needed to be reorganised to make it a genuine democratic body, because at present it was 'a dispenser of shoddy intellectual wares and an advocate of reactionary notions'.[22]

Before he left Queensland, however, he made another sustained intervention into working-class politics. In January 1919 he had published two long articles in the *Daily Standard* on labour ideals and strategies. These were tweaked and reprinted in Sydney's *Labor News* in February. A few weeks later he wrote to the *Daily Standard*, under the heading 'Some Questions for a Politician', a heading that hinted at his intent. Having begun his time in Queensland favouring political action, he was now redressing the balance by advocating the 'Newer Unionism', or what Cole called the Greater Unionism. This change was his response to the formation of the One Big Union. What should be the relationship between this organised expression of the industrialist impulse and Labor's parliamentarist politics? It was a question that now preoccupied labour intellectuals. The Queensland WEA, fearing it would be outflanked by the left, announced a series of lectures on workers' control in late August, and, at a subsequent meeting of the Central Council, Childe agreed to do two of them. But before we consider these writings by Childe we turn to his developing views about the role of intellectuals in the labour movement.[23]

---

22 *Daily Standard*, 19 September 1919; Jack Lindsay to Sally Green, date unclear but 1976, Jack Lindsay papers, Australian National Library, MS 7168, box 18.

23 Minutes of the WEA Central Council, 21 August 1919 (Childe agrees to give two lectures), OM 64-13, John Oxley Library, Brisbane.

Chapter 9

LABOUR'S MEDIATING INTELLECTUALS

On page one of *How Labour Governs* Childe declared that the labour movement in Australia 'takes on its specific character only from the date of its entry into the political arena'. That was in 1890. Twenty years later, when Labor parties began to form governments with parliamentary majorities, Childe chose this breakthrough as the starting point for his 'connected account' of how political and industrial labour would use state power to end 'the exploitation and enslavement' of the workers. Ten years later, at a moment of stasis in the class struggle, after splits, betrayal and misdirected militancy in the labour movement, he began to write this story. As he wrote, he had those three significant moments in mind, revealing his interest in the formation and transformation of insurgent social forces over a longish span. And these moments are also pointers to the analytical cast of his thinking about class: exploitation and emancipation; industrial and political wings; state power and capitalist power; combative practices from below but stubborn structures above; organisational discipline and unruly revolt.[1]

During these three decades, workers went to work, as of course they had to, and the educators and agitators, the labour intellectuals who were emerging organically from the working class, interpreted their class situation differently, avoiding the grand theoretical terms favoured by Childe. Whereas Childe, a traditional, trained intellectual, drew on the ideas of radical liberalism and socialism developed by thinkers in bourgeois public life, labour intellectuals focused on the defining experience of the working class, wage labour, and created a knowledge specific to the working class and a separate labour public. The two went hand in hand. To develop their attack on ruling-class ideology they needed a labour press, meeting halls, printeries, and a culture of labour

---

1   *How Labour Governs*, 1st edn, p. 1; Childe to Brereton, 21 December 1918, Brereton papers, Mitchell Library MSS 281 vol. 4, pp. 125–6.

ideas, trees of knowledge, festivities and rituals. To justify the energy required to set up this alternative public they had to be confident that their alternative labour ideology expressed a kind of knowledge that reflected specific working-class concerns, and therefore no other class, no well-meaning middle-class clergyman or politician, could be trusted to express it properly.[2]

The sphere of knowledge created by organic labour intellectuals drew on working-class experience in two big ways. First, it pointed to the constricting reality of living in a working-class situation, with limited choice, unequal chances and poor amenities. This emphasis on the real experience of wage-workers was a response to the unrelenting presentation in the capitalist press and by evangelicals in the Protestant churches of the abstractions of liberal individualism. The liberal story went like this: Why were workers demanding special rights when all were equal before God and the law? And could they not see that 'combination' – forming unions – was an interference with freedom of contract? What more could individuals want than having political rights as citizens of a constitutional government – rights that workers too would get when they were ready for it? The movement's leaders – organic labour intellectuals – saw this as unbelievable guff and responded by demanding practical policies to alter their members' actual situation. Working-class experience produced knowledge that was defiantly practical.

Second, labour intellectuals developed a specific political theory out of the experience of wage labour, a theory drawing attention to the unjust and oppressive aspects of that experience and the role of their work in creating the objects and techniques that society valued. This working-class inflected labour theory of value goes back many centuries. It appeared in the writings of the Ricardian socialists, the radical wing of political economy during the Industrial Revolution. It was inscribed on nineteenth century trade union banners as 'a fair day's work for a fair day's pay'. It has been credited as the underlying principle of labourism as well as a source for revolutionary politics in the form of the Marxist theory of surplus value.[3]

---

2   Irving and Scalmer, 'Labour Intellectuals in Australia: Modes, Traditions, Generations, Transformations', pp. 1–26.

3   Sean Scalmer, 'Being Practical in Early and Contemporary Labor Politics: A Labourist Critique', *Australian Journal of Politics and History*, vol. 43, no. 3, November 1997, pp. 301–11; Noel Thompson, *The People's Science: Popular Political Economy of Exploitation and Crisis, 1816–1834*, Cambridge, Cambridge University Press, 2002; Marc Mulholland, '"Its Patrimony, its Unique Wealth!" Labour-Power, Working-Class Consciousness and Crises: An Outline Consideration', www.academia.edu/356751/Its_Patrimony_its_Unique_Wealth_Labour-Power_Working_Class_Consciousness_and_Crises_An_Outline_Consideration, accessed 13 March 2018.

Childe was well aware of the labour public, writing for its press, speaking in its halls, socialising with its organic intellectuals, and lobbying, or working for, its leaders. Naturally he was familiar with the kind of knowledge, drawn from working-class experience, produced in the labour public, in particular the oppressive character of 'wagery' which he attacked in his 1919 *Daily Standard* articles. Yet his class background and training inevitably distanced him from that experience.

* * *

Childe and Norman Freeberg were born just a few weeks apart, they were both labour intellectuals, but in terms of class background they were very different. Freeberg's father, a Danish seaman who had jumped ship in Ballina in 1870, was an industrial militant on the wharves and a member of the Socialist Labour Party. His son Norman grew up in working-class Woolloomooloo, left school at age 12, and became a journalist. He described his self-education as:

> a ravenous consumption of everything political I could get my hands on, from muddle-headed Utopian literature to material and papers from the two IWW's ... I read every available pamphlet and book dealing with the working-class movement ... All the socialist classics, all the old bourgeois economists and philosophers ... everything of Marx and Engels that was translated, including the first volume of *Capital*.

In 1913, having added six years to his age, he was Financial Editor for the *Daily Standard*, the union-owned newspaper established after the defeat of a general strike in 1912. While in Brisbane he also worked on *The Worker* and, under a pseudonym, for *Knowledge and Unity*, the pro-Bolshevik paper of the Russian Association. He was already rehearsing, in the words of his biographer Marilla North, his 'double identity', his 'essential elusiveness' and 'carapace of ambiguity'. His career dipped in and out of working with the labour press — in the 1940s the Communist Party appointed him to manage its vast publishing operation — in between times working for the capitalist press. By this time, he had changed his name to Freehill. From the late 1940s he was the partner of the left-wing novelist Dymphna Cusack.[4]

---

4   This is Freehill's description of his role in CPA publishing; see Marilla North, 'Tinker, Tailor, Soldier, Sailor ... Who Was Norman Randolph Freehill?', *Overland*, issue 161, Summer 2000, pp. 36–42. Freeberg changed his name to Freehill in 1927.

In 1919, the year that Childe met Freeberg, he was working on the Brisbane *Worker*, and selling his self-published 138-page pamphlet *Socialism: What Is It? Word Pictures of Socialism in an Australian Frame*, a folksy guide on how to answer the common objections to socialism. Far more intellectually substantial was his 1919 paper, 'The University and Working-Class Education', which he wrote for discussion in the Queensland branch of the WEA, whose revolutionary socialists were aiming to sever the connection between the WEA and the university. Freeberg's arguments drew on developments in England, where socialist students at the trade-union supported Ruskin College in Oxford had seceded to form a labour college in London in order to promote class-struggle-oriented learning. But there were certain emphases in his paper that reflected the particular kind of hegemonic situation existing in Queensland, which was experiencing a high degree of militant working-class mobilisation and ruling-class desperation, overseen by a Labor government that, as Childe said, gave way to the militants while seeming, even to the Tories, not to.[5]

There was, firstly, a very clear assertion that bourgeois and proletarian culture were different. This situation arose as an expression of the different kinds of knowledge produced in class society – the experience-based practicality of working-class knowledge versus the abstraction and deceptive intent of bourgeois knowledge:

> Just as we can no longer accept the capitalist conceptions of political democracy so too must we discard the bourgeois culture which has grown out of the same social conditions which produce the gigantic sham and hypocrisy called by one class freedom but known to those of the other as wage slavery.

Secondly, he argued that the main thrust of working-class education was not simply to provide courses on industrial history and trade union organisation but to build a proletarian culture and mental attitude among the people. To this end courses on art, morality and religion should be taught in a way that

---

5   Norman R. Freeberg, *Socialism: What Is It? Word Pictures in an Australian Frame*, Brisbane, printed by *The Worker* newspaper, 1919. Norman R. Freeberg, 'Basis for Discussion: The University and Working Class Education', *Daily Standard*, 14 March 1919; P.F. Armstrong, 'The Long Search for the Working Class: Socialism and the Education of Adults 1850–1930', in T. Lovett, *Radical Approaches to Adult Education: A Reader*, London and New York, Routledge, 1988, pp. 35–58; Colin Waugh, *'Plebs': The Lost Legacy of Independent Working Class Education*, Wembley, UK, Post16 Educator, 2009; Jonathan Ree, *Proletarian Philosopher: Problems in Socialist Culture in Britain, 1900–1949*, Oxford, Clarendon Press, 1984; Childe to Brereton, 23 December 1918, Mitchell Library MSS 281, vol. 4, pp. 125–6.

showed their connection to the politics and economics of 'Scientific Socialism'. Needless to say, the bourgeois university failed in this regard. Thirdly, he said working-class education should be distinct from the propaganda produced by 'the rough and ready' needs of the class struggle. To develop working-class knowledge required 'systematic study', undertaken by the class's 'latent intellectuals', with the aim of producing 'an intelligence staff' for the proletariat.

Freeberg was in effect writing a manifesto for an independent working-class educational institution staffed by organic intellectuals of the working class. At the end of his paper he pointed to the recently formed Victorian Labour College as an example of what might be possible in Brisbane, and to the malign influence on the WEA of Meredith Atkinson as an example of why it had to be done.[6]

From a working-class background in England (his father was a blacksmith), Meredith Atkinson had won scholarships that took him eventually to Keble College, Oxford, where English philosophical idealism joined hands with the Anglican High Church tradition. After graduation he worked as a university extension lecturer in Durham, becoming a disciple of Albert Mansbridge, the founder of the WEA. When the University of Sydney decided to implement Mansbridge's scheme for adult education, Mansbridge recommended Atkinson for the position of Organiser of Tutorial Classes. In March 1914, Atkinson arrived in Sydney, where Childe, who was one of the first members of the NSW branch of the WEA, would have met him.[7]

But this was before Childe went to Oxford and discovered that orthodoxy was impossible for him. Meanwhile, in Sydney Atkinson was revealing how deeply orthodox he was. The war broke out soon after he arrived, and he supported it, as did most people in Australia. It was also orthodox to support conscription, although in his case, as a leader in the WEA, many of whose affiliates were against it, it would have been politic to keep his mouth shut. When he publicly associated himself with the campaign for conscription, as Secretary of the Universal Service League in 1915, there was consternation among union activists and labour intellectuals. The Sydney Labour Council withdrew its support from the WEA, and unions began disaffiliating, 17 of them in 1916. As the conscription crisis developed, the disruption of the union–WEA link spread to other states, and Atkinson, because of his

---

6   *Daily Standard*, 14 March 1919.
7   Helen Bourke, 'Worker Education and Social Inquiry in Australia 1913–1929', PhD Thesis, University of Adelaide, 1981, Ch. 3, 'Meredith Atkinson: Sociology in Australia'; Warren Osmond, 'Atkinson, Meredith (1883–1929)', *Australian Dictionary of Biography*, Vol. 7, 1979, pp. 121–2.

prominence in adult education and pro-war movements, was often blamed. How could he have been so indifferent to the political contests in the labour movement, the strength of the left, and the dynamics of class in Australia?[8]

The answer is that Atkinson's orthodoxy was more deeply rooted: philosophically he was a liberal who hated the idea of class struggle and could not believe that it was real. This was clear before the conscription crisis, as was his role in mobilising a group of like-minded liberal intellectuals to attack Australia's proletarian democracy and working-class militancy. In June 1915, under the auspices of the WEA, he organised a conference in Sydney on trade unionism, and later edited the published volume. Every paper was directed towards class collaboration. Atkinson's paper pushed the idea of unions cooperating with management through co-partnerships and profit-sharing, while the Victorian 'new liberal', Frederic Eggleston's twisted the ideal of cooperation, which had a long socialist and democratic history, currently embodied in a flourishing cooperative movement, into a managerialist day-dream in which 'efficiency in control should *alone* be considered. The idea that democracy is incompatible with leadership and authority or submission to expert control should be discarded'. I have italicised the key word to highlight his elitism, and the way it hid behind the neutral, technical idea of efficiency.

Apart from being elitist, the fetish for efficiency was also profitable, as Freeberg pointed out in his 1919 paper. The WEA intellectuals were not political economists, however; their ideological role was to undermine the idea of proletarian democracy. In Atkinson's contribution we see him explaining the absence of 'national efficiency' by pointing to the difficulty of ruling-class governance caused by the rising political power of the working class: 'The rapid growth of democratic institutions has certainly caused some loss of national effectiveness, chiefly by dissipation of control and government among the mass'. In Australia the problem was worse because of the ease of labour's conquest of the parliamentary state. Consequently, 'we must avoid the peril of mistaking advanced social legislation for advanced social efficiency.'

Efficiency was a buzzword at the time, used by liberal intellectuals working to move the offensive against popular democracy out of the sphere of electoral and parliamentary politics and into what they would later call 'industrial

---

8   Bourke, 'Worker Education and Social Inquiry', p. 83; Tim Rowse, *Australian Liberalism and National Character*, Malmsbury, Vic, Kibble Books, 1978, p. 60; Michael Roe, 'Robert Francis Irvine' in M. Roe, *Nine Australian Progressives: Vitalism in Bourgeois Social Thought, 1890–1960*, Brisbane, University of Queensland Press, 1984; Raymond Markey, *In Case of Oppression: The Life and Times of the Labor Council of New South Wales*, Sydney, Pluto Press, 1994, p. 148.

relations'. This book, *Trade Unionism in Australia*, which contains, on average, an endorsement of the need for efficiency every three pages, is not really what the title suggests – a survey of trade unionism by an organisation sympathetic to its history and class character. Instead, it is about the 'failure' of trade unionism to embrace the liberal ideal of worker–management partnership. More significantly it was an argument to shore-up the idea of rule from above, at work and in society at large.[9]

Before long the attack represented by the 1915 book on trade unionism had developed into a full-scale assault on proletarian democracy, mostly via the WEA, which set up a book series, but also with the involvement of the Anglican Church. R.F. Irvine, the Professor of Economics at the University of Sydney, edited *Organisation and National Efficiency* (1915). His colleague, G.V. Portus, who was Director of Tutorial Classes, wrote *Marx and Modern Thought* (1921). From Queensland, where Elton Mayo was Professor of Philosophy, came his *Democracy and Freedom* in 1919. Atkinson, publishing three more volumes, was unstoppable: *Capital and Labour: Co-operation or Class War* (1918); *The New Social Order: A Study of Post-War Reconstruction* (1919); and the edited volume, *Australia: Economic and Political Studies* (1920). And there were many lectures and conferences. Given the context of revolution and counter-revolution internationally, this outpouring of liberal ideology was very significant, and it has therefore attracted the attention of scholars. But reading their studies is like sitting on a see-saw without being able to see who is balancing you on the other end. In keeping with the books that they are discussing, these scholarly studies are vague on one crucial matter: who did the liberals think they were countering? It is as if Australia had no socialist intellectual life, no labour press, no Childe – just impersonal anti-liberal forces called 'Labor' or 'trade unionism'. No wonder Childe had such an animus against Atkinson.[10]

---

9   Meredith Atkinson (ed.), *Trade Unionism in Australia*, Sydney, Burrows and Company, 1915, pp. 84–5 (Eggleston), 12 (Atkinson); Rowse, *Australian Liberalism and National Character*, pp. 61–73 on 'efficiency'.

10   R.F. Irvine, *Organisation and National Efficiency*, Melbourne, Victorian Railways Printing Branch, 1915; G.V. Portus, *Marx and Modern Thought*, Sydney, WEA, 1921; M. Atkinson, *Capital and Labour: Co-operation or Class War*, Melbourne, Anglican Diocese of Melbourne, 1918; ditto, *The New Social Order: A Study of Post-War Reconstruction*, Sydney, Burroughs and Co., 1919; ditto (ed.), *Australia: Economic and Political Studies*, London, Macmillan, 1920; E. Mayo, *Democracy and Freedom: An Essay on Social Logic*, Melbourne, Macmillan and WEA, 1920; on the scholarly studies, see the works by Rowse, and Bourke, and Roe, cited in footnote 215; and Lucy Taksa, *Workers' Education* [sic] *Association and the Pursuit of National Efficiency in Australia between 1913 and 1923*, School of Industrial Relations and Organisational Behaviour, University of New South Wales, Sydney, Working Paper 111, March 1997.

* * *

According to R.S. Ross in 1918, 'Some Socialists seem to think that nothing good can come out of Australia in the way of writing, and so they import books and pamphlets wholesale. We need not disparage the imported matter in order to say a necessary word for the domestic product ... The traditional and strange notion that Australian writers are not equal to the treatment of socio-economic questions and problems is Stuff and Nonsense.' Ross was the editor of the *Socialist*, the weekly journal of the Victorian Socialist Party, and he wrote this defence of Australia's socialist intellectual life in an introduction to a short book by 'Radix' on the labour theory of value. Most of the 'domestic product' was not as erudite as the book by 'Radix' – whose name was A.E. Houston. Much of it was designed to inspire and mobilise, for example the books by Ernie Lane and Ernie Judd on the One Big Union (OBU). On the other hand, Childe and his friend Theodore Witherby, as well as J.H. Wood who wrote under the pen-name of John O'Rockie, were seriously trying to introduce Australian readers to the latest socialist thinking from abroad, and to adapt it to Australian conditions.[11]

While teaching his adult education students in Brisbane, and writing *How Labour Governs*, Childe was surrounded by this socialist intellectual life. In fact, he knew many of those contributing to it. He met Henry Boote, Vance Marshall and Ernie Judd in Sydney after returning from Oxford. In Brisbane he knew Freeberg, Ernie Lane, and Witherby. He would have known about 'John O'Rockie', who lived in Rockhampton, because his writings appeared the *Daily Standard*. He would certainly have read Bob Ross's book welcoming the Bolshevik Revolution, and perhaps Frank Anstey's. In Brisbane, he had collections of the most important labour newspapers to consult, both union-controlled, such as Brisbane's *Worker* and *Daily Standard*, and Sydney's *Australian Worker*, as well as those associated with political tendencies such as *Socialist* from Melbourne, and *Labor News*, *Social Democrat* and *Direct Action* from Sydney. This intellectual milieu was supportive, too. Witherby allowed him to use his excellent library; a fellow member of the Socialist League, Jennie Scott Griffith, was the Brisbane agent for *The Socialist*; and my guess is that Childe also was able to access the library of labour papers and conference documents in the office of the *Daily Standard*.[12]

---

11   'Radix', *Ability and Labour*, Melbourne, Ross's Book Service, 1918, p. 3 for Ross's introduction.
12   Childe to Stephensen, 29 December 1918, Mitchell Library MSS 1284, Y2150; R.S. Ross to Jennie Scott Griffiths, 17 May 1918, AA CRS CP 409/1Bundle 1 (QF 1081) re copies of *Socialist* for Brisbane.

It has to be remembered that this was a combative intellectual life. The socialist writers knew they were opposing dangerous elements of a powerful ideology: the collaborationist undertow of the national efficiency idea; the servility entailed in the statism of both the welfare schemes of new liberalism and the state enterprises of labourism; and the denial of popular self-government in liberal parliamentarism. Their writings were full of attacks on arbitration, 'wagery', and political betrayal. Atkinson was a particular bête noir. Both Frederick Sinclaire, the Christian socialist editor of *Fellowship* and President of the Victorian Labor College, and Le Gay Brereton were part of Childe's anti-Atkinson network. Reflecting on his lecturing to his tutorial class on economics, Childe chortled about the way he was able to use the study of Marx's *Capital* to refute Atkinson. And in the first edition of *How Labour Governs* he provided a bibliographical note, omitted from the second edition, to the effect that Atkinson's writing on Australia was biased and unreliable. This was the intellectually contentious environment in which Childe wrote, and for all his calculated air of ironic detachment he was not unaffected by it. In an appendix I have provided an additional index to the book, listing the pages on which all the usual terms of Marxist class analysis and socialist rhetoric appear. Why were they (mostly) omitted from the index as printed? Childe prepared the index – as is plain from its inclusion of his mordant inventions, such as 'Rats. *See* Treachery' – so we can only assume he fell in with the publisher's desire to use the book to beat the British Labour Party over the head with Australian examples rather than as a Marxist analysis of parliamentarism in a particular situation.[13]

* * *

Not long after Childe returned from Maryborough, Freeberg nominated him for co-option onto the Council of the Queensland WEA. Childe, as we have seen, had been involved with the WEA in Sydney in 1914, and

---

13 D. R. Walker, 'Sinclaire, Frederick (1881–1954)', *Australian Dictionary of Biography*, vol. 11, 1988, pp. 615–6; David Walker, *Dream and Disillusion: A Search for Australian Cultural Identity*, Canberra, ANU Press, 1976, Ch. 5; F. Sinclaire, 'Labor Colleges', *Daily Standard*, 20 February 1919, p. 3; Childe to Sinclaire, 20 August 1918, NAA CMF Intell. Files, MF 1628, 169/35-42; Childe to Brereton, 23 December 1918, Mitchell Library MSS 281, vol. 4, 125–6; Childe to Brereton, mid-May 1919, ditto, 127–8; see Appendix at end of this chapter, 'Subjects omitted from Childe's Index'.

again in 1918, but he also supported independent working-class education. In 1924 he published four book reviews in *The Plebs*, the magazine of the Plebs League, a British movement of labour colleges in opposition to the WEA. But his sympathies were clear much earlier. Indeed, when the Sydney University Senate rejected him for the tutorial classes job, he planned to set up a Labor College similar to the Central Labour College in London. He wrote to Frederick Sinclaire for urgent information about it, and he contemplated approaching the AWU and the miners' union for the cash to run it. In Brisbane, Freeberg and his socialist comrades were aiming at the same end, but going about it in a different way, by taking over the WEA and severing its connection to the university. If they were successful, they would have a ready-made organisation to re-purpose as a union-supported labour college. At a Council meeting in February Childe supported the proposal. At the conference Freeberg's proposal was defeated 21 to 39. Within a few weeks the socialists had set up the Workers' School of Social Science in opposition to the WEA. Childe did not participate. As we saw in Chapter 3, he took up a post, created especially for him, in the university's Tutorial Classes department teaching economics.[14]

Childe made a choice, but what kind of choice? The WEA was not monolithic. In Sydney, Brereton's support was qualified by his suspicion of university control. In Brisbane, the Acting Director of Tutorial Classes, Witherby, who wanted to maintain the university connection, was in trouble with the university for his sympathetic account of Bolshevism and his opposition to the prosecution of radicals for flying the red flag. He was also very critical of Atkinson's 1920 book, as was Adelaide's WEA face, Herbert Heaton. In Oxford, Rajani Palme Dutt was 'sabotaging' the WEA's class conciliation line by lecturing to its classes on the Marxist approach to the Russian Revolution. These examples indicate the existence of a tradition of trained, left-wing intellectuals working within the WEA, a tradition missed by writers focusing on its leadership, its official statements, its liberal celebrities and its sponsorship by the state. It was a tradition particularly strong in moments of working-class militancy. In relation to Australia in the 1920s and 30s, I think of Esmonde Higgins, Lloyd Ross, Norman Richmond, Percy Stephensen, Ken Dallas, Gordon Crane, and Fred Paterson – all of whom were influenced by communism. Possibly this tradition was stronger in Australia than in Britain, but, apropos Britain, recent scholarship has

---

14   Childe to Sinclaire, 20 August 1918, NAA CMF Intell. Reports AA 169/35-42; *Daily Standard*, 28 March 1919.

suggested that progressive intellectuals working in 'liberal' adult education in the early twentieth century were not aiming to 'incorporate' the working class into bourgeois society, and, what's more, they weren't able to.[15]

In a letter Childe explained his decision to side with the Queensland WEA in a mixture of self-deprecation and cheekiness, a style he liked to adopt in his private correspondence: 'They have started here a Workers School of Social Science. I've naturally thrown in my lot with [the] body that pays me, for as Marx remarks things without value like conscience and honor under capitalism take on the form of commodities and have an (irrational) price.' Then more seriously he continued: 'The Workers' School of Social Science will not get on very far owing to the incompetence of its staff and more to the inertness of the Australian workers'. It was a put-down, and in the short term he was wrong. The WSSS lasted five years, published a monthly journal and employed a secretary, J.B. Miles, who would go on to become a long-time secretary of the Communist Party. As for the inertness of the workers, this dismissive epithet was very common on the left at the time, reflecting the stalling after the war of industrial syndicalism. Childe used the term publicly, as did Jensen, who had supported the rebellious workers against the Administrator in Darwin, and Jock Garden, the leader of Sydney's 'Trades Hall Reds'. It was possible therefore to believe, as they did, in both the militant, even revolutionary, potential of the Australian working class, and the passivity induced by parliamentarist 'spoon-feeding' and bureaucratic unionism – an apparent conflict of beliefs, but actually a reflection of the hegemonic limits to mobilisation in their situation.[16]

---

15   Brereton to Hall, 0/4/1918, University of Sydney Archives, M235; University of Queensland, Correspondence, Reports etc, re Senate meeting, 10 October 1919, p. 26; *Daily Mail*, 11 April 1919, p. 6, and 28 April 1919, p. 5; Bourke, 'Worker Education and Social Inquiry in Australia 1913–1929', p. 86; Jones to Hall 25/6/1919, Childe's MI5 file; on Norman Richmond: https://teara.govt.nz/en/biographies/4r15/richmond-norman-macdonald; Michael Roe, 'Dallas, Kenneth McKenzie (Ken) (1902–1988)', *Australian Dictionary of Biography*, Vol. 17, 2007, pp. 294–5; Michael Roe, 'Higgins, Esmonde Macdonald (1897–1960)', *Australian Dictionary of Biography*, Vol. 14, 1996, pp. 449–50; Michael Easson, 'Ross, Lloyd Robert Maxwell (1901–1987)', *Australian Dictionary of Biography*, Vol. 18, 2012, pp. 369–70; Terry Irving, 'Rediscovering Radical History', http://asslh.org.au/hummer/vol-6-no-2/radica/; Ross Fitzgerald, *Fred Paterson, The People's Champion*, Brisbane, University of Queensland Press, 1997, pp. 28–33; Craig Munro, 'Stephensen, Percy Reginald (1901–1965)', *Australian Dictionary of Biography*, Vol. 12, 1990, pp. 70–1; Lawrence Goldman, 'Intellectuals and the English Working Class, 1870–1945: The Case of Adult Education', *History of Education*, vol. 29, no. 4, 2000, pp. 281–300.
16   Childe to Brereton, mid-May 1919, Mitchell Library MSS 281/4, pp. 127–8; R. Coates, 'Job Control in Theory and Practice – by "Turbot Street"', *Australian Left Review*, May 1972, pp. 27–30; Childe, 'The Newer Unionism and State Socialism',

Even before Freeberg's proposal was voted down at the WEA conference in March 1919, the leading protagonists knew that the ultimate aim of Freeberg and his comrades was to set up a Labor College. Witherby and Childe were in favour of this. As Witherby wrote to the WEA Secretary, he supported efforts to set up such a college, envisaging that the two arms of worker education would operate side by side. The college would be propagandist, while the WEA would continue to have a 'colder and more critical attitude', strengthening the workers' 'powers of thinking and make them able to sift the true from the false'. Witherby also believed that it was the duty of the workers in the WEA to try to reform the university, 'even to revolutionize it'. So, at the conference, Childe defended both forms of working-class education: university tutorial classes and a labour college, both of them necessary because the present pro-worker Labor government might be defeated in the future. In his speech, he expressly distinguished the WEA in Queensland from its sister branches in other states. And he was caustic in his denunciation of Australia's universities – producers of 'snobs, scabs and censors' – singling out for particular criticism the University of Sydney, where a loyalty battalion had taken the place of strikers. But Queensland again was different, for its university employed men of the calibre of Witherby. At the end of his speech the audience applauded. Among them was Professor Elton Mayo, who was so impressed that he supported Childe for the tutorial classes position.[17]

Childe took the post because he needed a job – it paid 50 shillings a class instead of the 10 shillings a day he received at the State Land Tax office – and because it enabled him to refute Atkinson in his lectures. To the Queensland militants he was not a vacillating liberal but a teacher who took a 'proletarian outlook' into worker education, according to a pamphlet, *Independent Working-Class Education and the W.E.A.*, issued by the Victorian Labor College. This infiltration of the WEA, made possible by an alliance of organic and trained intellectuals, continued after Witherby and Childe departed the state. From 1920, the pamphlet asserted:

> Keen young enthusiasts from University and Unions alike enrolled under [the WEA] banner. The WEA, probably for the first time in its existence in this or any other country, was providing a thorough-going

---

Daily Standard, 4 January 1919, p. 4; H.I. Jensen (letter), *Australian Worker*, 14 August 1919; Garden in Labor Council Annual Report, reported *Daily Telegraph*, 21 January 1921.

17   Witherby to J.B Roberts [WEA secretary], 1 March 1919, NAA CMF Intell. Reports 167/85-91; *Daily Standard*, 25 March 1919.

exposition of working-class History and Economics, and, what is more, influencing its students to study further along the same sound lines. Naturally, opinions were divided as to the fundamental unsoundness of the WEA, with its liberal constitution, setting out to be non-party, non-political, its University ties, and its Government subsidy, for signs were not wanting that its activities were being closely watched. To this, the enthusiasts for working-class education replied, 'Take advantage of it while you may. Use it until it ceases to serve the working class, and when it reverts to type, repudiate it.'

In 1926, that happened. One of the most successful of the tutors, a former protégé of Witherby, Gordon Crane, who had set up dozens of classes in Central Queensland, was dropped by the university and the WEA because of his support for striking railway workers. Retaliating, his classes resolved to break with the WEA, and at the beginning of 1927, under Crane's guidance, they formed a Plebs League in Queensland.[18]

* * *

Not until Childe returned to Australia in 1917, and experienced the relationship between intellectuals and workers, did he see it as a subject for reflection. Even then, mixing with students and academics while at St Andrew's, and limiting his political activity to the middle-class peace movement, he did not consider it an issue until the college got rid of him. Still smarting from that slap, he began to think about the attractions of the labour movement. It might be able to provide him with employment as an intellectual, and, if so, it would also serve as a rebuke to his academic tormentors. As we saw in Chapter 7, in June 1918 he wrote to his Oxford mentor Gilbert Murray, projecting a role for himself in Australia's liberal intelligentsia, even as he was being embraced by labour movement institutions, but he was careful not to reveal this to Murray. Instead he made a strong case for the kind of role that he had been moving away from since 1915: that of the liberal intellectual standing apart from class struggle, interpreting rival class movements to each other in the interests of avoiding revolution. Murray, incidentally, was Vice-President of the very-liberal

---

18   Victorian Labor College, *Independent Working-Class Education and the W.E.A.*, copy in University of Melbourne Archives; internal evidence suggests it was issued after 1927, and written by Gordon Crane, who had been at university with Stephensen and Paterson. For Childe as vacillator, see Evans, 'Social Passion', p. 21.

League of Nations Society. Did Childe hanker secretly after the status accorded to liberal intellectuals – despite delighting in labour's growing radicalism? And were not revolution and labour radicalism dangerously imbricated? In a personally unsettling moment, perhaps he was not thinking very clearly. What we can be more certain of is that he was hoping that English liberals would write embarrassing letters to Sydney's professorial jingoes. He had asked this of McGrath and Haverfield, but not of Murray, whose standing may well have persuaded him to take a more tactful approach. His letter opened by stating that Murray might be interested in an account of 'the "freedom of thought" allowed in colonial universities', a juicy bait for any liberal.[19]

In Brisbane, freedom of thought was not the issue – a progressive Labor government in Queensland was its guarantor. Working-class knowledge was safe in its own sphere; the problem was how to persuade bourgeois intellectuals of its validity. This was the import of his speech at the WEA conference in March 1919. It was framed by the idea that the universities and WEA in Britain, and elsewhere in Australia, 'were out of touch with the working-class movement'. Except in Queensland, where the university and the WEA were on a different, and radical, path, as shown by 'the work of the director [Witherby] who was able to freely state the views of the workers to the professional classes'.[20]

Childe made a third reference to the 'workers and intellectuals' relationship, this time in July 1924. He was in England, *How Labour Governs* was out, he was working on *The Dawn of European Civilization*, but he had not forgotten his four years of involvement in Australian politics. In a review in *The Plebs* he shaped up to the class collaborationist views of the proto-fascist, Judge Heydon. He begins: 'Employers of the Cadbury outlook are unusual in Australia and there are no publicists like the Webbs or the Coles to mediate between bourgeois and proletarian thought'.[21]

In each of these three references Childe is thinking of mediation to describe the process needed for the workers–intellectuals relationship, but, in each case, there is a different meaning. In the first case he highlights the possibility of compromise and conciliation between the conflicting movements of the capitalists and the working class. In the second, the emphasis is on communication, as he commends Witherby's capacity, because of his position in the university, to explain proletarian thought to the intellectuals – trained or in-training – of the ruling class. In the third case, Childe implies a role for trained intellectuals

---

19   Childe to Murray, 8 June 1918, shelfmark 376, ff. 44–6.
20   *Daily Standard*, 25 March 1919.
21   Childe, 'A Colonial Product', *The Plebs*, vol. 16, no. 7, July 1924, p. 288.

who operated in labour movement institutions (as the Webbs and the Coles did) *to clarify by mediating* the differences between bourgeois and proletarian thought. Each of them is an expression of the representational mode of labour intellectual work, in which labour intellectuals work for balance through mediating between forces in the movement and between the movement and the state. Together, however, these instances of his thinking about workers and intellectuals express flux and development. Mediation, so central to that representational mode, in Childe's thought becomes increasingly an active intervention in the interests of the proletariat as he becomes more exposed over time to the class struggle.[22]

Childe's socialist politics, like those of Gramsci, were formed far apart from the dominant mechanical Marxism of the Second International. In Chapter 10 we will look more closely at the influence on him of Cole's pluralism and democratic romanticism and of the English tradition of idealist philosophy. Those influences had inoculated him against the idea that the overthrow of capitalism was determined mechanically by laws of history. Instead, when in conjunction with Dutt he resumed his study of Marxism, he was drawn to the Italian Hegelians, Benedetto Croce and Giovanni Gentile, and he retained their interest in historical and scientific knowledge as a tool for practical knowledge for the rest of his life. By the time he reached Brisbane his view was that Marxism was a theory of working-class agency, not of universal laws; it was a theory of economic domination and subordination, approached and embraced by the subordinate class, but also a theory of the class's practice as it developed its ways of resistance to domination. Socialism was not inevitable; it had to be fought for by intelligence, alliance and contestation. That is why he taught Marx's *Capital* to his WEA/Tutorial Classes students in the light of Croce's Hegelian idealism.[23]

Brisbane provided Childe with a setting in which he could put into effect his ideas about the role of the labour intellectual, not just the tasks they would perform but their place in the process of creating working-class knowledge. His lectures, his articles in the labour press, and his WEA/tutorial classes on economics were not simply meant to bring ideas to the 'inert' masses but to agitate those that could be activated. They were deliberate interventions in the class struggle. In this sense he had struck out on a different course to

---

22   Irving and Scalmer, 'Labour Intellectuals in Australia: Modes, Traditions, Generations, Transformations', pp. 4–7.

23   See Ch. 10; Childe, 'Prehistory and Marxism', *Antiquity*, 1979, vol. 53, issue 208, pp. 93–5. This was written in 1949 and sent to *The Cambridge Journal*, whose editor, Grahame Clark, rejected it.

that of his Oxford exemplar G.D.H. Cole, whose 1913 book *The World of Labour* envisaged voluntary adult education of the WEA kind as necessary to produce 'sympathetic leaders' of the working class. This was too passive and too elitist for Childe. He and Cole were agreed that the object of working-class education was workers governing themselves, but Childe was looking for the practical ways to get there, by means of the workers' own actions, in a practice theorised by their own intellectuals.[24]

Appendix:
Political Terms in *How Labour Governs*

(Page numbers refer to the 1923 edition)

Bolshevism, 160
Bourgeois democracy, 2, 160–61, 197
Bureaucracy, 198–9, 204, 207
Class consciousness, 70, 133, 147, 152, 157, 159
Class war/struggle/conflict, 2–3, 116, 152–3, 157, 192
Dictatorship of the proletariat, 65, 160
Economic determinism, 155, 156
Fabianism, 172
Leadership, 21
Machine politics, 152
Marxism, 50, 130, 149
Masses, the, 160
Middle class, 74, 85, 117, 160
Nationalisation, 156
Oligarchy, 198
Palliatives, 116,119
Proletariat, 147, 149, 157
Revisionism, 198
Revolution, 129, 157, 159, 166, 192
'Right to work', 41
Social democracy, 73, 74
Socialisation, 129
Solidarity, 149, 150
Sovietism, 208
State, the, 42, 74, 156
State capitalism, 156–7
Syndicalism, 119
Unskilled workers, 150
Violence, 159

---

24   Cole, *The World of Labour*, pp. 16–18, 384, 425.

Chapter 10

THE WORLD OF LABOUR

In March 1919, the Brisbane labour paper, the *Daily Standard*, announced a lecture at the Trades Hall by Mr V.G. Childe on guild socialism, adding that 'he is a close associate of Mr G.D.H. Cole'. In Childe's writings traces of this implied intellectual dependence are not hard to find. *How Labour Governs* and his correspondence contain echoes of Cole's ideas – even phrases – as do many of his articles in the labour press, and, as we shall see in Chapter 11, Childe publicly asserted that 'the ultimate outcome' of the class struggle 'must be on the lines of Guild Socialism'. But Australia was not Britain; guild socialism in the Australian context might mean something different than in Britain. Here I examine Cole's *The World of Labour: A Discussion of the Present and Future of Trade Unionism* (1913), focusing on aspects of the argument that Childe might have noted as he thought about labour's situation in Australia. How might a 'study of workers' representation in Australia' contribute to the triumph of socialism in a world of labour where Australia was such a small player? In March 1919, Childe thought he knew. Although already engaged on the book that would become *How Labour Governs*, he had started another writing project, modelled on Cole's book, but on a smaller scale. At the same time, enthused by the opportunities presented to working-class politics by the formation of the One Big Union, he intervened in the internal affairs of Labor in two states by lobbying and publishing. Together, these theoretical and the practical forays pushed him to a distinctive conclusion: when the workers took to building socialism in Australia, they would do so on guild lines, but 'not necessarily by the syndicalist methods advocated under English bureaucracy'.[1]

* * *

---

[1] *Daily Standard*, 29 March 1919, p. 2; Childe, 'Some Questions for a Politician', *Daily Standard*, 7 March 1919; Cole, *The World of Labour*.

First published in 1913, *The World of Labour* was on sale in Sydney soon after, but it was Childe's experience of politics in Oxford that would have drawn him to the book. As Cole explained in the Preface, his book was a plea for a new type of workers' organisation, 'Greater Unionism'. It was his advocacy of this that would lead to his resignation from the Fabian executive, and the subsequent setting up in 1915 of the Oxford University Socialist Society by his followers, including Childe. We can be almost certain that Childe would have read it during that moment of left-wing schism, Childe's first, and that it contributed to his break with 'orthodoxy'.[2]

Cole's book is substantial – at 443 pages – and extensive, referring to labour developments in Britain and 14 other countries, with much attention given to France, America and Germany. There are descriptions of labour organisation, ideology and law, with some industrial history as context, but the aim of the book is always in sight. Cole wanted to steer Britain's labour movement away from three dangerous sandbars blocking the entrance to socialism: the antidemocratic dangers of Fabian collectivism, the inertia of the unimaginative 'head clerks' who ran the trade unions, and the 'sad failure' of the Labour Party. He wanted to redirect it towards a class-conscious unionism, one that was prepared in conjunction with a democratised state to abolish the wages system and take control of industry. In this book, Cole only hints at the pluralist philosophical bases of his argument, for he is mainly concerned to elaborate on it by comparing Britain's recent labour history with that of overseas countries. The impetus for his intervention, he writes, is the 'double labour unrest' that emerged in Britain after 1910: the revolt of workers against their employers and union leaders, and the 'intellectual unrest which may be called the Labour movement in search of a philosophy'.[3]

'For the moment', he writes, 'the working-class seems to have shown itself incapable of clear thinking', confused by a chaotic jumble of new ideas, but unable to advance beyond the utopianism of the revolutionaries and the pragmatism of the reformists. The revolutionaries are too often only half-educated, while the trade union leaders and labour politicians still adhere to the sterile vision of state socialism, or 'collectivism', which was imposed on the labour movement by Sidney and Beatrice Webb in the 1890s. According to this idea:

---

2   My copy of the 1913 edition of Cole's book has an Angus & Robertson ('Publishers to University') sticker inside the cover. The most recent edition (by Routledge) was published in 2017.

3   *The World of Labour*, p. 1.

the intellectual problem of labour was solved, and only the practical problems of labour remained: the Labour movement therefore became intensely 'practical', and, so far as the end in view was concerned, as fantastically fatalistic as the worst of the later followers of Marx. The progress of Labour was beautifully resolved into the gradual evolution of a harmony divinely pre-established by the Fabian Society in the early nineties

So, it is up to middle-class socialist intellectuals to play a bigger role. They alone can sort through these new ideas and direct labour onto a new path. They can staff the voluntary adult educational efforts that the working class needs if it is to produce its own class-conscious leaders. They can run the research departments that the trade unions need, collecting and analysing statistics, refining propaganda and developing policy for the movement. As almost the last sentence in the book has it: 'The present muddle in the world of labour comes partly from lack of educational opportunity, but mostly from intellectual indolence'.[4]

But intellectual intervention is pointless if the workers don't want it. Cole looks at the 'Great Labour Unrest' and discerns signs of self-activity and class-consciousness that suggest a fertile soil for new ideas: 'The labour unrest is real; that will be generally granted. But, over and above its reality, it is more than an inarticulate impulse: it possesses direction and determinateness, and this direction is Syndicalist'. The great attraction of Syndicalism to Cole is that it sees in the trade unions 'the germ of the future organisation of society'. Already trade unions, despite all their shortcomings, are sites where 'democracy is being given some chance to solve its problems for itself and in its own way'. When they are reorganised along industrial lines, as the British syndicalists propose, they will be able to play an even more daring role in the future, for after the democratic state has nationalised an industry it will be able to devolve its control to the 'industrial' or 'greater' union in that industry. In the meantime, syndicalist ideas encourage workers to press for workshop committees with power to control aspects of the work process in the factory. This experience will give workers a sense of responsibility for their work and prepare them for assuming the ownership and complete control of production.[5]

But what of the state? Here syndicalism makes both a positive and a negative contribution to socialist thought, according to Cole. Syndicalist ideas reinforce the labour movement's 'growing distrust of the State in all its forms',

---

4   *The World of Labour*, pp. 52–3, 246, 384, 425.
5   *The World of Labour*, pp. 24, 28, 33.

a sentiment to which Cole is sympathetic. But syndicalism, as a philosophy for producers, refuses to see that workers are also consumers: 'It does not recognise the function of the great league of consumers we call the State'. In fact, he writes, there is nothing in syndicalism that requires it to oppose all authority. Even in France the unions, 'syndicats', are more opposed to the state on pragmatic grounds than through any real commitment to anarchism. Cole wants it to be clear that he is not attracted to anarchist theory. In the future socialist society, there will certainly be a state, but it will be democratic, not 'bourgeois'.[6]

Scattered through the book are statements about how the transition to socialism will *not* occur. Obviously, the Fabian model won't work. Collectivism, he writes, presents its case against capitalism too narrowly, as a matter of business efficiency in order to justify state control of industry. Unfortunately, 'in endeavouring to persuade the world that Socialism was a "business proposition" it forgot that it must be a "human proposition" also; it found definiteness and Collectivism, and lost idealism, which is essential to real Socialism'. Moreover, it casts citizens in a passive role. Since the citizens would not be active, they could not control the state, which would then abuse its position. All that collectivist socialism would achieve would be a transfer of authority from the capitalist to the bureaucrat. Other models get a quick dismissal from Cole. The romantic socialists who have attributed a mythic status to the General Strike are wasting their time on something that is utopian and dangerous (because the ruling class will use its superior military force to cower the strikers). As for the revolutionary process envisaged by the Marxists of his time, in the manner of the Paris Commune of 1871, he regards the Commune as a localised revolt. Communism as a term he assimilates to anarchism, and it is telling that the index to his book contains no entry for 'revolution'.[7]

Yet, Cole is adamant that he embraces 'the revolutionary aspiration that should be present in every movement of the working class'. Clearly, he *does* want to encourage a transition to socialism, but in 1913 he is only able to see the process *in utero*, as developments in socialist ideas and strategies conceived in the intensified class struggle of the years since 1910. In the unions, the spirit of revolt was increasingly becoming the intelligence of will. Education and the Greater Unionism would feed into each other, making 'the worker realise his position and the remedy'.[8]

---

6   *The World of Labour*, pp. 4, 124–5.
7   *The World of Labour*, pp. 63, 193–204, 347.
8   *The World of Labour*, pp. 200, 414, 424–5.

So, what was Greater Unionism? In the first-place it meant consolidating and democratising union power in suitable areas of industry, but more importantly it meant extending that power at the expense of the employers. Cole is adamant that unions must never give up the right to strike, and that while they should continue to strike for increased wages and improved working conditions, they should use the strike weapon in a strategy of encroachment on managerial rights at work. Among those rights is the prerogative of hiring: unionists must refuse to work with non-unionists. As for strike-breakers:

> It is not as a rule wise to offer physical violence to 'blacklegs'; but there is nothing wrong about it, except in the eyes of the law and the middle class. The only argument against it, and also against militancy of other sorts, is that they do not pay.

But, as he also believes, sometimes militant violence does pay: 'The day of small unions is past; but the day of strikes has by no means gone with it'. Of course, some strikes will fail, and encroachment has limits, but the critical thing is that the union nurtures its capacity to fight. In short, Greater Unionism is powerful because it enables democratic control of the union, directed coordination of struggles ('a common brain'), the development of rank and file militancy, and, where workplace committees are in place, a sense of responsibility among worker-producers.[9]

Alone, however, Greater Unionism will never defeat the employers. 'If we are to wait for producers' control till the Unions have directly expropriated the employer and extended their power over all industrial conditions and processes, we shall wait for doomsday – and a little after. Trade Unionists do not, in the main, desire to control industry nowadays.' The critical step will have to be nationalisation, and that means a role for the state. As a critic of Fabian statist collectivism and the absolutist-state idea ('Prussianism') in social philosophy, Cole is careful about how he phrases the argument for this step. The state that Cole envisages does not have the expansive and interventionist character of the bourgeois state. It is democratic in the pluralist sense of acknowledging that other groups claim a share in the loyalty of citizens. Its role is not to control everything but 'to stimulate the demand for the "good life"', in this case 'to liberate and stimulate the energy' of the worker-producers to demand workers' control. But such a state does not exist, or rather it is only being created as worker-citizens realise their will to act through the group life of society. So,

---

9 *The World of Labour*, pp. 377–8, 404.

at the moment of nationalisation, the state is poised between its existing – if weakening – 'absolutist' inclination, and its emerging role as the moral sense of the community, with the aim of becoming 'a flexible instrument of the General Will'. On which side will it come down? Cole says that the state – and public opinion – will act sensibly – that is, morally, only if frightened.[10]

Someday, Cole says, 'we will have a revolutionary party imbued, not with the spirit of blind revolt, but with a real consciousness of what the State must be made'. The parliamentary Labour Party of 1913 was not such a party. It was tiny, it had achieved no useful legislation through its alliance with the Liberal Party, and it was 'capitalist in theory and outlook'. Its organisational links to the militant working class and the middle-class socialists were weak. Cole's advice was that it should purge itself of its Liberal members, approach the voters as a straight-out Socialist Party, and find a way to draw into the party those trade unions seeking a parliamentary voice.[11]

In the meantime, socialists in parliament would have to rely on 'fright': 'the weapon of organised protest' outside parliament. As the militancy of the working class increased so would socialist representation, and those representatives would be well positioned to assist in the transition to industrial democracy by supporting state action:

> As the control of industry cannot be assumed in a day, the State must preside over the process of transition, and it is of the first importance that the power should be in the hands of a strong, democratic Government capable of appreciating the working-class point of view. Parliament will have, in future, not merely to clear the ring for the industrial struggle, but to intervene more and more, and to take over from the capitalist the control which it will ultimately delegate to the workers.

Communicating the working-class point of view would be the job of the party as a 'subsidiary' of the trade unions, and to do so it must have the effective backing of the unions. It was an expression of the class's 'organised force', or it was nothing. 'As soon as, in becoming political, it ceases to be mainly economic in outlook its hold over the workers is gone, and it loses touch with the rank and file.' This is what 'a real Socialist Party' would be like: 'capable of voicing the aspirations of the workers', but also threatening capitalism with their organised power.[12]

---

10   *The World of Labour*, pp. 288, 381–2, 382, again, 421.
11   *The World of Labour*, pp. 395, 398–9, 422.
12   *The World of Labour*, pp. 399, 400–1, 423.

* * *

Childe would have noted that Australia was one of the countries Cole examined in order to develop his advice for England's labour movement. Given his suspicion of state capitalism, Cole was hoping to discover that Australia's attempt to outlaw strikes, to make arbitration compulsory, and to set minimum wages and working conditions, did *not* work. One of his heroes was Tom Mann, a socialist and engineering worker who had been one of the leaders of the London dock strike of 1889. In 1901 he went to Australia where, disillusioned with parliamentary socialism, he resigned from the Labor Party and founded the Victorian Socialist Party. He returned to England in 1910, just in time to play a prominent part in the Great Unrest, guiding it, according to Cole, into 'definite and constructive channels'. He came to national attention in 1911 as the Chair of the strike committee during the Liverpool transport strike, defying the Home Secretary Winston Churchill who sent an armed cruiser to the Mersey and 3,500 troops who killed two strikers and injured 350. But according to Cole, from the first, Mann

> knew his business well: he was aware that the English worker cannot be carried away by mere reasoning, and that the only way to get himself concerned with an idea is to show it to him actually at work. Tom Mann therefore began by organising strikes, and only preached the abstract gospel of the strike when he had already shown it could be realised in practice.

The gospel was syndicalism, which Mann promoted as the founder of the Industrial Syndicalist Education League. He was soon 'the most striking personality in the Trade Union world' due to 'his gift of oratory, and his strong personality and his vivid enthusiasm'.[13]

Best of all in Cole's eyes was that Mann had been to the 'social laboratory', as *The Argus* called Australia in 1910, and found that its experiments in social peace had failed:

---

13   *The World of Labour*, pp. 40–1; C. Tsuzuki, *Tom Mann 1856–1941: The Challenges of Labour*, Oxford, Clarendon Press, 1991; *Tom Mann's Memoirs, with a Preface by Ken Coates*, London, MacGibbon & Kee, 1967, Ch. XIII on the VSP; London Socialist Historians Group, 'The Liverpool General Transport Strike of 1811', http://londonsocialisthistorians.blogspot.com/2011/10/liverpool-general-transport-strike-of.html accessed 1 July 2018.

> In Australia and New Zealand he [Mann] studied the complicated systems of arbitration which are there in force, and gathered an impression highly unfavourable to arbitration as a whole. The industrial battle, he found, must, in spite of all State machinery, finally amount to a trial of strength and organisation between masters and men, a warfare which may be open or concealed, and which he would sooner have revealed in all its nakedness. He therefore returned to England with views upon the industrial question already strongly formed.

Cole devotes about 10 pages to the effects of the antipodean legislation dealing with compulsory arbitration and wages boards. He concludes that, although arbitration improved the position of workers employed for long hours at low wages in sweated trades, when the system was extended to other workers it was used by employers in an obstructive fashion to avoid dealing with their employees. The result was that workers resorted to direct action again: 'Compulsory legislation against strikes is breaking down all over Australia; compulsory regulation of minimum conditions is gaining ground'. Cole has a particular animus against wages boards. Since they set only minimum wages, workers strike for increases, but such strikes are easily stigmatised as immoral because subversive of 'agreed standards'. Their net result undermines the power of the working class. He sums up the discussion by drawing on his own socialist and pluralist views of industrial capitalism: 'Those who hold that labour is robbed, not merely where sweating survives, but wherever the wage system exists, can never accept the principle of State determination of wages'.[14]

* * *

The power of Cole's book lies in the underlying intellectual consistency of its argument, its unabashed insistence on the need for revolutionary change, and its range of historical examples. Childe could not have failed to be impressed for a number of reasons. As a former volunteer in NSW Labor's 1913 election campaign who had carried out secretarial work for the party's leader, he would have appreciated Cole's call for sympathetic middle-class intellectuals to engage with the movement. He would have been excited by Cole's demonstration of the international scope of the working-class militancy that he

---

14   *The Argus*, 6 August 1910; *The World of Labour*, pp. 40–1, 292–303.

observed in Sydney. He would have easily accepted Cole's perspective of the Greater Unionism leading from workshop control to socialism, because in the years before the Bolshevik Revolution what other strategy was there apart from bureaucratic Fabianism?

But in order to appreciate the relevance of Cole's argument to Australia, Childe needed to understand how its labour situation differed from that of other countries, an exercise if you like in the political sociology of revolutionary movements. The evidence that he was undertaking this exercise can be found in a letter from Witherby to Childe in February 1919. Although the war had ended over three months earlier, the censors were still prying, intercepting letters between leftists, including this one. The Brisbane Censor helpfully picked out the main points in Witherby's argument:

> 1. 'I, too, feel the need for some kind of Socialistic propaganda, not exotic. All propaganda seems exotic, e.g. the OBU, the IWW and now the Bolsheviki. Australia is wonderfully lacking in originality.'

> 3. 'What you say about responsibility, and responsibility through politics, backed up your quite illuminating distinction between Australian and European bureaucracy, is essentially to the point. The more I reflect the further I get into the conclusion ... that the political paddock is extremely worthy of cultivation.'

> 4. 'Industrial organisation of the Guild Socialist type is a policy of despair – only one degree less despairing than industrial organisation of the IWW type in Australia.'

> 5. 'It may be, though I do not think it, that both England and America are right in despairing of the political sphere.'

> 6. 'The Russians certainly were, but in Russia there was no political state to despair of. When autocracy fell the state fell with it.'

> 8. 'The only thing the working class, industrially organised, can do in Western Europe, is either to control or to alter the character of the existing political state. I do not know whether they can do this or not, but it is evident, as you point out, that this can be done in Australia. Australia differs from Europe in that its political state is relatively weak as compared to that of its parent state.'

9. 'But it differs from Russia in that its political state does exist and is extremely strong as compared with anything in Russia.'

10. 'The Australian worker must freely acknowledge the existence and necessity of the political state. He should further gladly see that its functions are varied and permanent, though not industrial, and he should be prepared, by careful and determined organisation in the industrial sphere to control this political state, while at the same time he obtains self-determination at his work.'

11. 'The example of Queensland should give Labour all over the world a great courage.'

12. 'The fact that, politically, the Labor Party is still so middle class, only means that it faithfully represents the population, for scratch the working man and you will find the bourgeois.'[15]

Two things stand out in this letter. First, there is the argument about the prospects for socialist revolution in countries with different kinds of connections between the ruling class and the state. Reading between the lines, it appears to be as follows. In Russia, as there were no political institutions separate from the Czarist autocracy, there was no alternative path for socialists but proletarian revolution of the kind led by the Bolsheviks. In Western Europe, where socialists face a strong political state controlled by the class enemy, socialists must either work within to control it, or oppose it industrially from the outside in order to alter it. In other words, the choice is either Fabianism or syndicalism. Finally, in Australia, where the political state is not as 'ancient' or as strong as in Western Europe, the working class can use its industrial strength to both control the political sphere and obtain industrial democracy at work. There is also a distinction made between bureaucracy in Western Europe and Australia which while it was illuminating to Witherby is unclear to us.

Second, the letter is concerned with what makes labour's prospects in Australia different. Witherby is not assuming that the labour movement, 'wonderfully lacking in originality' though it is, may by understood simply as part of a transnational movement. This approach reminds us, if you like, of historicity as a principle of analysis and of the tensions in centre-periphery relationships.

---

15   Witherby (Melbourne) to Childe (Brisbane), 21 February 1919, NAA CMF Intell. Reports, 167/85-91; see also 'Ideas under Socialism. Lecture by Mr T.C. Witherby', *Daily Standard*, 25 April 1919, p. 2.

Witherby is presenting his responses to something Childe has written. He refers in four places (in 1, 3 – twice, and 8) to a document or letter by Childe. None of Childe's publications, however, compares Australian working-class politics with those of other countries. So, was it a private letter to Witherby that is no longer extant? But then why did Witherby subject it to such close analysis? A few weeks after Witherby's letter, there is some further information. In a letter to Brereton, Childe discloses that he had sent Witherby a document meant for publication. After telling Brereton that he is delivering a course of lectures for the WEA on Marxist economics, Childe concludes:

> Witherby suggests that I should write a pamphlet on the lines of *The World of Labour* for the WEA. If the Federal Council [of the WEA] approve of this it will be something amusing to work at. I really have all the materials on hand already.[16]

Work on it Childe did, because it is referred to in a lecture by Witherby. In August, the Queensland WEA began planning a series of weekly lectures on 'The Control of Industry', culminating in a one-day conference on workers' control in the Queensland State Railways. Childe agreed to give two of the lectures, as did Witherby (one of his was to focus on Bolshevism). Other speakers included Gerry Portus from Sydney's Tutorial Classes Department, the American-born IWW militant Jim Quinton, and Mr Justice McCawley. Childe never got to deliver his lectures because he left for Sydney to become private secretary to Labor leader John Storey. Perhaps he was lucky. When Witherby's lecture opened the series, conservatives immediately characterised it as a call for revolution and demanded its author be sacked by the university and subjected to criminal charges. Witherby thought the best response was to have the lecture published, and persuaded the WEA to issue it under the title *Who Shall Control Industry?*[17]

It was an essay in ethical socialism; William Morris, not Marx, was his inspiration. Industry, Witherby said, existed not just to satisfy needs but 'to

---

16   Childe (Brisbane) to Brereton (Sydney), undated, but early April 1919, Brereton papers, MS MSS 281/4, pp. 127–8.

17   T.C. Witherby, *Who Shall Control Industry? Report of a Lecture ... Given in the School of Arts, Brisbane, Friday Sept. 12, 1919*, Workers' Educational Association of Queensland, 1919, 21 pages; for the lecturers in the series as delivered, see Minutes of the Fourth Annual Conference of the WEA of Queensland, 19 April 1920, in Records of WEA of Queensland, 1913–32, John Oxley Library, OM 64-13. The hostile reactions to the lecture are printed in the front of the published version. A second edition of *Daily Standard* 13 September 1919 was printed to provide 'a true report' of the lecture, see p. 5.

develop man's creative faculties, and his social relationships'. He then proceeded to show that neither capitalism nor state socialism recognised the importance of these functions – capitalism because of the autocratic nature of the wages system, and state socialism because the centralising tendency of the postwar state actually intensified the autocratic nature of 'wagery'. He identifies state socialism, with its European roots, as the program of the Queensland Labor government. But then he makes an important qualification:

> Here in Queensland, because we are in Australia and because we are under a Labor Government, the wage-earner's position has elements of strength not known in Europe. And this for three reasons. These reasons I owe to a pamphlet by Mr Childe. They are that the politician is more under the control of the industrialist [workers] than in other countries; the permanent official is not so far apart from the ordinary man as in the bureaucracy of Europe; and more consumers in this country are producers. However autocratic therefore State enterprise may appear to the worker in Queensland, there is here the possibility scarcely existing in Europe of a large share of workers control. It is only because of the indifference of the wage-earner on this matter that no advances have yet been made.

Compared to his letter in February to Childe, Witherby here reveals Childe's thinking on two additional points. First, that while bureaucracy in Europe has a remote, caste-like character, in Australia 'it is not so far apart from the ordinary man'. Second, in Australia 'more consumers are producers' – than in Europe presumably. Taken together these points reveal Childe's thinking about the Australian class structure: that it is not as stratified as in Europe, and that it has a larger working class ('producers') proportionately compared to Europe. Because he, like Witherby, believes that those worker-producers are quite bourgeois in their desires and 'bone-headedness', the implication here is *not* that this class structure elicits passivity and conservatism but that it is a basis for radical thinking and action, that 'the wage-earner's position has elements of strength not known in Europe'. If this appears hopeful rather than realistic, Childe would have pointed to his first 'element of strength': the power of militant unionism to control Labor politicians. But this too was more potential than actual.

In the remaining part of his lecture, Witherby looks critically at guild socialism and the OBU as schemes to transfer industrial control to the wage-earners. The former is too theoretical to attract mass support, the latter too centralised and undemocratic. He suggests that the attainment of industrial democracy on a wide basis will require industrial education but, more basically, industrial experiment. Following Childe's analysis in his *Daily Standard* articles (which we examine in the next chapter) he supports an amendment to the Labor platform to democratise the state industries and suggests that the railway workers and teachers in Queensland should be taking up the issue of workers' control with their respective government departments.

Witherby continued to champion Childe's pamphlet, proposing in October that the Queensland WEA should publish it. The meeting was divided. There were questions raised about the cost and some members thought it should be published by the Central Council. Finally, the suggestion of Central Council publication was withdrawn, and the meeting decided that the executive should report to the next meeting on the financial implications. By that time Childe's resignation from the Queensland WEA Council had been accepted. Whether it was because of objections to the content of the pamphlet or of Childe's absence from Queensland at the next meeting the matter was not raised. The reason might have been political, because at the annual conference in April next year a participant thought that 'the ultra-radicalism' of some members, including Witherby, might account for 'a certain lack of enthusiasm' in the WEA. Childe, the WEA Councillors would have remembered, was proposed as a Councillor by Witherby. Regarding the pamphlet, this was the end of the matter as far as the Queensland WEA was concerned. The manuscript, however, might have been sent independently to the Federal Council, either by Childe or Witherby, because a work by Childe was considered by its Reading Committee in 1920. This Committee decided that 'Mr Childe's book had been found unsuitable' for publication. That this book was the pamphlet and not *How Labour Governs* is suggested by the fact that it was Childe's intention to offer the latter to the Fabian Research Department, and by the timing. It is highly unlikely that Childe would have been able to complete *How Labour Governs* while working for Storey. At any rate, the pamphlet was never published, and its manuscript has not survived.[18]

* * *

---

18 Minutes of Queensland WEA Central Council, 23 October 1919, and Minutes of Adjourned Meeting of Council, 6 November 1919, and Minutes of Fourth Annual Conference, 19 April 1920, WEA of Qld Records 1913–32, OM 64-13, John Oxley Library, State Library of Queensland; *Australian Highway*, 1 February 1921, p. 4, and *Annual Report of the WEA 1920*, published 1921, held in Department of Tutorial Classes papers, University of Sydney Archives.

As an associate of both Cole and Dutt, Childe was thoroughly comfortable with the anti-state *zeitgeist* of the intellectual radicals, via English pluralism in Cole's case and Marxism's characterisation of the capitalist state in Dutt's. Yet, as he returned to Australia in 1917, he might have had reservations about this analysis. After all, when he had volunteered for the Labor Party in 1913 it was because the party had demonstrated its capacity to form majority governments in the Commonwealth as well as in New South Wales. By 1917 Labor had formed majority governments in three more states. These advances raise two questions: would Labor governments be able to carry out a socialist program, and more fundamentally would Labor parties, whether in office or not, be able to represent the class interest of the working class? One of the underlying assumptions of Cole's argument was that the Greater Unionism was worthy of support because it *did* represent the working class, and as we have seen Cole could demonstrate that the British Labour Party did *not* represent the working class. It was tied to the Liberals, it was dominated by capitalist ideas, and it had no organic connection with the organised expressions of class-conscious unionism and revolutionary intellectuals.

But in Australia? Childe would have known enough labour history to know that the Labor Party was formed after the great strikes of the 1890s, that unionists dominated its 'leagues', and that it had mechanisms to ensure, at least in form, that control of the party rested with the rank and file. Was Australian democracy therefore different to Britain's? Was the Australian working class more 'proletarian' (in the Marxist sense of being a class-for-itself) in character (if not in composition) than Britain's, and had it stamped its class imprint on the Labor Party? If the answer to these questions was 'yes', might workers' 'representation' in Australia take therefore a different, or at least a modified, form compared to that of Britain? Might it include a Labor-ratified devolution of sovereignty to producers' organisations along guild socialist lines but not by guild socialist or syndicalist methods? If so, the militant industrialism of the unions would need to suppress its syndicalist tendencies in order to contribute to the radicalisation of the Labor Party. When a new surge of One Big Unionism emerged in 1918–19 Childe saw an opportunity to achieve that end, as we will discuss in the next chapter.

Chapter 11

A STATE WITHIN THE STATE

When the German Social Democratic Party voted to support the war, its left-wing broke away to form the Independent Socialists. In February 1918 the breakaways issued a manifesto in Berlin urging German workers to join 'the struggle for peace, liberty and bread'. Their call was an echo of the Bolshevik slogan of November 1917: 'Peace, Land, Bread'. In Brisbane, Childe heard the echo. He repeated it in an article for *The Worker* called 'The Irrepressible Class Struggle', which he timed to appear as the first anniversary of the Bolshevik Revolution approached. Childe's aim was to refute the charge that recent British rail strikes, which were breaking the wartime industrial truce, were 'unpatriotic'. On the contrary, the railway workers were not in the least 'political'. They were not like the German workers, striking for 'peace, liberty and bread'. While workers in Berlin and St Petersburg were defying their rulers and confronting the war machine, British workers were 'loyal', and he scorned them for it.

The cables from Britain 'in the paid press', he wrote, were giving a confused and fragmentary picture. This strike, like others at the time, simply meant that the war between countries had not succeeded in suppressing the war between classes. He went on: workers were right to strike in order to redress the 'colossal robbery' they had suffered during the industrial truce, for the increased prices they were paying, as the cost of living rose represented 'the extra booty wrung from the working class by capitalists and profiteers'. Strikes of this kind were legitimate but also defensive.[1]

But what about the workers of Australia? He could not imagine political strikes of the German kind in Australia. How, then, would Australian workers actually abolish the system of class relations instead of merely defending themselves within it? Childe thought that the value of strikes was that they

---

1   Childe, 'The Irrepressible Class Struggle', *The Worker* (Brisbane), 17 October 1918. Childe followed European socialism closely. *The Ballarat Courier*, 25 June 1918, p. 3, had reported on the manifesto of the Independent Socialists in Germany.

were a constant reminder to the labour movement of the 'irrepressible' class struggle. This was their 'inner meaning'. But what workers learnt from the class struggle could be interpreted in several ways.

As he contemplated the progressive policies of the Ryan Labor government and the 'absurd optimism' of Brisbane's Leninists, he concluded that there might be a possible future for political action but none for an Australian revolution led by a class-conscious, Bolshevik-aping minority. But, if there were a promise of socialism in parliamentary political action, would defensive strikes burnish or dull that promise? And could nothing be salvaged for the advance to socialism from the militant industrialism that he had flirted with in Sydney? Where was the path forward? Then he thought he saw it, in the coming together of militant workers, left-wing union leaders and supporters of the ideas of the Industrial Workers of the World (IWW) in a movement to form the One Big Union (OBU) late in 1918.

For over a decade, the idea of the OBU had been at the centre of IWW practice of revolutionary industrial unionism. This was a form of working-class activity dedicated to direct action, democracy from below, and 'one big union' that would both lead the emancipatory struggles of the workers and, after their success, form a socialist government based on industrial rather than political power. The working-class militancy of the 1910s provided fertile ground for these ideas. The number of labour disputes more than doubled between 1913 and 1919, and working days lost increased more than eight times. There were newsworthy set-piece battles that rattled the ruling class and rallied the labour movement. Yet, if we look not at the great strikes but at the small strikes, a surprising picture emerges. Much of this activity should be characterised as working-class insubordination. It had little to do with 'the labour movement' in an institutional sense but much to do with the impulse among workers for collective resistance, with the process of workers constituting themselves as a class. As we saw in Chapter 2, there was strike action without the involvement of a union. There were strikes in which workers defied their unions and Labor Party politicians. Many of the strikers were 'atypical', if the typical worker is seen as male and blue-collar. There was lawlessness as strikers attacked scabs and police and destroyed property. When the soldiers returned from overseas there were military rebellions provoked by grievances that were unmistakeably working class. So pervasive was industrial unrest, both formal and informal, that the daily press used the term 'strike' to cover boycotts and other kinds of protests. Lastly, there was explicit 'anti-politicalism' expressed in attempts to break the nexus between the unions and the Labor Party or to set up new industrial labour parties. At this point in the process, the influence of the IWW was crucial.²

After the Commonwealth Government outlawed the IWW in 1916, rank and file 'Wobblies' (IWW members) who refused to disband their locals were gaoled or deported; others melted into the surrounding insurgency to agitate for job control and industrial unionism. As the value of real wages decreased and governments, both Labor and non-Labor, were unwilling to check or counter market forces, the Wobblies found receptive audiences in the existing unions, leaving an 'indelible mark' on them, according to Childe. Verity Burgmann, in her authoritative study of the IWW, discusses its influence in seven important disputes between 1916 and 1918. Childe pointed to the 'failure of the Labour Parties to gain tangible results'; by contrast, the rank and file insurgency was often successful.³

Disgusted by opportunistic politicians, outraged by the fines imposed on militants by arbitration courts, and aware of employers exploiting demarcation disputes between craft unions, militants in the state and regional labour councils were increasingly drawn to the idea of the OBU. The lead was taken by the recently elected left-wing leaders of the Sydney Labour Council who called a conference of NSW unions in August 1918. The delegates voted 83 to 9 to adopt a Preamble based on ideas first enunciated by the American IWW in 1905. It committed these unions to a class struggle view of working-class politics. Its challenge to the rest of the labour movement was clearest in the third paragraph:

> (3) Between these two classes the struggle must continue until Capitalism is abolished. Capitalism can only be abolished by the workers uniting in one class-conscious economic organisation to take and hold the means of production by revolutionary industrial and political action.
>
> 'Revolutionary action' means action to secure a complete change, namely, the abolition of capitalist class ownership of the means of production

---

2   Terry Irving, 'Rebellious Workers: Insubordination and Democratic Mobilisation in Australia in the 1910s', Keynote Address at a conference to celebrate Emeritus Professor Michael Quinlan's contributions, University of New South Wales, 7 September 2018, publication pending as Ch. 1 in Peter Sheldon, Sarah Gregson, Russell Lansbury and Karin Sanders (eds), *The Regulation and Management of Workplace Health and Safety: Historical and Emerging Trends*, London, Routledge, 2020; Verity Burgmann, *Revolutionary Industrial Unionism: The Industrial Workers of the World in Australia*, Cambridge University Press, 1995.

3   Burgmann, *Revolutionary Industrial Unionism*, pp. 165–80; Childe, *How Labour Governs*, 1st edn, p. 164 ('indelible') and 117 ('tangible results').

– whether privately or through the State – and the establishment in its place of social ownership by the whole community.

Long experience has proved the hopeless futility of existing industrial and political methods, which aim at mending and rendering tolerable, and thereby perpetuating, Capitalism – instead of ending it.

The conference decided that the OBU would be known as the Workers' Industrial Union of Australia (WIUA). In each state there would be six industrial unions or departments, each divided into divisions and subdivisions to cover the entire workforce. A structure of councils would reach from the bottom to the top of the union with delegates sent from lower to higher councils in each department, and from each department to State and National Conferences. At the same time in Brisbane similar decisions were taken, and a little later in Victorian and South Australia. Completing the scheme, a national conference of unions in Melbourne endorsed the WIUA in January 1919. At least on paper, Australia now had its One Big Union.[4]

In August 1918, Childe was concentrating on how to earn a living after St Andrew's College had forced his resignation and the university had rejected his application for a Tutorship. In September he moved to Queensland. In October he was lobbying government Ministers for employment. In November he was trying to teach while under attack from pea-shooters at Maryborough. Back in Brisbane in December, finally with regular remuneration from his job in the Land Tax Department, and no longer (since the Armistice) having to fight against war, he decided to write a book about the political and industrial labour movement, and to do it he needed to understand the immediate issues of working-class politics. On 2 January 1919 he sent to the *Daily Standard* a long article with the title 'The New Unionism and State Socialism'. It was the first of a series of four, written in the shadow of the OBU, designed to intervene in the Labor politics of two states. His object was to keep the political and industrial wings united.[5]

For this he has to appear even-handed:

[M]ay I say that as an Australian and a Socialist, I hail with delight and pride the One Big Union … The OBU marks an already overdue revival of attention to the industrial side of the movement which had

---

4   *The Australian Worker* (Sydney), 15 August 1918, p. 16, 'The One Big Union. Scheme to Be Launched on October 14 Next. New Preamble Adopted'.
5   Childe, 'The New Unionism and State Socialism', *Daily Standard*, 4 January 1919, p. 4.

too long relied upon 'spoon-feeding' by Parliamentarians. The Preamble, especially, indicates the enthronement of scientific socialism [an allusion to the well-known pamphlet by Engels, *Socialism – Utopian and Scientific*, the latter adjective referring to Marxism], and the overthrow of sentimental and servile Fabianism. Its endorsement by trades union congresses ranks with the Perth resolutions [for peace negotiations to end the war] in rehabilitating before the international [workers' movement], the reputation of Australian socialism … and rebuts the accusation levelled against Australian Labor that it lacks ideals.

Idealism, however, has its dangers: 'Australians, in common with other branches of the Anglo-Saxon race, are a painfully practical people … And we are, I fear, far too "democratic" to allow a Trotsky – even if we could produce one – to lead us into the one true democracy of the co-operative Commonwealth through a dictatorship of the class-conscious.' Meanwhile, the ordinary members of the OBU will see it as a way to obtain 'higher wages and better conditions', and in pursuit of these 'palliatives' the OBU will direct its energies to 'mending instead of ending the capitalist system'. The '"bone-head" majority will always drag [us] back into the old vicious circle'.

Moreover, when we talk of revolution, we leave it alluringly vague, 'as far as its initial stages are concerned', and we neglect 'the splendidly democratic machinery of the Labor party'. Speaking therefore as a revolutionary who wanted 'to go the whole hog', Childe insisted that some 'concrete form must be given – and given quickly – to the more modern ideas that industrialism grasps at', while at the same time the Labor Party must be brought 'into line with the more recent developments of constructive Socialism'. The industrialists, therefore, should work within the party to secure 'a mandate from [a Labor Party] convention in favor of "industrial democracy"'. There should be a plank in the party platform 'to give to the State employees a substantial share of the control of the industries in which they work'. Industrial democracy would make the state enterprises more efficient, as the British Whitley Report for Joint Industrial Councils in capitalist enterprises suggests, 'and point the way out of wagery'. Childe concludes:

> A working example will go further with the Australian temperament than endless fulminations against capitalism in the abstract and will encourage fellow-unionists to throw off the shackles of the private exploiter by their industrial might. Only by such an objective propaganda – which the substitution of industrial for craft unionism now renders practicable – can the membership of the OBU be prevented from falling

into a slumber of dreamy ideals, or a quite aimless militancy, and nerved to a strenuous effort 'to take and hold the means of production'.

He wrote a second article for the *Daily Standard* two weeks later, focusing on industrial democracy as a way of making superfluous the debate about direct action or arbitration. He saw each as a tactic of class warfare, and thus defensive and, in the light of the need to move forward to socialism, 'transitory'. Instead, we must attack the essential vices of capitalism: production for profit and wage slavery. The state enterprises, at least in Queensland, have eliminated the former by reducing prices to consumers, but their workers are still oppressed by 'the old coercive relationship of wagery':

> The worker is still a 'hand' to be engaged, supervised and dismissed by official foremen in whose appointment he has no direct voice and subjected to a code of working conditions which he can only control by the methods of the class struggle, whether it be arbitration or direct action. To the Socialist this is as ethically blameworthy and as economically unsound as any slavery.

Workers in that situation, anxious about their lack of self-government, answer to the appeal of 'fear and passion' voiced by agitators, but if, 'through their own organisations', they had 'control of the internal management' of their state-owned workplaces, the government might appeal to their 'reason and loyalty'. Then, as the 'continual irritant of the class war' disappeared, their productivity would increase – which would be a boon to the public. Finally, workers' control would provide 'a check on the possible treachery of unsympathetic and reactionary officials [i.e. public servants] and a safeguard for their well contrived plans should a fit of temporary insanity attack the constituency one election day'. Substituting 'democratic for bureaucratic management and discipline' would make 'workers in State industries ... live Socialists'.[6]

Within a few weeks the articles had caught the attention of labour notables in Sydney. Perhaps Gordon had sent copies to Bill McKell who then asked him to make the same argument in Sydney's labour press, because in February he did just that, writing a two-part article for the *Labor News*, the official organ of Labor's NSW State Executive but edited by a supporter of industrial militancy, Arthur Rae. The article, with the title 'Political Action and the Newer Unionism', reworked the material in the Queensland articles, but contained a stronger defence of political action and provided some details

---

6   Childe, 'Arbitration and Socialism', *Daily Standard*, 17 January 1919, p. 3.

about the form industrial democracy might take and state industries where it might be introduced. He begins with another warm endorsement of 'the splendid Preamble of the OBU, instinct [sic] as it is with the ideal of a true industrial democracy'. The growing support for the OBU is due, Childe wrote,

> to the quite legitimate dissatisfaction with the results of political action alone ... Still, it would be a tragedy if the reaction led to a neglect of political organization. I, too, came to Queensland doubting the possibility of achieving real progress through political channels. Four months study of the work of the Ryan Government have sufficed to convince me of the solid progress that can be made by a genuine Labor Government in the direction of real Socialism ...
>
> Yet, perhaps, it is just to this point that the criticism of the industrialists is most pertinently and menacingly directed. It may be said that the Collectivism which forms the objective of the A.L.P. is not Socialism but State Capitalism. Such arguments have certainly been used by the I.W.W. in reference to the activities of the Queensland Labor Party. Now, I do not believe it to be a correct statement of the case.

Childe's rebuttal has two prongs. The first is the case made in the *Daily Standard* articles that Queensland's state enterprises – 'The State Insurance Office, State Butcheries and Stations, the State Fish Supply, and the rest' – have reduced rates and prices to the consumers, making 'a revolution in the system of production'. Then Childe imagines the IWW responding that wagery still exists in the state industries, so he unsheathes his second prong:

> The 'State' of which we Laborites speak is conceived of as a State consisting wholly of producers – workers. Of course, as long as capitalism persists the State is really divided into two camps – the producers and the capitalists. But the Labor Party, founded as it is on the Industrial Unions, forms actually a 'State within the State'. When the Labor Party captures the machinery of government, and only then, is an approximation of the State of our objective realized. And under a real Labor Government it will be found that the workers, through their industrial organizations, can exercise considerable influence over the conditions of their employment.

Douglas Cole, writing about Britain, used the phrase 'state within the state' in *The World of Labour* to illustrate the weakness – from the point of view of replacing capitalism with socialism – of consumer cooperation and municipal socialism, spheres of working-class collectivism but within a state still dominated by capital's power. Childe is more positive about Australian Labor's 'state within the state'. He knew, in the first place, that unlike Labour in Britain, Labor in Australia had actually formed majority governments. In the second place – and this is something that he had not said before – since the industrial unions are the foundation of the party, 'Ministers, relying for re-election on the votes and financial contributions of unionists, must listen to the recommendations of their authorised representatives'.[7]

Childe gave examples to show that this strategy had already worked: during the 1917 mass strike and the Townsville meat strike, Ryan's government acquiesced in the railwaymen's refusal to carry black goods. But this form of workers' control is 'indirect and spasmodic', it leaves all responsibility to the government, and because the coercive wage relationship still exists, the IWW is still able to agitate for direct action or the 'go-slow'. So, instead of 'discussing fantastic notions for scrapping wholesale the existing [party] platform' and substituting the OBU Preamble, the industrialists should push for one new plank, 'the democratisation of State industries'.[8]

The second of his *Labor News* articles reused the arguments and phrases of the first of the *Daily Standard* articles: labour's idealism is always in danger of being betrayed by the 'bone-heads', the appeal of the revolutionaries is too vague and remote, and the Labor Party has democratic machinery that the industrialists should use. He is, however, a little more detailed about the form industrial democracy might take:

> The present machinery of Arbitration, as far as State-owned industries are concerned, might well be replaced by permanent committees representing on the one hand the organized workers, on the other hand the State – not as one among other employers, but as the representative of the organised consumers. On such bodies the workers must have real power, not the shadow offered by capitalist proposals for similar workshop committees which still leave the economic dominance of the private capitalist untouched.

And he makes a case for democratising a state enterprise known to New South Wales labour:

---

7   Cole *The World of Labour*, p. 345.
8   Childe, 'Political Action and the Newer Unionism' (Part I), *Labor News*, 15 February 1919, p. 6.

> A working example of an industry – even if it be only the Bombo quarries – successfully run by its employees under the direction of the State, will go much further with Australian temperament than endless fulminations against Capitalism in the abstract.[9]

Then finally he returned to his message, with a nod to his patron:

> If supporters of the Newer Unionism face the facts wisely and honestly, they will do nothing to imperil the union of the political and industrial wings of the Labor Movement, wherein, as Mr Theodore says the peculiar strength of the Movement in Australia lies[10]

* * *

A few days after the first instalment appeared (*Labor News* was a weekly), Gordon wrote a letter to the Secretary of the Darlinghurst Labor League, Reg Byrne, addressed not to his private address, which he had used in previous letters, but care of P.C. Evans, who was the General Secretary of the NSW party. Was it enclosed in a letter to Evans? There is a marginal note on the letter: 'Enclos. 436. 148.' It is possible that Gordon was indicating to the State Executive through this letter to Evans that he was interested in working for the parliamentary leader, a position for which McKell might have suggested him. In the letter to Byrne he wrote that he would be continuing his membership of the NSW ALP, because 'I am now expecting to come South in a month or two and not settle here [Brisbane] permanently'. He enclosed a subscription and concluded, 'I hope the trouble between the parliamentarians and the Exec will be settled in NSW. The two sides of the Movement must remain united.' A reassuring message for the State Executive, perhaps?[11]

---

9   Bombo is a small hamlet 74 km south of Sydney. Its blue metal quarry, purchased in 1911 by the NSW Labor government, later formed part of State Metal Quarries that was sold in 1935 by a conservative government. See *Sydney Morning Herald*, 31 August 1911, p. 4, for the minister's justification in terms of savings to the government's public works program.

10 Childe, 'Political Action and the Newer Unionism' (Part II), *Labor News*, 22 February 1919, p. 3.

11 Childe (Gowrie, Wickham Terrace, Brisbane) to Reg Byrne (Secretary of Darlinghurst Branch, ALP, c/o P.C. Evans) 18 February 1919, Meanjin Archive, University of Melbourne Library.

The immediate issue for the Labor Party was how it should respond to the Preamble of the OBU, the official version of which appeared after the Melbourne conference of the WIUA in January 1919. In Brisbane, Gordon heard that some local Labor parliamentarians, most notably Cuthbert Butler, were intending to lobby the state party to declare the Preamble heretical to Labor principles. In a letter to the *Daily Standard* Butler compared the Preamble and the Constitution of the Labor Party:

> The OBU says plainly and without confusion that it stands for syndicalism as against State ownership ... On the other hand, the Labor party has declared in favor of State ownership or nationalisation ... I fail to see how a person can remain a member of the ALP and subscribe to the constitution of the OBU.[12]

Childe and others on the left wing of the party detected a move to expel them. In March he wrote a long letter to the *Daily Standard*, which was published under the heading 'Some Questions for a Politician':

> Sir, – I must confess that it was with intense astonishment that I read of Mr Cuthbert Butler's 'discovery' that endorsement of the Preamble of the O.B.U. is incompatible with loyalty to the principles of the A.L.P. ... But what most amazed me were the confusions into which even so trained a thinker as Mr Butler can fall. May I then, through your columns, ask him in turn a few questions?

The first question: 'Is there no distinction between the State capitalism of the Preamble and the State Socialism of the Labor Party?' Of course there was, and it could be illustrated by the different purposes of the state railways in New South Wales and Queensland. In the former the 'Nationalist' government raised fares and cut wages in order to swell the general revenue and thus relieve capitalist taxpayers. In the latter the Labor government reduced fares and heaped taxes 'on the big capitalist'. Similarly, Queensland's state butcheries provided cheap meat for the people. Childe's second question was directed at Mr Butler's loose use of the term 'syndicalist'. Butler took it to mean a system in which groups of workers own various industries and thus are able to engage in profiteering in favourable conditions. Childe insisted

---

12   R.J. Cuthbert Butler to the Editor, *Daily Standard*, 5 March 1919, p. 6, 'A Politician's Questions'; D.B. Waterson, 'Butler, Robert John Cuthbert (1889–1950)', *Australian Dictionary of Biography*, Vol. 7, 1979, pp. 508–9.

that the Preamble intends workers to control the 'internal management of the industry' while 'the political state', representing the consumers, would ensure the interests of 'the whole community' were met. He noted in passing that this would mean that 'the politician would still have an industrial function whatever some industrialists might now say'.

> I believe, in short, that the ultimate outcome must be on the lines of Guild Socialism, though here not necessarily achieved by the syndicalist methods advocated under English bureaucracy. This would represent a common ideal to which the industrial and political wings can work together in harmony albeit by different methods ...

Thirdly, if our 'wise' leader, Mr Theodore, could distinguish between 'the reasonable claims for self-determination and responsibility that inspire the newer industrialism', and 'the exotic doctrines of sabotage and "go slow"' of the IWW, why couldn't Mr Butler? Fourthly, did Mr Butler really think it sensible to expel leaders of the party of the calibre of NSW's Mr A.C. Willis?

> If Mr Butler, instead of trying to act up to a dogmatic test of orthodoxy, would use his great abilities in considering the modification needed in the application of the wide principles of the A.L.P., to give effect to the newer ideals which experiments in State enterprises have called forth, he would do more to preserve our solidarity and earn the thanks of the workers.
>
> I am, etc.,
>
> V. Gordon Childe[13]

On the eve of the Queensland State Executive meeting to decide the party's response, Gordon interviewed the State President and Secretary. He pointed out that the OBU statement was not identical to the position of the IWW, which opposed all political action. On the contrary it made a commitment to political action (as long as it was revolutionary). This 'academic argument', to use his term to describe his intervention via the labour press, seemed to work, but no doubt there were other forces brought to bear on the executive. The executive's response accepted the legitimacy of industrial action, and the militants remained in the party.[14]

---

13   Childe, 'Some Questions for a Politician', *Daily Standard*, 7 March 1919, p. 4.
14   Childe to Reg Byrne, 14 March 1919, Meanjin Archives, Melbourne; on the preamble, see Childe, *How Labour Governs*, 1st edn, 192, and Ian Turner, *Industrial Labour and Politics*, pp. 183–6.

Gordon then turned his attention to resolving the dispute in New South Wales between the politicians, supported by the AWU-dominated State Executive, and the industrial militants, who operated through an internal party faction called the Industrial Vigilance Committee. As he explained to Reg Byrne,

> I shall very likely be down in Sydney before the ALP conference [in June]. I want to do anything I can to prevent a split in the Movement. I'm as keen as anyone on industrial unionism but I don't see why the ALP should be forced to swallow the – very fine – Preamble [to the OBU manifesto] which would so terrify the present bone-head electorate that a Labor Government will never get a show again ... Therefore, let the OBU recognize it is an industrial organisation and stick to the industrial field, and leave the ALP with its present mild objective to fix parliament.

Unable to get a delegate's ticket, he could not address the conference. Did he try to mediate between the two sides by interviewing the party heavyweights, as he had in Brisbane? It's very likely, and, if he did, this might have been the moment when John Storey gained a favourable impression of him. Whatever he did, it was not enough, for the outcome of the conference threatened to rupture the movement. The moderates staged a coup, and the militants walked out. There was talk of them forming a rival industrial socialist party.[15]

In July, the *Daily Standard* reported: 'Mr V. Gordon Childe returned from Sydney last night and will resume his lectures in economics (third year) at the WEA class rooms tonight. Mr Childe was a victim of influenza during his sojourn in Sydney, but has now fully recovered.' Lecturer, writer for the labour press, tutor, with access to leading party officials and parliamentary leaders, Gordon was becoming a celebrity in the left, and he took advantage of it. The next day he spoke about the conference to the paper, which headed the story 'Sydney Labor Quarrel – Prospects of Compromise – A Queenslander's Impression'. He also addressed a regular Sunday night meeting of the socialists at the Trades Hall, which Jennie Scott Griffith reported for the Melbourne *Socialist*.

---

15   Childe to Byrne (53 Bayswater Road Darlinghurst) 14 March 1919; *Australian Worker*, 12 and 19 June 1919; Turner, *Industrial Labour and Politics*, pp. 189–91; Michael Hogan, 'Template for a Labor Faction. The Industrial Section and the Industrial Vigilance Council of the NSW Labor Party, 1916–19', *Labour History*, no. 96, May 2009, pp. 79–100.

He was again even-handed in his approach. He castigated the 'moderates' for the 'unconstitutional' behaviour that had precipitated the walkout and regretted that the NSW Executive had not published a statement on the OBU along the lines of the one he had influenced in Queensland, 'recognizing the right of the left wing to full expression'. At the same time, he noticed the 'many foolish utterances' of 'the left' during and after the conference. In his view 'the split' was not as serious as the capitalist press asserted, for the leading militants were determined that the working class remain united, and Labor's parliamentarians were disinclined to expel the leading secessionists. Unity was crucial, and he appealed to the triumphant 'moderates' to seek a reconciliation with the left, and to the voters to elect wherever possible parliamentarians sympathetic to the socialist principles of the militant industrialists.[16]

A similar case for unity was made by Henry Boote in the Sydney *Worker* and by the editor of the *Daily Standard*. In Boote's words, the danger was that the new party would split the working class. This would leave progressives impotent and Labor denied the possibility of electoral victory. Rallying around the Labor Party was the only way forward. No parliamentary leader could have ignored such an argument, or the left-wing voices that were making it. Not surprisingly then, although Storey had publicly attacked the left's leaders in the past, he tried unsuccessfully to prevent the State Executive expelling three of them now: A.C. Willis of the coal miners' union; Jock Garden, Secretary of the Trades and Labor Council; and Arthur Rae, editor of *Labor News*. His message was that forming the next government would be impossible without party unity, for which he now campaigned strongly, including a widely reported speech to unionists at the Eight Hour Day Official Banquet.[17]

A few weeks before this speech Gordon had taken up his new position in New South Wales. Storey was a leader with whom he could work: politically adroit, popular in the electorate, and committed to party unity. As his private secretary he no doubt hoped to have another opportunity to mediate between working-class forces and state officials. But why did Storey take

---

16   Item on Childe's return, *Daily Standard*, 15 July 1919; Childe, 'Sydney Labor Quarrel – Prospects of Compromise – A Queenslander's Impression', *Daily Standard*, 16 July 1919; item on Childe's speech to the Brisbane socialists by Jenny Scott Griffiths, *The Socialist* (Melbourne), 8 August 1919.

17   Henry Boote, 'What is Going to Happen Now?', *Australian Worker*, 31 July 1919; editorial, *Daily Standard*, 24 July 1919; 'Eight Hour Day Official Banquet', *Sydney Morning Herald*, 6 October 1919, p. 5; Bede Nairn, 'Storey, John (1869–1921)', *Australian Dictionary of Biography*, Vol. 12, 1990, pp. 106–8; Christopher Cunneen, *William John McKell*, p. 63; Frank Farrell, 'Rae, Arthur Edward (1860–1943)', *Australian Dictionary of Biography*, Vol. 11, 1988, pp. 323–4.

Gordon – an intellectual, a sympathiser with the faction that was in discussions with anti-Labor socialist groups to form a rival party, a young man who had very little experience of day-to-day organising at the electorate level and no standing at all at the Trades Hall or the State Executive office – to be his private secretary? Clearly, Storey was reaching out to the left, but was he planning something else?

* * *

In 1919, Childe was the most politically influential of the labour intellectuals promoting a variant of guild socialism in Australia. In Melbourne some Christian socialists and members of the Victorian Socialist Party were expounding its ideas but they did not have Childe's political connections. In Brisbane Witherby's discussion of guild socialism in his pamphlet was fair, but privately he thought it too syndicalist to succeed. And he made a very revealing admission: 'Guild Socialism has been called by a certain section of the workers the last attempt of the middle-class mind to dominate the wage-earners'. Certainly, it was the latest attempt, and if the middle-class mind is excavated to its parliamentarist bedrock, it is not hard to see that guild socialism, in the Australian context of class struggle, provided an intellectual lifeline for labourism. Without endorsing the revolutionary solution favoured by the industrial militants, Labor intellectuals, under the cover of this new argument for socialism, could appeal to working-class activists with socialist reasons for supporting the Labor Party, including the possibility of industrial democracy in the state enterprises, at the same time as they were appeasing the power-hungry bosses of the AWU with their moderation.[18]

It was in this guild socialist milieu that Childe formulated the idea of a 'genuine Labor Government', a government enacting progressive policies for consumers, relying on organised militant unionism in the form of the OBU for electoral and financial support, and in return protecting and extending worker control of production. By the time he published *How Labour Governs*, having seen the New South Wales Labor government from the inside, he had to confront the limitations of his ideal government.

---

18   Witherby, *Who Shall Control Industry?*, p. 15.

Chapter 12

THE INTELLIGENCE DEPARTMENT

Gordon found lodgings in 'Kinneil', a rather grand Elizabeth Bay mansion not far from his uncle's home where he had lived while studying at the university. The political location was familiar too, for his Labor Party membership was still with the branch in the nearby working-class suburb of Darlinghurst. From Brisbane he had written friendly letters to the branch Secretary Reg Byrne, telling him about his plans and views on party matters, and when Gordon returned to Sydney Byrne wrote to congratulate him on his new post as private secretary to Labor's parliamentary leader. Replying on Parliament House letterhead, Gordon's tone was formal and distant. He promised to attend the next branch meeting and said he trusted that he would 'be able to do work which shall merit your confidence'. Six months earlier he had signed off his letter to 'Dear Comrade' Byrne, 'Yours for the revolution'. This time he wrote, 'Yours fraternally'. They were now moving in different political spheres.[1]

In his new sphere, Gordon had to tread carefully. After New South Wales Labor split in 1916, the parliamentarians supporting conscription had entered into an alliance with the conservatives, and campaigning as the National Party won a State election a few months later. Freed of its right-wing politicians, Labor continued its move to the left, as pacifists, industrial militants and socialists became more influential in the local branches of the party and its trade union affiliates. Meanwhile, as we have seen, the industrial militants, drawing on syndicalist ideas about the development of socialist consciousness, were reorganising the trade unions on industrial lines through the One Big Union to make industrial struggle the main thrust of the labour movement. This was a direct challenge to Labor's politicians who believed that forming Labor governments was the aim of the movement. Since becoming Labor's parliamentary leader in February 1917, John Storey had tried not to offend

---

1   Childe to Reg Byrne, 53 Bayswater Road, Darlinghurst, 14 March 1919; and Childe to Byrne, 28 September 1919, both letters in Meanjin Archive, University of Melbourne.

the party's left, but behind the scenes he was intriguing with the conservative Australian Workers' Union to head off this threat to parliamentarism. In public, his main argument was the foreignness of revolutionary Bolshevism and syndicalism, and the political uniqueness of Australia, 'where almost any reform can be gained by evolution' – a classic expression of Labor parliamentarism, or politicalism as Childe would call it in *How Labour Governs*.[2]

With a State election due in February 1920, Gordon's first task was to feed Storey material for his attacks on the Nationalist government led by the Labor rat W.A. Holman. According to Evatt, the 'concentrated pungency' of Storey's speeches and letters to the press suggested Childe's influence. He probably had in mind Storey's regular references to the odour of corruption and careerist deals hanging around Holman's administration, especially the resignation of Holman's Agriculture Minister during the Royal Commission into corrupt contracts at the State Wheat Office. Many of these references were underlined with the sarcasm typical of Childe's writings. Another possible indication of his influence was the barrage of facts and figures, drawn from official statistical reports, used by Storey to rebut attacks on state enterprises and to defend the wage levels of Australian workers. But regarding Labor's platform of policies for the election, Gordon had no influence, for Storey had presented all of them in a long speech a few weeks before Gordon reached Sydney. As the election came closer, however, Storey said that judges should be elected (influenced perhaps by the practice adopted in the United States), and the powers of the Legislative Council curtailed. He would set up a tribunal to examine the cases of the IWW 'twelve', the leading agitators of the banned organisation who had been gaoled under the Treason Act in 1916. Most pertinently, because Gordon had proposed this in his 1919 *Labor News* articles, Storey advocated the extension of state enterprises and employee participation in their management. Perhaps this increasing emphasis on democratising the state showed Gordon's influence.[3]

---

2   Storey's statement in reply to Holman's speech at the National Party conference, *Sydney Morning Herald*, 12 September 1919; Bede Nairn, 'Storey, John (1869–1921)', *Australian Dictionary of Biography*, Vol. 12, 1990, pp. 106–8; Jim Hagan, 'Storey, John' in David Clune and Ken Turner (eds), *The Premiers of New South Wales 1856–2005, Volume 2, 1901–2005*, Sydney, The Federation Press, 2006, pp. 141–52; on the emergence of the OBU, Ch. 8 in Ian Turner, *Industrial Labour and Politics: The Labour Movement in Eastern Australia 1900–1921*, Canberra, ANU Press, 1965, provides the ideological and organisational context; Childe, *How Labour Governs*, Ch. VIII, 'The Growth of the Reaction against Politicalism'.

3   H.V. Evatt, *Australian Labour Leader: The Story of W.A. Holman and the Labour Movement*, Sydney, Angus & Robertson, 1945, p. 489 for Childe, Ch. LXII for 'The Breath of Scandal' surrounding the Holman government; Storey reported in

Storey was pleased with Gordon's role in the campaign. A few weeks after the election – a narrow win for Labor – his government let it be known that 'Mr Storey will take with him to the Premier's office his own private secretary, in the person of Mr V.G. Childe'. Such a move would mean a new role for Gordon, as an officer of a government department, and a new line of reporting, to the Department Secretary. He would become a public servant in a position to which recruitment was controlled by the Public Service Board (PSB). When this information appeared in *The Sydney Morning Herald*, Storey had not yet written to the PSB. He was, no doubt, making sure that the PSB did not foist a Holmanite on him. Storey's tactic was justified because when he wrote officially to the PSB he received a very frosty response. The PSB indicated that there was in the Department an incumbent who had carried out secretarial duties for Holman, and anyway an ex-serviceman would have preference over Childe, who had not joined the military. Storey had to insist that no-one else could do the job; and then that Childe should have the same salary (394 pounds) as Holman's secretary. It took a month of pressure before the PSB accepted that only Childe 'had knowledge of Mr Storey's methods of working'. The use of this phrase helped the PSB come to terms with the fact that it had acquiesced in a political appointment, but, as we shall see, this was not enough to mollify the permanent public servants in the Premier's Department.[4]

Premier's was (and is) no ordinary department. Certainly, its Minister, as the head of the government, was the Minister most responsible for the political survival and re-election of the government. This, however, understates the department's significance. Its coordinating role in relation to other departments gave it a greater capacity to detect problems of policy implementation, to anticipate adverse public reactions, and to steer new directions in policy. This capacity relied on and in turn generated 'intelligence' about the government's impact on society. In that sense this capacity was political, but not in the sense of 'party political', because it was undertaken not so much on behalf of the *party* of government as of the government as an organ of *state* power, and not so much in relation to the electorate as to the main forces in society.

Sydney Morning Herald, 6 January 1920 (re Wade), 16 January 1920 (re State Wheat Office), 11 February 1920 (re jobs for cronies), 14 February 1920 (re silo contracts), 16 February and 20 February 1920 (wheat scandal); Storey using statistics as reported in *Sydney Morning Herald*, 26 November 1919 (re cost of living), 28 November 1919 (re defending state enterprises), 16 January 1920.

4 *Sydney Morning Herald*, 12 April 1919; NSW State Archives, Storey's letters to PSB 14, 16 and 20 April 1920, A21/1414 in 9/4864; Minute by Secretary of Premier's Department, 'The Case of V.G. Childe, B.Litt', 23/11/1921, A22/1477 in 9/4885.

The Premier's Department was the government's source of 'intelligence' about how to manage the changing array of divisions and tensions of capitalism, especially those that were economic. If Storey saw Childe as contributing to this form of 'intelligence', then his role was 'political' in an unexpected sense, and Childe's political activities must also be understood in terms of the development of the modern state.

* * *

The Premier's Department in New South Wales was set up by William Holman when he became Premier of an incoming Labor government in March 1914. It was the culmination of a process, beginning in the early twentieth century, of providing the Premier with an office to handle tasks that fell to the head of the government, such as communicating with other governments and taking responsibility for the two houses of parliament, the Executive Council, and the Cabinet. The process was in part an administrative necessity, a non-controversial element of state formation.[5]

There was, however, a section of the Premier's Office (and after 1914 in the Department) whose function was much more than administrative, the Intelligence bureau or department. The term 'intelligence' suggests vital information about the security of the state as a sovereign power. Since Federation that function was the preserve of the Commonwealth government, but in another sense of state security – the economic sovereignty of capitalist market relationships – State governments, irrespective of political complexion – required intelligence about their capacity to ensure an increasing supply of labour and capital, particularly when the birth rate was falling, and imperial capital markets were tightening. In the terminology of public policy, the intelligence was about immigration and tourism, but at a deeper level it revealed the working of state power in a white settler capitalist society.[6]

The Premier's Department grew rapidly during the war, from seven staff in 1914 to 213 in 1917. Much of the growth was the result of the challenge to

---

5   Public Service List, 1910, in *NSW Parliamentary Papers*, 1910, Second Session, Vol. 2, p. 103; K.N.J. Bernie, 'The Premiers' Conferences. An Historical Sketch from the Beginnings to 1930', *Australian Journal of Public Administration*, vol. 6, issue 8, December 1947, p. 410.

6   'The Premier's Department – Statement prepared October 1980', unpublished. I was given a copy of it in 1988 by Professor R.N. Spann, who presumably received it from his contacts in the New South Wales public service.

the labour supply created by military recruitment. The Department provided civilian oversight to recruiting campaigns. It staffed and serviced the State War Council, and the New South Wales Munitions Committee whose role was to advise local engineering companies about labour supply and methods. But it also provided intelligence about managing labour. It met the salaries of staff and other expenses of the Australia Day Amelioration Committee, which distributed relief to wounded ex-servicemen at a time when returned soldiers were a volatile, frequently armed and politically unpredictable mass, and the Voluntary Workers' Association, which existed to recruit and deploy scabs to break strikes in state enterprises and public services.[7]

Holman was fully aware of the significance of the enlarged role of intelligence in the State. In 1916 he encouraged moves to put the collection, assessment and use of intelligence in New South Wales on a systematic basis and to involve experts from outside government in this process. It was an idea whose time had come. Running parallel with it, and assuming a similar proactive role for the state, was the push from the manufacturing industry in Britain and Australia to bring science and industry together, a project that was thought to require government coordination. Holman planned to bring scientific and industrial research into the Premier's Department, by setting up an Intelligence Department as a central 'means of organizing information' on which to base legislation and administration. It would be staffed by the Premier's Department but overseen by a Board chaired by R.F. Irvine, who held the chair of Economics at the university.[8]

As far as we can discover, this board never met, presumably because the Intelligence Department itself never eventuated. No explanation for this survives in the archives. Perhaps the elections of March 1917, the mass strike beginning in September, and the second conscription referendum in December distracted Holman. Perhaps Irvine's radicalism – he was lecturing for the Labor Party in November – became too public for a Nationalist government. Something was salvaged, however, as later in 1917 a Publicity and

---

7   The staffing figures can be found in the Public Service Lists published in each year's *Parliamentary Papers*. The wartime activities of the department are referred to in 'The Premier's Department – Statement prepared October 1980', unpublished. On volatile returned soldiers, see Robert Bollard, *In the Shadow of Gallipoli: The Hidden History of Australia in World War I*, Sydney, New South Books, 2013, Ch. 8.

8   'Memorandum for Ministers – Re Secretariat to Premiers' Conference and Intelligence Department', no date but attached to Minute 7 March 1917 written by the Publicity Officer, E.F.H. Harpur. The memorandum reviews Holman's interest in setting up an Intelligence Department from December 1913. State Records of NSW, Premier's Department, Correspondence, B17/1437 in 9/4755.

Research Branch was set up in Premier's. In 1918 its tasks included assisting the government to deal with the repatriation of ex-servicemen. When Storey became Premier in March 1920, he was immediately able to promise a study of 'advanced democratic thought translated into legislative action', brandishing a list of overseas examples of industrial and welfare legislation provided by his department. So, the grand structure envisaged by Holman might not have come into being but the impetus for it, the need for 'intelligence', continued. Indeed, within a year Storey was contemplating a reorganisation of his Department for purposes that seemed uncannily similar to those driving Holman's vision, and the agent of change chosen by Storey was Gordon Childe.[9]

* * *

In 1920, prices were rising, jobs were scarce, and Storey was in trouble. In the parliament up on Macquarie Street a Labor faction was organising to replace him as leader. At the Trades Hall down the hill in Goulburn Street the militant unions were in control and trying to hold the government accountable, as Childe had advocated in Brisbane. The newly formed Communist Party had some influence among them. Flushed with organisational oxygen, the 'Trades Hall Reds' called for direct action: 'invade the food stores'. There were moments of turmoil on the streets. The unemployed invaded government offices in May 1920; the reds and the proto-fascists fought in the Sydney Domain in May 1921. Desperate to head off the communists, Labor's State Executive was insisting that the government create jobs, stop food profiteering, and appropriate unused land in the country to stimulate closer settlement.[10]

Storey had, in his words, only 'half a mandate'. Lacking a majority in the Assembly, the government relied on the support of independents and a conservative Speaker – and it had no money for a grand program of legislative reform. His response was twofold: to plan a trip to London to raise a

---

9 *Sydney Morning Herald*, 20 April 1920, p. 9 (Storey's promise); Irvine's lecture at IOOF Temple, 25 November 1917, NSW ALP, *Annual Report, 1918*, p. 27.

10 Terry Irving and Rowan Cahill, *Radical Sydney: Places, Portraits and Unruly Episodes*, Sydney, UNSW Press, 2010, Ch. 21; *Daily Telegraph*, 20 May 1920 (unemployed rush Cabinet); *Daily Telegraph*, 28 May 1920 (McGirr's conspiracy against Storey); *Sydney Morning Herald*, 15 January 1921 (State Executive versus Storey); *Daily Mail*, 11 May 1921, p. 15 (reds versus fascists); 23 August 1921 (commandeer the food stores) and 1 September 1921 (unemployed attack on government offices); Miriam Dixson, *Greater than Lenin? Lang and Labor 1916–1922*, Melbourne Politics Monograph, 4, no date, Ch. 4.

loan in the City, and to continue painting the big picture about the government's vision, emphasising nationalisation, efficient management of state enterprises, industrial democracy, price control and motherhood endowment. There was an international dimension to this vision, a dimension that was very likely brought to his attention by Gordon. In April 1920 Storey said in parliament that he was examining a digest of laws of other countries made by the Premier's Department, because many of them represented 'advanced democratic thought translated into legislative action'. Gordon had begun in the Premier's Department just a week earlier, so he probably conveyed this information to Storey. In May, Storey instructed him to travel the State and report on its resources and the work of the government-owned enterprises; he took a second trip in October. Storey had realised that, as well as a secretary, he had in Gordon an intellectual who understood the significance of Labor's program and the limits imposed on it by a hostile business community. Perhaps Gordon could also be the link between his government and the overseas world of 'advanced democratic thought'.[11]

Within the Premier's Department there was already a research unit, but its focus was on attracting investors and immigrants. Storey believed that it needed to focus on Labor's program of reform and popular democracy. Discussions ensued between McKell and Storey, and Gordon was consulted in order that the tasks envisaged were commensurate with his qualifications. Finally, in December 1920, as Storey was preparing to leave for London, he formulated the scheme: advertising and research in the Premier's Department was to be reorganised so as to provide 'by extended research, the framework of legislation and the basis of administrative reforms'. Childe was to be appointed as Research Officer until he could be sent to London to work in the NSW Agent-General's office. According to Storey, Childe was eminently suitable:

> He is a Fellow and Lecturer of Oxford University and has graduated with first class honours in arts and literature. He is an accomplished linguist, and reads, writes and speaks fluently several modern languages. He is the author of several standard works on industrial legislation and social welfare, some of them having been translated into other languages, and used as text books at European Universities.

---

11   Bede Nairn, 'Storey, John (1869–1921)' *Australian Dictionary of Biography*, Vol. 12, 1990, p. 108; *Sydney Morning Herald*, 20 April 1920 (Storey on advanced democratic thought overseas); Childe, letter in *New Statesman*, 6 May 1922 (his research trips in May and October 1920).

He has a wide knowledge of political economy, and a thorough grasp of the objects, aims and achievements of all political parties in the Commonwealth.

The author of this mixture of misunderstanding, hyperbole and invention was obviously not relying on direct knowledge. Gordon was never a Lecturer at Oxford; he might have been a strong applicant for a fellowship if he were in Oxford, but he was not; his language skills were untested, and he was not the author of text books on industrial and welfare matters, although Robin Page Arnot, who was the Secretary of the Labour Research Department (LRD), would later tell George Munster that Childe could have contributed the Australian material in *The Labour Year Book 1916*. The *Year Book* appeared, however, in December 1915, so Gordon would have had to have worked at the LRD in the summer of that year, which is possible, but we have no other record of this happening. Nor is there any evidence that the *Year Book* was translated into other languages. It is hard to imagine Gordon writing these misstatements about himself, but his friend Bill McKell might have, or Storey did, relying on notes passed to him by McKell.[12]

Already convinced that Gordon was a political appointment, the reaction of the Premier's Department to his new role was unsympathetic. The Acting Secretary tried to limit his advice to the government, insisting that 'as the policy of the Department is to submit plain statements of facts', he should not express opinions in his memoranda, except as footnotes. The Acting Secretary also resisted the proposed reorganisation of the research unit. The department had a research officer, E.F.H. Harpur, who prepared reports for other departments. The Acting Secretary assumed Gordon would work in cooperation with – that is, subordinate to – Harpur, but in a concession to the government allowed that Gordon's research might be 'for the benefit of Ministers personally'. The government was not satisfied, perhaps because Harpur was a Holman appointee. In Storey's absence (he had left for England

---

12   On discussions between McKell and Storey, see McKell to Sir George Fuller, 29 April 1922, State Records of NSW, Premier's Department Correspondence, A22/1477 in 9/4855. For Storey on Childe as Research Officer, see Storey's memo to PSB, 30 December 1920, State Records of NSW, Premier's Department Correspondence, A21/1414 in 9/4864. *The Labour Year Book of 1916*, London, issued under the auspices of The Parliamentary Committee of the Trades Union Congress, The Executive Committee of the Labour Party, and The Fabian Research Department, [1915]; for references to Australia, see pp. 422–3, 439, 497. R. Page Arnot, *History of the Labour Research Department*, London, LRD, 1926, p. 13. R. Page Arnot to George Munster, 21 April 1978, Munster papers, Mitchell Library MSS 7627.

a few weeks earlier), the Acting Premier, James Dooley, was even clearer about Childe's duties: he was to fulfil the needs of the Ministry. Dooley intervened directly in the management of the department, instructing the Acting Secretary that Childe 'would take over [Harpur's] work', that he would be free to reorganise the research office, and to decide the direction of its research. The Acting Secretary then decided that discretion was the better part of valour and made a further concession, announcing that Childe 'will engage in research work adapted to the special needs of the Government'. 'Special needs': a euphemism to describe the government's partisan understanding of its program and its reliance on a partisan public servant. Gordon was thereupon appointed as Research Officer with a salary of 439 pounds per annum.[13]

In London, Storey continued the process of defining Gordon's role as a political advisor. After consulting the Agent-General, Storey cabled Dooley that Gordon was to proceed to England to work in the office of the Agent-General as the government's Research and Publicity Officer at a salary of 525 pounds per annum. He also wrote a fuller memorandum, 'A Statement of Duties which it is proposed shall be discharged by Mr V.G. Childe, B.Litt, on his appointment to the office of the Agent General in London'. Gordon would be required to transmit regular reports on 'industrial legislation, social welfare movements, finance reports, new methods of taxation, new inventions of interest to the Government corporate bodies … It is desired that American, Canadian, New Zealand and German progression be especially noted.' Then there was a sentence that foreshadowed an input into policy formulation for Gordon: 'He may be regarded as having a clear idea of the nature of information required, and as possibly being able to extend usefully its scope'. And for those wedded to the bureaucratic ethos of the public service, the statement concluded with an inflammatory instruction: his reports were to come direct to the Premier, not via the Secretary of the Premier's Department, the 'question of the right of direct communication with the Secretary of the Premier's Department in Sydney' being reserved 'for future consideration'. In his new role, Gordon's loyalty was to be secured

---

13 Secretary of Premier's Department, Memorandum, 21 January 1921, State Records of NSW, Premiers' Department Correspondence, A21/1414 in 9/4864, and see also the Secretary's memorandum, 23 November 1921, 'The Case of Mr V.G. Childe, B. Litt', A22/1477 in 9/4885; Acting Premier Dooley to Acting Secretary Tremlett, 28 January 1921, B21/366 in 9/4875; Acting Secretary to Dooley, 31 January 1921, SRNSW, Premier's Department Correspondence, B21/366 in 9/4875; Acting Secretary of Premier's Department, Memorandum, 1 February 1921, B21/366 in 9/4875.

for Labor, not the liberal state, and there was no pretence that his advice would be that of a neutral expert operating in a sphere constituted above the contending classes of society.[14]

---

14 Storey's cable to Dooley, 14 April 1921, referred to by Sally Green, *Prehistorian*, p. 37; Secretary's memorandum, 23 November 1921, 'The Case of Mr V.G. Childe, B. Litt', State Records of NSW, Premier's Department Correspondence, A22/1477 in 9/4885; Storey, 'Statement of Duties', 1 May 1921, A22/1477 in 9/4885. We discuss Childe's London life in Chapters 14 and 15.

Chapter 13

THE PREMIER'S MINDER

Australia's intelligence community was keeping an informal eye on Gordon. Captain Eric Longfield Lloyd, who had spent the last years of the war with the Intelligence Section of the General Staff in Sydney, had joined the Pacific Branch of the Prime Minister's Department. In October 1920 he wrote to his superior, Major Edmund Piesse, formerly the wartime Director of Military Intelligence. Lloyd had heard that a former Censor in Sydney, Captain Arthur Lang Campbell, had some intelligence to impart to the Prime Minister about Evatt and Childe. They were known to Campbell because until 1917 he held the position of tutor and Vice-Principal of St Andrew's College: Evatt was a student and then a tutor at that time and Childe was probably Campbell's replacement on the college staff. Evatt had recently married Mary Alice Sheffer, the daughter of an American businessman, and was about to honeymoon in the USA. Campbell had heard that Evatt was to undertake a special assignment for the Prime Minister to investigate the assimilation of Japanese immigrants in California. This was a sensitive issue for the government. Japan's expansion in the Pacific, and its opposition in international meetings to the White Australia Policy, were major geo-political worries. Implicit in Lloyd's approach to Piesse was a doubt about whether Evatt could be trusted to hold the line. Did the Prime Minister not know of Evatt's dubious political associates? Lloyd conveyed Campbell's information: specifically, that 'Evatt came under most unfavourable notice during the war, and that both he and a friend of his named Childe were frequently reviewed in Censors' QF. He [Campbell] describes Childe as a noted Pacifist ... No doubt the D.C.C. Records with Jones will show something about him.'[1]

---

1   Eric Longfield Lloyd to Major Piesse, 27 October 1920, Piesse papers, National Library of Australia, MS 882, item 5/142; N.K. Meaney, 'Piesse, Edmund Leolin (1880–1947)', *Australian Dictionary of Biography*, Vol. 11, 1988, p. 227–9; Howard Zelling, 'Campbell, Arthur Lang (1869–1949)', *Australian Dictionary of Biography*, Vol. 13, 1993, p. 353–4; David Sadleir, 'Lloyd, Eric Edwin Longfield (1890–1957)',

There were other parties taking a dislike to Gordon. In June 1920 the Prince of Wales was in Sydney as part of a State Visit to Australia. Gordon was not caught up in the patriotic hysteria that gripped the city. We know this because 37 years later, when Gordon returned to Australia after his retirement, a Mr George Boss, JP, wrote to Prime Minister Menzies accusing Gordon of being 'a most disloyal British subject'. According to Boss, during the Royal visit Gordon engaged in 'disloyal actions in holding meetings and preachings against the Empire'. When these charges were made, ASIO interviewed Mr Boss, but, as their report has been redacted from Gordon's ASIO file, it is impossible to discover whether there was any factual basis for these allegations. But as an anti-imperialist Gordon might well have passed comments that disparaged the Prince and the obsequious press coverage of his visit, as the independent socialist Percy Brookfield did in parliament. Moreover, it is possible that Boss was reporting a view about Childe that was widely held in the public service, for he was the former manager of the State Bakery and an associate of D.R. Hall, Holman's Attorney-General and Minister for Housing. Any official who had served the Holman government would have resented Gordon's closeness to the Labor Premier and suspected his commitment to public service conventions of political neutrality.[2]

Gordon's tasks for the Premier in his first year would have confirmed the suspicions of the professional bureaucrats in the Premier's Department, for he did much more than arrange Storey's diary or act as the gatekeeper to his office. He diffused a dispute between rival clerical unions, one Holmanite, the other affiliated to Labor; he deflected an attempt by a patriotic paramilitary organisation (the King and Empire Alliance, led by Major General Sir Charles Rosenthal, D.H. Lawrence's model for the fascist Benjamin Cooley in *Kangaroo*) to embarrass the government by wooing its right-wing members; he dealt with employees from the State Dockyard in Newcastle annoyed that the government's promise of worker participation in its management had not occurred; he advised the government to open negotiations with the wrongly convicted Industrial Workers of the World prisoners about compensation (but the government decided not to); and he wrote the government's official

---

    Australian Dictionary of Biography, Vol. 15, 2000, p. 104–6. The censors' reviews were labelled QF; the D.C.C. was the Deputy Chief Censor; H.E. Jones was the Director of the Counter Espionage Bureau.

2   George Boss, J.P. to the private secretary of the Prime Minister, Mr R.G. Menzies, 15 April 1957, National Archives of Australia: 'Childe, Vere Gordon', A6126/24, ff. 2 and 3 (digital copy). For Boss's association with D.R. Hall: *Sydney Morning Herald*, 2 December 1914, p. 11, and 2 March 1916, p. 8. For the Royal visit, see *Sydney Morning Herald*, 19 June 1920 and later.

response to allegations that three of its members had taken bribes to close down a Royal Commission into the scandal-ridden Wheat Board, advising Storey to discredit the fixer to deflect attention from the parliamentarians. He performed similar tasks but none more openly partisan than these: he was managing the government's relationships with the labour movement, that swirling sea of factional intrigue, institutional power-plays and self-seeking leaders constantly trying to submerge the restive rank and file. He was a political minder before the term was invented.[3]

As such, he could hardly keep a low profile. He was well known to party and union officials who came to meet with the Premier at his office. They noticed him at the party's annual conferences which Gordon attended at Cabinet's request. When Ted Theodore (who was now the Premier of Queensland) passed through Sydney, *The Sydney Morning Herald* reported that Childe went to the wharf to meet him. A year after his appointment he was sufficiently notorious in political circles for *The Bulletin* to print a caricature of 'Gordon Childs [sic] B.A., B.Litt., sec. to NSW Premier Storey'.

And he kept in touch with his comrades on the left. One of them, Vance Marshall, wrote an account of watching a sketcher at work in Macquarie Street, where Gordon would have walked regularly between Parliament House and his office in the Chief Secretary's building. The subject of the sketch was Gordon Childe, but Marshall's account describes a slightly different image to the one printed in *The Bulletin*:

> It showed a tall, thin, somewhat stooped figure of a man, hat in hand, lolling almost affectedly upon a walking stick. A mop of curly hair was supposed to be tossed by imaginary breezes. But the face it was that held attention. Round, though not large, 'big boyish' rather than youthful, with lips pouting rather than suggestive of strength – a face set with the deep eyes of the thinker surmounted by the ungainly brow of the intellectual, but plain, homely, excessively, painfully so.

---

3   James Walter, *The Ministers' Minders: Personal Advisers in National Government*, Melbourne, Oxford University Press, 1986; 'Question of Ministers attending a Meeting of the United Bank Officers' Association', State Records of NSW, Premier's Department Correspondence, file B20/2344 in box 9/4856; memorandum by VGC on Sir Charles Rosenthal to the Premier, 1 September 1920, file B20/2845 in box 9/4858; re employees of State Works, file B20/2797 in box 9/4858; re compensation for IWW ex-prisoners, VGC's memorandum 17 November 1920, quoted in Ian Turner, *Sydney's Burning*, London and Melbourne, Heinemann, 1967, pp. 238–9; Lists of Matters Submitted to Cabinet 1917–1921, box 4/6259.3, for IWW items in April to November Cabinet meetings; VGC's memorandum on Mr Justice Pring's report on charges against Dooley, Mutch and Johnston, file B21/342 in box 9/4875. Robert Darroch, *D.H. Lawrence in Australia*, Melbourne, Macmillan, 1981.

With 'the ungainly brow of an intellectual' – Childe as the Premier's secretary, 1920. (Caricature by Len Reynolds, *The Bulletin*, 23 December 1920, p. 18, held by State Library of New South Wales, TN86A)

Marshall also described going to see Gordon at his office, but being unable to reach him because the stairs were blocked by a deputation of women wanting to complain to the Premier about the high price of food:

> In the midst of the excited throng stood Gordon Childe, striving to make his measured classroom voice audible above the medley … in a vain effort to coax them back to their homes by vague allusions to some more convenient day. His homely features were registering despair – but I knew that, deep within, his soul registered disgust. What did the price of potatoes matter to Gordon Childe? It was the cheapness of flesh and blood that stirred him.

Vance Marshall was, like Gordon, the son of a clergyman, but unlike Gordon he had fought on the front line as a union militant and pacifist, and had gone to prison twice as a result. His disparaging remarks about the women – he notes their 'high-pitched feminine cackle' – were typical of the left's sexism, and perhaps he knew Gordon shared this sexism, for he imagines Gordon saying to himself that they were 'a pack of female Neros fiddling while Rome was burning!'.

While it is clear from this account that Marshall admired Gordon – who had once led a deputation to the Minister of Justice on his behalf – it contains a whiff of condescension. It leaves the impression that Gordon's preoccupation with big ideas, with class struggle in the abstract, was at the expense of appreciating the mundane issues that stirred ordinary people, like the women on the stairs, and that ordinary people disgusted him. He looked, according to Marshall's interpretation of the caricature, like a homely, big boy who lolled about, with pouting lips, not a virile young man. Was Marshall thinking of the word 'effeminate'? In the *Bulletin* caricature Gordon is not holding his hat and he is not lolling on a walking stick. The mop of curly hair is missing. Perhaps Marshall saw the actual caricature as it was sketched but, a victim of his own imaginary breezes, misremembered it two years later to fit his own idea of Gordon. I think Marshall's description means that he, and perhaps others of Gordon's comrades on the male left, admired Gordon as a thinker, but not as a revolutionary. By contrast, as we have seen, a revolutionary woman thought he was one of the left's best people.[4]

There is another image of Gordon at this time that is perhaps closer to how his close friends saw him. A portrait photograph in sepia in the Evatt Papers, it is no doubt one of multiple copies given to friends and family, perhaps when he left Australia for the Agent-General's office in 1921. Clean-shaven, he wears a lightweight jacket, silk tie carefully knotted, a tiepin holding the collar's points neatly against the tie. From behind rimless glasses his eyes are clear and engaging. His forehead is high and broad; his hair wavy and full. It is an attractive face, with balanced features. It is certainly not an ugly face. The gaze, however, is disarming. This is a young man who is comfortable with his position in the world but not with himself. He seems to be seeking acceptance.[5]

---

4   'Mr Theodore in Sydney', *Sydney Morning Herald*, 10 September 1920; Childe attending Labor conference, his minute on Storey's memorandum of late January 1921, NSW State Archives, file A22/1477 in box 9/4885; caricature of Childe, *The Bulletin*, 23 December 1920; Vance Marshall, 'Gordon Childe – Scholar and Thinker', *Daily Standard*, 2 January 1924 (also in *Common Cause*, 17 January 1924).

5   The studio photo of Childe is in the Evatt Collection, Flinders University Library, Adelaide.

Childe as he would have liked his friends in the 1920s to remember him.
(Flinders University of South Australia, Evatt Collection Photographs:
Evatt_1510_050)

* * *

In January 1921, Storey left for London on SS *Orsova*, escorted down the harbour by a State launch, the *Premier*, carrying Labor Ministers and party supporters. Was Gordon on board the launch? If he were, he might have joined in the singing of 'Solidarity Forever', for he knew and loved the songs of the IWW. It had taken just five years for this one to travel from America to Australia, where its popularity in Labor circles reminded the party of its versatile founding myth: that the party was an expression of class solidarity as a result of the successful transfer of industrial strength into the political arena. Especially in 1921, after a decade of mutual hostility between the industrial and political 'wings', 'Solidarity Forever' was sung in tones of either subversive irony or bad faith, for nowhere in its six verses was there a hint of parliament or elections:

> When the union's inspiration through the workers' blood shall run
> There can be no power greater anywhere beneath the sun
> Yet what force on earth is weaker than the feeble strength of one
> For the Union makes us strong
> *Chorus*:
> Solidarity forever, solidarity forever
> Solidarity forever
> For the Union makes us strong.

To Storey, on the deck of the big ship, leaving Labor's divisions and intrigues behind, the singing was just 'a throaty rumble'. Gordon, filtering the words through guild socialist ideas, might have pondered the distinction between solidarity and unionism. In the Preface to *How Labour Governs* he would suggest that his aim was to reject the 'essential presupposition' of both trade unions and labour parties that formal organisation was the path to socialism. It was a position far more radical than his present emphasis on combining political and industrial struggles.[6]

As well as the general research project set out in Storey's December 1920 memorandum, Cabinet allocated various special tasks to Gordon,

---

6   *The Sun*, 22 January 1921, p. 7. For the words of 'Solidarity Forever', see Mark Gregory's website, 'Union Songs', http://unionsong.com/u025.html; on Childe's knowledge of IWW songs, see his letter to Mary Alice Evatt, 23 June 1931, Evatt papers, Flinders University Library. See the 'Preface' to *How Labour Governs* for Childe's criticism of 'formal perfection' in labour movements.

including attending the Labor Party's 1921 New South Wales conference. That was clearly a political task, as were the three tours of New South Wales that he undertook in the eight months between Storey's departure and his own in October. In April and May he went to the Riverina (which he had visited twice in 1920), inspecting the construction of the Burrinjuck Dam by the Public Works Department, the Murrumbidgee Irrigation Area supervised by the Water, Conservation and Irrigation Commission, the Forestry Commission's Bago State Forest, the Red Cross Sanatorium at Griffith where tubercular soldiers were trained to take up irrigation farms, the canning factory at Leeton, the Experimental Farm at Yanco, the Merungle Soldiers' Settlement, the first government irrigation scheme at Curlwaa, and Lake Menindie that supplied water to Broken Hill, where he descended the South Mine to the 1,270 foot level and inspected the Broken Hill Proprietary Company's concentrating and sulphuric acid plants. After this immersion in practical socialism, he caught the train to Adelaide and returned to Sydney by ship.[7]

Then a few weeks later he went north to Tuncurry State Forest, where a commercial pine plantation was ready to produce its first marketable timber. A fifth trip followed in September, again to the Northern Rivers, visiting soldier settlements in the Richmond/Tweed area. Having seen enough, he took the train to Brisbane where he met his old friends George Pearce, Ernie Lane and Mr Justice McCawley, and 'called upon' Labor notables Premier Ted Theodore and his Home Secretary Bill McCormack (who was much disliked by the left and the industrial militants). Gordon was also spotted by a *Brisbane Courier* reporter attending a recital by the Cherniavsky brothers at His Majesty's Theatre in the company of 'George Pearce and Miss Effie Pearce'.[8]

Gordon was clearly enjoying his role as an advisor and troubleshooter for Storey's government, the entrée it gave him to Labor's inner circles, and his notoriety in the anti-Labor press. In the public service, he was a kind of *enfant terrible*, but he embraced that role too because it was the reason that he was part of the State elite. He thus had to perform a delicate balancing act when reporting on his tours. They were 'fact-finding' investigations of

---

7   Childe, 'Report on the Resources of the State', 12 May 1921, NSW State Archives, Premier's Department Correspondence, file A21/1608 in box 9/4870.

8   31 August 1921, approval for Childe to visit soldier settlements, file A/2137 in box 9/1751. Childe to Alice Childe, June 1921, in Munster papers, Mitchell Library MSS 7627; *Brisbane Courier*, 6 September 1921, p. 9.

'the resources of the state' – terms sufficiently neutral to appease the public service mandarins. But at the same time, we can discern from his writings what he really thought he was doing. He was documenting the progress of state enterprises, comparing them to similar privately-owned activities, keeping an eye on health and safety standards in the silver and lead mines of the State's most powerful business, the Broken Hill Proprietary Company, whose 'dusted' mine workers had become a burden on the government, and making sure that the soldier settler schemes were working, because ex-soldiers were a potentially tumultuous anti-Labor force. Gordon had seen the violence of which they were capable in Brisbane's Red Flag riots in 1919, and only a few months earlier in Sydney when fascists attacked the reds in the Domain in the afternoon before rampaging through the city terrorising the left in its meeting halls at night.[9]

So, these were political tours, a fact underlined by his passing reference to a separate report on 'the question of filling the Sturt Vacancy' in his main report on his 1921 Riverina tour. This was an allusion to an embarrassing matter in Labor circles: the election of Percy Brookfield, representing a rival socialist party, the Industrial Labor Party (ILP), that had emerged after the 1919 Labor conference had expelled the left-wing militants. For 10 years Brookfield had been either an activist or the leading union official in Broken Hill (the major centre in the Sturt electorate) but he had died a few weeks earlier. He was killed while trying to disarm a deranged man at nearby Riverton railway station. In 1920 he had won 57 per cent of the vote in a three-member seat; now he was a martyr. How could Labor prevent another independent socialist winning this seat? Apparently, Gordon had a secret commission to discover the mood of the town if the government appointed a Labor candidate instead of the next in line on the ILP ticket. Gordon's report has not been found, but the government did appoint a Labor man, ignoring the complaints of the ILP that Labor was stealing the seat from them. One can imagine that Gordon had conflicted feelings about this manoeuvre. He stood by the principle of party unity, which meant getting behind the Labor banner, but, like Brookfield, Gordon was on the left, a position occupied by the ILP, and he could not have forgotten that Brookfield had lobbied politicians when Gordon was looking for a position in Queensland. In May 1921,

---

9   The Workmen's Compensation (Broken Hill) Act in 1920 provided for payments to 'dusted' miners, a major issue during the 1919–20 strike in Broken Hill; see Paul Robert Adams, *The Best Hated Man in Australia: The Life and Death of Percy Brookfield 1875–1921*, Glebe, Sydney, Puncher & Wattman, 2010, pp. 277–9; *Sydney Morning Herald*, 9 May 1921, p. 9.

Gordon would have taken the Labor line because, as he had said with just a little irony, writing to Brereton in 1919, he naturally threw in his lot with the body that paid him, 'for as Marx remarks, things without value like conscience and honour, under capitalism take on the form of commodities and have a (an irrational) price'.[10]

Perhaps to compensate for weakening the left on the Sturt vacancy issue, he persisted in advocating for the state enterprises even as they were losing their allure to Labor's parliamentarians in the financially strapped postwar years. Soon after returning from the Riverina, he wrote to the Acting Premier proposing the publication of a pamphlet summarising the work of the state enterprises, and suggesting the kind of data that should be collected from them, including the prices charged in comparison with private enterprises, the profits made, the approximate savings to the state by using the materials produced by the state enterprises, and the number of employees and the concessions made to them. Then he listed the state enterprises: brick works, timber yards, monier pipe works, metal quarries, trawlers, bakery, clothing factory, abattoirs, grain elevators, experimental farms and the Murrumbidgee Irrigation Area. There were others, as Murray Goot has recently shown. Dooley approved the collection on June 1, and the replies started to come in.[11]

In July, John Storey returned from England. In London he had visited Harley Street specialists to receive treatment for kidney disease, but as he resumed his duties in Sydney it was clear that he was still very ill. The health of the Labor Party was equally poor. Each of the factions was organising an event to welcome him: the industrial left with a banquet under the auspices of the Eight Hours Demonstration Committee; the AWU-dominated State Executive with a 'civic' reception (the Lord Mayor was also an AWU man); and the politicians at a classy restaurant. The State Executive, meeting at the AWU's McDonnell House, decided to make Storey 'toe the carpet', while Henry Boote, in an article widely republished in the country press, derided Storey's efforts to raise a loan. A satirical squib pictured him with a swelled head after visiting the King.[12]

---

10   Adams, *The Best Hated Man in Australia*, Chs 17 and 18; Childe to Brereton mid-May 1919, Brereton papers, Mitchell Library, MS MSS 281/4.

11   Childe: 'Memorandum for the Acting Premier – Summary of the Work of State Enterprises', 31 May 1921 State Records of NSW, Premier's Department Correspondence , file B21/1117 in box 9/4878; Murray Goot, 'Labor, Government Business Enterprises, and Competition Policy', *Labour History*, no. 98, May 2010, p. 81.

12   Jim Hagan, 'John Storey, 13/04/1920–05/10/1921', in David Clune and Ken Turner (eds), *The Premiers of New South Wales, Volume 2, 1901–2005*, Sydney, The Federation

It is true that Storey came home with the news that he had been able to arrange almost 20 million pounds of loans for New South Wales but later commentators neglect to say at what cost. This was what outraged Boote: to get the money, Storey had gutted one of the government's most radical proposals. In his 1919 policy speech, Storey had promised an Act to force big land-holders to subdivide by threatening them with a 'super tax', a public right of occupation, and resumption by the state if all else failed. As introduced, the Land Bill was (of course) less radical, providing for financial compensation, but it was still directed towards subdivision of large estates. In London, this was seen as expropriation. Leading financiers told Storey it was 'useless inquiring for loans if the Land Bill goes on the statute book of the State in its present form'. Storey compromised – land-holders would be bought out at market prices. In fact, he had been prepared for this outcome all along, taking with him to London a printed list of possible amendments to the Land Bill. 'Has our great Movement come to this', Boote thundered, 'that it must submit its legislation to a pack of interest-mongers over the seas?'[13]

* * *

As he prepared to leave the Premier's Department to take up his Research Officer post in London, Gordon reviewed the work of its Research Branch since he took over at the beginning of February and sent it to the Secretary. He said that in the main he had followed Harpur's approach, preparing memoranda and distributing them to government departments, who failed to use them. In future, he wrote, the Branch should focus on a particular topic, systematically collecting material on it, thus producing a document 'comprehensive and really useful'. He was no doubt thinking of his proposed publication on the state enterprises. When the Department Secretary sent the report to Harpur, the latter's resentment of Gordon was clearly displayed in his minute: 'I am afraid Mr Childe has based his remarks on an incomplete knowledge of the facts', as several departments had expressed appreciation of the work of the Branch.

Press, 2006, p. 149; *Sun*, 15 July 1921, 19 July 1921; *Sun*, 14 July 1921 (State Executive meeting); H.E. Boote, 'Storey in London', *Australian Worker*, 5 May 1921, p. 3, and also in *Canowindra Star, Lithgow Mercury, Temora Independent, Barmedman Banner; see Newcastle Industrial*, 12 May 1921 for squib.

13   Storey's speech at Mudgee: *Australian Worker*, 28 August 1919, p. 7; the Land Bill: *Australian Worker*, 5 May 1921, p. 9; London financiers: *Sunday Times*, 3 April 1921, p. 3; Storey returns: *Sun*, 20 July 1921, p. 7.

Then Harpur revealed what was really bugging him, writing that 'generally there has been a wide departure from the policy originally laid down by me'. This was a reference to the list of 153 memoranda appended to the report. Among the innocuous descriptions of labour conditions and government welfare programs there were memoranda that reflected Childe's political opinions. C.H. Hay had tried to suppress these by insisting on the relegation of opinion to footnotes, but Gordon had sidestepped this condition by selecting subversive topics to research. There were clusters of memoranda on industrial democracy in Britain, Italy, Germany, Norway and Austria (9 memoranda), profiteering in Britain (6), compulsory acquisition of land in Czechoslovakia, Portugal, Estonia and Mexico (3), and nationalisation in Germany and Canada (2).[14]

At the end of September, only a few days before he was due to depart, Gordon wrote another memorandum about the state enterprises, again to the Acting Premier. In the first of his 1919 *Daily Standard* articles, Childe had welcomed the OBU because it 'rebuts the accusation levelled against Australian Labor that it lacks ideals'; now he saw an opportunity to present Labor to the world as an exemplar of practical socialism. He told Dooley that Mr H.E. Holland, leader of the New Zealand Labor Party, had expressed interest in the progress of government enterprises in New South Wales, and therefore the State should publish an illustrated booklet about them. A discussion with Dooley took place and the next day Childe wrote a minute on his memorandum that the Acting Premier supported the idea and asked Childe to ask the publicity officer to look into the matter and report.[15]

But the timing was wrong. Storey died on 5 October, and Gordon left for England three days later. The government's interest in 'advanced democratic legislation', and the research to discover it, had lost its two main champions. By the time Childe reached London, Harpur had reported to Hay that 'It is not so much overseas visitors as our own people whom it is desirable to convince of the advantages of State Enterprise. In view of this and as the columns of the city and country press are available to us for local publicity, it is my opinion that expenditure on a booklet is unwarranted.' E.F.H. Harpur,

---

14   Childe, 'Report to the Secretary [of the Premier's Department] on the Work of the Research Branch during 1921', 22 September 1921, State Records of NSW, Premier's Department Correspondence, file A22/1477 in box 9/4885.
15   Childe, 'Memorandum for the Acting Premier – State Enterprises', 29 September 1921, State Records of NSW, Premier's Department Correspondence, file B21/1117 in box 9/4878.

was a Holman appointee who shared neither Gordon's internationalist vision nor his socialist ideals. Within a few years conservative governments had sold most of the state enterprises to private owners.[16]

Gordon's plan was to travel to England by the SS *Corinthic*, joining it in Wellington on 15 October, after discussions with officials of New Zealand's liberal government, and presumably with members of the small Labour Party. This schedule meant that he left Sydney in early October, for we know that he was still at his desk in late September. There was a ship leaving for New Zealand on 8 October, SS *Riverina*. Storey died on 5 October, so Gordon learnt of his death just before he boarded. He would have been in Sydney for Storey's funeral on the 7th.[17]

I like to think of him attending the funeral. It was a state funeral, with all the expected formal solemnities and public tributes – a line of cars two and a half kilometres long in the cortege – but the degree of popular mourning for the Labor leader was unexpected. Ten thousand people passed his coffin in St Andrew's Anglican Cathedral, and on the day of the funeral mourners gathered in immense crowds near the cathedral and lined the streets for the entire 13 kilometres to the cemetery. In the industrial suburbs, workers poured out of the factories and stood bare headed to show affection and respect for their Premier as the cars went by. Gordon would have had similar feelings. Was he able to attend? There is no mention of him in the list of mourners either from the Premier's Department or the Labor Party, but he might have joined the unnamed trade unionists – thousands of them – who assembled in Hyde Park to join the procession in George Street, and who walked as far as the technical college in Ultimo, 'where it became necessary to speed up the cortege because of the long distance to the Field of Mars cemetery'.[18]

In the press tributes, Storey was remembered most notably for his friendship with the Prince of Wales. To the *Sunday Times* he was 'a man of bright nature and normal talent … not a great man, but a man'. The journalists decided his administrative and legislative record was slight, which was true, but no-one, not even Gordon, sought to put on record that Storey had a vision for Labor as

---

16   Minutes by Childe 30 Sept 1921, and Harpur 21 October 1921 on the above memorandum by Childe, 29 September 1921.

17   *Sydney Morning Herald*, 8 October, 1921, p. 16; the daily press did not publish passenger lists for these voyages. SS *Riverina* was a Huddart Parker steamer, built in 1905, wrecked at Gabo Island 1927. Childe's departure: NSW State Archives, Premier's Department Correspondence, file A/22 1447; Green, *Prehistorian*, pp. 37–8.

18   *Sydney Morning Herald*, 8 October 1921, pp. 13–14; *Evening News*, 8 October 1921, p. 6.

a party of 'advanced democracy'. They saw instead a dying government, rent by factionalism, struggling to maintain its majority in the Legislative Assembly, facing a hostile upper house, and deprived by death of its only popular figure.[19]

* * *

In view of Childe's early scholarly promise and his later renown as a prehistorian, it might be thought that he was using his transfer to London as a ruse to escape 'the fatal lure of politics' and to re-establish himself in university circles. In the following year, when the Nationalists replaced Labor in government and sacked him, conservatives suggested this, as we shall see. But in October 1921 it is just as plausible to imagine him committing himself to work as a labour intellectual – in England or any other part of the world where there was the possibility of working-class power. Consider his recent experiences. He had been bundled out of Oxford in 1917 by the authorities in his college. In Australia, seeking to work as a scholar and teacher, he had been rebuffed three times by academic establishments. Why would he think that British academics would be more welcoming to someone with his subversive opinions? They wouldn't, a conclusion confirmed by the failure of Queens to ask him to apply for the Craven Fellowship after the war ended, as he thought the college authorities had promised in 1917. Given all this, why would he be contemplating a future in universities?[20]

On the other hand, after four years in Australia, immersed in the politics of labourism and socialism, he had established himself as a labour intellectual. He had advised trade union leaders and party officials about tactics, and with good effect. He had impressed intellectuals – labour and liberal – by lecturing and writing about labour's philosophy and its place in the unfolding postwar struggles for justice and popular democracy. Because of these accomplishments he had been taken into government as an advisor, a role that would continue in London. In his luggage he had an incomplete book about the organisation of the Australian labour movement, a book that he hoped would be of value to the movement 'in other Anglo-Saxon lands'. And in London the political

---

19   *Sunday Times*, 9 October 1921, p. 4.
20   On Childe's hopes for the Craven: Childe to Murray, June 1917, Murray papers, shelfmark 376, f. 157; Evatt to Childe, 3 December 1918, NAA CMF Intell. Reports 167/57-68; Irving and Scalmer, 'Labour Intellectuals in Australia: Modes, Traditions, Generations, Transformations', pp. 1–26.

friends from his Oxford days – Rajani and Clemens Dutt, Raymond and Margaret Postgate, Robin Page Arnot and Alan Kaye – were now significant figures in the movement, using the Labour Research Department, of which Douglas Cole was the honorary Secretary, to influence the leftward course of the British working class. Why wouldn't he see his intellectual future as being in left-wing politics? Why wouldn't he imagine himself making a contribution to this movement, and perhaps even making his home in England to do so?[21]

---

21 Childe, *How Labour Governs,* 1st edn, p. v for 'Anglo-Saxon lands'; Arnot, *History of the Labour Research Department.*

Part 3.
An Unknown Member of the Proletariat: London 1921–1926

Chapter 14

THE DISMISSAL

In November 1918 the war between the empires came to an end but in their European heartlands the war between the classes resumed. According to revisionist accounts of the origins of the Great War, in 1914 the ruling classes of Germany, Russia, Britain, France and Austria-Hungary thought war was desirable: 'Fearful of being swept away by those below, the ruling classes of Europe mistook democratisation for revolution, and brooded on "escaping forward" into war to head it off'. Industrial conflict and radical dissent did not disappear between 1914 and 1918 but wartime laws imposing conscription and boosting the state's emergency powers reduced the scope and effectiveness of resistance. So, when Germany surrendered, convulsions of suppressed working-class radicalism shook many parts of Europe.[1]

First there was Russia, and then, inspired by the Bolshevik triumph, there were revolutions and short-lived soviet republics in Berlin, Bavaria, Hungary, Slovakia and Italy between 1918 and 1921. Elsewhere workers took direct action in strikes that rattled the ruling class and put governments on the defensive. This was the situation in Britain, where the Liberal Prime Minister struggled to keep his coalition government together. The government faced crippling domestic and foreign debts, mutinous soldiers and striking policemen, not to speak of imperial turmoil as nationalist revolts flared in Ireland, India, Palestine and Egypt. In 1919 there were 50 mutinies in the British armed forces, some of them sparked by soldiers refusing to serve in the counter-revolutionary invasion of northern Russia. That was the year in which strike days rose to 35 million work-person days, six times more than in 1918.

Standing apart from the leadership of the trade unions, a national movement of Shop Stewards and Workers' Committees was demanding workers' control. In Glasgow the Clyde Workers' Committee led a political strike to reduce the working week to 40 hours. By January 1919, with 40,000 workers

---

1   Jack Beatty, *The Lost History of 1914. How the Great War Was Not Inevitable*, London, Bloomsbury, 2012, p. 3.

in the engineering and shipbuilding industries on strike, it had become a city-wide insurrection, further cementing the area's reputation as 'Red Clydeside'. Elsewhere, there were fierce industrial struggles involving railway men, cotton workers, dock workers, and especially coal miners. Facing cuts to wages when the government returned the coal mines to private ownership, miners began a series of bitterly fought strikes against wage cuts and for public ownership and worker control that went on until the General Strike of 1926. Elsewhere other kinds of issues were contentious. In London and Liverpool there were riots over resistance to police unionism, and in Luton ex-servicemen, enraged by the failure of local government to find jobs and housing for them, burned down the Town Hall. In response to this wave of rebellion from below, the labour bureaucrats had to act. The leaders of the mining, transport and railway unions re-formed the prewar 'Triple Alliance'. If it remained solid it could close down the economy and bring the country to a halt. No wonder the monarch, King George V, was in a funk 'about the labour situation and ... talking about ... the danger of revolution'.[2]

From the other side of the world Gordon and his socialist friends took a keen interest in these events. Some of them adopted positions at this time that lasted a lifetime. Bert Evatt, who would become the leader of the Federal Parliamentary Labor Party in the 1950s, told Gordon that he worried about the dismal performance in the 1918 general election of the divided British Labour Party – some candidates supporting the wartime government and recognised by it with 'coupons' (certifying the candidates' support for the war), others campaigning as former opponents of the war. He thought it was 'a terribly bloody' result overall, except in Ireland where Sinn Fein emerged as the largest party. When its members refused to take their seats in Westminster, this was the prelude to the actually bloody Irish War of Independence that began a few weeks later. Gordon also heard from Russell Pearce, who would move in Communist Party circles in the 1940s. He looked to Germany where he hoped the Socialists would get the upper hand 'and send fraternal greetings to Lenin and Trotsky'. A more measured response came from Theodore Witherby, who calculated the chances of a successful revolution in Western Europe and concluded that the only strategy that would work would involve

---

2   Simon Webb, *1919: Britain's Year of Revolution*, Barnsley, UK, Pen and Sword, 2016; Martyn Ives, *Reform, Revolution and Direct Action amongst British Miners*, Brill Online, 2016; Lindsey German and John Rees, *A People's History of London*, London, New York, Verso, 2012, Ch. 8; Chanie Rosenberg, *1919 – Britain on the Brink of Revolution*, London, Bookmarks, 1995; Andrew Rothstein, *Soldiers' Strikes of 1919*, London, Palgrave Macmillan, 1980. For digitised resources on Red Clydeside: http://gdl.cdlr.strath.ac.uk/redclyde/.

the working class organising industrially, like the syndicalists, and seizing control of the political state from redoubts built at work or in localities. This was when Gordon began to sign his letters, 'Yours for the revolution'.[3]

But what kind of revolution? Gordon was not a state socialist like Evatt; he thought the Australian democratic temperament was not suited to Bolshevik vanguardism; and he rejected syndicalist methods as selfishly pitting producers against consumers. At the end of 1918 he told Ted Theodore that he thought of returning to Oxford, but Ted warned him that 'if Bolshevism becomes a real menace to the governing classes, Oxford will become as intolerant as Sydney'. Gordon thought the warning was misplaced. It was inconceivable that Bolshevism would ever find enough support in the English working class, because '70% of the Labour Party are "loyal", [and] come to think of it', in comparison with British labour leaders, 'Ryan is an advanced socialist and Theodore a Bolshevik indeed!' Was Gordon just a bit too starry-eyed about Australian labour's tradition of 'proletarian democracy', as he called it in *How Labour Governs*? Rajani Palme Dutt thought so. He wrote from London, where 'even the cafes and tubes talk of industrial revolution coming'. Rajani could not understand why the revolutionary movement in Australia was 'so sentimental and nebulous'. He might have been thinking of Gordon's *Daily Standard* and *Labor News* articles, but perhaps Gordon had written to him along the lines of his unpublished pamphlet, explaining that the position of the working class was stronger in Australia than in Europe because of the history of the Labor Party. Rajani, about to join the Communist Party, would have thought such a view decidedly sentimental.[4]

Rajani also told Gordon that Britain was not quite ready for a successful revolution. He was right about that. In fact, these immediate postwar years now appear as the time of Britain's lost revolution. The radicals had only one major victory. Threatening a general strike supported by 350 'Councils of Action', the 'Hands off Russia' movement ended government support for the anti-Bolshevik intervention of the White armies. But at home 'non-party communism', the working-class political culture that historian Kevin Morgan has identified, formed by the cross-currents between syndicalism, communism

---

3   Evatt to Childe, 6 January 1919, NAA CMF Intell. Reports 167/69-76; Russell Pearce to Childe, 21 October 1918, NAA CMF Intell. Reports 167/56; Witherby to Childe, 21 February 1919, NAA CMF Intell. Reports 167/85-91; Childe to Byrne, 14 March 1919, Meanjin Archives.

4   Childe to Brereton, 23 December 1918, Mitchell Library MSS 281, vol. 4, pp. 125–6; Dutt's letter to Childe was intercepted by the censor and reported to MI5 in H.C. Jones to Colonel Hall, 25 June 1919, KV2/2148; Childe referred to the letter in his letter to Brereton, May 1919, Mitchell Library MSS 281/4, pp. 127–8.

and labour socialism, was squeezed out, pincer-like, by the advances of managerial social democracy in the Labour Party and Bolshevisation in the Communist Party. To this weakening of working-class counter-hegemony was added betrayal by union bureaucrats. In 1921 the leaders of the transport and railway unions refused to back the miners' strike against privatisation, thus ending the much-vaunted Triple Alliance. An economic recession that year told against the worker radicals too. Unemployment more than quadrupled over the previous year, rising to 16.9 per cent. The competition for jobs and housing contributed to the rekindling of racism among white workers, another fault line for class solidarity to cross. In 1919 there had been race riots in Liverpool and other port cities against coloured workers from Britain's African, South Asian and Caribbean colonies. In 1920 and 1921, it was Irish workers who were stigmatised, when the press confected a fear of Irish terrorists to justify the deployment of troops in Ireland to fight the Irish republicans. But mostly it was the more decisive weapons of military force and legal persecution that won the day for the government. There were gunships on the Mersey, tanks on the streets of Liverpool, soldiers fighting demonstrators in Glasgow, London and other towns and cities, and Special Branch raids on offices of revolutionary organisations.[5]

It was at this internally-conflicted and cheerless moment for the left that Gordon landed in England. It must have compounded his usual 'despondent irony'. Yet, although he was depressed by the faction-ridden labour movement he had left behind, he still hoped that it could rise above its destructive squabbles and European revolutionary models to create a distinctively Australian form of working-class power. In England there was even more reason to hope. As he had written to Brereton, he feared the class war was 'taking on a more definite shape' there, but England also had a culture in which middle-class socialist societies encouraged 'reconciliation and compromise' in the class war. His own political practice had been based on that model and

---

5   Kevin Morgan, *Harry Pollitt*, Manchester, Manchester University Press, 1993, Ch.1; Kevin Morgan's important argument about non-party communism provides the organising idea for his three books on 'Bolshevism and the British Left': *Labour Legends and Russian Gold*, London, Lawrence & Wishart, 2006; *The Webbs and Soviet Communism*, London, Lawrence & Wishart, 2006; and *Bolshevism, Syndicalism and the General Strike: The Lost Internationalist World of A.A. Purcell*, London, Lawrence & Wishart, 2013. Jacqueline Jenkinson, *Black 1919: Riots, Racism and Resistance in Imperial Britain*, Liverpool, Liverpool University Press, 2009. On 'Hands Off Russia': http://ourhistory-hayes.blogspot.com.au/search/label/Hands%20Off%20Russia; on unemployment, see James Denman and Paul McDonald, 'Unemployment Statistics from 1881 to the Present Day', *Labour Market Trends*, vol. 104, nos 15–18, 1996.

he looked forward to resuming it in a more thoughtful environment. He was about to discover, however, that political divisions on the left were creating suspicion and intrigue among his Oxford intellectual friends. This was the context in which he prepared *How Labour Governs* for publication, and in which reviewers would later find the book ambiguous and cryptic.[6]

* * *

In London, Gordon lived for five years at number 34 Cartwright Gardens, where his friend from Oxford, Robert Chorley, also had a room. A crescent of elegant, three-storey Georgian terrace houses, it was an address that had come down in the world; by the 1910s it was known for its shabby boarding houses and radical tenants. In 1917 Edward Carpenter, socialist and pioneer sex reformer, found number 18, where he would stay when he came to London – 'a friendly, companionable place, popular with Independent Labour Party members and trade unionists visiting London on political business'.[7]

The street and its semi-enclosed garden were named after John Cartwright (1740–1824), who lived at number 37 during the last years of his life. Cartwright was a naval officer and rural landowner who supported the American colonists in their War of Independence, and the English 'Jacobins' in their campaign for parliamentary reform and popular government. While contemporaries honoured him as 'the father of reform', Cartwright was part of a long tradition of radical democratic advocacy and practice, dating at least from the tithings of Anglo-Saxon England. This tradition continued through the struggle for democratic organisation in the medieval guilds, the debates among the radicals during the English Revolution, and the democratic style of the Hampden Clubs and reform movements that Cartwright was part of in the late eighteenth and early nineteenth centuries.

Cartwright aimed his proposals for reform at parliament, but the inscription on his statue in the garden opposite his house, using the demotic language of struggle, suggested that contemporaries saw his career in a more radical way. He was described as 'nobly refusing to draw his Sword against the Rising

---

6   Childe to Brereton, May 1919, Mitchell Library MSS 281/4, pp. 127–8 for 'class war taking on a more definite shape'; Childe to Murray, 8 June 1918, Murray papers, shelfmark 376, ff. 44–6.

7   Sheila Rowbotham, *Edward Carpenter: A Life of Liberty and Love*, London, Verso, 2008, p. 380.

Liberties of an oppressed and struggling People'. This was a reference to his removal as head of the Nottingham Militia – essentially a security force used against protesting rural and town labourers – because of his political opinions. The inscription continues: he was 'The Firm, Consistent and Persevering Advocate of UNIVERSAL SUFFRAGE, Equal Representation, Vote by Ballot and ANNUAL PARLIAMENTS'. These were four of the demands of Chartism, the mass working-class movement that emerged soon after Cartwright's death, and two of them – the most radical, equal representation and annual parliaments – are still rare or absent from our experience of representative government. In colonial Australia, Chartist ideas inspired the demand for popular control of representatives advanced by the workingmen's movement of the 1840s and 50s. Childe was continuing this tradition of radical democracy when he argued that Australia's 'proletarian democracy' and the Labor Party's 'novel theory of democracy' should be extended to include workers' control of industry.[8]

There were Sydney connections to the house – number 34 – where Gordon roomed. Robert Lowe, the barrister whom the working men elected to the Legislative Council of New South Wales in 1848, mistakenly thinking he was a radical, lived there in 1842. Returning to England in 1850 Lowe entered politics and became notorious as an opponent of further parliamentary reform. By Gordon's time, the house was called the Bloomsbury House Club, a place where, as he described it, 'briefless barristers and the black-coated proletariat sleep and eat'. One of those barristers would have been his friend Robert Chorley, who was tutoring part-time at the Law Society's School of Law. In 1928, a year after Gordon left the house, another radical Australian, the young Christina Stead, whose novel *The Seven Poor Men of Sydney* described the lives of the agitators and dreamers among whom Gordon had moved, took a friend to lunch there. Stead lived next door in number 33, 'a working women's club-house', in a street she described as 'a demi-lune of boarding houses'.[9]

---

8   Green, pp. 40–1; John W. Osborne, *John Cartwright*, Cambridge University Press, 1972; 'Cartwright Gardens (formerly Burton Crescent)', in www.british-history.ac.uk/survey-london/vol24/pt4/pp83-93 accessed 5 May 2017; Andy Blunden, 'On Political Representation', www.academia.edu/32316891/On_Political_Representation accessed 5 May 2017; Terry Irving, *The Southern Tree of Liberty: The Democratic Movement in New South Wales before 1856*, Sydney, Federation Press, 2006, Ch. 16.

9   Irving, *The Southern Tree*, Ch. 12; R.L. Knight, 'Robert Lowe (1811–1892)', *Australian Dictionary of Biography*, Vol. 2, 1967, pp. 134–7; Childe to J.L. Myres, 8 December 1923, Myres papers, Bodleian Library, box 8, f. 14; Hazel Rowley, *Christina Stead – A Biography*, Melbourne, Minerva, 1993, p. 90; Christina Stead,

From Cartwright Gardens Gordon could walk easily to the British Library, and to the 1917 Club in Gerard Street, Soho. The young rebels of the University Socialist Federation had long dreamed of a Socialist Club in London. In a moment of progressive exhilaration following the overthrow of Tsarist rule in February 1917, Leonard Woolf and other volunteers at the Fabian Research Department decided to make it a reality, but the club did not open its doors until December, after the Bolsheviks had ousted Kerensky's parliamentary liberals. From the beginning, therefore, according to Douglas Goldring, it attracted a heterogeneous membership, variously bohemian, artistic, labourist and revolutionary:

> Hindus, Parsees, puritans, free lovers, Quakers, teetotallers, heavy drinkers, Morris Dancers and Folk Song experts … members of the London School of Economics, Trades Union officials, journalists, poets, actors and actresses, Communists, theosophists. In short, every colour and creed, every 'ism' and 'ist' was represented.

Chorley was a member, so Gordon might have joined at the suggestion of his friend. He soon made himself comfortable, enjoying the company of fellow radicals such as his Oxford socialist comrades Cole and Postgate, and members of the Union of Democratic Control. Communists as well as prominent Labour Party figures mixed easily, taking lunch in the basement that smelled of cat's piss and gathering upstairs in the afternoon for challenging discussions on cultural and political topics. The club was dingy, jerry-built and draughty, but there were quiet spaces for writing letters, which Gordon took advantage of, and for reading. Gordon described the club as a place where 'déclassés, and Labour MPs meet, eat, play bridge and read the *Frankfurter Zeitung*'. He could have been thinking of himself and his own hobby and preferred reading – for he loved bridge and read German, and he felt, as he said in 1924, like 'a pauper colonial', without 'social qualifications … [and] status'.[10]

Until recently references to the 1917 Club were mainly concerned with its role in London's left-wing political and artistic life, but now it figures in

---

The Seven Poor Men of Sydney, London, Peter Davies, 1934; Christina Stead's description of Cartwright Gardens is in her novel, *For Love Alone*, New York, Harcourt Brace, 1944, p. 305.

10 Morgan, *Labour Legends and Russian Gold*, p. 64; Victoria Glendinning, *Leonard Woolf – A Life*, London and Sydney, Pocket Books, 2006, p. 210; Douglas Goldring, *The Nineteen Twenties*, London, Nicholson and Watson, 1945, p. 145; Helen Wussow, *The Nightmare of History: The Fictions of Virginia Woolf and D.H. Lawrence*, Lehigh University Press, 1988, p. 33; Green, pp. 41–2; Childe to Myres, 4 February 1924, Myres papers, Bodleian Library, box 8, f. 17.

the often-marginalised Queer history of London. Contemporary accounts, like the one quoted above, hinted at the club's association with transgressive sexual behaviour. Leonard Woolf, for example, described it as 'the zenith of disreputability'. It was after all situated in a red-light district, and prostitutes walked Gerard Street with their pimps, keeping an expectant eye on a doorway opposite the club, where Mrs Meyrick ran the most notorious of her nightclubs at number 43. But aside from its setting, the 1917 Club had its own 'radical socio-sexual hybridity', to use Anne Witchard's phrase. The painter John Armstrong, after visiting the club with Elsa Lanchester, wrote a verse about her that ignored completely its political origins:

> In nineteen one seven they founded a Club
> Partly as brothel, partly as pub,
> With membership mainly of literary bores
> Redeemed by a girl in Giotto-pink drawers.

The revolutionary urge, as Armstrong implies, could be as much about sexuality as politics. Indeed, according to Hermione Lee, 'After the war, the 1917 Club became largely bisexual', with the gay community moving between it and the more overtly queer Cave of Harmony set up by Elsa Lanchester in nearby Charlotte Street. The club's place in the history of gay London has also been noticed by novelist Alan Hollinghurst who imagines its more advanced members talking about 'libidos and orgasm'. Evelyn Waugh, during his 'acute homosexual phase', would often escape from Oxford to visit the club. Whether Gordon was similarly attracted by its atmosphere of sexual transgression we do not know, but he was certainly not repelled.[11]

* * *

---

11   Anne Witchard, 'Sink Street: The Sapphic World of Pre-Chinatown Soho', in Simon Avery and Katherine M. Graham (eds), *Sex, Time and Place: Queer History of London, c.1850 to the Present*, Bloomsbury Publishing, 2016; Andrew Lambirth, Annette Armstrong, and Jonathan Gibbs, *John Armstrong: The Paintings*, London, Philip Wilson Publishers, 2009, p. 19; Gay Wachman, *Lesbian Empire: Radical Crosswriting in the Twenties*, Rutgers University Press, 2001, p. 187; Hermione Lee, *Virginia Woolf*, Vintage Books, 1999, p. 384; Jane Marcus, *Virginia Woolf and the Languages of Patriarchy*, Indiana University Press, 1987, pp. 167–9; Paula Byrne, *Mad World: Evelyn Waugh and the Secrets of Brideshead*, New York, Harper Perennial, 2009.

Childe took up his position as Research and Publicity Officer in the London office of the Agent-General for New South Wales on 7 December 1921. John Storey might have thought that Childe would be able to send his reports direct to the Premier, but in the real world if one writes to 'The Premier, Parliament House, Sydney', the letter goes straight to the Premier's Department. So much for leaving the Secretary of the Department out of the loop. Further, although the Agent-General, Sir Timothy Coghlan, accepted that Childe was not working for him but for the Ministers in Sydney, Childe had to communicate with them through the Agent-General. Thus, at monthly intervals a batch of Childe's research memoranda would leave the office with a covering letter from Coghlan addressed to Premier Dooley. In Sydney, the letter would be opened by a Premier's Department clerk, logged and shunted off to another section of government or to a regular departmental file. Childe's research never escaped the oversight of Secretary Hay and Research Officer Harpur, and in time this would hasten the process of his dismissal.[12]

He commenced his work by collecting the pamphlets of the International Labour Organization, part of the recently formed League of Nations in Geneva, walking to its London office. He read in the London Library and the British Museum but was disappointed by the absence of documents from foreign countries in the latter. He must then have embarked on a tour of foreign consulates because in his memoranda he discusses the legislation of 18 countries, mainly in Europe and the Americas. There were 30 memoranda, usually about two typed foolscap pages, written at the rate of two or three every week. Although he was diligent it was hard to remain focused so far away from the political action in Sydney. He worried that his memoranda might not be useful; worse, that they might have no relevance at all if the Labor government fell, which seemed distinctly likely in December, just as he was taking up his position in London.[13]

In the meantime, he had to decide what was relevant, and some of his choices are revealing. As might be expected, there were statistical or technical memoranda on uncontroversial topics: the development of water power; refuse disposal in London; motor traffic in Britain; employment exchanges in Poland; unemployment in Denmark; and town planning in Salonika. But there were many other subjects that exposed the tensions of class conflict in postwar capitalism.

---

12   Childe's departure from Sydney and commencement of his duties in London noted in NSW State Archives, Premier's Department Correspondence, A22 1447.
13   Childe to Hay, 23 December 1921, NSW State Archives, Premier's Department Correspondence, file A/22 688 in box 9/4883; Childe to Hay 25 January 1922, ditto.

Exploitation by greedy profiteers? See how Argentina has legislated to prevent commercial fraud, to tax the profits of foreign banks and insurance companies, and to fix rents at current rates for two years. Farmers needing protection? Argentina had also fixed the minimum price of wheat and meat for export and enacted security of tenure of at least eight years on agricultural leases. Workers demanding industrial democracy? Japan had introduced social insurance in response to strikes for recognition of shop committees, and Argentina did the same for public employees with the added bait of employee representation. Workers demanding higher wages? Placate them with the social wage by legislating for insurance schemes covering accidents, unemployment, and superannuation, as in Holland, Argentina, Mexico, Uruguay, Sweden and Belgium. Childe noted, however, that union federations in Holland, France and Germany were cautious about supporting family allowances lest they depress wages. Cheap housing was another issue of concern in most of Europe after the war, and here too Childe showed that labour organisations preferred state enterprise to ameliorate working-class suffering – as in the public housing schemes of Sweden and Czechoslovakia – over financial benefits.[14]

* * *

The class struggle that Gordon reported on was not confined to the world outside Australia, and soon, on its parliamentary front in Sydney, his career would be derailed again. When the first batch of memoranda arrived in the Premier's Department, accompanied by his letter asking Secretary Hay for better 'political information', the Secretary immediately requested Harpur to evaluate them. Hay knew that the Labor government was about to fall. A month earlier it had been defeated in the Assembly, and the Governor of the State asked Sir George Fuller to form a government. It lasted seven hours before Jim Dooley returned as Premier leading a minority government weakened by widely reported factional fights. With a general election due early in 1922, the Nationalists were expecting an easy victory. Hay also knew that Childe's position would be terminated by a conservative government. In late November 1921 J.C.L. Fitzpatrick, Nationalist member for Bathurst and Holman's Treasurer before 1920, asked Premier Dooley

---

14   Childe's memoranda were sent in batches with covering letter from the Agent-General on 23 December 1921 (in Premier's Correspondence file A21/399 in box 9/1751), 16 January 1922 (ditto, 4883 A22/688), 25 January 1922 (ditto), 8 February 1922 (ditto), 22 February 1922 (ditto), 8 March 1922 (ditto), 23 March 1922 (ditto), 6 April 1922 (ditto), 20 April 1922 (ditto).

a series of questions about Childe. Had he been sent abroad and if so to what country? To what position had he been appointed, for how long, and at what salary and expenses? What were his duties? The answers must have been known already in parliamentary circles, even among Nationalists because of their friends in the Premier's Department. The point of the questions was to make Childe's role public, laying the ground for an attack on Labor's extravagance and political favouritism in appointments. All Secretary Hay had to do was provide the Premier with the appropriate information, but in addition he made public in coded words the information that would allow the Nationalists to sack Childe as a political appointee: Childe, he wrote, was required to 'undertake special research into matters remitted to him from time to time by the Premier'. Was it ominous that Hay gave his document answering Fitzpatrick's questions the title 'Case of Mr. V.G. Childe'?[15]

The elections were held in March 1922, the conservative parties secured a clear majority of seats, and Fuller became Premier. Five days later Hay again asked Harpur to evaluate Childe's memoranda. Harpur's reply to Hay's earlier request had been non-committal, so on this occasion Hay told him what to say: 'it seems to me that the work being done by Mr Childe is largely duplication'. In due course Harpur replied: none of Childe's memoranda provide new information, and moreover there are other, private channels for obtaining details of overseas legislation. On 18 April Hay sent Harpur's reply to Fuller with a minute recommending that Childe's services be dispensed with, after seeking Agent-General Coghlan's views. A cablegram was sent to Coghlan the same day.[16]

So far, no official decision about Childe had been taken, but unofficially it had. On 22 April the *Singleton Argus* carried this report:

> The work of lopping off unnecessary branches has begun by the new Government, and it came to a swift decision in regard to the so-called research work being carried out in London by Mr Gordon Childe. Mr Childe, a gentleman somewhat advanced in political thought and of brilliant scholastic attainments was at one time private secretary to the

---

15 Hay's minute on Attorney-General to Premier, 23 December 1921, in A21/399 in 9/1751; NSW Legislative Assembly, *Parliamentary Debates*, 29 November 1921; Hay's memorandum for the Premier, 23 November 1921, 'Case of Mr V.G. Childe', Premier's Correspondence, A22/1477 in 9/4885.

16 Michael Hogan, '1922', in Michael Hogan and David Clune (eds), *The People's Choice: Electoral Politics in 20th Century New South Wales, Volume One*, Sydney, Parliament of New South Wales and University of Sydney, 2001, pp. 235–68; Hay to Harpur, 30 March 1922; Harpur to Hay, 11 April 1922; and Hay to Premier, 18 April 1922 – all in A22/1477 in 9/4885.

late Mr John Storey ... Evidently the present Government did not assess the duties entrusted to Mr Childe at the same value put upon them by the previous Ministry, and the appointment has been terminated.

The source for this story was one of Sydney's major papers, *The Daily Telegraph*, which also circulated in Wentworth Falls. In 1912 the Rev. Stephen Childe had married Monica Gardiner, sold 'Chalet Fontenelle', and built another house, 'Coronel', in this Blue Mountains village. Concerned about his son's employment, he wrote from there on 21 April to the new Premier:

> Will you do me the kindness of telling me what are the terms of my son Gordon's dismissal; I mean whether he receives a month's or longer notice, and his return fare to Australia, or its equivalent. Of course, I am not surprised at your Cabinet's action for all my sympathies are with you and your party; but Gordon has always been a good son and is a generous helper of his invalid sister, making her a handsome monthly allowance from his salary. It is mainly on her account that I am seeking information as to how this [position] will terminate since my daughter has been largely dependent upon it.
>
> With hearty congratulations on your return to office, and with every good wish for a successful tenure.

Poor, caring Gordon: not even his father would say that he deserved consideration because he was performing the duties for which he had been engaged. His sister, Ethel, by the way, lived to the age of 92.[17]

In London, the Agent-General was in no doubt about the government's intention. He replied by cable on 26 April that he had given Childe notice of dismissal for 31 May, and Childe had accepted. Coghlan asked Hay if he could keep Childe on at a reduced salary of 250 pounds per annum (a cut of more than 50 per cent in his salary) to answer queries about New South Wales, at least until 1 August: 'He is very well informed and apparently harmless'. In a minute, Hay recommended this extension be granted, writing to the Premier that in his opinion the government was obligated to pay for Childe's return passage if he pressed the point. Hay probably hoped that the extra months would give Gordon time to find alternative employment in Britain; in fact, he suggested that Childe might be employed in a temporary capacity at a reduced salary beyond the start of August, if the Public Service Board agreed. Fuller

---

17 *Singleton Argus*, 22 April 1922; Rev. S.H. Childe to Sir George Fuller, 21 April 1922, A22/1477 in 9/4885.

approved and Coghlan was informed that the government had no objection to retaining Childe until August.[18]

A few days earlier Hay had written to Gordon's father at the Premier's request. Every important statement in this letter was misleading. He begins by denying that Gordon had been dismissed. This was correct in terms of administrative procedure. Hay then goes on to say that the government had asked the Agent-General if any good purpose would be served by retaining his services, neglecting to add that the government's cable reflected Hay's recommendation that Gordon be dismissed. Then he writes that the present government 'feels' that his appointment was made on political grounds and 'upon the decided understanding' that should Labor lose office 'there would be practically no prospect of its continuance'. This is what the conservatives preferred to believe, not what can be found in the archival record. In a similar fashion, Hay tells Gordon's father, for his 'confidential information', that Gordon 'was dispatched to London at his own request' so that he would be in a position to resume his career in scholarship. There is no documentary evidence of this either, and anyway the idea that a lowly public service officer could persuade the Premier of the State to send that officer to London for his personal advancement is risible. Finally, because the posting was made at Gordon's request, Hay writes that the government did not contemplate defraying the cost of Gordon's return voyage at the time, although Hay would tell the Premier three days later that if Gordon pressed the point the government would be obligated to grant him a return passage.[19]

Bill McKell has a different story of how Gordon was appointed. On April 29 he wrote to the Premier in response to the *Daily Telegraph*'s report. He said that he had known Gordon for many years and that he was 'a young man of high attainment and excellent character. Politically, he is regarded (wrongfully) by some as being violent, but knowing him as well as I do I can truthfully say he is quite harmless.' Gordon might have winced had he read this. His friend continued:

> The appointment of Mr Childe as Research Officer in London followed upon a suggestion made by Sir Joseph Carruthers to the late Mr John Storey to the effect that the State should have attached to the Agent-General's Office a man who could attend the different conferences that are held on the continent to report their relevance to NSW.

---

18 Coghlan's cable to Hay, 26 April 1922, A22/1477 in 9/4885; Hay to Premier, 27 April 1922, A22/269 in 9/4880.
19 Hay to Stephen Childe, 24 April 1922, A22/1477 in 9/5885.

Mr Storey mentioned the matter to me. Mr Childe, on account of his great knowledge of languages, immediately came to my mind, with the result that the Public Service Board on the recommendation of Mr Storey appointed Mr Childe to fill the office.

Conveniently omitting the political benefits of Gordon's role for Labor, McKell concluded by appealing to Sir George Fuller to take steps to retain 'such a highly qualified officer'.[20]

The 'Case of Mr V.G. Childe' continued to rumble on, fed by the radical press and most of all by McKell. In October he raised Gordon's dismissal in the Legislative Assembly, and in doing so shed further light on two aspects of Gordon's public service experience and the formation of his ideas about the state: first, the suspicion among Labor's socialists, of whom Gordon was one, that the state was not a neutral sphere standing above the contentions of politics, especially those arising from opposing class interests; and second, the consequent hostility that he faced from within the public service.

McKell's aim was not to strengthen the case for Gordon remaining in his London post, because having received a letter from Gordon in June he knew that Gordon had accepted his dismissal and was applying for a lectureship at the University of Leeds. Rather, his aim was to refute the conservative attack on the political nature of Gordon's appointment by insisting that Labor had followed proper Public Service Board procedure in making it, and to indict the conservatives for their motives in terminating it. Because no explanation had been offered, he said, the termination clearly 'was a political move on the part of the Government'.

This was clever, but it was never going to work because the conservatives knew too much about Gordon's politics. They reacted angrily to McKell's intervention. There were cries of 'His appointment was political', 'Is that the man who was in Queensland?', 'He is a most violent partisan', and 'You brought him into the service'. The last point was true, of course, and McKell had to explain it. He might have used the anodyne phrases of the PSB about Gordon's qualifications, but he chose to go on the offensive in parliament, implying that Labor did not trust the neutrality of public servants:

> MR McKELL: I would not be prepared to go into any department as Minister, and accept any clerk appointed to me by the Public Service Board.

---

20   McKell to Fuller, 29 April 1922 in A22/1477 in 9/4885.

MR OAKES: You would take a private citizen from outside and appoint him private secretary, and the Public Service Board would have no control over him?

MR McKELL: He is the Minister's officer; the Minister has control over him.

MR OAKES: But he has the run of the office!

MR McKELL: That is quite right, and the Minister would sooner have his own nominee with the run of the office than the nominee of the Public Service Board ... That officer handles the Minister's private and confidential correspondence, and the Minister should be able to repose confidence in him.

This line of argument called into question the liberal theory of the state by suggesting that state personnel could not be trusted to act in a non-partisan manner. Its ideological implications were too stark for McKell to use to advantage, for, as Storey had insisted in 1920, Labor was a self-proclaimed non-ideological party. McKell needed to get back to the main point of his intervention, that the dismissal showed that the conservatives were politically motivated. But, of course if, as McKell insisted, Gordon were just 'an excellent public servant', whom Sir Timothy Coghlan would be prepared to advise 'should be kept on', why was the government so vindictive? McKell presented a reason: 'there was a fly in the ointment' in Sydney, a man who continually spread misinformation about Childe. He had succeeded Gordon as Storey's private secretary, then worked for Dooley in the same capacity before resigning a few weeks before the 1922 general election. According to McKell, this man resented Childe from the moment Childe entered the service, 'and his resentment carried on to the time when he was appointed organizer by the National party a few weeks before the last general election' – 'the most dishonorable act I have ever known a civil servant to be guilty of ... I am prepared to say that this is the man who is responsible for the statements made about Mr Childe'.[21]

Although McKell did not name him it was not hard for contemporaries to discover that the man was W.J. Swan, an officer of the conservative National Association. In fact, Swan's resentment of Gordon might have arisen earlier

---

21 *The Federal Independent*, 1 June 1922; Premier's Office, Extract from Hansard, Thursday 11 October 1922, A22/1477 in 9/4885; re McKell receiving a letter from Childe: Hay to Rev. Stephen H. Childe, 23 June 1922, ditto.

than McKell indicated, because he had been Holman's private secretary before he was prevented from continuing in such a prestigious position with the succeeding Premier when Storey fought the Public Service Board to take Gordon with him into the Premier's Department in 1920. If Swan, with both a personal grudge and political animus against Gordon, had been making hostile remarks about him, the perception that Gordon's dismissal was political would be very hard to counter. Recognising the risk to his party, and to the idea of public service neutrality, Sir George Fuller instructed Hay to write to McKell. Hay told McKell that the government was not moved to act against Childe 'by any representations made by Mr Swan, late private secretary to the Premier, and now an Officer of the National Association'. A master at leaving a mistaken impression, Hay stopped short of saying that Swan did *not* make hostile representations about Gordon to the government. Assuming he did, we can be sure that he would have been attacking Gordon in wider public service circles as well.[22]

---

22   Hay to McKell, 19 October 1922, A22/1477 in 9/4885; *Canberra Times*, 13 February 1950, p. 2, 'Sudden Death of Mr W.J. Swan'.

Chapter 15

A PAUPER COLONIAL

The Fabian Research Department, where Gordon had volunteered in 1916 and 1917, became the Labour Research Department (LRD) in 1918. The change in name was more than symbolic. The LRD's research was at last receiving the recognition that it deserved: according to its Chairman, George Bernard Shaw, in his introduction to the 1918–19 annual report, 423 labour bodies were now affiliates of the department. At the same time its Honorary Secretary, Cole, who was advising the Labour Party on the administrative structure required by its 1918 constitution, brought the LRD closer to the parliamentary sphere of labour's politics. He was able to do a deal with the party: in return for some publicity work, the department would have rent-free offices in Labour's headquarters in Eccleston Square. But it was never a happy arrangement.

From the beginning there were ideological tensions. The department's volunteers and some of its staff had moved beyond their earlier guild socialist suspicion of top-down authority on the left to embrace the revolutionary perspective of the Communist Party. And there was also a profound disagreement about how left politics should be pursued, for the department saw itself as part of a loose movement, not of an institutionalised labour public becoming more centralised every day. Labour's opposing view, however, was that its hosting of a research body that was independent, both organisationally and financially, was simply not compatible with the party's new bureaucratic and professional orientation. In July 1921 the department received an ultimatum: dissolve itself into the new Trade Union Congress and Labour Party joint research department, or give up its offices in Eccleston Square. True to his democratic guild principles, and to his own stubborn individualism, Cole led the LRD out of the Labour Party's controlling embrace.[1]

---

1   Arnot, *History of the Labour Research Department*, p. 19; Morgan, *Labour Legends and Russian Gold*, pp. 71–2.

After finding the LRD in its new offices in Buckingham Palace Road, Gordon applied for membership, which was only open to individuals who were members of labour bodies. In February 1922, the Executive Committee elected him to membership, noting that his union was the National Union of Clerks. He brought with him the manuscript of his book, the 'connected account of labour history', hoping that the department would publish it. He had worked on the manuscript while on board ship, and he was still adding to it in London. Childe wrote in his Preface that the ending point for his study was 1921, when Australian labour 'passes into a new period of transition, the substantial tendencies of which are still obscure', but in fact there are references in the book to February, March, May and July 1922.[2]

These tendencies were already causing excitement among the communists of the LRD. In January, the *Labour Monthly*, nominally independent but actually subsidised by the Comintern, published the new program of the Australian Labor Party, including its socialist objective. In April, Esmonde Higgins, the only Australian in the LRD, was asked to write an article on Australian labour to act as a preface to 'a more or less elaborate study of Australian labour politics by a chap who used to be Storey's secretary but who is now in the NSW Agent-General's office here'. The article, 'The Rise and Fall of Australian Labour', appeared in the June 1922 issue of *Labour Monthly*. Its message was clear: postwar developments have shown that the Labor Party is unable to protect the workers from an employers' offensive to destroy 'every achievement of organised Labour'. It cannot use state enterprises to benefit the workers, it cannot protect the basic wage, it cannot prevent unemployment. But, 'the Industrialists', despite their 'nebulous' theory and their 'simple' strategy of the general strike, have nonetheless released the 'revolutionary will' and 'sincere hatred of the present order' of the working class. So, as the department contemplated the publication of Childe's manuscript, it had already decided how it was to be understood, as a critique of labour parliamentarism and a call to revolution.[3]

In July, the Executive Committee resolved to thank Childe 'for his offer of the manuscript of the book on Australian Labour together with all the rights therein, and their acceptance of it on the proviso that should a publisher be

---

2 Minutes of the Executive Committee of the LRD, 3 February 1922 (held by the LRD); Childe, *How Labour Governs*, 1st edn, pp. xvii, 85, 209–10.

3 Morgan, *Labour Legends and Russian Gold*, p. 36; Esmonde Higgins to his parents, 19 April 1922, E.M. Higgins papers, Mitchell Library MSS 740/6; E.M. Higgins. 'The Rise and Fall of Australian Labour', *Labour Monthly*, vol. 3, no. 5, June 1922, pp. 405–12.

found by the LRD for it, he would be entitled to a royalty or part royalty to be settled by arrangement between himself and the LRD'. By this time, he was working out the last weeks of his employment at half-pay with the Agent-General, so he would have felt some urgency about this proviso. He was also restoring his links to the network of radicals that he had been part of while at Oxford.[4]

A few weeks later he agreed to give a lecture to the LRD summer school in August, no doubt as a further stage in the department's plan to promote his book. According to Margaret Cole (Ray Postgate's sister), summer schools were a 'peculiarly Anglo-Saxon combination of holiday-making, sociability and more-or-less intellectual effort', and by the early twentieth century they had become a standing fixture in the calendar of young radicals. Students and tutors in the WEA, guild socialists, members of the ILP and the Fabian Society all looked forward to them. As the postwar radicalism gathered strength, so did the demand for the summer school experience. In 1920 a member of the Rowntree family – chocolate makers and Quaker philanthropists – purchased Cober Hill, a Victorian mansion in six acres of gardens on the edge of the North Yorkshire moors at Cloughton, setting up a trust to make it available to people working in adult education. This was the site for the LRD's 1922 school. It would last three weeks, with a week devoted to each of industrial questions, international problems, and working-class education. Gordon travelled there at the beginning of the second week, after lunching with Margaret at the railway cafeteria.[5]

We know a lot about this summer school. It features in published and unpublished sources, including two articles in *The Manchester Guardian* from a special correspondent, and, remarkably, we have Gordon's own account. Although he destroyed his personal papers near the end of his life, he overlooked this diary-style set of notes, with an entry for each day, no doubt because he wrote it in a research and readings notebook, one of many that he left to the Institute of Archaeology. On this occasion he recorded his impressions of the lectures (including his own), and noted the weather, his meals, and the recreations

---

4 Labour Research Department, Executive Committee Minutes, 7 July 1922, held by the LRD.
5 Margaret Cole, *Growing Up Into Revolution*, London, Longman Green, 1949, p. 117; Margaret Cole, *The Story of Fabian Socialism*, London, Heinemann, 1961, Appendix V; *Manchester Guardian*, 'The Labour Research Summer School', 30 August 1922, p. 12: Joseph R. Starr, 'The Summer Schools and Other Educational Activities of British Socialist Groups', *The American Political Science Review*, vol. 30, no. 5, October 1936, pp. 956–74. There had been an LRD summer school in 1921 at Herne Bay.

he participated in: bridge, tennis, walking, and acting in the traditional end-of-school revue. In a little over 200 words he mentioned 26 names of other attendees, some of them more than once. He names the two men whom he roomed with. He names those he played bridge and tennis with, and those he went walking with. He records his winnings at bridge: 15 shillings over four games. After one particularly long walk with two companions they were glad to stop for tea at the Beacon Cottage, where three other members of the school joined them. He notes who got drunk on Sunday night, the 'great crowd' with whom he travelled to York on the last day, and his fellow bridge players on the train back to London. Having been away from this milieu for five years, Gordon was looking for ways to be part of it again, and to build a network of friends and companions. On the evidence of this diary, a convivial young man (he was 30) had found his crowd.[6]

A smoko during the LRD summer school at Cloughton, 1922.
L to R: Ray Postgate, Maurice Dobb, Douglas Cole, Margaret Cole, Rose Cohen.
(E.M. Higgins, PXE 1085, in E.M. Higgins papers, MLMSS 740,
State Library of New South Wales)

---

6   *Manchester Guardian*, 30 August 1922, p. 12, and 15 September 1922, p. 6; J.G. Crowther, *Fifty Years with Science*, London, Barrie & Jenkins, 1970, pp. 19–21; Hugh Purcell, *The Last English Revolutionary: Tom Wintringham 1898–1949*, Stroud, Sutton Publishing, 2004, pp. 29–30; Esmonde Higgins to [his parents], 18 September and 29 November 1922, Higgins papers, Mitchell Library MSS 740/6; Childe papers, Institute of Archaeology, London, item 55 (notebook).

He was not choosy about his companions. He was often with friends from his Oxford days: walking with Margaret, playing tennis with Cole, rooming with Clemens Dutt (Rajani's brother, a maths honours graduate from Cambridge), and playing bridge with Ray Postgate. But he also interacted with the younger and newer rebels in the LRD: the Australian Esmonde Higgins, as well as Maurice Dobb, Rose Cohen and Hugo Rathbone, each of whom had joined the Communist Party. He also spent time walking with the venerable Fabian, George Bernard Shaw, and with Philip Snowden and Charles P. Trevelyan, both of whom were to have important roles in Labour governments. He played bridge with Barbara Gould, who had been gaoled as a window-smashing suffragette but was now making a career in the Labour Party, a little later in its National Executive Committee and after 1945 in parliament.

Nor was politics the only thing on his mind. He was staying in a region dotted with ancient burial sites, known as tumuli or barrows, dating from the Neolithic to the late Bronze Age. On Saturday he set out in the rain with Higgins to investigate the barrows in the Broxa forest. On Monday he walked to Scarborough, possibly to see North Yorkshire's most famous barrow, the Seamer Beacon. Wednesday was another dull and damp day but undeterred he walked in the woods to a circle of stones, recorded by him as the Druids Circle, a Bronze Age site near Cloughton Newlands. On Thursday he walked with four companions to Ravenscar via the village of Falcon. He no doubt wanted to see a carved rock from the Bronze Age that had been cemented into the wall of the Raven Hall Hotel.

Back in the lecture room, according to *The Manchester Guardian*'s correspondent, a 'Communist keynote … ran throughout most of the discussions'. This wasn't surprising because the 'left-wing' of communists, guild socialists and ILP-ers, still overlapping groups at this point, comprised 'the great majority' of those attending. There were some spirited discussions. The 'official, right-wing' Labour position was poorly represented, so the moderate Labour supporter, Trevelyan, received the full brunt of the left's attack on labourism. In the discussion following Trevelyan's second lecture, criticism 'came not only from the Communists but also from others, who thought that he expected too much from the parliamentary machine and underestimated the prospects of both constitutional and unconstitutional resistance by the propertied sections of the community'. On the left-wing, where there were also disagreements, the mood was hardening, and the correspondent detected it: 'Mr R. Palme Dutt presented the Communist position in two lectures, impressive in their effect despite the lecturer's undisguised contempt both for his audience and for all other points of view'. Rajani Dutt had a knack for sounding dogmatic; the other communists who delivered lectures – Robin Page Arnot, Clemens Dutt, Maurice Dobb and William Paul – perhaps because they adopted a more expository style, escaped the *Guardian*'s censure. Apart from the communists, the other political tendency most strongly in evidence in lectures was guild socialism. S.G. Hobson, the inventor of the term, explained the guild program of industrial control, while Cole gave no less than five lectures, including the opening and closing lecture. He called the latter 'A Plague on Both Your Houses', expounding guild socialism's 'differences from both the Parliamentarian and Communist positions'. His lecture on the guild strategy of industrial control elicited 'the best and briskest discussion of the week'.

In his diary Gordon did not respond positively to any of the lectures, but he did find five sufficiently interesting to make him want to record that he had heard them, and he made negative comments on four others. The lectures that he wanted to remember were by Dutt; by journalist Frank Horrabin and by Cole on the teaching of history to working-class students; by the editor of the *Communist Review*, William Paul, on communism; by Bernard Shaw on whether democracy was compatible with efficient government (the young communist Esmonde Higgins, however, thought Shaw 'painfully ridiculous'); and Cole's closing lecture. The ones he disliked were by the ILP journalist H.N. Brailsford on international problems ('bad lecture'); by Dobb on Marxian economics ('dull'); by Trevelyan ('dull'); and, then the lecture that he himself gave ('bad lecture').

His was not a dull lecture, in his mind, but a bad one: so its failure was down to something more than Gordon's usual lecturing style, a style that no-one ever described as stimulating. Was it the topic? In his diary Gordon wrote that it was on the One Big Union. This was a subject that he knew well, and that he had just been working on, because he discusses it in the last two chapters of *How Labour Governs*. The penultimate chapter is largely descriptive, the ultimate chapter is argumentative, so no doubt he based the lecture on the latter chapter. On the 'Contents' page of the book, he describes the chapter thus: 'The A.W.U. leaders opposed the O.B.U. as a threat to their positions and to their prospects of political advancement – The O.B.U. regarded the A.W.U. as structurally unscientific, as reactionary in policy, and as controlled by opportunists and boodlers – Examination of these contentions.' For this audience, union structure and politics were critical topics, and not out of line with the theme of the papers in the first week of the school: understanding why labour had lost the advantages it had held at the beginning of 1919. As *The Manchester Guardian* described the conclusion of that discussion, it was decided 'the problem was not primarily one of organisation, and ultimately it resolved itself into a question of spirit and attitude of the rank and file of the trade union membership. The failures of the recent years preceding the slump were traced back to a lack of the "will to go through with it". As so often in the minds of middle-class left intellectuals, the psychology of the workers was to blame.

But Gordon's analysis of the Australian situation was different. The OBU militants had plenty of will, but they misdirected it into a fight against existing unions, a fight that alienated the rank and file, their natural supporters. Meanwhile, the AWU bosses held off the challenge from the left by corruptly buying the support of the leaders of some smaller craft unions. Then they seduced the leaders of the main industrial unions with a proposal to set up something that looked like the OBU but under the banner of the AWU. And the 'industrialists' bought it, because the new body was allowed to use the notorious OBU 'Preamble' about class war! Gordon was disgusted. The so-called left leaders of the industrial unions were as self-serving as the AWU bureaucrats. In *How Labour Governs* he sums up the position in 1922: this apparent victory for the industrialists will cost them their ideals. The OBU will have to sacrifice its revolutionary idealism. It will become in all likelihood 'just a gigantic apparatus for the glorification of a few bosses. Such is the history of all Labour organisations in Australia, and that not because they are Australian, but because they are Labour.'[7]

If that were the argument of Gordon's lecture it is easy to see why the *Manchester Guardian* correspondent called it 'most depressing'. No-one at Cloughton wanted to be told that all labour organisations, even those that were idealistic and revolutionary, were prone to corruption, bossism, and betrayal of the working class. Such a message was not just depressing, it was a slap in the face. One can't imagine any positive reactions to it emerging from that audience. When Gordon reflected on this for his diary he came to the only possible conclusion: he had given a bad lecture.[8]

There was a further development resulting from his attendance at the summer school. On 22 September 1922, MI5 obtained a new Home Office Warrant to intercept the mail of one V.G. Childe who lived at 34 Cartwright Gardens, London. 'Childe is an extreme socialist who is closely connected with Postgate and other Communists; it is desired by means of this check to ascertain whether he is taking an active part in the revolutionary movement.'[9]

---

7   *How Labour Governs*, 1st edn, p. 210.
8   *Manchester Guardian*, 15 September 1922, p. 6.
9   Childe's MI5 file, KV2/2148, 169.

***

Gordon began looking for a job as soon as he knew that his position with the Agent-General was 'terminating', as he put it in his letter to Alice: 'I am hanging on for a bit and looking for another, but not very hopefully. They are rather rare. There is however a lectureship at Leeds which I am after at the present.' So, his first strategy was to fall back on his academic training. Between May 1922 and May 1923 he undertook four visits to museums in Central Europe, turning his research promptly into scholarly articles, which, according to the archaeologist Timothy Champion 'look like the resumption of unfinished business', because they continued the themes of Gordon's 1915 article and his BLitt thesis: the Indo-European influences on Greek prehistory, and the connections between the Neolithic cultures of south-eastern Europe. These six articles, published over roughly 24 months, brought him much needed recognition and valuable contacts in Britain and on the Continent. By November 1923 he was contemplating a book on the Neolithic and Bronze ages in Europe, a project warmly supported by the editor of the *Journal of Hellenic Studies*, John Forsdyke, who had published the first of those articles. This was the book that would make Gordon famous, *The Dawn of European Civilization*, published in 1925.[10]

His former Oxford college, Queen's, contributed funds for at least one of his research trips, but he needed well-paying employment to continue down this scholarly path. He had two powerful Oxford referees – John Myres, the Wykeham Professor of Ancient History, who had been his supervisor for the BLitt thesis, and Gilbert Murray, Regius Professor of Greek, whose advice he had sought in relation to the defence of conscientious objectors – but it was not until 1925 that he found a satisfactory scholarly position, with the Royal Anthropological Institute. Meanwhile, there were many knock-backs. As letters to Gordon have not survived (apart from those intercepted by British and Australian spy agencies) we have to rely on his letters to Myres and

---

10   Gordon to 'My dearest Alice', no date, but May 1922, in George Munster Further papers, 1908–2002, Mitchell Library Accession Record; Childe to Myres, 27 November 1923, Myres papers, Bodleian Library, box 8, f. 11; Timothy Champion, 'Childe and Oxford', *European Journal of Archaeology*, vol. 12, nos 1–3, April–December 2009, pp. 22–5; Attila László, 'The Young Gordon Childe and Transylvanian Archaeology: The Archaeological Correspondence between Childe and Ferenc László', *European Journal of Archaeology*, vol. 12, nos 1–3, April–December 2009, pp. 35–46; Bruce G. Trigger, *Gordon Childe: Revolutions in Archaeology*, London, Thames & Hudson, 1980, pp. 35–6.

Murray to get a sense of the disappointments of those years. The Leeds job eluded him. He was also thinking about a classics lectureship at Durham but whether he applied or not we do not know. We do, however, have his letters thanking Myres for advice and support for two college fellowships in Oxford, at Hertford and St John's, and an Open Senior Scholarship at New College. He failed to get any of them. Myres tried unsuccessfully to persuade him to take a position with the British School in Jerusalem, but the remuneration was inadequate and, according to Gordon, working 'in Jewry' would have been 'so unpleasant', with 'only the chosen to borrow from'. Anti-semitism was, it seems, one aspect of his Christian culture that he had not managed to throw off.[11]

The royalties from *How Labour Governs* were small – about £28 – or about the equivalent of three weeks of his former salary in the office of the Agent-General. He was able to arrange an advance on the legacy he expected when his father and stepmother died, but by July 1924 he had spent almost half of it, about £500. This meant that for two years he was living on less than half of his former salary. Green recounts that Robert Chorley, remembering how he and Childe would work together in the library of the Bloomsbury Club, and how abstemious Childe was at this time, worried that Gordon 'might die of semi-starvation' before finishing his 'great work'! Gordon was able to make some money out of his knowledge of languages, translating two books on archaeology from the French, but after his knock-backs he was not hopeful about finding a well-paid position. He told Murray that 'when one is 32 and qualified principally in archaeology, a subject which was remunerative only in civilized countries now defunct or moribund, one can't expect much'. But he had already explored his prospects in other fields. He enquired about jobs from his Oxford friend David Blelloch who was working for the International Labour Office in Geneva, and from the science journalist J.G. Crowther, whom he met at the LRD summer school in 1922, but neither was able to help.[12]

---

11   Pro-Provost of Queen's College to Myres, 25 January 1924, Myres papers, box 8, f. 16; Childe to Myres, 2 June 1922, Myres papers, box 8, f. 3 (Leeds and Durham); Childe to Myres, no date, but late May or early June 1922, Myres papers, box 8, f. 6 (Hertford); Childe to Myres, 4 February 1924, Myres papers, box 8, f. 17 (St John's); Childe to Myres, 22 July 1924, Myres papers, box 8, f. 25 (re New College); Childe to Myres, 16 October 1924, Myres papers, box 8, f. 28 (Jewry).

12   Labour Research Department, Minutes of the Executive Committee, 4 January and 4 April 1924; Childe to Myres, 22 July 1924, Myres papers, box 8, f. 25 (re legacy); Green, pp. 48 and 51; Trigger, *Gordon Childe*, p. 36 (re translations); Childe to Murray, 18 October [1924], Murray papers, shelfmark 48, f. 153; Childe to Blelloch, quoted in Green, p. 43; Crowther, *Fifty Years with Science*, pp. 19–20.

By then his political experience had secured him a more reliable if small income. After the general election of November 1922, he picked up part-time work as secretary to two Liberal politicians. Chorley introduced him to the newly elected MP for Taunton, John Hope Simpson. The other politician, Frank Gray, MP for Oxford, Gordon might have known from his Oxford days, and he would certainly have thought of him as a fellow radical. Although Gray was the wealthy son of a conservative Mayor and businessman in Oxford, he grew up hating the ruling class. He enlisted in the army but refused to take a commission and after the war published a book about his experiences as a private: 'Well, I do not wish to speak ungenerously or intemperately but my experiences taught me to believe that in fact we had no Leaders and no Generals'. He would allow tramps to stay overnight in his family mansion, and in the mid-1920s, dressed as a tramp, he worked in the Warwickshire mines and slept in the workhouses, collecting material for a book, *The Tramp: his Meaning and Being*. It is possible that he attended the summer school and, if so, Gordon would have met him there. Unfortunately, these secretarial duties did not last. Gray resigned from parliament, accused of corrupt electioneering, in May 1924 (he was later acquitted), and Simpson was defeated in the election of October 1924. Gordon at this point was really worried. Perhaps, he thought, his travels in Europe might qualify him for a position with the League of Nations Institute for Intellectual Cooperation. Ever the materialist, he wrote to Myres that his special knowledge of archaeology 'leads financially nowhere, and money is the ONLY thing moneyless people can consider'.[13]

Being a Marxist as well as moneyless, he naturally began to think about his position in the class structure. After his death, some commentators pointed to Gordon as 'an outsider'. This was a vogue term in the 1950s and 1960s, echoing the title of Colin Wilson's book of 1956. Its immense commercial success reflected the appeal of a crude popularisation of existentialism and a mood among young people of rebellion and alienation. In Peter Gathercole's influential article 'Childe the Outsider', Gordon is presented as alienated from British intellectual life because he was an Australian, a committed European, and a Marxist. He was all of those things, but the origins of the conflicted feelings that they provoked in him are in his political practice, and particularly in his first 'political' life up to 1922. So, we can be more specific. Gordon said in 1923 that he felt like 'an unknown member of the proletariat', 'a pauper

---

13   Green, p. 45 (re Simpson and Gray); Frank Gray, *The Confessions of a Private*, Oxford, Blackwell, 1920, p. ix; Gray, *The Tramp: His Meaning and Being*, London, Dent, 1931; Childe to Myres, 15 October 1924 (Myres papers, box 8, f. 27) and 18 October 1924 (f. 28).

colonial', phrases inflected by class analysis and his own dispositions. Highly trained, aspiring to professional status as an academic, Gordon's experience of work was in fact proletarian in the sense he sold his labour-power for a wage, clerking in a government department, administering a Premier's office, answering letters for politicians. He knew what proletarian labour was like: 'dull, mechanical, and monotonous', as he said, not to speak of underpaid. Servile too, although this was a term he applied to workers in general but never to himself. Still, he knew what he needed to escape from, and the title that he needed in order to obtain interesting, creative, and well-paid work. As he told Myres, he needed a job title that would denote him 'as a member of the ruling caste'. Within 18 months he was well on his way to entering that caste, and in subsequent years he enjoyed its privileges, but he never lost the feeling of being an outsider in the British class structure.[14]

Analysing his situation in this way, in terms of class and work, we see that Gordon was not about to leave politics behind. In 1924, as well as two scholarly articles, he published three political articles, one of them in *Labour Monthly* and two in the journal of the Plebs League, a Marxist-inspired workers' education movement. In 'A Fabian Judged by History', he makes a critical analysis of *State Experiments in Australia and New Zealand* by W. Pember Reeves, a liberal New Zealand politician who became a Fabian. A second impression of the book had just appeared, so Gordon was able to place it in the context of the 20 years that had passed since the first printing. His conclusion is damning: the strategy of state socialism ('Fabianism') has failed. It had not improved the condition of the workers and it had introduced corruption and division into the labour movement. Except, that is, in Queensland, where a 'real Labour government' has gone beyond the 'gentlemanly' tactics of the Fabians, propelled by the strength of 'genuine' unions, to introduce laws that actually improved the status of the workers. But even this situation had limits. A few months later he wrote about Premier Theodore's trip to the financiers of London to raise a loan to pay for Queensland's state enterprises. The title, 'A Labour Premier Meets His Masters', sums up his argument: the economic power of capital trumps the political power of the labour movement, at least when the movement follows the parliamentary path. Theodore and his Cabinet thus stand revealed, Gordon wrote, using a phrase from *The Communist Manifesto*, as nothing but 'a subservient managing committee for the bourgeoisie'. In the

---

14   Colin Wilson, *The Outsider*, London, Gollancz, 1956; Sarah Bakewell, *At the Existentialist Café: Freedom, Being and Apricot Cocktails*, London, Chatto & Windus, 2016, pp. 288–91; Gathercole, 'Childe the Outsider', pp. 5–6; Childe to Myres, 27 November 1923, Myres papers, box 8, f. 11.

third article, he ridiculed a book that advocated cooperation between workers and employers, as full of 'puerile abstractions' and '*in*voluntary ignorance'. Given his view of the reactionary nature of religion, Gordon would not have been surprised to discover that the author, J.K. Heydon, an Australian businessman and Catholic apologist, in the 1930s published a book eulogising fascism and Nazism as supposedly based in Catholicism. He also asserted that democracy was being forced on Britain by Satan through the medium of international finance.[15]

In 1925, Gordon's luck changed. With the help of Myres and Murray he was appointed as Librarian of the Royal Anthropological Institute in London. As Green explains, 'He was in charge of bibliographical work, and his personal contacts with prehistorians in other European countries resulted in a lasting relationship between their libraries and that of the RAI'. He was also now earning 750 pounds, about three times what he had been living on in each of the previous two years. This was the year, too, when *The Dawn of European Civilization* appeared, closely followed in 1926 by *The Aryans: A Study of Indo-European Origins*. In archaeological circles, he was clearly a coming man, and he knew it. In June of 1925, while he was still correcting the proofs of *The Dawn*, he told Myres that he was going to apply for a new Chair in archaeology at the University of Edinburgh.[16]

---

15   Childe, 'A Fabian Judged by History', *The Plebs*, vol. 16, no. 1, January 1924, pp. 12–13; Childe, 'A Labour Premier Meets His Masters', *Labour Monthly*, vol. 6, June 1924, pp. 282–5; Childe, 'A Colonial Product', *The Plebs*, vol. 16, no. 7, July 1924, p. 288; W. Pember Reeves, *State Experiments in Australia and New Zealand*, 2nd impression, London, Allen & Unwin, 1924; J.K. Heydon, *Wage Slavery*, London, The Bodley Head, 1924; J.K. Heydon, *Fascism and Providence*, London, Sheed & Ward, 1937, p. 142; Dan Stone, *Responses to Nazism in Britain, 1933–39: Before War and Holocaust*, Springer, 2003, p. 127.

16   Childe to Murray, 18 October [1924], Murray papers, shelfmark 48, f. 153; Green, *Prehistorian*, pp. 49–50; Childe, *The Dawn of European Civilization*, London, Kegan Paul, Trench, Trubner, 1925; Childe, *The Aryans: A Study of Indo-European Origins*, London, Kegan Paul, Trench Trubner, 1926; Childe to Myres, no date, but June 1926, Myres papers, box 8, f. 31.

Chapter 16

HOW LABOUR GOVERNS AND *THE DAWN*

How Labour Governs appeared in July 1923 under the imprint of The Labour Publishing Company (LPC). Although set up by the Labour Research Department a few years earlier, the LPC was a separate organisation, in separate premises, with a publishing list that was much wider than the pamphlets and books issued by the LRD. The manager of the company was Bernard Noel Langdon-Davies, son of a wealthy motor engineer, a conscientious objector during the war, and one of the founders of the National Council for Civil Liberties (NCCL). It was one of several publishers aiming for a readership in the labour movement, some of them quite profitable, but the LPC always struggled financially. A material point of difference between the LRD and the LPC was the source of funding. The capital of the LPC was raised from shareholders belonging to the progressive tradition of middle-class 'lettered fellow travellers' of the labour movement, whereas in 1923 the LRD was attached to the Soviet teat, sustained by Russian gold.[1]

Gordon had volunteered in the offices of the NCCL in 1916, so he might have used that connection to offer his manuscript directly to Langdon-Davies at the LPC. Or he might have approached the Twentieth Century Press, publishers of the journal of the Social Democratic Federation, *Justice*. Instead, he offered his manuscript to the LRD, where he had volunteered in 1916 and 1917, saying that he had written it 'as a result of his experiences in the Department'. It was an indirect indication of his intellectual and political debt to his Oxford friends who were now putting their mark on the LRD. Moving into the communist orbit now, they welcomed Childe and his book. We have seen that they instructed Higgins to prepare the ground for it by writing an article for *Labour Monthly*. From the beginning, then, Gordon's book was an

---

1   Pat Francis, 'The Labour Publishing Company 1920–9', *History Workshop Journal*, vol. 18, no. 1, 1984, pp. 115–23; Morgan, *Labour Legends and Russian Gold*, Ch. 3.

LRD project, an intervention into the politics of the British left. When at the 6th Congress of the Communist Party in May 1924 the Comintern emissary quoted from *How Labour Governs* to deride labourism, the LRD communists knew their intervention was appreciated.[2]

In January 1923, they were considering publishing the book itself. The reason for its publication by the LPC is unclear, although it was not uncommon for the LRD's publications, especially books with a more general appeal, to be issued from or jointly with the LPC. In March 1923, the Executive Committee approved a guarantee of up to 30 pounds to ensure its publication, and in April this was increased to 40 pounds. In the event, the guarantee was required, and Raymond Postgate, a member of the Executive Committee, stumped up the money.[3]

In its publicity the LPC described *How Labour Governs* as 'A masterly study of Labour politics and organisation in Australia by a former private secretary of an Australian Prime Minister. Full of lessons for Labour in this country.' Obviously, the publicist had not read Gordon's Preface in which he revealed his position with the Premier of New South Wales, nor the Special Note on p. x where he distinguishes between the Premier of a State and the Prime Minister of the Commonwealth. But this was not a mistake that would deter British readers. In appearance, the book was substantial: 216 pages plus 32 pages of preliminary matter (most of it in the Introduction), bound in hard covers, with the LPC's striking logo on the title page. There was a fold-out map of Australia, a short bibliography, a five-page chronological table of the main industrial events between 1879 and March 1922, and an index. The table of contents spread over two pages because each of the 12 chapter-headings had descriptive text attached. In the second edition published in 1964, this descriptive table of contents was omitted; just the chapter headings were given. The second edition also omitted Childe's bibliography. These omissions have hindered readers' understanding of his argument.[4]

Official Labour in Britain was gearing up for office. The title of Gordon's 1922 article 'When Labour Ruled' was meant to echo the title of the 1920 book by union leader and Labour MP Jimmy Thomas, *When Labour Rules*.

---

2   *Monthly Circular of the Labour Research Department*, October 1923; *Communist Review*, vol. 5, no. 2, June 1924 (on 1924 CPGB Congress).
3   Arnot, *History of the Labour Research Department*, Appendix VI, 'Publications'; Labour Research Department, Executive Committee Minutes, January, March and April 1923, and April 1924.
4   Pat Francis, letter to T. Irving, 18 April 1986, in the possession of the author (for LPC publicity); Childe, *How Labour Governs*, 1st edn.

Thomas became a 'labour rat' in 1931, when Labour Prime Minister Ramsay MacDonald led his followers into a National government, as did Philip Snowden, who published a book with a similar title, *If Labour Rules*, just a few months after Gordon's book. Both of these were about the policies that a Labour government would introduce, and both were meant to relieve the fears of the middle class. In Snowden's words: 'I am confident that a Labour Government will be less of a class Government than any other Government of the past has been'. In contradistinction, Gordon's book, as its subtitle revealed, was 'a study of workers' representation'; class government was exactly his focus, or, more exactly, his focus was the likelihood of a labour party governing in the interests of the *working* class. And this was how his book was understood at the time. In fact, the Labour Publishing Company made a revealing mistake when publicising the book: in the end-papers to Snowden's book, Childe's subtitle was rendered as 'A Study of Working Class Representation', instead of 'Workers' Representation'. Same meaning, but inserting 'class' suggested a different philosophical universe. Similarly, using 'Governs' in the title rather than 'Rules' clearly marked off his book philosophically from those by Thomas and Snowden, because on the anti-capitalist left – where Childe stood – governing is not the same as ruling.[5]

To state the obvious: Gordon's book was not written from a liberal perspective but with a class-based Marxist analysis. So dominant, however, is the liberal paradigm in political science and popular political commentary that from his day to ours his book is criticised for neglecting a discussion of Labor legislation and regulations. It is as if the only thing 'governs' can mean is what a government does, and how it does it. It is as if the question of 'Governing for whom?' cannot be asked. The question is either fatuous, because as equal citizens of the state the government supposedly governs for all; or dangerous, because it is likely to expose the self-interested, improper and sometimes criminal behaviour of a ruling class for whom liberal principles are cheap. So, it doesn't get asked, except by those who start, as Childe did, from an understanding of capitalism's class dynamics and their expression in the system of liberal representative government.

The book's Preface indicates Childe's intention: to 'give some account of the political and industrial organisation' of the movement. After an introduction that sketches Australia's historical background, geography and economic resources, the analysis of organisation falls into two halves. Chapters I to V

---

5   J.H. Thomas, *When Labour Rules*, London, W. Collins, 1920 (reprinted 1921); Philip Snowden, *If Labour Rules*, London, The Labour Publishing Company, 1923.

deal with 'politicalism', a term that Childe coined to describe the organisational steps required by the decision of the labour movement to fight in the parliamentary arena. Today, it would be called parliamentarism. Chapters VI to XII deal with the reaction against politicalism by the union militants, the 'industrialists' who sought a reorganisation of the workers along industrial lines. In the Preface he presents very briefly his argument. The object of a 'Labour Party' and a 'Trade Union', and the 'Labour Movement' of which they are part, is to alter the social structure of capitalism and thus end the exploitation of workers. Then he indicates his own view of this 'theory'. He has adopted it 'for expository purposes' but this 'must not be taken to imply my personal acceptance of the theory in question. On the other hand, the results of this book and the sequel, which I hope to publish subsequently on the work of Labour Governments, may be regarded as the most serious criticism of that whole position.'

This statement can be understood in different ways. Is he criticising the objective (that capitalist exploitation must be ended) or the party and union as organisational means for achieving that end, or the unnamed strategies – say, constitutionalist or revolutionary – chosen by party and union? And what of the anti-politicalist organisational method and strategy of the industrial unionists? As we shall see, Childe damns the One Big Union as well as the Labor Party in the last lines of the book. This has puzzled many readers, as has the cryptic explanation of his argument in the Preface.[6]

In Childe's account of politicalism, its object was to make the workers and not the capitalists the controllers of the state machine. This was to be achieved by three organisational steps. The first was to ensure that party policy was decided by the labour movement, hence the importance of the annual conference of delegates from the local labour leagues (that is, branches of the party in the electorates), affiliated unions and other bodies. The second step was to give the party executive the power to interpret the platform, and 'to grant or refuse endorsement to would-be Labour candidates' between conferences. The third step was to insist on the party voting solidly in parliament, and for this purpose the Caucus meeting of party members and the pledge made by members to vote as the majority of Caucus decided were essential. This system of 'triple controls' enabled Labor to claim that it was a party of the workers' movement, not a collection of individuals representing diverse constituencies.[7]

---

6   *How Labour Governs*, 1st edn, p. v.
7   *How Labour Governs*, 1st edn, Ch. 1, esp. pp. 6 and 11.

These steps, according to Childe, amounted to 'a novel theory of democracy'. It was a model, he wrote, that expressed the understanding of self-government developed by 'the proletarian democracy of Australia': that the 'issues to be submitted to the people must also be determined by the people'. Because it struck at the heart of liberal individualist notions of democracy, 'labour's novel theory of democracy' – this subordination of the party to the movement – has always outraged conservatives who invariably point out that it means that Labor parliamentarians 'are not representatives of the people but the tools of an irresponsible junta'. While Labor could shrug this off as right-wing outrage, it found it more difficult to answer critics on the left, such as Childe, who showed in *How Labour Governs* that Labor's model did not work.[8]

Childe began by arguing that Caucus control is illusory. Labor Ministers, even though elected by the parliamentary Caucus, 'undergo a mental transformation', coming to see non-ministerial Caucus members not as colleagues but as irritants. The Ministers manipulate Caucus, or ignore it, or the Premier threatens its members with a dissolution of the chamber leading to an election in which Caucus members might lose their seats. More serious was the fact that movement control of parliamentarians was counterproductive. Childe described how the workers' representative, 'surrounded by the middle-class atmosphere of Parliament', thought more of 'keeping his seat and scoring political points than of carrying out the ideal that he was sent in to give effect to'. Although many crises flowed from this opportunism, 'the machinery of checks and controls has succeeded in maintaining the solidarity and identity of the Party'. That is, the superior power of the movement functioned to maintain the party's working-class identity, even though it had lost the power to actually control the parliamentarians. So, time and again the movement's institutions, the conference and the executive, have found that they could not force a Labor ministry to comply with party policy, and, when they kept trying, revolts and splits occurred, leading ultimately to electoral defeat.[9]

The depressing analysis gets grimmer. One of the most far-reaching consequences of the movement's entry into parliamentary politics was that it attracted non-labour forces into the party. Childe showed the party changing its parliamentary strategy from offering support in return for concessions to opponents inside parliament to one of aspiring to major party status, and the formation of majority governments, by appealing for non-working-class allies in the electorate. He was merciless in his depiction of the serious conflicts

---

8   *How Labour Governs*, 1st edn, pp. 11, 41.
9   *How Labour Governs*, 1st edn, pp. 17, 23, 53.

of interest created within the party by the non-working-class elements – the middle-class democrats, Australian nationalists, small farmers, prospectors and shopkeepers, the Roman Catholic Church and the liquor trade. Through its ambition to govern the state, the Labor Party watered down its Labor-socialist objective, drowned the progressive espousal of internationalism in a tide of jingoistic militarism, and alienated unionists by its vacillating policy – all because it 'tried to govern in the interests of all classes instead of standing up boldly in defence of the one class which put them in power'. No wonder the model did not work: these non-labour recruits had diffused the movement's identity and made the parliamentary party more important than the movement that the model was meant to empower.[10]

In the second half of his book, Childe turned to the industrial wing of the labour movement. His object was to examine the effect of labour's entering parliament on unionism's fundamental need for coordination and solidarity, and on the organisational steps taken by the unions to regain control of the movement by reorganising on an industrial basis.

Here the story is just as sombre as in the first half of the book. Attempts to coordinate through union federations failed, not least because they were often seen as having the hidden aim of increasing the power of particular politicians. Forced to take direct action against the employers by the indifference and treachery of the parliamentarians, the unions turned to amalgamation, but what emerged was a giant, undemocratic body – the Australian Workers' Union (AWU) – that fell into the hands of 'opportunists and boodlers [those who accept graft]'. The most clear-cut strategy to confront politicalism was revolutionary industrial unionism. Gordon had considerable respect for the IWW: 'No body has exercised a more profound influence on the whole outlook of labour in Australia'. He admired its bravery, its understanding of proletarian psychology, its method of direct action, its internationalism, and its 'theoretical argument against political action'. Its influence continued into the One Big Union movement. But he was not uncritical of the Wobblies. The banning of their organisation by the Hughes government, the gaoling of 12 of its leaders for seditious conspiracy by the Holman government, and the determined hostility of employers and Labor parliamentarians disoriented the proponents of revolutionary unionism. In this repressive atmosphere they allowed trade union careerists in the AWU and other unions to appropriate its ethos. Soon revolutionary industrial unionism was associated with mistakes that alienated the rank and file.

---

10   *How Labour Governs*, 1st edn, p. 85.

Gordon focused on three: the attacks on the leadership of genuine industrial unions (such as those in mining and railways), the encouragement of mass strikes that could not be won (this was his conclusion concerning the 1917 strike) and the promotion of grandiose schemes for the One Big Union, schemes that neglected the stubborn predilection for self-government among the most class-conscious workers, a predilection, that is, for small local unions. By 1921 the revolt against politicalism – its leaders self-interested and bamboozled by the AWU, its activists attracted to the newly formed Communist Party – had lost its revolutionary potential.[11]

When Gordon looked back on this book in his 'Retrospect', written at the end of his life, he referred to it as 'a sentimental excursion into Australian politics'. He was describing his writing of the book, not his feelings about his four years of political involvement in Australian politics. An archaeologist, Jim Allen, has presented the contrary view in *The Australian Dictionary of Biography*: 'Thirty-five years later ... Childe dismissed these turbulent years as a "sentimental excursion into Australian politics"'. Not so. Gordon devotes his 'Retrospect' to the origins and development of his concepts and methods. It is about his intellectual life, not his sensuous life. He begins by describing his reading and his training in Classical-era archaeology at Oxford. He makes no mention of his return to Australia. Next, he discusses his development of a 'chronological framework' for Bronze Age Central European cultures, tracing his idea for this framework back to his training, and his subsequent study of the work of several scholars, and then mentions his own publications in 1925. It is in the middle of this discussion, having referred to his Oxford training, that he writes: 'Starting again from this point in 1922 – after a sentimental excursion into Australian politics – I got the idea of a chronological framework at least for central Europe'. Why did he start in 1922? Because in that year he completed the revision of the manuscript for *How Labour Governs*. That book was another manifestation of his intellectual life at the time, a book the writing of which elicited a sentimental mood – of a birth-country left behind, of ideals not realised. It was the book that was the sentimental excursion, not the political life that he experienced in those Australian years. Unfortunately, Allen's misinterpretation has contributed to the view that the young Childe was a political dabbler, and that he thought of himself in that way.[12]

---

11 *How Labour Governs*, 1st edn, pp. viii, 147, 155, 198.
12 Childe, 'Retrospect', p. 69; Jim Allen, 'Childe, Vere Gordon (1892–1957)', *Australian Dictionary of Biography*, Vol. 7, 1989, p. 636; see also Jim Allen, 'Aspects of Vere Gordon Childe', *Labour History*, no. 12, May 1967, pp. 52–9.

***

While Childe was re-immersing himself in the scholarly world of European prehistory, students of contemporary politics in Britain and Australia were reviewing *How Labour Governs*. In Britain, it was a favourable moment for the book. The Labour Party had emerged from the general election in November 1922 as the second largest party in the House of Commons. Throughout 1923, as divisions in the Conservative Party destabilised the government, a further general election seemed imminent, in which case Labour might emerge as the largest party. The mood in official labour circles was positive and hopeful. Two communists were also elected in 1922, a tiny success for revolutionary parliamentarism but a big quandary for communist strategy. In Australia, there was only one Labor government, in Queensland. In the Commonwealth and every other State, Labor was still recovering from a series of checks: the postwar recession, proto-fascist violence against the left, and newspaper hysteria about foreign reds, disloyal Irish, and rebellious workers, a propaganda that had successfully mobilised conservative voters. Labor's mood was defensive, and in the union movement there was uncertainty about whether to press forward with socialist militancy, in the spirit of the socialisation objective adopted by the unions and subsequently by Labor in 1921, or to concentrate on establishing stronger inter-union organisation.

The appearance of *How Labour Governs* was an opportunity for contemporaries to air two related clusters of ideas about the implications of mass politics for democracy, one cluster about the fears it raised, the other about the opportunities it created. The fear may be traced back to one of the most famous nineteenth-century works of political analysis, *Democracy in America* (1835) by the French aristocrat and anti-socialist liberal Alexis de Tocqueville. In the introduction to his book, he described 'the kind of religious terror' he felt as he contemplated the 'irresistible revolution' of democracy. 'Is it credible', he asked, 'that the democracy, which has annihilated the feudal system and vanquished kings, will retreat before tradesmen and capitalists?' Of course not; the bourgeoisie, too, will succumb to its dangerous levelling tendencies. During the nineteenth century, however, the 'science' of politics that de Tocqueville called for had developed and had nurtured the idea of government as a special profession understood only by those who make it work – the political class. In tandem, the practice of representation changed from being a way to create the general will of the people into a way of co-opting them for the defence of the values of market societies and to prevent the rise of democracy as popular rule. The success of representative government calmed the bourgeoisie's fear of the masses.[13]

But then in the last decades of the century the rise of the mass political party again aroused fears about 'the democracy's irresistible revolution'. Not levelling but directionless politics and destructive policies were now the worry. In the USA and Britain, according to a book by Moisey Ostrogorski, party 'bosses' and demagogues were supplanting educated property-owning men in the leadership of modern political parties. At the same time, political thinkers were perturbed by a book by Robert Michels who showed, using the German Social Democratic Party as a case study, that oligarchy was a necessary feature of complex organisations, a proposition that became known as the iron law of oligarchy. Not only was democracy impossible in the modern party, but the masses – the ordinary members of the party – actually desired to be led. By 1921, when James Bryce published *Modern Democracies*, liberal political thought was reconciled to the idea of the modern party as an aggregation of individuals inclined toward passion rather than reason in the determination of their political feelings.[14]

As they contemplated the rise of the masses, socialists imagined another political world was possible, and most of them thought parliament would play a role in achieving it. Since the 1890s the Fabians had been arguing in socialist circles against any form of popular democracy, such as delegation, direct election of experts, or referenda. Democracy to the Fabians was 'simply the control of administration by the freely elected representatives of the people' in parliament. The contrasting view, that a much fuller and direct democracy was a condition for socialism, rejected parliamentary methods to one degree or another. Among the most rejectionist were socialists, drawing either on the traditions of anarcho-syndicalism or 'impossibilist' Marxism; both hoped

---

13 See Bernard Manin, *The Principles of Representative Government*, Cambridge University Press, 1997, on elections as a mechanism to select pre-existing elites to rule through parliamentary assemblies; on the history of democracy as written by its 'outright opponents', see John Keane, *The Life and Death of Democracy*, New York and London, W.W. Norton & Co., 2009, pp. 880–1; for an argument that leaders use 'democracy' to mean rule *over* the people, see Luciano Canfora, *Democracy in Europe: A History*, Blackwell Publishing, Oxford, 2006; Andy Blunden, 'On Political Representation', www.ethicalpolitics.org/ablunden/pdfs/On%20Political%20Representation.pdf, accessed April 2017.

14 M. Ostrogorski, *Democracy and the Organisation of Political Parties*, London, Macmillan, 1902; R. Michels, *Political Parties: A Sociological Study of the Oligarchical Tendencies of Modern Democracy*, New York, Hearst, 1915; J. Bryce, *Modern Democracies*, New York, Macmillan, 1921; P. Pombeni, 'Starting in Reason, Ending in Passion: Bryce, Lowell, Ostrogorski and the Problem of Democracy', *The Historical Journal*, vol. 37, no. 2, 1994, pp. 319–41.

for a spontaneous proletarian revolt and spurned parliamentary reformism and Leninist vanguardism. Between these extremes were the socialists – and communists – who for principled or opportunist reasons expected to combine agitation outside parliament with the election of revolutionaries. In a special category were the guild socialists, or more accurately the followers of Douglas Cole, for whom state sovereignty was the problem, not parliament. If social power were decentralised and devolved, especially to the producers in industry, and the general will was expressed in the group life of society, then parliament could shed its statist arrogance and become just another group, one representing the producers in a different aspect of their social existence, as consumers.[15]

These hopes and anxieties about democracy were implicit – and sometimes explicit – in the reviews of *How Labour Governs*. Between its publication in July 1923 and the end of the year there were 10 substantial reviews and many shorter notices in Britain. The author and his book were mostly praised. W.N. Ewer, in the *Daily Herald*, then owned by the Trade Union Congress, thought the book 'invaluable', as did Douglas Cole in the guild socialist magazine *New Standards*. Ray Postgate, in *The Plebs*, called it 'a work of quite unusual importance'. The reviewer in *The New Statesman*, a weekly then close to the Fabian Society, wrote that 'Mr Childe has done his work well and patiently, and British Labour owes him a debt for his candour as well as his competence. His promised sequel, dealing in more detail with the actual work of the Australian Labour Governments, should be keenly awaited.' Liberal reviewers, however, such as Ramsay Muir in the *Weekly Westminster Gazette*, were not inclined to be so generous: 'This is a valuable, candid, bewildering, and depressing volume, full of useful and enlightening facts, set forth in a confusing way by an honest and rather cynical man'. Several other reviewers were similarly puzzled: What was the point of a labour supporter publishing such a critical book? Why did he write from a position that he disavows in his Preface? Cole was looking to put the book in the best possible light, but he was mystified that Childe would deny in the Preface that he wrote from the revolutionary standpoint, when it was obvious from the text that he did. For some reviewers, puzzlement turned to irritation. As the editor of *The Plebs*, Frank Horrabin, succinctly put it, after complaining that the printing, binding and paper were not worth 12 shillings and 6 pence: 'The title is not

---

15   Logie Barrow and Ian Bullock, *Democratic Ideas and the British Labour Movement, 1880–1914*, Cambridge University Press, 1996, see p. 32 for the words quoted from *Fabian Tract 70*; A.W. Wright, *G.D.H. Cole and Socialist Democracy*, Oxford, Clarendon Press, 1979.

the correct one for this first volume. The author's own attitude is inconsistent in various places, and always obscure.'[16]

According to the most thoughtful reviews, behind the book's irresistible surface story of 'the stink of corruption' (according to Postgate) and of 'cliques eager and greedy for place and pelf' (unsigned, *Saturday Review*) there was a discomforting message for political democracy: 'It would seem ... that the Labour leaders, political and industrial alike, do not always, or even as a general rule, represent the ideals and interests of the people who elect them. On the contrary, they quickly become a class apart with ambitions of its own.' The reviewer G.R. Stirling Taylor, writing in the liberal-conservative weekly *The Spectator*, saw it as a Michelsian problem that lay 'at the root of all political machinery'. Ramsay Muir agreed but blamed it on the 'jealousy of leadership' found among the mass membership of modern political parties. Democracy, he believed, could not exist without 'mutual trust between leaders and followers'. On the left, too, this theme appeared. In the *Daily Herald*, W.N. Ewer, a member of the Communist Party, worried about reconciling 'the essential power of the leaders and the equally essential power of the masses'. And then there was Cole, who tied the issue to the science of politics: 'Mr Childe's book' was 'a kind of Labour supplement to the work of Ostrogorski and Michels'.[17]

But was it? Both of those books were analyses of attempts to organise the newly enfranchised masses (i.e. workers), as was Childe's. Both books were negative about the results, as was Childe's. However, in *How Labour Governs* there is a countervailing idea that Cole overlooked: that the Labor Party was an expression of 'the proletarian democracy of Australia'. This was not the same as the machinery of conference, pledge and Caucus that Labor devised to represent workers as a class in a bourgeois parliament. That machinery, he showed, did not work. We will look at the tensions between the machinery

---

16   W.N. Ewer, 'When the People Come to Rule – Lessons from Australia of Labour's Problems when in Power', *Daily Herald*, 24 July 1923, p. 8; 'Ember' [G.D.H. Cole], 'Between the Lines – A Case for New Standards', *New Standards in Industry, Politics and Education*, November–December 1923, pp. 52–5; R.W. Postgate, 'How Labour Goes Wrong', *The Plebs*, vol. 15, no. 9, September 1923, pp. 396–8; unsigned, 'How Labour Governs', *New Statesman*, 18 August 1923, pp. 550–2; Ramsay Muir, 'How Labour Governs', *Weekly Westminster Gazette*, 11 August 1923, pp. 17–18; editorial footnote to Postgate's review, p. 396.

17   Postgate, 'How Labour Goes Wrong', p. 398; unsigned review, *The Saturday Review*, 22 September 1923, p. 332; G.R. Stirling Taylor, unsigned review, *The Spectator*, 25 August 1923, p. 257; Ewer, 'When the People Come to Rule', p. 8; 'Ember' [Cole], 'Between the Lines: A Case for New Standards', p. 52. Cole was referring to Ostrogorski, *Democracy and the Organisation of Political Parties*, and Michels, *Political Parties*.

and working-class democracy in the next chapter; here we need only note that it exposes the one-sidedness of the theories of Ostrogorski and Michels. Childe postulated a democratic impulse in the formation of the party, and he documented the democratic revolt against politicalism in its history. Even Michels, contradicting his own 'iron law' metaphor, knew that the masses rebelled from time to time. In fact, it seems that an oligarchical tendency in organisations works, in dialectical double-headedness, with a tendency to democratise from below.[18]

Ramsay Muir understood that the liberal idea of representative government and the 'class-conflict' character of Labour politics were incompatible. There was the problem of suspicion of parliamentary leadership as we noted above, but more basic was the 'materialist conception of politics' in which class interest overrode individual conscience. Thankfully, according to Muir, the book demonstrated that the Labour version of politics did not work: 'his book is in fact a very cogent argument for the Liberal conception of party organisation and of social aims against the Labour conception'. In the *New Statesman* a class-oriented labour party was also a worry:

> Early in the history of every workers' party … there arises the problem of control. Who is to determine policy, lay down programmes, decide what course the Parliamentary representatives of Labour are to pursue? Shall it be the body of constituents whom the Member is constitutionally supposed to represent, or the Union that put him forward and paid his expenses, or the party convention or conference as a whole? … As soon as Labour becomes Government it must be answered. Who is to nominate the Ministers? Who to decide the … order of precedence to be given to the various measures proposed? Is the Government's continuance in power to depend on the support of the party conference as well as on the possession of a Parliamentary majority?

The expulsion of Hughes and other Labor conscriptionists provided an answer to the last question, but how should the subsequent collapse of Labor governments be understood? A warning for parliamentary socialists against endorsing the class-conflict model for a labour party, or an indication to revolutionary socialists that extra-parliamentary working-class pressure needed to be stronger?[19]

---

18 Cole, 'Between the Lines', p. 52; Jodi Dean, 'Michels: The Rusty Iron Law of Oligarchy', https://jdeanicite.typepad.com/i_cite/2013/01/michels-the-rusty-iron-law-of-oligarchy.html, accessed 23 October 2018.
19 Muir, 'How Labour Governs', p. 18; unsigned, *New Statesman*, p. 552.

Childe would have been particularly interested in reviews by his associates on the left, Cole and Postgate, but also Esmonde Higgins and, in Australia, Percy Stephensen. Cole, apart from being bemused by the book's Preface, was also concerned that Childe's mood of 'anger and disgust' might be interpreted as cynicism. He was particularly disappointed in Childe's conclusion – that the OBU, like the Labor Party, would degenerate 'into a vast machine for capturing political power' for the benefit of individuals – because it seemed like 'an outburst of irritation' rather than 'a considered verdict in its truest sense'. Moreover, 'Mr Childe sometimes writes as if political corruption were an invention of Labour Parties'. Cole also found examples in the book that revealed his own perplexity about socialist advance. He highlighted Childe's statement that 'Democracy ... can by supreme exertions prevent politicians completely misinterpreting its aims but it cannot secure the achievement of them'. So, the political route was closed off, but even the industrialist reaction against the politicalist method, in which Cole found merit, was fruitless because it was part of a violent contest between 'opposing creeds', in which 'neither method can make headway' – a sentiment that Cole had voiced at the LRD summer school a year earlier. His genuine attempt to engage with Childe's analysis was hampered as much by his own political uncertainty as it was by Childe's cryptic Preface. The collapse of the guild socialist movement, already underway by 1923, left him 'theoretically and organisationally homeless', according to his intellectual biographer A.W. Wright.[20]

The review by Postgate, who had left the Communist Party by this time, was in the magazine of the Plebs League which was in conflict with the communists over the character of Plebs education. The communists in the League were insisting that working-class education should aim to build the party; the Plebs were just as adamant that it should aim to build the class, as 'independent working-class education' was always meant to do. This conflict made an opening for people who thought that fighting against the *limitations* of politicalism was beside the point; the movement needed to reject politicalism altogether. In his review, headed 'Where Labour Goes Wrong', Postgate embraced this syndicalist-leaning position. Naturally he relished Childe's stories of the corruption, splits and anti-working-class influence in Labor. He also gave more space than other reviews to the failure of the 'triple controls' of Caucus, pledge and conference. But it was Childe's account of the spirit of the IWW that Postgate was drawn to. 'For the first time there were men

---

20   'Ember' [Cole], *New Standards*, pp. 52–5; A.W. Wright, *G.D.H. Cole and Socialist Democracy*, Oxford, Clarendon Press, 1979, p. 4.

who urged the workers to fight for themselves alone. They carried the class struggle to its uttermost limit: sabotage, note-forgery, burning Sydney. They sacrificed themselves without question ... Here is something at last to admire.' Then he notes Childe's 'reluctant admiration' of the IWW.[21]

Douglas Cole in 1928, looking for the middle way.
(National Portrait Gallery, London; NPG x42851)

Unlike Postgate, Esmonde Higgins had remained in the Communist Party. Admitting that the revolution in Britain was a long way off, he told his parents in 1922 that 'these days the best thing for people like me to do is to criticise and to analyse the character of the present system; we've no chance to do anything but be maliciously destructive'. His four-page review, which was published in the Communist Party's *Labour Monthly*, aimed to destroy the reputation of Australian labour among sympathisers in Britain. He described the insubordination of Holman and other politicians to the movement, the graft paid for electoral advantage, the defection of Labor politicians to the

---

21 Postgate, 'How Labour Goes Wrong', pp. 396–8; Marc Mulholland, 'How to Make a Revolution. The Historical and Political Writings of Raymond Postgate', unpublished paper, www.academia.edu/30067214/How_to_Make_a_Revolution_The_Historical_and_Political_Writings_of_Raymond_Postgate_Postgate. Mulholland writes that Postgate was stronger on the agency of the common people than Cole.

conservative parties, and the anti-working-class policies of Labor governments. But he also took aim at Childe. He hoped the second volume would expose the absence of working-class ideals and aims in the movement, ignoring the evidence of this presented by Childe in Chapters III, IV and V. He criticised Childe for failing to evaluate the position of the workers after 30 years of labour organisation. Clearly, he wanted Childe to have written a different book. Worse, he accused Childe of holding a position that he would have found repugnant. Asking for the reason for the movement's demoralisation, Higgins asserts that Childe had a 'simple answer':

> The proletariat is utterly incapable of governing. It is ridiculous to expect a Labour Movement to have as its aim the alteration of the social structure to put an end to the enslavement of the workers. All attempts become only scrambles to secure benefits for individuals. With an Olympian superciliousness Mr Childe draws a sweeping moral to flatter what would appear to be a private habit of anarchic cynicism.

Thus, Higgins was another case of a reviewer understanding the Preface in a way that would have horrified Childe. At least Cole knew that Childe wrote from a revolutionary perspective. Higgins then heaped malice onto misunderstanding by referring to a supposed 'private habit' of supercilious thought. Did Childe annoy him so much at Cloughton that he had to resort to *ad hominem*?[22]

When Cole wrote that Childe was in danger of giving in to cynicism he set the dogs running. Higgins's review gave them a second run; there was to be a third in Australia a few months later. In the *Daily Standard*, Percy Stephensen – a former pupil and friend of Childe – wrote a review headed 'A Tired Cynic. Gordon Childe's Criticism of Australian Labour.' Stephensen, who had joined the Australian Communist Party in 1921, had obviously read the review by Higgins, and would have concluded that, as it appeared in an internationally distributed communist publication, it was expressing a communist position. So, like a good party member he repeated it. In Stephensen's words, Childe holds 'the opinion that Labour cannot govern'. He too could not resist the *ad hominem* shot: Childe was tired. But at least he was not a renegade; he was 'merely a cynical philosopher, driven to anarchistic despair by the dissensions and intrigues in the Labor movement'. Childe writes 'in a detached Olympian

---

22   E.M.H. [Higgins], Labour over the Threshold', *Labour Monthly*, vol. 5, no. 4, October 1923, pp. 243–6; Esmonde Higgins to parents, 13/7/1922, Higgins papers, Mitchell Library MSS 740/6. On Childe and Higgins at Cloughton, see Ch. 15.

manner' because he has only been 'an observer and experimenter', not a 'worker and fighter in the proletariat movement'. Stephensen was referring to the movement of which he was a newly-recruited member, a worker-fighter arousing the proletariat, in his case the pupils at Ipswich Grammar where he was teaching and wielding a terrifying weapon: the Rhodes Scholarship that would soon take him to Oxford.[23]

Vance Marshall, union official, anti-conscriptionist orator and socialist organiser, had better credentials for assessing Childe's contribution to the working-class movement than Stephensen, and he wrote a long response to the latter's dismissal of Childe's role. It was a series of personal sketches of him, printed under the heading 'Scholar and Thinker'. He recalled a street artist drawing Childe outside the Chief Secretary's Office at the height of his political career. He described Childe making an 'insistent, relentless' speech against the war in 1918. In a third sketch, he and Childe were in Martin Place watching unemployed men in broken boots gather on the edge of a recruiting rally while a band played 'God Save the King'. Childe turned to Marshall and said, 'It's a tragedy'. A fourth sketch showed Marshall unable to reach Childe because the stairs to his office were blocked by a deputation of women wanting to talk to the Premier about rising food prices:

> I had come to see him but I turned and went down the stairs ... I will get the book he sends to us from London and will read it. Not because the author was known to me will I do so, but because Gordon Childe, though he may on the surface play the part of tired cynic, is no fanatical cynic, but a thinker, a man who has rubbed shoulders with every phase of the working-class movement, and a man who will have weighed well his words before he set his pen to paper.

Stephensen replied three days later: 'Hats off to Childe for the stand he took at the university, and the good work he did by precept and example during the time he was associated with the rebel movement'. What precepts and examples? Why did he neglect to add Childe's two years working for Storey's government? Then he quotes Childe's Preface but omits the words referring to the Labor Party and the trade unions, so that it seems that Childe is rejecting the idea that exploitation and enslavement of the workers is involved in the present organisation of society. He reinforces this idea by quoting the last line

---

23   P.R.S. [Stephensen], 'A Tired Cynic – Gordon Childe's Criticism of Australian Labour – *How Labour Governs*', *Daily Standard*, 22 December 1923, p. 10. Craig Munro, 'Stephensen, Percy Reginald (1901–1965)', *Australian Dictionary of Biography*, Vol. 12, 1990, pp. 70–1.

of the book, concluding by repeating the travesty that he had copied from Higgins, that Childe thought that 'the proletariat is utterly unfit to govern'. Childe did not respond, but, as we shall see many years later, they met, and he told Stephensen that they were politically opposed.[24]

According to the *Daily Standard*, there was considerable discussion of *How Labour Governs* in Brisbane. A lengthy letter by 'Student' in the *Daily Standard* began by again raising the issue of Childe's limited experience in the labour movement, in particular the industrial movement. Citing Bryce, he nonetheless hoped that the industrial movement would make passive workers into active industrial democrats. Harald Jensen also read *How Labour Governs*, telling the *Standard* that school students should study labour and working-class history, in other countries as well as Australia, and that such a history should not avoid the scandals and corruption documented in Childe's book.[25]

The *Sydney Morning Herald* paid Childe's book the compliment of an editorial, but only to reinforce middle-class prejudices about individuals subjugating themselves to a cause. The editor of *The Australasian Decorator and Painter* – a trade magazine – was not so restrained. The movement's ideas, he wrote, are foisted on the workers by self-seeking demagogues and crazy idealists. The labour press is pitiful, its journalists circulating praise or blame as their bosses decide. Union ballots and party pre-selections are rigged. And so on. There was even a cartoon showing Mr Fat gleefully reading the book. It appeared in *The Worker* – which was owned by the AWU, the dominant force in the Queensland Labor Party – to illustrate its opinion that Childe's left-wing views were anti-Labor: 'The Childe of folly seems incapable of recognising that, if Labor has attained power, it has done so not by a "vacillating policy" or an attempt to please all parties, but by a programme submitted to the whole of the people'. George Black, one of the first Labor men elected to the New South Wales Parliament was livid that the book showed 'a tireless hatred of WA Holman and several of his Ministers, especially of myself'. Childe, he wrote, was like an 'insect which crawls laboriously from leaf to leaf' leaving 'a slimy trail' which needs to be wiped away with 'literary insecticide'.[26]

---

24   Vance Marshall, 'Gordon Childe. Scholar and Thinker. Personal Sketches of Author of *How Labour Governs*', *Daily Standard*, 2 January 1924, p. 8; P.R.S. [Stephensen], 'Gordon Childe, Cynical, Tired Philosopher', *Daily Standard*, 5 January 1924, p. 12.

25   'Student', 'How Labour Governs. Critics and Criticism', *Daily Standard*, 4 January 1924, p. 10; H.I. Jensen, 'Teaching History. Some Suggestions', *Daily Standard*, 21 January 1924, p. 8.

26   Unsigned editorial, 'How Labour Governs', *Sydney Morning Herald*, 15 September 1923, p. 14; unsigned review, 'How Labour Governs', *The Australasian Painter and Decorator*, 1 January 1924, pp. 86–7; 'Paul Pry', 'Out of the Mouth of a Childe',

Mr Fat reading *How Labour Governs*, by 'The Childe of folly'.
(*The Worker* (Brisbane), 26 July 1923, p. 5)

Childe made no response in print to the reviews. The hurtful ones from Australia he probably never saw, but perhaps Witherby, with whom he kept in contact, sent him the *Daily Standard* material. Nor is there is anything in his correspondence about the reviews. In December, however, the Executive Committee of the LRD considered a letter from him in which he suggests that the sequel to *How Labour Governs* should be offered to an outside publisher. Was there an understanding about the sequel that Childe wanted to break? Was he sparing the LRD the trouble and cost of the sequel? Or, having read the British reviews, was he writing out of a sense of dissatisfaction with his failure to make clear to readers what he had been trying to say in *How Labour Governs*? Had he written, as he said about his Cloughton lecture, a book that was 'bad'? Would a sequel about the work of Labor governments really be able to wipe away the confusion created by the cryptic Preface and the book's final sentence, a confusion that had produced the slur that he was cynical about the

---

The Worker (Brisbane), 26 July 1923, p. 5; George Black, 'How Labour Governs in Australia – A Book of Big Blunders', *The Australian Bystander*, 12 June 1924, pp. 9 and 29.

proletariat's capacity for self-government? As we saw in the previous chapter, in January 1924 *The Plebs* published a book review by Childe in which he insisted that 'the uncompromising policy' of the Labor Party in Queensland 'gave birth to a real Labor Government' which had improved the 'real status of the workers'. Childe must have had that view of what was possible for Labor in his mind as he wrote to the LRD in December. Then in June, in his *Labour Monthly* article, 'A Labour Premier Meets His Masters', he indicated his understanding of the limits of such a government. The last line of that article reminded his readers that Theodore's cabinet was now 'a subservient management committee for the bourgeoisie'. Together, the *Plebs* book review and the *Labour Monthly* article may be understood as a response to the reviews of his book. Childe was trying to set the record straight. Having shown it was possible, there was less pressing need for a sequel. Moreover, as we shall see in the next chapter, Childe had published an article in Britain before the appearance of the book, an article that argued for a socialist working-class movement that mirrored his experiences and built on his intellectual history.[27]

* * *

Even as the reviews appeared, he was hard at work on *The Dawn of European Civilization*, which appeared in 1925. *The Dawn* was not a slim volume, modestly designed to catch the interest of the gatekeepers of archaeology and prehistory. At 328 pages, it was a major contribution, with 148 illustrations, drawn by Childe, and four maps. It was also a handsome book in a prestigious series, 'The History of Civilization', published by Kegan Paul. It is interesting to consider how Gordon's manuscript found its way to this publisher. The series was edited by C.K. Ogden, three years older than Gordon, a Cambridge graduate, who joined Kegan Paul as a consulting editor in 1922. During the war, Gordon would have known about Ogden, because as the editor of the *Cambridge Review* he provided a weekly digest of the press in Germany and other foreign countries, digests which were an essential source for the anti-war movement. Ogden had friends in the Union of Democratic Control, and he was a member of the 1917 Club. No doubt Ogden, a brilliant editor, having read Gordon's articles, sought him out. For his part Gordon would

---

27 Minutes of the Executive Committee of the LRD, 14 December 1923; a year after publication the LRD Executive resolved to break up the type for Childe's book, see Minutes for 4 July 1924.

have recognised a political ally who could help him. Stamped and inset into *The Dawn*'s dark blue front cover was the logo of the series, a reproduction in gold of an ancient Athenian coin showing the owl of Athena, the goddess of wisdom. For this volume, it might well have been Tyche, the goddess of luck. Kegan Paul published many of Gordon's later books, and Green states that Gordon and Ogden were friends for many years.[28]

The Dawn appeared two years after *How Labour Governs*. Students of the history of archaeology, assuming that antipodean labourism and European prehistory are worlds apart, rarely ask whether the two books have anything in common. One who did was Peter Gathercole. In his article, 'Childe the "Outsider"' he pointed out that *The Dawn* and Gordon's later writings shared some characteristics with *How Labour Governs*, namely, 'a clearly expressed viewpoint from which the data are organized and expressed', 'a zeal to involve and fully convince the reader by demonstrating the importance of a large number of seemingly irrelevant facts to the substantiation of this viewpoint', and a 'sense of style'. I think we can go much further than this, but first let us see what *The Dawn* was trying to do.

It is called *The Dawn of European Civilization* because it was meant to counter the view that there was no prehistoric civilisation in Europe before the early Bronze Age. When Gordon wrote, this moment was dated to about 1,600 BC. He was relaxed about the idea that many civilising ideas and techniques were developed first in the Ancient East – the 'Orientalist' position of some archaeologists – and then diffused to Europe, so he did not subscribe to the racialism or sentimental nationalism of 'Occidentalists', for whom 'all the higher elements of human culture' appeared in Europe. His gut feeling was that in Europe a process of refinement and development of Eastern discoveries occurred. In his book, he set out to prove this. He reviewed the sequence of cultures in each of the several geographical regions of Europe and brought together the evidence of invasion, trade and migration linking them together over the previous 1,500 years. He showed that by 1,600 BC 'the principal regions of Europe were in the possession of peoples who were masters of their own food supplies, were elaborating their own schools of metallurgy and were linked together by certain commercial relations'. The world of the Neolithic food gatherers had been transformed into a food-producing civilisation, on a continental scale, characterised by 'energy, independence and inventiveness'.[29]

---

28   Green, *Prehistorian*, p. 51; W. Terrence Gordon, *C.K. Ogden: A Bio-bibliographical Study*, Lanham, MD, The Scarecrow Press, 1990, pp. 1–56, 'C.K. Ogden: A Biographical Essay'.

29   Childe, *The Dawn of European Civilization*, pp. xiii–iv, 302.

The book is therefore much more than a synthesis of existing research; it is propelled by a big idea, in much the same way as the failure of labourism as a strategy for liberating the working class was the big idea of *How Labour Governs*. So, it is not parallels between the two books that we are looking for but similarities that point to Childe's way of thinking. Consider in this regard his inductive approach to historical reasoning. In both books, he builds up a story – of a civilisation emerging in one case, and a political movement failing in the other – by presenting 'a large number of seemingly irrelevant facts' to substantiate the story. This is reflected in the organisation of the two books; the chapters deal with labour institutions, processes or movements in the earlier book, and with the cultures of the geographical 'provinces' and the diffusion of ideas and techniques in *The Dawn*. Of course, he is aware of change, but it is as if he is determined not to allow chronological models – turning points, epochs, etc. based on schema imported from philosophy or theology – to distort the investigation. There is, further, in both books a sense that he is involved in a quest to move beyond two opposing viewpoints – parliamentarism and industrial syndicalism in *How Labour Governs*, and Orientalism and Occidentalism in *The Dawn*. The European civilisation he discovers is not a compromise between the Orientalists and the Occidentalists but a new civilisation, 'a new and organic whole capable of developing on its own original lines'. Similarly, the socialist society he envisaged was not a compromise between parliamentarism and revolution but an entirely new form of popular democracy, even if at the time its opponents assimilated it to their respective political strategies.[30]

Raewyn Connell has suggested that Childe should be considered as 'a lost leader' of Australian sociology. She writes of reading *The Dawn*: 'There is a memory of structure here that is different from the concerns with racial ancestry, with national distinctiveness, or with schemes drawn from Engels, that preoccupied many of his contemporaries in archaeology'. As Childe wrote *The Dawn*, Connell implies, he was remembering *How Labour Governs*, a book that should be seen as a contribution to the kind of sociology that Australia failed to produce, an authentic engagement with the facts of settler society and its dependent relationship with the imperial metropole. For Connell, *The Dawn* thus has a deep Australian architecture, shown in the way Childe expresses in that book 'a powerful sense of space and distance, and his concern with the complexity of centre–periphery in the ancient world'.[31]

---

30   Childe, *The Dawn of European Civilization*, Preface, p. xiii; cf. Green, *Prehistorian*, p. 53 re 'compromise'.

31   Raewyn Connell, 'Antipodes: Australian Sociology's Struggles with Place, Memory and Neoliberalism', in Michael Burawoy, Mau-kuei and Michelle Fei-yu Hsieh (eds),

There is an insight in her remarks that deserves elaboration. What was the nature of Childe's Australian experience? In a phrase, it was a politics poised between metropolitan theorising and periphery-defined practice. The tension between his immersion in European political philosophy and his experience of Australian movement building and experiment *was* his experience of Australia. Of the two sides of this politics, the theoretical was the least important. As he wrote in 1919, Australians try hard to convince the mother country and 'the international', by which he means the world socialist movement, that its labour movement is based on ideas. But the real task is to convince the 'bone-head majority' in Australia that as workers they can practice socialism at work.[32]

So, let us turn to the practical nature of Childe's socialism. One of the themes of his intervention in the debate about the One Big Union was to caution the industrialists against relying on alluring but vague ideas about revolution. Instead he insisted on the value of practising collective self-management in state enterprises, even if it were only in the quarries at Bombo, a hamlet on the South Coast of New South Wales. Now we can grasp his idea of progress. This politics of revolutionary practice entailed an idea of progress that was not evolutionary, something emerging out of the preceding history of liberal self-government, as it was to the intellectuals of official labour. The idea of progress had to be taken away from them and reimagined as the creation of new values by a self-acting workers' movement, as a revolutionary and history-making 'alteration in the social structure'. This was the view of progress that his four years in the Australian socialist movement reinforced, and which in time underlay his archaeological theorising.[33]

There are echoes of this lesson in the Preface to *The Dawn*. Europe's prehistoric heritage might be revealed in the material evidence of archaeological cultures but in these 'monuments of early man' we may detect 'an organism that was once clothed with flesh'. This organism was a civilisation, an organism made by humans making themselves through their tools and their enterprise:

> Peasants with stone hoes and axes opened up its valleys to cultivation; hunters and herdsmen blazed the trail through primæval forests; mariners in dug-out canoes sailed the seas to the isles to the West; prospectors with picks of horn and flint revealed the treasures of the earth and crossed mountain passes in search of merchandise.

Facing an Unequal World: Challenges for a Global Sociology, Volume Two, Asia, Taipei, Academia Sinica, 2010, pp. 215–17.

32   Childe, 'The New Unionism and State Socialism', *Daily Standard*, 4 January 1919.

33   Childe, 'Political Action and the Newer Unionism – I', *Labor News*, 15 February 1919.

These were active, practical humans, and their discoveries were the preconditions of modern civilisation: 'Progress is an indivisible whole in which the invention of a new way of hafting an axe formed a necessary prelude to the invention of the steam engine or the aeroplane'. Embedded in Childe's words is a materialist concept of progress, and of history as a story of progress, a process created by practical activity, by human labour.[34]

What do we know about Childe's thinking at this time about history? He left no specific account, but there are scattered clues. Looking back on his life in 1957, he saw *The Dawn* as a history book. He wrote in 'Retrospect' that *The Dawn* 'aimed at distilling from archaeological remains a preliterate substitute for the conventional politico-military history with cultures, instead of statesmen, and migrations in place of battles'. And beginning in 1919 we can find a trail of references to Croce. In 1919, he told Brereton that in his adult education class on economics he was applying Croce's idea to his exposition of Marx's *Capital*, 'with brilliant results'. He was being self-deprecatory of course, but he was clearly fascinated by Benedetto Croce (1866–1952), an Italian neo-Hegelian philosopher who engaged critically with Marxism, bringing to the fore its cultural and historical structures. When Childe in 1923 was describing to Myres the kind of book he wanted to write, he called himself a neo-Hegelian, a person who could not imagine 'a fact altogether divorced from a theory or *vice versa*'. A few years after the publication of the book he defined himself as 'a Gentile-Crocian'. And there are further references to Croce in later years — 1945, 1947 and 1949 — that place his thinking in the Marxist tradition that would come to be called Western Marxism. For Childe, Croce was important because he understood historical knowledge as practical, furnishing rules for action, and because Croce removed from Hegel's 'grand conception' of the dialectical movement of history the supernatural character of the laws of history. In 1923, Childe was not able to formulate his debt in that way — as he did later — but *The Dawn* shows that he was already committed to an inductive approach to historical reasoning that amounted to the same thing.[35]

---

34   Childe, *The Dawn of European Civilization*, pp. xiv–xv.
35   Childe, 'Retrospect', p. 70; Childe to Brereton, no date, but mid-1919; Childe to Myres, no date, but late May/early June 1923; Green, *Prehistorian*, p. 83 (re Gentile-Crocian); Childe, 'Rational Order in History', *The Rationalist Annual*, London, C.A. Watts & Co., 1945, pp. 21–6; Childe, *History*, London, The Cobbett Press, 1947, pp. 45, 85; Childe, 'Prehistory and Marxism', *Antiquity*, vol. 53, issue 208, 1979, pp. 93–5 (written in 1949); Trigger, *Gordon Childe*, p. 43.

Clearly in 1923 he was familiar with Marxism's contribution to the debate between philosophical idealism and mechanical materialism. In the very first line of the Preface to *The Dawn*, he makes a distinction between the material basis of civilisation and its 'spiritual context', by which he meant not something ethereal but the practical interaction of humans with their environment out of which new values came – or 'the creative process' that is reality. This emphasis on 'spirit' as creative practical activity put him at odds with the 'scientific' economic determinist Marxists who dominated the Second International. The point is this: while scholars of the history of archaeology look in Childe's work for Marxist terminology and concepts, which they discover in his 1930s publications, they miss the organising ideas and methods that are present in his earliest works drawn from the 'idealist' side of that debate. These are also part of the tradition of Marxist thought, and they continued to ground his thinking right up to his last works.[36]

---

36   Thomas C. Patterson, *Marx's Ghost: Conversations with Archaeologists*, Oxford, New York, Berg, 2003, for 'Childe's Engagement with Marxist and Liberal Social Theory', pp. 42–53; Peter Gathercole, 'Childe, Marxism, and knowledge', *European Journal of Archaeology*, vol. 12, nos 1–3, April–December, 2009, pp. 181–92.

Chapter 17

'A MOVEMENT THAT WILL HAVE TO GO FURTHER'

In this chapter we ask not what *How Labour Governs* meant to its readers, but what Childe failed to make it mean. Part of the answer to this question can be found in the book, the rest of it in his London publications; in particular, a *Labour Monthly* article written soon after he returned from the Cloughton summer school feeling dissatisfied with his performance. Let's start with the book. Suppose you picked up a copy in which any reference to its title, and hence to governing or representation, had been removed. What is this book about, empirically? Organisation, obviously, of a labour party and of trade unions, but strikes as well. Thanks to digitisation, we know that there are 200 references to strikes in the book; in comparison, there are only 143 occurrences of the word 'movement', as in 'labour movement'. With this information, you might decide that the book is called *How Labour Strikes: A Study of Workers' Collective Impulse in Australia*. And Childe might have chosen that title had he been uninterested in questions of political theory. He was writing, after all, in the midst of a strike wave in Australia. In 1917, the year of the mass strike, five million working days were lost through strikes, but in 1919 the figure was 6,308,000. Even as the postwar recession hit, there were over 1.2 million working days lost on average each year between 1920 and 1922. But these figures are not in themselves important. The question is: what was the meaning of these strikes?[1]

Childe gave quite a lot of thought to this question, beginning during his year in Brisbane. As we saw in Chapter 11, emboldened by the One Big Union push in late 1918, Childe thought he had discovered an Australian path to

---

1 Strike references calculated from the digitised version of *How Labour Governs* at Australian Digital Collections, http://purl.library.usyd.edu.au/setis/id/p00052. Working days lost in strikes: Stuart Macintyre, *The Oxford History of Australia – Volume 4, 1901–1942, The Succeeding Age*, Melbourne, Oxford University Press, 1986, p. 194, based on *Labour Reports*.

socialism. If the industrial unionists could be persuaded to work through the Labor Party, and the party persuaded to alter its objective to include workers' control in the state enterprises – not just the railways and other public utilities but also the industries that Labor had colonised by setting up state-owned quarries, mines, trawlers, hotels, cattle stations, butcher ships, bakeries and so on – then a very big step towards a democratic form of socialism could be taken. Making this argument consumed his energies for most of 1919.

There was, however, another area where persuasion was needed, and it was the most intractable of all: in return for controlling their work, the workers in the state enterprises had to be persuaded that there was a bigger end in view than their local collective power. But here Childe took a misstep. In Childe's language, these workers had to accept 'responsibility' to the public and give up the right to strike. So for them the strike weapon had to be blackened, which he proceeded to do in nearly all of his 1919 publications. He described the strike as a purely defensive weapon, reinforcing the class struggle, whereas the aim should be to end it. Too often, he said, strikes were associated with aimless militancy, wielded with fear and passion. The strike was uncivilised, and however much it empowered wage-earners it alienated consumers – who were of course also wage-earners. Unable from his own experience to understand that workers could learn about collective strength from even the most trivial of disputes with the boss, Childe worried that the militancy demonstrated in strikes was aimless, that it taught nothing except how to survive the struggle. Strikes were in this new situation outmoded and inappropriate.[2]

Childe's strategy assumed that the sphere of state business activity could be expanded, existing enterprises maintained, and their workers securely employed and properly recompensed for their new responsibilities. It was a strategy that required investment, and this seemed available in 1919, before the postwar recession hit really hard. By 1922, in Britain, he had changed his mind about the viability of his strategy of introducing socialism via workers' control in the state enterprises. He was ready now to recognise that when 'the boom collapsed, the masters just closed down industry from which no more surplus value could be extracted'. Unemployment then increased, and the government's coffers were soon exhausted. The future of the state industries was in doubt. Observing Labor Premiers Theodore and Storey returning empty-handed from 'the City money-lenders' in London, he remarked with restrained irony that 'The State enterprises which were to replace capitalist

---

2   Childe, *Daily Standard*, 4 January 1919 (aimless militancy), 17 January 1919 (fear and passion); *Labor News*, 15 February 1919 (irresponsible agitators), 22 February 1919 (aimless militancy).

industry require loan money for their initiation. And for the destruction of industrial capitalism loan money has not been forthcoming.'³

* * *

Most of the 200 references to strikes in *How Labour Governs* are descriptive, sometimes mentioning a strike only in passing, which won't help us very much, and as well there are 25 references in the Chronological Table and five in the Table of Contents. Among those descriptive references are extended treatments of eight major strikes: the 1908 Sydney wharf labourers; 1909 Barrier miners strike in Broken Hill; 1909 coal strike; 1911 sugar workers strike; 1911–12 Hoskins steel strike at Lithgow; 1912 tramway strike that became a general strike in Brisbane; 1916 coal strike; and the 1917 'big strike'. If we need to be reminded: the extended focus on these strikes underlines Childe's stated intention, to write about labour's class 'ideals' and 'movements' rather than its 'legislative enactments' and electoral triumphs. And it is clear, especially when reflecting on Labor Premier McGowen's call for 'volunteers' to break the gas strike of 1913, that Childe stands by the view he expressed in 'The Irrepressible Class Struggle': that strikes are a legitimate defence against exploitation and oppression. But in *How Labour Governs* there is no more of that 1918 talk about workers in state enterprises giving up their right to strike. Instead, we can find indications of a more sympathetic attitude to strikes and glimpse his attraction to a revolutionary perspective in which to understand them.⁴

To start with a rather obvious contextual point, because it is a point that Childe makes: a sympathetic attitude to strikes has, as its obverse side, a contempt for arbitration. He makes this point in his discussion of the IWW's attitude to strikes, referring dismissively to the Arbitration Court as 'that pet creation of political Labour'. He goes even further. When pointing to the revolutionary purpose of strikes envisaged by the IWW, he contrasts it with Labor's evolutionary strategy for socialism, and writes that Labor's model was 'doomed by economic laws to futility'. This is the nub of the argument he makes in his 1922 article, 'When Labour Ruled – In Australia – By an Ex-Ruler', which we will look at later in this chapter. Here, we only need

---

3   Childe, 'When Labour Ruled – In Australia – By an Ex-Ruler', *Labour Monthly*, vol. III, no. 3, September 1922, p. 179; also, Childe, 'A Labour Premier Meets His Masters', pp. 282–5.
4   Childe, *How Labour Governs*, 1st edn, pp, 37 and 59 (re 1913 gas strike).

to note that every time Childe makes a positive point about strikes it is framed by the idea that Labor's alternative politicalism, its reliance on the constituted authority of parliament and courts, is a waste of time as far as socialism is concerned.[5]

The aspect of a strike that always elicits a positive response from Childe is its capacity to reveal the strength of class awareness among those workers taking part. And by positive, I mean admiration. So, he comments on 'the great spirit of solidarity' shown during the sugar strike of 1911. The Brisbane strike of 1912, even though it failed, was, as a general strike, 'historic', and the strikers 'preserved excellent order' for its duration. And one of his reasons for admiring the IWW was that it 'fomented … outlaw strikes' among shearers in 1916, defying the conservative AWU leadership. Further, the only positive thing Childe could manage to write about the mass strike of 1917 was that, because of the influence of the IWW, there was in 'existence … a general spirit of mass action – a sort of "let-us-try-a-general-strike" feeling'. OK – so it might be said that he is just reporting these manifestations of 'movement', but he was under no compulsion to use those sentiment-bearing adjectives: 'great', 'excellent', 'outlaw', and the vernacular appeal of 'let us try'. He is, despite himself, identifying with worker rebelliousness.[6]

Nor did he have to persist with his class analysis of strikes, his search for their 'hidden meaning'. A labourist would have smoothed away the awkwardness of strikes through connecting them to a story of union building and the progress of the parliamentary party. Childe, however, is drawn to the capacity of strikes to disrupt, and most of all to what they might reveal about the formation of collective consciousness. In *How Labour Governs*, after reporting the IWW's contempt for arbitration, he presents the organisation's view of strikes:

> The strike, on the other hand, it was held, by its concrete expression of solidarity and the spirit of comradeship in the struggle which it engendered, setting as it did the master class and the working class in opposite camps in open physical antagonism, embodied and symbolised the unseen struggle of the classes, promoted the class-consciousness of the proletariat, and so promoted the revolution.

Here we see the strike as a material thing: embodied, physical, an organised expression of one camp in the war of classes. This might well be enough to

---

5 Childe, *How Labour Governs*, 1st edn, p. 157.
6 Childe, *How Labour Governs*, 1st edn, pp. 73 (1890 maritime strike), 103 and 176–90 (1917 strike), 175 (1916 coal strike), 130 (solidarity in sugar strike), 134 ('historic'), 136 ('excellent' order), 165 ('outlaw') and 171 ('let-us-try').

establish its importance in revolutionary politics. But to Childe its significance is also mental, expressed as a spirit, a capacity to symbolise the struggle, and promote the kind of collective consciousness without which revolution is impossible.[7]

He is not positive about all strikes. When strikes fail, as the maritime strike of 1890 did, they reveal the limitations of direct action; and he thought the 1917 mass strike was badly led. The 1916 coal strike succeeded because the miners 'supposed' their leader, Willis, had 'planned the whole campaign'. Did Willis plan it? We don't know. All we know is that the miners thought he had, and that was sufficient to ensure their victory. Childe draws our attention to the mental sphere again, to class consciousness, pointing to its critical role in successful working-class struggle.[8]

But was class consciousness enough? Not in 1917 Australia. After explaining the success of the 1916 strike, he writes:

> The antithesis – the uselessness of a strike, however widespread and popular, when the forces of labour lack organisation and unitary control – was cruelly demonstrated the next year ... [in] the Great Strike of 1917.

In other words, class consciousness was not enough. Also needed were organisational effort and 'unitary control', achieved through strong leadership. Worse, the IWW's concentration on developing class consciousness through 'strikes, riots and acts of defiance towards the established social order' meant that it gave less priority to 'constructive plans for the future'. Lastly there was the danger that the IWW's advocacy of violence, as in sabotage, to embroil the workers with the authorities, would inspire only 'blind mass action'. What was the point of a revolution if the workers could not see where they were going?[9]

These were the problems in the IWW's practice, but in its theory could be found a solution. The IWW, according to Childe, saw itself as a class-conscious minority, organised to 'carry along with them' the mass of 'inert' working-class 'bone-heads'. In other words, its philosophy 'foreshadowed' the 'Bolshevik dictatorship of the proletariat'; it would lead, plan for, and mobilise the working class. It was already a fighting organisation, and it aspired to build a single, centrally-controlled union of all workers that would replace

---

7   Childe, *How Labour Governs*, 1st edn, p. 157.
8   Childe, *How Labour Governs*, 1st edn, p. 176.
9   Childe, *How Labour Governs*, 1st edn, p. 159 (constructive plans; blind mass action), 176 (the antithesis).

bourgeois parliamentary democracy with industrial democracy. This, as he said, was the 'positive, constructive side of I.W.W. philosophy'.[10]

Childe admired the purposive, directive character of this philosophy. Moreover, he could relate to it not just ideologically, that is, for its 'workerist' inflection, but because it functioned in the realm in which he preferred to act – the mental realm. He wanted to contribute to a movement that took ideas seriously, that had a role for thinkers like him, trained, traditional intellectuals, as well as for the IWW's organic working-class intellectuals. He wanted to believe that the merging of socialist intellectuals and a militant proletariat agitating for workers' control in industry could push 'a real Labor Government' beyond parliamentary democracy. As we shall see, this was close to the orthodox Marxist understanding of 'the road to power' – the title of Karl Kautsky's 1909 book that captured the imagination of socialists, including Lenin, before the Bolshevik Revolution.[11]

* * *

Desperately short of food, fighting a civil war, and repelling invading Allied military forces, the Bolsheviks in 1919 set up the Communist International to protect their revolution by spreading it to other countries. At the founding congress in Moscow, Lenin presented a set of theses on 'bourgeois democracy and proletarian dictatorship'. In those countries where Soviet power was not established, the chief task of communists, he said, was to 'explain to the broad masses of the working class the historical meaning of the political and practical necessity of a new proletarian democracy which must replace bourgeois democracy and parliamentarianism'. The theses were a succinct statement of the argument that he had developed in *The State and Revolution: Marxist Teaching on the State and the Task of the Proletariat in the Revolution*, written in 1917. A few years later, in London, Childe was completing the manuscript of *How Labour Governs*, disappointed by having lost his job as an advisor to Labor in New South Wales. He was disillusioned by the 'crooks and cabals' of the Labor Party and the stuttering efforts of the militant industrial unionists. Yet in the first few pages he reached for a positive perspective on

---

10 Childe, *How Labour Governs*, 1st edn, pp. 160–1 (Bolshevik; class-conscious minority; industrial democracy).

11 Karl Kautsky, *The Road to Power*, first published 1909; first English translation, 1909: www.marxists.org/archive/kautsky/1909/power/.

labour's Australian history, a perspective on its search for 'true' democracy. Self-government to 'the proletarian democracy of Australia' meant that the 'issues to be submitted to the people must also be determined by the people'.[12]

Although both Lenin and Childe used the term 'proletarian democracy', each gave it a different meaning. For Lenin, proletarian democracy was a system of rule. Soviets in Russia, workers' councils in Germany, and shop stewards' committees in Britain were all examples of proletarian democracy because they drew 'working people' into organisations of self-government that abolished top-down power relationships (of employers, capitalist state officials and union bosses) and foreshadowed the withering away of the state. In the revolution, such forms of worker power constituted the dictatorship of the proletariat, and as such they made bourgeois parliamentary democracy irrelevant and counter-revolutionary. For Childe, proletarian democracy described something elemental: the desire for self-government of the working class. In this respect Childe was not at odds with Lenin. His framing idea, however, did not have the Leninist aim of protecting and extending the proletarian revolution. Rather, because he was trying to understand a labour movement facing well-established parliamentary institutions (frequent elections, and universal adult male suffrage exercised under the protection of the secret ballot), Childe frames the problem of proletarian democracy as one of developing a form of representation that would protect its integrity within the existing bourgeois parliament. Hence, the system of checks and controls over Labor's political representatives. Of course, he is well aware of the limits of parliamentary democracy, describing its ministries and anti-Labor parties as 'bourgeois'. He presents the IWW's criticisms of parliamentary democracy fully and fairly. The evidence for this is in *How Labour Governs*. And in 1919 he was advocating workers' control in the state industries, which would have impressed Lenin.

Different meanings, but understandable as responses to the different situations that confronted the Russian and Australian working classes. So, this difference is no basis for treating Lenin as a bold revolutionary and Childe as a cautious dabbler in working-class politics. Indeed not, because in Childe's thought there is evidence that there was a growing affinity with Lenin's revolutionary perspective. Take his use of the terms 'proletarian' or 'proletariat'. Before the publication of *How Labour Governs*, he hardly used these words at all – and never in his publications. In a letter to Murray he

---

12 Lenin, 'Theses on Bourgeois Democracy and Proletarian Dictatorship', *Communist International* (London), no. 1, May 1919; Childe, *How Labour Governs*, 1st edn, p. 5.

mentioned 'proletarian movements' and in letters to Brereton he referred ironically to the British trade union leader J.R. Clynes as 'a great proletarian leader', and angrily to the intention of the Allied capitalist governments to exterminate the Russian proletariat. In contrast to these descriptive uses, in Childe's book there are nine references to proletariat/proletarian, each of which draws on Marxism's theory of class struggle. He uses each of these words to refer to the proletariat's desire for self-government (twice), its system of rule ('dictatorship') over the bourgeoisie (twice), its rebelliousness, psychology, culture, consciousness, and thought. Then, in three of his London articles he continues the same Marxist perspective. He criticises the Labor Party for relying on a cross-class alliance of proletarian and non-proletarian interests, thus confusing 'the fundamental issues of the class war'; he applauds the Ryan Labor government for being 'on the side of the proletariat' when class-struggle issues arose; and he recognises that the proletariat and the bourgeoisie live in different mental universes. All this suggests a stiffening of Childe's revolutionary commitment, and it makes it more than likely that he was thinking about Lenin's idea of proletarian democracy. Would he have known about it? Very possibly, because the Australian Socialist Party published Lenin's *The State and Revolution*, in Sydney in 1920, and his theses for the Communist International were printed in London in 1919. They would have been available in the LRD library, and possibly also in the reading room of the 1917 Club.[13]

In 1913 Lenin published in *Pravda* a very short article, 'In Australia', responding to the news of Labor's defeat in the 1912 federal elections. 'What a peculiar capitalist country is this', he wrote, in which Labor can form governments 'and yet the capitalist system does not suffer any danger!' Moreover, the Labor Party does not even call itself a socialist party: 'As a matter of fact it is a liberal bourgeois party'. But this was a temporary situation caused by Australia's immature, dependent form of capitalism. It was abnormal. In

---

13   Childe, *How Labour Governs*, 1st edn, pp. 5, 65, 74, 143, 152, 159, 160 (twice), 207; Childe, 'When Labour Ruled', p. 175; Childe, 'A Labour Premier Meets His Masters', p. 282; Childe, 'A Colonial Product', p. 288; Lenin, 'Theses on Bourgeois Democracy and Proletarian Dictatorship'. As far as I can determine, although Marx wrote about democracy and the proletariat and the kind of rule that would emancipate the working class in *The Eighteenth Brumaire* and *The Civil War in France*, he never coupled the two terms and wrote specifically about 'proletarian democracy'. This coupling was even less likely to occur in the revisionist and orthodox currents of pre-war European social democracy; both stressed the importance of socialist electoral success as the basis for a proletarian revolution, not soviets, workers' councils or shop stewards' committees. Only in Russia, in October 1917, where the State was collapsing and revolutionary committees were exercising political authority by force, was it necessary, as Lenin found, to give Marxist legitimacy to their rule as 'proletarian democracy'.

time, he wrote, the Labor Party, jointly with the conservative parties, would complete the task of developing the country into an independent capitalist state with a central government. When this was achieved the class struggle would enter a new stage, the workers would develop a socialist consciousness, and the 'Liberal Labor Party' would make way for a 'Socialist Labor Party'.[14]

Lenin's purpose in this article was to kill any illusions among Russian liberals that their country might follow the Australian example and avoid class war. What was happening in Australia, he insisted, was exceptional. But would Childe have agreed? Surely the question was not whether Australia was 'exceptional', but to what extent? Was there really no class war in Australia? Were there no socialists in the Labor Party? Lenin's information was second- or third-hand, and he was not interested in advising Australian socialists about their tactics in relation to a 'Liberal Labour' party. But Childe was. He knew that in Queensland the Labor Party was socialist from the start, and federally that the party had amended its objective to strengthen its socialist commitment in 1912 and 1915. He knew about the big strikes, the insubordination that characterised the prewar wave of little strikes, and the rise of the industrialists in the party. He knew about the expulsion of Hughes, Holman and their moderate followers in 1916 and observed the split to the left in New South Wales that produced the Industrial Socialist Labor Party in 1919. He welcomed the formation of the OBU and advised the party how to deal with it. Then, in 1921 the Labor Party at a national congress altered its objective to include 'the socialisation of industry, production, distribution and exchange', as well as workers' representation in the management of nationalised industries. It seemed as if Lenin's prediction that Labor would become a 'Socialist Labor Party' was being fulfilled. Would Childe make a similar prediction? In London, between 1922 and 1924, as British Labour formed a government and his former Oxford friends were deciding whether to stay in or leave the Communist Party, Childe had to clarify his thinking about socialist advance in Australia, or at least about Labor's role in that process.[15]

* * *

---

14   Rick Kuhn, 'Lenin on the A.L.P. – The Career of 600 Words', *Australian Journal of Politics and History*, vol. 35, no. 1, April 1989, pp. 29–49.

15   Terry Irving, 'Socialism, Working-class Mobilisation and the Origins of the Labor Party', in Bruce O'Meagher (ed.), *The Socialist Objective: Labor and Socialism*, Sydney, Hale & Iremonger, 1983, pp. 32–43; Ian Turner, *Industrial Labour and Politics: The Dynamics of the Labour Movement in Eastern Australia, 1900–1921*, Canberra, ANU Press, 1965, pp. 217–26; Kuhn, 'Lenin on the ALP', p. 30.

When Childe arrived in London, Rajani Palme Dutt was the editor of *Labour Monthly*, a communist journal aimed at labour movement activists outside the party. The September 1922 edition carried a substantial article, 'When Labour Ruled – in Australia'. It was attributed to 'An Ex-Ruler', but those who attended the LRD summer school at Cloughton would have recognised Childe as its author. The school ended in late August, so he must have written it there or in London soon after. At nearly 4,000 words, it was his attempt to explain the meaning of *How Labour Governs*, which was already with the publisher, or, more correctly, the meaning that he failed to get across in the book. It was also an important statement of how he expected the Australian socialist movement to develop, the first that he had made since his Brisbane articles. The impetus for writing it we can only infer. Was it triggered by the disappointing reaction to his lecture? Was it the result of listening to Dutt's lectures on the communist position and deciding that he had to emulate his old friend by rejecting 'all other points of view'? Perhaps Dutt offered Childe some bracing private advice. These questions arise because Childe stated a position in this article much further to the revolutionary left than anything he had hinted at before.[16]

Childe begins by noting the dismal record of Labor governments, both federally and in the States, over the previous 12 years. They were voted into office 'on high hopes and boundless promises' but their performance fell so short of expectations that the workers lost faith in them, 'whereupon they have been defeated at the polls or ceased to be Labour'. The latest failed Labor government was the Dooley administration in New South Wales which was defeated in March by 'an unprecedented turnover of votes'. This was the Labor government in which he had served as secretary to its Premier and researcher for its Ministers. Did he feel a duty to protect its reputation? Not at all, for his assessment of the government was scathing. Its legislative program was 'unfruitful', it had neglected to fulfil its 'solemn' pre-election promises to the industrialists, it had cut wages by three shillings, and it had left the State with 'an enormous deficit' and 'an unprecedented volume of unemployment'. Its defeat at the polls was not due to fear of socialism or the activities of anti-Labor industrial unionists but to the apathy of disappointed wage-earners whose sense of class solidarity with the government had been broken: 'The Australian workers are disillusioned of political action on the old lines. This is not surprising to those who know the facts; what needs explanation is why they were so slow to realise the futility of old political fetishes.'

---

16   'When Labour Ruled', pp. 171–80.

This was the question that he should have raised in *How Labour Governs*. Despite his choice of words, he is not looking to explain why it took so long 'to realise the futility', but why the 'the old political fetishes' were so futile in the first place. He finds the answers by reviewing the origins and contradictions, both political and economic, of the Labour program.

Part one of 'When Labour Ruled', called 'The Labour Programme and its Origins', tells a familiar story. Labour Parties are formed after the defeat of 'the great strikes' of 1890–94 in order to rehabilitate unionism 'by the capture of political power'. This phrase is central to his argument. Choosing to make capturing parliament the main aim of the movement 'left a deep impression on the Labour platform, and has, in fact, set the key for all subsequent developments'. This was where politicalism began. Every proposal to rehabilitate unionism required state action: laws to regulate hours of work and factory conditions, interventions in the management of state utilities to 'set the tone of the labour market', extensions of public works to absorb the unemployed. And from this 'capturing' impulse flowed state arbitration with its legally enforceable contracts, the White Australia Policy to protect the employment of white workers, and Federation so that the same conditions for labour would exist nationally. Moreover, the capture of political power also affected how socialism was understood. Labour socialism would be achieved simply by the extension of public ownership from the existing utilities to the major industries.

There is another aspect of his story of origins, one that points to something hitherto unfamiliar in his thinking. Providing detail missing from the treatment in *How Labour Governs* of 'the great strikes' of the 1890s, Childe highlighted the violence in the state's response: 'Strike breakers had been armed and protected by the police; savage sentences had been inflicted upon unionists; while scabs had been given *carte blanche* to shoot them down; special legislation had been passed to suppress strike camps and disarm bush unionists.' Three years earlier in Brisbane he had skipped quickly over the sharp stones in the path of class struggle in order to direct attention to Labor's idealistic horizons, its democratic machinery and the possibility of a Labor government introducing workers' control without any nasty reaction from the state and paramilitary organisations. But then he saw close up the 1919 Red Flag riots in Brisbane and the 1921 proto-fascist anti-Labour riots in Sydney. By the time of writing 'When Labour Ruled' he is ready to acknowledge the violence endemic to class struggle, and to contemplate its use by the working class in self-defence.

The second section of 'When Labour Ruled' is called 'The Political Contradictions in the Labour Programme'. It summarises the material in Chapter V of *How Labour Governs*, 'Heterogeneity of the Elements within the Labour Party', but in the interval between book and article the idea of difference has become the idea of contradiction. Both article and book explain that in order to control the legislature Labor had to appeal to small producers and the 'general democratic sentiment'. Both emphasise the way the party consolidated its cross-class support by placing a nationalist clause above the socialist clause in its 1905 objective. But in the book the effect on the party program is described as producing 'inconsistencies' and vacillation in policy, whereas in the article the tone is much harder. In office, Labour politicians betray their working-class supporters; at election time they display 'more anxiety about the bourgeois vote than about the wage-earners' [vote] … And, in fact, it was largely on the votes of the little farmers, cockroach capitalists, and black-coated "patriots" that Labour climbed into office in the Federal Parliament, in New South Wales, in South Australia, and in Western Australia in 1910 or thereabouts.' The article insists that the interests of the 'heterogeneous' elements clash with those of the proletariat, and that the 'bribes' offered to such elements 'are mutually contradictory'.[17]

'Naturally', there was a backlash by the 'wage-earners who form the nucleus and backbone of the Party'. In New South Wales it led to the formation of the 'industrial section' within the party. The industrialists, however, were wrong to ascribe the failures of Labour to personal foibles and the 'undue respect' of the politicians for the middle-class vote. There were deeper reasons. These Childe discusses in the third section of his article under the heading 'The Economic Contradictions of the Labour Theory'.

The labour theory asserts that the conditions of the workers will improve when wages are raised by administrative enactment or arbitration court decisions. Childe calls this a 'revisionist' tactic, because it reminded him of the peaceful, incrementalist case for socialism deployed by the Marxist 'revisionists' led by Eduard Bernstein in the German Social Democratic Party. Childe counters the theory with an assertion of fact: wages were increasing before the arbitration system was set up. Moreover, when the courts did order a wage rise, the capitalists passed on the increase in wage costs to the consumer, thus revealing 'another secret of capitalist dominion'. Anyway, since 1908 real wages have fallen, leading to an epidemic of strikes.

Then the war began, and the true economic reasons for the politicians' failures were hidden by their 'evident treachery' over conscription: the 'inherent defects in the Labour programme were attributed to the personal baseness of its parliamentary exponents'. And the war created 'a fictitious prosperity'

---

17   Childe, *How Labour Governs*, 1st edn, p. 85.

which hid the incompatibility of the 'unionist ideal' and 'the continuance of the capitalist system'. It was during this exceptional wartime period that the Ryan Labor government, 'with commendable zeal', was able to appease the appetites of Queensland's workers, or, in Childe's less-flattering words, to give 'the workers just those palliatives which they had been induced to crave'. But when the boom collapsed the capitalists were able to circumvent Labor's pro-worker 'devices'. They closed industries, locked out the meat workers, the most militant section of the unionists, and persuaded overseas shipping companies not to call at Townsville because it was a union town. This new situation illustrated 'the reserve weapon of capitalism'.

With tax receipts falling, the Labor government needed to borrow money for a big public-works program, 'the accepted Labour panacea for unemployment':

> So, in 1920, Mr Theodore, as Premier of Queensland, came to London in quest of a loan. And then he and the unionists of Queensland learnt what is the real power behind Governments. Theodore was plainly told that he could not get a penny unless he was prepared to throw overboard several planks of the Labour platform. So he sailed home empty handed, and the Labour Government was forced to embark upon a scheme of retrenchment among public servants that a Tory Minister might envy.

For Childe, the meaning of this debacle was only too plain: 'the illusion of the old Labour-Unionist wage theory had vanished'.

There was a second economic contradiction in labour theory. It arose because the theory assumed that 'the whole [social] organism will peacefully pass into the co-operative commonwealth by a slow process of duly compensated expropriation'. The 'absurdity' of this 'wider theory of the socialist transformation of society' through state enterprises was also revealed by the government's financial crisis: 'And for the destruction of industrial capitalism loan money has not been forthcoming'. This was clear as early as 1912 when the New South Wales Labor government could not raise money from the banks to establish a state iron and steel works. Then comes his damning summing up of the futility of 'political action on the old lines': 'Hence, while the Labour platform can give the workers no real improvement in position under capitalism, it offers them no escape from capitalism'.

But what if working-class political action could be envisaged on new lines? At the end of this article Childe writes a short paragraph which should be as much associated with his contribution to labour ideology as the notorious *How Labour Governs* conclusion about labour organisations degenerating, 'not because they are Australian, but because they are Labour':

It is the realisation of this dual contradiction that has alienated the Australian workers from the old Labour Party and has induced the more intelligent to make the breakaway which has led to the adoption of the new objective at Brisbane and Melbourne last year. The new objective will not solve the situation; but it is the beginning of a movement which will have to go further, under the pressure of the same powers that brought it into being. The old chapter is closed; a new chapter of Australian Labour history is opening.

* * *

Between 1917 and 1924, Childe held three positions on socialist strategy in Australia. In Sydney in 1917 his student friends assumed that he supported the anti-political, direct action methods of the IWW. In Brisbane he became a convert to political action; that is, he thought the industrialists should work through the Labor Party in the expectation that 'a real Labor Government' would encourage workers' control in the state enterprises. Then, in London, he rejected his Queensland position, revealing the contradictions of 'the labour theory' to prove the futility of capturing 'political power', by which he meant having majority support in the parliament. This was the message of 'When Labour Ruled'. And later in 'A Fabian Judged by History' and 'A Labour Premier Meets His Masters' he reaffirmed this message. 'A real Labour Government' could only improve 'the status' of the workers when the economy was booming. When that moment passes, capital would use 'fascist violence' and create unemployment to protect itself – as had happened during the Theodore government, which in the end was only 'a subservient management committee of the bourgeoisie'. Thus, it was fatuous to promise, as Labor did, to transform capitalism by evolutionary means.[18]

But there was a positive side to the situation. He noted the 'savage criticism' meted out to the Theodore government by Queensland's unionists. While working for Storey he registered the rise of the Trades Hall 'Reds' in Sydney. Then in 1921 a national conference of union delegates recommended a new objective for the Labour Party, a socialist objective. The leadership of the

---

18   Censor's comment on Witherby to Childe, 21 February 1919, 167/85-91; Childe, 'A Fabian Judged by History', pp. 12–13; Childe, 'A Labour Premier Meets His Masters', pp. 282–5.

labour movement was shifting leftwards. Childe's response was qualified. The objective in itself, he said, would not be enough to emancipate the working class; the movement that produced it would have to go further.[19]

By the early 1920s the revolutionary wave had receded. In Britain the Communist Party was tiny, bureaucratic and unable to reach the working class through the Labour Party, which continually rebuffed its overtures for affiliation. Childe meanwhile was developing his 'chronological framework' for the origins of a Bronze Age civilisation in Europe. By late 1924, *The Dawn* was about to be published and he knew he was in line to become the Librarian at the Royal Anthropological Institute. By what means the international working-class movement could go further, he does not know, but he has a sense of the academic path that will ensure his own progress.

---

19   Childe, 'A Labour Premier Meets His Masters', p. 283 ('savage criticism'); for the Trades Hall Reds, see Miriam Dixson, *Greater than Lenin? Lang and Labor 1916–1932*, Melbourne Political Monographs, no date.

Part 4.

What Happens in History: 1927–1957

Chapter 18

SCIENCE AS COMMUNISM

After two years as Librarian at the Royal Anthropological Institute in London, in 1927 Childe went to Edinburgh University to take up the Abercromby Professorship of Archaeology, which was financed by an endowment under the will of Lord Abercromby, one of the founders of Scottish archaeology. As well as its annual salary of 700 pounds, for most of his years at the university Childe received a further 200 pounds as the Munro Lecturer, a position funded by a trust set up by another amateur Scottish archaeologist to pay for an annual series of lectures in archaeology and anthropology. His earnings were not as great as those of the average Professor in the Arts Faculty who was paid 1,000 pounds, but compared to the penury of his early London years he was now very well off. He could afford to buy a 'Chummy', a baby Austin 7. Apparently, his taste in cars quickly matured, for in the early 1930s he traded up to an open-topped Terraplane, a powerful six-cylinder version of an eye-catching US marque. Later in the 1930s, or perhaps after the war, he owned a Morris 14, a saloon, and then there was another open-top, a Bentley. These were his only extravagances, for he lived simply, and he never bought any real-estate. He acquired cars as markers of his increased social standing; they were signs of his pleasure in having made it despite being a colonial and a radical. In the same way, he enjoyed being invited to stay in some of Scotland's grand houses, and of being a member of exclusive gentlemen's clubs, such as the Athenaeum in London. He knew what this looked like to his friends. As he was departing for Edinburgh in 1927, he told Rajani Dutt 'that he would have chosen revolutionary politics but he found the price too high, and anyway he preferred what he termed the *bios apolausticos* (fleshpots) of professional status'.[1]

---

1   Ian Ralston, 'Gordon Childe and Scottish Archaeology', *European Journal of Archaeology*, vol. 121, nos 1–3, 2009, pp. 47–90; R.P. Dutt, letter to the *Times Literary Supplement*, vol. 3, no. 304, 1965, p. 359, quoted in Peter Gathercole, 'Childe, Marxism and Knowledge', *European Journal of Archaeology*, vol. 121, nos 1–3, 2009, p. 182.

And one could always undercut the hubris of status with a little whimsy. After several years lodging at a house in suburban Liberton, to the south of the city, he made a typically idiosyncratic decision about his next private space: two rooms in the Hotel de Vere. Built in the 1870s, this hotel in the Western New Town was part of an elegant terrace of town houses on Eglinton Crescent, curving around one side of a private communal garden. Until 1938 he was only required to lecture for two terms, so he was able to spend half of each year supervising excavations, travelling to foreign archaeological sites and museums, or living in London, where he sometimes rented a flat in another comfortable Victorian residence in Kensington with a name that tickled his fancy, the Moscow Mansions. His eccentric dress served the same end: shorts in summer, a mackintosh in winter, the broad-brimmed hat always, and a red tie when some advance of revolutionary politics needed recognition.[2]

Beset with the demands of a new career, and missing the excitement of 'the movement', he liked to keep up with the progress of his political friends. In 1931 he wrote to Mary Alice Evatt that he would 'love to come to Australia to see you and Bert and Billy McKell and Jack Lang, not to speak of [uncle] Sir Alexander [Gordon], the Sydney Bridge and Canberra'. Bert Evatt was now a Justice of the High Court of Australia, the youngest ever appointed, McKell was Minister for Justice in Lang's second government in New South Wales, while Uncle Alexander had recently retired from the Supreme Court bench. Childe then told Mary Alice, 'And really I could afford it if only I felt I'd earned a holiday by getting Scottish prehistory onto its legs. At the moment it's very backward and I have to dig which I loath [sic] a good part of the summer (so-called).'

And dig he did, at 20 Scottish sites in the 19 years of his Edinburgh professorship, including most famously at the Neolithic village of Skara Brae on Orkney. He also published at least one article a year on Scottish archaeology, delivered addresses almost every year to the Edinburgh League of Archaeologists, a student club that provided labour power for his digs, and participated in the Society of Antiquaries of Scotland as a Councillor from 1930. At the university he gave three lectures a week for two terms as well as running a seminar for honours students. Initially his course was offered only to Arts students but in 1933 he successfully manoeuvred the Science Faculty into setting up a bachelor's degree in Physical Anthropology and Prehistoric Archaeology.

---

2   Ralston, 'Gordon Childe and Scottish Archaeology', pp. 58–9; Green, *Prehistorian*, p. 74.

Childe as the well-dressed professor in the 1930s. (By Andrew Swan Watson (Edinburgh) from National Library of Australia. The original held in the Evatt Collection, Flinders University of South Australia: Evatt 3025)

Meanwhile he was consolidating his reputation internationally. He made a research trip to Germany and Central Europe in the Spring of 1933, and then to India and Iraq later in the year. He went to Russia in 1935 to investigate Marxist ideas in archaeology, and to the USA to receive honorary degrees in 1936 (Harvard) and 1937 (Pennsylvania State), and again in 1939 for research at the University of California. Yet, despite these varied and continuing responsibilities, he found time to write substantial works of scholarship, including *The Most Ancient East* (1928), *The Danube in Prehistory* (1929), *The Bronze Age* (1930), *The Prehistory of Scotland* (1935), and a revised edition of *The Dawn of European Civilization* (1939). By the mid-1930s, his contributions to the science of archaeology, and to Scotland, could no longer be ignored, and he was elected to the Royal Society of Edinburgh by Scotland's intellectual elite in 1935.[3]

One might imagine that Childe spent all his waking hours in academic or scholarly circles, but tantalising scraps of evidence suggest otherwise. About to leave London to take up his new post in Edinburgh, he ran into the communist, Robin Page Arnot. Did they meet at a pub near the Labour Research Department, where Robin was still the secretary? With visiting political friends from Australia, Childe was the convivial companion. In 1929, Percy Stephensen was in London where he was publishing the scandalous paintings of D.H. Lawrence and mixing with artistic communists. Witherby, who was also in London, sent him a note: 'Inky, you blighter. Let us dine a la Australienne. Childe will be dining with me on Sat night next at 7 sharp (he leaves at 9.00 for north of the River Tweed). Will you join us, Communist?' In 1931 Childe wrote to Rajani Dutt that Allen Hutt was 'the only one of your colleagues I meet nowadays'. By colleagues Childe meant members of the Communist Party. Hutt, a journalist with the *Daily Worker*, at that time might have been researching for his book, *The Condition of the Working Class in Britain*. Did they meet in Edinburgh or London, and why was Childe meeting him? And was it more than a coincidence that in 1932 the Marxist and lecturer in Classical Archaeology, Cathcart Roland (Roly) Wason, lived at the De Vere Hotel? The association was brief, however, because Roly abandoned archaeology to become a Labour Party organiser in County Argyll. Later he was a shop steward, socialist organiser and bus driver, before publishing in 1976 his *Rebel Scotland: The History of Democracy in Scotland*. Childe kept in touch with Wason, mentioning at a Left Book Club meeting in 1936 Wason's idea of securing world peace by ending colonialism.[4]

It seems likely, on the basis of this evidence, that the Communist Party was following Childe's progress. After all, if MI5 were, why not the communists?

---

3   Childe to Mary Alice Evatt, 23 June 1931, Evatt papers, Flinders University, file on Childe; Ralston, 'Gordon Childe and Scottish Archaeology', passim.

4   R.P. Arnot to Peter Gathercole, 4 February 1960 [copy sent to me by Gathercole]; Craig Munro, 'Stephensen, Percy Reginald (1901–1965)', *Australian Dictionary of Biography*, Vol. 12, 1990, pp. 70–1; Witherby to Stephensen, September 1929, Stephensen papers, Mitchell Library MSS 1284, Y2150; Childe to Dutt, 4 April 1931, Dutt papers, CPGB (Communist Party of Great Britain) Archives, Labour History Archive and Study Centre, People's History Museum, Manchester; for Hutt, see Graham Stevenson, www.grahamstevenson.me.uk/index.php?option=com_content&view=article&id=290:alan-hutt-&catid=8:h&Itemid=109; Childe MI5 file, 17 November 1936 re Left Book Club; For Wason, see Graham Wason, 'Obituary, Roly Wason', *The Independent*, 24 January 1998; C.R. Wason, *Rebel Scotland*, Hicksville, Exposition Press, 1976.

But between 1923 and 1930 there are no entries in Childe's MI5 file. How should we explain this absence? Of course, he is preoccupied with getting Scottish prehistory 'onto its legs', and he has new academic responsibilities to discharge. He has not, however, become apolitical, as is clear from his continued contacts with his British and Australian left-wing friends. Moreover, as we shall see, he was developing in these years a prehistory of human progress and change that resonated with the current revolutionary hopes of the left. But he was not associated with left-wing organisations, because otherwise MI5 would have picked those things up. In terms of his personal life, this is all we can say. To this limited evidence, however, the collective life of the revolutionary left adds an extra layer of meaning.

Childe as a member of the LRD in the early 1920s was part of what might be called non-party communism, a surprisingly well-connected political culture found in a broad range of labour institutions, currents of ideas and radical agitation, a culture created by and supportive of the Russian Revolution and the Soviet 'experiment'. Kevin Morgan has delineated it in his three-volume study of *Bolshevism and the British Left*. Although it was fluid and shape-shifting, lodging temporarily in organisations and struggles, it always remained anti-statist and radical democratic when it encountered the older traditions of British socialism. It was boosted by the 'Hands off Russia' campaign, whose Councils of Action frightened the British Government into ceasing to support the 'Whites' during the Russian Civil War. It drew on a deep sentiment of working-class solidarity strengthened by the slaughter of workers during the First World War. And it expressed the progressive dreams of middle-class intellectuals not just for a better world but one that was qualitatively different from the 'new liberal'/labour-collectivist vision of the first quarter of the twentieth century.

It was an impulsive culture, however, one that could not survive the Bolshevisation of the Communist Party and official labour's bureaucratic manipulation of working-class politics. Both these developments occurred during the 1920s. By 1924, for example, the LRD was fully controlled by the Communist Party. The most debilitating moment, however, was the defeat of the General Strike of 1926. According to Morgan, the strike failed because Ernest Bevin imposed on it a centralised top-down strategy that dampened rank and file militancy, opened the way for the right-wing union leader Jimmy Thomas to betray the strikers in his negotiations with the government, and consolidated the hold of labour socialism in the trade unions. Thus, working-class insurrectionism died not because it ran out of steam but because its fire was doused by its supposed leaders. By the early

1930s, non-party communism in Britain had been squeezed out of the labour movement, pincer-like (to use Morgan's phrase), by the machinations of Labour's 'managerial social-democracy' and British communism's imposition of Bolshevism on the revolutionary left.[5]

And then came the 1930s, fabled decade of left-wing revival among British intellectuals and artists. Childe was part of this, according to his MI5 file. He is detected joining organisations – the Scottish–USSR Society (President of the Edinburgh branch in 1932–3), the Left Book Club, the India League (Chairman in 1938), and the Association of Scientific Workers (Chair in 1938). He made speeches to the Cambridge Anti-War Group and the National Council of Labour Colleges, in the case of the latter perhaps disturbing its usual right-wing conversations. In response to the rise of fascism he spoke out against racialist ideas in archaeology. Yet he was cautious about identifying himself with the Communist Party or the Labour Party. The trouble with these leading organisations was that they were caught up in the process that began in the 1920s when they suppressed non-party communism. The political logic unfolded inexorably. For the Communist Party, it was the move to 'class against class', the strategy imposed by the Comintern in 1929 to direct working-class militancy against official Labour in order to expose reformism. It led to sectarian isolation and declining membership. For the Labour Party, it was to continue the policy of compromise with the state. It led to betrayal, when in 1931 Prime Minister Ramsay MacDonald, facing a revolt by a section of his Cabinet over cuts to public spending, kept his parliamentary majority by taking his followers into a National government with Labour's enemies. Writing soon after to Mary Alice, Childe explained that 'I and everyone else is thoroughly sick of Macdonald and Co. But there is no alternative less bad, the CP being quite hopeless here. We have become politically agnostic.' When he was an active player in the Australian movement, the need to keep it united as well as socialist had been one of his clearest messages.[6]

* * *

---

5 Morgan, *Labour Legends and Russian Gold*; Morgan, *The Webbs and Soviet Communism*, London, Lawrence & Wishart, 2006; Morgan, *Bolshevism, Syndicalism and the General Strike: The Lost Internationalist World of A.A. Purcell*, London, Lawrence & Wishart, 2013.

6 Childe to Mary Alice Evatt, 23 June 1931, Evatt papers, Flinders University, file on Childe; Childe's MI5 file, entry for 29 July 1931; Macintyre, *A Proletarian Science: Marxism in Britain, 1917–1933*, pp. 78–9.

We know that Childe corresponded with Jack Lang in Sydney because he told Rajani Dutt about it in April 1931. Dutt had asked him to write an article for *Labour Monthly* explaining Lang's recent actions as Premier of New South Wales, where the economic depression had created a financial crisis in the State. Lang's response – using populist rhetoric with anti-imperial flourishes – was to refuse to pay the interest on the state's overseas loans, most of which were to British banks. He did not foresee that this would make an opening for revolutionary agitation by the local communists against capitalism as a system. In order to outflank them, Lang's supporters in the Labor Party proclaimed him as 'Greater then Lenin', and produced plaster mini-busts of him inscribed with the words 'The People's Champion'. A year earlier, Labor's left had set up 'Socialisation Units' in the local party leagues. The climax of this populist/left shift in the NSW party was its historic decision at the 1931 Annual Conference to pledge itself to 'socialism in our time' through a five-year plan of socialisation. That never happened, of course; the next day the factional numbers had changed, and conference rescinded the vote.[7]

But on the day the conference in Sydney voted for this objective, Childe in London replied to Rajani – on the letterhead of the Royal Societies Club in St James's. He was 'awfully bucked', he wrote, to hear from him again, but alas he was not in a position to write the article. There were 'new developments since I left and new names that I do not know' and he was too busy even to go to Australia House and read the *Labor Daily*.

Nonetheless, he gave Dutt a briefing on the chances for socialist revolt in Australia. He began by considering whether Australia could survive economically without borrowing cheap money from overseas: 'in other words are her secondary industries sufficiently developed to make her independent of <u>real</u> foreign capital. If the answer is in the affirmative (I've no means of judging) then the only sensible course is a bold Soviet policy – repudiate foreign loans and take over the secondary industries like the BHP steel works etc.' Here he is, confounding our expectations, suggesting that a communist revolution in Australia might be 'sensible'.

But, he asks, 'is there anyone with the brains to do it?' He runs through the qualities displayed by certain Labor leaders. The Premier of NSW, Lang, 'is (or was) a very honest man and strong willed (or at least obstinate). But I doubt whether he was really brilliant, and now and then a very small quantity of liquor would make him drunk.' T.J. Garden of the Sydney Labor Council

---

7   Nick Martin, 'Bucking the Machine: Clarrie Martin and the NSW Socialisation Units, 1929-35', *Labour History*, no. 93, November 2007, pp. 177–95.

'is an ex-parson and a mere gasbag'. Ted Theodore is 'really rather conventional' and 'more or less capitalised, too. For a politician he is honest, ie he is clever enough only to take bribes for what he would do anyway, but remember how he capitulated over the Pastoral Leases?' Here Childe confuses Leninist vanguardism with the politicalists' fetish for strong leaders.

Then he turns to the workers. He 'can't imagine [them] getting constructively revolutionary'. The skilled workers are 'kept in reasonable comfort' through the living wage policy of the industrial courts. They 'would certainly be worse off for a while under a Soviet regime (unless run by a super Lenin) [and they] probably guess this'.

> To me the questions are (i) state of secondary industries (ii) leaders (iii) temper of proletariat, and I'm really unable to answer them. Australia is an ideal country for a Soviet system when the economic conditions are ripe but as long as the Tories can rely on the active co-operation of (a) the small farmers (b) the black-coated proletariat, and (c) a section of the skilled unionists they would probably win if it came to fighting. The 'cockies' are hefty chaps and the capitalists generally have better organising power and better leadership.

Perhaps he was remembering the 'cocky' farmers brought in from the country areas by the proto-fascists to beat up the reds in the Sydney Domain in 1921.

The letter concludes by suggesting that Dutt ask Esmonde Higgins, no doubt because Childe knew or guessed that Higgins was a communist. Childe was not, but he hesitated to take a position opposed to Dutt's, his friend, and the person who had introduced him to a revolutionary perspective on socialist politics. Sometimes Childe told people what he thought they might like to hear.[8]

* * *

In 1933 Childe was outraged at the distortion of archaeological knowledge by the Nazis to justify their expansionism. In Germany earlier that year, he had witnessed Hitler's coming to power. He told his students that in the name of discredited racialist theories 'men are being exiled from public life and shut up in concentration camps, books are being burned and expressions of opinion

---

8   Childe to Dutt, 4 April 1931, Dutt papers, CPGB Archives.

stifled just as, in the name of religious ideas, they were during fifteen long centuries of darkness'. In a 1934 letter to Professor Myres he wrote that he would not visit Germany because of its National Socialist government, and that he hated fascist ideas, especially in British archaeology and anthropology. Childe knew that the racialist moment in British science was passing. Scientists including anthropologists were rejecting the racial cleansing of eugenics, pointing out problems with the definition of race, and moving away from the social Darwinist interpretation of history as a struggle of races through natural selection. But not in Germany, where archaeology numbered among its founders Gustaf Kossinna (1858–1931), who argued that archaeological cultures were traces of an ethnic past, and that archaeology had discovered the origins of a unified German race dating back to proto-Indo-European peoples. By the 1930s, apologists for the Nazis were celebrating Kossinna as the scientific father of their racial doctrines, claiming, as Kossinna himself had, the superiority of the Nordic race, and Germany's right to expand its borders to cover much of Central Europe, including Poland.[9]

During the 1930s, using the latest findings from anthropology, genetics, philology and prehistory, Childe went on a crusade against this false science. To expose its political use, he translated a pamphlet on the teaching of history and prehistory in German institutions by the Nazi Minister of the Interior, Wilhelm Frick, and published it in *Nature*, before arranging for copies to be sent to leading archaeologists in Europe. He addressed the Edinburgh League of Prehistorians on 'Aryan Nonsense' and wrote a short piece for *The Plebs*. A more substantial refutation appeared in *History*, under the title 'Races, Peoples and Cultures in Prehistoric Europe'. Message: cultures and languages correspond to peoples, not races. His 1934 article in *Discovery*, 'Anthropology and Herr Hitler', a longer version of the same argument, ended with a warning that 'it is not only in Germany that sentimental considerations are liable to disturb the objectivity of scientific judgement. Amongst an imperial people ruling over subjects of diverse hue the racial theory of history has a powerful emotional and economic appeal.' In 1936, *Nature* carried his short note exposing the financial connection between an international congress in Edinburgh on ethnology and the German state: its object was to promote the idea of an Aryan race; and in *Man Makes Himself* he rubbished 'fascists like Dr Frick'

---

9   Childe to Myres, 27 February 1934, Myres papers, Bodleian Library, box 120, f. 90; Paul Rich, 'The Long Victorian Sunset: Anthropology, Eugenics and Race in Britain, c 1900–48', *Patterns of Prejudice*, vol. 18, issue 3, 1984, pp. 3–17; B. Arnold, '"Arierdämmerung": Race and Archaeology in Nazi Germany'. *World Archaeology*, vol. 38, issue 1, Race, Racism and Archaeology, 2006, pp. 8–31.

who try to prevent the advance of historical science. In 1938, there were two articles based on his Presidential Address to the Anthropology Section of the British Association for the Advancement of Science. His subject, 'The Orient and Europe', was given a brief summary and then a fuller version in *Nature*. Childe then recycled the material for 'The Oriental Background of European Science', an article which he wrote for the first issue of the Communist Party's *The Modern Quarterly*. The most important task of prehistory, he wrote, was to 'trace out in ever greater detail the paths and mechanisms whereby the great discoveries of the Ancient East ... were transmitted to the savages and barbarians of Cisalpine Europe'. So much for Nordic arrogance.[10]

But it was not enough to write and speak against fascism. As a member of the Association of Scientific Workers, he took the opportunity to participate in its project of assisting refugee scientists fleeing Nazism. In 1935 he was helping to publish the work of a German emigré, Gertrude Hermes, who was an expert on the Indo-European origins of the light war chariot. He told Myres that she would probably be thrown into a concentration camp when she returned to Germany. In 1938 Gerhard Bersu arrived in England, having lost his job as Director of Germany's premier archaeological institute in Frankfurt because of the 1935 Race Laws. Under the auspices of The Prehistoric Society, which Childe had helped to form a few years earlier, Bersu carried out excavations in Little Woodbury, Wiltshire. He was interned on the Isle of Man when the war broke out, but with Childe's support he was permitted to undertake some excavations with the help of other internees. Sometimes Childe was unable to help. In 1937, the University of Barcelona archaeologist Pere Bosch Gimpera, who had earlier stayed in Childe's Edinburgh apartment, became the Minister of Justice in the Catalan Republican government. When the Francoist fascists defeated the Republicans in 1939, Gimpera had to flee. Myres arranged a temporary job for him, but when it ended Childe had to tell Myres that he was too committed to supporting Bersu and his wife

---

10   On the Frick translation, see Margarita Diaz-Andreu, 'Childe and the International Congresses of Archaeology', *European Journal of Archaeology*, vol. 12, nos 1–3, 2009, pp. 97–8; the address to the League of Prehistorians is listed in Ralston, 'Gordon Childe and Scottish Archaeology', p. 87; Childe, 'Where Did Culture Arise?', *The Plebs*, vol. XXV, 1933, pp. 268–71; Childe, 'Races, Peoples and Cultures in Prehistoric Europe', *History* (NS), vol. 18, October 1933, pp. 193–203; Childe, 'Anthropology and Herr Hitler', *Discovery*, vol. 15, 1934, pp. 65–8; Childe, 'International Congress on the Science of Man', *Nature*, no. 137, 1936, p. 1074; Childe, 'The Orient and Europe', *Nature*, no. 142, 1938, pp. 557–603; Childe, 'The Oriental Background to European Science', *The Modern Quarterly*, no. 1, 1938, pp. 105–20.

to offer any assistance. Gimpera managed to get to Mexico where he had a distinguished archaeological career.[11]

* * *

After Childe's death his colleagues remembered their relationships with him as 'friendly and comradely', but not close. They felt he kept one at a distance, never revealing his private feelings. They knew of no partner, no regular companions, no intimates. There was, however, one friend, O.G.S. Crawford, who might have contradicted this conclusion, had he wanted to. They had met in 1925, when Crawford was the Archaeology Officer attached to the Ordinance Survey office, where he was pioneering the use of aerial photography in archaeology. In 1927, he founded the quarterly journal *Antiquity*, positioning it according to his biographer 'somewhere between the learned societies and the popular press', in order to strengthen the shift of archaeology away from wealthy amateurs and narrowly focused academics. He edited it for the next 30 years. Childe warmly supported this move to 'democratise archaeology'. He contributed an article and three reviews to the first issue, and in succeeding issues up to the end of 1939 he published another nine articles and no less than 50 reviews. In 1933, Crawford heard that Childe's introductory lecture to that year's archaeology students had caused a stir, and he immediately obtained Childe's permission to print it. He gave it the title 'Is Prehistory Practical?'. In 2019 its message still resonated with a group of younger archaeologists at the Annual Conference of the European Association of Archaeologists. Reminding us that Childe's question was a response to the rise of fascism, they designed a session with the same title in order to open up a discussion about archaeology as 'a place for practical invention' and of resistance to what the EAA President called 'the pressing threats that challenge an inclusive and progressive Europe'.[12]

---

11   Childe to Myres, 27 March 1935, Myres papers, box 8, f. 57; re Bersu: Green, *Prehistorian*, p. 88, and Heinrich Härke, 'Archaeology and Nazism: A warning from Prehistory', in V. Mordvintseva, H. Härke and T. Shevchenko (eds), *Archaeological and Linguistic Research: Materials of the Humboldt-Conference (Simferopol, Yalta, 20–23 September, 2012)*, Kiev, Stilos, 2014, pp. 32–42; Childe to Crawford, 11 May 1940, Crawford papers, box 66; re Fraulein Hermes: Martin Bernal, *Black Athena: Volume II: The Archaeological and Documentary Evidence*, Rutgers University Press, 1987, p. 348; on Bersu and Gimpera, see Margarita Diaz-Andreu, 'Childe and the International Congresses', pp. 97–100.

12   Kitty Hauser, *Bloody Old Britain: O.G.S. Crawford and the Archaeology of Modern Life*, London, Granta Books, 2008; P. Gathercole, 'Childe in History', *Bulletin of the Institute*

Osbert Guy Stanhope Crawford democratising archaeology.
(O.G.S. Crawford Photographic Archive, print 35.32.
Courtesy of the Institute of Archaeology, Oxford)

Crawford admired Childe's political commitment as much as his learning. Although six years older than Childe, his background was not dissimilar. Born

---

of Archaeology, London, no. 31, 1994, p. 27, for the terms used to describe Childe's personality by his associates; Childe, 'Is Prehistory Practical?', *Antiquity*, vol. 7, no. 28, December 1933, pp. 410–18; on 'democratising archaeology', see Childe to Crawford, 8 March 1942, O.G.S. Crawford, General Correspondence, Bodleian Library, Oxford, box 67, f. 40; on 2019 EEA Conference, see www.e-a-a.org/eaa2019 and Joanna Alves-Ferreira, main organiser of session no. 360, 'Is Archaeology Practical?'.

in India, Crawford was another child of the empire; after his parents died, he was brought up in a pious household by his father's sisters in England; as a young man he rejected religion and came to despise the British ruling class. A visit to Germany led to a hatred of fascism. Sometime in the 1930s he became a socialist, visited the Soviet Union in 1932, declared that he was a Marxist and flirted with the Communist Party. He worked on a project to photograph the houses and pubs associated with Marx and Engels in nineteenth-century England; the result was probably exhibited at the Marx Memorial Library in London. When the Bersus family needed financial support in exile, he shared the expense with Childe. As to Childe's learning, in *Antiquity* he recorded that Childe's *Man Makes Himself* (1936) was 'the book Marx himself would have written had he had access to all the knowledge discovered in the fifty years since his death'.[13]

* * *

The Communist Party became seriously interested in Childe as an 'asset' as early as 1931, according to his MI5 file. In that year the party considered Childe, Professor Lancelot Hogben (a zoologist) and Professor Hyman Levy (a mathematician) as members of a 'wider Board of Contributors' for a proposed 'Marxist Theoretical Journal'. This is interesting. According to political Marxism's commentary on Childe, he was never a Marxist, and when the archaeology discipline searches for Marxism in his works, he was not a Marxist until four or five years after this date. Clearly, the Communist Party based its assessment on different criteria – a matter to which we will return in the next chapter. Nothing came of this proposal at the time, but in 1937 the party decided to publish 'a Marxist Quarterly', and once again Childe was mentioned. He was approached, and he agreed to serve on its 'editorial committee'. *The Modern Quarterly*, as it was called, appeared a year later. Childe remained one of its editors until May 1951, and contributed in that time three articles, including one, as we have seen, in its first issue.[14]

---

13 Hauser, *Bloody Old Britain*, Chs 1–4, and 174 on 'the book Marx would have written'; Childe to Myres, 24 March 1940, Myres papers, box 8, doc. 69, Bodleian Library.

14 Childe's MI5 file, 29 July 1931, 4 January 1937, 9 November 1937, 13 January 1950, and 10 May 1951; Neil Faulkner, 'Gordon Childe and Marxist Archaeology', *International Socialism*, issue 116, 2007, http://isj.org.uk/gordon-childe-and-marxist-archaeology/#116faulkner_41 accessed 30 April 2019; Humphrey McQueen, 'Historians – V. Gordon Childe', www.surplusvalue.org.au/McQueen/hist_ns/

During that time the party continued to cultivate Childe, but very carefully. In April 1943 Childe's MI5 file contains the transcript of a telephone call between Cyril Claydon, a leading cadre in the Young Communist League (YCL), and William Robson, the party official responsible for 'cultural matters'. The YCL had persuaded Childe to write a pamphlet on historical materialism for young workers – it would become *The Story of Tools* (1944) – but Claydon was now critical of the manuscript. It was too factual; the style was too professorial. Should Claydon write a statement adding the correct Marxist formulae? How should the YCL proceed? Robson said no to any addition, cautioning Claydon against upsetting Childe:

> Childe is an important fellow and one we have to keep on good terms with … My opinion is that your criticism is valid, but it is so useful to get a man of this status to write and to identify himself with [the YCL's efforts to educate young workers] that it would be better not to offend him if possible. … His approach has always been along those lines and not along ours, but I believe he is sympathetic to our approach. … Gordon Childe is quite an important fellow, you know.

In the next chapter we will see how this difference of approach worked out.[15]

In 1938, encouraged by its success in getting Childe involved with *The Modern Quarterly*, the party deputed Rajani Dutt to find a further organisational role for Childe. He reacted badly, writing to Dutt:

> I have been considering in a rather calmer way the subjects of our conversation on Monday last. On the first, I regret to say I have come to the following conclusion. I cannot see what really useful purpose would be effected by a prehistorian, resident in Edinburgh, joining the Faculty of Marx House as a historian. The only practical effect would be to tie round my neck a label and I don't like labels, especially if they are liable to be misleading. This probably is. To me Marxism means effectively a way of approach to and a methodological device for the interpretation of historical and archaeological material and I accept it because and in so far as it <u>works</u>. To the average communist and anti-communist alike

---

historian_v_gordon.htm; Leo S. Klejn. 'Childe and Soviet Archaeology: A Romance', in David R. Harris (ed.), *The Archaeology of V. Gordon Childe: Contemporary Perspectives*, Melbourne University Press, 1994, p. 76.

15   Childe's MI5 file, 12 April 1943. On Robson, http://grahamstevenson.wwwtest.co.uk/2008/09/20/robert-robson/; on Claydon, see www.pressgazette.co.uk/cyril-claydon-a-dedicated-campaigner-and-trade-unionist/.

(and presumably it is only for their benefit that this piece of labelling is necessary), Marxism means a set of dogmas – the words of the master from which as among medieval schoolmen, one must deduce truths which the scientist hopes to infer from experiment and observation ...

Rajani Palme Dutt in 1943 – 'We don't want sugaring'.
(Portrait by Howard Coster, National Portrait Gallery, London. NPG x11531)

The second subject was easier for Childe to agree to: 'On the question of annotation of The Family, State and Property I remain delighted and indeed very anxious to cooperate – and on a concrete issue like that which is not just a question of an empty label you could count on me'. This was a reference to Engels's 1884 book, *The Origin of the Family, Private Property, and the State: In the Light of the Researches of Lewis H. Morgan*. Morgan was an American anthropologist whose book *Ancient Society* (1877) was closely studied by both Marx and Engels because it expanded the study of social evolution by linking kinship with technological development, property relations and government. Through its publisher, Lawrence & Wishart, the party wanted to bring out a new edition of Engels's work, and had asked Dutt 'to secure the collaboration of Childe and … to exercise some check on him'. The need for this check seemed necessary after Childe had referred to communists treating Marxism as a set of dogmas. So Dutt was anxious to ensure, even before the actual annotating of the text began, that Childe understood that the purpose of the new edition was 'to help readers to understand and master the Marxist method of social analysis'. He wrote to Childe in June 1939 urging him 'to write me some indication of how you see the approach as a whole, or any general problems … so that we can see if there are any questions of principle we may need to tackle first and see if we can reach agreement on'.[16]

When Childe replied to Dutt he was in Berkeley, at the University of California, reading Engels in the original German edition. He began by stating his conclusion about the project: he was 'pessimistic of evolving therefrom a really useful or reliable synthesis [because] the elements of permanent value in his book are very small compared to its glaring shortcoming'. It was a long letter – almost a thousand words – in which he gave examples of the empirical and analytical shortcomings of the book. It was not just handicapped by its ignorance of the knowledge produced by the preceding 50 years of archaeological research, ethnography and economic analysis of Greece and Rome, 'to say nothing of the earlier oriental empires', but also by its reliance on Morgan. This meant that the book did 'not even illustrate the MCH [Materialist Conception of History] as I understand it'. Childe then briefly gave his definition of the MCH: 'the dominance of the machinery of production (techne)[17] and the economic system in which the productive machine functions as determining such "ideal" manifestations as political-social organisation, religion and art'.

---

16   Childe to Dutt, 14 October 1938; Dutt to Garman, 18 July 1939; Dutt to Childe, 17 June 1939 – all the preceding letters are in the Dutt papers, CPGB archives.

17   'techne' (from classical Greek philosophy) means practical knowledge, or knowledge that is practically applied.

But Morgan, said Childe, 'was not primarily interested in material culture or equipment. Though he nominally makes material culture the <u>criterion</u> of his several stages, he fails to show the dependence of the sociological forms on the material and in practice uses the sociological criterion instead of the economic'. Moreover, for Morgan his 'material-economic criteria ... are based on observations of New World primitives: they are absolutely incompatible with the data provided by Old World archaeology and are often purely formalistic'. As a consequence of Morgan's interests, 'a quite undue proportion of [Morgan's book] Ancient Society is devoted to (what I must frankly call speculations about) the form of the family and kinship relations which from an economic standpoint are often secondary or even irrelevant and about which in prehistoric times we can know nothing <u>directly</u>'.

Childe then moved to a devastating question: '*Quae quum ita sint* [Since these things are] what shall we tell the would-be readers of U F P S [*Der Ursprung der Familie, des Privateigenthums und des Staats*]? To read it like a modern Xian reads his Bible, as a collection of inspired parables describing darkly what did not happen? ... If I had anything to do with the new edition of Engels the substance of above would have to be incorporated, naturally in more sugared terms in Intro.'[18]

Dutt reacted angrily: 'We [the party] don't want sugaring', he told Douglas Garman at Lawrence & Wishart, 'Let's drop the project'. Of course, another outcome was possible, making the new edition's criticisms – Childe's criticisms – an example to the world that Marxism was a method that could submit even its own productions to scientific scrutiny. In fact, the publisher at Lawrence & Wishart was leaning towards that suggestion, pointing out to Dutt that Childe was really attacking Morgan. Dutt, however, would not hear of this. Childe's remarks, he told Garman, 'give the effect of hostile, non-Marxist criticism'. They were not, but to Dutt the book's ideological role, its 'party-purpose', was all that counted. Science had to be subordinated to politics. So, he wrote to Childe that their project had been dropped, but Lawrence & Wishart would proceed with another editor. Would Childe be willing to advise if that project went ahead? Childe said yes.[19]

* * *

---

18 Childe to Dutt, 5 July 1939 in Dutt papers. Emphases are in the original letter.
19 Dutt to Garman, 18 July 1939, in Dutt papers; Garman to Dutt, 21 July 1939, in Dutt papers; Dutt to Childe 25 July 1939, in Dutt papers; Childe to Dutt, 28 July 1939, in Dutt papers.

Intellectuals who decided to serve the working class usually found that in order to be accepted they had to join a trade union. In Brisbane, Childe joined the Australian Clerical Association, retaining his membership when he moved to Sydney. In London, he joined the National Union of Clerks in 1922. In Edinburgh he was 'actively concerned' with the founding and building of the Edinburgh branch of the Association of Scientific Workers (AScW), serving as its Chairman between 1939 and 1946. Moving to London, he was active in the Central London branch and then served for three years on the AScW's national Executive Committee. The AScW was an organisation of natural scientists. It had been formed in 1918 as the National Union of Scientific Workers, in order to represent the economic interests of applied scientists in government and industrial laboratories. How, then, did Childe, a prehistorian trained in classics, skilled in 'interpretative concepts' rather than in 'brilliant excavations' – that is, in the labour (as a proletarian would understand it) of an archaeologist – become one of its office bearers?[20]

The answer lies in the changing way science came to be understood. Although the 1914–18 experience of 'total war' had underlined the growing importance of science and technology in warfare and industry, nonetheless a university-based 'scientific aristocracy' dominated the field of science and defined its meaning. In its view, the pursuit of scientific truth was a purely intellectual exercise, fortified by hard experimental data and untainted by utilitarian considerations. Accordingly, any other understanding of science was speculative, the social sciences were beyond the pale, and pure science was, naturally, above politics. The effects of this view were stultifying to science policy and disastrous for scientific culture. Applied science was pushed to the margins and the idea that science should be understood in its social relations was regarded with incomprehension. Even after the establishment in 1923 of the Department of Scientific and Industrial Research, with its numerous scientific advisory committees, this 'High Science' view prevailed. Unable to imagine how to overcome this situation, the National Union of Scientific Workers languished in the 1920s.[21]

In the 1930s, however, science and peace, as political causes for social action, became intimately connected. In response to the rise of fascism, and under pressure from the left, the peace movement shifted from a humanist

---

20 W.A. Wooster, 'Professor V. Gordon Childe. 1892–1957', *Association of Scientific Workers' Journal*, vol. 4, no. 1, January 1958, p. 16; Childe's MI5 file, 31 July 1947 and 18 August 1949.

21 Gary Werskey, *The Visible College: A Collective Biography of British Scientists and Socialists of the 1930s*, London, Free Association Books, 1988, Ch. 1.

and Christian pacifism, opposing rearmament and collective security, to a more interventionist pacificism, calling for a popular front against fascism and its aggressive States. For radical scientists there was a comparable move from quite narrow concerns such as the militarisation of science to broader assertions about the capitalist social relations of science. Behind these developments lay domestic and international developments.

In Britain during the Great Depression, the Unemployed Workers' Movement organised regular 'hunger marches' that not only dramatised the suffering of the unemployed but prompted sympathetic scientists to consider how they might use their expertise to allay it. Internationally, there were worrying military interventions by fascist governments in Manchuria (1931), Abyssinia (1935), Spain (1936–39), Austria (1938) and Czechoslovakia (1938–39). The response of the governments of Britain, France and the USA was to appease these aggressive regimes, a policy that was interpreted by the Soviet Union as a signal to the fascists to direct their aggression against it. Accordingly, in 1932 the Comintern established the World Committee Against War and Fascism in order to defend the Soviet Union in this threatening international environment.[22]

The revival of scientific-worker organisation occurred against this background, as part of an awakening of radical activism. Members of the AScW agitated for peace, socialism, progressive education, and culture for the people. As Gary Werskey has shown, Cambridge was the crucible. In 1932 its radical scientists, led by the communist J.D. Bernal, formed the Cambridge Anti-War Group which later made a name for itself trying to demonstrate the scientific weakness of the government's advice on Air Raid Precautions. They also revived the local branch of the Association of Scientific Workers (the name adopted in 1927), in the process calling on scientists to accept that they were engaged in a social practice, impacted negatively by market and government decisions, and capable of redirecting science to solve humanity's problems. In the here and now, they said, scientists could play a part in anti-capitalist social struggles – showing working people how to protect themselves from aerial bombardment, how to improve their nutrition, and most of all how to free their thinking from the shackles of irrationality.[23]

In 1939, Bernal published *The Social Function of Science*, setting out at length not only science's present imperfections and misuse by fascist governments

---

22   Richard Davis, 'The British Peace Movement in the Inter-War Years', *French Journal of British Studies*, vol. XXII, no. 3, 2017; Werskey, *The Visible College*, pp. 216–19.
23   Werskey, *The Visible College*, pp. 223–37.

and private corporations, but also what it could do – its role in social transformation – to realise its true social function. He encouraged scientists to join the AScW. And he ended with a paragraph introduced by the heading 'Science as Communism':

> Already we have in the practice of science the prototype for all human common action. The task which the scientists have undertaken – the understanding and control of nature and of man himself – is merely the conscious expression of the task of human society. The methods by which this task is attempted, however imperfectly they are realized, are the methods by which humanity is most likely to secure its own future. In its endeavour, science is communism.

Or, to put it another way, for left intellectuals unwilling to identify as members of the Communist Party, science might be seen as a substitute. They could identify as communists by proclaiming themselves as scientists. Childe is a case in point. In 1938, as we have seen, Rajani Dutt tried to persuade him to join the faculty of the Communist Party's Marx House, but Childe resisted because it would label him as a communist. He explained to Dutt that for him Marxism was 'an approach and a methodological device', and that he wanted to be thought of as a scientist, inferring truths from 'experiment and observation'. At exactly the same time, he was involving himself with running the Edinburgh branch of the AScW, becoming its Chairman in fact, thus happily identifying himself with Bernal's science-inspired common action as communism.[24]

* * *

Childe had the last word on the run-in with Dutt about Engels's *The Origin of Family*. In 1940, Lawrence & Wishart did publish a new translation of the book, and Childe reviewed it. He chose to publish it in *The Scientific Worker*, the periodical of the AScW. There it might escape the notice of experts in the field but would certainly get the attention of intellectuals awakened to communism by the new 'scientism' of the left. The book he said was a classic of the Marxist method, that is 'the correlation' of 'social and political institutions' – such as the family and the state – with 'methods of production and

---

24 J.D. Bernal, *The Social Function of Science*, London, George Routledge & Sons, 1939, pp. 415–16; Childe to Dutt, 14 October 1938, Dutt papers, CPGB archives.

economic stages'. To the student, he offered this advice: read Chapter IX – and by implication ignore the other chapters – because this chapter, where Engels discussed the division of labour, commodity production, and the state in the transition from barbarism to civilisation, offered a 'general outline' of the Marxist method. Then apply it to 'the richer and more reliable data now available'. But 'it would be a tragedy if [the book] were mistaken for a canonical account of what actually happened in human history'. Here we see a prefiguring of the organising principle of the book that would make him famous with the general public – *What Happened in History* (1942). Its genesis was his 1938 dispute with Dutt on the Engels project and more generally his insistence to Dutt that he approached Marxism as a scientist inferring truths 'from experiment and observation'. In the 1940s he would work out his idea of history by projecting that idea onto the evidence of the past, as we shall see in the next chapter.[25]

---

25   Childe, review of Engels, *The Scientific Worker*, vol. 12, 1940, p. 100; and see P. Gathercole, 'Childe in History', p. 42; Childe to Dutt, 14 October 1938, in Dutt papers, CPGB archives.

Chapter 19

A GRAND AND HOPEFUL EXPERIMENT

In 1937 Childe published 'War and Culture', a chapter in an edited book called *Eleventh Hour Questions*. He wanted to refute the 'alleged deductions from the sciences of biology, anthropology and history that war is beneficial to the human species and is even necessary for continued progress'. Characteristically, as a newly identifying scientist, he began by using reason and evidence in order to pull away the biological underpinnings of pro-war arguments. The progress of the human species might be analogous to the evolution of non-human species, but it did not proceed through the same mechanisms. The Darwinian concepts of natural selection and survival of the fittest could not be applied to humankind. Then he moved to the counter-argument. 'It is intelligence and its use in converting experience into science and science into extra-corporeal organs [tools and machines] that has been the mainspring of human progress.' Then the deduction: fitness in the human species was not a hereditable trait but an aspect of culture. And the political point: cultures 'are not competitive but complementary. The survival of the fittest culture cannot be secured by war which can only destroy culture.'[1]

This work by Childe is interesting less for its ideas (for he had been drawing on similar arguments in his attacks on racialism) than for the story behind the book in which it appeared. In June one of the editors, Rev. J.E. McIntyre, arranged for the 4th International Congress of Anti-Militarist Ministers and Clergymen to be held in Edinburgh. He told the congress that he was a Christian Pacifist, but also said to them that it wasn't enough. During the session on communism he entreated the assembled Ministers to 'de-class themselves' by studying economics and sociology. 'Marx taught that our opinions are due to our financial status. Until we got rid of our system,

---

1   Childe, 'War and Culture' in W.B. Tavener et al., *Eleventh Hour Questions – Articles on Peace by Various Authors*, Edinburgh and London, Moray Press, 1937.

we should have war.' This mental challenge to bourgeois Edinburgh became physical a few weeks later when fighting broke out in the city. Among the anti-fascists arrested for trying to break up a meeting of fascists were two people associated with the book, a contributor, Wendy Wood, an artist and militant Scottish nationalist, and an editor, Fred Douglas, one of Edinburgh's leading communists. Part of this mood of questioning and tumult was the lead editor, Wallace Tavener, who taught philosophy and political theory to WEA classes. He was the Minister of St Mark's Unitarian Church in Edinburgh where he introduced the congregation to humanistic theology and ran Sunday evening discussions on social and political matters.[2]

Subtitled 'Articles on Peace by Various Authors', this book was the product of a committee of intellectual and political radicals, the literature committee of the Scottish Peace Council. The Council's work reflected both the quickening of interest in collective security as the threat of war increased and the long tradition of pacifism in Britain maintained by organisations such as the Women's International League for Peace and Freedom, and more recently the Peace Pledge Union. It was not a communist front. When the Secretary, Mrs Mary Baxter, addressed a conference of the Co-operative Women's Guild about the Council's policy, she made no mention of fascism or war, despite the existence since 1933 of the Comintern's peace movement, the World Committee Against War and Fascism. The range of contributors also points to the book's non-communist focus. Among them were Sir Norman Angell, a former Labour MP who had received the Nobel Peace Prize in 1936 and was now an executive member of the World Committee; Robert Boothby, a Conservative politician and one of the founders of a movement in 1936 to bring Britain's political parties together in a 'popular front' against fascism; Sir Archibald Sinclair, an anti-appeasement Liberal MP who was a friend of Churchill; as well as William Gallacher, the Communist MP.[3]

The Edinburgh that produced this book was Childe's Edinburgh. No doubt the editors approached him because of his scholarly reputation but they could well have known him personally. Childe chaired meetings of the Left Book

---

2   On Tavener: edinburgh-unitarians.squarespace.com/our-story/; on Douglas, see www.grahamstevenson.me.uk/index.php/biographies/d-f/d/1472-douglas-fred; on J.E. McIntyre, www.peacepalacelibrary.nl/pmfiles/A30-3-003.pdf.

3   On the 'Popular Front', see Kevin Morgan, *Against Fascism and War: Ruptures and Continuities in British Communist Politics, 1935–1941*, Manchester University Press, 1989, Ch. 2; and David Blaazer, *The Popular Front and the Progressive Tradition: Socialists, Liberals and the Quest for Unity, 1884–1939*, Cambridge University Press, 1992; and Davis, 'The British Peace Movement in the Inter-War Years'; for Mary Baxter's speech, see *Linlithgowshire Gazette*, 16 June 1939.

Club, which at its height had 57,000 members and 730 local groups, and of the Society for Cultural Relations with the USSR. His picture appeared in an Edinburgh daily newspaper, hobnobbing at a local garden party with the Soviet Ambassador, Ivan Maisky. His circle of acquaintances extended to include Donald Mackenzie, a Scottish folklorist who wrote a gossip column for a Glasgow newspaper. Edinburgh was a small city of about 400,000, and its radicals – socialists, pacifists, liberal Christians, worker educationists, Scottish nationalists, as well as revolutionaries – would have intermingled at meetings, pubs, churches or university extension classes. The editors of this book were part of that milieu, and so was Childe. This suggest a less snooty, if not quite bohemian, side of Childe's social life, one that should be put in the balance against his oft-remarked liking for the attractions of Scotland's grand houses. He might have been just as much at home among Edinburgh's radicals.[4]

* * *

Childe was not an opponent of war as a matter of principle; he was not a pacifist in that sense. He became part of the anti-war movement in 1915 as a socialist and civil libertarian; indeed, it was the government's censorship and cruelty towards political conscientious objectors, and the warmongering of the press, that really cemented his opposition to the First World War. This was still his motivation in the 1930s, as he contemplated the rise of fascism. After Hitler's invasion of the Sudetenland, the German-speaking part of Czechoslovakia, in September 1938 he wrote a letter to the *New Statesman*, whose editor published it under the heading 'War for Democracy?' Childe had a question for middle-class progressives: yes, another war 'must, in fact, destroy all that in Britain still deserves the name civilisation', but will not the creeping fascism of the British Government destroy it even more completely? The government's appeasement of Hitler in Czechoslovakia and elsewhere in Europe must have repercussions at home, and these are already visible. The 'docile press' is calling 'Hitler's terms Chamberlain's peace plan', a sign of government influence, he wrote. The next step will be to brand 'criticism of

---

4   Ben Pimlott. *Labour and the Left in the 1930s*, Cambridge University Press, 1977, Ch. 16; Maisky and Childe photo, *Edinburgh Evening Dispatch*, 22 June 1936; for Mackenzie, see Howard Kilbride-Jones, in Harris (ed.), *The Archaeology of V. Gordon Childe*, p. 136.

Hitlerism' a disloyal embarrassment to 'the Government's mission of reconciliation' with Nazism. Then will come the denial to critical voices of access to the press and the gradual exclusion of Marxists in universities. This will occur without provocative legislation but through the working of 'government controls', such as financial support for universities. Britain was about to follow Germany down the path of fascism, but in less overt ways:

> German intellectuals who hailed Hitler as their saviour from Marxism are now helpless to protest against the consequent sterilisation of science and art. British intellectuals who preferred peace in alliance with Hitler in preference to war in alliance with the U.S.S.R. may all too easily have cause to wonder whether the bombed ruins of London and Berlin would not have been better than the skeleton of a civilisation condemned to stagnation by the denial of free enquiry.

Childe was already prepared to support a war against fascism, if and when it came.[5]

A fortnight later, after Prime Minister Chamberlain had signed the notorious Munich Agreement with Hitler and Mussolini, he made the same point in a letter to Dutt. He railed against the 'blasted governing class' which is at present content with 'muzzling the Press, the pictures [the cinema], and inspiring the BBC to praise the Nazi regime and vilify all its critics'. But later the ruling class would get around to imprisoning Jews and prohibiting anti-Nazi ideas. He declared, no doubt to please Dutt, that he had 'swung back to the Left again'. Subsequent events would test his commitment.[6]

Childe spent the summer of 1939 as a Visiting Professor at the University of California. He was glad to get away from the threat of war in Europe. As his visit drew to a close, he began to worry about returning to Edinburgh if war began. He told Bert Evatt that he was looking for a job at Harvard. In earlier visits to the USA he had deposited funds in a Boston bank, and now he added to them. He considered delaying his return to the United Kingdom, and he left a locked suitcase with his colleague Hallam Movius, telling him he might return if Edinburgh was attacked. While aboard ship, he heard that the Soviet Union had signed a non-aggression pact with Nazi Germany, thus betraying his hope that a war against fascism would be fought in alliance with the Soviet Union. 'No doubt Stalin's action will accelerate the spread of

---

5   Childe, 'War for Democracy', letter to *New Statesman and Nation*, 24 September 1938, pp. 451–2.
6   Childe to Dutt, 6 October 1938, Dutt papers, CPGB Archives.

Communism ... but it does not consolidate my wavering faith that that is the best hope for humanity', he wrote in a private letter. He thought of jumping overboard. He was still considering a retreat to the USA on the day after he stepped off the ship, warning Jack Lindsay about 'the coming catastrophe'. By early September, Britain was at war with Germany; the Soviet Union remained neutral.[7]

His despondency continued into the early months of 1940. Bill Peace talked to one of his students, R.B.K. Stevenson, who recalled an afternoon walk into Edinburgh with Childe in 1940:

> We were talking about the dangers all around, the collapse of France and so on. He said his name would certainly be on some Nazi list for extermination. He said he would drown himself in a canal before they came for him. It was a matter-of-fact statement, that this was going to happen in the circumstances of an invasion.

He talked to Crawford about what he was planning. He would later say that Crawford talked him out of it, but perhaps the fact that a publisher was discussing the possibility that he might write a book – for Penguin Books – helped too.[8]

But would he support the war? The British Communist Party's initial position was to urge the British working class to fight on two fronts, against both the German aggressors and the reactionary Chamberlain government. The Comintern, however, soon pulled the party into line, and Childe's friend Rajani Dutt was elevated to head a new secretariat to replace Harry Pollitt who had retained his integrity by opposing the Comintern. The new line was that this was an imperialist war between two blocs of imperialist powers. Communists should oppose their government's war policies and demand a negotiated peace and a people's government. The *Daily Worker* announced this new line on 7 October 1939. A week later, it ran a front-page feature on the responses of Bernard Shaw, H.G. Wells, Beatrice Webb and other 'men and women prominent in public life' – including Professor V. Gordon Childe of Edinburgh – to a questionnaire (devised by the paper) about the need for peace negotiations, an armistice, the lines a settlement should take, and how it might be enforced.

---

7 Peace, 'Vere Gordon Childe and the Cold War', pp. 131–3; Childe to Sir W. Lindsay-Scott, 1939, quoted in Green, *Prehistorian*, p. 89.

8 Peace, 'Vere Gordon Childe and the Cold War', p. 132 (interview with Stevenson); Childe reflected on this moment in a letter to Crawford at a later date: Childe to Crawford, 14 February 1941, Crawford papers, box 67.

Childe's response was rather less than enthusiastic. He endorsed negotiations but only if they did not give Hitlerism 'another Munich victory'. To the second question (on an armistice) he responded that he could not see the point of it 'as the war has not effectively begun'. This was the period of the 'Phoney War'. He was more forthcoming on the kind of settlement that should end the war: colonialism must be abolished (by handing over colonies to an international administration) and Britain should lead by offering this concession in relation to its own colonies; Germany must give up its racialist doctrines; the USSR should be a participant in the settlement; and independence restored to the Czechs and Poles. Lastly the League of Nations, revised and strengthened to give the smaller democracies more influence, should take over the world's colonies and the air forces of the Allies and Germany. Clearly, he had thought about the kind of international order that might be possible after the war, but logically the war would have to be fought first. On the actual war the Communist Party had nothing to say, a want of political will and moral backbone that Childe noted.[9]

This 'Phoney War' continued for another seven months. It ended in May 1940, when German forces advanced through Holland and Belgium and into France. By this time Soviet forces had invaded and defeated Finland and annexed parts of Poland and the Baltic states, and German forces controlled Denmark. A German invasion of Norway was underway. The German navy and air-force were attacking British warships in the North Sea. It was suddenly clear that the Germans were winning. In the British Parliament, confidence in the ability of Chamberlain's government to defend Britain collapsed. When Chamberlain resigned, Churchill formed a National government on 10 May 1940. The next day, Childe wrote to Crawford: now that Chamberlain had gone, he supported the Allies resolutely. He had underestimated, as he told Movius, 'the pressure that democracy is still able to exert in Britain'. But then, in a sombre mood after the fall of France in June: 'night is falling over Europe'. Only countries such as Finland 'permit a little flame of unrestricted thought' to burn 'unshrouded by the dogmas of "Marxism-Leninism" and "Hitlerism". I suspect history has been moving too fast.' We must expect a dark age to follow, dominated by Hitler and Stalin, but it will at least 'lop off the tall stalks', and in about '2700 years or so' a more widespread crop of large ears will grow.[10]

---

9   *Daily Worker*, 14 October 1939, pp. 1 and 6; Monty Johnstone, 'The CPGB, the Comintern, and the War, 1939–1941: Filling in the Blank Spots', *Science and Society*, vol. 61, no. 1, Spring 1997, pp. 27–45.

10 Childe to Crawford, 11 May 1940, Crawford papers, box 66; Childe to Crawford, 1 June 1940, box 67; Childe to Movius, 27 January 1942, quoted in Peace, 'Vere Gordon Childe and the Cold War', p. 133.

He meant that we can fight fascism – as we have to – but we might not win – except when we imagine a very distant communist future. In the meantime, one had to survive. In early July he was predicting that Britain would be annexed to Germany. Six months passed but the prospect of Germany's defeat still seemed remote. Then his focus shifted to the political movement – the communists – on which he was relying to lead the underground resistance to German rule in Britain. They were doughty fighters, but they were also a danger to democracy. He confessed to Crawford that 'I've now definitely become anti-totalitarian'. In personal interactions Childe like to strike a pose, hence the 'definitely', for he had always believed in democracy as a dialectic between leadership and pressure from below. The occasion for this bit of personal theatre was his reading of Arthur Koestler's *Darkness at Noon* – a fictionalised account of the experiences of an old Bolshevik arrested during the Soviet purge of Stalin's opponents in the late 1930s. Childe wrote that he recognised the book as anti-Soviet propaganda, but its picture of the communist true believer was 'psychologically intelligible'. Knowing Dutt, Childe was able to recognise the mental and emotional tricks needed to survive as a Stalinist. But at the same time, Childe knew that if it came to a choice between the contending dogmas, he would choose Marxism-Leninism; he had told Dutt that in 1938.[11]

While Childe was preparing himself for cooperation with Dutt and the Stalinists in the necessary resistance to Hitler's triumphant regime, Crawford was not feeling so resilient. Childe wrote to him in February 1941: 'I can honestly repeat the advice you gave me at Blairgowrie in September 1939. While I think it will be the only thing in the end, I am glad I did not suicide then. Prehistoric communities [the title of a book by Childe published in 1940] may or may not be any good but it was tremendous fun to write and quite a lot of people read it.' Childe concluded by telling Crawford: 'Do fight the brass-hats – for the past's sake not your own'. As we shall see, Childe and Crawford had a vision of history as a useable past, a weapon in the fight for socialism and democracy.[12]

* * *

---

11   Childe to Crawford, 1 July 1940, Crawford papers, box 67.
12   Childe to Crawford, 22 February 1941, Crawford papers, box 67.

Childe had been associated with efforts to promote cultural exchanges with the Soviet Union since the early 1930s. There were two organisations in this field. The British–Soviet Friendship Society, known as the Friends of the Soviet Union, was formed by the Communist Party in 1927 to attract sympathisers from the working class. It aimed at a large membership and operated as a cheer-squad for the policies of the Russian state. The Society for Cultural Relations with the USSR (the SCR), by contrast, was an elitist organisation, founded in 1924 by a group of influential liberal intellectuals still elated by the success of the 'Hands Off Russia' campaign. Its first President was Professor L.T. Hobhouse, while among its Vice-Presidents were the novelists E.M. Forster and Virginia Woolf, the economist J.M. Keynes, the philosopher Bertrand Russell and the biologist Julian Huxley. None of these intellectuals was starry-eyed about Russia's new system of rule, its ideology or its geo-political ambitions, but to one degree or another they were seduced by the romanticism of revolution and intrigued by the possibility that its happening was a sign of civilisation moving to a higher plane of cooperative social relations. To satisfy such interests the SCR encouraged scientific and cultural exchanges between the two countries and promoted knowledge of the Soviet Union through exhibitions, lectures and film shows. While Crawford was a member of the Friends of the Soviet Union, Childe favoured the SCR, becoming the President of its Edinburgh branch in 1932, and continuing in this position until 1946.[13]

Childe visited Russia in 1935 in the interests of archaeological science, but, when the Allies had to respond to Germany's invasion of Russia in June 1941, he began to see a different role for the SCR. In July, Britain and Russia signed a mutual aid treaty, and in August Britain and the USA issued the Atlantic Charter, a declaration of war aims, soon endorsed by Stalin. The Soviet Union was now an ally. Childe wrote to Crawford: 'Our Russian friends are putting up a fine show. I wonder how our fellow members [of the Prehistoric Society] who in 1939 "would rather be allied with Hitler" are feeling about the compulsory alliance with Stalin?' A few days later, when chairing a meeting of the Edinburgh SCR, he took the opportunity to praise the 'amazing performance' of the Russians in resisting Hitler's military might. In the following months there were setbacks but in January 1942 the Russians began their winter offensive. In February, he wrote to his sister Alice:

---

13   Emily Lygo, 'Promoting Soviet Culture in Britain: The History of the Society for Cultural Relations between the Peoples of the British Commonwealth and the USSR, 1924–45', *Modern Language Review*, vol. 108, no. 2, April 2013, pp. 571–96; Childe's MI5 file for 5 December 1932, 17 July 1936.

> I send a photo of myself with the Lord Provost [the Mayor of Edinburgh] opening an exhibition illustrating the Soviet's war effort and cultural background. I have for years been branch President of the Society for Cultural Relations with the U.S.S.R., a position that was anything but reputable in the past, especially during the Finnish War. But now the Society has become terribly respectable all of a sudden and Ministries and Mayors gladly assist our work. Russia is the one bright spot in the military situation at the moment and everybody is quite anxious to learn how and why. Having always believed that the Soviet Union was a grand and hopeful experiment at least, we can tell them something more reliable than the lies that have hitherto been dished out by most authors and papers …

From his time in Brisbane, Childe had accepted that the Bolshevik Revolution was led by socialists seeking to validate Marx's prediction that class society would end when the proletariat overthrew the capitalist system. And this is what the Stalinists claimed they had achieved. But should he believe them? Childe had reservations. In 1936 he described the Stalinist state as totalitarian, and in 1939 he deplored the Russian invasion of Finland. The Bolshevik state, it seemed, had become a new form of 'oriental despotism' – the term Childe used for Asiatic totalitarian regimes. How then to explain the magnificent resistance of its people to Hitler's invasion? Perhaps after all Russia's revolution had released the creative energies of the empire's rural and urban workers; perhaps in that limited sense it was a sign of human progress, or at least a hopeful experiment. In which case, the SCR was a useable tool to force the pace a little. From 1942 this was Childe's position, and he set out to justify it intellectually by a series of works attempting to put the materialist conception of history – the theory which explained the significance of the Russian Revolution to Marxists – on a scientific footing. To understand his thinking, we need to go back to 1936, when Childe's *Man Makes Himself* appeared.[14]

* * *

---

14   Childe to Crawford, 12 August 1941, Crawford papers, box 67; Childe's MI5 file, 17 August 1941; Childe to Alice Childe, February 1942, quoted in Green, *Prehistorian*, p. 103; Childe to Hallam Movius, 3 December 1939, quoted by Peace, in Gathercole, Irving and Peace, *Childe and Australia*, p. 131.

Childe wrote *Man Makes Himself* (1936) and *What Happened in History* (1942) not for scholars but for 'the bookstall public', the 'wider democratic circles that I imagine buy 6d [sixpenny] books', as he told the publisher, Allen Lane. In terms of copies sold they were a great success. There were five reprints in England of *Man Makes Himself* during Childe's lifetime and four after his death. Overseas, it was printed twice in his lifetime and 10 times in the next 30 years. As for *What Happened in History*, Childe declared proudly in 1957 that it had sold 300,000 copies. It is worth remembering when thinking about these books that he had been trying to influence 'democratic circles' since his return to archaeology in the mid-1920s, writing his first review for *The Plebs* in 1923. In the 1930s there was only one year when he did not publish a review or an article in this magazine of the National Council of Labour Colleges. As an archaeologist he was no less concerned with empowering the masses through education than he was as a labour intellectual in Australia.[15]

But what would be the content of this education? Of course, it would be the story of prehistory, but it would be a mistake to consider these books simply as 'major works of *haute vulgarisation* by the outstanding prehistorian of his generation'. When considered in relation to his other works between 1944 and 1947 a different and more significant content emerges. In 1944 there was the pamphlet *Tools*, which presented history as 'essentially the history of production'. In the same year, *Progress and Archaeology* aimed 'to describe the progressive tendencies of mankind during the last 50,000 years'. In 1945, 'Rational Order in History' discussed the concept of historical laws. *Scotland before the Scots* in 1946 applied 'universal laws', ostensibly Marxist, to the prehistory of Scotland. He soon realised that his attempt was unconvincing. He had, like the Soviet archaeologists, relied on too few instances, ignored awkward facts, and distorted the laws of historical development into pseudo-scientific statements. The Soviet scholars were influenced to look for uniformities in social evolution by the work of linguist N.Y. Marr, and in the 1950s Childe would make several critical references to the weaknesses of 'Marrism'. But even in 1947 Childe could see that the 'laws of motion' discovered by Marx and Engels did not describe history as a mechanical order. This was his conclusion in his book *History*, which summed up his ideas on human progress and its economic foundations, placing them in an historiography culminating in the materialist conception of history. So, *Man Makes Himself*, which aimed to show that progress is the content of history, and *What Happened in*

---

15   Peter Gathercole, 'Childe among the Penguins', *Australian Archaeology*, no. 50, June 2000, pp. 7–11.

History, which argued that progress 'is real if discontinuous', were in a series of works in which Childe attempts to understand the connections between science, society and history. His attempts would continue after 1947, but we will pick them up in a later chapter. As far as these works are concerned, we should note that only the book on Scotland had a mainstream commercial publisher, that one was published by Penguin, whose books were regarded by 'more thoughtful' readers during the war 'as a kind of template of their aspirations', while two were published by the Communist Party and three by the Rationalist Press Association.[16]

Childe wrote *Man Makes Himself* at the invitation of Hyman Levy, the Professor of Mathematics at Imperial College, London. Three years older than Childe, Levy came from a working-class Jewish family in Edinburgh, where he became a socialist at university. He pursued his mathematical studies in Göttingen, developed an interest in aerodynamics, and during the war enlisted in the Royal Flying Corps. After the war, while working in the National Physical Laboratory, he became an activist in the National Union of Scientific Workers and the Labour Party. He frequented the 1917 Club in Soho and taught courses for the Plebs League. His biographer describes him at this time as 'doubly class-conscious': of the exploitation of the proletariat that he knew about from his childhood, and of the stranglehold of aristocratic High Science on socially conscious scientists, something that he experienced in his work. He was exactly the kind of left-wing activist intellectual that Childe wanted to be, and it is highly probable that they met in the 1920s. In 1930, Levy tired of the Labour Party's indifference to science and became an open member of the Communist Party. Childe was not, but from the party's point of view they were equal in their usefulness, as we saw when the party in 1931 considered them together as contributors to a projected Marxist intellectual journal.[17]

Levy, a superb teacher and populariser of science, was able in the early 1930s to reach a wider audience through a series of BBC radio broadcasts, often in conversation with other prominent scientists, about science and social needs. Their success encouraged him to look for a publisher, and 1934 he

---

16 For 'haute vulgarisation', see Alan Saville, book review essay, *European Journal of Archaeology*, vol. 12, nos 1–3, 2009, p. 248; on 'thoughtful readers', see Peter Gathercole, 'Allen Lane's Archaeological Bestseller', *The Penguin Collector*, no. 46, July 1996; these were Richard Hoggart's words; see Childe, 'Archaeological Organisation in the USSR', *Anglo-Soviet Journal*, vol. 13, no. 3, 1952, pp. 23–6, for a short critique of the 'Marrist' methods of Soviet archaeologists that he had applied in *Scotland Before the Scots*.

17 Werskey, *The Visible College*, pp. 44–52, 115–27, and 166.

persuaded C.A. Watts, the Rationalist Press Association publisher, to issue a series under his editorship called 'The Library of Science and Culture'. It aimed to offer the 'general reader a picture of the world, both of action and of thought, as science is shaping it'. Or, in other words, culture was being shaped by science, just as science itself was a cultural phenomenon. His own contribution to the series – a collection of his interviews, *The Web of Thought and Action* (1934) – by its title alone signalled an implicitly Marxist dialectic. Its front endpaper listed the other books in the series, including number five, Childe's *Man Makes Himself*.[18]

This means that Childe was committed to this book before he went to the Soviet Union in 1935. It also means that he was far more intellectually attuned to the world of British left-wing 'scientism' in the 1930s than our earlier discussion of the AScW and Bernal might suggest. Then we focused on the radicalisation occurring among British scientists in terms of their political and trade union activity, but their ideology was equally important for the left. In 1932, Levy's book for The Thinker's Library, *The Universe of Science*, contributed to this ideology by presenting science as both a social movement of individuals and institutions, and, like the universe, an infinite system that was finitely discoverable. Science 'begins and ends with common sense. Its knowledge is essentially democratic. It cannot remain for ever the privilege of any special class.' Nor should science be seen as having an aim:

> There are no objects in science; there are results. There are the vast changes it has effected in production and in social life. There is an achievement in the form of a body of agreed knowledge, and there are accepted modes of demonstrating the 'truth' of that knowledge. These modes expand with the body of knowledge.

This book had a lasting effect on Childe. We know that he read it because he refers to it (but not by name!) in *Man Makes Himself*. Levy's argument that science begins in social practice and that its progress is the content of history ran parallel with Childe's thinking. They are central to *Man Makes Himself* and a continuing preoccupation in later works as he looked for a way to formulate a scientific basis for materialist history.[19]

---

18 Werskey, *The Visible College*, pp. 170–1.
19 H. Levy, *The Universe of Science*, London, Watts & Co., 1932, pp. 181–2, 188–9; Childe, *Man Makes Himself*, London, Watts & Co., 1941 edition, p. 2.

By this time there were commentators on Marxism who had caught on to the fact that its Hegelian roots were important. As Douglas Cole put it in his book *What Marx Really Meant* (1934), the term 'materialist' could be misleading to non-Marxist philosophers. 'The conception of history' in Marx, he wrote, is not materialist because in philosophy materialism means the supremacy of matter over mind, whereas in Marxism mind is understood as a formative force in history as it becomes embodied in things, 'changing their shape and potency, and combining them into relations and systems whose changing phases are the basis of the history of mankind'. The same point had been made by the economist Maurice Dobb in an article in the *Communist Review* in 1922 when he relied on the neo-Hegelian, Benedetto Croce, to argue that Marxism was 'a realist' not a materialist theory of history. This was the term Cole used: 'The Realist Conception of History is so far from representing men as really merely the sport of things that it stresses more than any other theory the creative function of men in making the world after the pattern of their own knowledge'. Childe had used the same neo-Hegelian approach in his 1919 lectures in Brisbane, but it was not until 1935 that he adopted the term 'realist' to describe it. In his Presidential Address to the Prehistoric Society he said:

> [The writing of history] has recently become much less political – less a record of intrigues, battles and revolutions – and more cultural. That is the true meaning of what is miscalled the materialist conception of history – realistic conception would as Cole says be better – [because] it puts in the foreground changes in economic organisation and scientific discoveries.

And in *Man Makes Himself* he restated the point. History as once taught was chiefly political history. Marx, however, insisted on the importance of the economy, the social relations of production, and the application of science, as the factors of historical change. 'His realist conception of history is gaining acceptance in academic circles remote from the party passions inflamed by other aspects of Marxism.'[20]

---

20   G.D.H. Cole, *What Marx Really Meant*, London, Victor Gollancz, 1934, pp. 15, 20; Maurice Dobb, 'Communism or Reformism – Which?', *Communist Review*, vol. 2, no. 4, February 1922, pp. 273–98; Childe, 'Changing Methods and Aims in Prehistory: Presidential Address for 1935', *Proceedings of the Prehistoric Society*, vol. 1, no. 1, 1935, pp. 1–15; Childe, *Man Makes Himself*, illustrated edition with an introduction by Sally Green, Bradford-on-Avon, Wiltshire, 1981, pp. 30–1.

A Grand and Hopeful Experiment

At the time of writing *Man Makes Himself*, Childe was convinced that he had pulled off a marvellous Marxist coup. He thought of it as an example of why 'white-anting' worked better than openly professing Marxism, telling Rajani Dutt in 1938:

> I want to get good Marxist ideas across to my colleagues and students and in that I have had some success, but they would not listen if I <u>began</u> as a Marxist (in Man Makes Himself the class struggle is disclosed as a deduction from an imposing looking array of facts).

And there's another piece of evidence that Marxism framed his thinking as he wrote it. In 1934 he received an invitation from Bernal to contribute the prehistory chapter to a Marxist history of science. That project fell through, but the fruits of his work for it are in the book's very dense Chapter VII, 'The Revolution of Human Knowledge'. It described in detail the development of mathematics, astronomy and medicine of Egypt, Babylonia and the Indus Valley. His object was a materialist one, to make the 'quite respectable' point that 'the lore, successfully applied by craftsmen, has contributed quite as much to modern Natural Science as the rather futile speculations of literate astrologers, hepatoscopes [who practised divining with the entrails of slaughtered animals] and alchemists'. Science, he concluded, 'did not and could not spring directly from either magic or religion'. This chapter was not based on his own research but on the 'translations and commentaries by competent authorities cited in the notes' – a rare case of Childe having to acknowledge the work of other scientists – since he confessed that he did not 'attempt to master hieroglyphic or cuneiform' to read the ancient written sources.[21]

Looking back on *Man Makes Himself* in 1957, Childe was pleased that he had made the story of prehistory into 'genuine history' but also critical of his analysis. It was not sufficiently Marxist. He had shown the facts of progress in history as revealed in the archaeological record, emphasising two revolutionary transitions, the first from a food-gathering to a food-producing economy, and the second to an urban economy. He had shown the origins of science in 'the practical crafts', rather than in magic and religion. And he had linked the history of 'laws, institutions, religion and art' to the history of these successive economies. But he had made them into a superstructure, a 'secondary' analytic element. While this would have received an approving

---

21   Childe to Dutt, 14 October 1938, Dutt papers, CPGB Archives; Gathercole, 'Childe in History', p. 33; Childe, 'Retrospect', p. 72; Childe, *Man Makes Himself*, p. 173 (edited by Sally Green), and 'Preface', p. v.

nod from most Marxists at the time, there were others such as Jack Lindsay and Edward Thompson who would have been sceptical. In 1945, in an internal Communist Party debate, Childe supported their arguments against this orthodox and mechanistic view. Later, in *History* (1947) he would formulate his understanding of 'base' and 'superstructure' dialectically, as an interrelationship, as Lindsay and Thompson would have wished. We will come to that in due course.[22]

It is in *Man Makes Himself* that Childe recognises for the first time that politics and ideology can impede or even halt historical progress. His last chapter, 'The Acceleration and Retardation of Progress', counted the many scientific discoveries made in the two millennia before the Urban Revolution and the relatively few made as a result of it, and concluded that it seemed 'to mark not the dawn of a new era of accelerated advance, but the culmination and arrest of an earlier period of growth'. How could this be? Well, because of the internal and external contradictions of this new urban economy and culture. The internal contradiction was the creation of a class structure that impoverished farmers and craftsmen, out of whose practical interaction with non-human nature science arose, while enriching a ruling class that relied not on science but on superstition (magic and religion) to sustain its rule. Science was hampered in other ways, too. The 'new middle class' of scribes, learned men and priests, cementing their adherence to the ruling class, upheld 'vain superstition', neglecting 'experiment and observation of the living world' for 'mere book-learning'. The external contradiction arose from the imperial conquest that the new city states were forced to embark upon because of their need to secure imports (especially metals). On the one hand, these empires facilitated the continued accumulation of wealth, and through trade and communications diffused the benefits of the Urban Revolution, but on the other they were unstable polities, plagued by revolts and wars that destroyed civilisation and peoples.[23]

Childe's contempt for oriental despotism's sycophantic professionals paralleled his hatred of Britain's anti-democratic and cliquish learned class – expressed in a 1940 letter to Crawford. His negative picture of ancient imperialism was framed by his own experience of war in the modern age of imperial wars. On both fronts he was expressing the frustrated hopes of the community of radical scientists of which he was part. The mixture of hope for progress with pessimism at the impediments it faced was not ironic, as

---

22   Childe, 'Retrospect', p. 72.
23   Childe, *Man Makes Himself*, pp. 175–6.

Childe scholar Bruce G. Trigger suggested, but the result of writing history that was both scientific and politically committed.[24]

What Happened in History is *Man Makes Himself* on a larger stage. Indeed, Childe initially intended to continue the story up to the Industrial Revolution of the late 18th century, but the manuscript grew too long, and he found it difficult to read sources for the Dark Ages while he carried out emergency, war-threatened digs in the north of Scotland, where security was strict. He contemplated dividing the story and writing a sequel, but in the end only a single volume appeared, its final chapter called 'The Decline and Fall of the Ancient World'. His thinking about the book began in 1939, after Penguin's interest in re-publishing *Man Makes Himself* collapsed when C.A. Watts refused to give up its copyright. Allen Lane of Penguin then suggested to Childe that he might write another 'general book', but Childe was busy preparing a revised edition of *The Dawn* (it appeared in 1940 but most copies were destroyed during an air attack on London) and writing a text for Chambers on *Prehistoric Communities of the British Isles* (1940). So, it was not until the first half of 1941 that he turned to writing a new book. He told Allen Lane about it in June 1941, adding that he would like to call it 'What Happened in History'. Lane was delighted, the manuscript was completed in October 1941, and the book duly appeared in November 1942.[25]

While he was writing *What Happened in History* Childe declined an offer from the Clarendon Press (the publisher for Oxford University Press) because, as he told Allen Lane, 'what I really want to do this time is to reach the wider, more democratic circles that I imagine buy 6d books and show that archaeology is after all not so useless and dull'. Not just archaeology, but a scientific and materialist approach to the history it revealed, for as he explained in 'Retrospect' (1957) this new book continued the 'conceptual framework and explicative mechanisms' of *Man Makes Himself* – and also of course the democratic and rationalist implications of that book. His 'Retrospect' also stated that he wrote the new book 'to convince myself that a Dark Age was not a bottomless cleft in which all traditions of culture were finally engulfed. (I was convinced at the time that European Civilization – Capitalist and Stalinist alike – was irrevocably headed for a Dark Age.)'. This suggests that the book was written in despair. That might have been the case when he began it in the first half of 1941, but thereafter he was not only more optimistic about the progress

---

24   Childe to Crawford, 1 November 1940, Crawford papers, box 67; Trigger, *Gordon Childe: Revolutions in Archaeology*, p. 104.
25   Gathercole, 'Childe among the Penguins', pp. 7–11.

of the war but also about the role of active, popular democratic forces in the winning of it. As he told Crawford, he was almost certain that a workers' state would emerge in the future and it was their duty to see that a democratised archaeology survived until then. MI5 reported at the time that he was telling audiences that democracy required every citizen to be a politician by speaking out. In a letter to his sister Alice, he declared that saving archaeology depended on saving the world, and only the masses could do that. The last sentences of the book express his optimism that this was possible:

> Progress is real if discontinuous. The upward curve resolves itself into a series of troughs and crests. But in those domains that archaeology as well as written history can survey, no trough ever declines to the low of the preceding one, each crest out-tops its last precursor.

As Gathercole stated, '*What Happened in History* was Childe's particular, and as it turned out, highly successful, contribution to the war effort'.[26]

But it was a contribution to something besides the war effort. In his Preface, Childe wrote that he was offering an answer to the question of whether mankind had progressed 'in the several hundred thousand years' of its existence on the Earth'. But he was just as conscious that the story he was telling was one of discontinuities, of progress thrown into a trough. The external contradictions between states, and the internal contradictions between classes, are everywhere in his story. War is an insistent theme, as is class conflict. Interestingly, there are no Marxist references in the text. Once again, he was 'white-anting', presenting class struggle as capable of being deduced from 'an imposing array of facts'. And it is this smuggled version of materialist history that gives the book its distinctive flavour. Consider this paragraph from the chapter on the early iron age:

> Finally, the Greek 'industrial cities' were not only cleft internally into contending classes, but were also opposed to one another as autonomous States continually dissipating real wealth in internecine wars that benefitted only the slave-dealers. It is this state of perpetual internecine warfare, itself partly due to the class struggle (in as much as slavery prevented the productive employment of surplus population [which

---

26   Gathercole, 'Childe among the Penguins', p. 9, for Childe's letter of 21 July 1941 to Lane, and the role of the book in the war effort; Childe, 'Retrospect', p. 73; Childe to Crawford, January 1952, box 67/39; MI5 file on Childe, May 1942; Childe to Alice, quoted in Green, *Prehistorian*, p. 98; Childe, *What Happened in History*, London, Penguin Books, 1942, p. 252.

then had to look for military employment]) and in turn aggravating it (by replenishing the slave-market), that appears in history as the occasion for the ruin of the classical economy and the collapse of the polity it supported.

Or consider his damning account of the Roman ruling class: 'In the last century of the Republic Senators and capitalists amassed vast fortunes ... acquired not as the reward for organising industry and commerce, but as the plunder of war and the proceeds of extortion, usury and financial manipulation'. Meanwhile, the peasantry had been driven from the land by debts and conscription. 'The dispossessed peasantry could find no rehabilitation in industrial employment; for the urban working class too were being impoverished and socially degraded by the competition of slaves ... The imperial city contained within her the material for civil war.' And he continued his exposure of the role of superstition in controlling the masses; he noted the violence that erupted in the struggles of rich versus poor; and he introduced the idea of totalitarianism to describe the system of rule in certain Hellenistic states. If this was how history happened, it would not be difficult for some readers – quite a few perhaps, given its sales – to be reminded of the recent history of British class relations and imperialism, and of the present world war. *What Happened in History*, we might say, contributed to the anti-establishment mood that defeated the Churchill government three years later.[27]

In 1944, in *Progress and Archaeology* and *The Story of Tools*, Childe continued his analysis of history as a story of progress, but now he organised it not as a narrative but as a study of the fields of material life in which archaeology has discovered progress. The former book, the second of Childe's works for The Thinker's Library, has chapters on the food quest, tools, warmth and shelter, funerals, temple building and the diffusion of culture. In *Tools*, written as we saw earlier at the invitation of the Young Communist League, what appears as 'a history of production' is actually a class analysis of successive stages of human economic and social organisation. The descriptions of changing tools and techniques in each book are not what the reader will remember – because they are technical and detailed. Rather it is the history in which Childe embeds them, a history of scientific knowledge and consciousness as central to progress. As he put it in *Progress and Archaeology*, while 'the growth in ability to make and do things' has been his central theme, this ability is only a reflection of 'the growth of knowledge of the world' – that is, science. In *Tools*, through a series of sketches of the history of invention

---

27   Childe, *What Happened in History*, pp. 179, 232–3.

we are led into a history of the relations of production and the way scientific knowledge determines, or is determined by, them. His account starts from 'primitive communism' and ends with a modern collective farm in the USSR, using agricultural machinery to 'lighten toil and increase output per head' for the benefit of the community. The two books are complementary, the first about progress in the instruments of production, the second about the social context of progress. In each Childe understood progress as a scientist would, as something to be observed, validated, and made understandable through a theory of change – historical materialism.[28]

Since 1936 he had written four books to popularise materialist history as science and scientific archaeology as a method for understanding it. He had highlighted democracy, progress, class conflict, rationalism, imperialism and warfare: all themes that were agitating the minds of people in the 1930s. These books were just his latest experiment in scholarly activism. A few months later, Russian forces entered Berlin, the Allies assumed control of Germany, and in May 1945 the war in Europe was over. Within weeks, Childe was on a plane to the Soviet Union to see how that 'grand and hopeful experiment' in history-making was faring.

---

28   Childe, *Progress and Archaeology*, London, Watts & Co., 1944; Childe, *The Story of Tools*, Brisbane, Building Workers' Industrial Union (Queensland branch), 1965 (first published, London, Cobbett Press, 1944).

Chapter 20

AN ABSOLUTELY SINCERE APPROACH TO THE PARTY

A few weeks before his death, Childe sent to Grahame Clark, the Professor of Archaeology at Cambridge, an 'autobiographical note' about his intellectual development. Clark sent it to *Antiquity* where it was published in 1958 under the title 'Retrospect'. For students of Childe's thought it is an essential document, a final statement of his thoughts on his contribution to archaeology, which he sums up as 'interpretive concepts and methods of explanation'. It is also an account of his intellectual progress, beginning with his interest in comparative philology, proceeding through Marxism and functionalism, and ending with the sociology of knowledge. In fact, it devotes quite a lot of space to his archaeological encounters with Marxism – over a third of the article.

But students of Childe should ask whether this document answers all the questions about the origins and significance of Marxism in his thought. Should we not, for example, consider the situation in which it was written and to whom it was sent? He wrote it after he became aware of Stalin's crimes and after the Soviet invasion of Hungary, an event that deeply disturbed him. He sent it to Grahame Clark, surely the archetypical ruling-class-supporting don, whose political beliefs have been described as 'lying well to the right' of Margaret Thatcher. Why not send it to the socialist John Morris, editor of *Past and Present*, with whom Childe corresponded during his last months, or to Stuart Piggott, who succeeded him in the Abercromby Chair? It would seem that he wanted to distance himself in 1957 from anything suggestive of communism. Before 1957, however, his commitment to left-wing politics was notorious, and from the 1930s that included organisations associated with the Communist Party. As Ruth Tringham explained in 1983: 'Childe ... was a highly political person; he was aware of the world about him, and felt strongly about political issues, and throughout his career, incorporated these feelings into his choice of what he wrote and where he published it'. But there is little of that in 'Retrospect'. There is barely a hint of his early and continuing interest in rationalism and socialism, the two ideological shafts that guided him to Marxism. He gives no clue to the reason he began to use the language of Durkheimian functionalism in the late 1940s – to avoid using Marxist terms. It would seem that in this 'autobiographical note' Childe deliberately steers the reader away from Marxism as a political aspect of his intellectual life, and thus away from questions about the impact of his politics on his scholarship. Certainly, Childe lived in the world of European archaeology, but between 1943 and 1955 he also lived intellectually in the world of British communism.[1]

Many of his archaeological peers found this difficult to believe. Sure, they could see the outward signs, the *Daily Worker* on his desk, and the red tie, but anything intellectually meaningful? Impossible, especially when the Cold War got under way. As Max Mallowan, Childe's professorial colleague at the Institute of Archaeology, wrote in his memoirs: 'Few of us took his political ideas seriously'. And in a *British Archaeology* notice of Childe's name appearing on George Orwell's 1949 list for the Foreign Office of Soviet 'fellow travellers', the editor reported that 'Archaeologists mostly dismissed Childe's interest in politics and Marxism; Stuart Piggott called it an intellectual joke.' To MI5, however, Childe was no joke, especially in the 1940s and 1950s. In 1947 the spy agency believed that he was a member of the Communist Party, based on 'a reliable but delicate source', although in 1953, unable to find any concrete evidence, it decided that it was safer to describe him as a sympathiser. On the other side of the barricades, the Communist Party had regarded him as an important asset in 'the struggle of ideas' since 1931. But in 1938 he had rebuffed the party over the Marx School and the new edition of Engels. By 1943 the party had to accept that it was unable to control him politically. In that year, the leading party cadre concerned with its educational and intellectual work, Emile Burns, who knew Childe from his time in the LRD, was recorded by MI5 as saying that Childe was not a party member, and that once

---

1 Childe, 'Retrospect', pp. 69–74; Brian Fagan, *Grahame Clark: An Intellectual Biography of an Archaeologist*, Boulder, CO, Westview Press, 2001, p. 240; Ruth Tringham, 'V. Gordon Childe after 25 Years: His Relevance for the Archaeology of the Eighties', *Journal of Field Archaeology*, vol. 10, no. 1, Spring 1983, p. 89; re Childe and Durkheim, see W.J. Peace, 'Vere Gordon Childe and the Cold War', in Gathercole, Irving and Melleuish (eds), *Childe and Australia*, pp. 141 and 234. Peace acknowledges that Bruce Trigger made the same point in his 'Marxism and Archaeology' in Sydney Mintz et al. (eds), *On Marxian Perspectives in Anthropology*, Malibu, Undena Publications, 1984, p. 70; more recent studies by archaeologists of Childe's Marxism include: Randall H. McGuire, *A Marxist Archaeology*, Orlando, Florida, Academic Press, 1992, and Thomas C. Patterson, *Marx's Ghost: Conversations with Archaeologists*, 2005.

or twice had said he did not like the party. On the other hand, Burns said, 'he always discusses his work with Party members ... and has an absolutely sincere and sympathetic approach to the Party'.[2]

* * *

During the war against fascism, Childe feared that, as in the First World War, there would be attempts to restrict political liberty and free enquiry. When Defence Regulations were used in 1941 to ban the *Daily Worker* and *The Week* (edited by Claud – 'Believe nothing until it has been officially denied' – Cockburn) his fears were realised. He wrote to Crawford that the ban was 'a blow to freedom', and he lent his name to the campaign to reverse it. But he was just as apprehensive about threats to civil liberties from the left. In 1943 he wrote to the Communist Party's Glasgow office refusing to join a protest against the release from detention of a British fascist, pointing out that the regulation under which he was detained was obnoxious. That should be the issue: the regulation could be used just as easily by the government against the left. Looking abroad, Childe saw the German resistance to fascism as an instance of the same struggle for liberty, becoming patron of an organisation called 'Allies within Germany' in 1943. And given his characterisation of the Soviet Government as totalitarian, he would have felt the same way about the suppression of dissent in Russia, which explains a statement he made in a letter in June 1945 to John Lewis, who edited *The Modern Quarterly* for the Communist Party. Having just returned from a visit to Moscow to attend the Jubilee celebrations of the Soviet Academy of Science, Childe wrote: 'Russia was swell, though it left doubts on certain points'.[3]

He felt the state's juggernaut personally, because he assumed – correctly – that he was under surveillance. In 1943, he was examining archaeological sites in northern Scotland's high-security military area with Angus Graham, who was secretary of the Royal Commission on the Ancient and Historical Monuments of Scotland. Childe was angry that the security and military forces were obstructing their important scientific work. Graham recalled in his

---

2   Max Mallowan, *Mallowan's Memoirs*, London, Collins, 1977, p. 234; 'Archaeologists Fingered by Orwell', *British Archaeology*, issue 73, November 2003; Childe's MI5 File, 26 February 1943, October 1943, 21 August 1948, October 1953.
3   Childe to Crawford, 14 February 1941, box 67; Childe's MI5 file, 12 September 1941, 29 November 1943, 26 July 1945.

memoirs Childe's hatred of all forms of authority – police and lairds included. There was an incident when Childe wanted to post a letter. Believing that his mail was being opened, Childe took a day-long train journey so that he could post it outside the security zone.[4]

As the war in Europe was ending in Spring 1945, Childe walked to a lectern in London to deliver a lecture on Engels at the Marx Memorial Library and Workers' School, the institution he had refused to join in 1938. A few weeks later he was elected to its General Council. A strange reversal, but there were various earlier signs that it would happen. In 1941 he told Crawford that he was coming around 'a long way to orthodox Marxism'. This was when he was lecturing on Russian prehistory using the approach of Soviet archaeologists. Then came the success of *What Happened in History*. By 1945, so established was his public standing as a Marxist with both scientific and political credentials that he had been approached by Wolfgang Foges, an Austrian emigré and innovative publisher (he introduced the concept of 'book-packaging' to British publishing) to edit a series of 'Marxian' books for Foges's company, Adprint. Nothing came of this approach, but it would have confirmed his view, formed after discovering the 'reasonable tone' adopted by George Thomson in his *Aeschylus and Athens* (1941), that Marxism as a method of historical enquiry was now so acceptable that its proponents had no need of polemic – or, we might add, of the jargon of Soviet Marxism. Thomson, the Professor of Classics at Birmingham University, had joined the Communist Party in 1936.[5]

Childe's friendship with Crawford was crucial to both his decision to identify as a Marxist and to his interest in developing it as a science of history. Crawford sent him books to review in *Antiquity*, knowing that Childe would bring 'a Marxist perspective' to them. Childe used Crawford as a sounding board for his ideas about validating Marxism as a science of the past, because he knew Crawford shared this interest. He told Crawford that the present was chaotic. 'Reformers' came out with 'infallible remedies' whose results were very different from what they promised. So, let's avert our eyes from 'the collapse of civilisation' as a result of this current war, and focus on the past, 'wherein we may discern an order' – and, he might have added, revolutionary

---

4   Angus Graham, 'In Piam Veterum Memoriam', in A.S. Bell (ed.), *The Scottish Antiquarian Tradition*, Edinburgh, 1981, p. 224.

5   *Marx House Bulletin*, March–April 1945, p. 3 and June 1945, p. 7 – Childe's lecture part of a series to commemorate the 50th anniversary of the death of Engels. I am grateful to the staff and volunteers at the archives of the Marx Memorial Library for this information. Childe to Crawford, 3 June 1945, box 67/69; Childe to Crawford, 15 June 1941, box 67/31.

transformations. Look what I have done at the National Museum of Antiquities in Edinburgh (where he became interim Director in 1944). I have rearranged the exhibits to illustrate a materialist approach to history in a popular way, so as to make Marxism more easily understood by the people. Childe's belief in reason as a popular force was a touching aspect of his humanism.⁶

Childe became a member of the Marx Memorial Library's General Council in 1945. (Image courtesy of Marx Memorial Library and Workers' School, London)

---

6   Childe to Crawford, 30 April 1942, box 67/41; Childe to Crawford, December 1943, box 67/51; Childe to Crawford, 14 December 1944, box 67/66; Ralston, 'Gordon Childe and Scottish Archaeology', p. 63.

'Rational Order in History', which Childe published in *The Rationalist Annual* for 1945, was his first attempt to explain the existence of order in history in a scientific way. Why was this necessary at this time? Because physicists were predicting disorder, chaos, and entropy as the future of the earth. Meanwhile, biology was predicting the opposite: higher organisation and greater complexity. At least since 1859, when *On the Origin of Species* appeared, 'biology had become an historical science, for if Darwinism made human history part of natural history it equally gave nature a history'. Species evolved through historical events; that is, mutations. 'The old static order [of 'neat hierarchies of immutable species and genera'] was dissolved, but by that very fact there was displayed a new sort of order – an historical order – no less rational.'[7]

We could say, with just a little exaggeration, that Childe was setting himself the task of doing for human history what Darwin had done in the broader field of natural history: to reveal that it was an orderly process of social evolution, a history of change, proceeding on principles that could be understood. Of course, others had trod that path, as Childe would note at the end of the article. But his concern was that history was being written in ignorance of their work. The philosophers of history were as reluctant as natural philosophers to admit 'the reality of change'. Instead, in historiography there have been 'persistent efforts to find behind the constant flux ... a permanent reality exempt from change ... a transcendent unity above the struggling mob of events.' He then examined three of these persistent efforts. First came religion, which he traced from the Sumerians to the Christians, who assumed a 'divine plan for the redemption of the world and man and the establishment of the Kingdom of God'. He commented: 'The order discovered by such assumptions is neither historical nor rational'. Then he considered various cyclical theories of history, before moving to attempts to make history dependent on three branches of the exact sciences: geography/meteorology (H.T. Buckle), physical anthropology ('blood and soil' racialism) and classical economics ('economic man' and the immutable laws of the market). His assessment was that 'such theories must eliminate all novelty in the historical process. The "laws" are there unchangeable, and apparent events are merely cases of their application, instances of their immutability. It is significant and scarcely accidental that they have habitually been used in the interests of political reaction.'[8]

---

7   Childe, 'Rational Order in History', *The Rationalist Annual, 1945*, pp. 21–6; for the references to science and biology, pp. 21–2.
8   Childe, 'Rational Order in History', pp. 22–3.

So where should progressive historians look for theories that allow for novelty and potentialities in the evolution of mankind? They should start with G.W.F. Hegel, who 'really tried to present the history of man and the universe as a creative process in which genuinely new values ... and novel events emerged'. Hegel failed because 'he could conceive of the unity of the process only as transcending it ... the self-manifestation of the Absolute Idea, acting in accordance with its own eternal nature ... The absolute was thus raised above the process like a sort of deity.' Failing Hegel, they should look to his heirs, the dialectical materialists on the one hand, and the idealists such as Croce and Gentile on the other. They had purged Hegel's theory 'of its quite unnecessary trappings of supernaturalism and transcendentalism'. Childe noted that the 'title of Signor Croce's latest book is *History as the Story of Liberty*'. The English edition appeared in 1941. He says no more about the book; apparently its title alone conveyed the point Childe wanted to make: mankind has a history because it has the liberty to make its own laws.[9]

The conclusions Childe drew from this study he would amplify in later works. First, the historical process is 'untrammelled by any external laws but creates its own laws' and although it does not conform to 'any rigid mathematical order' it nonetheless 'manifests a growing order which reason can partially comprehend'. Second, the historical order is not just harder to grasp than the abstract orders represented say by mathematics or mechanics, but it is never complete. Third, from the laws of the historical order one cannot deduce a particular event, but 'merely ... clues for disentangling order in seeming chaos. With the aid of such conceptions the historian can define *tendencies*, not uniformities.' These are conclusions about how to think about the laws of history, not about their substance. He is giving historians a lesson in the kind of logic they need to use – a dialectical logic. But he still had to describe such an order to clinch his case.[10]

* * *

In Jack Lindsay's papers there is a snipped-off slip, about 7 cms in height, a carbon-copy of a typed message. It reads:

---

9   Childe, 'Rational Order in History', pp. 24–5.
10 Childe, 'Rational Order in History', pp. 25–6.

18 Lawn Road Flats, NW 3. 22/9/46

> A Childeish professor invites you to inspect its new nursery and such prehistoric liquors as survive on Thursday, October 3 at 6 p.m.

RSVP. Belsize Park tube or no. 24 bus.

Childe was glad to get out of Edinburgh, a move that he had been hoping for since December 1944 when a member of the selection committee for the post of Director of London's Institute of Archaeology unofficially approached him with the news that he would be appointed subject to the availability of funds. He took up his post in the summer of 1946 and moved into his flat in early September. The drinks to which Lindsay was invited – and their informality and the inclusion of radicals like Lindsay – suggest Childe was in an up-beat mood, pleased with the success of his career and relaxed about his left-wing reputation. The address itself was also significant. His Lawn Road flat was in the Isokon Building, one of London's few pieces of architecture built to the modernist principle that 'form follows function'. In Sydney, London and Edinburgh he had been content to live in overwrought Victorian piles. Having rejected bourgeois politics 30 years earlier in Oxford, was he now at last turning his back on the bourgeois tastes of his family and the city where he had grown up?[11]

The Isokon Building was an example of 'a machine for living in', Le Corbusier's ideal for residential architecture. Designed by Wells Coates, it was opened in 1934. On four levels with external galleries, it was streamlined – like an ocean liner, according to Agatha Christie – and its 32 flats were small, airy, unornamented, and compact, with built-in cupboards, cooking and washing facilities. The smaller flats were just 25 square metres. Some residents, presumably, liked living in the cabin of a ship. 'We cannot burden ourselves', wrote Coates in 1933, 'with permanent tangible possession as well as our real new possessions of freedom, travel, new experience – in short what we call life'. Childe might have taken that to heart because he had few possessions to dispose of when he left London 10 years later. Isokon was also an experiment in communal living. On the ground floor was a restaurant-cum-club room. Residents could eat there or have their meals delivered by dumb-waiter to

---

11 Jack Lindsay papers, National Library of Australia, MS 7168, box 18; David R. Harris, '"A new professor of a somewhat obscure subject": V. Gordon Childe at the London Institute of Archaeology, 1946–1956', *European Journal of Archaeology*, vol. 12, nos 1–3, 2009, pp. 14–126; Childe to Crawford, 14 December 1944, 67/66.

their flat. The gardens provided other common spaces, including a garden on the roof. Residents could use the communal laundry, have their windows cleaned and even their shoes polished.[12]

Situated on the lower slopes of Hampstead, the Isokon was soon home to people typically attracted to that suburb – artists and intellectuals – especially if, like Henry Moore and Maxwell Fry, their sensibility was modernist. As fascism spread, they were joined by modernists from Europe, including two of the Bauhaus alumni, Walter Gropius and Marcel Breuer. Among these anti-fascist refugees were several communists with connections to Soviet intelligence organisations, including Arnold Deutsch who recruited the 'Cambridge Five' – Blunt, Burgess, Cairncross, Maclean and Philby. During the late 1930s and early 1940s there was much coming and going between these emigré spies and local communists. But the Isokon's moment as Soviet spy-central was over by 1946.

It may have been through his connection with Mallowan that Childe chose to live at the Isokon, as Mallowan and his wife Agatha Christie were already in residence. Childe lived in one of the small flats until he moved to a larger one in 1949. In residence also was a manager/chef who would serve drinks in the cleverly named ground-floor 'Isobar'. Since the late 1930s the restaurant had built a reputation for reasonably priced good food and fine wines that were available both to residents and to a dining club of outsiders organised by Raymond Postgate and celebrity chef Philip Harben. Childe took full advantage of the Isobar's restaurant, inviting friends to dine, and of its club-like atmosphere. He played bridge with Agatha Christie there, and entered a competition to define High Dudgeon, Huff and Umbrage. He wrote:

> Beneath the shadow of his beetling brows,
> stiff Umbrage glares, roused by some fancied slight.
> Huff simply sulks, and flounces off,
> his temper ruffled by the merest trifle.
> But Dudgeon stalks away, his head held high,
> his unrequited merit to defend.

The Isokon in Childe's life was like a second iteration of the 1917 Club. Certainly, Hampstead was not as revolutionary or louche as Soho, but it was even more learned and liveable. Best of all for Childe, while it was bourgeois in its personal relationships – because they existed within a commodified

---

12 'Wells Coates: Architect and Designer', www.wellscoates.org/lawnroadflats.htm, accessed 6 February 2019; David Burke, *The Lawn Road Flats: Spies, Writers, and Artists*, Woodbridge, UK, Boydell Press, 2014.

tenant–landlord structure – it was anti-bourgeois in its communal setting and impersonal modernity.[13]

* * *

'An artist whose creations have never been appreciated as beautiful by any society is not an artist at all.' No artist can say exactly what his creation will be like; no intellectual can predict that his ideas will have any effect. Meaning is a social matter, and only history will reveal if these creations, these ideas, matter, and in history nothing is predictable. Childe made this point – as he had made it before in *What Happened in History* – in a letter to Jack Lindsay in 1945.

The ideas that Childe and Lindsay discussed in 1945 were novel, at least on Britain's left. At a meeting where they presented them to a wider audience, they were rubbished. The ideas were then forgotten, or at least buried. It looked as if they would be without historical significance. Twelve years later, other thinkers thought the same thoughts, but now they were taken up widely and they became part of something historically important – the New Left. These later thinkers made no reference to Childe or Lindsay – which, ironically, might prove Childe's point about the social determination of ideas – except that one of the people who participated in the 1945 discussion became, 20 years later, a luminary of the New Left, by articulating those very ideas. His name was E.P. (Edward) Thompson.

This is how Childe and Lindsay's premature New Leftism began. By 1945, Lindsay had made a name for himself as a cultural activist on the left. After the Fanfrolico Press collapsed he moved to Cornwall in 1930 to devote himself to writing, which he did with manic intensity, publishing 28 books in the next 10 years. There were novels, including a trilogy set in the Roman Republic, a very popular 'mass declamation' in verse called *On Guard for Spain*, literary biographies and poetry. He joined the Communist Party in 1939. Returning from war service, he threw himself into the party's contributions to a wider progressive effort to create a people's culture. Lindsay had always been interested in both ideas and art – he had begun as a writer under the influence of his father's Nietzschean philosophy – so his move to the left elicited a keen interest in Marxism's philosophy of art and culture. What he

---

13   Burke, passim and p. 196.

discovered worried him. Although the *Economic and Philosophic Manuscripts* of the humanistic 'young Marx' had delighted Lindsay, revealing a philosophy that placed 'all possible emphasis on the dialectically directive powers of the spirit', the Marxism of the Communist Party was flat-footed and mechanical. It aped Stalin's Marxism but made it more formulaic. Lindsay was particularly affronted by the party's use of the concept of 'reflection' in cultural matters, as in the formula that the 'superstructure' of ideas and art simply reflected society's economic 'base'.[14]

Colonial gadflies – Jack Lindsay and Percy Stephensen at the Fanfrolico Press, London, in the 1920s.
(Fryer Library, University of Queensland; papers relating to P.R. Stephensen, box 2)

Lindsay attacked this formula in a paper for the party's Cultural Committee. He argued that base and superstructure interacted, and that 'spirit and consciousness were a necessary element in productive activity'. He prefaced his paper with a quote from Childe's *What Happened in History*: 'The reckoning

---

14 Robert Mackie (ed.), *Jack Lindsay – The Thirties and Forties*, University of London Institute of Commonwealth Studies, Australian Studies Centre, Occasional Seminar Paper No. 4, November 1984; Jack Lindsay, *Marxism and Contemporary Science, or The Fullness of Life*, London, Dennis Dobson, 1949, p. 197.

may be long postponed. An obsolete ideology can hamper an economy and impede its change for longer than Marxists admit.' He sent a copy to Childe who called it

> a very useful paper. The collection of relevant passages from M and E [Marx and Engels] are in themselves most valuable. I agree that 'reflection' is not a happy term. 'Umgesetzt und übergesetzt' does not = 'reflected'. 'Determined' (bestimmt) must not be taken in a mechanistic ie transcendentalist sense ...

Then followed some criticisms of Lindsay's use of anthropological terms and a suggestion about how a materialist should define 'symbol' and 'idea', a point he would take up in his penultimate book, *Society and Knowledge* (1956). Finally, Childe regretted that he would miss the meeting of the Cultural Committee. Presumably, because Childe was not a member of the party, Lindsay had received permission to invite him. But the meeting was postponed a month and Childe was able to attend. He and Lindsay had dinner and then went in together to the meeting.[15]

There was a furious attack on Lindsay at the meeting by the party's Stalinists. The only person to support Lindsay was a young history student: Edward Thompson. Childe, who attended as Lindsay's guest, diplomatically said nothing, but later in *History* (1947) he would write: 'a superstructure – institutions, faiths, ideals – is actually indispensable for the productive process itself ... Relations of production must ... be lubricated with sentiment. To provide motives for action they have to be transformed in the human mind into ideas and ideals.' Lindsay expanded his 1945 argument into a book, published in 1949 as *Marxism and Contemporary Science*, an attack on the vulgarisation of Marxism by both Stalinists and anti-Marxists. A notable feature of the book is its attention to the question of Marxist morality, which would also become a theme in Edward Thompson's essays in the 1950s. A decade before the first New Left, Lindsay and Childe had breached the walls of 'orthodox' Marxism.[16]

Twelve years after he had defended Lindsay at the Cultural Committee meeting, Thompson published a long essay in *The New Reasoner*, the journal of dissident British communists. Ten thousand of them had exited the party, appalled by the revelations in Khrushchev's 'secret speech' and the Soviet invasion of Hungary, and Thompson was their most eloquent spokesperson.

---

15   Childe's letters to Lindsay, 27 May 1945 and 1 October 1945 are in the Lindsay papers in National Library of Australia, MSS 7168, box 18; Lindsay provided only parts of the letters when he wrote the Foreword to Green's book, see pp. xii–xiv.

16   Lindsay, 'Foreword' to Green, *Prehistorian*, p. xiv.

In this essay, 'Socialist Humanism', Thompson demolished the distortions of Stalinism, especially its over-simplified version of economic determinism in history that belittled 'the part played by men's ideas and moral attitudes in the making of history'. It was the nearest the New Left got to a manifesto, exposing Stalinism as an ideology of a bureaucratic elite, insisting that Marxism must have an 'ethical sensibility', and reintroducing its 'lost vocabulary' of agency and moral choice. According to Cal Winslow, 'Socialist Humanism' is 'still the most discussed (and criticised) of his contributions in these years'. It contains no mention of either Lindsay or Childe.[17]

Writing about Lindsay's ideas in the 1940s, Victor N. Paananen said: 'Publication of his theoretical work proved difficult at times, and small press runs and lack of an academic platform meant it was overlooked'. But Thompson was present in 1945. And it is simply impossible to believe that Thompson was unaware of Childe's popularising in the 1940s of a non-orthodox Marxist theory of history as a creative process. As a communist, did he not read Childe's 1947 book *History*, published by a party press? Why did he fail to acknowledge their ideas? Lindsay was unwilling to join the revolt in the British Communist Party, and Childe, who was not a member, was unable to. In 1957 he retired to Australia and committed suicide. His body was found at the bottom of a cliff in the Blue Mountains, just a few months after Thompson's essay on 'Socialist Humanism' appeared. Yesterday's men of the Old Left, Lindsay and Childe could be ignored.[18]

* * *

There are two aspects of Childe's *History* that are nearly always overlooked: its title and its publisher. First, consider the hubris revealed by the title. Not, 'A Contribution to the Study of ...', or 'An Interpretation of ...' but just one word, the name for an area of human thought that has been practised for millennia, and the name for an academic discipline with a long tradition of scholarly methods and principles. Childe clearly intended to signal that he wanted to be regarded as an authority on history. Second, consider the circumstances

---

17 Cal Winslow (ed.), *E.P. Thompson and the Making of the New Left*, New York, Monthly Review Press, 2014.
18 Victor N. Paananen, *British Marxist Criticism*, London, Garland, 1999, p. 56. It was not until 1973 that Thompson acknowledged that Childe was working within the tradition of Marxist history: Thompson, 'An Open Letter to Leszek Kolakowski', *Socialist Register*, London, Merlin Press, 1973.

of its publication. The book was published by the Cobbett Press as number six in their series 'Past and Present – Studies in the History of Civilisation Designed to Show How History Can Help'. The General Editor was the Irish communist and classicist Benjamin Farrington, and Childe was another of the editors. Cobbett Press was owned and controlled by the Communist Party, but it was not set up to be merely a voice for party members or sympathisers. As Farrington explained to Bernhard J. Stern, the anthropologist who edited the independent American Marxist journal *Science and Society*,

> the series will not be announced as specifically Marxist. It looks as if about 50% of the writers would be Marxists, and there is of course no ban on references to Marxist literature. But our non-Marxist collaborators are chosen for their eminence in their subjects, and our confidence is that if they are true scientists they can not help assisting the development of Marxist thought.

Childe could have chosen a different publisher; after all he had published a best-seller with Penguin Books and a very successful book with the Rationalist Press Association, with whom he would publish a further book. If his aim, however, was to get Marxist ideas into the mainstream of scientific discussion, Cobbett Press was a better choice. It also kept him in the communist intellectual milieu.[19]

Arriving in London from Edinburgh, Childe was soon drawn into its network of communist intellectuals. Many of them, including Bernal and Levy, he would meet, or renew contact with, as a member of the executive of the Association of Scientific Workers, to which he was elected in 1946. The Communist Party, intensifying its efforts to embed Marxism in Britain's intellectual life and to keep an eye on its own intellectuals, set up loosely constituted (but secretly controlled) bodies of intellectuals in several fields. To these, after vetting, non-party intellectuals could be invited. The Engels Society, the Social Philosophy Group, and the now notorious Historians Group: these were established by the party in 1947 and Childe was associated with all of them – in the sense that each of them claimed he was a member. The Engels Society planned either a book with eight chapters or a series of booklets on 'the materialist approach to the world we live in'. Bernal's area would be chemistry and physical change, while Childe's would be 'savagery, civilisation and society'. This was in April; the manuscripts were required

---

19   Farrington to Bernhard J. Stern, 1 August 1945, Bernhard J. Stern papers, University of Oregon, quoted by Peace, 'Vere Gordon Childe and the Cold War', p. 233.

by October. It is possible therefore that *History*, which is only 83 pages, was written for this project. And, of the three party-controlled bodies mentioned above, the Engels Society was the only one that Childe refers to in his correspondence, in a 1948 letter to the Glasgow branch of the Communist Party summarising his forthcoming lecture on 'Marxism and History'.[20]

About this book, *History*, it is also never said that it is highly quotable. It gleams with pithy statements and confronts the reader with attitude. It is not a potboiler but a considered distillation of his thinking about scientific history, a project that he had been engaged on since the mid-1930s. What is history? It is the scientific study of both archaeological and written sources. 'It should yield a science of progress, though not necessarily an exact science, like physics, nor an abstract descriptive science like anatomy. It should, in other words, disclose if not mathematical laws or a static general scheme, an order, in its own way as intelligible as that of astronomy or anatomy.' The purpose of the book was 'to show by a review of various theories of historical order what kind of order you may really expect to find in history and how its study can be useful'. But first, Childe provides an illustration of an historical order, by 'isolating one factor in the historical process' – the tools and machines of production. Other factors have to be reckoned with, but 'in the long run the technological is decisive'. Then follows an analysis similar to the one in *The Story of Tools*, but with a conclusion that is more intellectually challenging. There is direction in the process: 'Each step has in fact resulted in the extension of rational human control over brute nature and enhanced society's independence of the non-human environment'. But it has not been directed: 'The historical character of a process lies precisely in its self-determination'. Moreover, this is a social process: 'An invention that no one uses or knows of is not an historical event at all … In practice all tools are made and used socially.' This adds a complication, because it is obvious that we now have to explain 'the vagaries and fluctuations' in the history of invention in different parts of the world. To do that we need to study a different social order: the 'social, economic, political, juridical, theological and magical institutions, customs and beliefs' that 'have acted as spurs or brakes on men's inventiveness'.[21]

Childe next devotes four chapters to historiography, specifically those that make the intellectual move of imposing a transcendental order on history, that is, a history ordered from without. This section of the book amplifies the

---

20 Childe's MI5 file, 27 April 1947, 3 May 1947, 26 September 1947, 24 October 1948.
21 Childe, *History*, pp. 1–15. The book had five reprints between 1953 and 1957 in the USA, Japan, Argentina and Iran – but none in Britain.

discussion in 'Rational Order in History'. His theme is clearer now: that those traditions always produce a history that supports the power of the ruling class; even in 'contemporary Britain where literacy is universal, the principal market for history-books is formed by the ruling class and its favoured dependents and imitators in the middle classes. Naturally, publishers are more willing to disseminate histories that are interesting from the standpoint of the ruling class.' Did he imagine at this point his own feelings if this book had been rejected by a mainstream publisher? His response: 'It is just no good demanding history shall be unbiased. The writer cannot help being influenced by the interests and prejudices of the society to which he belongs – his class, his nation, his Church.' Then he dismisses the theological conception of Divine Government because it presents history's order as 'comparable to that of existing society', and because God's Will 'cannot be demonstrated by history or deduced from it. It is apprehended by faith, not by reason.' Then he looks at 'magical historiography', opening with his oft-quoted definition: 'Magic is a way of making people believe they are going to get what they want, whereas religion is a system for persuading them that they ought to want what they get'. The 'Great Man' theory is an example of magical history. Its fundamental defect is that ignores the social environment, the economic context and the technological basis from which great men arise. Childe then moves on to a critique of historical theories that impose models from the natural sciences, a form of transcendental naturalism, and of Spengler and Toynbee for ignoring precisely those human activities – science and technology – that are 'unambiguously cumulative and revolutionary'.[22]

The final chapter on 'History as a Creative Process' differs from 'Rational Order' because its account of how it was possible for a 'creative' or dialectical historical theory to move beyond Hegel omits the role played by the Italian idealist philosophers Croce and Gentile. Childe must have realised that while they were significant for someone coming to Marxism, as he had, during the Edwardian revolt against British empiricism, this was no longer the case. Instead the chapter goes directly into a discussion of 'dialectical materialism', using historical and everyday examples, and citing selected writings by Marx, Engels, Lenin and Stalin. His embrace of their ideas is positive, but he warns that these ideas have to be understood in a way that does not obscure the complexity of the process of history-making. Although he does not say explicitly, there is no doubt that he is building an alternative account of Marxism to that of its friends and enemies who distort it into a form of

---

22   Childe, *History*, pp. 16–66.

economic determinism. He stresses firstly the possibility of a 'tragic discrepancy' between 'progressive technology' and the existing property relations. Secondly, the necessary adjustment of the relations of production (in such a case) requires a supportive superstructure: 'relations of production must ... be lubricated by sentiment'. So, a battle of ideas needs to be fought: 'new slogans and banners are required' because the superstructure has 'a certain independent historical reality'. Action, organisation – both understood as social phenomena – are needed. And if they do not occur? Well, as he says, progress is not inevitable; socialism may not come, because our civilisation 'may vanish like the Mayan'; and (remembering no doubt that he writes in the shadow of Hiroshima and Nagasaki) *Homo sapiens* may become extinct.[23]

The last pages of *History* are hugely positive. Childe insists that analysed 'from the standpoint of dialectical materialism, history will show how institutions and beliefs have, in fact, in the past been related to technological and scientific developments'. But 'this will not explain the precise form assumed in particular instances'. It reveals only the patterns. The 'laws' of historical materialism do not 'constitute the order of history but help us to recognise those interrelations between events that do constitute it'. Scientific history 'makes no claim to be a sort of astrology to predict the outcome of a particular race or an individual battle ... Its study, on the other hand, will enable the sober citizen to discern the pattern the process has been weaving in the past and therefrom to estimate how it may be continued in the immediate future.' Thus, Childe is neither pessimistic about social evolution nor 'scientistic'. He leaves room for class struggle. His emphasis, however, is on the creative character of the 'rational order in history', including class struggle, so that he can counter mechanistic accounts of historical materialism. The final sentence in the book refers to Stalin as a 'great statesman' who has successfully 'foreseen the course of world history'. In the light of what we know now about Stalin and Stalinism, this is embarrassing for students of Childe. We need to remember, however, that Childe never endorsed Stalinism as a system of rule, and that he had never joined the Communist Party and submitted to the undemocratic centralism required of its members. It was not Stalin's personal role in events that Childe was referring to. Instead he was treating Stalin as a symbol for 'the course of world history' towards an imagined 'wholly rational historical order' through socialist cooperation and scientific advance. The liberation of Europe from fascism, Russia's role in it, and the sense that ordinary people – especially those in Russia – had shown their capacity for resistance and their

---

23 Childe, *History*, pp. 67–81.

desire for change during the war, seemed to bring that imagined future closer for Childe as it did for the left all over the world. Their mood was caught by Edward Thompson: 'all of Europe … was moved by a consensual expectation of a democratic and peaceful postwar continent. We supposed that old gangs of privilege, money and militarism would go. Most of us supposed that the nations of West and Southern Europe would conduct their anti-fascist alliances towards some form of socialism.'[24]

* * *

Of course, it wasn't to be. The Soviet Union and the USA faced off, and each adopted an increasingly aggressive stance towards the other. It was soon apparent that in the competition for global dominance the superior military and financial power of the USA would force the Soviet Union onto the defensive. Superior cultural power too, which Churchill understood and took advantage of when he declared in 1946 that the Soviet Union had had to build an 'iron curtain' around its satellites in Eastern Europe to stop them finding out about the liberal West. Communists and their supporters in the West could hope to counter this by engaging the apologists for capitalism on the ideological field, until in 1947 the Truman Doctrine sent a stream of money for anti-communist propaganda into the coffers of Western governments. Then in 1949 US military forces were permanently deployed in Europe under the North Atlantic Treaty Organization. In response to these setbacks, the world communist movement began a 'peace offensive' against the 'warmongering imperialists' and their atomic weapons, but even its most ardent proponents knew the purpose was to compensate for Russia's weaker Cold War position. In domestic politics the story was similar. In 1947 Communist Ministers were summarily dismissed from the governments of France and Italy. In Greece, the communist-led partisans lost the civil war in 1949. In the elections of 1950 the socialist Labour Government in Britain, which had secured a landslide in 1945 against Churchill, was returned with a majority of just seven. In the USA, the McCarthyite witch-hunts were terrorising the left into silence. In fact, when Childe was writing *History* the retreat of the European and North American left had already begun.

---

24 Childe, *History*, pp. 81–3; Edward Thompson, *The Heavy Dancers*, London, Merlin Press, 1985, p. 199, quoted in Mike Makin-Waite, *Communism and Democracy: History, Debates and Potentials*, London, Lawrence & Wishart, 2017, p. 162.

How should we understand Childe's response? Of course, he could not fail to be affected by the anti-communism of the Cold War. He knew that the American edition of *History* was rejected by two mainstream publishers – Holt, and Barnes & Noble – before it was published in 1953 by a start-up press. In 1948, when the American anthropologists Leslie A. White and Duncan Strong collaborated to invite him to lecture at their universities, he replied that he was 'very doubtful whether, under the present regime of anti-communist hysteria (though I am not a member of the party), I should be granted a visa, and, even if I were, whether I might not find myself suddenly kidnapped by some official or unofficial body'. About the visa, Childe was correct. White and Strong discovered that the government would indeed refuse to issue the visa and that if they persisted with the invitation the reputation of their universities would suffer – not to speak of their own careers. They dropped the invitation.

Then there was a snub closer to home. In 1949 the archaeologist Glyn Daniel referred to Childe as an exponent of 'Marxist prehistory' in *The Cambridge Journal*, an organ of the academic establishment. The adjective, in Childe's view, was meant to be pejorative, and, as Daniel did not provide a description of what he was dismissing, Childe wrote a short article for the journal. In it he explained how Marxists used theory to deduce 'a working economic organization' from an archaeological culture; how Marxists assume that the transmission of material cultures is also a process by which ideas are spread, for his main concern was to refute the idea that Marxism was mechanistic. Certainly, the determining processes according to Marxism were materialistic, but their relationship with social institutions and ideas was dialectical, just as it was between the events of a situation. The editor of *The Cambridge Journal* was the conservative philosopher Michael Oakeshott, well-known for his hostility to Marxism. He rejected the article. To his credit, when Daniel was editor of *Antiquity*, he published Childe's short piece in 1979.[25]

Childe had experienced this kind of oppressive ruling-class behaviour before, in 1918 and 1919, so he was not unprepared. His fall-back position was to disguise his intellectual debt to Marxism, as he explained to White in 1950:

> [I]n spite of the extreme reaction, you and Stern and co. are managing to get across a lot of good Marxism ... Here where the Party is formally unrestricted, it insists on publishing exclusively in what the bourgeoisie call 'Marxist jargon'. Many quite intelligent people are so repelled thereby

---

25 Childe, 'Prehistory and Marxism', *Antiquity*, vol. 53, issue 208, July 1979, pp. 93–5; Green reprinted it in her book at pp. 79–83.

that they never read any Marxism at all. I believe in sugar-coating as in the Hobhouse lecture. With my own avowedly Marxist work hardly anyone gets beyond the preface.

His only 'avowedly' Marxist work, so described in its Preface, was *Scotland before the Scots*. The Hobhouse Lecture, 'Social Worlds of Knowledge', delivered in 1948, is remarkable for the complete absence of references to Marxism (although Benjamin Farrington and Christopher Caudwell, the Marxist polymath who died in Spain, are footnoted). Instead, the central figure in its exposition of the social worlds of history and thinking – the former materialist, the latter dialectical – an exposition that would have been quite familiar to readers of 'Rational Order in History' or *History*, is Durkheim.[26]

Yet his political profile in this period contradicted this academic cautiousness, for he vigorously promoted it and seemed indifferent to its alignment with Russian interests. Consider his attitude to the Soviet Union's development of atomic weapons. He joked with Crawford in December 1945 that, 'I'm sure we'll soon have a better bomb than the Yanks. We have lashings of U [uranium] in the Kazak and Usbek FSR's. Yours till it explode …'. More seriously, and more indicative of how he connected 'the bomb' with socialism and scientific progress, he spoke out against the USA's 'monopoly of the bomb', and of the probable desire of big business to profit from atomic energy as the reason. This happened a few months later at a conference of the Scottish–Soviet Friendship Society. In the same speech he referred heatedly to the British Government denying visas to a group of scientists wishing to visit the USSR. So, this won't come as a surprise: in 1947, on the thirtieth anniversary of the Bolshevik Revolution, one of the speakers headlined for the celebration was Professor V. Gordon Childe.[27]

He could be quite provocative in his political activities. In 1950 the World Peace Council, a communist front organisation with many supporters among leading artists and intellectuals, issued its Stockholm Peace Appeal which called for the outlawing of atomic weapons. Childe, as a sponsor of the British Peace Council, sent the appeal with a covering letter to members of the Royal Anthropological Institute, seeking their signatures. This was not only impolitic, it was very bad form. One of the members, Dr W. Fagg of the British Museum,

---

26 I draw here on the work of William J. Peace, 'Vere Gordon Childe and the Cold War' in Gathercole, Irving and Melleuish (eds), *Childe and Australia*, pp. 128–43; Childe, *Social Worlds of Knowledge*, L.T. Hobhouse Memorial Trust Lecture, No. 19, London, Oxford University Press, 1949.

27 Childe to Crawford, December 1945, 67/74; Childe's MI5 file, 23 March 1946. Note: 'FSR's' means 'Federated Socialist Republics'.

sent an anonymous letter complaining about Childe's introduction of politics into scholarly circles to *The Manchester Guardian* and *The Daily Telegraph*. (It was not difficult for MI5 to discover the name of the writer.) Childe was not discomforted. A few months later, his name appeared in *The Times* appended to a jointly-signed letter from Australians living in Britain protesting at the Australian Government's decision to cancel the passports of 29 Australian peace delegates. A newly introduced government policy banned Australians from visiting communist countries. The delegates were already in Britain but on their way to Warsaw whither the Peace Congress, originally scheduled for Sheffield, was forced to relocate after the British Government refused to admit many overseas delegates. In 1955, he sponsored the Hampstead delegate to another World Peace Council meeting, this time in Helsinki.[28]

For his part, Childe had no qualms about visiting 'the socialist heaven', as he called it when writing to Crawford, crossing the Iron Curtain to Czechoslovakia in 1949, Russia in 1953, Hungary, Romania and Bulgaria in 1955, and Russia again in 1956. In similar fashion he publicly supported the international gatherings behind the 'iron curtain' of communist-led movements, such as the World Student Conference and the World Peace Council. He protested against the restrictions placed on a delegation to Britain from the newly formed People's Republic of China by the British Government in 1950, and in 1952 became a Vice-President of the Britain–China Friendship Society. He was also willing to lecture to the Bulgarian–British Friendship Society in 1955. All of this was in addition to his active role in the Society for Cultural Relations with the USSR (the SCR). His visit to Russia in 1953, at the head of a delegation of 11 'cultural workers', was under the auspices of the SCR. On its return, Childe, on the BBC and in the press, rejected the charge that the delegates were unable to go where they wished, and also that in Central Asia the local cultures were suffering under a policy of Russification.[29]

His public statements and actions in the postwar years convinced MI5 that he was a communist, and it is a record that might convince someone still imprisoned by the binary logic of the Cold War to lump him in with the Stalinists. But if we remember his earlier political experiences a different picture emerges, one that is not incompatible with the defensive, 'sugaring' strategy that he adopted in his writings. From 1915 he was deeply committed to the right of free intellectual exchange and reacted viscerally when

---

28 Childe's MI5 file, 17 August 1950, 18 January 1951, 15 August 1951.
29 Childe to Crawford, 19 November 1952, 76/114; Childe's MI5 file, 1 May 1950, October 1950, June 1952 (China), 24 May 1955, 2 June 1955 (Bulgaria), 22 August 1953 (Russian trip), 7 September 1953, 15 September 1953.

governments abridged or denied that right. In 1951 he was elected to the Executive Committee of the National Council for Civil Liberties. It was his opposition to governments building walls around scientific knowledge and to the power of corporations to exploit the fruits of that knowledge that drove his political involvement in these years. And there was an intellectual parallel to this commitment, discovered as he developed his arguments about the cooperative element in social evolution, the practical basis of scientific knowledge and rational order in history.

In his political thinking during the Cold War, 'friendship' was the equivalent of 'diffusion' in his scholarly thinking. Progress in history was dependent on the role of invention and the spread of scientific knowledge through trade, migration and conquest. Moreover, his explanation for 'why Europe behaved in a distinctively European way', even in the Bronze Age, was because its specialist metallurgical craftsmen, 'smiths', began 'a tradition of independence' that protected them from 'relegation' to the exploited class and allowed them to roam freely across Europe. That was how in 1957 he described to John Morris the argument of his last book, *The Prehistory of European Society*. The role of the independent, creative and mobile smiths may be taken as analogous to the position he and other radical intellectuals had to adopt in the Cold War of the Atomic Age.[30]

Childe was determined not to be 'relegated' by anti-communism or discredited by Stalinism. 'Sugaring' remained his default mode of left-wing intellectual activity up to his death. In 1950 the Communist Party decided that it would start a new 'serious' journal. *The Marxist Quarterly* had been resurrected after the war as *The Modern Quarterly*. The party now wanted a journal quite free of the taint of party-control, rather like the 'Past and Present' series put out by the Cobbett Press. John Morris, of the Communist Party Historians Group, had been pushing for this since 1949. Childe was asked if he would agree to be associated with it. Demonstrating his 'absolutely sincere approach to the party', albeit on his terms, he said 'yes', and then resigned from *The Modern Quarterly*. Two years later the first issue of *Past and Present* appeared. It was run by an editorial collective comprising members of the Historians Group, but it was free of party control and dedicated to forging a popular front with non-Marxist historians. Childe, 'as the most distinguished name in Marxist history anywhere', and crucially not associated with any party journal, was

---

30   Childe's MI5 file, 22 April 1951; Childe to John Morris, 19 April 1957 (from Sydney), from a typed copy sent to me by Peter Gathercole of the Childe–Morris correspondence provided by Morris to Gathercole. Childe, *The Prehistory of European Society*, London, Penguin Books, 1958, p. 9 and Ch. 10.

invited to join its board. Early meetings, in fact, were held in his flat. He remained an active board member of this 'journal of scientific history' – as its subtitle proclaimed – sending to it one of his last articles just a few weeks before his death.[31]

---

31   Childe's MI5 file, 2 December 1950, 10 May 1951; Childe to Morris, 17 August 1957; Christopher Hill, R.H. Hilton and E.J. Hobsbawm, 'Past and Present – Origins and Early Years', *Past and Present*, no. 100, August 1983, pp. 3–14.

Chapter 21

1956

Childe's complicated relationship with the Soviet Union would be tested in 1956. Until that year, his support for Russia's 'grand and hopeful experiment' had been very public; only in his private correspondence had he criticised the Soviet Communist Party's totalitarian rule and Stalin's deal with Nazi Germany. How would he react to '1956'? That is the term used on the left for the moral and mental confusion it experienced trying to make sense of that year's double-whammy: Khrushchev speaking at length about Stalin's crimes, and the invasion of Hungary by Soviet troops.

In June, the press in the capitalist West printed in full the 'secret speech' that Nikita Khrushchev, Secretary-General of the Soviet Communist Party, had delivered earlier that year at its 20th party conference. Khrushchev blamed Stalin's 'flaws' for the 'Great Purges' of the late 1930s, the violations of collective leadership, the imposition of a 'socialist realist' straight-jacket on culture, the murder of thousands of 'Old Bolsheviks', and for other crimes too numerous to list. In horror, communists in the West defected from their parties in droves, or else they were expelled for agitating for a wider and more honest debate about the 'cult of personality' and what they were now ready to call 'Stalinism'. Among them was Childe's friend Hyman Levy who insisted on publishing his highly critical first-hand investigation into the oppression of Jews in the Soviet Union. The second blow was the invasion of Budapest and other parts of Hungary by Soviet tanks and soldiers in early November to suppress an anti-communist uprising. The *Daily Worker* sent Peter Fryer to cover the uprising but, when the paper censored or suppressed his dispatches, he left the paper and wrote a book, *Hungarian Tragedy*, for which he too was expelled by the British party.[1]

In November 1956, *Past and Present* carried an article by Childe that referred to '1956' and also to 'Stalinism'. It took the form of a review article of

---

1   Hyman Levy, *Jews and the National Question*, London, Hillway Press, 1958; Peter Fryer, *Hungarian Tragedy*, London, Dennis Dobson, 1956.

1956

Geoffrey Barraclough's *History in a Changing World*. It was a book of essays in which Barraclough developed his approach to comparative history, which was a topic that Childe had covered, and criticised, in *History*. His line of attack then (mainly against Arnold Toynbee) he now used against Barraclough: that comparativists mistakenly focus on items on a list of historical developments, in different times and places, that are subjectively chosen by the historian, and about the relative merit of which there will always be disagreement. Meanwhile, they ignore 'just those human activities that in history are unambiguously cumulative and revolutionary', and the scientific and technological knowledge they produce. Without this practical knowledge there would be no civilisations for historians to compare.

Barraclough had been an early non-Marxist co-editor of *Past and Present*, but he had resigned because he found the board 'intolerable'. Perhaps this irritated Childe, but it was more likely that he found it intolerable that Barraclough had failed to engage with the arguments in *History*. Childe opened fire: Barraclough's history had 'contemptuously ignored the indispensable foundation [of society] and considered only the superstructure erected thereon'. Worse, Barraclough was condescending about the idea 'that history is a tale of progress'. Childe was firing true: Barraclough's idea of progress was 'shallow, subjective and *a priori*', a 'steady approximation' to 'a preconceived goal'. He pointed out dismissively that such preconceived gaols are only those 'within easy reach' of the imagination of the movement that subscribes to them, or to the historian who chooses to study them. Barraclough had smuggled in 'the old determinist view'.[2]

Then Childe makes his political point: goals such as the welfare state (of the labourists), and communism (of the Stalinists) are chosen by their societies for political reasons. 'It was particular preconceptions that were exploded in 1946 and 1956 and with them should go the whole idea of history as a predetermined process leading to an appointed end.' To underline his argument he called the article 'The Past, the Present, and the Future'. Why 'the future'? Printed by the editors at the front of the journal to emphasise its importance, Childe's argument encapsulated the political position of the journal: the future was open, historical materialism was incomplete, and Marxist intellectuals needed freedom from party diktat. Marxist and non-Marxist historians should be searching for 'the values to which history is approximating'. On such a view who could say that the future was communist? History should

---

2   Childe, *History*, pp. 64–5; Childe, 'The Past, the Present, and the Future', *Past and Present*, no. 10, 1956, pp. 3–5; on Barraclough's resignation, see Hill, Hilton and Hobsbawm, 'Past and Present – Origins and Early Years', pp. 9 and 10.

not be interrogated with predetermined ends in mind. Those who say that communism was Childe's ideal are certainly wrong if they mean by 'ideal' an end to which history is moving.[3]

In this publication Childe is using the events of 1956 to reaffirm the materialist basis of scientific history. Unlike Communist Party members, he is not beating his breast about being deceived by Russia's communist regime, because deceived by it he never was. He is not feigning ignorance about the regime's brutal repression, because, as we shall see, he publicly imagined how its victims might be affected. Nor was he about to rat on his comrades, whom he had always been careful to address as fellow Marxist intellectuals, not as party cadres. So, his 'sincere approach' to the party continued. It was a difficult path to tread, especially as Crawford in 1950 had declared to a friend (not Childe) that he had become 'fanatically anti-Soviet, anti-communist'. He and Childe continued to correspond, although not so regularly. After 1938 there were even fewer letters between Childe and Rajani Dutt, but nonetheless in July 1956 he agreed to move the main toast at the dinner to celebrate Dutt's 35 years as editor of *Labour Monthly*. Dutt was a recalcitrant when it came to Stalin's contribution to socialism, referring in the May issue of the journal to Stalin's crimes as 'spots on the sun'. Childe curbed his tongue on this occasion, recalling instead their early friendship in Oxford. It was therefore quite typical that, as he prepared to return to Australia, he gave an informal talk to the Cambridge University Graduate Branch of the Communist Party.[4]

In the Northern spring of 1956, Childe paid a last visit to his fellow archaeologists in the Soviet Union. He had been reading their publications since 1926, experimenting with their ideas in his studies of Scotland's prehistory, and applying their 'democratic' arrangement of archaeological items ('to unmask the reality of class conflict'), as used in the Moscow Museum, to the displays in the Edinburgh Museum. In 1942 he had written about 'The Significance of Soviet Archaeology' in *Labour Monthly*, praising it for relying on 'the co-operation of the workers and peasants' to preserve and collect the 'prehistoric treasures' that lay 'buried in the soil of socialised Eurasia'. He had noted approvingly that the Communist Party's adherence to the materialist conception of history meant that it 'recognised the historico-scientific value

---

3   Green, *Prehistorian*, p. 121.
4   Hauser, *Bloody Old Britain*, p. 252. Callaghan, *Rajani Palme Dutt*, p. 269; Green, *Prehistorian*, p. 121; Gathercole, 'The Relationship between Vere Gordon Childe's Political and Academic Thought', in Gathercole, Irving and Melleuish (eds), *Childe and Australia*, p. 95.

of archaeological material – consisting as it largely does, of the instruments of production devised and used by societies of the past'.

None of this was enough for certain Soviet colleagues. During his lifetime, Childe remained, in the eyes of the leaders of official Soviet archaeology, 'a bourgeois scholar', albeit a 'progressive' one who was 'not afraid to call himself a pupil of Soviet archaeologists', according to A.L. Mongait in the early 1950s. In their eyes he was not a Marxist; his materialism was mechanical, he neglected to deduce the structures of social relations from archaeological cultures, and he was 'a dogmatic orientalist'. None of these charges is valid, as we have seen, but many of the books in which Childe presented arguments that would have rebutted them, including *Man Makes Himself*, *What Happened in History*, and *History*, were never translated into Russian – deliberately, of course.[5]

When Childe discovered Mongait's assessment, he used to point it out delightedly to his British colleagues. Fancy being criticised for my Marxism by British colleagues and for not being a Marxist by the Russians? He didn't have to worry about his reputation in Britain; after all, who among his British colleagues had written a book that sold hundreds of thousands of copies? But why were the Russians, with whom he supposedly shared a common commitment to historical materialism, so unwilling to embrace him, so disdainful indeed of his ideas? He left no record of his understanding of this situation but as a long-time member of the Society for Cultural Relations with the USSR he must have been involved in discussions – privately one must assume, given the privileged status of the organisation in Russia – about the regime-imposed limits on its intellectual and cultural life. If he accepted those limits, and we must assume that he did, it was because he thought they were offset by communism's 'democratisation' of archaeology and recognition of its 'historico-scientific' function. But there were limits to his tolerance and they were reached during his 1956 visit to Russia.

His attempts to ask questions about the experience of coping with the regime while on private outings with Soviet archaeologists did not get very far because his companions overwhelmed him with their own gripes! What his specific reservations were, we do not know, but there was an incident when the wretched state of Soviet intellectual life really came home to him. One of the archaeologists whose work interested Childe was E.Y. Krichevskii. According to Childe in 1942, Krichevskii's work on Danubian societies, using

---

5 Childe, 'The Significance of Soviet Archaeology', *Labour Monthly*, November 1942, pp. 341–3; Leo S. Klejn, 'Childe and Soviet Archaeology – a Romance', in Harris (ed.), *The Archaeology of V. Gordon Childe*, pp. 75–93.

the officially approved focus on internal class-related dynamics, was incredibly important because it helped to refute the Nazi nonsense about an immigration of 'Nordic Indo-Germans' bringing civilisation to the region. Childe could also see the weakness in his work: 'one sometimes felt ... that Krichevskii was talking about an abstract, generalised and therefore imaginary society'. In 1956 Childe heard that Krichevskii had completed a manuscript before he was killed in the siege of Leningrad. Motivated by scientific curiosity and perhaps a sentimental wish to honour Krichevskii's sacrifice, Childe called on his widow. She refused to give up the manuscript, fearing that her contact with a foreigner would be construed as disloyalty to the regime.[6]

Returning to England, where the anti-communist mood was stronger than ever, Childe could have won approving nods from his fellow clubmen, and even from some of his left-wing associates, had he made critical remarks to the press about his experiences. Instead he did what he had done once before, in 1917, at a moment of personal crisis: he wrote a long private letter. Dated 16 December and personally typed by Childe at the Athenaeum Club, it has no salutation, and addresses no recipients. As a result of Leo Klejn's investigations, we know that he sent it to at least three of the leading archaeologists in the USSR. In five closely-typed pages he destroyed the reputation of Soviet archaeology. There were the general deficiencies: its primitive dating techniques, its neglect of aerial photography, its crude pollen analyses, and its inadequate understanding of the evidence needed to establish an archaeological culture. To this he added a detailed rubbishing of poor excavation techniques and inadequate plans of excavations. Altogether he referred to 13 studies by Soviet scholars and many by Western archaeologists for comparison. Note, however, that he made no attack on historical materialism in his critique, an absence which has puzzled archaeologists who assume that to abjure the Soviet system was to reject the Marxist framework of the system. What disappointed Childe was not the theory but its human exponents. They had made a mess of their chance to make history. This letter was Childe's '1956' moment – a steely recording of his disgust with the Stalinist regime's disastrous impact on the science to which he had devoted his life.[7]

---

6   Childe's assessment of Krichevskii is in his 1942 *Labour Monthly* article; the events of Childe's 1956 visit are recounted by Klejn, in Harris (ed.), *The Archaeology of V. Gordon Childe*, pp 75–93.

7   The letter by Childe, 16 December 1956, is printed on pp. 94–100 of Harris (ed.), *The Archaeology of V. Gordon Childe*.

1956

* * *

In late November 1956, Childe wrote to his cousin in Sydney, Alexander Gordon, informing him of his retirement from the Institute of Archaeology and of his plan to visit Australia. And then he said, 'I am sending you a copy of a book I published in USA (despite McCarthy!). It is not archaeological and not Marxist (at least my Soviet colleagues would not recognise it as such though old Marx might have) so should not be too repellent.' This book was *Society and Knowledge*. He does not refer to it by name in 'Retrospect', but it is there implicitly. Since 1913, he wrote, he had been fascinated by philosophy, a subject that had led him to 'a sociological approach to epistemology and the discovery of Durkheim and a deeper appreciation of his master, Marx'. He does not say when this interest in epistemology began, and it is tempting to see it as an expression of something new and non-Marxist in his intellectual life, and then to connect it to '1956' as another sign of political disillusionment. In fact, he had been rehearsing the questions raised in this book all his adult life.[8]

I doubt that writing *Society and Knowledge* was Childe's idea. It was in a series, 'World Perspectives', edited by the American ethical philosopher Ruth Nanda Anshen (1900–2003), who had a 'lifelong obsession' with solving the world's problems by finding 'a unitary principle' to bring together mankind and nature, knowledge and life. In pursuit of this metaphysical ideal she edited several series of books for major publishers, including 'The Science of Culture', 'Perspectives on Humanism', 'Religious Perspectives', as well the series of which Childe's book was part. Her quest began while attending the Harvard Tercentenary in 1936, which Childe also attended. She listened to the representatives of the various divisions of knowledge discoursing in isolation of each other's ideas, including perhaps Childe's paper on the diffusion of prehistoric knowledge from the Near East to Europe. But what personal vision did they bring to their studies? So, she approached them to find out, and seemed to have no difficulty persuading Albert Einstein, Alfred North Whitehead, Niels Bohr, Erich Fromm, Thomas Mann and maybe a hundred other leading thinkers to write for her. By the early 1950s, Childe would have been in her sights. He was a best-selling author, an invited lecturer for prestigious intellectual trusts, and the pre-eminent thinker in the discipline

---

8   Childe to Alexander Gordon, 20 November 1956, Munster papers, State Library of NSW; Childe, *Society and Knowledge*, New York, Harper & Brothers, 1956; also, London, George Allen & Unwin, 1956. References below are to the British edition.

of archaeology. Better still, by treating archaeology as a branch of history, he had transcended the narrow specialism of the field. It is not difficult, therefore, to imagine Ruth Anshen deciding to commission him for her current series. And how could he resist an invitation to write about his beliefs, the subject of the last chapter in the book, after the *Cambridge Journal* blocked publication of his article on Marxist archaeology in 1949?[9]

He began writing the book in the first half of 1954, and it was probably finished in 1955. It is not therefore stained by the mental and psychological turmoil of '1956'. But it is framed by his repugnance for the Cold War. Discussing the existence of patterns in our methods of communication, he illustrates it by pointing to Morse Code:

> You have all read stories about the prisoner confined in a dungeon by the Gestapo or the NKVD. He notices … a tapping noise and then suddenly he realises that there is a recurrent rhythm in the noise … He is excited to recognise a familiar pattern, a key signal in the Morse Code. (Unlike the present writer, the imaginary prisoner has always happened to serve as a telegraphist or something equally improbable.) … And so he establishes communication with the victim in the next cell. They expatiate at length on the iniquities of Hitler or Stalin and then proceed to plan their escape.

At another point in the book, Childe shows how the two-camps mentality of the Cold War damaged the possibility of discourse. To illustrate the way that words have both an indicative and an imperative aspect, he writes that it is confusing when a word which is primarily imperative is used as if its meaning were descriptive.

> 'Communist' once meant a man who had joined a political party with a clearly stated political and economic program and was thereby committed to work for the realisation of this program. It is [now] applied to an old fashioned liberal, not of course to describe his political and economic views which are diametrically opposed to Communism but as an opprobrious epithet to prevent his employment. 'Fascist' is abused in precisely the same way in Communist circles!'

Childe's socialism was infused with the principles of individual freedom and popular self-government, but he knew he was often described as a communist.

---

9   Susan Wyckoff, 'Ruth Nanda Anshen', in 'Jewish Women's Archive', https://jwa.org/encyclopedia/Anshen-Ruth-Nanda, accessed 23 March 2019.

If he was thinking of himself as an 'old fashioned liberal' it was because he hated the totalitarian direction that Stalinist socialism had taken in the USSR.[10]

In this book he writes about knowledge as both public and 'capable of being translated into successful action', a view of knowledge that is compatible with historical materialism. To validate this view of knowledge as a reproduction of reality 'serviceable for co-operative action thereon', he sets out to answer three philosophical questions: in what sense does knowledge correspond to reality, how is knowledge communicated, and how does the experience of reality turn into knowledge? It is this last question that is most important for him. He is determined not to be seen as dithering around with the perennial philosophical problem of mind and matter, the 'spirit' on the one hand and a world 'external to my head' on the other. He does not want to be labelled 'a naive realist', a person believing in a world of things 'in themselves', just waiting to be known. On the contrary, knowledge not only corresponds to reality, 'but is a part or an aspect of, or moment in, Reality. Its pattern not only corresponds to, but by that very fact, coincides with, the pattern – or at least a pattern – of Reality ... In acting, men do not act on Reality, but participate in the activity that is Reality.'[11]

There are elements in this book that make one think of earlier moments in his intellectual life. In Chapter IX he discusses the difference between 'truths', the propositions in which a society believes, and 'trueness', 'the correspondence of the conceptual reproduction of reality with the external reality it should reproduce'. Remembering his letters to *Hermes* and Watt, it would seem that he was grappling with the difference in 1917. There is also an echo of the definition of 'spirit' in *The Dawn* – 'energy, independence and inventiveness' – in his use of 'spirit' to describe the creative activity of reality in *Society and Knowledge*. There is a more substantive similarity when Childe begins his engagement with the theory of history in the 1930s. In his 1938 discussion with Dutt he apologised for venturing into metaphysics:

> I do not believe that there are uniformities in history of the kind from which one can make such predictions as work in natural science. I believe that the historical process as a whole is the actual creation of genuinely new values and that is why I am neither a Christian or a Hegelian. I am not sure whether Marx got beyond Hegel in this; I suspect he did but his commentators have successfully missed the point.

---

10 Childe, *Society and Knowledge*, pp. 37, 65, and 22–3, 41 (in the order in which the points are made in the paragraph).
11 Childe, *Society and Knowledge*, pp. 4, 54, 128.

In *Society and Knowledge*, Childe insisted that reality is an activity creating 'genuinely new values'. In both cases he was thinking about the implications of his definition of knowledge as public and useful. Result: history is rational; reality is historical. Two further parallels: Chapter IV, on 'Symbols and Their Meaning', is a topic that he was mulling over in 1946 when he discussed it with Jack Lindsay. His old friend C.K. Ogden had published *The Meaning of Meaning* (with I.A. Richards) in 1923, so it is likely that Childe had been thinking about the philosophical as well as the evolutionary function of language for some time. Finally, in Chapters VIII and IX he deals with the consequence of there being separate social worlds of knowledge, the subject of his 1948 lecture for the Hobhouse Memorial Trust.[12]

It is not the book's newness that strikes one so much as what it fails to say. In 1951, Childe sent greetings to the 30th Anniversary edition of *Labour Monthly*, congratulating it for keeping alive 'the positive vision of a classless and peaceable society as the logical culmination of the historical process'. This way of specifying his vision is noticeably missing from *Society and Knowledge*. It is not an absence that might have been encouraged by Ruth Anshen's woolly brief for the series, printed as a nine-page Foreword to the book, for Childe in this book expressly denies religious revelation as a basis for truth, not to speak of his denial of eternal values and the possibility of perfect knowledge. It is rather, as he implied in his letter to Alexander Gordon, that he did not want this to be a *Soviet* Marxist book. Yet it does have a vision: any idea accepted by society can become 'objectified' by the continual removal through cooperative action of impediments to the cumulative process of knowledge-making. The 'result at any time represents the pooled experience of mankind'. Rejecting predetermined ideas of Perfect Knowledge and the Ideal Society, Childe declares that *sufficient* knowledge is attainable. What kind of knowledge? Knowledge that recognises progress in history, and this includes knowledge about 'the determining influence of the economic pattern', with his usual qualification that this is not a mechanical process. Although he no longer asserts that there is 'a logical culmination' to the process, one can see why his belief in reality as creative process would have pleased 'old Marx'.[13]

---

12   Childe to Dutt, 14 October 1938, Dutt papers, CPGB Archives; Childe, *Society and Knowledge*, pp. 123, 128; Childe, *Social Worlds of Knowledge*; C.K. Ogden and I.A. Richards, *The Meaning of Meaning – A Study of the Influence of Language upon Thought and the Science of Symbolism*, London, Kegan Paul, Trench, Trubner, 1923.

13   Childe, 'From Professor V.G. Childe', *Labour Monthly*, vol. XXXIII, July 1951, p. 342; Childe, *Society and Knowledge*, pp. 61, 102–3, 126.

The last lines of the book make an uncanny forecast of an issue that has come to preoccupy concerned scientists of the Anthropocene:

> Already it is possible to see why the Humanist ideal is not absolute or final. It is possible to imagine a society comprising more than humanity. Indeed, scientists have hinted that humanity may owe a duty to non-human nature, and that not only in the generally recognised utilitarian sense of conserving natural resources for more economical human exploitation.[14]

* * *

In early 1956 Childe gave notice to his colleagues that he would retire a year early. His ostensible reason was that the Institute was about to move into new premises in the centre of London in Gordon Square, and he wanted to allow the new Director space to set his mark on the move from the beginning. But he also acted as if he was in a hurry to bring to an end several of his intellectual paths. *Society and Knowledge* was on his philosophy and history path, a path that he had been following since the mid-1930s. Two other books published in 1956 saw him step back on to the path of archaeological method and theory: *Piecing Together the Past: The Interpretation of Archaeological Data*, and *A Short Introduction to Archaeology*. The third path was the quest for Europe's uniqueness in prehistory, that he had been treading since *The Dawn*. He revised it for a sixth edition which appeared early in 1957, and then distilled its argument for his last book – fittingly in view of his democratic aspirations, a Pelican Book – *The Prehistory of European Society*, which appeared posthumously in 1958. None of those paths for him was possible of further extension, and there are no hints that he had a new project in mind.

In other ways, too, he showed that he was contemplating an intellectual as well as an institutional retirement. He had decided to return to Australia. Apart from visiting his sisters and the Evatts, what would he do there? Europe was his focus as an archaeologist. Maybe he contemplated returning to England? He told John Morris that he was going back to Australia on a reconnaissance to see if he could bear living there or not. But in December 1956 he cleared out his flat in the Isokon building, and sorted his extensive

---

14   Childe, *Society and Knowledge*, p. 131.

library into books that he would gift to the Institute and those that he would sell. He left his notebooks at the Institute and destroyed his personal papers. When a colleague at the Institute, Edward Pydokke, asked 'what plans he had for accommodation when he returned from Australia ... he replied that he doubted he would return from Australia and that he would in all probability throw himself over some convenient cliff'. His successor as Director of the Institute, W.F.Grimes, had a similar conversation with Childe, as did Professor Wooldridge of King's College, London. When Grimes asked him why he would jump off a cliff, Childe said, 'I have a horror of a prostate operation'. It looks as if he was contemplating a decision about mortal retirement, about ending his life.[15]

In his last months in England his mood fluctuated. At his final lecture he executed a Childeish joke, introducing himself as the Institute's Director who then for an hour entertained the audience with the achievements and missteps of the Professor of Archaeology, one V.G. Childe. When he officially left the Institute in the summer, there was a big party for him, a dinner, and a Festschrift in his honour. He was grateful. A few months earlier he had been touched to receive the Gold Medal of the Society of Antiquaries. In December, having been invited by the Indian Government to be its guest at the annual Science Congress, he left by air for New Delhi, via Athens where he visited the British School of Archaeology whose library he had used in 1915. In January 1957, however, back in England, depressed by Crawford's isolated and comfortless existence in a remote cottage in Hampshire, he worried about his own future. He claimed that he had never saved any money. He thought his pension would not be sufficient to meet his needs when he became ill, and he lamented his lack of family members to look after him in his old age. And he was not looking forward to being under surveillance from the security service while in Australia. An invitation in February to stay with a former student, Celia Topp, and her husband in Gibraltar raised his spirits. He lectured there, visited archaeological sites, played a lot of bridge, went to parties and generally had a good time. When Jack Lindsay met him in London in early March, he was in a genial mood. Interestingly, it was at a political meeting, and as this is Jack's description of it, he meant that it was a communist inspired or supported meeting. A few weeks later, about to sail on

---

15   John Morris's typed notes of his 1957 correspondence with Childe, in my possession, see note on letter of 29 May 1957; I have relied on Green, *Prehistorian*, pp. 142–5 for this account of Childe's last months in England, including a letter from Pydokke to Celia Topp (on p. 145); for Grimes and Wooldridge, see *Antiquity*, vol. 54, no. 210, March 1980, p. 1.

the SS *Oronsay* for Sydney, he told Crawford that as he was now quite poor, he would have to cancel his subscription to *Antiquity*. He had decided that he had nothing more to contribute to the democratisation of archaeology.[16]

As the *Oronsay* drew nearer to Australia, he would have remembered that his contribution to its ideas about democracy and socialism was never popular, even within the labour movement. Still, he must have wondered whether those or similar ideas had become 'objectified'. Was Australia still a proletarian democracy? After many Labor governments, how much socialism was there in Australia?[17]

---

16 Green, *Prehistorian*, pp. 142–5; Jack Lindsay to Sally Green in 1976: carbon copy, no date, in Lindsay's papers in the National Library of Australia, MS 7168, box 18; re surveillance: as John Morris recalled in an interview with Bill Peace, and reported in letter to me from Bill Peace, dated 14 September 1988; Childe to Crawford, 16 March 1957, Crawford papers, box 67, f. 136. He made the claims about his lack of savings and the inadequacy of his pension in his suicide note, discussed below.

17 Childe, *Society and Knowledge*, pp. 129–30.

Chapter 22

A SENTIMENTAL EXCURSION

In 1955, at a party in the roof-garden of the Isokon flats to celebrate the building's 21st birthday, a photographer, recording the event, snapped Childe with a nearly empty glass of wine in his hand. We see him side-on, against a crowd of male backs, each covered in a tailored jacket over a white shirt. Childe, however, is jacket-less, his spotted tie just visible beneath the collar of his dark shirt. Dressed comfortably but unconventionally, his face nonetheless betrays a person not quite at ease. He has failed to simulate the affected smile of the frequent party-goer; perhaps he is feeling uncertain about whether he will find someone to talk to.[1]

Childe in 1955, at the 21st birthday celebration of the Isokon Flats, Hampstead. (Image courtesy of University of East Anglia, Pritchard papers. Photographer unknown)

---

1   David Burke, *The Lawn Road Flats*, p. 216 and photographs after p. 170.

Among his academic peers Childe wore a different face. In May 1956 he was a panellist in a half-hour episode of a quiz show on BBC television called 'Animal, Vegetable, Mineral?'. Most of the episodes of the show, which ran for seven years, are lost, but this episode survived in the BBC archives, and has been copied to YouTube. The idea of the show was that the panel would compete with a museum to identify a sample of objects provided by the museum. On this occasion the objects were brought to London from the National Museum of Prague by a friend of Childe, its director Jîri Neústupný. He was in the studio with Childe, the Host, archaeologist Glyn Daniel in a bow-tie, as well as the other panellists, both well-dressed archaeologists, Sir Mortimer Wheeler and Professor Séan P. Ó Ríordáin. Wheeler had a huge reputation at the time, both as an archaeological entrepreneur and as a media star – he was voted TV personality of the year in 1954 – but he is not so highly regarded today. He was a cheat – if the opportunity arose, he would investigate objects before the show by finding out what the museum had withdrawn from its collection – a bully when in charge of excavations, and a serial philanderer. He was quite a contrast in personality to Ó Ríordáin, whose early death in 1957 depressed Childe. Daniel wrote of him later that he was 'lovable, kindly, learned, sincere and essentially Irish'.[2]

The atmosphere was formal but relaxed, the Host setting the tone with some self-deprecating remarks about his attempts to pronounce the names of the Czech and Irish visitors. The museum objects were passed around amid scholarly banter, each panellist addressing the others by their titles and surnames. Childe was in his element, ready to show off his familiarity with Central European artefacts, an expertise which the other panellists accepted, Ó Ríordáin chuckling at one point, 'Professor Childe is always right'. Of the eight objects in the competition he successfully identified seven, and as his success rate rose Daniel's impersonal moderation faltered and he referred to the show's star as 'Gordon', before correcting himself. Gordon, visibly more relaxed than the others, ignored the formalities of the occasion to shove a wad of paper into the top pocket of his suit coat. When two paleolithic ritual fertility objects were under discussion he was noticeably readier than Wheeler and Ó Ríordáin to avoid euphemism, saying of a stick-like object with two protuberances that 'its sexual parts are conspicuous', and of a pot shaped to suggest the female figure that 'it's a lady pot; you shouldn't look too closely at its back side; its breasts are quite conspicuous, and its arms are

---

2   Daniel, Glyn, 'Professor Sean O Riordain: An Appreciation', *University Review*, vol. 2, no. 1, 1960, 59–61; Gabriel Moshenska and Tim Schadla-Hall, 'Mortimer Wheeler's Theatre of the Past', *Public Archaeology*, vol. 10, no. 1, 2011, pp. 46–55.

up but not in surrender'. Scientific description was more important to him than offending the sentiments of a middle-class TV audience, and with his croaky, accent-less voice – so different from the soft brogue of the Irishman, the well-modulated voice of the Welsh host, and the upper-class accent of the knighted archaeologist – he could get away with it.[3]

* * *

In the *Communist Manifesto*, Marx and Engels wrote about the bourgeoisie destroying 'ancient prejudices' such as 'philistine sentimentalism' and tearing away the 'sentimental veil' from the family, thus revealing its material role in the history of production. They also ridiculed the 'sickly sentiment' used by socialist rivals in Germany to prettify their windy abstractions. In Childe's writings there are also many moments when he showed his scorn for sentiment in public life. Was he channelling Marx and Engels?[4]

Childe's public attack on sentimentality as a tool of rulers and deceivers began during the First World War, when, with tongue in cheek, he embraced Sydney's jingoes for renouncing the 'silly sentimentality' of the brotherhood of man. As an opponent of the war's imperialist character, he also had to expose the so-called civilising mission of colonialism. It was really just 'sentimental gilding' for exploitation by the mother country's investors. And he had a job to do on pro-war socialists: Fabian doctrines were 'sentimental', because they failed to encompass the precepts of 'scientific socialism'. The Labor Party had also taken the wrong path. When it identified with 'the sentiment of Australian nationalism' it became captive to the myth of 'racial purity' and the 'sentimental flag-waving that savours of jingoism'. By the 1930s racialism was his target. In the British empire as well as the German it rested on 'sentimental considerations' because it rejected the lessons of 'scientific judgment' about human diversity. In *Man Makes Himself* he was scathing about 'sentimental' historians who, confronted with unpleasant truths in the documents, 'close their eyes in utter horror'. He presented his book as a defence of the idea of progress against 'sentimentalists and mystics', while in 'Rational Order in History,' to make the same point, he reminded us that naturalists do

---

3   'Animal, Vegetable, Mineral?', 3 May 1956, accessed 12 August 2019, www.youtube.com/watch?v=RdI6T-74E_o.

4   Karl Marx and Friedrich Engels, *The Communist Manifesto*, edited by Frederick L. Bender, New York and London, W.W. Norton & Company, 1988, pp. 57–8 and 81.

not 'sentimentalise over the hardness of the dinosaur's fate'. Historians were again in his sights in 1945: if they deny their prejudices they fall into 'mere sentimentalism', a condition brought on by trying 'to put the other side'. There were no 'sides' in science.[5]

Of course, not all sentiment was bad. Progressive sentiments – a love of science, a hatred of exploitation and oppression, or the awe inspired by humankind making itself in prehistory – were fine. Indeed, they were crucial for revolutionary politics. As he pointed out in *History*, 'relations of production' needed to 'be lubricated with sentiment. To provide motives for action, they have to be transformed in the human mind into ideals and ideas.'[6] At this point a question arises: what was the role of sentiment in motivating Childe's actions? More generally, there are questions about Childe as a person. How did he manage his personal relationships? How intimate were they?

In the years following his death many of those who knew him – archaeologists, mainly – attempted to answer those questions in memoirs and at conferences. After listening to reminiscences about him at the Childe Centenary Conference in 1992, Colin Renfrew formed the impression that there was a side to Childe's personal life that was 'elusive'. Don Brothwell at a 2007 conference opined that Childe lacked 'intimate relationships and friendships'. Some colleagues remembered him as kindly and approachable, others saw him as remote and uncomfortable in company, and as possessing a notably ugly face. Yet in photographs his face is attractively proportioned. A close associate thought his temperament was unstable, another said he liked to put down his enemies; indeed, he had more enemies than friends. To his students at the Institute, Childe was both a distant scholar and genial associate – Uncle Gordon – who could share jokes and tea, drive them with terrifying incompetence to archaeological sites on the weekends, and invite a fortunate few to accompany him to the Festival Hall or the Communist Party's Unity Theatre. A common memory was of his sweet tooth and love of alcohol. From these reminiscences emerged a Childe whose personality surprised because it seemed contradictory. For archaeologists, Childe as a person was a mystery, just as in archaeology Childe's Marxism was a puzzle.[7]

---

5   Childe, 'Conscientious Objectors', May 1917; Childe, 'The German Colonies in the Pacific', February 1918; Childe, 'The New Unionism and State Socialism', January 1919; Childe, 'When Labour Ruled', September 1922; Childe, *How Labour Governs*, 1923, 1st edn, p. 85; Childe, 'Anthropology and Herr Hitler', March 1934; Childe, *Man Makes Himself*, 1936, p. 36; Childe, 'Rational Order in History', 1945; Childe, *History*, 1945, p. 23.

6   Childe, *History*, p. 75.

7   Colin Renfrew, 'Concluding Remarks – Childe and the Study of Culture Process', in Harris (ed.), *The Archaeology of V. Gordon Childe*, p. 121; Don Brothwell, 'Childe, His

In Childe's correspondence, his usual closing salutation was 'V. Gordon Childe'. There were revealing exceptions, however, suggesting a degree of intimacy that was uncommon in his professional relationships. In letters to Dutt, whom he addressed as 'My dear Raji', he would sign off as 'Yours ever, Gordon', and he used the same closing phrase when writing to Crawford, Jack Lindsay, John Morris and Robert Stevenson. And then there are the letters and cards that he signed in Cyrillic. An affectation, certainly, but also a double intimacy; that is, not 'Gordon' in the familiar Roman alphabet but 'Gordon' hidden behind an unfamiliar script. He would have had to have felt certain that his correspondent would get the joke: the supposed pro-Russian 'commie' telling his closest friends that he did not care what the state and narrow-minded people thought. He used the Cyrillic signature when writing to Stevenson and Crawford.

Childe's relationship with Robert Stevenson, a former student who became a close friend is of particular interest if we are discussing his capacity for intimacy. In the mid-1930s, Stevenson spent a year studying with Childe as part of his postgraduate classics degree in Edinburgh. He did well in the course and Childe began to mentor him, inviting him to join a dig at Larriban in Northern Ireland in 1935, and entrusting him with proofreading the 1939 edition of *The Dawn*, and his 1940 book *Prehistoric Communities of the British Isles*. Stevenson also read the proofs of the 1947 edition of *The Dawn*, in the preface to which Childe highly praised Stevenson's research on Neolithic pottery in Italy, where Stevenson was stationed during the war. By the late 1930s they were walking together in Edinburgh's Braid Hills, a custom that continued after the war. By this time Childe had ensured that Stevenson was appointed the Keeper of the National Museum of Antiquities of Scotland (while Childe was its Acting Director). After Childe moved to London in 1946, he stayed with Robert, his wife and their children when he needed to visit Edinburgh.[8]

Childe's tone in his correspondence with 'My dear Robert' (or 'Caro Roberto' when in Italy), was unguarded, commonplace and intimate. He described his walks in 'enchanting' Umbria, the cost of a trattoria meal, his drinking habits ('yours intoxicatedly'), his companions, and his impressions of conferences ('quite instructive'). When he was overseas, he told Robert he looked forward to seeing

---

Student and Archaeological Science: An Epilogue', *European Journal of Archaeology*, vol. 12, nos 1–3, April–December 2009, p. 199; Charles Thomas (a recollection) in Harris, *The Archaeology of V. Gordon Childe*, p. 135; Green, *Prehistorian*, pp. 115–17.

[8] Alice Stevenson, '"Yours (unusually) cheerfully, Gordon": V. Gordon Childe's letters to R.B.K. Stevenson', *Antiquity*, vol. 85, issue 330, November 2011, pp. 1454–62.

him even if it meant exchanging Umbrian sun for Scottish ice. But above all he was playful. In February 1945, he joked about how Robert's appointment as Keeper might be arranged after the 'brave Red Army' had 'liberated' Scotland in 1946, having driven its tanks over the frozen North Sea. The position would be advertised in *Pravda* and *Izvestia*, museum labels would be transcribed in Cyrillic, supplemented by 'appropriate extracts from ENGELS and STALIN'. Childe imagined himself pulling the strings, presumably as a 'Friend of the Soviet Union'. This elaborate riff was only funny on the surface. A few weeks earlier, Poland had been 'liberated' by the Red Army and placed under a puppet government, despite the protests of Russia's allies. Would liberated Scotland be 'Russified' – a fate suggested by Childe's imagined details of Stevenson's appointment? There is irony in Childe's joke – showing a loss of political certainty, perhaps? – and yet he signs off 'Yours (unusually) cheerfully, Gordon'. Was he cheerful because of the advance of the Red Army, or the impending end of the war and Robert's appointment? When he was in Moscow in 1953, having flown over the Aral Sea to Tashkent, his postcard to Robert was equally cryptic: 'Having a heavenly time in USSR'. Clearly, with Stevenson, Childe felt that he did not have to hide the uncertainty beneath his irony.[9]

With Crawford, Childe's relationship, although close, was more formal: like many professional men of that era they addressed each other by their surnames. Despite this element of formality, Childe was able to confide in Crawford. In Childe's last letter to him, written a few weeks before he died, he admitted that he was introverted, a confession more easily made because (he said) he detected the same failing in his friend – although to a lesser degree. Reflecting on this letter after the news of Childe's death reached him, Crawford remembered several occasions when they were alone and Childe unburdened himself. In 1936, when Crawford was visiting Edinburgh, Childe invited him on a Sunday drive. In the Pentland Hills, south of the city, they left the car and began a strenuous walk. As they climbed Childe explained that he had to do this at regular intervals for his mental and physical health; Crawford decided it was a 'deliberately formed habit acquired for a definite purpose'. Later that year, Crawford went to Southampton to farewell Childe before he sailed for New York on the SS *Manhattan*. On board, in luxurious comfort, they drank, and Childe became 'a little tight and unusually expressive'. He turned to Crawford and said, 'I've got the hell of an inferiority complex'.[10]

---

9 Stevenson, 'Yours (unusually) cheerfully', pp. 1454–62.
10 Childe to Crawford, 26 August 1957, Crawford papers, Bodleian Library, box 67, f. 140; Crawford to Harold Edwards, 23 October 1957, Crawford papers, Bodleian Library, box 76, ff. 151–2 (for this letter I am grateful to Beth Hodgett, Institute of

This term was invented in the early twentieth century by the Austrian psychoanalyst Alfred Adler. Along with Sigmund Freud and Carl Jung, Adler was one of the founders of psychoanalysis; each would develop his own school. In 1912, Adler broke with the Freudian and Jungian schools, setting up his own version of psychoanalysis called 'Individual Psychology', which stressed that the individual should be understood holistically and socially. Adler, a socialist (his wife was a friend of Trotsky) and a refugee from Nazism, believed society was moving towards communal and egalitarian ideals. In their practice, Adler's followers were democratic, doing away with the therapist's couch, and concentrating on the dynamic of superiority/inferiority as it manifested itself in the patient's behaviour. The 'inferiority complex' is not (as it is in popular idiom) just an expression of feeling inadequate but also of needing to compensate by power-seeking, egocentric behaviour. In psychotherapy, this 'will to power' could be used to create a healthier personality. Adler's approach to personality attracted socialists because it helped them imagine a social order in which psychological wellbeing and social equality were mutually reinforcing. At the same time, it armed them with a critique of totalitarianism as an expression of the warped personalities of Hitler and Stalin.[11]

From early 1920s, Adler lectured almost continually in Britain, Europe and the USA, and from the mid-1930s he had an energetic promoter of his ideas in Britain, Ernan Forbes-Dennis, so there was plenty of opportunity for Childe to learn about Adler. In fact, we know from Childe's correspondence with Jack Lindsay that he closely followed developments in psychoanalysis. He was suspicious of the 'introspective' method of the 'Freudians and Jungians', their 'nebulous imagery', and their ignorance of the science of the brain. This kind of psychoanalysis, he said, was a reactionary development. Meanwhile, in Moscow, the State Brain Research Institute under S.A. Sarkisov was 'on the fruitful track'. Founded in 1928, it focused on developing neuroscience in two directions: cytoarchitectonic (by brain dissection) and electroencephalogical (by monitoring the brain's electrical activity). Then Childe made a remark to Lindsay that suggests why he was interested in psychoanalysis: Russia's scientific approach, especially through the use of the electroencephalogram, would help us understand 'bi-poles'.[12]

The bipolar condition involves mood swings between mania and depression, and it appears that Childe was interested in its cure. Did he think he was

---

Archaeology, Oxford).
11   Phyllis Bottome, *Alfred Adler*, New York, Vanguard Press, 1957.
12   Pam Hirsch, 'Apostle of Freedom: Alfred Adler and his British disciples', *History of Education*, vol. 34, no. 5, pp. 473–81; Childe to Jack Lindsay, 27 May 1945, Jack

bipolar? He never said so, but why would he? We do know that Crawford and Le Gay Brereton thought he was often depressed, that Brothwell noted occasions when he was inarticulate, and Kilbride-Jones thought he was nervous in company. More pertinently, we have Crawford's evidence that Childe believed he was introverted, had a mental health issue, and that he had an 'inferiority complex'.[13]

So, what did Childe mean when he referred to his inferiority complex? Adler's psychotherapy was premised on the idea that psychological wellbeing was achieved by facing up to three 'life tasks': occupation/work, society/friendship and love/sexuality. As regards the first of these challenges, Childe's extraordinary work ethic, publication rate and academic achievements would surely have seen him pass at the highest level, and indeed that was his own assessment of his career. In his 'Personal Statement' of 1918 he reminds us that he was 'the first Sydney man' to obtain a First Class Honours in 'Greats' at Oxford. He told the readers of the *Maryborough Chronicle* that he was 'a Medalist' [sic] of Sydney University and formerly a Research Student of Queen's College, Oxford. In the *Brisbane Courier* a few months later, when advertising his coaching skills, he described himself as 'Medalist [sic], Honorman [sic] in Classics and Philosophy (Sydney and Oxford)'. The left was happy to accept this self-promotion – the Australian Peace Alliance wrote about his 'unique brilliance' – but what the Censor in Brisbane detected was 'unbounded intellectual pride'. A psychotherapist might have concluded that there was an element of overcompensation in Childe's approach to this 'life task'.[14]

A psychotherapist might have come to the same conclusion about how Childe faced up to the second 'life task', that his dedication to social responsibility was a bit forced. Childe had a long history of joining committees, in some of which he assumed an organisational role. Once again it was Childe who drew attention to this aspect of his life in the aforementioned 'Personal Statement', where he proudly noted his secretaryship in the Oxford University Socialist Society and his presidency of the Oxford Union of Democratic Control. Earlier

---

Lindsay papers, Australian National Library, Canberra, MS 7168, box 18; Jochen Richter, 'Pantheon of Brains: The Moscow Brain Research Institute 1925–1936', *Journal of the History of the Neurosciences*, vol. 16, 2007, pp. 138–49.

13   H. Kilbride-Jones, 'The Experience of Knowing Childe and Wheeler', *Archaeology Ireland*, vol. 4, no. 3, 1990, pp. 18–20.

14   Childe, 'Personal Statement', in Childe to Murray, 8 June 1918; Childe, 'Who is Mr Childe?', *Maryborough Chronicle*, 29 November 1918; Childe, advertisement, *Brisbane Courier*, 26 April 1919, p. 1; Australian Peace Alliance, press release, 12 September 1918, MF 1805 169/9-16; Censor's note on Childe to Pearce, 28 October 1918, MF 1805 168/30.

at Sydney he had held office in the Men's Christian Union, sat on two of the committees of the University of Sydney Union, and joined the Council of the WEA. Returning to Australia after Oxford he was the Assistant Secretary of the Australian Peace Alliance in Sydney and a member of the Council of the WEA in Brisbane. In Edinburgh in the 1930s he was Chair or President of the Scottish–USSR Society, the local branch of the Association of Scientific Workers, and the Scottish branch of the India League. Moving to London he continued to hold offices in the Society for Cultural Relations with the USSR and the Association of Scientific Workers, but as well he accepted official positions in the Marx Memorial Library, the National Council for Civil Liberties and the Britain–China Friendship Association. And at different times in these years in Britain he also served on the editorial boards of *The Modern Quarterly* and *Past and Present*.

If Childe were overcompensating, what deficit was he trying to reduce? Love/sexuality was the third of Adler's 'life tasks'. Did Childe discover Adler's terrifying views on homosexuality and apply them to himself? Homosexuality, according to Adler, was a form of inferiority complex, a lack of courage to face up to the challenge of sexuality, a form of feeling inferior in relation to one's gender. Today, such ideas are 'chiefly of historical interest, as instances of stereotyped judgmentalism and reified folk belief of a kind not uncommon among professionals of [Adler's] day'. They may, however, have seemed plausible to Childe in 1936, assuming homosexuality was his sexual orientation.[15]

When Sally Green published her biography of Childe she omitted any reference to his sexual orientation, but she did ask Jack Lindsay about it. We know this because a carbon copy of Jack's reply exists in his papers, which was:

> I don't want to be too emphatic about homosexuality. Certainly his main effect was of someone withdrawn, with no apparent sexual responses to either man or woman. However, he did have this student with him for a while and his attitude certainly had more of a personal touch than I had noted in any other of his relations. But beyond that of course I cannot go.

We can go a little further. As a young man Childe hated sport and warfare, which set him apart from the hegemonic masculinity of the time. At Oxford

---

15   R.W. Connell, *Masculinities*, 2nd edn, Cambridge, Polity Press, 2005, pp. 15–6; Ward Hauser, entry on Adler in *Encyclopedia of Homosexuality*, Vol. 1, edited by Wayne R. Dynes, Routledge, 1990, p. 14.

his affection for a fellow student was noted by the authorities in his college. In Maryborough, he befriended one of his young tormentors, the handsome Percy Stephensen. We know that he read a novel of homoerotic love among schoolboys, and that he was a member of a radical club in London where transgressive sexuality was sometimes on display. In the 1930s, one of his friends was a Cambridge don at Clare College, Mansfield Forbes, who was openly gay. In the 1940s, according to the archaeologist Paul Ashbee, Childe would often spend a day or two with Siegried Sassoon in his house, Heytesbury, near Stonehenge. Sassoon was bisexual. Much later, after his death, a former student, Don Brothwell, 'sensed' Childe was homosexual – as did Jack Lindsay, who knew Childe, on and off, for almost 40 years. Yet there is no evidence in Childe's life of a homosexual relationship or lifestyle. For this there are three possible explanations. First, that as it was a criminal offence during his lifetime to engage in homosexual acts, Childe might have decided to avoid the judicial and social punishments that would follow his being caught for breaking the law, by remaining celibate. Second, that Childe might have preferred the intimacy of non-sexual friendships. Third, that the truth is a mixture of both explanations.

In another letter to Sally Green in 1976, Lindsay wrote:

> I think Childe had a very deep feeling of fellowship – expressed in a general way in his socialism, in a personal way in his response to those who had at all got past that difficult mask of remoteness. His tragedy was in his inability to follow up in a fully satisfying way this need for friendship. His sardonic mask was the mask of his fear, the inability to reveal what he really felt in the way he would have liked to.

But who is to say what a 'fully satisfying' friendship is? Perhaps it is enough to say that Childe was naturally friendly, as we have seen, or, better, that he was comradely. It is striking that, with the exception of Robert Stevenson, the friends to whom he was really close – the Evatts, Dutt, Margaret Cole, Crawford, Lindsay, Morris – were all men and women of the left.[16]

In 1922, Childe finished writing *How Labour Governs*, a task which, as you may remember from Chapter 16, he described as 'a sentimental excursion into Australian politics'. It was the book that was the sentimental excursion, not

---

16   Jack Lindsay to Sally Green, no date on carbon copy, but 1976, in Lindsay papers, National Library of Australia, MS 7168, box 18; for the speculation about Childe's relationship with Forbes and Sassoon, see Gathercole to Irving, 21 September 1999, in the possession of the author.

the political involvement on which it was based. In 1957, Childe returned to his native land for good. This was an *actual* sentimental excursion. As we will see, it elicited strong feelings about Australia, as he rediscovered its natural beauty, experienced its cultural failings and analysed its lost socialist promise.

Chapter 23

'AUSTRALIA TODAY IS FAR FROM A SOCIALIST SOCIETY'

Arriving in Sydney on 14 April 1957, his 65th birthday, Childe immediately posted a letter to John Morris. On board, he had been working on the manuscript of *The Prehistory of European Society* and the first thing he wanted to do was to tell Morris that he had found a way to succinctly explain why European Bronze Age societies differed from other barbarian societies and from the totalitarian Asiatic and North African societies. He had nailed it in class terms; he was excited. In a nutshell: first, the trade in metals, machinery and knowledge from Mesopotamia and the Indus Valley could easily reach Europe; and second, because the Urban Revolution, in Europe's smaller, less priest-bound societies, did not produce a class division, therefore 'the specialist craftsmen it released were not there at once and ipso facto relegated to the exploited class but could build up a tradition of independence, "welcomed everywhere" in Homer, which was never quite lost'.[1]

It sounds just like the proletarian ideal of economic independence that inspired Australia's colonial radicals during the gold rushes. Childe had to come home before the Australian roots of his habitus, his disposition to look for signs of resistance to oppression, might be inferred. As one newspaper would headline his story, probably not recognising its layers of meaning: 'A Digger is Home'.[2]

Why had he returned? He needed to get his story straight. He told *The Sydney Morning Herald* that he was on holiday and that he might stay six months, returning to Britain after he had finished his book on European prehistory. To the reporter from Sydney's *Daily Telegraph* he said that he liked Sydney 'and may even decide to live here'. In August, there was an awkward

---

1   Childe to John Morris, 14 April 1957 (from Morris's notes on his correspondence with Childe, 1957).
2   *Melbourne Herald*, 19 September 1957.

moment – which we will come to – when he let slip the possibility of jumping off a cliff. In September he told the Melbourne *Herald* that he had come back just to look at his native land, and in the same month, when Brian Fitzpatrick asked him about his plans, he replied that he intended to return to Britain to work on epistemology. The longer he stayed the more likely he was to say that he would return to Britain.[3]

Another question: why had he left all those years ago? It was a question he was rarely asked, but, when it was, he played down the academic victimisation that had pushed him into full-time political involvement. Speaking with Russel Ward he laughed about being 'persuaded' to resign from Sydney University – he meant St Andrew's College – but made no mention of his subsequent failure to get teaching positions at the universities of Sydney and Queensland. For the *Daily Telegraph*, he indicated that he had worked for Premier John Storey but described his political dismissal in 1922 as a voluntary resignation. Politics, he told the reporter, was not his metier. True, but he did retain an interest in it, so another question he might have feared: was he a red? As far as we know he was never asked this, but early on he headed it off by claiming that his interest in the Soviet Union was because of its archaeology. It was of course, but it was also much more.[4]

From the ship, Childe went to stay with Bert and Mary Alice Evatt. Ten days later the University of Sydney awarded him its Honorary Doctorate, an award which Evatt, as a member of the University Senate, may have organised. Bert, Gordon's oldest friend, admired his work, and Gordon reciprocated. Evatt and his 'great ability and unusual vision' were often on his mind, and he praised Evatt to other people, which was unwise given Evatt's public notoriety after his performance at the Petrov Commission and his efforts to expel members of the secret Catholic 'Movement' from the federal Labor Party. He wrote about him to Morris; he told John Mulvaney that 'Evatt had been very badly done by, and it was shocking'; he eulogised his achievements and political courage in a public lecture in Melbourne; and must have mentioned their friendship to the Sydney University archaeologist James R. Stewart, with whom he stayed in early May.[5]

---

3   'Professor Home after 36 Years', *Sydney Morning Herald*, 15 April 1957, p. 4; *Daily Telegraph* (Sydney), 23 April 1957; Brian Fitzpatrick, 'V. Gordon Childe – In Memoriam', *Overland*, no. 11, Summer 1958, p. 23.

4   Russel Ward, 'Death of Professor V.G. Childe', *Outlook*, vol. 1, no. 4, November–December 1957, p. 11.

5   'University Honours Sydney-born Professor Who Won Fame Abroad'. *Sydney Morning Herald*, 25 April 1957, p. 1; Childe to John Morris, 17 August 1957; John Mulvaney on *The Science Show*, 22 January 2005, on ABC Radio National website,

Outside the Great Hall, University of Sydney, 24 April 1957. Evatt is opposite Childe, and the university's former Professor of Anthropology, A.P. Elkin, is between them. (Photograph by J. Tanner; National Archives of Australia; A1200:L22900)

Stewart lived at Mount Pleasant outside Bathurst, a regional city 200 kilometres north-west of Sydney. He was descended from Major-General William Stewart who in 1825 founded the world's first mounted police force to hunt escaped convicts and suppress Aboriginal resistance. This force raided local Aboriginal camps and carried out multiple executions of Aboriginal prisoners. Through free grants and purchases he became a large landowner, building a mansion called Mount Pleasant. His descendant, James Stewart, was a 'gentleman farmer' and expert in Near Eastern archaeology whose work Childe respected. On several occasions in 1957 he spent a week or so there, enjoying the hospitality of Stewart and his wife Eve, also an archaeologist. At Mount Pleasant, there were two farmhands, a young Swedish woman, Laila Haglund, who was Jim Stewart's assistant, upwards of 20 indoor and outdoor cats, and at certain times of the year a handful of students who were expected to spend time studying Stewart's archaeological collection in his

---

accessed 1 May 2011; for the public lecture, see below.

home laboratory. In May he wrote to the distinguished French archaeologist Claude Schaeffer, imploring him to find a way to get Eve and him 'away from this country, which I hate'. He concluded:

> Gordon Childe is using us as his headquarters. Although he represents politically everything that I loathe, he is a very pleasant guest, and we like him. But I'm afraid I do not regard him as a great archaeologist, and can only assume that many of his ideas are conceived in his sleep! Anyway our cats get on well with him, so he must be a pleasant character! I am always amazed by the vastness of his knowledge, and at the same time by the narrowness of his interests. At the moment he is away in Canberra with that traitor Evatt, who appears to be a great friend of his. Most decent Australians would like to shoot Evatt.

Apparently, Childe was not making an effort to disguise his political views.[6]

On the day after his return from Britain, George Boss, whom we met in Chapter 13, wrote to the Prime Minister about Childe's supposed disloyalty in 1920. The letter was sent to ASIO, which decided the news was 'of little or no relevance to Professor Childe's present day activities'. Not that the spy organisation was indifferent to Childe's return; it had sent to its trusted right-wing media a summary of Childe's career, including the wrong information that he was secretary to Premier Holman in the 1910s. *The Bulletin* ran the ASIO handout as news. On the same day as George Boss sent his letter, Percy Stephensen wrote to Childe. Since they had met in 1919 in Brisbane, Stephensen had moved across the political spectrum, from communism to anti-communism, but his letter to Childe in 1957 was welcoming, if tongue in cheek: 'What an opportunity you will now have to complete How Labour Governs, sere perennius ['durable plant']'. He reminded Childe of their friendship in Maryborough, where 'the ideas you then planted helped me to attain a satisfactory contra mundum outlook, which I still retain in some measure'. 'Inky', however, was at pains to show that he and Childe were 'contra' now. He recounted his career since 1926, including being interned in 1942 as a member of the proto-fascist Australia First organisation for three and a half years by Evatt who was the wartime Attorney-General:

---

6   R.S. Merrillees, 'Stewart, James Rivers Barrington (1913–1962)', http://adb.anu.edu.au/biography/stewart-james-rivers-barrington-11769, accessed 16 April 2019; James R. Stewart to Professor Claude Schaeffer, 12 May 1957, CAARI Archive, Nicosia, Cyprus, kindly provided by Bob Merrillees.

I am an Australian Nationalist ... I am the only Nationalist in Australia ... I gather you are some sort of Leftist ... You will be pleased to observe that pedestrians in Sydney are now regulated to keep to the left. I consider this reform to be due to your influence with John Storey, or was it Jim Dooley? Anyway, you contributed something practical to Australian regimentation. Yours for Australia First, affectionately, PRS.

Childe's reply was playful but firm. He warned Percy not to try to convert him 'to Australian or any other kind of Nationalism. I remain a near Comy [sic].' In June they had lunch in a restaurant in the city.[7]

In the Australian vernacular, a communist was a 'commo'; 'commie' was the American term. Within 10 days of stepping ashore, Childe had framed his understanding of Australian manners and values as American. 'Sydney had gone ahead remarkably and is quite Americanized, except in matters of service', he told the *Telegraph*'s reporter. Childe had a soft spot for America. In 1940, soon after returning from the USA, he had told Crawford that he much preferred the 'democratic character' of that country's 'learned classes' to Britain's elitist academics. Australia, of course, had a democratic character, and, as in the USA, the trains were good, but where were the porters? Unable to carry heavy luggage, he wore the same clothes until they fell to pieces and then bought others, as he told Crawford, but 'it is a nuisance when it gets cold abruptly as woollens are too heavy to carry and not easy to buy. And very few hotels have any sort of heating. I stay in the Carrington [in the Blue Mountains town of Katoomba] because it is centrally heated.' Did he reflect on the irony of a socialist appreciating good service in the USA, where underpaid waiters and porters relied on gratuities, but complaining of poor service in Australia where strong trade unions and labour market regulation resulted in relatively good wages for unskilled workers?[8]

He was surprised to find that even in middle-class families there were no cooks, maids or gardeners. Thinking of his own situation – an old, single, professional man on a small pension, and fearing a prostate operation – he decided he would not be comfortable living in Australia. Worst of all he did not like Australia's culture. To Crawford in August he wrote:

---

7   Childe's ASIO file (NAA, A6126/24) has the George Boss letter and the file note on Childe's role with Holman; *The Bulletin*, 8 May 1957; P.R. Stephensen to Childe, 15 April 1957, Stephensen papers, Mitchell Library MSS 1284; Childe to Stephensen, 31 May 1957, Stephensen papers.
8   *Daily Telegraph*, 23 April 1957; Childe to Crawford, 1 November 1940; Childe to Crawford, 26 August 1957, Crawford papers, box 67.

You really ought to come out and look at Australia. You might dislike it less than I do (the scenery I love, but not the mess my countrymen make nor the heat). You are less introverted, less exacting of material comforts, quite partial to beer (actually, Australian wine is excellent but hard to get and far too dear). The value systems seem to be proletarian – but of an uneducated proletariat. Icelandic and Soviet standards, which could also be called proletarian in different senses, suit me better.

In Armidale, Russel Ward explained to him the argument of his forthcoming book, that the national mystique, or 'Australian Legend', arose and developed among the bush workers of the nineteenth century pastoral industry. Afterwards, Childe wrote to Morris:

Ward is a very intelligent person and his views on Australian history quite interesting. Actually, I don't think he's got the whole story. Australian society is dominated today by values that Zweig takes as typical of the BRITISH working class. What is demanded by people who stay in hotels and what is offered by advertisers in the beastly papers is sport and beer and new motor cars.

Childe of course was a very intelligent person, but he had misunderstood Ferdynand Zweig's *The British Worker*, a Pelican book of 1952. Zweig was a Polish-born, liberal social psychologist. His book, based on life-history interviews, was about workers as individuals in social settings. At the heart of the book were its chapters on sport as the worker's religion, and his gambling, drinking and indifference to saving. It was one of the earliest documentations of what would come to be known as 'the affluent worker' thesis in British sociology. Underlying its method was a search for the social average. Its findings may be called *typical* only if the British working class is understood as an aggregation of individuals, not as a collectively acting, historical class. Childe himself had made this distinction in his exhortations to fellow archaeologists to move from studying archaeological cultures to imagining historical cultures. As Ward would point out in the Foreword to the second edition of *The Australian Legend* (1965), his argument that the national mystique was typical was not refuted by insisting that the average person in Australia today was a bundle of atypical traits. In listening to Ward, why did Childe forget his own arguments?[9]

9   Childe to Morris, 17 August 1957; F. Zweig, *The British Worker*, London, Penguin Books, 1952; Russel Ward, *The Australian Legend*, Foreword, pp. vi–vii, London, Oxford University Press, 1966.

In 1919, Witherby had made a similar finding to Zweig's when he said that by scratching an Australian worker one could find a bourgeois, and Childe had agreed. In September 1957, he had a chance to reconsider Australia from the point of view of class analysis when he addressed the Melbourne branch of the Australasian Book Society. This was a left-wing group of writers and intellectuals, formed under the auspices of the Communist Party and dedicated to publishing books – novels mainly – about Australia's tradition of militant struggle. Its Secretary was Ian Turner, who was a close associate of the writer and editor of *Overland*, Stephen Murray-Smith. Childe had corresponded with Murray-Smith in London when the latter had tried to persuade him to buy shares in a proposed Australian communist daily newspaper. They were in the audience with Brian Fitzpatrick, the poet David Martin, and other luminaries of Melbourne's intellectual left, keenly awaiting his address. What would the author of *How Labour Governs* say about labour and working-class politics today? Childe, understanding their expectations, wrote a paper specially for the occasion. His opening words did not disappoint: 'Australia today is far from a socialist society'. The next sentence was acceptable, 'As far as State governmental intervention is concerned, it is less a welfare state than Great Britain', for that was common ground for both Laborites and communists. The third sentence, however, was perplexing: 'But the working classes as a whole have got what they want'. In the manuscript for the address, Childe had scratched out 'the working class as a class has got what it wants'. By making the change to 'working classes' Childe was reminding himself that he understood the difference between the analysis of class dynamics and the description of the average social behaviour and beliefs of workers, and that his address would be mainly about the latter.[10]

What had 'the working classes' ... got? First, there were the material benefits that came mainly from high wages (home-ownership, good clothes, motor cars, liquor, sport and gambling) but also from state provision of education and leisure facilities (especially the 'national parks'). Second, working-class tastes had, surprisingly, become the tastes of the nation. According to Childe, in dress, one could not tell the classes apart; they attended the same amusements, listened to the same radio stations and read the same newspapers. So, was there any class distinction in Australia? Yes, and it was fostered by private schooling. But this distinction of status had not hardened into a ruling elite for

---

10 Witherby to Childe, 21 February 1919, NAA CMF Intell. Reports, 167/85-91; Childe to Stephen Murray Smith, 1 June 1949, Childe's MI5 file, KV2 1 2148; Childe, 'Australia Today is Far from a Socialist Society', *Labour History*, no. 58, May 1990, pp. 100-2, from the original manuscript in the Library of the Institute of Archaeology, London.

several reasons: because of the relatively even distribution of monetary and other rewards throughout the workforce; because education offered little incentives for upward mobility ('teachers are worse paid than miners and cooks can earn more money than scientists'); and because of the effects of a strong political labour movement. In the upper reaches of the state – the public service and parliaments – individuals of working-class or lower-middle-class origin were distinctly visible due to its influence. He mentioned Evatt and McKell in this connection. 'Political and trade union activities, and success in sport ... were better passports to success in Government and I think in industry' than the old school tie or 'recommendations from select dons'. At this moment there were Labor governments in three states, while, in Queensland, Labor had only recently lost office after it split on the issue of anti-communism.

Mention of Labor took him into class analysis. He said it was a credit to the working class that it had remained loyal to Evatt despite the virulent attacks on him by the press and its political backers. These attacks showed how dangerous he was to the ruling class. Childe also noted the displacement of graziers from the leadership of the ruling class by urban businessmen, and lamented the absence of an intelligentsia, 'which was not really a class'. And that was as far as he ventured. Yet there was an implicit argument in the address about class relations. In the early 1920s, as a result of his association with the British left, he had finally and definitively exposed the contradictions in Australia's 'labour theory', and concluded that 'politicalism', the capture of political power, would be futile, even if carried out by 'a real Labor government' under orders from a militant industrial movement. He had hoped that the leftward shift of the labour movement in 1921 would go further than simply inscribing a socialist objective on its banner – to the point of making a revolution. Clearly it had not. Instead, a compact between a state recognising labour's rights and a strong union movement had 'got the workers', not the working class, 'what they wanted' – not socialism but a 'wage-earners welfare state', in which basic needs were provided by a national statutory wages system, backed up by a highly organised working-class movement, rather than by universal social security. This was the class analysis that Childe's address was pointing towards, but it never got there. 'Australia today is far from a socialist society' thus had two meanings: a social-democratic meaning defined as the absence of universal social security, and a second meaning, unrealised in class relations as well as in Childe's address – namely, the absence of revolutionary proletarian democracy.[11]

---

11   See conclusion to Ch. 17; F.G. Castles, *The Working Class and Welfare: Reflections on the Political Development of the Welfare State in Australia and New Zealand, 1890–1980*, Sydney, Allen & Unwin, 1985.

'AUSTRALIA TODAY IS FAR FROM A SOCIALIST SOCIETY'

***

Among Childe's letters in Crawford's papers there are some containing hints of a long personal relationship, one that was close enough for them to discuss their mutual feelings about suicide; namely, that it was an acceptable way to end one's life if civilisation retreated as barbarous dictatorships advanced. That moment (it was 1939) passed for each of them, but in 1957, residing on opposite sides of the world, in a different political situation, at a different stage in their corporeal lives, a decision to commit suicide appeared rational again to one of them. Crawford, who had never married, was living alone in an isolated, comfortless house in England, and he was ill. As news of his decline reached Australia, Childe became depressed. He tried to persuade Crawford to come to Australia, writing, 'You might dislike it less than I do'. Trying to give a sick friend something to plan for, Childe's disarming statements about his homeland made the real point of the letter, its gift of understanding, easier to make. On receiving it in England, Crawford marked it 'last letter written to me'. When news of Childe's death reached him, he knew instinctively that it was suicide: 'everyone has the right to end their lives if and when they want to', he wrote. Crawford died a few weeks later in his bed.[12]

Understanding Childe's life in his final six months requires us to keep in focus our knowledge of the manner of his death. If it were Childe's intention to 'go over a cliff', why did it take him so long to act on it? Obviously, he was curious to see his native land again and meet with his family and friends, but why should that take six months? The answer may be that he was struggling with how to control the meaning of such an act. When he told his friends and associates what he intended to do, perhaps it was not to shock or hurt but to elicit wonder and fellow feeling. At the same time, he did not want to be so specific about timing and means that they might try to prevent his carrying it out. He needed empathy but also distance. So, he set up several false trails about the academic work that he was doing or would be doing – epistemology, for example – even though he also said that his work was over. And on top of that confusion of message, he had to decide how to do it and when. Did he indeed have the will to do it? Three months after he arrived in Australia, Childe startled a dinner party by announcing that he would jump off a cliff in Katoomba.

---

12   Lindsay to Green, April 1976, Jack Lindsay papers, National Library of Australia; Hauser, *Bloody Old Britain*, pp. 92 and 258.

Since his return, the University of Sydney had awarded him an Honorary Doctorate, important newspapers had treated him like a celebrity, the Australian Broadcasting Commission had commissioned him to present a 'Guest of Honour' talk, and history teachers in Sydney and academics in Adelaide had invited him to give lectures. Now it was Canberra's turn to hear his account of European prehistory. The left-wing academics at the Canberra University College were excited to have an eminent Marxist scholar on campus. They decided to organise a private dinner for him at the home of Robin Gollan, a labour historian who had been until recently a member of the Communist Party. The guests no doubt expected that a man of such achievements, who had been receiving positive attention in Australia, would be at ease in their company, but at the dinner Childe was quiet. As Gollan recalled, to get conversation going, he turned to Childe and said:

> What are you going to do now? There's obviously Australian archaeology, still in its infancy, and you could no doubt make a great contribution to it. And he said: Well, my work is finished. I'm not going to do any more work and I think I'll go over a cliff at Katoomba. That was the greatest conversation stopper I've ever experienced.

During the dinner Childe also said that his homecoming was not a happy one because he was disappointed that there was less socialism in Australia than when he left it half a lifetime earlier, the theme he would develop for his talk to the Australasian Book Society.[13]

Until his retirement, Childe had been a constant traveller, looking for evidence, exchanging ideas, observing and deducing as he thought about history as science and archaeology as history. Returning to Australia his journeys around the country were of a different kind, sentimental rather than scientific, revealing restlessness rather than purpose. He spent a fortnight in Sydney, before going to Bathurst. In mid-May he went to Canberra. At the end of May he was on a train to Broken Hill, where the Barrier District Council, the peak union body, controlled civic life. He said later that he liked proletarian Broken Hill because it was 'vibrant and culturally conscious'. Resuming his journey, he arrived in Adelaide where he lectured and met fellow historians. He was back in Sydney in mid-June to lunch with Percy Stephensen and attend a production of *Hamlet*. The next day he took a train to Brisbane to

---

13 Childe's ASIO file A 6126/24 for the Gollan dinner; R.A. Gollan, in *The Science Show*, 22 January 2005, on ABC Radio National website, accessed 1 May 2011; Gollan's review of *How Labour Governs*, in *Labour History*, 7, 1964, pp. 61–2.

visit his sisters Alice and Ethel, and his niece Mary. This entailed a trip to the Darling Downs. Then he stopped in Armidale on the way back to Sydney to visit Russel Ward. In July he visited Canberra again, where he lectured, and dined at Robin Gollan's. In early August he was in Katoomba, staying at the Carrington, and taking a short trip to the Jenolan Caves. It was probably during this Katoomba visit that he went to Wentworth Falls to visit 'Coronel', the former family home. He also took a trip to Bowral in the Southern Highlands in August. In the middle of September, he was in Melbourne, bemusing comrades in the ABS. John Mulvaney, then a young archaeologist at the University of Melbourne, drove him to the Dandenong Ranges east of Melbourne in a fruitless search for lyre birds. From Melbourne he flew to Tasmania for several days of bushwalking. Next, he was back in Melbourne to lecture. Then he travelled by train to Sydney and lunched with his cousin Alexander Gordon. There was another trip to the Stewarts in Bathurst. From 11 to 19 October he was at the Carrington in Katoomba, hiring a taxi to take him around to various cliff-top sites on the edge of the Grose Valley.[14]

He was often writing. He sent off the manuscript of *The Prehistory of European Society*, entrusting the task of seeing it through the press to his former colleague at the Institute, Dr Isobel Smith. He sent the lectures based on the book's argument to Morris in August for publication in *Past and Present*. Then in late September or early October he turned his mind to writing about himself in three documents that were published only after his death. Two of them were meant for publication. There was 'Retrospect', which we discussed in Chapter 20, that he sent to *Antiquity*, and there was a long review of archaeology in Britain as he had observed it over 40 years, and the main tasks confronting it. This was a very communist thing to do. It was like Rajani Palme Dutt's 'Notes of the Month' in *Labour Monthly* – a survey of the forces for and against progress followed by a series of concrete proposals for action – except that Rajani did not number his paragraphs, and to his credit avoided the use of exclamation marks. In the document, Childe revealed that his materialist vision for archaeology was undimmed – 'what Marxists call the relations of production' must be a central inference for archaeologists – and his distaste for idealists who insist on vainly searching for motives and emotions in the archaeological record was cutting: 'The collection and interpretation of mother-goddesses is just a harmless outlet for

---

14   John Mulvaney, 'From "The Dawn" to Sunset: Gordon Childe in Melbourne, 1957', *Australian Archaeology*, no. 30, June 1990, p. 30; State Records of NSW, Coroner's Inquests, 13/8459, 57/2389: 'Inquest into the death of Vere Gordon Childe, 1957', evidence of Henry Newstead, taxi driver, p. 10.

the sexual impulses of old men'. This was a dig at Glyn Daniel and Crawford who were captivated by the idea of a Neolithic religion in Europe devoted to a mother goddess. Archaeologists were, and should be, 'predisposed to a sort of materialism', but they can never be 'complete' materialists, for archaeological data are the 'expressions and symbols of human thought' that transcend the particular archaeological datum and the individual actor/thinker because these expressions and symbols are 'social and therefore eminently immaterial!' He sent it for publication in *The Bulletin of the London Institute of Archaeology*, where it appeared under the title 'Valediction', in 1958.[15]

The third document was an essay on ageing, in effect his suicide note, written at the Carrington in the days – or on the day – before his death. He sent it with an accompanying letter to Professor W.F. Grimes at the Institute:

Dear Grimes,

The enclosed contains matter that may in time be of historical interest to the Institute. But now it may cause pain and even provoke libel actions. After ten years it will be less inflammable. So I earnestly request that it be deposited in the archives and be not opened until January 1968, supposing that year ever arrives.

Yours sincerely,

V. Gordon Childe

Childe dated the letter '20 October 1957', but in fact he died on the 19th. The mistake may have been deliberate, suggesting that he intended to die after the 20th, but it may have just reflected his mental turbulence. I lean towards the latter, especially when his writing of it is placed in the context of his other actions in his last days. He told his cousin Alexander, on the day that he had left Sydney for Katoomba, that he would cancel his sea passage and fly back to Britain where he would take up his archaeological studies. In the meantime, he would finish his paper on the geology of the Blue Mountains. At the Carrington he wrote again to Alexander discussing his plans and

---

15 Childe to John Morris, 17 August 1957; Childe, 'Valediction', *The Bulletin of the London Institute of Archaeology*, no. 1, 1958, pp. 1–8; Andrew Fleming, 'The Myth of the Mother-Goddess', *World Archaeology*, vol. 1, no. 2, 1969, pp. 247–61. I owe the joke about exclamation marks to Humphrey McQueen's 'What happened to Childe?' https://labourhistorycanberra.org/2018/06/what-happened-to-childe/#more-1957, accessed 5 October 2019.

complaining about the heat. He also wrote to the Evatts, promising to see them next week. He took a trip to Bathurst to see the Stewarts either from Katoomba (a journey of two hours by train) or from Sydney earlier in the month. During this visit, Laila Haglund recalled, a friendly neighbour invited them for dinner one evening when the Stewarts were away. Childe became quite tipsy drinking rum and milk, and after dinner they stumbled home in the dark 'between rabbit holes and tall tussocks'. 'What a nice lady, what a pleasant evening', he kept repeating. Earlier, he told her about his exploration of the mountain valleys and peaks around them, and she concluded that he was studying them in a professional capacity. Back at the Carrington, he had befriended the receptionist, who is only identified in the sources as 'Mrs C', telling her about Mount Pleasant and his plan to write a book about the geology of the Blue Mountains. She enjoyed his company. On the evening of 18 October, Childe left the private bar to avoid some rowdies whom he thought were making 'cruel jokes' (in Mrs C's words) about his appearance, and went to the reception desk for a chat, in the course of which he offered Mrs C his typewriter as a gift. She politely refused but he insisted, so she accepted the typewriter, thinking that he meant her to mind it and that he would ask for it back.

The next morning, he went out early and never returned. Later that day, glasses, a hat and a compass with some papers were found outside the fence at Barrow Lookout, within 30 centimetres of the edge of the cliff. On the 20th his body was found at the bottom of the cliff, near Bridal Veil Falls.[16]

The placing of those objects performed the same function as his last letters and meetings. They were not meant to confuse people about his intention, for there was no longer any need for that. Rather, he wanted, as a last gesture of fellowship, to ease the pain felt by friends and colleagues when they learnt of his death. They were meant to suggest that it was an accident, or if they learnt that he was contemplating suicide, that he had not intended to die at that particular moment. After all, Childe could not be certain what the Coroner would conclude about the manner of his death. For all he knew, Gollan, Grimes, Pyddoke or Wooldridge might provide evidence of his statements about throwing himself off a cliff, leading the Coroner to make an open

---

16 Childe to Professor F.W. Grimes, 20 October 1957, *Antiquity*, vol. 54, March 1980, p. 1; Inquest into death of V.G. Childe, evidence of Alexander Gordon and James Morey, Constable; Kylie Tennant's statement to Bill Peace re Childe's letter to the Evatts, contained in Peace to Irving, 19 March 1988; Laila Haglund, 'Memories of Gordon Childe', *Australian Archaeology*, no. 30, June 1990, pp. 33–5; John Low, 'New Light on the Death of Gordon Childe', *Hummer*, no. 8, February–March 1985, www.labourhistory.org.au/hummer/no-8/gordon-childe/, accessed 3 October 2019.

finding about his death, or even to find suicide as its cause. And Childe knew that he was about to write a suicide note, and that in 10 years' time it would be opened. When that happened, he hoped his friends and associates would remember his last letters and conversations, and that they would understand that he had acted in dying as he had in living, in a positive and creative frame of mind. This would give them some emotional relief, but something else as well. He wrote the suicide note in the hope that it would carry their understanding beyond emotion to reason. He wanted them to understand that in his chosen way of dying he was defiantly continuing his commitment to progressive and humanist values. His death was not only a performance but a meaningful act, a fatal political act.[17]

His suicide note was not published until 1980, when the Institute's Director sent it to *Antiquity*, whose editor Glyn Daniel published it, untitled, in his editorial, calling it an 'essay'. It was an appropriate description because Childe focused less on what we might expect to find in a suicide note – a statement of an existential crisis – and more on his social situation, and what kinds of social regression and individual suffering his suicide might diminish. He began with an argument about generational justice: 'The progress of medical science has burdened society with a horde of parasites – rentiers, pensioners, and other retired persons whom society has to support and even to nurse. They exploit the youth which is expected to produce for them and even to tend them.' Or, if 'persons over 65' continue to work, they block the progress of their younger and more efficient successors. Even in retirement, these 'venerable counsellors', 'hanging around the fringe of learned societies or university institutions', can slow down progress and 'blast the careers' of younger and innovative thinkers who challenge theories and procedures that were formerly 'original and fruitful'. 'For all in all persons over 65 – there are of course numerous exceptions – are physical less capable than their juniors and psychologically far less alert and adaptable.' So, 'I have always considered that a sane society would disembarrass itself of such parasites by offering euthanasia as a crowning honour or even imposing it in bad cases, but certainly not condemning them to misery and starvation by inflation'.[18]

---

17 For Childe's suicide as performance, see Billy Griffiths, '"The Dawn" of Australian Archaeology: John Mulvaney at Fromm's Landing', *Journal of Pacific Archaeology*, vol. 8, no. 1, 2017, p. 102.

18 An alternative, idealist account of Childe's state of mind can be found in Martin Thomas, *The Artificial Horizon: Imagining the Blue Mountains*, Melbourne, Melbourne University Press, 2003, 'Passage Five – Gordon Childe and the Abyss of Time'. Thomas relies on philosophy and psychoanalysis to suggest Childe experienced an 'epistemological crisis' at the end of his life.

Then he wrote about his own condition. His memory has begun to fail and 'new ideas rarely come my way'. He admitted that he saw 'no prospect of settling the problems that interest me most – such as that of the "Aryan cradle" – on the available data. In a few instances I fear that the balance of evidence is against theories that I have espoused or even in favour of those against which I am strongly biased.' Moreover, he has become 'too dependent on a lot of creature comforts – even luxuries – to carry through some kinds of work for which I may still be fitted'. He would like to travel again in the USSR and even in communist China, but now lacks 'the will power to face the discomforts and anxieties' to do so. He gets ill too easily ('every little cold in the head turns to bronchitis') and has never saved any money. When his pension runs out, he will become 'a burden on society as an invalid. I have always intended to cease living before that happens.'

Finally, comes the statement of how he intends that it should happen:

> The British prejudice against suicide is utterly irrational. To end his life deliberately is in fact something that distinguishes *Homo sapiens* from other animals even better than ceremonial burial of the dead. But I don't intend to hurt my friends by flouting that prejudice. An accident may easily and naturally befall me on a mountain cliff. I have revisited my native land and found I like Australian society much less than European for I have lost faith in all my old ideals. But I have enormously enjoyed revisiting the haunts of my boyhood, above all the Blue Mountains. I have answered to my own satisfaction questions that intrigued me then. Now I have seen the Australian spring; I have smelt the boronia, watched snakes and lizards, listened to the 'locusts'. There is nothing more I want to do here; nothing I feel I ought and could do. I hate the prospect of the summer, but I hate more the fogs and snows of a British winter. Life ends best when one is happy and strong.[19]

What did Childe mean when he wrote that he had lost faith in all his old ideals? He spent the last six months of his life haunted by the memory of his youthful idealism for 'a real Labor government', and for a working-class movement that might have 'gone further' and achieved a democratic and socialist Australia. In 1957, Australia's economistic proletarian culture and its consumerist workers, who had 'got what they wanted', had sullied those old ideals. It was his hope for an ideal Australia that he had lost, for he was still

---

19 Childe, his essay sent to Grimes, reprinted without title, and introduced by the editor, Glyn Daniel, *Antiquity*, vol. 54, issue 210, March 1980, pp. 1–3.

an historical materialist, and a socialist globally and ideologically – a 'near Commie' in fact. He would have liked to travel to communist China to see if its workers had taken control of their lives and built a proletarian culture like Iceland's or Broken Hill's. Would theirs be the values to which history was approximating? In the meantime, content with his long-time commitment to reality as a creative process but facing up to his own mortality, he desired only that his ideas might be accepted by society and thus become 'objectified', and part of 'the pooled experience of mankind'.

His personal experience of politics was real enough, and it elicited creative impulses without which his ideas could not have taken shape. During the First World War, he had opposed militarism in Oxford, Sydney and Brisbane. Like other radicals at that time, he had been electrified by the working-class struggles for popular democracy in the years before the Bolshevik Revolution, struggles that convulsed Europe and North America as well as Australia. He then set himself the task of understanding whether a parliamentarist labour party could represent the interests of Australia's rebellious workers and decided that the lure of parliamentarism would be fatal to those interests. He observed the signs of an old state-order, with its hateful colonialism, collapsing around him, and as a result decided to work for a more humane and democratic order of which the Russian Revolution claimed to be the precursor. And he opposed the rise of fascism that threatened to prevent it emerging.

He became through these experiences a revolutionary intellectual – a thinker about revolutions and a revolutionary thinker. He believed in historical progress and in revolutions as necessary for progress. But when he died, this understanding of his life was obscured by Cold War passions. On 6 December, the same day as the Coroner delivered his verdict that Childe had 'died from injuries accidentally received … when he fell from a clifftop', ASIO's NSW Regional Director reported on his inquiries into possible counter-espionage elements in Childe's death. This report has been redacted from the public version of the ASIO file, perhaps because it raised doubts about the Coroner's finding.

* * *

Three days after his body was found, Bert Evatt and Alexander Gordon organised a funeral service at St Thomas's, North Sydney. It was attended by more than 60 mourners, among them parliamentarians, judges and Sydney

University contemporaries. Did any of them think to ask whether he should be commemorated in this way? Already they were distorting his legacy by associating it with religion, although he had been moving away from religion since the First World War, decrying it as a superstitious impediment to the development of scientific knowledge in prehistory, and mocking it in *History*. The travesty continued. When his body was released in December it was taken to Northern Suburbs Crematorium. Somebody, presumably Alexander Gordon, decided that he should be memorialised, but no separate memorial niche or plinth was created. Instead a version of his name that he never used was added to an existing plaque, in a small collection of tree memorials at a spot recorded by the Crematorium as NT 451A. Perhaps it was an act of family piety, or just kindliness. The plaque reads: 'Marion H. Shannon – Died 28th October, 1940', and then below her name: 'Vere G. Childe – Died October 19th, 1957'. Marion Shannon was the sister of Alexander Gordon's wife. These two individuals, Marion H. Shannon and Vere G. Childe, had never met. Regarding the careless attitude shown in these events to preserving Childe's memory, some people might be disappointed, but they are on the wrong path.[20]

In *Society and Knowledge*, at the end of the chapter on 'My Beliefs', there is a passage that reveals how he understood the value of his contribution to knowledge, and why he felt positive about ending his life:

> The creative process that I call Reality is completely self-contained and self-sufficient. Outside of it there can be nothing. Therefore, it is not made of anything, whether matter or spirit, nor anyone called God or the Absolute. Apart from the process there are no individuals, no persons. Yet to the process, each individual, though a part, can yet contribute and thus can actively participate in creation itself. For we have seen that there can be no person outside society and no society not composed of persons. At the same time, Society is immortal, but its members are born and die. Hence any idea accepted by Society and objectified is likewise immortal. In creating ideas that are thus accepted, any mortal member of Society attains immortality, yes, though his name be forgotten as completely as his bodily form dissolve. Personally, I desire no more.

Childe would have been happier had there been no memorial at all to his cremated bodily form.[21]

---

20   *Sydney Morning Herald*, 24 October 1957; Huw Barton, '*In Memoriam* V. Gordon Childe', *Antiquity*, vol. 74, issue 286, December 2000, pp. 769–70.
21   Childe, *Society and Knowledge*, pp. 129–30.

David Martin, in a poem called 'Gordon Childe', caught Childe's sense of immortality. His poem is different in intent from two other poems about Childe. Stuart Piggott wrote 'Ballade to a Great Prehistorian' in the mid-1930s, ending each stanza with a tribute to Childe's *The Dawn of European Civilization*. In the early 1960s, Jack Lindsay, reflecting on Childe's death, remembered their time together climbing Mount Tambourine while Childe demolished Lindsay's certainties with complicated truths. David Martin, who did not know Childe personally, remembered instead his intellectual legacy for the left. Hungarian-born Martin was a veteran of the Spanish Civil War, a refugee from fascism who had arrived in Australia in 1950, imbued with the revolutionary left's hopes for historical progress. He saw that hope in Childe's work, incorporating into his poem the title of *Man Makes Himself* and the last words of *What Happened in History*:

> From this far, late-country that still keeps
> A primitive and ancient dream he drew
> That which is name- and changeless. Here he grew
> And, all his work accomplished, here he sleeps.
> ...
> And so, come home, he closed the book and cast
> Upon the fertile wind his unwrit page.
> Dying, the hills stood round him, age on age,
> Man makes himself. Each crest out-tops the last.[22]

---

22   Stuart Piggott, 'Ballade to a Great Prehistorian' is reprinted in Green, *Prehistorian*, pp. 158–9; Jack Lindsay's poem is in the same book, pp. xvi–xvii; David Martin's poem is in *The Penguin Book of Australian Verse*, edited by Harry Heseltine, 1972, p. 178.

CODA

Childe's Revolutions and the Fatal Lure

In Childe's life, revolution – a 'real' phenomenon affecting 'all departments of human life', as he wrote in 1935 – presented itself at three moments. By the end of his life, these moments had produced the sense of a single phenomenon, but during his life he apprehended them as a logical order. First, there was the revolution he desired for Australia: proletarian democracy. Then there was the revolution he watched from a distance: communism. And lastly there was the transformative process that he discovered in prehistory, a process of two parts that he named the Neolithic and Urban revolutions.[1]

When the Bolsheviks seized power in November 1917, Childe had just returned to Sydney from Oxford. He had to find a job, the war that he detested was still going on, there was a place for him in the growing local resistance to it, and Russia was a long way away. He scarcely registered the tremors from what John Reed called 'the ten days that shook the world'. It was not until he joined the exodus of Sydney radicals to Brisbane a year later that he mixed with socialists who were sympathetic to Bolshevism. But he was not sympathetic; Australians, he said, would not have a bar of Trotsky's working-class dictatorship. His focus in Brisbane was on Australia's tradition of proletarian democracy, whereby the 'issues to be submitted to the people must also be determined by the people'. He saw its potential for producing a revolutionary socialism that avoided both the complexity of the guild socialist blueprint and the tendency of syndicalism to ignore the interests of consumers. The key factor would be the election of a 'real' Labor government that was committed to workers' self-management in the state enterprises as a result of pressure from the 'newer unionism', whose germs he detected in the militant industrial unions. Such a commitment would be the first step on Australia's path to socialism. When he signed his letters from Brisbane, 'Yours for the revolution', it was not a Bolshevik revolution that he had in mind.[2]

---

1   Childe, 'Changing Methods and Aims in Prehistory – Presidential Address for 1935', *Proceedings of the Prehistoric Society* (NS), vol. 1, no. 1, 1935, p. 7.
2   John Reed, *The Ten Days the Shook the World*, New York, Boni & Liveright, 1919.

When did he become interested in Bolshevism? The mordant tone of *How Labour Governs* suggests that he was open to a different model of revolutionary politics. But was it possible to imagine proletarian democracy apart from the parliamentary system, whose failings to represent the interests of workers he had observed at first hand while working for Storey and Dooley? Two aspects of his life in England in the 1920s pointed him towards the Russian experiment. First, he was mixing with progressive intellectuals in the milieu of non-party communism, a political culture that was harnessing British sympathy for the Russian revolution and government by soviets. Some of his closest friends, including Dutt and Postgate, had gone further, joining the recently formed Communist Party. Second, in the course of completing *How Labour Governs*, and reassessing his experience of working-class power in New South Wales and Queensland, he saw more clearly its failures and shortcomings. The result was the first attempt in the world to analyse parliamentary socialism.

His book about the history of the labour movement in Australia revealed the debilitating effect of its cabals and corruption, as well as the sapping of its socialist purpose by parliamentarians 'spoon-feeding' workers with palliative reforms. He followed it with articles demolishing the theory of socialism that Australian labour relied on. In the face of capitalist intransigence, the movement's leaders were powerless to enhance the working lives of their followers, let alone being in command of a state machine that could expropriate the capitalists and move Australia towards socialism. The effects of this development in his thinking were immediate. Writing during the 1920s, his commitment to class analysis became clearer, including the realisation that revolution involved not just ideological warfare but physical violence. By 1931, with the capitalist world suffering the effects of another economic depression, he was gingerly embracing revolutionary communism. Australia, he said, was an ideal country for a Soviet system, but it would need a 'super-Lenin' to achieve it.

Childe's scholarly methods and his cynical view of the uses of sentimentality in ruling ideologies prevented him becoming starry-eyed about Russia. He visited on several occasions but never endorsed its totalitarian system of government; indeed in private he called Stalinism a dictatorship. In his eyes, the revolutionary aspect of the Soviet Union was that it was an experiment in applying science to understanding and changing society. He thought it might be a harbinger of a new communist stage in history, dominated by proletarian and rational values, but he anticipated that the process of creating it would take many centuries. Meanwhile, developing the materialist conception of history would have positive effects; he particularly admired the work of Soviet museum directors because they were able to illustrate it in their displays. He promoted Soviet archaeology until he worked out that it was misconceived ('Marrism') and just plain sloppy – that is, unscientific.

He allowed himself to be associated with communism through his support for communist causes and front organisations, but he never joined the Communist Party. In fact, he was critical of it, sometimes in public, but mostly in private. The bewildering history of Childe's relationship to communism makes sense when we place him in the story of the changing fortunes of the left and analyse his thinking about socialist politics. But there is a much simpler way to understand it. Revolutionary communism was Childe's secular faith, the Communist Party was his church, and the Soviet Union was his promised land. He understood this and joked about it. That he made this leap of faith is unsurprising, given his upbringing in the Church of England. That he could imagine himself as a heretic within it is also not surprising, given the disagreements about worship and spirituality in the Sydney diocese during his father's time at St Thomas's. So, in his secular faith, as in official religion, it was possible to disagree with the actions of its institutions and leaders, and to question whether its ideology was effectively bringing the day of liberation closer.

There was nothing peculiar about Childe's reconstituting revolutionary ideas and behaviour as pillars of a secular faith. The writings of the left are replete with Christian imagery. Labour's 'trees of knowledge' – lifted from the book of Genesis – are a case in point. Formed socialist intellectuals, those described by Gramsci as being trained in the higher education institutions of bourgeois society before they convert to the left, are particularly prone to see themselves as secular followers. They need the sense of fellowship with the proletariat – and its organic intellectuals – which they can only find by defining their own way of belonging to revolutionary institutions. They may be estranged technically from these institutions, and loudly proclaiming their differences with them, but at that moment more than ever they need to find Gileads in the revolutionary movement, safe places of testimony where they can affirm their continued connection with the faith. So, they write for the left's internal journals, turn up for the iconic celebrations of historic labour struggles, and take nominal leadership positions in 'friendly' organisations, as Childe did.

The theology of Childe's secular faith was, of course, Marxism. He discovered it before the Bolshevik revolution, in Sydney as a sociology of classes and the state, and then in Oxford (talking with Dutt) as a dialectical philosophy of structures and revolutionary ruptures. In his two earliest books, revolution hovers in the background. In *How Labour Governs* it is 'an alteration in the social structure'. In *The Dawn* it is 'the several stages of the transformation of the world of food-gatherers' during the Bronze Age – the revolutions of prehistory before he gave them their names. He was already thinking as an historical materialist, thinking structurally. The same kind of thinking is present in *The Most Ancient East* (1928) and *New Light on the Most Ancient East* (1934), the latter containing a reference to the 'Two great revolutions in human culture'. The first is named as the Neolithic revolution in his 1935 presidential address to the Prehistoric Society; the second is referred to there as 'an economic revolution'. Then in *Man Makes Himself* (1936) the familiar terms Neolithic and Urban revolutions appear as chapter headings.[3]

So, there is no Marxist moment of revelation in this story of his discovery of the two revolutions. His interest in the transformation of social structures originated in his prior involvement in revolutionary politics. It is the character of his thinking, not his use of Marxist terms, that we should concentrate on, remembering that his neo-Hegelian tradition of Marxism was a philosophy of critique not a science of universal laws codified in the terminology of Marxism-Leninism, and that he admitted to 'sugar-coating' his Marxism – avoiding its jargon – to make it more accessible to his readers.

This discussion of Childe's revolutionary involvement prompts a final thought. There was an early moment in his life when politics might have become a fatal lure for his scholarly career. But if politics was a foundational aspect of his thinking, we might just as well ask whether his politics suffered from the fatal lure of scholarship. No doubt the more orthodox British and Russian Marxists who criticised his books thought so. Thus, Childe's experience of revolutionary politics has a double significance for understanding his legacy. It reminds us of his intellectual contribution to the study of human cultural evolution, as well as highlighting a problem all radical intellectuals face, namely how to combine intellectual and political work in the service of changing the structures of society.

---

3   Tringham, 'V. Gordon Childe after 25 Years'; Peter Gathercole, 'Childe's Revolutions', in Colin Renfrew and Paul Bahn (eds), *Archaeology – The Key Concepts*, London, Routledge, 2004; Kevin Greene, 'V. Gordon Childe and the Vocabulary of Revolutionary Change', *Antiquity*, vol. 73, no. 279, March 1999.

ACKNOWLEDGEMENTS

Peter Gathercole died in 2010, but his influence is everywhere in this book – in its ideas, sources and even words ('Childe's revolutions'). A friend for over thirty years, he shared his copies of Childe's letters and publications and encouraged me to investigate Childe's political commitment as the key to his life and thought. This book is my attempt to write the political biography of Childe that Peter always wanted to write. Through Peter I met William J. (Bill) Peace, an expert on Childe and American anthropology. Bill was equally generous with his discoveries about Childe. He guided me around New York and put me up in his family home on several occasions. Sadly, he died just as this book was in press. Another significant collaboration was with Gregory Melleuish who was one of the organisers in 1990 of the Childe Centenary Conference at the University of Queensland. Together with Peter Gathercole, we would later co-edit the papers from the conference, under the title *Childe and Australia*.

At that time, I was contemplating a book on Childe's 'first life' – as a political intellectual in Australia and Britain - in order to contribute to the lively discussion among archaeologists about marxism in his scholarly 'second life', and to assess Childe's ideas on Australian democracy and socialism. For help with Childe's archaeological career and thought I am grateful to Mike Berry, Robin Derricourt, Robert Merrillees, Michael Rowlands and Peter White. I would also like to acknowledge the help I received from the late Andrew Sherratt, the late Bruce Trigger, and of course Peter Gathercole, in overcoming my archaeological ignorance. My thinking about Childe as a labour intellectual was assisted by the advice, leads and encouragement that I received from Margaret Allen, Peter Beilharz, Jennifer Broomhead, Christopher Cunneen, Barbara Dale, Raymond Evans, Pat Francis, Murray Goot, Michael Hogan, David Howell, Ann-Mari Jordens, Marie de Lepervanche, Stuart Macintyre, Ben Madison, Roger Milliss, Michael Roe, Malcolm Saunders, Sean Scalmer and Gary Werskey.

After Peter Gathercole's death I decided that I should write about Childe's entire life. Rowan Cahill warmly supported my new approach, keeping me focused and encouraging my political intentions for the book. Every page of this book has been read carefully and sympathetically by him. Raewyn Connell and Humphrey McQueen helped with suggestions about sources and ideas, and they read early versions of the manuscript, as did Sarah Irving-Stonebraker,

Sean Scalmer, Geoffrey Sherington, and Anne Whitehead. Their feedback was positive, and I have tried to follow their advice.

There are many others who had fleeting roles – convenors of university seminars, organisers of academic conferences, and most kindly remembered, friends and colleagues in the Australian Society for the Study of Labour History who discussed the papers I delivered at its branch meetings and conferences. The Labour History Society is a most valuable means for developing historical awareness through championing radical history of all kinds. Which reminds me that my interest in Childe began in the 1980s when I was lecturing to undergraduate students at the University of Sydney in a course on working-class politics. It was their quizzical reaction to *How Labour Governs* that persuaded me to look more closely at Childe's political life and thought.

Librarians and archivists were of course essential facilitators of this book. There are too many to name individually, but I would like to mention the special attention that I received from Karin Brennan at the University of Sydney Archives; Bridget Gillies at the University of East Anglia Library; Beth Hodgett of the Crawford Photographic Archive at the Oxford Institute of Archaeology; Meirian Jump and Monica Brown at the Marx Memorial Library (London); John Merriman at the Blue Mountains City Library; Emma Quinlan at the Nuffield College Archives (Oxford); and Simon Sheppard at the Labour History Archive and Study Centre, People's History Museum (Manchester).

At Monash University Publishing, Nathan Hollier took the manuscript on board. Joanne Mullins, Sarah Cannon and Les Thomas guided it through to book form, while John Mahony was its painstaking copy editor. I am grateful to each of them, as I am to Nick Irving who compensated for my digital illiteracy in my dealings with Monash University Publishing.

Throughout the long period of this book's gestation, I have benefitted from the love of my family: Sue Irving, Sarah Irving-Stonebraker, Nick Irving, and in recent years John Stonebraker and my grandchildren, Madeleine, Charlotte and James. But without Sue's love this book would not have been completed. I owe her everything.

BIBLIOGRAPHY

Works by Childe
Manuscripts
Government sources
Newspapers and periodicals
Primary sources – books, articles and chapters
Secondary sources – books
Secondary sources – articles, chapters, and websites
Theses

* * *

Works by Childe

'A Colonial Product', *The Plebs*, vol. 16, no. 7, July 1924.
'A Fabian Judged by History', *The Plebs*, vol. 16, no. 1, January 1924.
'A Labour Premier Meets His Masters', *Labour Monthly*, vol. 6, June 1924.
'Anthropology and Herr Hitler', *Discovery*, vol. 15, 1934.
'Arbitration and Socialism', *Daily Standard*, 17 January 1919.
'Archaeology in the U.S.S.R.', *Anglo-Soviet Journal*, vol. 5, no. 2, 1944.
'Australia Today is Far from a Socialist Society', *Labour History*, no. 58, May 1990.
'Australian Demand for Negotiation', *Labour Leader*, 22 August 1918.
'Bronze Age Economics Created European Society', *ABC Weekly*, 13 November 1957.
'Changing Methods and Aims in Prehistory: Presidential Address for 1935', *Proceedings of the Prehistoric Society*, vol. 1, no. 1, 1935.
'Conscientious Objectors', *Hermes*, vol. 23, no. 1, May 1917.
'Editorial note', *Past and Present*, vol. 4, no. 1, 1953.
'From Professor V.G. Childe', *Labour Monthly*, vol. XXXIII, no. 7, July 1951.
History, London, The Cobbett Press, 1947.
How Labour Governs: A Study of Workers' Representation in Australia, London, Labour Publishing Company, 1923; second edition, Melbourne, Melbourne University Press, 1964.
'International Congress on the Science of Man', *Nature*, no. 137, 1936.
'Is It the Black Hundred?', *Daily Standard*, 27 March 1919.
'Is Prehistory Practical?', *Antiquity*, vol. 7, no. 28, December 1933.

[letter to Professor F.W. Grimes], 20 October 1957, *Antiquity*, vol. 54, March 1980.
[letter to Soviet archaeologists], 16 December 1956, in David R. Harris (ed.), *The Archaeology of V. Gordon Childe: Contemporary Perspectives*, Melbourne, Melbourne University Press, 1994.
Man Makes Himself, London, Watts & Co., 1936.
'On the Date and Origins of Minyan Ware', *Journal of Hellenic Studies*, vol. 35, no. 2, 1915.
'Political Action and the Newer Unionism' (Part I), *Labor News*, 15 February 1919.
'Political Action and the Newer Unionism' (Part II), *Labor News*, 22 February 1919.
'Prehistory and Marxism', *Antiquity*, vol. 53, issue 208, 1979.
'Priest and Proletarian in Prehistoric Times', *The Plebs*, vol. 16, 1924.
Progress and Archaeology, London, Watts & Co., 1944.
'Races, Peoples and Cultures in Prehistoric Europe', *History* (NS), vol. 18, October 1933.
'Rational Order in History', *The Rationalist Annual, 1945*, London, C.A. Watts & Co., 1945.
Response to questionnaire, *Daily Worker*, 14 October 1939.
'Retrospect', *Antiquity*, vol. 32, issue 126, 1958.
[review of F. Engels, *The Origin of the Family, Private Property and the State*], *Scientific Worker*, vol. 12, 1940.
Scotland before the Scots, London, Methuen, 1946.
Social Evolution, London, C.A. Watts, 1951.
Social Worlds of Knowledge, L.T. Hobhouse Memorial Trust Lecture, No. 19, London, Oxford University Press, 1949.
Society and Knowledge, New York, Harper & Brothers, 1956; also, London, George Allen & Unwin, 1956.
'Some Questions for a Politician', *Daily Standard*, 7 March 1919.
[suicide note], *Antiquity*, vol. 54, issue 210, March 1980.
'Sydney Labor Quarrel – Prospects of Compromise – A Queenslander's Impression', *Daily Standard*, 16 July 1919.
The Aryans: A Study of Indo-European Origins, London, Kegan Paul, Trench Trubner, 1926.
'The Coming Crisis in Australia', *New Statesman*, vol. XIX, 6 May 1922.
The Dawn of European Civilization, London, Kegan Paul, Trench, Trubner, 1925.
'The German Colonies in the Pacific', *Australian Worker*, 7 February 1918.
'The Irrepressible Class Struggle', *The Worker* (Brisbane), 17 October 1918.
'The Need for Clear Thinking', *Australian Worker*, 28 March 1918.
'The New Unionism and State Socialism', *Daily Standard*, 4 January 1919.
'The Orient and Europe', *Nature*, no. 142, 1938.
'The Oriental Background to European Science', *Modern Quarterly*, no. 1, 1938.
'The Past, the Present, and the Future', *Past and Present*, no. 10, 1956.

The Prehistory of European Society, London, Penguin Books, 1958.
'The Significance of Soviet Archaeology', *Labour Monthly*, vol. 24, no. 11, November 1942.
'The Sociology of Knowledge', *Modern Quarterly*, new series, vol. 4, 1949.
The Story of Tools, Brisbane, Building Workers' Industrial Union (Queensland branch), 1965 (first published, London, Cobbett Press, 1944).
'Treatment of Political Prisoners', *Daily Standard*, 28 April 1919.
'Valediction', *The Bulletin of the London Institute of Archaeology*, no. 1, 1958.
'Visitors to Russia', *The Times*, 15 September 1953.
'War and Culture' in W.B. Tavener et al., *Eleventh Hour Questions: Articles on Peace by Various Authors*, Edinburgh and London, Moray Press, 1937.
'War for Democracy', *New Statesman and Nation*, 24 September 1938.
What Happened in History, London, Penguin Books, 1942.
'When Labour Ruled – In Australia – By an Ex-Ruler', *Labour Monthly*, vol. III, no. 3, September 1922.
'Where Did Culture Arise?', *The Plebs*, vol. XXV, 1933.
'Who is Mr Childe?', *Maryborough Chronicle*, 29 November, 1918.
'30th Birthday Greetings', *Labour Monthly*, vol. 33, 1951.

Manuscripts

Bodleian Library, Oxford

Crawford, O.G.S., papers.
Murray, Gilbert, papers.
Myres, J.L., papers.
Oxford University Fabian Society, records.

Cyprus American Archaeological Research Institute, Nicosia

Schaeffer, C.F.A., papers.

Flinders University Library, Bedford Park, South Australia

Evatt, H.V., papers.

John Oxley Library, Brisbane

Worker's Educational Association of Queensland, records 1913–1932.

Labour History Archive and Study Centre, People's History Museum, Manchester

Communist Party of Great Britain archive, papers of R.P. Dutt.
Labour Research Department collection.

London Metropolitan University, Trade Union Congress Library Collection

Labour Research Department Archive.

Mitchell Library, Sydney

Australian Peace Alliance, papers.
Brereton, John Le Gay, papers.
Higgins, Esmonde, papers.
Munster, George, papers.
Scott, Rose, correspondence.
Stephensen, P.R., papers.

National Library of Australia

Coghlan, Sir T.A., papers.
Evatt, Mary Alice, oral history interview.
Hall, H. Duncan, papers.
Lindsay, Jack, papers.
Piesse, E.L., papers.
Watt, R.G., papers.

Nuffield College, Oxford

Cole, Dame Margaret, papers.

University College London, Institute of Archaeology

Childe, V. Gordon, notebooks.

University of Melbourne Archives

Meanjin Archive.

University of Queensland Archives

Minutes of Joint Committee for Tutorial Classes.
Minutes of Senate.

University of Queensland, Fryer Library

Stephensen, P.R., papers.
Walker, S.E.A., 'School Days with Percy' (typescript).

University of Sydney Archives

Anderson, Sir Francis, papers.

Brereton, John Le Gay, papers.
Childe, Vere Gordon, personal file.
Department of Tutorial Classes, Annual Reports and Minutes of Joint Committee.
Minutes of the Senate.
Minutes of the Undergraduates' Association.
Registrar's Letter Book.
University of Sydney Union, Debates Committee minutes.

University of Sydney, Fisher Library, Rare Books Library

Chadwick, Nora, special collection.

University of Texas at Austin

Bridge, Ann, papers.

Government sources

National Archives of Australia

Australian Security Intelligence Organisation, 'Childe, Vere Gordon', A6126/279; A6126/24.
Commonwealth Military Forces, Intelligence Report Files, 'Enemy trading or other suspicious acts', MP95/1.

National Archives (UK)

Military Intelligence Section, 'Childe, Vere Gordon', 2005 KV2/2148 and 2005 KV/2149.

State Records of New South Wales

NRS 12060, Premier's Department Correspondence, Letters Received, 1907-25 (9/4683-4931; 9/2167-68).
NRS 12060, Premier's Department Correspondence, Special Bundles, List of matters submitted to Cabinet, 1917–1921, 4/6259.3.
NRS 12060, Attorney-General's Department, Report of Royal Commission into Trial of IWW members, 4/7592.
NRS 12060, Premier's Department, Correspondence, Special Bundles, Royal Commission of Inquiry into Administration of State Wheat Pool, 1919–21, 7/5927-28.

Parliamentary Debates and Papers

Commonwealth of Australia, *Parliamentary Debates*, House of Representatives, No. 49, 1960.
New South Wales, *Government Gazette*, no. 71, 22 April 1914.
New South Wales, *Journal of the Legislative Council*, 1903.
New South Wales, *Parliamentary Debates*, Legislative Assembly, second series, 1918, 1921.
New South Wales, *Parliamentary Papers*, 1910, Second Session.

Newspapers and periodicals

A.B.C. Weekly (Sydney).
Age (Melbourne).
Alert (Maryborough).
Argus (Melbourne).
Australian Highway (Sydney).
Australian Worker (Sydney).
Brisbane Courier.
Bulletin (Sydney).
Bulletin of the University Socialist Federation (UK).
Call (London).
Canberra Times.
Common Cause (Sydney).
Communist International (London).
Communist Review (London).
Daily Herald (Adelaide).
Daily Standard (Brisbane).
Daily Telegraph (Sydney).
Edinburgh Evening Dispatch.
Evening News (Sydney).
Fabian News (UK).
Federal Independent (Sydney).
Fellowship (Melbourne).
Glen Innes Examiner (NSW).
Guild Socialist (London).
Herald (Melbourne).
Hermes (Sydney).
Labour Leader (London).
Labour Monthly (London).
Linlithgowshire Gazette.
Manchester Guardian.
Maryborough Chronicle.
Marx House Bulletin (London).

Millions Magazine (Sydney).
Modern Quarterly (London).
Monthly Circular of the Labour Research Department.
Oxford Magazine.
Plebs (London).
Ross's Monthly (Melbourne).
Singleton Argus.
Social Democrat (Sydney).
Socialist (Melbourne).
Socialist Review (London).
St Andrew's College Magazine (Sydney).
Sydney Morning Herald.
Times (London).
Times Literary Supplement (London).
Torchbearer (Sydney).
Truth (Sydney).
Worker (Brisbane).

Primary printed sources: books, articles and chapters

Arnot, R. Page, *History of the Labour Research Department*, London, LRD, 1926.
Ashley, M.P. and C.T. Saunders, *Red Oxford: A History of the Growth of Socialism in the University of Oxford*, Oxford, Oxford University Labour Club, 1930.
Atkinson, M., *Capital and Labour: Co-operation or Class War*, Melbourne, Anglican Diocese of Melbourne, 1918.
Atkinson, M., *The New Social Order: A Study of Post-War Reconstruction*, Sydney, Burroughs & Co., 1919.
Atkinson, M. (ed.), *Australia: Economic and Political Studies*, London, Macmillan, 1920.
Barker, Ernest, *Political Thought in England from Herbert Spencer to the Present Day*, London, Williams & Norgate, 1915.
Black, George, 'How Labour Governs in Australia: A Book of Big Blunders', *The Australian Bystander*, 12 June 1924.
Bridge, Ann, *And Then You Came – A Novel*, London, Chatto & Windus, 1948.
Bridge, Ann, *The Dangerous Islands*, London, Chatto & Windus, 1964.
Bryce, J., *Modern Democracies*, New York, Macmillan, 1921.
Cole G.D.H., [writing as 'Ember'] 'Between the Lines: A Case for New Standards', *New Standards in Industry, Politics and Education*, November–December 1923.
Cole, G.D.H., 'Introduction' to J.J. Rousseau, *The Social Contract & Discourses*, translated with an Introduction by G.D.H. Cole, London & Toronto, J.M. Dent & Sons, 1913.
Cole, G.D.H., *The World of Labour*, London, G. Bell & Sons, 1913.
Cole, G.D.H., *What Marx Really Meant*, London, Victor Gollancz, 1934.

Council of Soldiers' and Workers' Delegates, *What Happened at Leeds*, London, Pelican Press, 1917.
[Crane, Gordon?], *Independent Working-Class Education and the W.E.A.*, Melbourne, Victorian Labor College, 1927 [?].
Dobb, Maurice, 'Communism or Reformism: Which?', *Communist Review*, vol. 2, no. 4, February 1922.
Dutt, R.P., letter to the *Times Literary Supplement*, vol. 3, no. 304, 1965.
Ewer, W.N., 'When the People Come to Rule: Lessons from Australia of Labour's Problems when in Power', *Daily Herald*, 24 July 1923.
Freeberg, Norman R., *Socialism: What Is It? Word Pictures in an Australian Frame*, Brisbane, printed by *The Worker* newspaper, 1919.
Fryer, Peter, *Hungarian Tragedy*, London, Dennis Dobson, 1956.
Gollan, Robin, review of *How Labour Governs*, in *Labour History*, 7, 1964.
Gray, Frank, *The Confessions of a Private*, Oxford, Blackwell, 1920.
Gray, Frank, *The Tramp: His Meaning and Being*, London, Dent, 1931.
Heydon, J.K., *Fascism and Providence*, London, Sheed & Ward, 1937.
Heydon, J.K., *Wage Slavery*, London, The Bodley Head, 1924.
Higgins, E.M., *David Stewart and the WEA*, Sydney, Workers' Educational Association of New South Wales, 1957.
Higgins, E.M., 'Labour over the Threshold', *Labour Monthly*, vol. 5, no. 4, October 1923.
Higgins. E.M., 'The Rise and Fall of Australian Labour', *Labour Monthly*, vol. 3, no. 5, June 1922.
Hobhouse, L.T., *Democracy and Reaction*, London, Fisher Unwin, 1904.
Hobhouse, L.T., *The Metaphysical Theory of the State: A Criticism*, London, Routledge, 1918.
Hobhouse, L.T., 'The Soul of Civilisation', *Contemporary Review*, 108 (1915).
Hobson, J.A. and A.F. Mummery, *The Physiology of Industry*, London, Murray, 1889.
Hobson, J.A., *Democracy after the War*, London, George Allen & Unwin, 1917.
Hobson, J.A., Hobson, *Imperialism: A Study*, London, Nisbet, 1902.
Hobson, J.A., *Problems of Poverty*, London, Methuen, 1891.
Hobson, S.G., *National Guilds: An Inquiry into the Wage System and the Way Out*, London, Bell & Sons, 1914.
'How Labour Governs', *Australasian Painter and Decorator*, 1 January 1924.
'How Labour Governs', *New Statesman*, 18 August 1923.
'How Labour Governs', *Sydney Morning Herald*, 15 September 1923.
Irvine, R.F., *Organisation and National Efficiency*, Melbourne, Victorian Railways Printing Branch, 1915.
Jensen, H.I., 'Teaching History. Some Suggestions', *Daily Standard*, 21 January 1924.
Jensen, H.I., *The Rising Tide: An Exposition of Australian Socialism*, Sydney, The Worker Trustees, 1909.
Kautsky, Karl, *The Road to Power*, first published 1909; first English translation, 1909: www.marxists.org/archive/kautsky/1909/power/.

BIBLIOGRAPHY

Kilbride-Jones, H., 'The Experience of Knowing Childe and Wheeler', *Archaeology Ireland*, vol. 4, no. 3, 1990.

Labor Party (New South Wales branch), 'Early Conference and Executive Reports of the Labor Party of New South Wales,' edited by Michael Hogan as *Labor Pains Volume II (1906–11)* and *Volume III (1912–17)*, Sydney, The Federation Press, 2008.

Lenin, V.I., *Imperialism: The Highest Stage of Capitalism*, London, Communist Party of Great Britain, 1916.

Lenin, V.I., 'Theses on Bourgeois Democracy and Proletarian Dictatorship', *Communist International* (London), no. 1, May 1919.

Levy, Hyman, *Jews and the National Question*, London, Hillway Press, 1958.

Levy, Hyman, *The Universe of Science*, London, Watts & Co., 1932.

Lindsay, Jack, *Marxism and Contemporary Science, or The Fullness of Life*, London, Dennis Dobson, 1949.

Lloyd, Mary E., *Sidelights on Two Referendums, 1916 and 1917*, Sydney, William Brooks, 1952.

Mallowan, Max, *Mallowan's Memoirs*, London, Collins, 1977.

Mann, Tom, *Tom Mann's Memoirs, with a Preface by Ken Coates*, London, MacGibbon & Kee, 1967.

Marshall, Vance, 'Gordon Childe. Scholar and Thinker. Personal Sketches of Author of *How Labour Governs*', *Daily Standard*, 2 January 1924.

Marx, Karl and Friedrich Engels, *The Communist Manifesto*, edited by Frederick L. Bender, New York and London, W.W. Norton & Company, 1988.

Mayo, E., *Democracy and Freedom: An Essay on Social Logic*, Melbourne, Macmillan and WEA, 1920.

Michels, R., *Political Parties: A Sociological Study of the Oligarchical Tendencies of Modern Democracy*, New York, Hearst, 1915.

Montefiore, Dora, *From a Victorian to a Modern*, London, E. Archer, 1925.

Muir, Ramsay, 'How Labour Governs', *Weekly Westminster Gazette*, 11 August 1923.

Ogden, C.K. and I.A. Richards, *The Meaning of Meaning: A Study of the Influence of Language upon Thought and the Science of Symbolism*, London, Kegan Paul, Trench, Trubner, 1923.

Ostrogorski, M., *Democracy and the Organisation of Political Parties*, London, Macmillan, 1902.

'Paul Pry', 'Out of the Mouth of a Childe', *Worker* (Brisbane), 26 July 1923.

Pember Reeves, W., *State Experiments in Australia and New Zealand*, 2nd impression, London, Allen & Unwin, 1924.

Pombeni, P., 'Starting in Reason, Ending in Passion: Bryce, Lowell, Ostrogorski and the Problem of Democracy', *The Historical Journal*, vol. 37, no. 2, 1994.

Portus, G.V., *Marx and Modern Thought*, Sydney, WEA, 1921.

Postgate, R.W., 'How Labour Goes Wrong', *The Plebs*, vol. 15, no. 9, September 1923.

Pulsford, Frank E., *A Leave-time Study of the Democratic Control of Industry*, Sydney, The Worker Print, 1918.

Pulsford, Frank E., *Co-operation and Co-partnership*, Sydney, The Worker Print, 1913.
Pulsford, Frank E., *The Society of Tentmakers*, Sydney, Bible House, 1909.
'Radix', *Ability and Labour*, Melbourne, Ross's Book Service, 1918.
Snowden, Philip, *If Labour Rules*, London, The Labour Publishing Company, 1923.
Somerville College, Archives (Oxford), 'Somerville and the Great War', online.
Stephensen, P.R., 'A Tired Cynic – Gordon Childe's Criticism of Australian Labour – *How Labour Governs*', *Daily Standard*, 22 December 1923.
Stephensen, P.R., 'Gordon Childe, Cynical, Tired Philosopher', *Daily Standard*, 5 January 1924.
'Student', 'How Labour Governs. Critics and Criticism', *Daily Standard*, 4 January 1924.
Sydney University Christian Union, *The University of Sydney Students' Handbook*, Sydney, G.B. Philp & Son, 1913.
The Labour Year Book of 1916, London, issued under the auspices of The Parliamentary Committee of the Trades Union Congress, The Executive Committee of the Labour Party, and The Fabian Research Department, 1915.
Thomas, J.H., *When Labour Rules*, London, W. Collins, 1920.
University of Sydney, A Short Description Prepared for the Use of the Congress of the Universities of the Empire, published by the university in 1912.
Wason, Graham, 'Obituary, Roly Wason', *The Independent*, 24 January 1998.
Waugh, Alec, *The Loom of Youth*, London, Grant Richards, 1917.
Workers' Educational Association, *Annual Report of the WEA 1920*, Sydney, WEA, 1921.
Witherby, T.C., *Who Shall Control Industry? Report of a Lecture ... Given in the School of Arts, Brisbane, Friday Sept. 12, 1919*, Workers' Educational Association of Queensland, 1919.

Secondary sources

Books

Aarons, Mark, *The Family File*, Melbourne, Black Inc, 2010.
Adams, Paul Robert, *The Best Hated Man in Australia: The Life and Death of Percy Brookfield 1875–1921*, Glebe, Sydney, Puncher & Wattman, 2010.
Australian Dictionary of Biography, Vols 1–18, Melbourne, Melbourne University Press, 1966–2005.
Bakewell, Sarah, *At the Existentialist Café: Freedom, Being and Apricot Cocktails*, London, Chatto & Windus, 2016.
Ball, Desmond and David Horner, *Breaking the Codes: Australia's KGB Network, 1944–1950*, Sydney, Allen & Unwin, 1998.
Barrow, Logie, and Ian Bullock, *Democratic Ideas and the British Labour Movement*, Cambridge, Cambridge University Press, 1996.

Beatty, Jack, *The Lost History of 1914: How the Great War Was Not Inevitable*, London, Bloomsbury, 2012.
Bernal, J.D., *The Social Function of Science*, London, George Routledge & Sons, 1939.
Bernal, Martin, *Black Athena, Volume II: The Archaeological and Documentary Evidence*, Rutgers University Press, 1987.
Bevir, Mark, *The Making of British Socialism*, Princeton and Oxford, Princeton University Press, 2011.
Blaazer, David *The Popular Front and the Progressive Tradition: Socialists, Liberals and the Quest for Unity, 1884–1939*, Cambridge University Press, 1992.
Bollard, Robert, *In the Shadow of Gallipoli: The Hidden History of Australia in World War 1*, Sydney, New South Publishing, 2013.
Bottome, Phyllis, *Alfred Adler*, New York, Vanguard Press, 1957.
Bridge, Ann, *The Dangerous Islands*, London, Chatto & Windus, 1964.
Brodsky, Isadore, *North Sydney 1788–1962*, Municipal Council of North Sydney, 1963.
Buckley, Ken, Barbara Dale, and Wayne Reynolds, *Doc Evatt: Patriot, Internationalist, Fighter and Scholar*, Melbourne, Longman Cheshire, 1994.
Burgmann, Verity, *Revolutionary Industrial Unionism: The Industrial Workers of the World in Australia*, Cambridge University Press, 1995.
Burke, David, *The Lawn Road Flats: Spies, Writers, and Artists*, Woodbridge, UK, Boydell Press, 2014.
Byrne, Paula, *Mad World: Evelyn Waugh and the Secrets of Brideshead*, New York, Harper Perennial, 2009.
Cable, Leonie, *Cable Clerical Index to Australian Anglican Clergy*, online.
Callaghan, John, *Rajani Palme Dutt: A Study in British Stalinism*, London, Lawrence & Wishart, 1993.
Canfora, Luciano, *Democracy in Europe: A History*, Blackwell Publishing, Oxford, 2006.
Carey, Hilary M., *Believing in Australia, 1851–1900*, Sydney, Allen & Unwin, 1996.
Carpenter, L.P., *G.D.H. Cole: An Intellectual Biography*, Cambridge, Cambridge University Press, 1973.
Castles, F.G., *The Working Class and Welfare: Reflections on the Political Development of the Welfare State in Australia and New Zealand, 1890–1980*, Sydney, Allen & Unwin, 1985.
Ceadel, Martin, *Pacifism in Britain, 1914–1945: The Defining of a Faith*, Oxford, Clarendon Press, 1980.
Cole, G.D.H., *Communism and Social Democracy 1914–1931, Part II*, London, Macmillan, 1958.
Cole, Margaret, *Growing Up into Revolution*, London, Longmans, 1949.
Cole, Margaret, *The Life of G. D. H. Cole*, London, Macmillan, 1971.
Cole, Margaret, *The Story of Fabian Socialism*, London, Heinemann, 1961.
Coleman, Peter, *Australian Civilization: A Symposium*, Melbourne, Cheshire, 1962.
Connell, R.W., *Masculinities*, 2nd edn, Cambridge, Polity Press, 2005.

Crawford, R.M., *'A Bit of a Rebel': The Life and Work of George Arnold Wood*, Sydney, Sydney University Press, 1975.
Crowther, J.G., *Fifty Years with Science*, London, Barrie & Jenkins, 1970.
Cunneen, Christopher, *William John McKell: Boilermaker, Premier, Governor-General*, Sydney, UNSW Press, 2000.
Darroch, Robert, *D.H. Lawrence in Australia*, Melbourne, Macmillan, 1981.
Day, David, *Andrew Fisher: Prime Minister of Australia*, Sydney, Fourth Estate, 2008.
Dixson, Miriam, *Greater than Lenin? Lang and Labor 1916–1922*, Melbourne Politics Monograph, 4, no date.
Dobbyn, D., *A Sense of Time Past and Future: The Building of St Thomas's Anglican Church, North Sydney*, The Church, 1971.
Duncan, Robert and Arthur McIvor (eds), *Militant Workers: Labour and Class Conflict on the Clyde 1900–1950*, Edinburgh, John Donald, 1992.
Ellem, Bradon (ed.), *The Great Labour Movement Split in New South Wales: Inside Stories*, Sydney, Australian Society for the Study of Labour History, 1998.
Evans, Raymond, *The Red Flag Riots: A Study in Intolerance*, St Lucia, Queensland, University of Queensland Press, 1988.
Evatt, H.V., *Australian Labour Leader: The Story of W.A. Holman and the Labour Movement*, Sydney, Angus & Robertson, 1945.
Fagan, Brian, *Grahame Clark: An Intellectual Biography of an Archaeologist*, Boulder, CO, Westview Press, 2001.
Fitzgerald, Ross, *Fred Paterson: The People's Champion*, Brisbane, University of Queensland Press, 1997.
Freeden, Michael, *J.A. Hobson: A Reader*, London, Unwin Hyman, 1988.
Gathercole, Peter, T.H. Irving and Gregory Melleuish (eds), *Childe and Australia: Archaeology. Politics and Ideas*, Brisbane, University of Queensland Press, 1995.
Glendinning, Victoria, *Leonard Woolf: A Life*, London and Sydney, Pocket Books, 2006.
Goldring, Douglas, *The Nineteen Twenties*, London, Nicholson & Watson, 1945.
Graham, Malcolm, *Oxford in the Great War*, Barnsley, UK, Pen and Sword Military, 2014.
Green, Sally, *Prehistorian: A Biography of V. Gordon Childe*, Bradford-on-Avon, UK, Moonraker Press, 1981.
Hauser, Kitty, *Bloody Old Britain: O.G.S. Crawford and the Archaeology of Modern Life*, London, Granta Books, 2008.
Hinton, J., *The First Shop Stewards Movement*, London, Allen & Unwin, 1973.
Hirst, Paul Q. (ed.), *The Pluralist Theory of the State: Selected Writings of G.D.H. Cole, J.N. Figgis and H.J. Laski*, London, Routledge, 1989.
Horne, Julia and Geoffrey Sherington, *Sydney: The Making of a Public University*, Melbourne, The Miegunyah Press, 2012.
Horner, David, *The Spy Catchers: The Official History of ASIO, 1949–1963*, Sydney, Allen & Unwin, 2014.
Irving, Terry, *The Southern Tree of Liberty: The Democratic Movement in New South Wales before 1856*, Sydney, Federation Press, 2006.

Irving, Terry and Rowan Cahill, *Radical Sydney: Places, Portraits and Unruly Episodes*, Sydney, UNSW Press, 2010.
German, Lindsey and John Rees, *A People's History of London*, London, New York, Verso, 2012.
Gordon, W. Terrence, *C.K. Ogden: A Bio-bibliographical Study*, Lanham, MD, The Scarecrow Press, 1990.
Ives, Martyn, *Reform, Revolution and Direct Action amongst British Miners*, Leiden, Brill, 2016.
Jack, R. Ian, *The Andrew's Book: St Andrew's College within the University of Sydney*, St Andrew's College, 1989.
Judd, Stephen and Kenneth Cable, *Sydney Anglicans: A History of the Diocese*, Sydney, Anglican Information Office, 2000.
Keane, John, *The Life and Death of Democracy*, New York and London, W.W. Norton & Co., 2009.
Kendall, Walter, *The Revolutionary Movement in Britain, 1900–21*, London, Weidenfeld & Nicolson, 1969.
Lambirth, Andrew, Annette Armstrong, and Jonathan Gibbs, *John Armstrong: The Paintings*, London, Philip Wilson Publishers, 2009.
Lee, Hermione, *Virginia Woolf*, Vintage Books, 1999.
Lindsay, Jack, *Life Rarely Tells: An Autobiography in Three Volumes*, Ringwood, Vic., Penguin Books, 1982.
Macintyre, Stuart, *A Proletarian Science: Marxism in Britain 1917–1933*, London, Lawrence and Wishart, 1980.
Macintyre, Stuart, *The Oxford History of Australia, Volume 4, 1901–1942: The Succeeding Age*, Melbourne, Oxford University Press, 1986.
Mackie, Robert (ed.), *Jack Lindsay: The Thirties and Forties*, University of London Institute of Commonwealth Studies, Australian Studies Centre, Occasional Seminar Paper No. 4, November 1984.
Makin-Waite, Mike, *Communism and Democracy: History, Debates and Potentials*, London, Lawrence & Wishart, 2017.
Manin, Bernard, *The Principles of Representative Government*, Cambridge, Cambridge University Press, 1997.
Manne, Robert, *The Petrov Affair: Politics and Espionage*, Sydney, Pergamon Press, 1987.
Marcus, Jane, *Virginia Woolf and the Languages of Patriarchy*, Indiana University Press, 1987.
Markey, Raymond, *In Case of Oppression: The Life and Times of the Labor Council of New South Wales*, Sydney, Pluto Press, 1994.
McGuire, Randall H., *A Marxist Archaeology*, Orlando, Florida, Academic Press, 1992.
McKnight, David, *Australian Spies and their Secrets*, Sydney, Allen & Unwin, 1994.
Meynell, Francis, *My Lives*, London, The Bodley Head, 1971.
Michels, R., *Political Parties: A Sociological Study of the Oligarchical Tendencies of Modern Democracy*, New York, Hearst, 1915.

More, Bill, *Sheffield Shop Stewards 1916–1918*, Pamphlet 18, Communist Party History Group, London, 1960.
Morgan, Kevin, *Against Fascism and War: Ruptures and Continuities in British Communist Politics, 1935–1941*, Manchester University Press, 1989.
Morgan, Kevin, *Bolshevism, Syndicalism and the General Strike: The Lost Internationalist World of A.A. Purcell*, London, Lawrence & Wishart, 2013.
Morgan, Kevin, *Harry Pollitt*, Manchester, Manchester University Press, 1993.
Morgan, Kevin, *Labour Legends and Russian Gold*, London, Lawrence & Wishart, 2006.
Morgan, Kevin, *The Webbs and Soviet Communism*, London, Lawrence & Wishart, 2006.
Munro, Craig, *Inky Stephensen: Wild Man of Letters*, Melbourne, Melbourne University Press, 1984.
O'Lincoln, Tom, *Into the Mainstream: The Decline of Australian Communism*, Melbourne, Red Rag Publications, 2009 (2nd edn).
O'Meagher, Bruce (ed.), *The Socialist Objective: Labor and Socialism*, Sydney, Hale & Iremonger, 1983.
Osborne, John W., *John Cartwright*, Cambridge University Press, 1972.
Paananen, Victor N., *British Marxist Criticism*, London, Garland, 1999.
Patterson, Thomas C., *Marx's Ghost: Conversations with Archaeologists*, Oxford, New York, Berg, 2003.
Pimlott, Ben, *Labour and the Left in the 1930s*, Cambridge University Press, 1977.
Postgate, John and Mary, *A Stomach for Dissent: Life of Raymond Postgate 1896–1971*, Keele, UK, Keele University Press, 1994.
Purcell, Hugh, *The Last English Revolutionary: Tom Wintringham 1898–1949*, Stroud, Sutton Publishing, 2004.
Ree, Jonathan, *Proletarian Philosophers: Problems in Socialist Culture in Britain, 1900–1949*, Oxford, Clarendon Press, 1984.
Richards, Jeffrey, *Happy Days: The Public Schools in English Fiction*, London, Manchester University Press, 1988.
Roe, Michael, *Nine Australian Progressives: Vitalism in Bourgeois Social Thought, 1890–1960*, Brisbane, University of Queensland Press, 1984.
Rosenberg, Chanie, *1919: Britain on the Brink of Revolution*, London, Bookmarks, 1995.
Rothstein, Andrew, *Soldiers' Strikes of 1919*, London, Palgrave Macmillan, 1980.
Rowbotham, Sheila, *Edward Carpenter: A Life of Liberty and Love*, London, Verso, 2008.
Rowley, Hazel, *Christina Stead: A Biography*, Melbourne, Minerva, 1993.
Rowse, Tim, *Australian Liberalism and National Character*, Malmsbury, Vic., Kibble Books, 1978.
Scott, Ernest R., *Australia during the War: Vol. XI of the Official History of Australia in the War of 1914–18*, Sydney, Angus & Robertson, 1936.
Stead, Christina, *For Love Alone*, New York, Harcourt Brace, 1944.
Stead, Christina, *The Seven Poor Men of Sydney*, London, Peter Davies, 1934.

Stone, Dan, *Responses to Nazism in Britain, 1933–39: Before War and Holocaust*, Springer, 2003.
Svensen, Stuart, *Industrial War: The Great Strikes 1890–1894*, Wollongong, NSW, Ram Press, c. 1995.
Swartz, Marvin, *The Union of Democratic Control in British politics during the First World War*, Oxford, Clarendon Press, 1971.
Taksa, Lucy, *Workers' Education [sic] Association and the Pursuit of National Efficiency in Australia between 1913 and 1923*, School of Industrial Relations and Organisational Behaviour, University of New South Wales, Sydney, Working Paper 111, March 1997.
Tennant, Kylie, *Evatt: Politics and Justice*, Sydney, Angus & Robertson, 1970.
Thomas, Martin, *The Artificial Horizon: Imagining the Blue Mountains*, Melbourne, Melbourne University Press, 2003.
Thompson, Edward, *The Heavy Dancers*, London, Merlin Press, 1985.
Thompson, Noel, *The People's Science: Popular Political Economy of Exploitation and Crisis, 1816–1834*, Cambridge, Cambridge University Press, 2002.
Trigger, Bruce G., *Gordon Childe: Revolutions in Archaeology*, London, Thames & Hudson, 1980.
Thwaites, Michael, *Truth Will Out: ASIO and the Petrovs*, Sydney, Collins, 1980.
Turner, Ian, *Industrial Labour and Politics: The Dynamics of the Labour Movement in Eastern Australia 1900–1921*, Canberra, ANU Press, 1965.
Ian Turner, *Sydney's Burning*, London and Melbourne, Heinemann, 1967.
Turney, Clifford, Ursula Bygott and Peter Chippendale, *Australia's First: A History of the University of Sydney, Volume 1, 1850–1939*, Sydney, University of Sydney, 1991.
Tsuzuki C., *Tom Mann 1856–1941: The Challenges of Labour*, Oxford, Clarendon Press, 1991.
Wachman, Gay, *Lesbian Empire: Radical Crosswriting in the Twenties*, Rutgers University Press, 2001.
Walker, David, *Dream and Disillusion: A Search for Australian Cultural Identity*, Canberra, ANU Press, 1976.
Walker, Jeannie (convenor), *What God Has Done: 150 Years at St Thomas's Anglican Church, North Sydney*, The Church, 1996.
Walter, James, *The Ministers' Minders: Personal Advisers in National Government*, Melbourne, Oxford University Press, 1986.
Ward, Russell, *A Radical Life: The Autobiography of Russell Ward*, Melbourne, MacMillan, 1988.
Ward, Russell, *The Australian Legend*, Melbourne, Oxford University Press, 1958.
Wason, C.R., *Rebel Scotland*, Hicksville, Exposition Press, 1976.
Watson, Don, *Brian Fitzpatrick: A Radical Life*, Sydney, Hale & Iremonger, 1979.
Waugh, Alexander, *Fathers and Sons: The Autobiography of a Family*, London and New York, Penguin Random House, 2008.
Waugh, Colin, *'Plebs': The Lost Legacy of Independent Working Class Education*, Wembley, UK, Post16 Educator, 2009.

Webb, Simon, *1919: Britain's Year of Revolution*, Barnsley, UK, Pen and Sword, 2016.
Werskey, Gary, *The Visible College: A Collective Biography of British Scientists and Socialists of the 1930s*, London, Free Association Books, 1988.
Whitehead, Anne, *Paradise Mislaid: In Search of the Australian Tribe of Paraguay*, Brisbane, University of Queensland Press, 1997.
Whitmarsh, Tim, *Battling the Gods: Atheism in the Ancient World*, London, Faber & Faber, 2016.
Wilkins, Lola (curator and editor), *Stella Bowen: Art, Love and War*, Canberra, Australian War Memorial, 2002.
Wilson, Colin, *The Outsider*, London, Gollancz, 1956.
Winslow, Cal (ed.), *E.P. Thompson and the Making of the New Left*, New York, Monthly Review Press, 2014.
Wright, A.W., *G.D.H. Cole and Socialist Democracy*, Oxford, Clarendon Press, 1979.
Wussow, Helen, *The Nightmare of History: The Fictions of Virginia Woolf and D.H. Lawrence*, Lehigh University Press, 1988.
Zweig, F., *The British Worker*, London, Penguin Books, 1952.

Articles, chapters and websites

Allen, Jim, 'Aspects of Vere Gordon Childe', *Labour History*, no. 12, May 1967.
'Archaeologists Fingered by Orwell', *British Archaeology*, issue 73, November 2003.
Archer, Robin, 'Labour and Liberty: The Origins of the Conscription Referendum', in Robin Archer, Joy Damousi, Murray Goot and Sean Scalmer (eds), *The Conscription Conflict and the Great War*, Clayton, Vic., Monash University Publishing, 2016.
Armstrong, Mick, 'Disturbing the Peace: Riots and the Working Class', *Marxist Left Review*, 4, Winter 2012.
Armstrong, P.F., 'The Long Search for the Working Class: Socialism and the Education of Adults 1850–1930', in T. Lovett, *Radical Approaches to Adult Education: A Reader*, London and New York, Routledge, 1988.
Arnold B., '"Arierdämmerung": Race and Archaeology in Nazi Germany', *World Archaeology*, vol. 38, issue 1, Race, Racism and Archaeology, 2006.
Barton, Huw, '*In Memoriam* V. Gordon Childe', *Antiquity*, vol. 74, issue 286, December 2000.
Béliard, Yann, 'Introduction: Revisiting the Great Labour Unrest', *Labour History Review*, vol. 79, no. 1, April 2014.
Bernie, K.N.J., 'The Premiers' Conferences: An Historical Sketch from the Beginnings to 1930', *Australian Journal of Public Administration*, vol. 6, issue 8, December 1947.
Bongiorno, Frank and David A. Roberts (eds), special issue on 'Russel Ward: Reflections on a Legend', *Journal of Colonial Australian History*, vol. 10, no. 2, 2008.

Bongiorno, Frank, 'Why did Australians Get So Emotional over Conscription during World War I?', unpublished paper, National Archives of Australia, 4 November 2016.

Brodney, M., 'Militant Propagandists of the Labor Movement', *Labour History*, 5, November 1963.

Brothwell, Don, 'Childe, His Student and Archaeological Science: An Epilogue', *European Journal of Archaeology*, vol. 12, nos 1–3, April–December 2009.

Brown, Nicholas, 'Enacting the International: R.G. Watt and the League of Nations Union', in Desley Deacon, Penny Russell and Angela Woollacott (eds), *Transnational Lives: Australian Lives in the World*, Canberra, ANU E Press, 2008.

Blunden, Andy, 'On Political Representation', www.ethicalpolitics.org/ablunden/pdfs/On%20Political%20Representation.pdf.

Champion, Timothy, 'Childe and Oxford', *European Journal of Archaeology*, vol. 12, nos 1–3, April 2009.

Coates, Ken, 'Introduction' to *What Happened at Leeds*, Nottingham, The Russell Press, 1974.

Coates, R., 'Job Control in Theory and Practice, by "Turbot Street"', *Australian Left Review*, no. 5, May 1972.

Cohn, Nora, 'Welles Coates: Architect and Designer' at www.wellscoates.org/.

Cole, Margaret, 'Guild Socialism and the Labour Research Department', in Asa Briggs and John Saville (eds), *Essays in Labour History – 1886–1923*, London, Macmillan, 1971.

Collini, Stefan, 'Hobhouse, Bosanquet and the State: Philosophical Idealism and Political Argument in England 1880–1918', *Past and Present*, no. 72, 1976.

Connell, Raewyn, 'Antipodes: Australian Sociology's Struggles with Place, Memory and Neoliberalism', in Michael Burawoy, Mau-kuei and Michelle Fei-yu Hsieh (eds), *Facing an Unequal World: Challenges for a Global Sociology, Volume Two, Asia*, Taipei, Academia Sinica, 2010.

Daniel, Glyn, 'Professor Sean O Riordain: An Appreciation', *University Review*, vol. 2, no. 1, 1960.

Darling, Elizabeth, 'Finella, Mansfield Forbes, Raymond McGrath, and Modernist Architecture in Britain', *Journal of British Studies*, issue 50, January 2011.

Davis, Richard, 'The British Peace Movement in the Inter-War Years', *French Journal of British Studies*, vol. XXII, no. 3, 2017.

Dean, Jodi, 'Michels: The Rusty Iron law of Oligarchy', https://jdeanicite.typepad.com/i_cite/2013/01/michels-the-rusty-iron-law-of-oligarchy.html.

Denman, James and Paul McDonald, 'Unemployment Statistics from 1881 to the Present Day', *Labour Market Trends*, vol. 104, nos 15–18, 1996.

Derricourt, Robin, 'The Making of a Radical Archaeologist: The Early Years of Vere Gordon Childe', *Australian Archaeology*, vol. 79, December 2014.

Diaz-Andreu, Margarita, 'Childe and the International Congresses of Archaeology', *European Journal of Archaeology*, vol. 12, nos. 1–3, 2009.

Duncan, Robert and Arthu McIvor (eds), *Militant Workers: Labour and Class Conflict on the Clyde 1900–1950*, Edinburgh, John Donald, 1992.

Estèves, Olivier, 'Bertrand Russell: The Utilitarian Pacifist', *Revue Française de Civilisation Britannique* [Online], XX-1, 2015.
Evans, Raymond, '"Social Passion": Vere Gordon Childe in Queensland, 1918–19', in Peter Gathercole, T.H. Irving and Gregory Melleuish (eds), *Childe and Australia: Archaeology, Politics and Ideas*, University of Queensland Press, St Lucia, 1995.
Faulkner, Neil, 'Gordon Childe and Marxist Archaeology', *International Socialism*, issue 116, 2007, http://isj.org.uk/gordon-childe-and-marxist-archaeology/#116faulkner_41.
Fitzpatrick, Brian, 'In Memoriam: V. Gordon Childe', *Meanjin*, vol. 16, December 1957.
Fitzpatrick, Brian, 'In Memoriam: V. Gordon Childe', *Overland*, no. 11, January 1958.
Fleming, Andrew, 'The Myth of the Mother-Goddess', *World Archaeology*, vol. 1, no. 2, 1969.
Forsyth, Hannah, 'Knowledge, Democracy and the Russell Ward Case', unpublished paper, 2011.
Foster, Alan J., 'O'Malley, Sir Owen St Clair (1887–1974)', *Oxford Dictionary of National Biography* online edition accessed 21 June 2011.
Francis, Pat, 'The Labour Publishing Company 1920–9', *History Workshop Journal*, vol. 18, no. 1, 1984.
Gathercole, Peter and Terry Irving, 'A Childe Bibliography: A Hand-list of the Works of Vere Gordon Childe', *European Journal of Archaeology*, vol. 12, nos. 1–3, 2009.
Gathercole, Peter, 'Allen Lane's Archaeological Bestseller', *The Penguin Collector*, no. 46, July 1996.
Gathercole, Peter, 'Childe among the Penguins', *Australian Archaeology*, no. 50, June 2000.
Gathercole, Peter, 'Childe in History', *Bulletin of the Institute of Archaeology, London*, no. 31, 1994.
Gathercole, Peter, 'Childe, Marxism, and Knowledge', *European Journal of Archaeology*, vol. 12, nos 1–3, April–December 2009.
Gathercole, Peter, 'Childe's Revolutions', in Colin Renfrew and Paul Bahn (eds), *Archaeology – The Key Concepts*, London, Routledge, 2004.
Gathercole, Peter, 'Childe the "Outsider"', *Royal Anthropological Institute News*, 17, 1976.
Gathercole, Peter, '"Patterns in Prehistory": An Examination of the Later Thinking of Vere Gordon Childe', *World Archaeology*, vol. 3, no. 2, 1971.
Gathercole, Peter, 'The Relationship between Vere Gordon Childe's Political and Academic Thought', in Peter Gathercole, T.H. Irving and Greg Melleuish (eds), *Childe and Australia: Archaeology, Politics and Ideas*, Brisbane, University of Queensland Press, 1995.
Goldman, Lawrence, 'Intellectuals and the English Working Class, 1870–1945: The Case of Adult Education', *History of Education*, vol. 29, no. 4, 2000.

Goot, Murray, 'Labor, Government Business Enterprises, and Competition Policy', *Labour History*, no. 98, May 2010.
Graham, Angus, 'In Piam Veterum Memoriam', in A.S. Bell (ed.), *The Scottish Antiquarian Tradition*, Edinburgh, 1981.
Gregory, Mark, 'Union Songs', http://unionsong.com/u025.html.
Green, Sally, 'Introduction' in V.G. Childe, *Man Makes Himself*, illustrated edition, Bradford-on-Avon, Wiltshire, Moonraker Press, 1981.
Greene, Kevin, 'V. Gordon Childe and the Vocabulary of Revolutionary Change', *Antiquity*, vol. 73, no. 279, March 1999.
Griffiths, Billy, '"The Dawn" of Australian Archaeology: John Mulvaney at Fromm's Landing', *Journal of Pacific Archaeology*, vol. 8, no. 1, 2017.
Griffiths, Phil, 'Labor's Tortured Path to Protectionism', in Robert Hood and Ray Markey (eds), *Labour and Community*, Australian Society for the Study of Labour History, Illawarra Branch, Wollongong, 1999.
Hagan, Jim, 'Storey, John' in David Clune and Ken Turner (eds), *The Premiers of New South Wales 1856–2005, Volume 2, 1901–2005*, Sydney, The Federation Press, 2006.
Haglund, Laila, 'Memories of Gordon Childe', *Australian Archaeology*, no. 30, June 1990.
Hanak, H., 'The Union of Democratic Control during the First World War', *Historical Research*, vol. 36, issue 94, November 1963.
Härke, Heinrich, 'Archaeology and Nazism: A Warning from Prehistory', in V. Mordvintseva, H. Härke and T. Shevchenko (eds), *Archaeological and Linguistic Research: Materials of the Humboldt Conference (Simferopol – Yalta, 20–23 September 2012)*, Kiev, Stilos, 2014.
Harris, David R., '"A new professor of a somewhat obscure subject": V. Gordon Childe at the London Institute of Archaeology, 1946–1956', *European Journal of Archaeology*, vol. 12, nos 1–3, 2009.
Hauser, Ward entry on Alfred Adler in *Encyclopedia of Homosexuality*, Vol. 1, edited by Wayne R. Dynes, Routledge, 1990.
Hill, Christopher, R.H. Hilton and E.J. Hobsbawm, 'Past and Present: Origins and Early Years', *Past and Present*, no. 100, August 1983.
Hirsch, Pam, 'Apostle of Freedom: Alfred Adler and his British disciples', *History of Education*, vol. 34, no. 5, 2005.
Hogan, Michael, 'Template for a Labor Faction: The Industrial Section and the Industrial Vigilance Council of the NSW Labor Party, 1916–19', *Labour History*, no. 96, May 2009.
Hogan, Michael, '1922', in Michael Hogan and David Clune (eds), *The People's Choice: Electoral Politics in 20th Century New South Wales, Volume One*, Sydney, Parliament of New South Wales and University of Sydney, 2001.
Horton, Jim, 'The First Shop Stewards' Movement', *The Socialist*, 16 November 2011.
Imperial War Museum, Conscientious Objectors' Register, https://livesofthefirstworldwar.org.

Irving, Terry and Sean Scalmer, 'Labour Intellectuals in Australia: Modes, Traditions, Generations, Transformations', *International Review of Social History*, vol. 50, part 1, April 2005.

Irving, T.H., 'New Light on *How Labour Governs*: Re-discovered Political Writings by V. Gordon Childe', *Politics*, vol. 23, no 1, May 1988.

Irving, T.H., 'On the Work of Labour Governments: Vere Gordon Childe's Plans for Volume 2 of *How Labour Governs*', in Peter Gathercole, T.H. Irving and Gregory Melleuish (eds), *Childe and Australia: Archaeology, Politics and Ideas*, Brisbane, University of Queensland Press, 1995.

Irving, Terry, 'Rebellious Workers: Insubordination and Democratic Mobilisation in Australia in the 1910s', in Peter Sheldon, Sarah Gregson, Russell Lansbury and Karin Sanders (eds), *The Regulation and Management of Workplace Health and Safety: Historical and Emerging Trends*, London, Routledge, 2020.

Irving, Terry, 'Rediscovering Radical History', http://radicalsydney.blogspot.com.au/p/rediscovering-radical-history-essay-by.html.

Irving, Terry, 'Socialism, Working-class Mobilisation and the Origins of the Labor Party', in Bruce O'Meagher (ed.), *The Socialist Objective: Labor and Socialism*, Sydney, Hale & Iremonger, 1983.

Jackson, Peter, 'The Russian Revolution and the British Working Class', *International Socialism*, issue 156, October 2017, online.

Jensen, H.I., 'The Darwin Rebellion', *Labour History*, no. 11, November 1966.

Johnstone, Monty, 'The CPGB, the Comintern, and the War, 1939–1941: Filling in the Blank Spots', *Science and Society*, vol. 61, no. 1, Spring 1997.

Jordens, Ann-Mari, 'Anti-war Organisations in a Society at War, 1914–18', *Journal of Australian Studies*, vol. 14, no. 26, 2009.

Klejn, Leo S., 'Childe and Soviet Archaeology: A Romance', in David R. Harris (ed.), *The Archaeology of V. Gordon Childe: Contemporary Perspectives*, Melbourne University Press, 1994.

Kuhn, Rick, 'Lenin on the A.L.P.: The Career of 600 Words', *Australian Journal of Politics and History*, vol. 35, no. 1, April 1989.

Laurent, John, 'Tom Mann, R. S. Ross and *Evolutionary Socialism* in Broken Hill, 1902–1912: Alternative Social Darwinism in the Australian Labour Movement', *Labour History*, no. 51, 1986.

László, Attila, 'The Young Gordon Childe and Transylvanian Archaeology: The Archaeological Correspondence between Childe and Ferenc László', *European Journal of Archaeology*, vol. 12, nos 1–3, April–December 2009.

Lindsay, Jack, 'Foreword' in Sally Green, *Prehistorian*, Bradford-on-Avon, Wiltshire, Moonraker Press, 1981.

London Socialist Historians Group, 'The Liverpool General Transport Strike of 1911', http://londonsocialisthistorians.blogspot.com/2011/10/liverpool-general-transport-strike-of.html.

Low, John, 'New Light on the Death of Gordon Childe', *Hummer*, no. 8, February–March 1985.

Lygo, Emily, 'Promoting Soviet Culture in Britain: The History of the Society for Cultural Relations between the Peoples of the British Commonwealth and the USSR, 1924–45', *Modern Language Review*, vol. 108, no. 2, April 2013.

Mangan, J.A., 'Conformity Confronted and Orthodoxy Outraged: *The Loom of Youth*: Succès de Scandale in Search of a Wider Reality', *The International Journal of the History of Sport*, vol. 29, issue 12, 2012.

Martin, Nick, 'Bucking the Machine: Clarrie Martin and the NSW Socialisation Units, 1929–35', *Labour History*, no. 93, November 2007.

Matthews, Frank, 'The Ladder of Becoming: A.R. Orage, A.J. Penty and the Origins of Guild Socialism in England', in David E. Martin and David Rubinstein (eds), *Ideology and the Labour Movement: Essays Presented to John Saville*, London, Croom Helm, 1979.

McQueen, Humphrey, 'Historians: V. Gordon Childe', www.surplusvalue.org.au/McQueen/hist_ns/historian_v_gordon.htm.

Miliband, Ralph, 'Marx and the State', in R. Miliband and J. Saville (eds), *The Socialist Register 1965*, London, The Merlin Press 1965.

Moore, Gregory, 'The Super-Hun and the Super-State: Allied Propaganda and German Philosophy during the First World War', *German Life and Letters*, vol. 554, no. 4, October 2001.

Morison, Patricia, 'J.T. Wilson and the Fraternity of Duckmaloi', *Clio Medica*, vol. 42, 1997.

Moshenska, Gabriel and Tim Schadla-Hall, 'Mortimer Wheeler's Theatre of the Past', *Public Archaeology*, vol. 10, no. 1, 2011.

Mulholland, Marc, 'How to Make a Revolution. The Historical and Political Writings of Raymond Postgate', unpublished paper, www.academia.edu/30067214/How_to_Make_a_Revolution_The_Historical_and_Political_Writings_of_Raymond_Postgate_Postgate.

Mulholland, Marc, '"Its Patrimony, its Unique Wealth!" Labour-Power, Working-Class Consciousness and Crises: An Outline Consideration', https://www.academia.edu/356751/Its_Patrimony_its_Unique_Wealth_Labour-Power_Working_Class_Consciousness_and_Crises_An_Outline_Consideration.

Mulvaney, John, 'From "The Dawn" to Sunset: Gordon Childe in Melbourne, 1957', *Australian Archaeology*, no. 30, June 1990.

North, Marilla, 'Tinker, Tailor, Soldier, Sailor … Who Was Norman Randolph Freehill?', *Overland*, issue 161, Summer 2000.

Patzia, Michael, 'Zenophanes (c.570–478 BCE)', *Internet Encyclopedia of Philosophy*, http://www.iep.utm.edu/xenoph/ accessed 1 April 2016.

Peace, W.J., 'Vere Gordon Childe and the Cold War', in Peter Gathercole, T.H. Irving and Gregory Melleuish (eds), *Childe and Australia: Archaeology. Politics and Ideas*, Brisbane, University of Queensland Press, 1995.

Penny, Keith, 'The Origins of the Prime Minister's Department, 1901–1911', *Australian Journal of Public Administration*, vol. XV, issue 3, September 1956.

Ralston, Ian, 'Gordon Childe and Scottish Archaeology', *European Journal of Archaeology*, vol. 121, nos. 1–3, 2009.

'Red Clydeside', *Wikipedia*, https://en.wikipedia.org/wiki/Red_Clydeside.
Renfrew, Colin, 'Concluding Remarks: Childe and the Study of Culture Process', in David R. Harris (ed.), *The Archaeology of V. Gordon Childe: Contemporary Perspectives*, Melbourne, Melbourne University Press, 1994.
Rich, Paul, 'The Long Victorian Sunset: Anthropology, Eugenics and Race in Britain, c 1900–48', *Patterns of Prejudice*, vol. 18, issue 3, 1984.
Richter, Jochen, 'Pantheon of Brains: The Moscow Brain Research Institute 1925–1936', *Journal of the History of the Neurosciences*, vol. 16, nos, 1–2, 2007.
Rickwood, Peter, 'Forensic History: Professor Childe's Death near Govett's Leap – Revisited', *Blue Mountains History Journal*, issue 3, September 2012.
Saunders, Kay, 'Masters and Servants: The Queensland Sugar Workers Strike, 1911', in Ann Curthoys and Andrew Markus (eds), *Who Are Our Enemies? Racism and the Working Class in Australia*, Canberra, Hale & Iremonger, 1976.
Scalmer, Sean, 'Being Practical in Early and Contemporary Labor Politics: A Labourist Critique', *Australian Journal of Politics and History*, vol. 43, no. 3, Nov. 1997.
Smith, Kylie M., 'Subjectivity, Hegemony, and the Subaltern in Sydney, 1870–1900', *Rethinking Marxism*, vol. 19, no. 2, April 2007.
Starr, Joseph R., 'The Summer Schools and Other Educational Activities of British Socialist Groups', *The American Political Science Review*, vol. 30, no. 5, October 1936.
Stevenson, Alice, '"Yours (unusually) cheerfully, Gordon": Vere Gordon Childe's letters to R.B.K. Stevenson', *Antiquity*, vol. 85, 2011.
Stevenson, Graham, *Encyclopedia of Communist Biographies*, https://grahamstevenson.me.uk/category/commiepedia/.
Thompson, E.P., 'An Open Letter to Leszek Kolakowski', *Socialist Register*, London, Merlin Press, 1973.
Toporowski, Jan, '*Imperialism*, with Special Reference to J.A. Hobson's Influence on Lenin', *Bulletin of the Marx Memorial Library*, 133, Spring 2001.
Tregenza, Ian, 'Are We All Socialists Now? New Liberalism, State Socialism, and the Australian Settlement', *Labour History*, no. 102, May 2012.
Trigger, Bruce, 'Marxism and Archaeology', in Sydney Mintz et al. (eds), *On Marxian Perspectives in Anthropology*, Malibu, Undena Publications, 1984.
Tringham, Ruth V., 'Gordon Childe after 25 Years: His Relevance for the Archaeology of the Eighties', *Journal of Field Archaeology*, vol. 10, no. 1, Spring 1983.
Ward, Russell, 'Death of Professor V.G. Childe', *Outlook*, vol. 1, no. 4, Nov–Dec 1957.
White, Stephen, 'Soviets in Britain: The Leeds Convention of 1917', *International Review of Social History*, vol. 19, no. 2, August 1974.
Willis, K., 'The Introduction and Critical Reception of Marxist Thought in Britain, 1850–1900', *The Historical Journal*, vol. 20, no. 2, June 1977.
Witchard, Anne, 'Sink Street: The Sapphic World of Pre-Chinatown Soho', in Simon Avery and Katherine M. Graham (eds), *Sex, Time and Place: Queer History of London, c.1850 to the Present*, Bloomsbury Publishing, 2016.

Wooster, W.A., 'Professor V. Gordon Childe. 1892–1957', *Association of Scientific Workers' Journal*, vol. 4, no. 1, January 1958.

Wyckoff, Susan, 'Ruth Nanda Anshen', in 'Jewish Women's Archive', https://jwa.org/encyclopedia/Anshen-Ruth-Nanda.

Theses

Bourke, Helen, 'Worker Education and Social Inquiry in Australia 1913–1929', PhD Thesis, University of Adelaide, 1981.

INDEX

1917 Club, 207–8, 247, 319

Abercromby, Lord, 271
Absolutists, 58, 60, 68
Adler, Alfred, 352, 353–4
Agent-General (of NSW), 180, 182, 209
Alert, The, 118
Allen, Clifford, 55
Allen, Jim, 235
Anarchist/anarchism, 108, 109, 119, 124, 149
Anarcho-syndicalism, 98, 237
And Then You Came, xxiii
Anderson, Sir Francis M., 44, 54, 92, 95–6
Anshen, Ruth Nanda, 339–40, 342
Anstey, Frank, 137
Anthropocene, 343
Anti-communism, x
Anti-conscription, 33, 66
Anti-politicalism, 29, 30, 31
Anti-totalitarian, 298
Anti-war movement, 56
Antiquity, 281, 314, 329
Arbitration, 255, 263
Armistice, 88, 96
Armstrong, Pro-Provost Edward, 69, 70, 79
Armstrong, John, 208
Arnot, Robin Page, 61, 181, 198, 222, 274
Ashbee, Paul, 355
Association of Scientific Workers, 276, 280, 288, 290, 303, 324
Atheism/Atheist, 58
Athenaeum Club, 338
Atkinson, Meredith, 134–5, 136, 138

Australasian Book Society, 363, 367
Australia First, 360–1
Australian Clerical Association, 288
Australian High Commissioner (London), 66, 85, 92
Australian Labour Federation, 122
Australian Legend, The, 36
Australian Military Intelligence, 85, 92
Australian Peace Alliance, 89, 91, 97
Australian Security Intelligence Organisation (ASIO), xiii, xix, xx, xxi, xxii, xxiv, 360, 372
Australian Socialist Party, 260
Australian Union of Democratic Control, 89, 92
Australian Worker (Sydney), 34, 86, 92, 104, 105
Australian Workers' Union, 36, 139, 171, 173, 175, 193, 222–3, 234

Bakunin, Mikhail, 119
Barff, Henry Ebenezer, 86, 92, 94
Barker, Ernest, 53
Barraclough, Geoffrey, 335
Bauhaus, The, 319
Bax, Belfort, 37
Baxter, Philip, xvii
BBC, 347
Bellamy, Edward, 37, 116
Bernal, J.D., 289–90, 303, 305, 324
Bernstein, Eduard, 264
Bersu, Gerhard, 280
Bevin, Ernest, 275
Black, George, 245
Blackheath, xiii
Blelloch, David, 58, 59, 225
Bloomsbury House Club, 206, 225
Blue Mountains, xiii, 11, 15, 371

Boer War, 100
Bollard, Robert, 8
Bolshevik/Bolshevism, 98, 154, 175, see also Russian Revolution (November 1917)
Boote, Henry, 84, 86, 137, 172, 193–4
Boss, George, 185, 360
Bourgeois democracy, 258
Bourgeois knowledge, 133
Bowen, Stella, 49
Bowling, Peter, 19–20, 30–1
Brailsford, H.N., 222
Brereton, John Le Gay, xiv, 83, 85, 95, 116, 117, 120, 121–2, 126, 138, 139, 156, 193, 251, 353
Bridal Veil Falls, xiii
Bridge, Ann, xxiii
Brisbane, 115, 120
British Association for the Advancement of Science, 280
British Communist Party – *see* Communist Party of Great Britain
British intelligence service - *see* MI5
British Socialist Party, 51, 103
British-Soviet Friendship Society, 299
Brockway, Fenner, 55
Broken Hill, 191, 366, 372
Broken Hill Proprietary Company, 191, 192, 277
Brookfield, Percy, 91, 113, 185
Brothwell, Don, 349, 355
Bryce, James, 237, 245
Bulgarian-British Friendship Society, 331
Bulletin, The, xii, 186, 360
Bureaucracy, 154, 157
Burgmann, Verity, 162
Burns, Emile, 312
Butler, Cuthbert, 169
Byrne, Reg, 168, 171, 174

Cairns, Jim, xix
Callaghan, John, 60
Cambridge Anti-War Group, 276, 289

Cambridge Journal, The, 329, 340
Campbell, Arthur Lang, 184
Canberra University College, 366
Carpenter, Edward, 205
Cartwright Gardens, 205
Cartwright, John, 205–6
Carruthers, Sir Joseph, 213
Catts, James H., 93
Caucus, 232–3
Caudwell, Christopher, 330
Central Labour College (London), 95, 139
Chamberlain, Neville, 295, 297
Champion, Timothy, 57, 224
Chartism/ist, 206
Chaundy, Theodore, 55
Childe, Alice, 9, 11, 224, 299–300, 308, 367
Childe, Ethel, 9, 11, 212, 367
Childe, Harriet, 9, 12
Childe, Lawrence, 8, 9
Childe, Marion ('May'), 9
Childe, Mary, 8, 367
Childe, Rev. Stephen H., 4, 8, 9–11, 212
Childe, Vere Gordon
  Alcohol, 117, 349, 350, 369
  The Aryans: A Study of Indo-European Origins, 228
  'Arbitration and Socialism', 165–7
  Cars, 271
  Childhood, 8
  Clubs, 42, 43, 271, 277, 338
  Cremation, 373
  The Dawn of European Civilization, 247–252
  Death, xi, xiii, xiv, xxi, 365, 368, 369–70, 371
  Debating, 42–43
  Dress, 272, 346, 361
  'A Fabian Judged by History', 227
  History, 301, 306, 322, 323, 325, 328, 329, 330, 335, 349
  Homosexuality, *see* Sexuality

INDEX

How Labour Governs, xii, xv, 3, 18, 23, 49, 85, 116, 130, 137, 158, 173, 205, 222, 223, 229–250, 260, 355
Inferiority complex, 351, 353, 354
'The Irrepressible Class struggle', 160, 255
'Is Prehistory Practical?', 281
'A Labour Premier Meets his Masters', 227–8, 247
Man Makes Himself, 279, 283, 300, 301, 302–7, 348
Memorial, 373
Mental health, 351, 352–3, 365
'The New Unionism and State Socialism', 163–5
'On the date and origins of Minyan ware', 68
Pacifism, 47
'The Past, the Present, and the Future', 335–6
Personal relationships, 50, 65–6, 349–50
Physical health, 361, 371
'Political Action and the Newer Unionism', 165–6
'Prehistory and Marxism', 329
The Prehistory of European Society, 332, 343, 357, 367
Progress and Archaeology, xii, 301, 309
Publishing statistics, ix
'Rational Order in History', 301, 316, 326, 330, 348
Religion, 12–4, 373, 377
'Retrospect', 235, 307, 311
Scotland Before the Scots, 301, 330
Sexuality, 126, 354–5
'The Significance of Soviet Archaeology', 336
Social Worlds of Knowledge, 44, 330
Society and Knowledge, 44, 322, 339, 341–2, 373
'Some Questions for a Politician', 169–70
Student career, 15, 43–4, 45, 57, 67

The Story of Tools, 284, 301, 309, 325
Sugar coating / sugaring, 330, 331, 332, 378
Suicidal thoughts, 296, 298, 344, 358, 365–6, 368, 371
Typewriter, 369
'Valediction', 368
Voice, 348
Walking, 14, 15, 124, 220, 367
'War and Culture', 292
'War for Democracy', 294
What Happened in History, 291, 301, 307–9, 320, 321
'When Labour Ruled – in Australia, by an ex-ruler', 230, 255, 262–266
White-anting, 305, 308
China, 331, 372
Chorley, Robert, 48, 55, 205, 206, 207, 225, 226
Christian Social Union, 12, 41
Christian socialism/ists, 39, 41, 173
Christie, Agatha, 318, 319
Church of England, 7, 11
Churchill, Winston, 297, 328
Clark, Graham, 311
Class analysis, 41, 227, 363, 364, 376
Class collaboration, 135
Class conflict/struggle/war, 3, 61, 65, 77, 78, 90, 135, 162, 165, 210, 240, 256, 260–1, 263, 276
Class consciousness, 147, 257
Clayton, Wally, xix
Cloughton, 219, 223, 243, 246, 253, 262
Clyde Workers' Committee, 75, 201
Coates, Wells, 318
Cobbett Press, 324, 332
Cockburn, Claud, 313
Cockroach capitalists, 264
Coghlan, Sir Timothy A., 211, 212, 213, 215
Cohen, Rose, 221
Cold War, x, xii, xv, xviii, 312, 328, 329, 332, 340, 372

Cole, Margaret – 219, 221, 355, *see also* Postgate, Margaret
Cole, G.D.H., 53, 54, 55, 59, 80, 87, 105, 107, 109, 110, 121, 129, 145, 146–154, 159, 166, 198, 207, 217, 221, 222, 238, 239, 241, 242, 304
Collectivism, 39, 40, 41–2, 103, 147, 149, 166
Collingwood, R.G., xxiv
Colonialism, 297
Commemoration Day (Sydney University), 24–6
Commune of 1871, 149
Communist International (Comintern), 49, 50, 258, 276, 289, 296
Communist Manifesto, The, 227
Communist Party Historians Group, 324, 332
Communist Party of Australia, xiv, xix, 87, 124, 132, 179, 235, 243, 363, 366
Communist Party of Great Britain, xv, 48, 49, 78, 103, 204, 217, 230, 267, 274–5, 276, 283, 296, 297, 299, 302, 306, 312–3, 320–1, 323, 336, 349, 377
Communist Party of the Soviet Union, xix, 334
Connell, Raewyn, 249
Conscientious objectors, 58, 60, 62, 72, 78
Conscription, 111, 115, 264
Conscription referendum 1916, 66, 67
Conscription referendum 1917, 86
Cooperatives, 40
Cooperativism/cooperation, 40, 41, 135
Councils of Action, 203, 275
Counter-espionage, xxi, xxii
Cowley Barracks, 60
Crane, Norman, 139, 142
Craven fellowship, 68, 197
Crawford, O.G.S., 78, 281, 282–3, 296, 297, 298, 299, 306, 308, 314, 331, 336, 344, 345, 350, 351, 355, 361–2, 365, 368
Croce, Benedetto, 144, 251, 304, 317, 326

Crowther, J.G., 225
Cullen, Chancellor Sir William, 96, 113
Cusack, Dymphna, 132
Cyclical theories of history, 316

Daily Standard, 115, 126, 132, 137
Daily Worker, 312, 313
Dallas, Ken, 139
Dangerous Islands, The, xxii–xxiii
Daniel, Glyn, 329, 347, 368, 370
Darlinghurst, 14, 87, 168, 174
Darwin (N.T.), 36
Darwin, Charles, 37, 316
Davidson, Morrison, 37
Davies, Leila, 49, 55, 79
Davies, Philip Taliessen, 48, 49, 53, 58, 61, 68–70
Demaine, William (Billy), 118, 122
Democracy (in political philosophy), 98, 100, 104, *see also* Labour's novel theory of democracy
'Democracy, The', 104, 236
Democratic Labor Party, xviii
Democratic movement, 105
De Tocqueville, Alexis, 236
Deutsch, Arnold, 319
Dialectical materialism, 317, 326, 327
Diffusion, 332
Direct action, 116, 165
Dobb, Maurice, 221, 222, 304
Domain, Sydney, 4, 179, 192
Donnelly, Ignatius, 116, 122
Dooley, James, 182, 193, 195, 209, 210, 262, 361
Dorchester prison, 68
Douglas, Fred, 293
Durkheim, Emile, 312, 330, 339
Dutt, Clemens, 47, 198, 221, 222
Dutt, Rajani Palme, xv, 49, 50, 51, 55, 59–60, 61, 65, 70, 78, 79, 102, 110, 113, 139, 159, 198, 203, 221–2, 262, 271, 274, 277, 278, 284, 286–7, 290–1, 295, 296, 298, 305, 336, 350, 355, 367, 376, 377

Index

Economic depression, 4
Economic determinism, 327
Economic protection, 101
Edinburgh, 292–4, 295, 296, 318
Edinburgh League of Archaeologists, 272, 279
Edward, Prince of Wales, 7, 185
Efficiency, 135
Eggleston, Frederic, 135
Elizabeth Bay, 14, 15, 174
Elkin, A.P., 359
Engels, Friedrich, 110, 164, 286, 287, 290–1, 314, 322, 326, 348, 351
Engels Society, The, 324–5
English, John, 120
Epistemology, 339, 358
Espionage, xviii-xix, xx, xxi, *see also* Counter-espionage
Ethical socialism, 39
Euthanasia, 370
Evangelicals, 10–12
Evatt, H.V., xv, xvii, xviii, xix, 15–6, 32, 39, 44, 45, 89, 121, 175, 184, 202, 272, 295, 355, 358, 359, 360, 364, 369, 372
Evatt, Mary Alice, xvii, xxii, 184, 272, 276, 355, 358, 369
Ewer, W.N., 238
Ex-servicemen, 178

Fabian Research Department, 59, 61, 70, 121, 207 *see also* Labour Research Department
Fabian Society – 50, 52, 107, 237 *see also* Oxford University Fabian Society
Fabianism, 155, 227, 348
Fagg, W., 330–1
Farrington, Benjamin, 324, 330
Fascism, 228, 263, 266, 279, 283, 288, 293, 294–5, 298
'Fellow travellers', xx
Finland, 297, 300
First World War, x, 18, 71–5, 102, 201, 275, 294, 348

Fisher, Andrew, 34
Fitzpatrick, Brian, xv, xvi, 358, 363
Fitzpatrick, J.C.L., 210
Foges, Wolfgang, 314
Forbes, Mansfield, xxiii, 355
Forsdyke, John, 224
Freeberg, Norman, 116, 126, 132–3, 135, 137, 139, 141
Freehill, Norman, *see* Freeberg
Frick, Wilhelm, 279
Frodsham, Bishop George, 104
Fryer, Peter, 334
Fuller, Sir George, 94, 210, 211, 216

Gair, Vince, xviii
Gallacher, Willie, 75, 293
Garden, T.J. (Jock), 87, 140, 172, 277
Garman, Douglas, 287
Gathercole, Peter, 48, 226, 248, 308
Gentile, Giovanni, 144, 317, 326
George, Henry, 37
German Social Democratic Party, 64, 98, 107, 160, 237, 264
Germany, 64, 72, 73, 273, 278, 279
Gilruth, John, 36
Gimpera, Pere Bosch, 280–1
Glasgow, 75
Glenn Innes, 45, 117
Goldring, Douglas, 207
Gollan, Robin, xv, 366
Goot, Murray, 193
Gordon, Alexander QC (1815–1903), 9
Gordon, Alexander (Childe's cousin), 339, 342, 368–9, 372
Gordon, Anne, 9
Gordon, Sir Alexander (1858–1942), 9, 12, 272
Gould, Barbara, 221
Govett's Leap, xiii-xiv
Graham, Angus, xxiv, 8, 313–4
Graham, Ethel, xxiv
Gramsci, Antonio, 144, 377
Gray, Frank, 226
Greater unionism, 147, 149–50, 154

Greece, 57
Green, Sally, 8, 354
Griffiths, Jennie Scott, 84, 91, 115, 126, 137, 171
Grimes, W.F., 344, 368
Gronlund, Louis, 37
Guild socialism/ist, 52, 53, 61, 100, 146, 154, 157, 159, 170, 173, 222, 238, 241

Haglund, Laila, 359, 369
Hall, D.R., 185
Hall, Hessel Duncan, 70–1
Harben, Philip, 319
Hardacre, Herbert F., 118, 128
Harding, G.Y., 118
Hargreaves, Leonard, 75
Harper, Dr Andrew, 92, 93, 95
Harpur, E.F.H., 181–2, 194–5, 209, 210, 211
Hartwell, R.M., xvii
Harvard University, 273, 295, 339
Haverfield, Francis J., 97
Hay, Clifford H., 195, 209, 210, 211, 212, 213, 216
Health and safety, 192
Heaton, Herbert, 139
Hegel, G.W.F., xv, 54, 63, 71, 108, 109, 110, 251, 317, 326, 341
Hegelian/ism, 62, 63, 71, 144, 304
Hermes, 23–4, 62, 341
Hermes, Gertrude, 280
Heydon, Judge J.K., 143, 228
Higgins, Esmonde, xvi, 79, 139, 218, 221, 222, 242–3, 278
High Church, *see* Tractarians
Historians Group, *see* Communist Party Historians Group
Historical materialism, xx, 44, 286, 300, 303, 304, 310, 327, 335, 337, 338, 341, 372, 376, 378
Hitler, Adolph, 278, 295, 297, 298, 352
Hitlerism, 297
Hobbes, Thomas, 107, 108
Hobhouse, L.T., 63, 299

Hobson, John A., 53, 99–103, 105
Hobson, S.G., 222
Hogben, Lancelot, 283
Holland, H.E., 195
Hollinghurst, Alan, 208
Holman, William, xiii, 32, 33, 44, 66, 104, 122, 175, 176, 178, 179, 181, 185, 360
Holme, Professor E.R., 86
Holmes, Arnold, 115
Homosexuality, 125, 354–5
Horrabin, Frank, 222, 238
Hotel de Vere, 272, 274
Houston, A.E. ('Radix'), 137
Hughes, William Morris, xiii, 27, 33, 66, 240
Humanism/ist, 315, 343, 370
Hungary, 311, 322, 334
Hutt, Allen, 274

Icelandic culture, 362, 372
Idealism/ist (in philosophy), 63, 71, 252, 317, 367
Imperialism, 99–100, 105
Independent Labour Party, 51, 87, 121
Independent Working-Class Education, 139, 141, 241
India, 344
India League, 276
Indian nationalism, 59
Indiana Jones, ix
Individualism, 103
Industrial arbitration, 153, 165, 167
Industrial conscription, 56, 74
Industrial democracy, 41, 53, 147, 148, 155, 164–5, 167, 180, 195, 257
Industrial Labor Party, *see* Industrial Socialist Labor Party
Industrial revolution, 131, 307
Industrial Socialist Labor party, 192–3, 261
Industrial syndicalism, 140
Industrial unionists / 'industrialists', 87, 98, 126, 223, 232, 254, 262

Industrial Vigilance Committee, 122, 171, 264
Industrial Workers of the World (IWW), 90, 122, 123, 127, 154, 161–2, 166, 167, 170, 175, 185, 190, 234, 241, 255, 256–8
Institute of Archaeology, 312, 318, 343, 344, 349
Intellectuals
  As mediators in class struggle, 87, 113
  Dissenting intellectuals, x
  Labour intellectuals, 44, 83, 130, 132, 173, 197
  Left intellectuals, 83
  Liberal intellectuals, 87, 112, 135, 143
  Marxist intellectuals, 336
  Organic intellectuals, 131, 132, 134, 377
  Radical intellectuals, 378
  Rootless intellectuals, 101
  Socialist intellectuals, 148
  Trained intellectuals, 98, 130, 377
  Working-class intellectuals, 52
Intelligentsia, 364
International Labour Office/Organisation, 59, 209, 225
Irish War of Independence 1920–1, 201, 202, 204
Irvine, Professor R.F., 96, 136, 178
Isokon building (Lawn Road flats), 318–9, 343, 346

Japan, 184
Jensen, Harald Ingemann, 34–7, 38, 42, 140, 245
Jews, 225
Jingoism/Jingoes, 348
Joint Committee for Tutorial Classes, 91, 95, 109
Joint Industrial Councils, 164
Jones, Luke, 84, 91
Judd, Ernest (Ernie), 86, 87, 137

Katoomba, xiii
Kautsky, Karl, 257
Kaye, Alan, 58, 59, 61, 198
Kendall, Walter, 52
Keynesianism, 99
Khrushchev, Nikita, xix, 322, 334
Kilbride-Jones, H., 353
King and Empire Alliance, 185
King George V, 202
Kingsley, Charles, 39
Klejn, Leo, 338
Koestler, Arthur, 298
Kossinna, Gustaf, 279
Krichevskii, E.Y., 337–8
Kropotkin, Peter, 37, 119
Knowledge and Unity, 132

Labor News, 129, 165
Labor Party, 38, 39, 66, 80, 90, 254, 261, 348
Labor Party (NSW), xi, 30, 31, 35, 39, 42, 48, 86, 87, 97, 103, 107–8, 111, 112, 171–2, 173, 277
Labor Party (Qld), 37, 115, 261
Labor's novel theory of democracy, 206, 233
Labour Club (University of Sydney), xii
Labour Council, Sydney, 4, 6, 27, 84, 86, 88, 114, 134, 162, 179, 266
Labour historians, xv-xvi
Labour History (journal), xii
Labour intellectuals, *see* Intellectuals, labour
Labour Leader, 87–8
Labour Monthly, 218, 336, 342
Labour Party (Britain), 86, 102, 204,, 217, 236, 276, 302
Labour public, 130
Labour Publishing Company, 229–231
Labour Research Department (London), xvi, 181, 198, 217–219, 229, 246, 275
Labour theory of value, 131, 137
Labourism/ist, 131, 173, 230, 249, 256

Lanchester, Elsa, 208
Lane, Allen, 307
Lane, Ernest (Ernie), 137, 191
Lane, William, 116, 122
Lang, J.T. (Jack), 272, 277
Langdon-Davies, Bernard N., 229
Larrikin 'pushes', 6
Lawrence, D.H., 185, 274
Laurent, John, 37
League of Nations Institute for Intellectual Cooperation, 226
League of Nations Union, 71, 112
Lee, Hermione, 208
Leeds Convention, The, 76–7, 79
Left Book Club, 274, 276, 293–4
Lenin, V.I./Leninism, 100, 104, 238, 258, 259, 260, 261, 278, 326
Levy, Hyman, 283, 302–3, 324, 334
Lewis, John, 313
Liberal/Liberalism, 54, 62, 99, 131, 135, 182, 226, 231
Liberty, 73, 106, 108
Liebknecht, Karl, 64
Lindsay, Jack, 124, 129, 296, 306, 317–8, 320–3, 342, 344, 350, 352, 354, 355, 374
Lloyd, Eric Longfield, 184
Lloyd George, David, 104
Locke, John, 108
Lowe, Robert, 206
Loyalists – *see* Scabs
Luxemburg, Rosa, 64

MacCallum, Sir Mungo, 85–6, 94, 96
MacDonald, Ramsay, 231, 276
Mackenzie, Donald, 294
MacLaurin, Sir Normand, 22, 25
Magic, 305, 306, 326
Magrath, John R., 97
Maisky, Ivan, 294
Mallowan, Max, 312, 319
Manchester Guardian, The, 89, 219, 331
Mann, Tom, 152
Mannix, Cardinal Daniel, 95

Mansbridge, Albert, 134
Marr, N.Y., 301, 377
Marshall, Vance, 84, 88–9, 91, 92, 112, 127, 137, 186–8, 244
Martin, David, 363, 374
Marx, Karl, 321, 322, 326, 341, 342, 348
Marx/Marxism/Marxist, xi, xv, xvii, 44, 98, 102, 103, 110, 124, 131, 140, 144, 156, 159, 226, 231, 237, 251, 252, 273, 283, 287, 290, 295, 304, 305, 311, 312, 314, 324, 326, 329, 330, 336, 349, 377 *see also* Western Marxism
Marxism-Leninism, 297, 298, 342, 378
Marx Memorial Library, 283, 284, 314, 315
Maryborough, 118, 360
Maryborough Boys' Grammar School, 117, 118, 122, 123
Maryborough Chronicle, 118, 119
Materialism/ist, 252, 256, 304, 305, 367–8 *see also* Historical materialism
Maurice, F.D., 39
Mayo, Elton, 128, 136, 141
McCawley, Judge T.W., 156, 191
McCormack, William, 191
McCristal, Timothy William, 31–2
McGowen, James, 19, 32, 122, 255
McIntyre, Rev. J.E., 292
McKell, William, 89, 93, 94, 106, 165, 168, 180, 181, 213, 214–5, 216, 272, 364
Mediation, 113, 143–4
Men's Christian Union (University of Sydney), 14, 39, 41
Menzies, R.G., xix
Metal craftsmen, 332
Meynell, Francis, 76
MI5, xxi, xxiii, 69, 70, 80, 85, 223, 275, 283, 308, 312, 331
Michels, Robert, 237, 239, 240
Michie, Professor J.L., 128
Middle class, 204, 234

Miles, J.B., 140
Miles, William J., 90, 113
Militant Propagandists of the Labour Movement, 90
Military recruitment, 178
Military Service Acts, 55, 56, 57
Military Service Tribunals, 55 *see also* Oxford University Military Tribunal
Mill, J.S., 105, 109
Mill, James, 105
Minyan ware, 68
Mockbell's café, 90
Modern Quarterly, The, 280, 283, 284, 313, 332
Mongait, A.L., 337
Montefiore, Dora, 77, 102
Morby, W., 86, 87, 88
Morgan, Kevin, 203, 275–6
Morgan, Lewis H., 286–7
Morris, John, 311, 322, 343, 350, 355, 357, 358, 362, 367
Morris, William, 116, 156
Moscow Mansions, 272
Motherhood endowment, 180
Movius, Hallam, 295, 297
Muir, Ramsay, 238, 240
Mulvaney, John, 358, 367
Munster, George, 181
Murray, Sir Gilbert, 47, 55, 58, 59, 60, 61, 67, 79, 87, 110–1, 142–3, 224, 228
Murray-Smith, Stephen, 363
Myres, Sir John, 224–5, 226, 227, 228, 251, 279, 280

Nation, The, 89
National Council for Civil Liberties, 55, 61, 229, 332
National Council of Labour Colleges, 276, 301
National Museum of Antiquities (Edinburgh), 315, 336, 350
National Party, 174, 197, 210, 211, 215
National Union of Clerks, 218, 288
Nationalisation, 180, 195

Nationalism/ist, 264
Nelson, Harold, 36
Neo-Hegelians, 99, 378
Neústupný, Jiří, 347
New Age, The, 52, 53
New Guinea, 104
New Left, 320
New liberalism, 38, 39, 40, 100
New protection, 102
New Statesman, The, 238
Newer unionism, 122, 129, 168
Newington College, 120
Nicholson, Professor George G., 86, 96
No-Conscription Fellowship, 55, 56, 59
Non-party communism, 203, 275–6
North, Marilla, 132
North Sydney, 3, 7
North Sydney Preparatory School, 8
Northern Territory, 36

Oakeshott, Michael, 329
Occidentalist, 248
Ogden, C.K., 247, 248, 342
O'Malley, Sir Owen St Clair, xxiv
One Big Union (OBU), 36, 122, 129, 137, 146, 154, 157, 159, 161, 163–4, 166, 169, 170, 173, 174, 222, 223, 234, 235, 250, 253, 261
Opportunism, 233
Orage, A.R., 52
O'Reilly, Very Reverend M.J., 95
Oriental despotism, 300, 306
Orientalist, 248
Ó Ríordáin, Seán P., 347
Orwell, George, xxiv, 312
Ostrogorski, Moisey, 237, 239, 240
Outlook (journal) xvi
Outsider, The, 226
Overland (journal), xvi, 363
Oxford, 46, 95, 110–1
Oxford Magazine, 56
Oxford Military Service Tribunal, 48, 58
Oxford Movement, *see* Tractarians

Oxford University Fabian Society, 48, 50, 53
Oxford University Socialist Society, *see* Socialist Society (Oxford University)

Paananen, Victor N., 323
Pacificism, 289
Pacifism/ist, 56, 77, 87, 115, 128, 184, 289, 292, 294
Palmer, Helen, xvi
Parliamentarism, 38, 218, 376
Parliamentary socialism, 376
Past and Present, 311, 332, 334–5
Paterson, Fred, 139
Patriarchy, 23
Paul, William, 222
Peace, William J. (Bill), 296
Pearce, George, 90, 117, 191
Pearce, Russell, 90, 202
Pennsylvania State University, 273
People – 'the people' (in political philosophy), 101
Permeation, 102
Petrov, Vladimir, xix
Piesse, Edmund, 184
Piggott, Stuart, 311, 312, 374
Plebs, The, 139, 143, 279, 301
Plebs League, 142, 227, 241
Pluralism/pluralist, 53, 102, 150, 159
Political action, 116
Politicalism, xi, 23, 175, 232, 263
Pollitt, Harry, 296
Popular democracy, *see* radical democracy
Popular sovereignty, *see* radical democracy
Portus, Garnet Vere (Jerry), 91, 92, 95, 109, 136, 156
Postgate, Margaret, 59, 198 *see also* Cole, Margaret
Postgate, Raymond, 49, 53, 55, 58, 59, 61, 198, 207, 221, 230, 238, 239, 241–2, 319, 376

Practice/practical activity/praxis, 250, 251
Prehistoric Society, The, 299, 304, 378
Premier's Department, 176–183, 194, 209
Price control, 180
Prince Albert, 7
Profiteering, 195
Progress, 250–1, 306, 309–10, 325, 326, 332, 335, 348, 372
Proletarian culture, 133, 260, 362, 366, 372
Proletarian democracy, 135, 136, 206, 233, 239, 259, 345, 364, 375, 376
Proletarian dictatorship, 257, 258
Prussian-Australianism, 99, 101
Psychoanalysis, 352–3
Public Questions Society, 90
Public Service Board, 176, 214
Public sphere, 130, 131
Pulsford, Frank E., 39–42
Pydokke, Edward, 344

Quaker/s, 219
Queen's College, Oxford, 46, 47, 48, 49, 67
Queer history, 208
Quinton, Jim, 156

Race riots, 204
Racialism/ist, 88, 276, 278, 279, 297, 348
Radical democracy, 40, 52, 53, 180
Radical liberalism, 130
Rae, Arthur, 165, 172
Rat, 336
Rathbone, Hugo, 221
Rationalism/ist, 90, 312
Rationalist Association of NSW, 90
Rationalist Press Association, xii, 117, 302, 303, 324
Red flag riots, 126–7, 192
Reed, John, 375
Reeves, W. Pember, 227

Religion, 106, 305, 306, 316, 326
Renfrew, Colin, 349
Representative government, 29, 231, 237
Returned soldiers, *see* Ex-servicemen
Revolution, 78, 98, 108, 160, 162–3, 164, 203, 218, 236, 372, 375–9
Revolutionary democracy, xi
Revolutionary industrial unionism, 234
Richmond, Norman, 139
Rivett, Rev. A., 91
Robson, William, 284
Rosenthal, Major-General Sir Charles, 185
Ross, Lloyd, xv, 139
Ross, R.S., 137
Rousseau, Jean-Jacques, 106–7, 108, 110
Royal Anthropological Institute, 224, 228, 267, 271, 330
Royal Society of Edinburgh, 274
Ruskin College, 133
Russell, Bertrand, 55, 72, 299
Russia, xx, 154–5, 273, 297, 299, 300, 310, 313, 328, 330, 331, 334, 336, 338, 341, 358, 376
Russian exiles, 126
Russian Revolution (March 1917), 56, 65, 69, 76, 77
Russian Revolution (November 1917), 36, 77, 98, 117, 126, 160, 201, 203, 300, 330, 375, 376
Ryan, Thomas J. (Tom), 115, 122, 166, 167, 265

Sabotage, 3
Sarkisov, S.A., 352
Sassoon, Siegfried, 355
Saturday Review, The, 239
Scabs, 20, 84, 150, 178
Schaeffer, Claude, 360
Science, 288, 302, 305, 316, 325, 327, 349
Science and Society, 324

Scientific history, 333, 336
Scientific socialism, 348
Scottish Peace Council, 293
Scottish-USSR Society, 276, 330
Second International, 252
Second World War, 102, 296, 297
Secular faith, 377
Sentiment, 322, 348, 349, 366
Sexism, 188
Shannon, Marion H., 373
Shaw, George Bernard, 217, 221, 222, 296
Sheffield Workers' Committee, 75
Shop-stewards' committees, 56, 76, 201, 259
Siedleckie, Stefania, xiv
Sim, Arthur, 30
Simpson, John H., 226
Sinclaire, Frederick, 138, 139
Skara Brae, x, 49, 272
Small producers, *see* Cockroach capitalists
Smith, Isobel, 367
Smiths, *see* Metal craftsmen
Snowden, Philip, 221, 230
Social Darwinism, 37
Social democracy, xi
Social Democratic Federation (Britain), 229
Social Democratic League, 84, 88, 90
Social Democratic Party of NSW, 32
Social gospel, 12
Social Philosophy Group, 324
Socialist Labour Party, 132
Socialist League, Brisbane, 137
Socialist/socialisation objective, 236, 266
Socialist Society (Oxford University), 53, 54, 61, 78, 79
Socialist Society (Sydney University), 23–4, 38–9, 42
Socialists, 4, *see also* ethical socialism, state socialism, Socialist Society (Sydney University), Social Democratic Party of NSW

Society for Cultural Relations with the USSR, 294, 299, 300, 331, 337
Society of Antiquaries of Scotland, 272, 344
Soho, 80
South Brisbane, 126
Soviets, 259
Soviet Union, *see* Russia
Spencer, Herbert, 37
Spengler, Oswald, 326
St Andrew's College, 15, 45, 85, 90, 92, 93
St Thomas's church/rectory, 4, 5, 7–8, 10, 11, 372
Stalin, J.V. /Stalinism/ists, xx, 295–6, 297, 298, 299, 307, 311, 321–3, 326, 327, 334, 336, 341, 351, 352, 376
State capitalism, 152, 166, 169
State enterprises, 122, 166, 169, 175, 180, 192, 193, 195, 254, 255
State socialism, 39, 102, 147, 157, 169
State, The (in political philosophy), 53, 54, 63, 64, 98, 101, 106–7, 108–9, 148–9, 150–1, 154–5, 166, 176–7
Stead, Christina, 206
Stern, Bernhard J, 324
Stephensen, Percy ('Inky'), 90, 122, 123–4, 139, 243–5, 274, 321, 360, 366
Stevenson, R.B.K. (Robert), 296, 350–1, 355
Stewart, David, 91, 95
Stewart, Eve, 359
Stewart, James R., 358–60
Stewart, Major-General William, 359
Storey, John, xii, 87, 88, 129, 156, 172–3, 174, 175, 176, 177, 179–80, 190, 193–4, 195–6, 209, 215, 266, 358
Stott, W.B., 68
Strikes
 1890s, 3, 5
 1900s, 255
 1910s, 26–7, 255, 256, 257
 Gas strike 1912, 18–20

General strike, 149, 202, 256, 275
Mass strike 1917, 83, 87, 98, 167, 235, 253, 255, 256, 257
Strong, Duncan, 329
Sturt electorate, 192
Suffragette, 127
Superstructure, 305
Surplus value, theory of, 131
Swan, W.J., 215–6
Swann, Isabel, 89, 91
Sydney Church of England Grammar School ('Shore'), 7, 12–3, 85
Sydney Morning Herald, 5, 20
Syndicalism/syndicalist, 102, 148–9, 152, 155, 169, 174, 175, 203, *see also* Industrial syndicalism

Taylor, G.R. Stirling, 239
Tavener, Wallace, 293
'The democracy', 104, 236
Theodore, Edward (Ted), 95, 120, 126, 128, 168, 170, 186, 191, 203, 227, 265, 266, 278
Third Interstate Peace Conference, 92, 103, 112
Thomas, Jimmy, 230, 275
Thompson, E.P. (Edward), 306, 320, 322–3, 328
Thomson, George, 314
Thorpe, Margaret, 115
Todd, Professor Frederick Augustus, 86, 96
Topp, Celia, 344
Totalitarian, 300, 309, 313, 341
Townsville, 167, 26
Toynbee, Arnold, 326
Tractarians, 10–12
Trade Union Congress, 74
Trades and Labour Council, *see* Labour Council (Sydney)
Trades Hall (Brisbane), 115, 116, 120, 171
Trades Hall (Sydney), *see* Labour Council (Sydney)

Index

Treachery, *see* Rat
Trevelyan, Charles P., 221, 222
Trigger, Bruce G., 307
Tringham, Ruth, 311
Triple Alliance, 202, 204
Trotsky, Leon, 164
Truth, 71, 72
Turner, Ian, 363

U.S.A., 67, 70, 273, 328
U.S.S.R., *see* Russia
Ullman, Cleeve, 115
Undergraduates' Association (Sydney University), 23, 25, 26
Unemployed/unemployment, 4–5, 254, 262
Unemployed Workers' Movement, 289
Union of Democratic Control, 56, 65, 77, 78, 91, 99, 103, 112, 207, 247
United States of America, *see* U.S.A.
Universal Service League, 134
University Club (Sydney), 86
University of California, 273, 286, 29
University of Edinburgh, 228, 271
University of Melbourne, 90
University of Oxford, xv
University of Queensland, 117, 124, 129
University of Sydney, x, xi, 12, 14, 15–6, 22–6, 34, 111, 113, 141
University of Sydney (Men's) Union, 24–5, 42, 43
University of Sydney Professorial Board, 25–6
University of Sydney Senate, xiv, 22, 24, 25, 26
University of Sydney Socialist Society, *see* Socialist Society (Sydney University)
University Socialist Federation, 50, 61, 207
Urban Revolution, 306

Venona (US counter-intelligence operation), xix
Victorian Labour College, 95, 134, 138, 141
Victorian Socialist Party, 152, 173
Violence
  by state organisations, 6, 263
  by strikers, 20, 28–9
  by suffragettes, 127
Voluntary Workers' Association, *see* Scabs
Volunteers, *see* Scabs

Wade, Charles G., 22, 24, 31
Wage labour, 130, 131, 147, 227
Wagery, 23, 132, 157, 164, 165
Wages boards, 153
Wages system, 153, 157
Wallace, A.R., 37
Walshe, Bob, xv
Ward, Russel, xv, xvi-xvii, xx, 358, 362, 367
Warsaw Peace Congress, 1951, 331
Wason, Cathcart Roland (Roly), 274
Watt, Raymond G., 70–1, 74, 79, 105, 341
Waugh, Alec, 125–6
Waugh, Evelyn, 208
Webb, Beatrice, 147, 296
Webb, Sidney, 147
Wells, H.G., 296
Wentworth Falls, 11, 12, 15
Werskey, Gary, 289
Western Marxism, 251
Wheat Board, 186
Wheeler, Sir Mortimer, 347
White, Leslie A., 329
White-anting, 305, 308
White Australia Policy, 184, 263
Wickham Terrace, 120
Williams, Fred, 90
Willis, Albert C., 170, 172, 257
Wilson, Colin, 226
Wilson, President Woodrow, 104

Winslow, Cal, 323
Witchard, Anne, 208
Witherby, Theodore C., 117, 124, 128, 137, 139, 141, 143, 154–6, 158, 202, 246, 363
Womanhood Suffrage League, 102
Wood, George Arnold, xiv
Wood, J.H. ('John O'Rockie'), 137
Wood, Wendy, 293
Wooldridge, Professor S.W., 344
Woolf, Leonard, 207, 208
Worker (Brisbane), 34, 132, 245, 246
Workers' control, 129, 165, 173, 206, 254, 259
Workers' councils, 259
Workers' Educational Association, 44, 86, 91, 108, 110, 111, 128, 129, 133, 134, 138, 139, 140, 141, 145, 156, 158, 171
Workers' Industrial Union of Australia, 163, 169
Workers' School of Social Science, 139, 140
Working class education, 145
Working class insubordination, 27–8, 74, 161
Working class knowledge, 133–4, 143–4
Working class militancy, 135, 151
World Committee Against War and Fascism, 289, 293
World of Labour, The, 87
World Peace Council, 330, 331
World Student Conference, 331
Wurth, Wallace, xvii-xviii

Xenophanes of Colophon, 12–4

Young Communist League, 284, 309

Zweig, Ferdynand, 362

ABOUT THE AUTHOR

Terry Irving, radical historian and educational radical, is Honorary Professorial Fellow at the University of Wollongong, Australia. His books include *Radical Sydney* (with Rowan Cahill), *Childe and Australia* (edited with Peter Gathercole and Gregory Melleuish), *Class Structure in Australian History* (with Raewyn Connell), and *The Southern Tree of Liberty*. He was editor of *Labour History: A Journal of Labour and Social History* and a founder of the Free University (Sydney).
www.terryirving.net